THE BASIC PAPERS OF
George M. Humphrey

GEORGE MAGOFFIN HUMPHREY
Secretary of the Treasury 1953–1957

THE BASIC PAPERS OF

George M. Humphrey

AS SECRETARY OF THE TREASURY

1953-1957

EDITED BY NATHANIEL R. HOWARD

The Western Reserve Historical Society

CLEVELAND, OHIO

The Western Reserve Historical Society Publication Number 119

Copyright 1965
by The Western Reserve Historical Society

Library of Congress Catalogue Card Number 65–17514

Printed in the United States of America

Foreword

One of the purposes of a historical society is to conserve the evidences of the past, not only the artifacts of yesteryear, but also the written record. For nearly a century The Western Reserve Historical Society has collected manuscripts relating chiefly to events or citizens of this northeast section of Ohio that was once the Western Reserve. In recent years much has been done to increase the size of this collection and to make it more readily available to scholars.

Many manuscripts in the collection relate to distinguished citizens, who themselves took a prominent part in shaping events. Of particular interest and value are the papers of the Honorable George M. Humphrey relating to the period when he was Secretary of the Treasury under President Dwight D. Eisenhower. These papers give us insight into the financial policies of our Federal Government during an important period of our history. We are most fortunate and very grateful to have received them.

Publication of the basic documents in these papers conforms to the general policy of this Society of making the documents and papers in its custody more usable. The Society, therefore, is pleased to present to the public *The Basic Papers of George M. Humphrey* as its publication for 1965.

The editor, Nathaniel R. Howard, is particularly well qualified for the task. As a newspaperman during the Eisenhower Administration, he was in an exceptionally good position to observe firsthand events on the national scene.

THE WESTERN RESERVE HISTORICAL SOCIETY

Herman L. Vail, *President*
Meredith B. Colket, Jr., *Director*

Preface

In 1962 George M. Humphrey turned over to The Western Reserve Historical Society his collection of public papers—statements, actions, and procedures—as Secretary of the Treasury for four and a half years, 1953–57. The Historical Society promptly acted to publish sufficient of these to record in detail in Mr. Humphrey's own contemporary words a career in the two administrations of President Dwight D. Eisenhower which was singular in many respects.

Most of the papers conveyed by Mr. Humphrey are included here. The few not published (deposited in the Humphrey Collection at the Society in Cleveland) are either of routine or repetitive character.

To the collection published within these covers have been added a representative number of the Secretary's statements and testimony before committees of Congress. The editor was directed by the Historical Society to, and did, make all selections himself, for the purpose of an all-around profile of Secretary Humphrey and his public service. It seems logical to refer to this publication as "Basic Papers" of the four and a half years' service.

Mr. Humphrey came from a private career in the business world in which he had neither sought nor had experience in public affairs. Yet he developed into one of the most articulate, most listened-to, most quoted Treasury Secretaries in our history. His total of public appearances and expression are near 200, far more than the self-exposure of most Secretaries of the Treasury.

In part, this was the result of his bringing to his office several faiths in certain fixed truths and policies which are credo to the broadly successful business leader. In his Treasury service he never deserted these fundamental personal faiths. Most of his public words are for their exposition and understanding.

To this character he added a rapidly acquired conviction that the people of America would better understand their government if told more details of its operation. He became the antithesis of a secretive or privately minded official; he addressed himself fervently to the purpose that the people know all there was to know of fiscal government and the proper choices of fiscal principles.

This had much to do with the high level of esteem in which Secretary Humphrey was held by members of Congress and the press and the frequency with which they interviewed him. He never appeared a reluctant, always a willing, spokesman.

Many of the Secretary's speeches, statements, and articles are herein presented in full. Some have been abridged of salutations and minor discursive asides. Some are excerpts from longer speeches or statements which make the point and register the effect for which the statement was intended. Testimony and conversation in Congressional hearings and public panels have been edited only where repetition or non-sequiturs seemed worth avoiding. There is one exception to this pattern. Secretary Humphrey's final fourteen-day performance on the stand before the Senate Finance Committee has been condensed by excerpting to about half of his total words. The total of that hearing would have required an additional volume.

Ellipses inform the reader where as much as a single phrase has been deleted.

The papers are divided into eight general classifications of topic for the sake of easier reference. These classifications naturally spill over into each other; yet in the main each constitutes an identifiable section of Secretary Humphrey's view in a specific area of government and interests. While the "Basic Papers" do not in any sense serve as a biography of the Secretary during his federal service, they have a superiority to a biography in being his own words—in many ways, more revealing of the man and the statesman.

The cartoons reproduced are a selection from the collection of original cartoons relating to George M. Humphrey, ninety-six of which are on permanent display in the George Magoffin Humphrey Room of The Western Reserve Historical Society.

The editor gratefully acknowledges help and counsel by Meredith B. Colket, Jr., director of The Western Reserve Historical Society, and John Large, Jr. and others of the Society staff; the

Public Affairs Office of the Treasury Department and Nils Lennartson, formerly of the Department of Defense; the reference staff of the Cleveland Public Library; and Benjamin M. McKelway, editorial chairman of *The Washington Star*. He likewise wishes to thank Christine Kuehn, Kermit Pike and Taylor Gaither for their indispensable work in proofreading and indexing.

N.R.H.

Copyright Acknowledgments

"The Way to Check Inflation" is reprinted from "Sound Money is Continuing Policy," in *Nation's Business*, January, 1955; copyright, 1955, by *Nation's Business*, Washington.

"Credit Restraint Equally Necessary" is reprinted from "The Future—Sound as a Dollar," in *Fortune* magazine, April, 1955; copyright, 1955, by Time, Inc.

"No Threat of Dangerous Inflation—Now" is reprinted from "We Are Spending Too Much Money," in *U. S. News and World Report*, published at Washington, February 8, 1957; copyright, 1957, by U. S. News and World Report, Inc.

The copyright permissions granted pertain only to the material published in this book and do not include any further reproduction. For these copyright permissions, The Western Reserve Historical Society is grateful.

Contents

	Page
List of Papers	xv
List of Illustrations	xxiii
A Brief Biography	xxv

The Basic Papers of George M. Humphrey

I. The Secretary's Background	1
II. Fiscal Management and the Sound Dollar	33
III. Taxation	353
IV. International Policy	445
V. Public Policy	487
VI. Government and Business	545
VII. The President	577
VIII. General and Personal	607
Chronological List of Public Appearances and Statements	627
Index	635

List of Papers

Page

I. THE SECRETARY'S BACKGROUND

Statement and testimony, Senate Finance Committee, on
confirmation of his appointment. January 19, 1953   3

II. FISCAL MANAGEMENT AND THE SOUND DOLLAR

Remarks, luncheon of Cleveland Chamber of Commerce.
February 17, 1953   37

Remarks, Advertising Council of America, Washington.
April 1, 1953   43

Statement, Treasury Department, announcing thirty-year 3¼
per cent bond issue. April 13, 1953   47

Speech, annual luncheon of Associated Press, New York.
April 20, 1953   48

Television panel interview, Meet the Press, Washington.
May 24, 1953   55

Statement and testimony, House Ways & Means Committee. June 1, 1953   63

Remarks, television panel at White House. June 3, 1953   76

Article, *U.S. News & World Report,* "What Sound Money
Will Mean." June 12, 1953   79

Television panel interview, Man of the Week, Washington.
June 21, 1953   90

Radio panel interview, Reporter's Round-up, Washington.
June 22, 1953   94

Statement, Treasury Department, Federal Reserve Board
discount rate. June 24, 1953   99

Statement, Treasury Department, analysis at end of fiscal
year. July 19, 1953   101

News conference, White House, debt limit. July 30, 1953   102

Speech, National Conference of Governors, Seattle. August 4, 1953   103

Page

Interview, *U.S. News & World Report*, debt limit. August 7, 1953   108

Interview, *Newsweek*, honest-money policy. August 10, 1953   110

News conference, Treasury Department, budget. August 27, 1953   112

Speech, National Press Club luncheon, Washington. September 16, 1953   113

Speech, American Bankers Association, Washington. September 22, 1953   118

Speech, New York Clearing House Association, New York. October 5, 1953   127

Speech, Union League Club, Philadelphia. October 30, 1953   132

Speech, Investment Bankers of America, Hollywood, Florida. December 1, 1953   138

Interview, *Newsweek*, higher living standards. January 4, 1954   143

News conference, Treasury Department, analysis of 1954 budget. January 20, 1954   145

Speech, American Society of Newspaper Editors, Washington. April 15, 1954   148

Remarks, National Farm-City Conference, New York. May 25, 1954   152

Article, *U.S. Coast Guard Magazine*, "The Sound Dollar." June, 1954   155

Statement, Treasury Department, deficits. September 14, 1954   156

Article, *The New York Herald-Tribune*, "The Fiscal Gains of Twenty Months." October 7, 1954   157

Speech, American Bankers Association, Atlantic City. October 19, 1954   159

Statement, Joint Committee on the Economic Report, bond interest. December 7, 1954   163

Article, *Nation's Business*, "Our Continuing Policy." January, 1955   168

Article, *Washington Post and Times-Herald*, "Keep Inflation Dead, Goal of Humphrey." January 2, 1955   171

Speech, Chamber of Commerce of Greater Philadelphia. February 16, 1955   173

Page

Speech, National Canners Association, Chicago. February 19, 1955 — 178

Article, Fortune magazine, "The Future: Sound as a Dollar." April, 1955 — 187

Statement and testimony, House Ways & Means Committee, debt limit extension. June 24, 1955 — 191

News conference, Treasury Department, budget prospect. August 25, 1955 — 206

Statement, Treasury Department, prospect of budget balance. September 29, 1955 — 218

Speech, Republican finance dinner, Philadelphia. October 4, 1955 — 219

Article, *Washington Post and Times-Herald*, "Future Promising, Humphrey Writes." January 4, 1956 — 225

Statement, Treasury Department, balanced budget. January 14, 1956 — 227

Television panel interview, Meet the Press, Washington. January 22, 1956 — 229

Statement, Joint Committee on the Economic Report, prosperity. February 3, 1956 — 230

Statement, House Ways & Means Committee, reduce national debt. June 19, 1956 — 231

Speech, Economic Club, Detroit. October 8, 1956 — 232

News conference, Treasury Department, 1958 budget. January 15, 1957 — 236

Television panel interview, Meet the Press, Washington. January 27, 1957 — 254

Testimony, Joint Economic Committee. February 4, 1957 — 263

Statement, House Ways & Means Committee, excise tax rates. February 6, 1957 — 265

Interview, *U.S. News & World Report*, taped. February 8, 1957 — 267

Speech, Republican meeting, Masonic Temple in Detroit. March 6, 1957 — 279

Remarks, National Industrial Conference Board, New York. April 18, 1957 — 283

Speech, Republican meeting, Des Moines, Iowa. May 7, 1957 — 286

Page

Statement, Subcommittee on Fiscal Policy of the Joint Economic Committee. June 14, 1957   292

Statement, House Committee on Post Office and Civil Service. June 24, 1957   295

Statement, Senate Committee on Finance, Investigation of the Financial Condition of the United States. June 18, 1957   298

Testimony, Senate Committee on Finance. June 19 to July 12, 1957   330

III. TAXATION

Remarks, American Society of Newspaper Editors, Washington. April 16, 1953   355

Remarks, White House Conference of State Governors, Washington. May 5, 1953   357

Statement, Treasury Department, general sales tax. September 30, 1953   360

Article, *Nation's Business*, "More Tax Cuts Are Essential." January, 1954   361

Statement, Joint Committee on the Economic Report. February 2, 1954   365

Statement, Treasury Department, tax exemption proposals. February 25, 1954   378

Speech, League of Republican Women, Washington. March 1, 1954   379

Article, *Life*, "How New Tax Bill Can Promote Prosperity." March 15, 1954   382

Letter to Speaker Joseph W. Martin, Jr., tax revision bill. March 17, 1954   387

Television panel interview, Youth Wants to Know, Washington. March 28, 1954   389

Speech, Republican Women's Centennial Conference, Washington. April 7, 1954   393

Letter to Subcommittee of the Senate Judiciary Committee, opposing tax limitation. April 27, 1954   398

Speech, Full Employment Conference of the Congress of Industrial Organizations, Washington. May 11, 1954   398

Page

Speech, Tax Institute of the University of Texas, Austin, Texas. October 1, 1954   405

Article, *The Saturday Evening Post*, "What the New Tax Law Does for You." October 2, 1954   410

Interview, *The New York Herald-Tribune* Forum, New York. October 21, 1954   418

Statement, Senate Finance Committee. February 28, 1955   425

Statement, Senate Finance Committee. May 11, 1955   428

Statement, House Government Operations Committee, tax write-offs. July 18, 1955   430

Statement, Senate Committee on Finance, tax write-offs. May 7, 1957   434

IV. INTERNATIONAL POLICY

Remarks, World Bank and International Monetary Fund meeting, Washington. September 9, 1953   447

Statement, House Ways & Means Committee, reciprocal trade treaties. May 4, 1953   449

Statement, Senate Foreign Relations and House Foreign Affairs Committees. May 5, 1953   450

Remarks, Capehart Government Study Commission, Washington. September 15, 1953   454

Panel discussion, meeting of the International Bank for Reconstruction and Development, prospects for private international investment. September 28, 1954   457

Speech, Inter-American Economic Conference, Rio de Janeiro. November 23, 1954   464

Statement, House Ways & Means Committee, reciprocal trade treaties. January 18, 1955   475

Statement, Senate Banking Committee, world investment agency. June 6, 1955   477

Remarks, International Monetary Fund and World Bank meeting, Istanbul, Turkey. September 12, 1955   481

Remarks, meeting of the Governors of the International Monetary Fund, Washington. September 24, 1956   483

Remarks, Pennsylvania Society of New York, New York. December 8, 1956   484

Page

V. PUBLIC POLICY

Speech, Economic Club, Detroit. November 9, 1953   489

Statement and testimony, Senate Public Works Committee,
highway financing. March 22, 1955   496

Statement, House Committee on Public Works, highway
program. May 16, 1955   513

News conference, Treasury Department, bomb alert.
June 16, 1955   516

Speech, National Grange, Cleveland. November 19, 1955   521

Statement and testimony, Senate Finance Committee, highway financing. May 17, 1956   526

Statement, House Judiciary Committee, item veto. May 27,
1957   542

VI. GOVERNMENT AND BUSINESS

Statement, Treasury Department, current economy. November 1, 1954   547

Speech, New York Chapter of the Investment Bankers Association, New York. October 21, 1954   548

Statement and testimony, Senate Banking and Currency
Committee, stock market. March 15, 1955   555

Speech, American Petroleum Institute, San Francisco. November 17, 1955   572

Speech, Mercantile Trust Company, St. Louis. December 7,
1955   574

VII. THE PRESIDENT

Statement, Treasury Department, reassurance after the President's heart attack. September 26, 1955   580

Remarks and news conference, Lowry Air Force Base, Denver. October 15, 1955   580

Speech, Citizens for Eisenhower dinner, Madison Square
Garden, New York. January 21, 1956   593

Speech, Republican dinner, St. Louis. October 22, 1956   599

Letter of resignation by Secretary Humphrey to President
Eisenhower. May 28, 1957   603

Letter of President Eisenhower accepting Secretary Humphrey's resignation. May 29, 1957   604

Page

VIII. GENERAL AND PERSONAL

Remarks, Civic Dinner in the Secretary's honor, Saginaw
Michigan. November 10, 1953   609

Remarks, Thoroughbred Racing Associations of the United
States, New York. December 3, 1953   613

Remarks, welcome to first iron ore cargo through the St.
Lawrence Seaway, Cleveland. September 4, 1954   618

Remarks, Pennsylvania Society of New York award dinner,
New York. December 11, 1954   619

Preface to President Eisenhower's Cartoon Book published
in 1956   621

Remarks, dedication of the Hanna Pavilion of University
Hospitals, Cleveland. April 14, 1956   621

Remarks, Republican meeting, The Plains, Virginia. October 14, 1956   626

List of Illustrations

PHOTOGRAPHS

Opposite page

George Magoffin Humphrey, *frontispiece*

The Secretary on a trip in California   4

New Cabinet appointees   4

Secretary Humphrey at his Treasury desk, 1955   5

How to sell bonds   36

LL.D. at Harvard, 1956   36

With the President at Thomasville   37

EDITORIAL CARTOONS

Page

"Dan Reed in Charge."   66
Jim Berryman in *The Washington Star*, 1953

"Just don't let'er blow up, boys!"   100
Fitzpatrick in *The St. Louis Post-Dispatch*, 1956

"I always run into this same Byrd. . . ."   109
Jim Berryman in *The Washington Star*, 1955

"And MY price has gone up, too! . . ."   114
Jim Berryman in *The Washington Star*, 1953

"Waiting at the Church."   154
Canfield in *The Newark Evening News*, 1954

"It used to be a very bad crossing!"   170
Dowling in *The New York Herald-Tribune*, 1955

"Boy, oh boy! A pair of thrillers!"   176
Alexander in *The Philadelphia Bulletin*, 1954

"Three years late already!"   180
Orr in *The Chicago Tribune*, 1955

Page

"Finally got the genie back in the jar!"   213
Dowling in *The New York Herald-Tribune*, 1956

"If they want to add the finishing touch!"   220
Parrish in *The Chicago Tribune*, 1955

"Wait a while—I think I have it!"   226
Fischetti for the NEA Service, 1956

"Bring me the black ink!"   228
Berryman in *The Washington Star*, 1956

"A neat trick if he can make it fit!"   234
Marcus in *The New York Times*, 1954

"Speaking of Reds!"   239
Reg Manning, McNaught Syndicate, 1954

"Whose hair, George?"   253
Fitzpatrick in *The St. Louis Post-Dispatch*, 1957

"Baby sitter."   284
Seibel in *The Richmond Times-Dispatch*, 1957

"Ever think of pleading the Fifth Amendment?"   297
Berryman in *The Washington Star*, 1957

"The curl he left behind."   329
Warren in *The Cincinnati Enquirer*, June 30, 1957

"There goes my strong right arm!"   342
Russell in *The Los Angeles Times*, 1957

"Beautiful—and not a lame duck in the flight!"   592
Crockett in *The Washington Star*, 1956

"And if you were in my boots, George?"   604
Haynie in *The Greensboro News*, 1957

"It won't be the same without you, George!"   605
Poinier in *The Detroit News*, 1956

A Brief Biography

George Magoffin Humphrey—Secretary of the Treasury, 1953–57, under President Dwight Eisenhower—was born in Cheboygan, Michigan, March 8, 1890, to Watts Sherman and Caroline Magoffin Humphrey. Watts Humphrey was a distinguished and widely known Michigan citizen who in the Civil War enlisted almost as a boy in the First Michigan Cavalry, served in Custer's Brigade in the Virginia campaigns, and was wounded at the Battle of the Wilderness. On return to Michigan, where he had had three years' schooling at Michigan Agricultural College, he enrolled in University of Michigan Law School and was graduated in 1867 in one of that school's earliest classes.

Building a law practice at Cheboygan, Watts Humphrey served as county prosecuting attorney and other public posts and in 1890 went to the larger city of Saginaw to join the law firm of McKnight, Humphrey & Grant. He was president for two years of the Michigan State Bar Association.

George Humphrey's mother was descended from the Union Civil War governor of Kentucky, Beriah Magoffin.

Young George attended elementary and high schools of Saginaw; he was twice vice president and twice president of his school class, and played on a state championship high school football team. The gift of a pony when he was a small boy led to his becoming an expert horseman in youthful years, and in adult life to owning, breeding, and racing horses.

Following high school graduation in 1908, he went to the University of Michigan to study engineering, but switched to his father's field of law. On graduation—after having won his LL.B., being elected to Phi Delta Phi, and editing the Michigan Law Review—he passed the state bar examination and became a partner in his father's firm, Humphrey, Grant & Humphrey. Among his clients were the Michigan Central and Grand Trunk railroads, and he was on the verge of also entering the banking business in Saginaw when Richard F. Grant, general counsel for M. A. Hanna Company in Cleveland, invited him to become his assistant. The Hanna firm was a partnership founded in 1885 by Marcus Alonzo Hanna, later the famous senator and sponsor of President William McKinley. Late in 1917 Mr. Humphrey was made general counsel for Hanna; in 1920 he was made a partner in charge of the Hanna iron ore properties and operations, and in a short time learned the iron ore business with nation-wide perspective.

When the Hanna enterprise fell on unprofitable years in 1921–23, Mr. Humphrey designed a reorganization of its assets and operations which included incorporating the enterprise in 1922 as a company. He became vice president and shortly thereafter executive vice president and in 1924 the Hanna Company returned to profitable operation which never again faltered. In 1929, at the age of 39, he was made president and held the position until 1952 when he became chairman of its board.

During his executive leadership M. A. Hanna Company invested in, promoted and managed steel and iron, coal, ore and other kinds of enterprises leading to its identity today as one of the country's largest industrial holding companies. In the late 1920's Mr. Humphrey, with George Fink and Ernest T. Weir, put together the National Steel Corporation; and in 1945 he effected the combination, with George Love, resulting in the Consolidation Coal Company. National Steel became famous for producing earnings throughout the depression of the 1930's and Consolidation Coal has become the largest coal producing company in the world. In recent years it has also become a large stockholder in Chrysler Corporation. M. A. Hanna Company maintains large interests in iron ore, steel, and coal corporations as well as in fibre, plastics, copper, petroleum, shipping, and banks.

Benjamin F. Fairless and Mr. Humphrey (for the coal industry) in 1945 negotiated a national miners' wage contract with John L. Lewis, president of the United Mine Workers.

Mr. Humphrey served as board chairman of Consolidation Coal; chairman of the executive committee of National Steel; president of the Iron Ore Company of Canada (organized by the Hanna interests at Mr. Humphrey's initiative to tap the vast rich iron ore of Quebec and Labrador and provide important new resources for the steel industry); chairman of the executive committee of Industrial Rayon Corporation; and a director of all these and of Phelps, Dodge Corporation, National City Bank of Cleveland, and Canada & Dominion Sugar Company. He resigned from all these positions for his term of office and service in Washington, at the end of which he returned to M. A. Hanna Company as its honorary chairman and to National Steel as chairman of its board.

He was chairman of the Business Advisory Council of the United States Department of Commerce and a trustee of the Committee on Economic Development formed to study the future of the American economy after World War II. He was chairman of the Special Committee of the United States Economic Co-operation Administration charged with revision of reparations and the dismantling of captive war plants in Germany. It was the task of his committee to separate the necessary peace-time functions of West German enterprises from their war-making potential, and during this service he became acquainted with General Lucius Clay, American high commissioner for Germany. General Clay is credited with having nominated Mr. Humphrey to President-elect Eisenhower for Secretary of the Treasury.

The proffer of this cabinet portfolio came to Mr. Humphrey as an intense surprise. He had had no prominent role in the Eisenhower campaigns and had just moved to the Hanna chairmanship with a view to a less strenuous life. At the same moment, the President-elect invited Charles E. Wilson, president of General Motors, and an old friend of Mr. Humphrey, to be Secretary of Defense; and Mr. Humphrey's first tidings of impending selection came from Mr. Wilson (whom the President had likewise surprised). Mr. Humphrey's first visit to talk with General Eisenhower in New York was surrounded with anonymity because the press hardly knew of his identity. Mr. Humphrey took two days to think about the offer and to talk further with Mr. Wilson. On November 20, 1952, the President-elect announced Mr. Humphrey's acceptance of the Treasury secretaryship.

* * *

The high spots of Secretary Humphrey's service might be inscribed as follows:

An immediate reduction, under his guidance, of governmental expense; cutting of the impending first fiscal year deficit to half its expectancy; a tax reduction in the second year for all the people of the country; at the end of the second fiscal year a cash balance in the Treasury and a further reduction in the book deficit; then two actual balances of the budget for the third and fourth years.

In these four years, the nearly 50-per cent drop in the value of the dollar between 1930 and 1950 was virtually halted; the variation in its value in these four years was less than one cent.

Unexpected developments compelled the Secretary to return to private life in 1957 and he resigned on May 30—after a considerably longer service than he had contemplated when he took the post. He departed expressing less than complete satisfaction with achievement of his aims and some concern over the mounting of government expenditure which he had helped to check.

Mr. Humphrey was chairman of the Joint Committee for the Advancement of Medical Education and Research of Western Reserve University School of Medicine and Affiliated Hospitals. He was a member of the Visiting Committee of Harvard University Graduate School of Business Administration; chairman of Rainbow Hospital (Cleveland) finance committee; a director of the Ford Foundation Fund for Adult Education; and a life member of the Massachusetts Institute of Technology Advisory Council, School of Industrial Management.

In 1947 he was awarded the Charles F. Rand Medal by the American Institute of Mining and Metallurgical Engineers for distinguished achievement in mining administration. In 1948 Saginaw High School, with affectionate words for him as boy and man, gave him its Distinguished Alumni award. Honorary degrees bestowed on him include the following:

Doctor of Laws—Western Reserve University, 1950; University of Michigan, 1953; John Carroll University, 1953; Ohio Wesleyan University, 1953; University of Rochester, 1953; Brown University, 1954; Lehigh University, 1954; University of Pittsburgh, 1954; West Virginia University, 1955; Yale University, 1955; Williams College, 1955; University of Notre Dame, 1956; Harvard University, 1956.

Doctor of Engineering—Case Institute of Technology, 1951. (Case in 1955 also awarded him its Diamond Jubilee Medal.)

Among other honors were the Bank of France Award, 1957; Alexander Hamilton Award by the United States Treasury, 1957; Benedict Crowell Medal of Cleveland Post of the American Ordnance Association, 1955; Brotherhood Award of the National Conference of Christians and Jews, 1958; Cleveland Chamber of Commerce Distinguished Service Award, 1953; Research Institute of America Medal, 1958; Governor Handley Award, 1958.

Mr. Humphrey is an advisory committee member of the George C. Marshall Research Foundation of Lexington, Virginia, and was instrumental in the establishment of the Dwight David Eisenhower Library of Abilene, Kansas, and the John Foster Dulles Library of Princeton, New Jersey.

Mr. Humphrey was married in 1913 to Miss Pamela Stark at Saginaw; they had been friends since elementary school days. Their children are Mrs. Royal Firman, Jr.; Gilbert Watts Humphrey, present chairman of M. A. Hanna Company; and Mrs. John G. Butler.

THE SECRETARY'S

BACKGROUND

The Secretary introduces himself

*Statement and testimony by Secretary-Designate
Humphrey before the Senate Finance Committee,
Washington, sitting to consider confirmation
of the President's Cabinet appointments. Senator
Eugene D. Millikin of Colorado, chairman.*

January 19, 1953

MR. HUMPHREY. In 1890 I was born at Cheboygan, Michigan. I went
to the public schools and to high school in Saginaw.

From 1908 to 1912 I was an undergraduate in the Law School at the
University of Michigan. I obtained a law degree in 1912. I was a member
of Psi Upsilon fraternity, Phi Delta Phi law fraternity, *Michigan Law
Review,* and the Order of the Coif. I was admitted to the Michigan
bar in 1912.

From 1912 to 1917 I practiced law at Saginaw with the firm of
Humphrey, Grant, & Humphrey.

In 1913 I was married to Miss Pamela Stark, of Saginaw.

In 1917 I joined M. A. Hanna & Company at Cleveland as general
counsel. From 1920 to 1922 I was a partner in the partnership of M. A.
Hanna & Company.

From 1922 to 1925, when the business was incorporated, I became
vice president of the M. A. Hanna Company. From 1926 to 1929 I
served as executive vice president of the M. A. Hanna Company and
from 1929 until 1952 was the president of the company. In 1952 I
became chairman of the board.

As of the 18th of November last, I held these positions:

Chairman of the board, the M. A. Hanna Company

Chairman of the board, Pittsburgh Consolidation Coal Company

Chairman of the executive committee, National Steel Corporation
Chairman of the executive committee, Industrial Rayon Corporation
President, Iron Ore Company of Canada
Director of the M. A. Hanna Company, National Steel Corporation,
    Pittsburgh Consolidation Coal Company, Industrial Rayon Corpo-
    ration, Phelps Dodge Corporation, National City Bank of Cleve-
    land, Canada and Dominion Sugar Company, Iron Ore Company
    of Canada.

I was a member and former chairman of the business advisory council
of the United States Department of Commerce and a trustee of the
Committee for Economic Development.

I was chairman of the industrial advisory committee of Economic
Cooperation Administration for Revision of Reparations and Dismantling of Plants in Germany.

I was also a member of the Academy of Political Science, Tax Foundation, American Iron and Steel Institute, American Institute of Mining
and Metallurgical Engineers, Newcomen Society of England, National
Industrial Information Committee, United States Council of the International Chamber of Commerce.

I have resigned from all of those offices now. I have none of them
and none of those connections. . . .

When General Eisenhower asked me to become Secretary of the
Treasury in his Cabinet, I reviewed my situation, in consultation with
counsel, to determine the applicable legal and other requirements. As
the result, I have resigned all my offices and directorships in the businesses with which I have been connected. I am on leave of absence
without pay as an employee of Industrial Rayon Corporation, which
permits me to retain certain group insurance and also as an employee
of the M. A. Hanna Company, which continues my rights under its
provision for retirement of employees. While I am in the Treasury, I
will not receive any salary or bonus of any kind from any source other
than from the United States Government.

My securities, which I expect to retain, consist now, and have always
consisted, almost entirely of common stocks of four companies with
whose management I was associated. These are the M. A. Hanna Company, Hanna Coal & Ore Corporation, National Steel Corporation, and
Pittsburgh Consolidation Coal Company. I have accumulated these
interests over the period of my connection with these companies, which,

The Secretary on a trip in California. The news photographer who snapped this picture had chatted for a half hour with the Secretary at the airport without realizing his identity—then made an extra effort with his camera to "catch up."

New Cabinet appointees. The Secretaries-designate with President-elect Eisenhower on the U.S.S. Olympia in late 1952; left to right, Secretary of Interior Douglas McKay; Attorney-General Herbert Brownell; Secretary of Defense Charles E. Wilson; the President; Secretary of State John Foster Dulles; Secretary Humphrey.

Secretary Humphrey at his Treasury desk, 1955.
The posture is characteristic of his news conferences.

in the case of M. A. Hanna Company, goes back almost 35 years. The M. A. Hanna Company in turn owns substantial stock interests in National Steel Corporation, Pittsburgh Consolidation Coal Company, Industrial Rayon Corporation, Standard Oil Company of New Jersey, Phelps Dodge Corporation, Seaboard Oil Company, Iron Ore Company of Canada, Durez Plastics & Chemicals, Incorporated, Hanna Coal & Ore Corporation, and smaller interests in a few other companies.

I am advised by counsel that there is no legal reason why I should not continue to hold the securities which I now own.

I shall, of course, advise my immediate assistants to see to it that I have no participation in the decision of any case or transaction involving any of the companies in which, through stock ownership, I am directly or indirectly interested.

I think that sets forth my situation as briefly and as pointedly as I am able to do it.

CHAIRMAN MILLIKIN. Mr. Humphrey, you have stated that before you accepted the invitation to become Secretary of the Treasury that you and your lawyers studied the applicable laws of the job, and therefore I assume you are familiar with that provision of the law which is Section 243 in 5 United States Code reading as follows:

No person appointed to the Office of Secretary of the Treasury, or Treasurer, shall directly or indirectly be concerned or interested in carrying on the business of trade or commerce, or be owner in whole or in part of any sea vessel, or purchase by himself, or another in trust for him, any public land or other public property, or be concerned in the purchase or disposal of any public securities of any State, or the United States, or take or apply to his own use any emolument for gain for negotiating or transacting any business in the Treasury Department, other than what shall be allowed by law.

Let me ask you, are you personally interested in the ownership of any sea vessel?

MR. HUMPHREY. I am glad to explain this. My understanding is that there is a ruling that the ownership of stock in a corporation is not directly or indirectly engaging in business. The M. A. Hanna Company owns stock in the Iron Ore Company of Canada, which in turn owns a small stock interest in a steamship company which is building two ocean-going ships in England at the present time. Those ships are three times removed from me through stock ownership.

THE CHAIRMAN. Could you tell us what percentage is your stock ownership in any of these companies? Give us your greatest stock ownership in any of the companies that you have mentioned.

MR. HUMPHREY. It is less than 5 per cent and in most cases substantially less.

THE CHAIRMAN. So you have no control, actual or practical, over the companies that you have mentioned?

MR. HUMPHREY. That is correct.

THE CHAIRMAN. The law says you shall not directly or indirectly be concerned or interested in carrying on the business of trade or commerce. You have stated that rulings have said that a stock ownership of the type you have mentioned does not come in conflict with that provision. While you are Secretary of the Treasury will you engage in any business or trade or commerce personally, directly or indirectly?

MR. HUMPHREY. I will engage in no business whatever personally or indirectly.

THE CHAIRMAN. The meaning of that law I think is well summarized at the end of what I have read. There is a prohibition against taking or applying to your own use any emolument or gain for negotiating or transacting any business in the Treasury Department other than what shall be allowed by law. Do you or do you not expect to take or apply to your own use any emolument or gain for negotiating or transacting any business in the Treasury Department other than what shall be allowed by law?

MR. HUMPHREY. I will have no income of any kind from any company other than is permitted by law, which I understand includes dividends. That is all.

THE CHAIRMAN. Will you attempt while you are Secretary of the Treasury to prosecute or to help forward or to continue or to carry on any of the businesses with which you have been identified?

MR. HUMPHREY. I will not. I am completely out.

THE CHAIRMAN. Do you have any ownership in public lands affecting public lands?

MR. HUMPHREY. I have not.

THE CHAIRMAN. Do you have any interest in brokerage firms or dealers in public securities?

MR. HUMPHREY. I have none.

THE CHAIRMAN. Will you be good enough to advise us your authority for the opinion that having a stock interest of the type that you have described is not in violation of the prohibitions of this law?

Mr. HUMPHREY. I have the opinion of our counsel, Jones, Day, Cockley, and Reavis, who have given a great amount of consideration which goes into great detail which I will be glad to file with the committee if the committee desires to have it.

SENATOR EDWARD MARTIN (Pennsylvania). Where is that firm located?

Mr. HUMPHREY. In Cleveland, Ohio. They are our regular counsel, Senator Martin.

THE CHAIRMAN. I assume you are familiar with the fact that Secretary Mellon was challenged on the ground of stock ownership, that the then Attorney General gave an opinion that his stock ownership did not disqualify him for the office of Secretary of the Treasury, and that in connection with that opinion cases were cited including an opinion of the United States Supreme Court from which it might be concluded that a stock ownership particularly of the magnitude that you have does not run against any of the prohibitions of the statute.

Mr. HUMPHREY. Our counsel are familiar with that and mentioned it in their opinion, I believe, and it is partly on that and partly on their own study of the law that they have given an opinion.

THE CHAIRMAN. I think you have stated it with sufficient clarity but I want to make it clear again, you do not intend to influence any of these companies in any way in the conduct of their business while you are Secretary of the Treasury?

Mr. HUMPHREY. I will have no connection with the management of these businesses.

THE CHAIRMAN. I do not recall any instance where the Secretary of the Treasury would have any direct contractual relations with any of those companies. Do you know of any case of that kind that might come up?

Mr. HUMPHREY. I do not know of any but, of course, you never know. That is the reason why I will give to my immediate juniors the authority on the instructions to handle any such matters, whatever they may be.

THE CHAIRMAN. Tax matters, for example, will probably begin and end in the office of the Commissioner of Internal Revenue, will they not?

MR. HUMPHREY. They will end with my juniors, wherever they may be.

THE CHAIRMAN. If any tax question came up that should penetrate up to your level, you would disassociate yourself from the decision?

MR. HUMPHREY. That is correct. It will not be up to my level. It will be stopped before it gets there.

THE CHAIRMAN. I suggest that most tax questions will probably go no further than the Commissioner of Internal Revenue and his staff.

MR. HUMPHREY. I think that is correct.

I might add, Senator, that I am very pleased and very proud of the men who have consented to join me in the operation of the Treasury Department. And they are very competent people to handle whatever matters arise.

THE CHAIRMAN. Will you state their names?

MR. HUMPHREY. Mr. Marion Folsom is the Under Secretary, Mr. Randolph Burgess is the Special Assistant, Mr. Chapman Rose is the Assistant Secretary, Mr. Tuttle will be our General Counsel, Mr. Andrews will be the Commissioner of Internal Revenue. Mr. Overby will be in charge of international finance. Mr. Parsons is the Administrative Assistant.

THE CHAIRMAN. This committee is well acquainted with Mr. Folsom and I think we probably know all of those people.

MR. HUMPHREY. I am very proud, indeed, of that organization.

SENATOR HARRY F. BYRD (Virginia). The Commissioner of Internal Revenue is appointed by the President; is he not?

MR. HUMPHREY. What I mentioned were all Presidential appointments made on the recommendation of the Secretary-designate.

SENATOR BYRD. I would like to ask a question in regard to Law 434 which was briefly referred to by the chairman:

"Interested persons acting as Government agents:

"Whoever being an officer, agent, or member or directly or indirectly interested in the pecuniary profits or contracts of a corporation, joint-stock company or association, or any firm or partnership, or of a business entity, is employed or acts as an officer or agent of the United States for the transaction of business with such business entity, shall be fined not more than $2,000 or imprisoned not more than two years or both."

Did your attorneys who investigated the matter consider this law too?

Mr. HUMPHREY. Yes, that is quoted in their opinion.

SENATOR BYRD. As I understand it, if you owned stock in a company that would give you a pecuniary interest then you are prohibited from making a contract with that company. Does the Secretary of the Treasury make any contracts or have reason to make any contracts with a business corporation, that you know of?

Mr. HUMPHREY. So far as I know, from the point of view of purchasing or anything of that kind, I think not. Contracts, of course, can be broadly interpreted, but contracts for purchases and that sort of thing the Treasury has nothing to do with.

THE CHAIRMAN. You do not contemplate—I think I asked you the same question before—engaging in any procurement business or anything of that kind as Secretary of the Treasury with any of the companies that you have been associated with?

Mr. HUMPHREY. I myself will not have any dealings of any kind with any of the companies that I have been formerly associated with. Any dealings of any kind that the Treasury has with companies that I have formerly been associated with, my aides will be advised of, and I will personally have nothing to do with any of it, whether it is a contract or a tax settlement or any association or any connection whatever.

THE CHAIRMAN. I am trying to make the point, Mr. Humphrey, that the Secretary of the Treasury does not make procurement contracts—at least I do not know of any procurement contracts that he makes—and that he does not engage in business with anybody.

In reviewing the situation of the Secretary of the Treasury, I cannot recall any contractual relationships of any importance that the Secretary of the Treasury engages in.

Mr. HUMPHREY. I cannot either, Senator. I do not know of any.

SENATOR BYRD. I would like to ask further as to the independence of the Commissioner of Internal Revenue. He is appointed, of course, by the President and is confirmed by the Senate. To what extent can you overrule or control his actions in relation to tax rebates and things like that?

Mr. HUMPHREY. I am afraid I cannot tell you that in detail, Senator Byrd. Of course, by and large he handles his own department and handles it entirely independently. Whether or not there are some provisions where an appeal might be taken or something of that kind, I am not prepared to state at this time.

SENATOR BYRD. Can an appeal, so far as you know, be taken by a taxpayer?

MR. HUMPHREY. If any such thing did occur and an appeal was taken in any way, it would come before one of my assistants before it came to me and it would stop with the assistant.

SENATOR BYRD. I have been under the impression that the Commissioner of Internal Revenue was more independent as a subordinate officer than other agency heads.

MR. HUMPHREY. He is more independent than in an ordinary case.

SENATOR BYRD. If it should come before you, it would only come before the Treasury Department as an appeal from the taxpayer or some question like that?

MR. HUMPHREY. That is correct.

SENATOR BYRD. In other words, it does not come before the Treasury Department unless there is some special reason for it?

MR. HUMPHREY. Some special occasion.

THE CHAIRMAN. I doubt whether an opinion that might be given at your level would be called a transaction of business any more than a judicial decision or a quasi-judicial decision is called a transaction of business. I think there is a distinction there between what might come up to your level and what might be a transaction of business which is contemplated by the statute.

SENATOR EDWIN C. JOHNSON (Colorado). Mr. Humphrey, you have stated that should any occasion arise where a decision had to be made as between some of these companies with which you had a former connection and the Treasury, that you would delegate that function to your aides. These aides are, of course, beholden to you and work for you and naturally would be prejudiced. Do you not think that if a case of that kind should come, some outside person not connected with your department at all, selected by the President, should pass judgment?

MR. HUMPHREY. Senator Johnson, if the law were changed to provide for some such thing as that it would, of course, be a very satisfactory arrangement so far as I am concerned.

As it stands now, my own feeling, and speaking of the aides that I have, is that there would be no reason for it. I am expressing no opinion about the desirability or nondesirability of some new law. At the present time I just do not see how that could be accomplished because action would have to be taken by authorized people.

SENATOR JOHNSON. Of course, I think the action of one of the persons serving under you would be the same as if you acted yourself.

MR. HUMPHREY. I do not feel that way myself.

SENATOR JOHNSON. I do not see that there would be any difference.

MR. HUMPHREY. I do not feel that way, myself, in talking about this particular situation. These men are all men of distinction and independent action who have established for themselves independent reputations and have very high standings in their respective fields.

Frankly, if it had any effect on them whatever, it would be to lean over backward, in my opinion.

SENATOR JOHNSON. That may very well be and probably you are correct. However, in our Government we have to be very careful about maintaining and holding the confidence of the people. I do not think the people, generally speaking, would have confidence in a decision made by someone under you where you did not feel competent to make the decision yourself.

MR. HUMPHREY. Your judgment would be better than mine. These gentlemen have all come under great personal sacrifices. None of them are there for any purpose except to try to do a job. I cannot believe that any of them are sufficiently interested in the job except for the sake of doing a good job that they would be so influenced whatsoever.

SENATOR JOHNSON. We understand that, of course. I do not know that the people generally would understand it or appreciate that.

MR. HUMPHREY. That might be.

THE CHAIRMAN. Do you anticipate any questions of that kind coming up to you?

MR. HUMPHREY. I do not anticipate anything. I do not anticipate the slightest difficulty.

SENATOR ROBERT S. KERR (Oklahoma). I came in a little late, Mr. Humphrey. Did you furnish the committee with a list of your holdings in the various companies with which you have been associated?

MR. HUMPHREY. I did not, but I will be glad to do so if you would care to have me. I will file it with you.

THE CHAIRMAN. He didn't furnish us a list, but he was asked the question of the largest percentage of stock that he holds in any company in which he is interested. I think he said some 5 per cent.

He said also in his testimony that he would not attempt because of his stock ownership or relationships with those businesses in the past to influence their policy or attempt to direct them in any way whatsoever.

MR. HUMPHREY. That is my direct holdings. There are some family holdings in addition to that, but that is my direct holdings.

THE CHAIRMAN. If you added your family holdings?

MR. HUMPHREY. It would be less than ten.

SENATOR KERR. Did I understand you to say you would be glad to furnish the committee such a list?

MR. HUMPHREY. I will.

SENATOR KERR. The statute referred to by Senator Byrd, as I understand it, had reference to the transaction of business with such a business entity. I take it that you would understand that to be a broader scope than what might be implied in language referring only to procurement?

MR. HUMPHREY. I do not know just what you mean, Senator.

SENATOR KERR. The general term "transaction of business" is a broader term than the term "procurement," do you not think?

MR. HUMPHREY. I think it is.

SENATOR KERR. Do any of the companies with which you are associated have any matters pending or imminent in the way of tax settlements or controversies with the Government?

MR. HUMPHREY. I do not know of any controversies, but of course they all file tax returns and tax returns are always subject to examination and there are always some minor questions.

SENATOR KERR. There are sometimes some major questions, from my own experience.

MR. HUMPHREY. So far as I know, there are none of major importance pending at this time.

SENATOR KERR. I was interested in your remarks that you would have decisions which the law places responsibility for upon the Secretary of the Treasury made by someone under you. Let me say that I am glad you are coming down here and I am just as interested in your eligibility for this position as you are.

But I have some difficulty in my own mind visualizing a procedure whereby a decision could be made for which, under the law, you are responsible by anybody else in such a way as to relieve you of the responsibility placed upon you under the law.

MR. HUMPHREY. Well, Senator, I am coming down here for just one reason. I had no idea, as you well know, of taking this job. It was suggested to me and I spent three or four days thinking of all the reasons why I should not do it. I wanted to refuse. My wife and I talked it over and we finally concluded that we really had no decision to make, that when we were asked to try to assist in this program it was a duty and a responsibility that we could not refuse.

I do not want to come here unless everyone is satisfied and happy about it and the feeling is not exactly not only in accordance with the letter of the law but in accordance with the spirit of it and with the confidence of the people. I do not want to do it under any other circumstances.

SENATOR KERR. I want to say to you that I am concerned about the same considerations that you have expressed there and am exploring it only in order that I may have a clearer understanding of it myself and also that such a showing may be made as will result in what you have just described as being your own objective.

MR. HUMPHREY. And I want that as much as you do.

SENATOR KERR. But I come back to the question which, frankly, in my own mind, I have not resolved, and that is how a man charged by the law with certain responsibilities can assign them to others and meet the responsibility fixed by the law.

MR. HUMPHREY. I do not think that I assign them, necessarily. The Under Secretary, by law, is authorized to act for the Secretary.

SENATOR KERR. For the Secretary?

MR. HUMPHREY. In almost all instances where the Secretary is unavailable for the purpose.

SENATOR KERR. He signs the Secretary's name and when the Secretary permits him to act does it not then become the act of the Secretary? That is the question that is in my mind.

MR. HUMPHREY. Well, is that not a legal distinction rather than a factual one?

SENATOR KERR. I would say it is the legal matters with which we are dealing.

MR. HUMPHREY. That is correct. Well, not entirely. What you are trying to get at as I see it and what I am trying to get at as well as you, is what is the right thing here, with respect to the influence that might be had on the activities of a man. While the action of the Under Secretary might be legally the act of the Secretary, the considerations which lead to it are the Under Secretary's situation rather than the Secretary's.

It seems to me that unless you are to take the position that anybody who owns anything cannot fulfill this job that you are in a position where you have to accept some such reasoning as that.

For instance, suppose I sold everything that I had. I have thought of that, of course. It would be a tremendous hardship and whether it could be done or not is a problem, but suppose you did. How would you account for what you received for it? Would you leave it in cash in the bank? If so, would you then be under the compulsion of perhaps favoring in some way that bank because, of course, the Secretary deals with that bank in one way or another. Would you put it in Government bonds? If so, there is nothing that the Secretary of the Treasury could so influence by his conduct as Government bonds.

I can, as Secretary of the Treasury, have more influence on the price of Government bonds and the value of them, a whole lot, than I can on the value of M. A. Hanna common stock when I am no longer an officer, representative, or connected with the firm.

Now you get yourselves into a situation where, if you do not be practical about this thing that you can so draw the laws that you just cannot have a Secretary of the Treasury unless he is a man who has nothing.

SENATOR BYRD. Of course, the purchase of Government bonds is specifically prohibited.

MR. HUMPHREY. I thought it was the dealing in Government bonds that was prohibited.

THE CHAIRMAN. These concern the purchase or disposal of any securities of the United States.

MR. HUMPHREY. Probably if I sold out everything I had before I bought the bonds and then sat and held them I might technically comply, but there is a problem.

SENATOR BYRD. You could not purchase any while you were Secretary of the Treasury.

MR. HUMPHREY. Or sell them; that is correct.

I think this is a subject that has two sides to it. Just selling one set of securities and buying another does not answer the question at all. I may jump from the frying pan into the fire.

SENATOR KERR. I would hope that you were faced with neither of those unfortunate alternatives.

MR. HUMPHREY. I would too.

SENATOR KERR. What I was trying to determine from that was whether you could be in any other status.

MR. HUMPHREY. Well, that is what I hoped.

SENATOR RUSSELL B. LONG (Louisiana). Mr. Humphrey, all of us are faced with the problem you are discussing in one aspect or another. We are in difficult positions as Senators since the only people who can raise our salaries are ourselves. I am chairman of a subcommittee who raised the salary of everybody except United States Senators and Congressmen. Almost anything you do in a position that you have may have some bearing upon you as an individual or upon your family or upon the public generally. That is particularly the case with regard to our tax problems. In your capacity you would be required to make recommendations as to possible tax reductions in the event that that were possible, would you not?

MR. HUMPHREY. I would.

SENATOR LONG. What is your view on that? Do you believe that we should undertake to reduce taxes while we are still running with a Government deficit?

MR. HUMPHREY. Senator, I have had the feeling that it was inappropriate and perhaps a little presumptious on my part to start out saying what I thought we were going to do before I was in a position to do something about it and really know more about it than I do today so it is a little difficult for me and I think probably not quite right for me to talk about where we are going and what we are going to propose.

I will say this, however, that I think our first job should be to attempt to balance the budget.

SENATOR LONG. I take it you are not in favor of deficit financing but you are in favor of tax reduction if it is possible?

MR. HUMPHREY. I certainly favor a tax reduction at the earliest practical, possible time. I think our present tax system is more burden than this country can bear over any extended period.

SENATOR LONG. Do you have a view on the excess profits tax?

MR. HUMPHREY. If you don't mind I think it is proper for me to—don't you think we better wait for those discussions until I—when, if and as I am confirmed? I am in the unfortunate position at the moment of being neither an American citizen who can talk as he pleases, or an officer of the Government who can talk with authority. I am just between hay and grass.

SENATOR LONG. I am frank to say that whether you are for or against the excess profits tax I don't believe it should affect the judgment of this committee but I do feel we are entitled to know your views on that subject if you have a view.

MR. HUMPHREY. I will put it this way: I think the excess profits tax in principle is a bad law. I think it induced all sorts of activities that are not to the best interests of the country. I think in balancing out how you apportion the taxes that are to be raised, it is a problem that requires the most serious consideration and I think one of the very first jobs that the Treasury has upon it is a study of the entire tax situation, not necessarily with just reduction, which very frankly I fear is not in the immediate future—I hope but I fear is not in the immediate future. I think that in balancing that out we ought to try if possible to find some better means than the excess profits tax as it now exists.

SENATOR LONG. I believe it is the prevailing view of the majority of Congress—I know it is my view and of course I reserve the right to change it if I can be persuaded otherwise—I think any fair-minded man should—that the excess profits tax is not a proper peacetime tax; that it is not consistent with our form of government in peacetime.

Do you generally subscribe to that point of view?

MR. HUMPHREY. I hope we can find a method of eliminating the excess profits tax and still raise the funds that are required.

SENATOR KERR. You know the present excess profits tax expires in a few months, at June 30.

MR. HUMPHREY. I know that.

SENATOR KERR. And the indication is that there will be no legislation reimposing it.

MR. HUMPHREY. Yes.

SENATOR LONG. I take it you are in favor of a general reduction in income tax when possible?

MR. HUMPHREY. As soon as the expenses can be adjusted to permit it.

SENATOR LONG. You were president of M. A. Hanna Company prior to your appointment?

MR. HUMPHREY. I was chairman in the last few months but I have been president for 25 years.

SENATOR LONG. Then you were no longer president immediately prior to the time you were appointed?

MR. HUMPHREY. I was chairman of the board at that time.

SENATOR LONG. Does that position carry a salary?

MR. HUMPHREY. Yes, indeed.

SENATOR LONG. Would you object to telling us what the salary was in that position?

MR. HUMPHREY. I received salaries from several directions. I suppose what you are interested in is my total salary and bonuses that have been canceled or that I no longer receive.

SENATOR LONG. Yes.

MR. HUMPHREY. They exceeded $300,000 a year.

SENATOR LONG. How much does this position you have here pay, $22,500; I believe?

MR. HUMPHREY. I believe so.

SENATOR LONG. We felt it should have been more at the time we raised it. I think you are entitled to more and I think it should be raised again.

THE CHAIRMAN. Do you have any bonus arrangement which will require you to do anything while you are Secretary of the Treasury in behalf of any of your companies?

MR. HUMPHREY. I have no bonus. My bonus stopped with December 31, 1952. I have no bonus, I have nothing. It is all cut off.

SENATOR LONG. Mr. Humphrey, I have known one or two very capable businessmen who were persuaded to serve with the Government who came here having made a decision that they could stand the financial sacrifice for a limited period of time. Is that your feeling?

MR. HUMPHREY. That is my feeling.

SENATOR LONG. If you would rather not say why I will not press you; but is it your intention to serve out the term of the incoming President?

MR. HUMPHREY. That will have to depend upon circumstances, Senator. I have no commitment to do that.

SENATOR LONG. In other words, you reserve the right to go back to private industry?

Mr. Humphrey. That is correct.

Senator Long. You perhaps are contemplating serving out the four years as you take the position.

Mr. Humphrey. That will entirely depend upon circumstances.

Senator Long. As president and chairman of the board of M. A. Hanna Company, did you take any interest in the proposal for the construction of the St. Lawrence Seaway?

Mr. Humphrey. Yes, sir. I appeared before committees of Congress and I was very active in attempting to persuade the Congress to approve action on the St. Lawrence Seaway.

Senator Long. Do you believe that interests of that company would be greatly advanced by the construction of the seaway?

Mr. Humphrey. I believe the interests of the entire country would be advanced by it.

Senator Long. Do you believe the interests of that company would be more advanced than perhaps the average company dealing in the steel industry?

Mr. Humphrey. That company is of course interested. There are a number of other companies equally interested and I think it is to the great advantage of the entire country that the raw materials which are required for the steel industry, which is the base of our American economy, be obtained for existing plants in the steel industry at as low a cost as possible. I think that is just axiomatic for the benefit of the entire country among industries who are based on steel.

Senator Long. Will you give us some idea of the extent of the Hanna Company's holdings in Labrador ore?

Mr. Humphrey. Yes. It owns about—well, it is just a little complicated—the underlying leases are owned by some Canadian companies. The company that is developing a portion of the ore, which is that part which is now under development and for which the railroad is being built is the Iron Ore Company of Canada. That is the present active company. In the future there will be some others who will also develop production up there, but at the moment it is the Iron Ore Company of Canada, and the Hanna Company in one way or another has approximately a quarter interest—I think it is 27 per cent interest in the Iron Ore Company of Canada.

Senator Long. Are there other American companies holding an interest in that also?

Mr. Humphrey. Both American and Canadian.

SENATOR LONG. Will you give us an idea of what the other companies are who hold such interest?

MR. HUMPHREY. Republic Steel, National Steel, Youngstown Sheet & Tube, Armco Steel, and Wheeling Steel, and the Canadian companies are Conger Consolidated Gold Mines, the Labrador Mining & Exploration Company, and the Quebec-North Shore Exploration Company.

SENATOR LONG. Will you give us some idea as to what percentage of the steel industry is represented by the American companies who are interested in that Labrador ore?

MR. HUMPHREY. I cannot do it accurately. I think I could add it up in my head. I would say roughly those are five of the larger independent steel companies and I would say that roughly it is between 15 and 20 per cent.

SENATOR LONG. It represents between 15 and 20 per cent of American steel production.

MR. HUMPHREY. Of total steel production. I would say 15 to 25 per cent because I just haven't added it up but it is in that range.

SENATOR LONG. The largest steel companies in the Nation then are not concerned?

MR. HUMPHREY. The United States Steel Corporation, which is the largest, is not concerned. Bethlehem is not a stockholder in the business but purchases a substantial tonnage of ore.

SENATOR LONG. And most of these steel mills are located in the Great Lakes area, I take it?

MR. HUMPHREY. And if you include Bethlehem in that it would raise it to perhaps 30.

SENATOR LONG. Does Bethlehem own an interest in this?

MR. HUMPHREY. No, but it purchases a substantial tonnage. It controls 1.5 million tons a year for 25 years.

SENATOR LONG. Most of the steel companies in this development then are in the Great Lakes area?

MR. HUMPHREY. That is correct, they are in the Middle West.

SENATOR LONG. And that today would advocate the construction of a seaway?

MR. HUMPHREY. That is correct.

SENATOR LONG. Is it necessary that such a seaway be constructed to get ore from the Labrador area to the steel companies?

MR. HUMPHREY. No, the ore will move whether there is a seaway or whether there isn't . . . You can't move as much in volume and it will cost more, probably.

SENATOR LONG. What is the extent to which the present canal system could be used?

MR. HUMPHREY. To a very limited extent. It only takes boats that are about 2,600 to 2,700 tons. They are small boats, and the facilities are not modern. The aids to navigation are not modern and it can be used—we estimate that you can move in small boats somewhere from 1.5 to 3 million tons a year through the existing facilities.

SENATOR LONG. How much ore do you estimate the maximum movement of Labrador ore might be if we had facilities that would permit unlimited use?

You could not use it for five months in any event, could you?

MR. HUMPHREY. That is right. The Labrador operation will be similar to our lake operation. Our best estimates are that it will be less than a month difference. We operate on the Great Lakes between seven and eight months and we expect to operate here between six and seven.

SENATOR LONG. How much do you estimate the additional movement of ore might be? That would have to depend upon your capacity to use such ore as that, or the capacity of mills who own it in the Great Lakes area and mills who might not own it but might purchase it?

How much could your capacity be expanded there in the movement of ore?

MR. HUMPHREY. Our present program is for 10 million tons a year. I think it is all laid out to double and I think it can be trebled rather easily.

SENATOR LONG. Now, the ore produced in Labrador could be brought to port mills such as the Bethlehem mill at Sparrow's Port, of course, by ordinary ocean shipping, could it not?

MR. HUMPHREY. That is correct.

SENATOR LONG. But most of the companies interested in that ore do not have any mills against the sea—that is in New England or Pennsylvania or Maryland.

MR. HUMPHREY. The way the movement is at the present time, it will move down the eastern seaboard and then ex-ocean by rail to Pittsburgh or points in the Middle West, or it will go up in small boats through the canal or it may move all rail from Montreal.

SENATOR LONG. Now here is a question that concerns me. Of course, frankly, I have always reserved judgment on the seaway. I voted to recommit it but I may be persuaded some day. Perhaps an expert like yourself might persuade me sometime.

MR. HUMPHREY. You are going to get me in a position where I am going to be in trouble with all these other gentlemen because I am working for the company, I think, but I am also working for the United States, so I will be working for them.

SENATOR LONG. You would be in this difficult position as a member of the President's Cabinet. There is a major project that if it is undertaken, would be the major public works project of the present administration. You are an enthusiast for the project, one because you believe in it in the national interest, and you would also be subject to being accused of being interested as a stockholder in M. A. Hanna Company.

Do you feel you could express yourself or give your judgment on that to the President's Cabinet in a discussion of that type thing, or do you feel that your position and your interests require you to remain almost completely mum on the subject?

THE CHAIRMAN. Senator Long, may I interject on that point? Senator Frear asked me to ask a question which I think points up the whole subject. You are aware that this is a highly controversial subject?

MR. HUMPHREY. I am.

THE CHAIRMAN. It says: "Do you intend to use the powers of your new office to advance or encourage legislation leading to the participation of the United States in the construction of the St. Lawrence Seaway?"

MR. HUMPHREY. Well, Senator, I think I can answer the whole thing in one word, and I think it just stands to reason. If I were trying to advance my own interests or the interests of any of these companies, I don't believe I would be here at all and I don't believe that anybody would think that I would be here at all.

It is perfectly obvious, if I were trying to advance my own interests or the interests of the companies as against anyone else, I would stay with them. We have done pretty well as we were doing it.

I am here for just one purpose and that is to try to do a job for our country.

THE CHAIRMAN. Coming back to the specific question, do you intend to use the powers of your new office to advance or encourage legislation leading to the participation of the United States in the construction of the St. Lawrence Seaway?

MR. HUMPHREY. I do not.

SENATOR MARTIN. Senator Frear brought up this question. I do not suppose there is anybody in the Congress of the United States who has opposed, for a longer period of years than I have, the construction of the St. Lawrence Seaway. I want to make this observation.

Knowing Mr. Humphrey by reputation, I do not think that he will let his past interests interfere with his judgment in making recommendations to the Eisenhower administration as it relates to the St. Lawrence Seaway. It does not seem that that is a matter of interest and I am one of the folks very much opposed to the construction of the St. Lawrence Seaway. I am as you are, Mr. Humphrey. I do not think you have advocated it because of your interest in the M. A. Hanna Company, or anything else.

I believe you feel that it would strengthen the United States. Personally, I feel it would weaken the United States. We differ. I am not fearful in your becoming Secretary of the Treasury that you will be too much interested in that.

THE CHAIRMAN. Mr. Humphrey has just said he would not use the powers of his office to advance or encourage legislation in behalf of the St. Lawrence Seaway.

SENATOR LONG. I have no desire to embarrass the witness. I only feel that we should make a record here, not only for the Nation in connection with this appointment, but as a precedent and as a guide for other Secretaries in the future and for other men of public affairs when they have business connections.

The fact that a man is successful in business indicates in itself that he is well qualified for a high position. The record indicates already that Mr. Humphrey is making a very large financial sacrifice to take the position. There is no doubt in my mind that if Mr. Humphrey were primarily interested in seeing the St. Lawrence Seaway constructed, he would not take a Cabinet position. He would use his position in private business to do everything he could to persuade the Government that it was in its interest to construct the seaway, rather than to come to Washington to take a position serving the Nation in a public capacity.

I would like your views, Mr. Humphrey. You are an attorney and obviously a good attorney.

MR. HUMPHREY. I used to be years ago.

SENATOR LONG. You say you are a member of the Order of the Coif. I am a member myself and I think one would have to be a pretty good student of the law to merit that distinction.

You say you have given some thought to this matter of ethics, certainly as an attorney. I would like your views as an individual, not only for guidance of those of us here, but for the guidance of members of the President's Cabinet and possibly Senators and Congressmen in the future.

What is your view as to what your conduct would be with regard to such a project which you in your personal capacity believe to be a very good project in the national interest, which you have publicly advocated long before you took the position, and which you could speak to as a member of the President's Cabinet, which prospect also now involves you somewhat financially when you hold a public position?

MR. HUMPHREY. I think, Senator Long, what you have to do in all these cases is to do the normal and the right and fair thing.

I think in this particular case, I am so thoroughly convinced and so honestly believe that the seaway is very definitely in the national interest that I should be at liberty to say that in Cabinet meetings.

I think that as a public advocate of the seaway I should not participate. I think I should no longer be an advocate of it for that reason. I think to honestly state my views and opinions is the only proper thing for me to do.

SENATOR LONG. Oftentimes it seems to me that a person has to withhold judgment on an issue because he is in some way interested and does not deceive anyone.

MR. HUMPHREY. If you do not proceed on that theory, you can only conceive having someone working for the Government who has nothing, someone who has done nothing.

SENATOR KERR. And has no intention of doing anything.

MR. HUMPHREY. That would be going too far.

SENATOR LONG. Regarding your stock ownership in various companies and your proposal that your assistants or Under Secretaries would make a decision involving any company in which you are interested, there is not much doubt in my mind that your companies would make out better with them deciding than they would with you.

I believe you would be reluctant to give any company in which you held a financial interest the benefit of the doubt. You would feel that in justice to yourself you should protect yourself from favoring your financial interests.

MR. HUMPHREY. That is a normal inclination.

SENATOR LONG. It does seem that perhaps in such an instance it might be well that there be some measure for advice. That is that perhaps certain members of the Committees on Finance and Ways & Means might be advised that here was a matter that the Treasury had to decide and that in fairness if they did not want it to be a closed matter just in the Treasury files, those who might have some criticism if they knew about it, could know what the decision was and what the elements there involved happened to be.

MR. HUMPHREY. If the committee desired anything of that kind we would be delighted to supply it.

SENATOR LONG. Thank you very much.

SENATOR MARTIN. I understand you have taken this up personally from a legal standpoint as to whether or not you can qualify as the Secretary of the Treasury and also with your personal counsel and that you and they have determined that you are qualified?

MR. HUMPHREY. That is right, Senator Martin, and I have an opinion from them which I would be very glad to file with the committee.

SENATOR MARTIN. That is what I understood.

MR. HUMPHREY. That is correct.

SENATOR MARTIN. It is not only your intent to comply with the law but also, as I understand you, to conform with the spirit of the law?

MR. HUMPHREY. That is correct.

SENATOR MARTIN. I might ask him some things relating to currency and so forth, Mr. Chairman, but I think that would take unnecessary time.

Probably you and I will agree on this: That the first thing we have to do is cut down the cost of Government.

MR. HUMPHREY. That is correct.

SENATOR MARTIN. After we get that done we can take up the matter of reducing taxes and decide what taxes shall be reduced and that you will give us your recommendations and opinions and, of course, it will be up to the Ways & Means Committee and the Finance Committee of the Senate to determine what they shall be because that is, after all, our responsibility.

MR. HUMPHREY. That is right.

SENATOR MARTIN. You can advise but it is our final responsibility.

MR. HUMPHREY. We will give it the benefit of our considered advice and then we will perform as you direct.

SENATOR MARTIN. I would like to ask this question which gets into the matter of currency.

Just a short time ago I heard a man make this statement. He said, "I want you to understand that I am not an economist. I am a research man."

He said, "I have gone into the history of the countries of the world and any country which goes off a sound money currency only lives 42 years."

Have you given any thought to that?

We have been off a sound money currency for 19 years.

Have you given thought as to what you might be able to recommend to the Congress along that line?

MR. HUMPHREY. Senator, I have given a great deal of thought to it because that is one of the basic and fundamental things. I am not prepared to state to the committee today what I do recommend, but it is a subject that is going to be given further consideration.

SENATOR MARTIN. You have given it consideration?

MR. HUMPHREY. Yes, sir; and it will have our most earnest consideration because it is one of the most important questions that face us.

SENATOR MARTIN. Mr. Chairman, I think the big problem is whether or not Mr. Humphrey can comply with the spirit of the law as it now exists. I feel from what you have said that you have taken that up, explored it personally with your own counsel and you do feel that you can.

MR. HUMPHREY. That is my feeling.

SENATOR JOHN J. WILLIAMS (Delaware). Mr. Humphrey, as Secretary of the Treasury, would you feel you had a right to take part in any decisions which were made by the Tax Commissioner's office?

MR. HUMPHREY. Well I will certainly take no part up through the authority of the tax people. I am not prepared to discuss this because it is a legal matter but, if there are any places where appeals can be taken above the Tax Bureau or something of that kind that come to the Treasury, of course, the law would have to be complied with in that respect.

SENATOR WILLIAMS. Only as they will appeal to you through the process of law?

MR. HUMPHREY. We will only have them where absolutely required and necessary.

SENATOR WILLIAMS. How would you feel about a separation of the tax collection service?

MR. HUMPHREY. I would not like to say. I am not prepared on so much of this but I am not in office yet.

THE CHAIRMAN. You would show a certain degree of rattle-headedness if you had all your policies down pat before you warmed your chair.

MR. HUMPHREY. Thank you for that. I would be very hesitant about it and that is as far as I would want to go into it.

SENATOR WILLIAMS. Thank you.

SENATOR RALPH E. FLANDERS (Vermont). Well, Mr. Humphrey, most of the things I had in my mind have been taken care of in previous questions and answers.

There is one thing I have always been interested in which is a subsidiary matter.

As I remember, you said that your salary included your dividends as well.

MR. HUMPHREY. No, it does not include dividends.

SENATOR FLANDERS. That does not? That does not include dividends?

MR. HUMPHREY. That does not.

SENATOR FLANDERS. That would run around $300,000.

MR. HUMPHREY. It exceeded that.

SENATOR FLANDERS. I do not know whether you can answer that or not. In a sense it is not important and in a sense it is.

Whenever these large figures are mentioned in public and get into the press and are read by ordinary citizens of the country, they do not often stop to think that only a minor part of that is available to you.

MR. HUMPHREY. That is correct.

SENATOR FLANDERS. I think whenever these large sums are mentioned, if possible some indication should be given as to what part of that is available to you and what part of it goes to the support of the Government of the United States.

SENATOR KERR. Will the Senator yield there for a moment?

SENATOR FLANDERS. I yield to the Senator of Oklahoma.

SENATOR KERR. Do you not think, if you showed that exactly and showed the amount the Government was going to pay for this gentleman's services, they might send him back to work?

SENATOR FLANDERS. That is just what I am getting at. My State is a dairy State and they take good care of their herds. Over the years they have continually raised the output of milk per cow and the output of cream per gallon of milk.

Here, we have this herd of dairy cows supporting the Government of the United States. The question is whether we want to strew them around the pasture or whether we want to recognize that the Government has an interest in the earnings of business, particularly in view of the fact that it is taking so much of it—two bites: one from business taxation and second, out of whoever gets the remaining portion of the profits of the company.

It has been a matter of concern to me, Mr. Chairman, whenever $300,000 or some other sum, insignificant in the requirements of the Government but tremendously significant to the individual—whenever those sums are mentioned, it would be a good thing if we could accompany them with some statement as to how much of the sum the Government is getting out of it.

Might I ask if you are able to do that right offhand?

MR. HUMPHREY. I cannot do it right offhand but I will supply it to you. I will be very glad to.

THE CHAIRMAN. You are in a high percentage bracket; are you not?

MR. HUMPHREY. That is correct.

SENATOR WALLACE F. BENNETT (Utah). Will the Senator yield?

SENATOR FLANDERS. Yes.

SENATOR BENNETT. Do you think there is a chance that if this particular cow is taken off production, that other cows who can produce approximately the same tax return will be substituted?

SENATOR FLANDERS. There is, of course, a continuous process of retiring the aged dairy cows and providing new ones and I think that will still go on.

Yet the point I raised is apropos to the general policy or understanding of realizing where the income comes from that our Government spends so lavishly and freely.

SENATOR GEORGE W. MALONE (Nevada). Mr. Humphrey, I am glad to see you here. I am interested in the way that everybody takes it for granted that we are going to fix the appropriations and then the tax rate.

Do you think that is the way we should go about it, fix all the appropriations and then fix the tax rate or do you think it might be well to read the menu backward and figure out what we can pay and then fix the appropriations?

MR. HUMPHREY. I think this is a little unorthodox for a prospective Secretary of the Treasury, but you do "do it backward."

The way we do it in business, the way you do it backward.

SENATOR MALONE. In other words, a businessman figures out what his company can do and then goes about it.

MR. HUMPHREY. Every citizen in the home does it that way. Every business that survives does it that way.

SENATOR MALONE. Do you think it would hurt to move some of that into the Government?

MR. HUMPHREY. I have wondered how you ever did it the way you do.

SENATOR FLANDERS. I would like to say that the Senator from Colorado, who sits across here, has a bill in the Congress providing for just that type of fiscal management of our country and I certainly am in sympathy with it.

SENATOR MALONE. I knew the distinguished Senator from Colorado when he was Governor of Colorado. I was State engineer in Nevada and we had about the same ideas, I can say at this point.

Another thing, we have a policy here in Government that when a thing becomes overproduced and we have too much of it, we appropriate the taxpayers' money to hold the price up.

A merchandiser, anyone from my State, would fix a price so he could sell it.

What would you think would be a good policy?

MR. HUMPHREY. That is what we have always done in business.

SENATOR MALONE. That is the way I thought. That is the reason you are still in business.

MR. HUMPHREY. That is one of the reasons.

SENATOR MALONE. Now I suppose there is no argument that through the first policy of setting up appropriations for everything everybody wants and fixes a tax rate, we have had inflation, here, that has practically stolen one-half of the wages and one-half of the savings and a half of the insurance.

Now you can raise the wages, but you cannot do anything about the savings. Is that true in insurance?

MR. HUMPHREY. That is right.

SENATOR MALONE. So we take the savings and insurance and spend it all over the world.

I just wondered what your idea would be. We might just once take a look at the peoples who are doing the work, like miners and stockmen and ranchers and a little industry out in Nevada, and see how much they could pay before we fixed this appropriation.

MR. HUMPHREY. I think it is essential that at some point the giveaway be reduced and that we get on to a basis of what this country can take in taxes, and that we cut our cloth to fit.

Now when you have on your hands as we have at the moment, a world condition and a requirement for preparedness, just how you balance out what the country can afford to pay with having a suitable preparedness and balance those two things together and how that preparedness is developed, presents a very complex problem.

SENATOR MALONE. What we have done so far, we have overbuilt industry in Europe. I suppose you know that.

Many of the people there compete with our industry here in America.

There have been some differences in the two parties for 75 years. One of them is sound money and having a measuring stick for money. It has been known as the gold standard.

There may be some better way. There is a measuring stick for money just like a measuring stick for cloth.

What do you think about the situation?

MR. HUMPHREY. I think, Senator, our very first job is to retard and stop further depreciation of the dollar.

SENATOR MALONE. That might be by establishing some measuring stick for the money.

MR. HUMPHREY. One thing is to eliminate these continuing deficits which is a tremendous job in itself. And then these other things follow.

SENATOR MALONE. The gold standard?

MR. HUMPHREY. These other things follow, that is correct.

SENATOR MALONE. Should it follow?

MR. HUMPHREY. It must follow.

SENATOR MALONE. Thank you.

MR. HUMPHREY. At the appropriate time.

SENATOR MALONE. Well, the appropriate time is while we have ahold of it, is it not?

MR. HUMPHREY. As soon as conditions can be developed to take it.

SENATOR MALONE. Well, I should say if you turn this Congress loose for another few years without any safeguard whatever in appropriations, it will be too late to do anything.

MR. HUMPHREY. It will be entirely too late, yes, sir.

SENATOR MALONE. You would be in favor of getting at this measuring stick for money at the earliest opportunity?

MR. HUMPHREY. At the earliest possible time.

SENATOR FRANK CARLSON (Kansas). I want Mr. Humphrey to know that we appreciate Mr. Humphrey making a sacrifice in this time of trials and tribulations. I am looking forward to serving on this committee with you as Secretary of the Treasury.

I hope this committee recommends his confirmation and the Senate confirms you.

I served on the House Ways & Means Committee for eight years and during that entire eight years, we always raised taxes and never reduced taxes once.

Your statements during your appearance before this committee are quite refreshing.

MR. HUMPHREY. I appreciate that very much.

SENATOR BENNETT. I have a question and perhaps you would prefer to reserve answer to it but have you come to any conclusion in your attitude on the independence of the Federal Reserve Board?

MR. HUMPHREY. Yes, I have. I think the Federal Reserve Board should be independent of the Treasury. I think, however, the two should work very closely together for a common purpose. I am very happy to say that with the present set-up that is exactly what is going to happen.

SENATOR BENNETT. You do not feel you have any power to overrule the decisions of the Board acting within its own legal province?

MR. HUMPHREY. I do not and I do not think we should.

SENATOR BENNETT. Thank you. That is my only question.

SENATOR MALONE. Mr. Humphrey, do you think the Congress of the United States should operate independently of the executive department?

Mr. Humphrey. I certainly do.

The Chairman. Any further questions?

Have you anything further to say, Mr. Humphrey?

Mr. Humphrey. I have one thing. I would not want to leave this meeting without referring to one thing that really is not germane to the subject at all but it has been mentioned in the newspapers and I think it should be brought out here before you.

The Hanna Coal & Ore Corporation is opening a nickel deposit out on the west coast under a deal with Defense Minerals and that arrangement has all been made and it is completed and they are opening a nickel deposit in Oregon. That is made under Government contract for the sale of nickel.

I just want to bring it up. As I say it has no connection with me except that it is a thing that has been in the newspapers and I think it should be mentioned. I have no connection with it whatever.

The Chairman. Thank you very much. We will excuse you and thank you for coming.

✄ The Committee immediately voted unanimously to confirm the appointment of the Secretary of the Treasury.

FISCAL MANAGEMENT
AND THE
SOUND DOLLAR

The first of the papers collected under this heading are concerned with, and were a part of, the first battle in which the Secretary of the Treasury found himself after taking his office. Curiously, it was not a partisan fight but a disagreement among Republicans of Administration and Congress from the opening day of the new Eisenhower Administration.

On the first day of Congress, January 3, 1953, Rep. Daniel Alden Reed of New York, who had become head of the Ways & Means Committee, introduced "House Bill No. 1" to reduce income taxes by 11 per cent the following July 1 instead of the subsequent January 1, 1954, date specified in 1950 by the authors of the tax increase for Korean War financing. The excess profits tax provision of that legislation was originally marked to expire July 1, 1953. In that Eighty-first Congress, Reed and most of the Republican representatives had fought both tax increase and excess profits provision, and, coming to power in 1953, deemed it a solemn duty (as Reed and others had declared in their election campaigns) to get rid of both war tax measures.

When the Secretary took office on January 17, he was already in the midst of discovering the Government's precarious fiscal position. He found that Korean War orders totaling $81 billion over and above a peace-time Government operation, for which no funding requirements had been made, would be coming due to be paid in the next few years. The departing Administration also had overestimated income for the 1953 fiscal year's operation, and, instead of the announced $9 billion expected deficit, there would be forecast an $11 billion deficit. The war was still on and growing more expensive; the anomalous attitude of Soviet Russia toward the Korean outbreak had hardened the menaces of the so-called "cold war"; it was impossible to make the vaguely great immediate cuts in Government operating cost about which some of the 1952 Republican campaigners had spoken in large terms. As candidate for President, Gen. Eisenhower had discussed the need for reduction of Government costs and taxes, but he had put ahead of these the more serious issue of getting Government income and outgo more closely into or toward balance, which had to be done if the Government credit were to be maintained and the value of the sinking dollar stabilized for the benefit of everyone in the United States of America.

Secretary Humphrey's managerial eye swept the scene and he reported at once to the President that to get national income and outgo closer, at once, without the sweeping cost cuts not at once possible the Government needed to hold the tax income line where it was. The President so reported in his Budget Message to Congress late in January, asking that the tax reduction be postponed through the calendar year 1953 and that the excess profits tax be continued for the full year. Chairman Reed and a

Republican majority of the Ways & Means Committee paid no heed to this appeal. Without having held any hearings on their proposal, they reported out House Bill No. 1, 21–4, on February 16 to proceed with the tax reduction.

A little less than a billion dollars in income (with the plus or minus valence of $2 million) swung on this Republican disagreement. Secretary Humphrey naturally became the public spokesman for the budgetary position instead of the reductions. On February 17, both the President and he issued public statements challenging the Ways & Means course and haste. Chairman Reed thereupon defended his course as an issue of keeping public faith. Reed was a 34-year veteran of the House, representing a rock-ribbed western New York district; before his first election to Congress in 1918, he had been Cornell University's football coach. The duel between him and Secretary Humphrey was classic for the respect and courtesy with which they treated each other while battling with all the political powers they could summon.

The chronology and outcome of the battle may serve to interpret more deeply Secretary Humphrey's words and tactics on the issue. When he had a bill introduced by another Republican to extend the excess profits tax through the remainder of 1953, he was countered by Chairman Reed's public announcement that the bill would never emerge from the Ways & Means Committee (February 17). The President and his Secretary appealed at once to the party leadership of the House majority, with the result that House Bill No. 1 was carefully shelved in the Rules Committee.

On March 13, Reed appealed to the Rules Committee in vain to let House Bill No. 1 come on the calendar; Chairman Leo Allen (Illinois) of the Rules Committee said it could not possibly be dealt with before May 15. "In 34 years, what have I done to deserve such treatment?" demanded Reed. On April 13 he filed with the Rules Committee a petition signed by 25 ranking Republicans to have the bill released on grounds that "a promise made is a promise to be kept." Finally on June 1 Reed consented to hold Ways & Means Committee hearings on the excess profits tax extension. He produced scores of business men and organizations as witnesses demanding the end of the excess profits levy. Secretary Humphrey was before the committee to appeal for the extender June 1, 3, and 4 in a memorable performance. He had meantime taken the issue to platform and television panel, pounding away at the Administration line that to put income and expense into Government balance was more important to business and its dollar than a six months' delay in tax reduction.

The Secretary further became the champion of the "little taxpayer"; he gained momentum with the reiteration that to give a first tax reduction to

How to sell bonds. The Secretary with a group of industrialists whose enterprises he had enlisted in the payroll savings-thrift campaign for the sale of Government bonds, 1955.

LL.D. at Harvard, 1956. Secretary Humphrey is seated between President Nathan Pusey of the University and the commencement speaker, the then United States Senator and later President John F. Kennedy.

With the President at Thomasville. President Eisenhower, convalescing from his 1955 heart attack, as he and the Secretary set out (in the hunting wagon) for a chance at some birds, February 24, 1956.

a minute minority of the country's wealthiest taxpayers was unjust and un-democratic, that when taxes could be reduced at all they must be reduced to the smallest taxpayer at the first juncture. His program became, a tax re-duction for every one in January, 1954, and then a wholesale revision of the whole tax structure for every one; meantime saving the effect of $2 bil-lion income for the Government's most precarious fiscal year.

By June Chairman Reed could see that House Bill No. 1 was not going to come forth to the floor, and concentrated his fight against the excess profits six-month extension. He took the floor of the House July 10 with a motion to recommit the bill to the Ways & Means Committee (from which it had been pried by the House leadership). His motion was de-feated 275–127, after which the House approved the excess profits ex-tension by a voice vote. In the Senate the following day, the extension survived an attempt at amendment by Senator John Williams (Delaware) to exempt certain small enterprises from the extended tax, by a 52–34 vote, and the Senate then passed the bill by voice vote.

This was Secretary Humphrey's most spectacular political victory of his entire service. The effective $2 billion income enabled him to reduce the expected 1953 budget deficit from the expected $11 billion to a cash deficit of $5.3 billion.

"The problem is to know the facts"

Remarks by Secretary Humphrey before a luncheon of the Cleveland Chamber of Commerce at the Carter Hotel, Cleveland, on the occasion of the award of Distinguished Service medals to him and to Clifford Hood, president of the United States Steel Corporation.

February 17, 1953

I just cannot tell you how overwhelmed I am with this turnout today for "Cliff" and me, and with this award that has been made. I had no idea anything of this kind was going to be done. I thought I was just coming to a simple meeting of the Chamber, and that they were very nice indeed to ask "Cliff" and myself to attend.

You know, when it came to leaving Cleveland, my wife and myself went through a lot of agony. We had our friends here; we had business here; we had everything we wanted here, and it was a terribly difficult thing to make up our minds to leave. We were feeling pretty bad about it, but sometimes things are brought home to you by a chance remark, or, very often, a remark of a child, a simple thing that brings it to your mind.

One day, when we were feeling particularly bad about leaving, one of our grandchildren said to my wife: " 'Hummy,' don't feel so bad. When you die and go to Washington, I'll look after your garden for you."

We decided that, as long as we were going to go to Washington, we were going to put everything in it that we had; we were going to do everything we could to do a job; and we were going to get as much pleasure and enjoyment out of it as we could while we were doing it. . . .

I do not have a prepared speech, and I do not want to attempt to make one; not because the occasion does not justify it, but because there have been so many requests for speeches that I have had to just say that I would not make any for six months, and I do not want to break that rule because I would be in trouble in a lot of other places. With your permission, what I would like to do is just sort of gossip with you about some of the things that have happened, and some of the things that have developed as I have seen them in my long experience in Washington of almost thirty days.

Right here for just a minute I would like to interrupt the speech to put in a commercial. The Treasury is in the savings bond business. I would just like to impress upon you the fact that getting the debt spread into these savings bonds is one of the most important jobs there is in the country. The more investors there are in America, the better America is going to be, and anything that any of you can do to campaign to liven up and build up the savings bond campaign, and the payroll deduction campaign, and make a mark, and a record, for Cleveland, in that regard certainly will not only be doing a great job for the country, but it will be greatly appreciated by everyone concerned.

I would like to get to one or two things that have been talked about in the newspapers. It is a little dangerous to do that, but I am sure you are interested particularly in the things that are going on that have been under discussion here in the last couple days, such as this matter of the precedence of tax reduction or budget balancing.

The figures down there are stupendous. When they talk about them, and you see these figures working out with all these zeros stretching clear across the page, it just takes your breath away. I made up my mind that after all there are only ten digits, and if you forget the zeros and talk about one, two, three, four, I can understand that. I can get the relationship of those things one to another.

I try to think, to see what is a billion dollars. You cannot touch a billion dollars. You cannot see it. I wondered how in the world you could get an idea of what a billion dollars is. I thought, as I so often do, of Cleveland, and I wondered what the assessed valuation of Cleveland was, what Cleveland is worth. Well, I checked it up, and Cleveland is worth about $2 billion, Pittsburgh is worth about $2 billion, Youngstown about $.5 billion, Detroit about $3 billion. That is $7.5 billion if you take Cleveland, Pittsburgh, Youngstown, and Detroit.

The Truman budget that has been presented, that we are trying to struggle with to see what reductions can be made in it, starts out with $9.9 billion deficit of expenditures over income with as high and liberal statement as you can make. So if we were to cut out of that budget enough items to build Pittsburgh, to build Youngstown, to build Cleveland, to build Detroit—and you admit that is quite a lot of building—if we cut out all of that, we would only cut out $7.5 billion, approximately, and out of the $9.9 billion we would still have $2.4 billion to work on to balance the budget.

When you talk about balancing a budget, and when you talk about these figures, it is a real job.

This Administration, and the American people, want tax reduction. The Administration wants tax reduction. It is committed to tax reduction. It is also committed to balancing the budget. It is committed to attempting to slow down and stop this inflationary tendency that has been going on for all these years that has reduced the value of your dollar down to 53¢ or 54¢, or something of that kind.

I want to call your attention to the fact that it is the history of all these inflationary moves—and you can follow them everywhere; you can see them in all the countries of Europe; you can see them all over the world, not only now, but in times past—that they start slowly, and they gain speed with momentum, and they keep going, and the first half of the loss is the slowest half of the loss, and then if it continues, if it is not stopped, it goes much faster.

If something is not done to slow this down, and to bring it to a stop, this country is in for just the sort of catastrophe that we have seen going on in all the countries, well, practically all the countries in Europe and the rest of the world. So it is a dedication of this Administration to do what it can to stop this drive, this rush that we are in that has been increasing toward inflation, and to get back, if we can, and as soon as we can, to a sound dollar and a sound dollar base.

The problem is a problem of precedence; it is a problem of timing; it is a problem of knowing what are the facts. The Truman budget, as I said before, was presented with a proposed deficit of $9.9 billion, which is almost $10 billion. If somebody said, "One hundred million dollars," you would just round that off and forget that. But that $10 billion, by comparison you can see what an enormous amount of money that is. That budget has been taken apart and been sent back to all the departments, and everybody in every department is working to see what reductions can be made.

We have no quarrel at all with the desire of the Republicans in Congress, the Republicans everywhere, for wanting a tax reduction. We are just as strong for a tax reduction as anybody can be, just as strong as they are, and we want it just as soon as it can be had; but I have always found in all business experience—and I am sure that all of you are exactly the same way—that when you have a disagreement as to timing, or disagreement as to results, that very largely you find it is because the facts aren't known; that if you really have the facts, an awful lot of your troubles disappear, and if you really know what you are talking about, your decisions, as a rule, become pretty simple. That is what is desired here.

This movement for a quick reduction of taxes is perfectly all right. The happiest thing in the world would be if the facts, as they are finally developed, would justify it, and if everybody could get behind it, and it could go through. We do not want to take any position with respect to it. We only hope that it can be justified; but the thing that we do not want to have done is that it be pushed through and enacted into law, or for people to be so committed on it they cannot change their minds in the event the facts do not justify it.

Those facts are going to be coming out within the next couple months, and within two or three months we are going to see what the real facts indicate as a possibility of reduction of expenditures. If the expenditures can be sufficiently reduced so as to balance the budget, and take up some of the slack, or all of the slack, that would follow this proposed reduction in taxes, or any other reduction in taxes, then we are immediately for that reduction in taxes, and for it just as soon as it can possibly be enacted, but until that time comes, until we can see a balance, and an opportunity to get a balance in the budget, any tax reduction, or move to reduce taxes, is premature. Because the dangers of not doing it far outweigh the advantages and the desirability of getting it done.

In this matter of cutting expenses, I just want to bring to your attention this thing that I had not appreciated as fully when I was here, just engrossed in business; that I had not appreciated nearly as fully as I do now. I had not appreciated fully how very definitely there is a direct chain of events between the foreign policy of this country and a man working for the success of a business in the city of Cleveland. It is a direct chain of events that goes right from one to the other.

Let me illustrate it in just this way—and it has very largely to do with the reduction of the budget and the reduction of expenditures, because about two-thirds of the budget is for security, military preparedness or economic aid. On top of that you have about 20 per cent of the budget, or, perhaps, even a little more, that is in fixed items; they are in interest charges; they are in definite agreements to support State activities; they are in obligations to veterans, and they are in obligations of all sorts of things that are committed and where there is no chance for a change or reduction in those items.

So when you get right down to it, somewhere from 80 to 90 per cent of the budget has nothing to do with just firing employees, or reducing what you may think are wasteful expenditures, but has to do with our security. . . .

In the security field you are confronted with a terribly serious problem. If somebody asks you what you will spend to save your life, it is a terribly difficult problem to answer. What we have to do, as I see it, and the great problem we have before us, is to weigh what you are willing to spend to save your life, that is, what you are willing to spend for military security, and what you think you have to reduce in order to save your economic security in order to keep America in business, to keep America strong, and to keep us from having a tax burden that we simply cannot bear, and that will just dry up all our activities. . . .

Getting back to the thought of the direct chain of events of foreign policy with jobs and business activity in Cleveland, which is very direct, just think of this: When our Secretary of State takes a position with respect to some foreign problem—I mean, an important one—he cannot just play a pair of deuces. We have gone along in a dillydally sort of way with our foreign positions about as long as we can go. When we take a position with respect to some foreign question or situation, our Secretary of State, and our country behind him, has to be able to back up that position. It has to be prepared, in the event that position is challenged, to meet the challenge, whatever it may be.

That means that when the Secretary of State decides to take a position, he must tell the Secretary of Defense that he must be prepared to back that position.

That means the Secretary of Defense has to decide what is required to be in position to meet that position if it is challenged.

That means spending money. He tells me how much money he is going to spend, which has to go into the budget, which is two-thirds of all the money we are spending in total, and that, in turn, very largely determines what the tax rates are going to be, what our total fiscal policies are going to be; and the tax rates and the fiscal policy are the things that determine how many people work and how business progresses right here in Cleveland....

In trying to determine what your expenditures are, and what your expenditures are going to be, you start with this big end of your expenditures, which is dependent upon your foreign policy, and it comes right back to your fiscal policy. If the expenditures for defense or for security are so great that they are going to force at the other end of the line fiscal policies and taxation policies that are going to destroy our economy, you might just as well be killed from one end as destroyed from the other....

Now, the policy of this Administration, as you have already seen, is to do everything possible to turn this country back to the citizens; to have as free an economy as it is possible to have; to permit the citizens all the freedom of activity that they can possibly have, which is the way the citizens operated during the years (and the period) during which this country became great and developed our present standard of living.

That does not mean laissez faire; that does not mean you are going to tear everything down. It simply means the citizens must be as free as possible to pursue their own ends; to develop themselves in their own way; to develop their business in their own way so long as they do not tramp upon or injure the rights of others. . . .

Freedom does not come free. Freedom comes with freedom. Every time you get an additional freedom, you get an additional responsibility, an individual personal responsibility. . . . The Administration will attempt to do what it can, but the real job has to be done by you gentlemen and all of the citizens of Cleveland, and all of the citizens of the United States, each one in his own way of doing what is right by himself. And the cumulative effect of that is what will make America strong and free.

✒ Secretary Humphrey's first gentle warning that the tax reduction expected from Congress might not come through.

"Deficits should be avoided like the plague"

Remarks by Secretary Humphrey to the annual
Washington meeting of the Advertising Council
of America at Hotel Statler, Washington.

April 1, 1953

You have been so effective in helping with governmental activities in the past that I want to take the liberty of suggesting something more that you can undertake now which is of even greater importance to our country than your many previous fine accomplishments, for which we are all so very grateful.

We are facing a deficit in this country for this present fiscal year of an estimated $12 billion. The Administration is now in the process of fine-tooth-combing the requests of the various departments of government in preparation for the budget for the next fiscal year, 1954. Requests for expenditures, as is always the case, start out by substantially exceeding the current year's expenditures. Hours and hours of painstaking analysis are spent in balancing the urgency of the many requests in each department, and also of department with department, before a proposed budget can be presented.

There is a widespread feeling abroad in the land that we must face another deficit year and perhaps even deficits year after year, and that it is of small consequence if we do. That we might as well get used to it. That it really doesn't matter. Now, you know and I know that there is nothing further from the truth. It is threatening to our way of life. But millions of our fellow citizens do not know this or understand the dangers. President Eisenhower has recently again pledged his every effort in a relentless fight against unnecessary spending and loose handling of our fiscal affairs, and he said, "That kind of spending must stop or the United States of America is in the most serious trouble."

Both the President and the Treasury have recently reaffirmed their dedication to responsible fiscal policies. This can be achieved best by strict adherence to these simple but essential objectives:

(1) Control and reduction of over-all federal spending, which is a prerequisite to

(2) Much needed general federal tax reduction as soon as it appears that the near future may produce a sufficient increase in income over expenditures, and

(3) The established practice of living within our federal means with balanced budgets.

The accomplishment of these objectives means fiscal responsibility for our Government.

The accomplishment of these objectives also means the accumulation of capital to provide the added modern tools of production to make jobs for the millions of new and present workers in our growing population, with competitive production, which is the only means of sustaining and increasing our present national scale of living.

It means the growth of national as well as international trade and the ability to protect our competitive position in world trade.

It will reverse the trend during the past several years of deficits in our balance of payments with the rest of the world and will help to replenish our declining reserves.

It means orderly and receptive markets for Government securities.

It means stability in our cost of living and renewed strength in the value of our dollar, which means protection for the savings of our people and the worth of their pensions, insurance and resources.

It will increase the incentives to work and to save and to be self-sufficient and provide for our own and our families' futures—to take risks with new enterprise and to make more and more and always better jobs and opportunities.

It gives meaning to our heritage of America as the land of opportunity for which our country stands throughout the world.

It requires effective unification of our military activities with resulting savings of duplication and in deployment, which will increase our strength to maintain, for whatever period may be required, an adequate posture of military defense to deter attack from any foreign source.

These objectives are in sharp contrast to our present deficit position and to that long period of deficit policy of previous administrations, which was pursued with artificial markets for our Government securities and a resulting reduction in the worth of our dollar by more than half, with a corresponding increase in the cost of living for our people. However, these objectives cannot be obtained by the most strenuous efforts of our representatives in Government unless they are supported steadfastly by the people themselves.

We have built up in this country over the past 25 years a built-in vested interest in Government spending in large and powerful interested groups widely spread throughout our land. These groups as a general policy all favor Government economy and the reduction of federal spending for every one but themselves. They each prosper or benefit from the federal purse, and will mightily resist any action that threatens the reduction of their particular participation in the Government spending.

These groups include many business concerns which serve the Government with billions of dollars' worth of material each year—communities which enjoy employment of their citizens either by the Government directly or through Government business or purchases—farmers and others receiving subsidies of various kinds—schools—housing and real estate developments—hospitals—veterans and the several million persons either directly in military service at home or abroad or those that serve them, as well as the foreign lands to whom Government loans and grants in aid are made. In many case, active organization and regular lobbies are maintained to protect their continued participation in federal funds.

I do not infer that any of these vested interests are improper. But I do insist that the extent to which each is absolutely necessary and urgent must be kept under searching scrutiny and relentless pressure for control and reduction of their expenditures to make the whole pattern of spending come within limits that our people can afford.

When the justifiable total is determined by the final authorities of Government then the current cost should be currently paid in taxes and not passed on through deficits to rob future years and generations of their chance in life. Deficits and the theft of inflation which results should be avoided like the plague, and the pressures of the vested interest pressure groups should be limited to only most urgent national necessity. All excesses should be denied and disallowed with resulting benefit for all the people and the maintenance of our way of life.

How can this be done? It's a tough assignment and takes tough originating treatment by those in direct control of governmental processes, as President Eisenhower has recently said. But even then government can only succeed when backed by wholehearted intelligent public support.

Now this is where the Advertising Council comes in. This is the great job that you are better qualified to perform than any other group on earth. You have the know-how and the means. You have the dedication to public service which you have so abundantly demonstrated by your loyalty and support of Government activities. You merit and have the everlasting grateful thanks of every department and servant of the Government which you have so generously helped.

The people of this country must be educated not only to the benefits, but also to the compelling necessity for the adoption of these fundamental objectives for fiscal responsibility. They are essential to the preservation of individual opportunity and freedom of choice, incentive and protection which this country has given past generations of our people and which the great majority of Americans want preserved for their children and the generations to come. The education of the masses of our people is a huge but essential task, and equally with it must come an awareness of the pitfalls of the siren songs and easy ways of reckless spending, deficit financed, which all too late will be found to be the destruction of all that we hold dear.

That is the job I suggest to you. It's worth a mighty effort, and a mighty effort it will take, but you are a mighty, powerful influence in this country. I hope you will undertake it.

Bless you, and many thanks.

🖎The Advertising Council of America, formed years ago by advertising media interests, agencies, and federations to offer services to worthy national causes, had been both advisory and administrative in promoting the popular advertising for U. S. Treasury Bonds sold directly to the public and business; and it was to their consideration of a new public service in this connection that the Secretary threw out this suggestion of a national campaign of education in fiscal governmental probity and balance.

Looking for "longer-term investors"

Statement by Secretary Humphrey from the
Treasury Department.

April 13, 1953

The new issue of 30-year 3¼ per cent bonds is one step in a program "of extending part of the debt over longer periods and gradually placing greater amounts in the hands of longer term investors" announced by President Eisenhower in his State of the Union Message.

The concentration of short-term debt in the banks by the previous Administration was one of the causes of inflation in the cost of living which has cost the American people billions of dollars. A gradual placing of more securities in the hands of non-bank investors is a necessary step for economic stability.

The sale of long-term bonds to these investors carries a somewhat higher interest rate, but this cost will be offset many times over if it lessens the cost and disorganization of inflation. The increased interest cost is partly recovered in taxation. To the extent that the interest on these bonds goes to insurance companies, savings banks, pension funds, and other forms of the people's savings, it will benefit the millions of families who have been most damaged by inflation and by inadequate return on savings because of artificially low interest rates.

As far as deflation is concerned, while a few prices have declined recently, the cost of living is near its post-war high, employment is higher than ever before and unemployment is very small. With continued heavy military expenditures, the Government is still operating at a deficit.

🖎 Nine senators had raised an issue on the Senate floor concerning the new bond policy following the Treasury's announcement of the 30-year bonds at 3¼ per cent interest. This was the longest-term bond issue, at correspondingly higher interest rates, since the 1930's and as previously noted was the Administration's wall against any inflation of prices when the last controls were dropped. This statement was labeled as a reply to "the nine senators."

"Competition . . . has made our American system"

Speech by Secretary Humphrey before the luncheon of the annual meeting of the Associated Press membership at the Waldorf-Astoria Hotel, New York.

April 20, 1953

There is no reason to fear peace.

We are not headed for depression.

Some people in this country are talking as though they were afraid of peace. Peace is what we are working and striving to attain. To achieve peace we are helping our friends and strengthening our own defenses, on the theory that an ounce of prevention is worth a pound of cure. In peace, America grew great. It was in peace that we grew strong and rich and accumulated the homes, plants, farms, mines and transportation, that saw us through two wars.

It was wars that brought us debt and taxes and inflation.

Why then should any one fear peace? The reason as I understand it is that some people fear for the strength of our own economic position if Government spending for defense is reduced. They fear a free economy devoted to the pursuits of peace. Such thinking is entirely unjustified. We are not going to have a depression in America whether we have an armistice, a real peace, or continue to develop a proper and balanced posture of defense. There is no reason for a depression unless we fail ourselves to do the things we ought to do and lack the courage and foresight to do them.

There will be readjustments, of course. There are always readjustments taking place in any active economy, sometimes to the advantage or detriment of one group and sometimes to another. But depression, no. We cannot preserve our way of life through another long, deep depression and we must never permit it to occur.

The resources and the resourcefulness of our country are such that the dismal days of depression need not occur unless we ourselves, we American citizens, fail to have the strength and fortitude to avoid the excesses of speculative boom and deal with readjustments when they are necessary.

For several years past we have been treading a dangerous path, one from which we have now turned. It is not too late to make the turn and avoid the inevitable consequences for which we were directly headed.

For twenty years we have been consistently following unhealthy policies that induced inflation, depreciated our currency and threatened to exhaust our credit. Over that period our dollar has shrunk from the 100 cents we started with to approximately 50 cents today. We have artificially manipulated our interest rates and have actually printed billions of dollars of current indebtedness which is only narrowly removed from printing money.

As a result of vacillating foreign policies we found ourselves at war in Korea and in the midst of a feverishly improvised program of vast military spending. . . . We now find ourselves with over $267 billion in total indebtedness.

Of this amount, $32 billion matures every ninety days, and there are over $175 billion of total maturities in less than five years. We have inherited outstanding obligations and unsatisfied authorizations to spend government funds of $81 billion which will have to be paid in revenues in 1954 and future years.

We were handed a proposed budget for next year's expenditures in excess of $78 billion, which involves a $10 billion deficit over the anticipated revenues. In addition to deficit of $4 billion in 1952; $6 billion in 1953 and $10 billion in 1954, we found that the proposed future programs contemplated billions of dollars of deficits in each of the next several years.

We have a tax structure that is already so high that it is adding tremendously to our cost of living and threatening to destroy the incentive to work and save and invest. This is our legacy. This is what we face today.

It is far from a pretty picture. But it is by no means an impossible one, in view of the great strength of our country and the vigor and resourcefulness of our people. Our inheritance of obligations both immediate and planned is staggering, but not yet beyond our powers of control. Accumulations of twenty years cannot be removed in ninety days. It will take rigid self-discipline and determined action. But over a period of time, if we resolutely hold our course to definite objectives, it need give us no fear.

What is it we have been so hurriedly preparing to preserve? Is it just our lives? No. What we are really trying to preserve is our American way of life. That is what we have fought for over the years. That is what we must always preserve and always protect. Confronted with a crisis, we hastened to protect it from outside aggression without regard to cost in a feverish rush to preparedness. But we must not forget that our way of life is threatened, not from one, but from two sources at the same time. It can be lost just as completely by economic deterioration from within as by aggression from without. In fact, economic deterioration will not only destroy our way of life, but it will destroy the very means by which we seek to protect it from aggression. It is the economic strength of America that has supplied the sinews for ourselves and for our allies to fight two great wars.

We are confronted, not with a problem, but with a dilemma, which simply means two problems at the same time. We must seek and find that delicate balance which will give us the necessary military preparedness for defense against outside attack while always continuing to maintain our economic strength at home. Those are dual problems and must be simultaneously solved.

The first step in solving them is to achieve a sound currency. History demonstrates that, whenever currency deterioration has started it tends to continue at an ever increasing rate, the faster the further it goes. Unless courageous, determined corrective action is taken in time it finally speeds entirely out of control and finishes in utter collapse.

The first half of the depreciation of our dollar has already occurred. The programs and conditions which this Administration inherited would have accelerated that pace. Stopping that spiral is imperative.

One essential to accomplish this goal is to bring our federal expenditures under control and at the earliest possible time balance them with our income. This cannot be done in a minute with such large future obligations already contracted for. But it is not too late, if we are tough enough, to make real and early progress in that direction and start at once. . . .

More defense for less money is perfectly practical and a possible accomplishment. Neither can this be done in a minute, but it is in the cards and on the way. Deliberate, not timid, carefully planned objectives, with price tags attached and efficiently pursued both for ourselves and our allies will provide a posture of defense against outside aggression that can and will be maintained over whatever period may be required. This will protect us more adequately from threat from abroad than blowing first hot and then cold in extremes of emotion as we have been doing since World War II.

Talk of truce in Korea, or even an actual truce, will not have an early important influence on the rate of military spending. We have a big program to complete in any event to attain a proper, permanent posture of defense for America.

Control of our expenses is vital to our success, but that is only part of the task. Equally important in balancing the budget is the amount of income we have to spend. That involves taxes, and that is more a matter of my own immediate concern. Also, that is where the American people must do their part.

Taxes should not be reduced until expenses are under control. Both should come down together, but only as a balance is obtainable. There is no easy way to correct our fiscal excesses of past years. We must stand and take it all along the line.

However, that does not mean that no relief from present taxation, which is far too high, can be anticipated. Just the opposite is true. Taxes must come down. It's simply a matter of timing geared to reduction of expense. Both are too high and both must be reduced. In addition there must be a radical revision of our tax system to better provide the incentives for the creation of more jobs for more people and for the making of more better and cheaper goods for all the people.

Taxes are all included in the cost of living, no matter what form they take, but they are more destructive of initiative in some forms than others. Taxes today contribute greatly to high costs and the high prices of everything we buy. The present tax system threatens to stifle initiative, expansion and ultimately jobs. A better balanced system is required.

The reduction of taxes, moreover, is one of the best guarantees we have against the fear of depression, in the event that peace makes possible curtailment of Government defense spending. It is essential that, as Government expenses are brought under control, as waste is eliminated, and as Government spending is gradually reduced, that taxes must also be reduced as rapidly as Government spending declines. If we return to the citizens as rapidly as possible the savings we make in Government expenses, the people will have the money to spend for themselves in their own way what the Government has been spending— or wasting—for them.

The people can spend their own money for their own account and in their own way for what they want much better than the Government can spend it for them. . . .

After the last war, we decreased the rate of total Government expenditures in just two years from $98.7 billion in 1945 to $39.3 billion in 1947. Our deficit was decreased in the same period from a deficit of $51 billion in 1945 to surpluses in 1947 and 1948.

Defense spending itself was reduced from $90.5 billion in 1945 to $16.8 billion plus about $5 billion of foreign aid in the same two years. We have no such tremendous reductions to contemplate or gaps to fill now. Our plant is already geared to increased civilian production.

Full production in many lines where plant capacity has been recently so greatly increased will require real sales effort and bring highly competitive times in several lines.

But do we fear competition? That is what America stands for. Competition is the life of trade. It is what has made our American system. More and better goods at less cost for more people is our national slogan. Our greatest pride is our imagination, resourcefulness and ingenuity in production, sales and distribution. Let's all prepare to give them a chance under whatever the conditions may be and see if again they will not produce the brightest day we have yet seen in America.

An equally important fundamental to preserve the soundness of our money and flourishing trade is the management of our huge debt. The way in which it is handled can also have an important bearing upon economic conditions and the creation of good or bad times. A stable currency is essential to an ever-expanding level of employment and a sound prosperity.

If the debt is so managed as to increase unduly the available money supply, foster the over-extension of credit and depreciate the value of the dollar it can contribute greatly toward pushing us right back into the inflationary spiral of recent times.

If, on the other hand, the debt is so managed that it drains the savings of the people too rapidly and in too large amounts so as to unduly restrict credit, depress prices and deprive industry of the funds required for full operation and expansion, then it can contribute to depression. Here again balance and timing are of first concern, and wise and careful handling of refinancing our enormous debt structure is of the greatest importance.

This Administration believes in the American way of life and in a free market economy. It believes that a most powerful influence over the years has been the accumulated effect of the industry and efforts of so many of our people to advance their own interests independently and in their own ways. This way of life has withstood wars and political manipulations and experiments of all kinds. It will overcome all of our burdens of today. It is because of the accumulative desires and the ambitions of the vast number of our citizens to so live their lives, that by their own endeavors they continually advance their own positions that we are what we are today. We are in good hands as long as the great American consumer is free from artificial restraint and can freely decide what he will buy, when he will buy and what prices he is willing to pay. That means that the productive and inventive power and the ingenuity of all America is in competition for that consumer's dollar and must devote itself to the creation of more and better things at less cost in vying for his favor.

However, freedom for an individual or for a nation must be jealously guarded and carries with it corresponding obligations. The Golden Rule still is fundamental in human relations. Freedom for the citizen involves equal responsibility of the citizen, each for himself to see that he wholly fulfills it. He must use this freedom for his own advancement only to the extent that it does not trample upon the rights of his neighbor and enhances the common good. It is the responsibility of every citizen of this country, of businessmen, farmers, labor and all of you here today in accepting your freedom to accept the responsibility that goes with it. If the American people really want stability they must all contribute to it, in the prices they charge, in the wages they demand and in everything that they do. They must exercise self-restraint from making quick turns to the detriment of others and promote in every way possible the long-term thinking and planning that is for the ultimate good of all the people. . . .

Peace is what we all want. It is nothing to fear, nor is there any reason for depression. Adjustments, yes. But not depression. So long as we maintain the soundness of our money; attain that nice balance between achieving security from aggression and maintaining economic strength; eliminate waste and handle our fiscal affairs with wisdom, America can look forward to good jobs at good pay and real advances in our scale of living. We can have a stronger economy based on sounder fundamental conditions and with greater opportunity for individual and collective future security than we have known in many years.

🖝 The "story behind" this speech is reflective of the non-oratorical business man who developed from his public service into one of the most popular speakers of his years in Washington. This speech to the annual Associated Press meeting was the first public speech, prepared for such, in Secretary Humphrey's life. He was assigned to it by President Eisenhower, who was asked to the AP assembly after he had accepted a somewhat conflicting speaking date before the Society of Newspaper Editors; the Secretary's dismay was met head-on by a friend of the President's, Roy A. Roberts, editor of the *Kansas City Star* and a director of the AP. "I'll help you," said Mr. Roberts. "I know the audience. It is not the kind you stand up to tell how pleased you are to be here and what a privilege it is for you —these are newspaper owners and editors who can't stand that kind of pleasantry. They want to be told something quickly."—"Such as what?" asked the Secretary.—"Well, you tell me," said Roy Roberts, "whether we're going to have a bad depression this year. Out my way things are rather poor and people are worried."—"We're not going to have bad times.

This is going to be a pretty good year."—"Tell them that, say just that. Now, then, are we going to have any more war?"—"No, we're not, and the Korean thing is going to be over pretty soon."—"Is peace going to bring us some hard times?"—"It shouldn't. We should get back to good business on a peace-time basis very quickly."—"Tell them that," said the editor. "Just stand up in front of them and say, there isn't going to be any more war and there isn't going to be any depression. Don't waste any words getting those statements out."

The Secretary did just that, as note his opening words: "There is no reason to fear peace. We are not headed for depression."

"The most wholesome prospect in twenty years"

*Remarks by Secretary Humphrey on Meet the Press
television panel in Washington. Miss Martha Rountree,
moderator; Richard Wilson, Cowles Publications;
Frank O'Brien, Associated Press; Robert Riggs,
Louisville Courier-Journal; Mrs. May Craig,
Maine Papers.*

May 24, 1953

MISS ROUNTREE. Welcome to another session of Meet the Press. Our guest today is the Secretary of the Treasury, the Honorable George Humphrey. Mr. Secretary, if you are ready I think we're going to start with Mr. Riggs.

MR. RIGGS. Mr. Humphrey, as Secretary of the Treasury you are the chief financial officer in an Administration which is elected chiefly, or in a great deal, on a promise to reduce taxes. Now your Administration has taken a position opposed to immediate reduction; on top of that it has asked for extension of some taxes which means people will pay almost a billion dollars more this year in taxes. Do you feel your party has repudiated its pledge?

SEC. HUMPHREY. Mr. Riggs, I don't feel we have repudiated any pledge. The reason taxes are not being reduced at this time are two. The first is that the condition in which we found the Treasury and our obligations, was in much more difficult shape than we had anticipated. Second, and most important is the security of our country is involved in the question of what we do about reducing taxes and reducing expenditures, both have to go together.

MR. RIGGS. Are you saying that things have changed since last fall, or that your knowledge has changed since last fall?

SEC. HUMPHREY. Our knowledge has changed very materially since last fall and I think perhaps the knowledge of most everyone concerned has changed considerably in realization of the obligations that have been created and the situation in which things were.

MR. RIGGS. Do you feel that there was a definite promise in the campaign to reduce taxes now?

SEC. HUMPHREY. The President never made a promise of any kind. I think that perhaps some of the candidates did, I'm not sure about that, but the President himself never made a promise.

MR. RIGGS. We have all accepted the view that the President himself never said it, but just last week I ran across this quotation from an Eisenhower campaign speech. I take it for granted this is what the man said: "They say you can't cut taxes, what kind of stuff is that, don't and can't? Of course we can and will, that is what the people want now. They want lower taxes." Do you feel that is a pretty definite promise?

SEC. HUMPHREY. Those are exactly the same words that can be repeated today. We want to reduce taxes, we're going to reduce taxes, but we have to reduce expenditures before we reduce taxes and the matter of reducing expenditures involves the security of our country.

MRS. CRAIG. Mr. Secretary, at your press conference the other day you said that, along with other possible taxes you were considering a federal sales tax, is that right?

SEC. HUMPHREY. We are considering all sorts of tax bills; the brand new tax bill, the big tax bill is what you are talking about now, which we expect to have ready for submission to Congress next January.

MRS. CRAIG. Since you are already in the Federal Government taxing most of the luxuries, would you not have to tax the necessities of life in order to get any money out of such a tax?

SEC. HUMPHREY. No, we would not, and we would not expect to tax the necessities under any bill that might be any form of excise bill that might be developed. What we expect to do and what we're planning to do, and in fact it's going on now with both the Ways & Means Committee and other members of Congress, and in our own office, we're studying every form of taxation, we have made up our mind to accept none, and a sales tax or further excise taxes are simply one of the many things. As a matter of fact, we anticipate reducing a good many of the excise taxes, we think a good many of them are too high.

Mrs. Craig. Have you considered the political effect of putting on what the Democrats and labor unions always call a poor man's tax, the political effect of it?

Sec. Humphrey. Mrs. Craig, what we are trying to do is find out what is the right thing to do for America. We are not trying to determine what is political or political expediency, we're trying to seek what is the right way to raise the money that is required to run this Government properly and to provide sufficient security for our country....

Mrs. Craig. Do you think you could get Congress to vote for it in an election year?

Sec. Humphrey. I believe that Congress will vote for what they think is right....

Mr. O'Brien. Mr. Secretary, interest rates have been rising to I believe the highest levels in two decades. What has brought this about, and what are the likely economic effects of it?

Sec. Humphrey. The thing that has changed the interest rates was the ending of the manipulation of rates which had been going on for many years by the Treasury and the Federal Reserve Board. They had manipulated the rates, they had manipulated the money over a period of a good many years to depress interest rates and we have not had a free market in interest rates for a long time. About a year and a half ago there was quite a difficulty between the Federal Reserve Board and the Treasury and finally the Federal Reserve Board won out and took its hands off and stopped the manipulation. When that manipulation stopped, the free market began to operate and gradually from that time on there has been a change in the interest rates, which have increased. They're still low, but they have increased over what they were under the manipulated practice.

Mr. O'Brien. It's true that in the last few weeks several large business firms have withdrawn from financing programs that they had contemplated? ... Do you think that the rise in interest rates will cause enough of this sort of economic postponement to have a general effect on the economy?

Sec. Humphrey. I don't believe that it will. I think as a matter of fact that it's a very wholesome thing to have that occur. I'm not sure how many business firms have postponed. I'm not sure how many political entities like counties and municipalities have postponed, but I think that, with the full employment that we have at the present time, with the very active business we have at the present time, it's a very wholesome thing not to have further pressure on prices at this time.

Mr. O'Brien. Mr. Secretary, if you were still a businessman and not Secretary of the Treasury, what view would you take of the business outlook under present governmental policies and what actions would you be taking as a businessman?

Sec. Humphrey. It's a little hard of course for me to differentiate myself and go back with a business hat and I hope you won't think this answer prejudiced; but I would think, if I were in business today, I was enjoying the most wholesome prospect I had seen at any time in the past 20 years. . . .

Mr. Wilson. I would like to ask you whether you think inflation or deflation is likely to be the bigger problem in the next 12 months?

Sec. Humphrey. I think right at the moment that we have many inflationary pressures. I think that they're continuing in a stronger way than we had anticipated. I hope that we're going to be bothered neither with a wide inflation nor a wide deflation, and I don't believe we will, if we continue sound practices and continue our free markets in a sound way.

Mr. Wilson. Some of the labor economists—I think some of them very able economists—disagree with you on that point and say that you should be more concerned in the immediate future with the problems of deflation due to the slowing down of the defense program.

Sec. Humphrey. Well, the thing they neglect to take into account is that the defense program at the moment is not slowing down. We are going to spend our budget; our budget that has been presented to Congress provides for the spending of as much money this year as was spent last year. Now we hope to make some savings in that, but the savings that we can make over the next 12 months will not be so great in our opinion to radically upset that position. Furthermore, we are advocating a tax reduction to take effect in January and it's our belief that the tax reduction to be made in January will at least offset the savings that we expect to make between now and then, so that, when the money is slackening off because of savings going out for war materials, it will be handed in tax savings to the people so that they will have it themselves to spend, and there will be as much money available in expenditure in the whole economy as there is today.

Mr. Wilson. Would you limit the tax reduction which will come in January to the 10 or 11 per cent which would be provided by going back to the old rate?

Sec. Humphrey. That is correct. . . . The reason that we are advocating it at this time, that it should be given, is because we believe that we can make some savings between now and then which will justify it.

Mr. Wilson. That doesn't apply to the excess profits tax however? You feel that you need the revenue—I mean, the same situation applies, you need the revenue from the excess profits tax?

Sec. Humphrey. There are two things about the excess profits tax. First we need the revenue, but the bad, the vicious features of the excess profits tax continue over the year whether the law is repealed or whether it isn't. . . . The excess profits tax, if figured in a way which takes into account earnings for the entire year, also takes into account expenditures for the entire year so that, even though the law expires in July, the earnings and expenditures for the half of the year that goes on after the tax is out, is still taken into account in computing the tax you pay. So long as all of the vicious things with respect to the excess profits tax are going to be into effect for the whole last half of this year anyway, we think that it's highly desirable that we get the billion dollars approximately that will be available to help the balancing of the budget, and to bring our expenditures and our income more easily or more nearly into balance during that same period.

Mr. Wilson. There seems to be a strong feeling at the Capitol that there is very little prospect that you will get an extension of the excess profits tax even for six months.

Sec. Humphrey. I do not believe it, I think we'll get it. I think that when Congress thinks of the deficit that we have, when Congress thinks of the great desirability and the great wish of the American people to have sound money, to have a sound dollar and to stop these inflationary pressures and the depreciation of the dollar, I believe that Congress will see that it is the wise, sensible thing to do and that we will get an extension of the excess profits tax for that six months.

MR. WILSON. You think the people will want Congress to follow President Eisenhower?

SEC. HUMPHREY. I believe they will, because I believe it's the right thing to do. I think the President has picked the right course and I believe the people follow what is right.

MISS ROUNTREE. You think Congressman Reed and his committee will see it that way?

SEC. HUMPHREY. I don't know whether Congressman Reed will or not. He and I have discussed this matter many, many times together. We see it differently, we believe the effect may be somewhat different. We hope there will be enough members of his committee who will see it our way so it will carry through.

MISS ROUNTREE. If they held it up and it was debated beyond the June 30 date could anything be done?

SEC. HUMPHREY. I think it would be unfortunate if they did that, I think they'd be making a mistake and it would be unfortunate for the country if that happened.

MR. RIGGS. Mr. Secretary, I think it's become obvious if President Eisenhower is going to get an extension through the House or at least through the Ways & Means Committee he's going to have some Democratic votes. Yet on two occasions, last Tuesday in his radio speech and in the message to Congress, he each time said one reason he couldn't reduce taxes now was the Democrats had left things in such a bad shape. The Democrats in Congress are not very happy about that. I wonder if you think that's a good way to get this bill through Congress, to blame it on the Democrats?

SEC. HUMPHREY. I don't think you want me to comment upon tactics. The fact is that we were left in bad shape. The fact is that there were $81 billion of bills, goods bought to be paid for COD. The purchases had been made and we had to pay for the goods when, as, and if received, and that's going on and will go on over this year and all of next year.

MR. RIGGS. Is it the position of this Administration that was due to bad management?

SEC. HUMPHREY. I will speak for myself; I think it was due to bad management particularly for this reason: In my business experience, on two or three occasions I've had to spend a lot of money, I don't think people generally realize how hard it is to spend a lot of money and to do it rapidly and to get value received for it. . . .

Mr. O'Brien. Mr. Secretary, how could the defense program have been set up and planned and carried out unless there had been very large appropriations made ahead?

Sec. Humphrey. The way you do that in business is to get yourself organized and not get your spending ahead of your organization. You get more results, you'll get more finished security, more real safety for America by money that's spent wisely with organization all perfected and with good planning in the spending than simply by just spending a lot of dollars. . . . You can develop your organization and develop the amount of money they can spend wisely both at the same time and let the two go hand in hand, and the result over a period will get you more security every day you go, will get you more for your money, and will have more security currently provided than you will simply by going out and spending your money broadcast and going into waste and uneven expenditures where you're all unbalanced and you have nothing finished but just a lot of things in process.

Mr. O'Brien. In line with that, you are a member of the National Security Council as Secretary of the Treasury, is that right? . . . As a member of that Council and as Secretary of the Treasury, you have had a hand in the cuts that have been made both for appropriations for the military and planned spending cuts for the military?

Sec. Humphrey. They have been submitted to the Security Council, that is correct.

Mr. O'Brien. Is it your opinion that the country will now and in the future get the same defense in terms of planes, tanks, men, and ships, as if these cuts had not been made?

Sec. Humphrey. In my opinion, we will get more real security and we'll get it faster under the present program than has obtained before.

Mr. O'Brien. And you mean in the hard terms of men, planes, and ships?

Sec. Humphrey. That's correct; that are fully equipped and ready to perform. I think we've had a lot of paper goals that were entirely unattainable in the period that they were provided for and I think a balanced program of expenditure, well organized will give us every day from now on more defense for less money and better defense than at any time in the past.

Mr. O'Brien. Are you saying then, sir, that the cuts you have made are merely cuts in an imaginary thing, that these were goals that would never have been reached, money that wouldn't have been spent anyway?

Sec. Humphrey. These goals couldn't have been reached within the periods provided for them by any stretch of the imagination. . . .

Mrs. Craig. Mr. Secretary, I want to ask you about the old age insurance. Do you think it is fair for the Government to force the workers to pay the payroll tax for old age insurance and then if they earn a little bit on the outside to eke out that tiny pension then you don't give them back the money they put in?

Sec. Humphrey. Mrs. Craig, the old age insurance is not in my department. We look after the money but we do not provide that and that is a problem of Congress and other departments. . . .

Mrs. Craig. You have no opinion then as to practice of penalizing anybody for earning money on the outside?

Sec. Humphrey. That's not part of my job.

Mrs. Craig. Is it not true that you've already spent all the money we turned in and all we have is Government IOU's for the billions we've collected so far?

Sec. Humphrey. That is not true and I'm very glad you raised that question, Mrs. Craig, because what we have done is this: As the money was collected for these pension funds and other funds of the Government, it's been the practice right along to take that money out of most funds and put these funds in Government obligations, Government bonds. One day a businessman said to me, isn't that practically thievery? Aren't you just reaching in there and stealing that money? He was operating a large company pension fund of his own. I said to him, What have you got your pension funds in? He said, Ours are invested in Government bonds. I said, So are ours.

Mr. Wilson. Can you tell us when you aim to balance the budget?

Sec. Humphrey. I'll be very glad to tell you when I aim to do it. It's my hope and ambition and I believe we will accomplish a balance of this budget by June of 1954. We are starting out with a deficit in 1954; it's a very great disappointment to me that we have been unable to balance the budget now at this time, but I'm sure that we're on the right track and I believe that we will during the 14 months that remain between now and the first of July, 1954, make sufficient reductions so that by that time our income and our outgo will be in balance.

MR. WILSON. Provided we don't get deeper into the war, is that correct?

SEC. HUMPHREY. I always have to, Mr. Wilson—except foreign complications or the bringing on of a war.

Time "to get control of the budget"

Statement and testimony by Secretary Humphrey
before the House Ways & Means Committee.
Representative Daniel A. Reed of New York,
chairman.

June 1, 1953

The immediate problem is the extension of the excess profits tax for six months through December 31. I am here to urge this extension in spite of the fact that I dislike the excess profits tax and think it is a bad tax.

The basic problem is that of national security—which means military security and economic security. The country must be kept safe from aggression from abroad. And further inflation must be stopped and the dollar must be kept sound to provide a solid base for a healthy economy.

Military security and economic security are the chief responsibilities of the nation. They must take precedence over everything else.

A few financial facts will show just what we are up against.

Last January the budget filed for the fiscal year 1954 showed total estimated receipts of $68.7 billion and expenditures of $78.6 billion, with a prospective deficit of $9.9 billion. On the basis of our present information, it appears that revenue receipts will be $1.2 billion less than had originally been estimated for that year. This would make the deficit $11.1 billion.

In his message of May 20 to the Congress, President Eisenhower showed a reduction of $4.5 billion in the proposed expenditures; this would bring the projected deficit down to $6.6 billion. I personally am disappointed that we have not been able to make greater reductions in expenditures.

I had hoped until a few weeks ago that it would be possible to cut back Government spending fast enough to justify a reduction in individual income taxes and the end of the excess profits tax on July 1. Unfortunately, that is not possible.

I am confident that further cuts can be made as the year progresses. But I am also satisfied that the reductions now proposed are all that can be made safely at this time.

We live, as the President has said, in an age of peril. The danger of an atomic Pearl Harbor is real. Reductions in defense spending must be made only after full account is taken of all the security factors involved. We can, in time, secure more defense for less money. Action to date gives me confidence that this result can be accomplished.

In business, a management can drastically cut back on some activity and later rebuild it if the original cut turns out to be too large. On matters affecting national security, we cannot take this risk. The chance for second guessing may never come. Much though we dislike the level of Government spending and taxation, we are not willing to gamble with the nation's defense by too rapid cuts in defense outlays which might leave us open to attack.

There is a second gamble we cannot take. With a deficit of $6.6 billion, it is not safe to gamble with the country's economic security by making immediate cuts in taxes. This would simply increase the deficit, again build up inflationary pressures and further postpone the time when a sound economy, sound money and a balanced budget can be attained.

The projected deficit of $6.6 billion for fiscal 1954 is after taking into account four major tax reductions which are scheduled to occur under present law during the year. The sequence of these reductions was fixed by legislation adopted some time ago, without reference to the military or economic situations which might exist when the tax cuts were to become effective. A sensible financial plan cannot possibly be made now out of such a schedule in view of present conditions.

At the start of the next fiscal year, that is, on next July 1, the excess profits tax expires. This will involve a loss of revenue of $2 billion in a full year and $800 million in fiscal 1954.

The individual income tax rates are planned to go down at the beginning of next January by amounts ranging from about 10 per cent in the lower and middle brackets to between 1 per cent and 2 per cent in the highest brackets. This will involve a loss of $3 billion on a full-year basis and $1.1 billion in fiscal 1954.

On April 1, 1954, the normal corporation income tax is to be reduced from 30 per cent to 25 per cent, with the surtax remaining at 22 per cent. This will reduce the total regular rate on the bulk of corporate income from 52 per cent to 47 per cent. It will mean a loss of $2 billion in a full year, with only a small loss in fiscal 1954.

At the same time, April 1, 1954, various excise taxes are also scheduled to be reduced, for a loss of $1 billion on an annual basis and $200 million in fiscal 1954.

These reductions all add up to $8 billion for a full year and $2.1 billion for fiscal 1954.

Two things are wrong with this schedule of tax reductions. First, with a deficit of $6.6 billion, no immediate tax reduction can be safely made. And second, there are many inequities and hardships which occur from various provisions of the several tax laws. These affect many corporations and a great many individuals. In the present situation, it does not seem fair to let the first reduction benefit only a relatively small group of corporations at least six months ahead of any relief for any other taxpayers.

Individual income taxes need to be reduced. There are many defects in the excise taxes and many inequities affecting both corporations and individuals under many provisions of the tax laws which need to be corrected. Much though I dislike the excess profits tax, it should not be singled out as the only one for special treatment now.

On the basis of all of these facts, and taking into account the need for maintaining military security and economic security, the President has made the following recommendations to the Congress concerning immediate tax legislation. In his message to the Congress of May 20, the President said:

"(1) The excess profits tax should be extended as now drawn for six months beyond its present expiration date of June 30. This action seems necessary in spite of the fact that this is an undesirable way of taxing corporate profits. . . .

Dan Reed in charge.

Jim Berryman in *The Washington Star*, 1953

"The scheduled expiration of the tax in June would be misleading in its consequences. It would simply mean that the tax would be applied at half the full rate, 15 per cent, to all of this year's business income. Therefore its bad effects in penalizing efficiency and encouraging waste will continue through this year in any event. The extension of the tax through December 1953 would maintain the full 30 per cent rate for the entire year and would produce a gain in revenue of $800 million in the fiscal year 1954.

"(2) The reduction in the regular corporate tax rate from 52 per cent to 47 per cent, now scheduled to go into effect on April 1, 1954, should be rescinded. A continuation of these extra five percentage points on the corporate tax will bring in about $2 billion a year, about the same amount as will be lost annually by the expiration of the excess profits tax at the end of this calendar year.

"Though a 52 per cent corporate tax rate is too high for the long run, the budget will not now permit a reduction in both individual and regular corporate tax rates. A reduction in individual taxes must come first, for the benefit of the entire economy.

"(3) The increase in the old-age insurance tax from 1½ to 2 per cent on both employees and employers, now scheduled to go into effect next January 1, should be postponed until January 1, 1955.

"The old-age and survivors trust fund has now reached almost $18 billion. Receipts at present tax rates are currently well in excess of expenditures. The further addition to the fund which would flow from the projected tax increase is not required. . . .

"(4) The wide variety of existing excise rates makes little economic sense and leads to improper discrimination between industries and among consumers. Specific proposals for a modified system of excise taxation will be included in the recommendations for tax revisions that will be submitted to the Congress next January.

"The reductions in excise taxes, which would take place next April 1 under present law, should be rescinded pending the development of a better system of excise taxation.

"(5) I believe that a reduction in personal income taxes can and should be made effective next January 1. . . . A reduction will be justified next January only because of reductions in proposed expenditures which the present Administration has already been able to make and because of additional economies we expect to achieve in the future."

In the same message, the President referred to the need to revise the whole tax structure "to remove existing inequities, . . . simplify the needless complications which have developed over the years in tax laws, and generally secure a better balance of tax revenues. . . . At the same time, we must develop a system of taxation which, to the greatest extent possible, will not discourage work, savings and investment, but will permit and encourage initiative and the sound growth of our free economy."

As you have said on various occasions, Mr. Chairman, the present system has developed in a patchwork manner over many years. It needs a thorough overhauling. We are pleased to know that you have directed your staff and the staff of the Joint Committee to work on this revision.

We in the Treasury are also hard at work on the same subject. We appreciate the opportunity for cooperation in various ways. We already have set up ten joint committees with representatives of your staffs and the Treasury. . . .

It should be clear from the President's statement that we disapprove in principle of so-called excess profits taxation. I shall not elaborate on the disadvantages and bad effects of this form of tax. They are familiar to all of us. It will be a relief when the tax is off the books. I want to emphasize that the recommendation is for a six-months' extension. We would object to any extension beyond that time.

In considering the excess profits tax, it is important to see what corporations pay it. Complete data on returns filed in 1951, for 1950 income, show that 50,200 corporations paid an excess profits tax. This was less than 12 per cent of the 424,000 corporations with taxable income in that year. Preliminary figures for returns on 1951 income, filed in 1952, show that the percentage was even smaller in that year.

Most of the tax was paid by large companies. The 1950 returns showed a total excess profits tax of $1.385 billion. Of this total, $1.234 billion were from corporations with net incomes of more than $250,000 each. This means that only $151 million or 11 per cent of the total tax came from companies with incomes below $250,000. . . .

The significant point to me, from these figures, is that, though the tax is a very serious barrier to growth for rapidly expanding small companies, it does not affect the vast majority of companies. It falls most heavily on profitable large companies.

I want to be sure that my position on this point is clear. The present distribution of the corporate tax burden is bad because of the tax barriers to growth and the tax penalties on efficiency. But for the rest of this calendar year, most of the bad effects are present anyway.

As the President has noted, the expiration of the tax on June 30 would be misleading in many respects. Regardless of the date of expiration, the tax is computed on a full-year basis. Even though it expires on July 1, its provisions are applicable to the rest of the year. The expiration of the tax in the middle of the year simply means that the rate is lower on the income for the entire year. Thus, if a company lost money through June and made large profits in the last part of the year, it would still be subject through December to all of the peculiar, damaging effects of excess profits taxation on business judgments, even though the tax had supposedly expired some months previously.

Since the vast majority of companies are on a calendar-year basis, the end of the calendar year is the logical time for the tax to expire. I would feel entirely differently about extending the tax even for one month into another year.

A while ago I mentioned the fact that we had had to reduce the earlier estimates of tax receipts. For this year, with only a month left, we know that receipts will be at least $1.5 billion below the estimate made last January. For next year, the reduction is $1.2 billion. Our figure for next year's receipts differs by only $100 million from that made independently by the staff of your joint committee.

The reductions in estimates do not mean that tax collections are falling off. It just means that the original estimates were too high. Collections this year will be several billion dollars more than in any previous year in the history of the country. Next year, even with the tax reductions proposed in the President's program, receipts will be higher than this year.

The extension of the excess profits tax for six months, without modification or amendment, is a necessary first step towards economic security. It will give us time to get control of the budget. It will help in maintaining a sound dollar. It will make it possible for tax reductions and revisions affecting everyone to take place at the same time next year. It will lessen a gamble with national economic security.

We are convinced that this is a sound program. The overwhelming editorial support from all sections of the country is very gratifying. We are satisfied that the country as a whole is back of the President's program. I urge, therefore, that the tax be extended without modification for six months and that we then get rid of it once and for all. In the meantime, we will devote ourselves to further reducing current expenditures so that the reduction in individual income taxes for all the people can justifiably be made a reality. . . .

Cross-examination of Secretary Humphrey

CHAIRMAN REED. I want to thank you very much for your testimony. I think you made a fine case from your point of view. But I would like to explore your views a little further. You do believe, do you not, that the excess profits tax tends to limit the growth of production both for civilian and defense purposes?

SEC. HUMPHREY. I think the excess profits tax very definitely tends to limit the growth of small companies.

CHAIRMAN REED. And you also believe it tends to prevent business expansion and increases in the standard of living for all?

SEC. HUMPHREY. I think it does, Mr. Chairman. . . . I don't want to defend it. I don't think it is a proper form of taxation.

CHAIRMAN REED. Just what assurance can you give that this will not be extended again?

SEC. HUMPHREY. I can only give you my own assurance and the assurance of the President that we will oppose any further extension of this tax beyond December 31. He has said so, and I have just said so now. That is definite Administration policy.

CHAIRMAN REED. You do believe that when the excess profits tax is added to the normal and the surtax rate it encourages extremely wasteful business practices?

SEC. HUMPHREY. I agree to that, yes, sir. . . .

CHAIRMAN REED. I understand Senator Robert A. Taft was quoted as saying the other day that the excess profits tax was a vicious tax. Do you agree with the Senator?

SEC. HUMPHREY. Yes, I think I would say the same thing. . . .

REP. THOMAS A. JENKINS (Ohio). On page seven of your statement, you say: "It will give us time to get control of the budget. It will help in the maintaining of a sound dollar. It will make possible for tax reduction and revision affecting every one to take place at the same time next year." Do you really think that just a continuation of this excess profits tax bill will do all of these things?

SEC. HUMPHREY. Mr. Jenkins, I did not say it will do them all. I said it would help in all; and the billion dollars that this will save will be a very great help in all those things. . . .

MR. JENKINS. As I understand you now, you mean if this bill will bring in $800 million it will be to that extent only a very great help in all those things?

SEC. HUMPHREY. I think to both extents, Mr. Jenkins. I think it brings in, in round figures, nearly a billion in money and I think it shows a fair way of dealing with taxpayers. It does not single out a small group for early treatment ahead of the rest. It puts all taxpayers into the same basis and it shows the determination of the Administration to move forward. I think if the Administration has the courage to come in here and ask you gentlemen to extend this tax it is the firmest good-faith showing that we are determined to balance the budget and to accomplish sound economy. . . .

REP. JERE COOPER (Tennessee). What do you think of providing a new general relief section similar to Section 722 of the World War II excess profits tax law?

SEC. HUMPHREY. Mr. Cooper, I am opposed to any amendments for this short period of time. I think if you were to put in an amendment such as the 722 you might very well open up a mass of cases that might take more income, or a large part of the total income this tax will provide during this period, and the very purpose of taking this step would be defeated. More than that: I think if amendments are once started you can't make a good tax out of it no matter what you put in. I think it would be a great mistake to attempt to patch it up for a six-month period. . . .

I would be very strongly opposed to any amendment of any kind. I think you have this tax in force for what is really an improper length of time. You have a calendar year which for some reason not before us now was cut off on July 1. All that means is that the tax is in effect today for the entire twelve months, but you cut the rate in half by making it a July tax expiration date instead of a December 31. What we are asking for, what I think is the right thing for the country, is to have the full rate on the full year for the tax that now exists, and that by so doing you will not be starting out giving relief to a small group of taxpayers six months ahead of when you give relief to all taxpayers. I think all taxpayers are entitled to consideration at the same time; I do not think you should pick out a favored few and give them a particular advantage. . . .

When I first came down here in the spring, I hoped we could be back of House Bill No. 1. Nothing could have been better from my point of view than to have been able to come into this meeting and say, "Mr. Chairman, the Administration is 100 per cent behind your Bill No. 1. . . ." The difficulty with it is just this: As we met during the early spring I took the position that the Administration could make no commitments until it first learned the facts; that our desires might be one thing but that we had to find out what cuts could be made, how nearly we could come to balancing the budget, what expenditures we had to provide income for.

As those facts developed, we got farther and farther from this desire to join in support of House Bill No. 1. We found we simply could not make the cuts in expenditures that were required to balance the budget, or to see our way clear toward balancing the budget at this time, and take on an additional large reduction in income. As those facts came together, we found the delay in cutting security, military, and other expenses that we could not cut, make cuts in the security program of sufficient amount to eliminate this $11 billion deficit proposed by the preceding budget. Eleven billion dollars was just too much to be cut in so short a time without taking some chance in affecting security.

We did not feel justified in taking a chance when it came to the security of your country. When it comes to just cutting expenditures of a department, I think we could swing a broad ax and cut it to any extent desired, and would not hesitate to do so. I have had to cut expenses in business a number of times and I have not hesitated to cut expenses to do what was required and bring them down. You have to get them down before you can start on a sound basis.

But when you deal with the security of your country; when you are as aware as you all must be that you can have a Pearl Harbor in America, that we have overhanging us a war in Korea, that we have a threat no other country in history has ever faced; never has the chance for annihilation of as great a number of people at one fell swoop existed in the history of the world as it exists today.

When you face that condition, you cannot take a chance in just slashing billions off a program that has already been devised and is under way—too many billions of dollars. You have to be very sure what you are doing. . . .

We are justifying, we are making a reality, out of something that was just a paper hope. That becomes reality as these individual tax cuts become effective January 1.

Mr. Cooper. You emphasize that you not under any condition recommended an extension of this excess profits tax beyond the period here recommended by you?

Sec. Humphrey. We not only will not recommend it, we will come here and oppose it. . . . If the world situation is bad and we have to have more money, if we get into full mobilization, or into more difficulties, I think we can have a better, a fairer tax than the excess profits tax that will raise the necessary money.... I think the purpose can much better be done by renegotiation of the war contracts than by an excess profits levy.

MR. COOPER. What do you think is the likelihood the Administration will recommend a (sales) tax?

SEC. HUMPHREY. I can't tell you a thing about it except that we are studying, in collaboration with you gentlemen and your staffs, every sort of tax we can study....

REP. CARL T. CURTIS (Nebraska).... To a considerable extent, the expenditures in various foreign programs are not due to decisions made in the last few months, is that correct?

SEC. HUMPHREY. You might be interested in a little discussion of the Mutual Security Administration program. The MSA this year contemplates expenditure of about $6.5 billion. That is cash out in fiscal 1954. Of that amount, about $5 billion is for military procurement, purchasing of military end items that are shipped abroad to arm people to fight for us in lieu of sending American boys over there.... Out of the $1.5 billion remaining, about $1.1 billion has to do with defense financing in Europe or the war in Indo-China. About $400 some odd million has been granted France to contribute to financing the war in Indo-China France is carrying on, which is directly connected with defense....

MR. CURTIS. Even something classified as military, you have to hunt to find somebody that can spend dollars running into billions, do you not?

SEC. HUMPHREY. It is a terribly hard job, Mr. Curtis, to spend a billion dollars and get your money's worth.... I said the other day that one of the hardest things in the world is to spend a lot of money rapidly and get your value for it. It is harder... than it is to make money.... It is my private opinion that, the money appropriated to be spent and the time we stepped out to spend it in, it could not have been spent efficiently by any group of men on the face of the earth.

REP. JOHN W. BYRNES (Wisconsin). We voted against the excess profits tax in 1950. How do you suggest we can rationalize ourselves and justify our voting for it now? ...

Sec. Humphrey. I think you were correct when you voted against it at that time. I do not think it is a good tax. But so long as you have now got it ... and so long as the only fair and decent thing is to try to reduce everybody at the same time, I think you would make another mistake if you voted against it now. ...

Rep. Wilbur D. Mills (Arkansas). Are you gambling on whether you will actually have your tax structure ready by the time you get to the point of the savings in expenditures?

Sec. Humphrey. We are actually recommending to you that individual taxes be reduced January 1. To have that a sound procedure, we have got to make some savings in expenditures before we get to January 1. We believe we can do that, and we will do it. ...

Mr. Mills. Mr. Chairman, let me comment for the record that in my opinion Mr. Humphrey makes as good a witness as we have had before our committee. You disarm us and you leave us perfectly helpless to resist anything you propose.

Chairman Reed. I do not share Mr. Mills' views on that last point.

Sec. Humphrey. I am sorry, Mr. Chairman.

Chairman Reed. I want to comment on one thing. Unless we make the tax cut well in advance of the so-called cutting of expenditures it would not be quick enough to pick up the jobs that are necessary to preserve our free enterprise . . . I am following the lines of Prof. Schlichter and others who advise that these cuts come well in advance . . . During the 1920's when we cut taxes four times we had full employment during that time. We cut four times and we raised more money than we had raised before with the highest tax rates. That was Mr. Mellon's philosophy. ...

Sec. Humphrey. Mr. Chairman, I think I agree entirely with your statement. I think you are entirely correct that you must anticipate savings and reduce taxes ahead of time. ... But it is a matter of judgment as to how far ahead you can discount your ability to cut. And that brings in something that did not bother Mr. Mellon, and I wish to God it did not bother us now, and that is the fear of atomic attack.

🖎 Within 24 hours, the Committee had heard from important business organizations and leaders that they supported the President and Secretary Humphrey in their tax program; and Secretary Humphrey on June 3 was recalled to the stand by Chairman Reed and quizzed about possible "lobbying" for his program (Mr. Reed having previously stated in a press conference that "there was too much lobbying going on, and there are laws to cover that sort of thing.") The Secretary said he had talked informally to a business partner about his testimony of June 1, but had done nothing— nor had any of his staff—to prod any business organizations to speak up. The Secretary also answered some further questions of other members of the committee on ground he had covered in his June 1 discussion; the committee, a majority of which still was patently opposed to extending the excess profits tax, then resumed hearing witnesses opposed to extending the provision.

Testimony by Secretary Humphrey before the House Ways & Means Committee.

June 3, 1953

. . . REP. NOAH MASON (Illinois). Both the Treasury and the President have recommended to the Congress that we freeze the social security tax, that it be left at 1½ per cent in January instead of going to 2 per cent. That means a loss to the Treasury of about a billion dollars. How can you afford to lose a billion in tax from that source and not afford to lose $800 million in cash on this excess profits tax?

SEC. HUMPHREY. In the first place, it is not a billion, it is about $400 million this year. . . . The second thing is, when you say "loss to the Treasury," what you mean is this money is collected and put in a trust fund. . . . The only way that cash can be used for Treasury purposes is to take the money out of that trust fund and put it into the general fund.

MR. MASON. And then IOU's are put into the trust bonds.

SEC. HUMPHREY. We call them bonds, we put them into the trust funds. That has been a current practice for a long time. There has been great criticism of that. I do not think it is entirely bad. It is not what I think we ought to do. Frankly, what we ought to do is, when those trust funds get into that, when the money is paid into the trust fund, then the trust fund ought to take the money and go out and buy bonds from the public and bring those bonds into the trust fund, so that we are not increasing, but decreasing, our outstanding bonds in public hands. We are taking them away from the public and putting them in the trust fund where they will be available for use when you later want to sell those bonds and turn them into cash.

If we do it the other way, what we do is put those bonds into the trust fund, take out the cash. We would get exactly the same cash if instead of putting those bonds into the trust fund we put them in the hands of the public. We are just selling that many more bonds, that is all, so we do not lose any money by reduction of this at all, all we do is make it a little easier to sell some bonds to a trust fund instead of selling them to the public. We are selling bonds in either event.

Tax reduction for everyone

Remarks by Secretary Humphrey in a television report to the American people by the President and other members of his Cabinet, Conference Room of the White House.

June 3, 1953

THE PRESIDENT. . . . Over here in this corner you see a basket of mail. This is a portion of one day's mail at the White House. We have been averaging over 3,000 letters a day in an average week—heavy weeks it's more. Now from this whole mass, I am going to read to you just parts of one letter, to show you what one citizen in our country is thinking about, and it's sort of a challenging letter.

"Dear Mr. President," this lady from Pawtucket, Rhode Island, writes, "I am writing you to ask some questions that have me deeply worried. I am a housewife with four children, and though I don't know much about the budget you and your people have to worry about, I do know something about running my own family budget. That is why I have so many questions, when I read about all the money you have to spend for guns and planes, and all the problems that you must have when you try to balance our country's budget.

"The sums are so huge I really find it almost impossible to grasp them." (And I might tell the lady, so do I.) "I wonder how you even know where to begin. Won't you please explain to me, in words I can understand, just how you are going to have our money keep its value, and at the same time make our country strong and secure?"

I chose that letter because it brings up this great problem of security, and the money that it costs. Now, it's a good starting point, and I want to tell you, before Mr. Humphrey takes over to discuss something about finances, we must remember this: During 17 of the past 20 years we have gone into debt.

Borrowing cheapens money. That's like water in your coffee—it just doesn't go very far and isn't worth much. So I have asked Mr. Humphrey and our Director of the Budget, Mr. Dodge, to get after this thing in order to keep spending under the amount we take in so that your dollar will still buy what it should buy. That's his job and now he is going to tell you about it.

SEC. HUMPHREY. Mr. President, I think the woman from Rhode Island was right. I think it is a lot harder, a lot tougher job to balance the national budget than it is your own home budget, because we owe so much money nationally, and we are spending so much money every single year.

Let me just take this chart that I have here and show you where all that money goes. Seventy-three per cent of the total money we spend goes for defense; 15 per cent goes for fixed charges—that is, things like interest, and all sorts of things that the Congress has voted that we pay, like State aid and all that sort of thing. It only leaves 12 per cent for the ordinary running of the Government.

Now, then, our job is to balance this budget. Our job is to get our income even with our outgo. That can be done in two ways, either by raising more taxes or by cutting expenses. Well, of course we don't want to raise taxes—we want to reduce taxes—so the way left is to cut expenses.

And that involves two serious problems. The first problem is that we can't so cut our expenses that we interfere with security. As you have said, we have got to maintain the security of this country. The second big problem is this—over the last year or two a great many materials, war materials and other materials, have been bought COD. They are delivered now; as the deliveries come, we have to pay for them in cash.

I would just like to show you another chart, here, that will illustrate to you the way in which our spending and our income are growing apart as planned for the next few years—the program that we found when we came. Here you will see this line going way up here is spending, and here you will see this line way down here is income.

In between the two is a widening difference, a widening spread which is a deficit. Now that deficit has got to be stopped. Unless it's stopped we are going to be right back on the old merry-go-round of inflation.

THE PRESIDENT. Well, now, George, we know we are going to stop it. But as an ex-soldier I have promised the American people two things; they are going to be secure, and, next, these expensive military establishments are going to be maintained in the most economical way possible. You are going to get one dollar's worth for every dollar we spend. And I am going to keep that promise.

SEC. HUMPHREY. That's just right, Mr. President. What we are going to do is to cut these expenses slowly. We are going to study every month what can be done. We have made a good start already, but we are going to continue every month as we go along and make further reductions in those expenses.

By that sort of process, I think we will be well balanced out by June in 1954, provided we do not have a much worse condition in the world develop. Of course, something could happen in Russia that would upset our plans.

To accomplish that purpose, we have set up a new tax bill. Now in that new tax bill, we ask for an extension of the excess profits tax for an additional six months to carry it from July, when it would expire, to the first of January. The reason we do that is because it is grossly unfair to relieve just a few—the relatively few corporations— who pay an excess profits tax and give them tax relief before we give relief to all the other corporations and to all of the people.

If the Congress will pass the bill we have before them, the bill that we are recommending to them, with the savings that we have already made, with the savings that we are going to make in the next 14 months and with this tax money—this excess profits tax money that we can use to reduce the deficit—it will justify a reduction on the first day of January for taxes for all the people of the country—individual tax reductions.

That will mean that every one will get a tax reduction at the same time. There will be no favorite few. It will help to balance the budget. It will help to stop inflation. It will help to keep sound money. It will help to keep business active, and more jobs, and it will provide better living for all.

⚑ Also presented by the President on the telecast were the Secretary of Agriculture; the Secretary of Health, Education, and Welfare; and the Attorney General.

No "quick checkup" in government

Taped interview with Secretary Humphrey published by U. S. News & World Report, headlined "What Sound Money Will Mean."

June 12, 1953

QUESTION. We have had "cheap money" these last twenty years and now we are going into a period of hard money. What's the objective in trying to get hard money?

MR. HUMPHREY. We've been in this long period of manipulated currency—manipulated money, manipulated credit—and I think that during that period what's happened is that we have saved a small amount of interest on the debts that we had. In the last several years I would say that the interest rates have hardened about ¾ per cent. During that same period of manipulated currency we lost just about half of our dollar.

QUESTION. If you tighten up you don't necessarily see unemployment on a large scale?

MR. HUMPHREY. No, I do not. In fact, I think that the surest way to avoid unemployment on a large scale is to harden this money and have it stabilized. . . .

QUESTION. When do you think we will have a "sound dollar?"

MR. HUMPHREY. I think you have it today. I think the dollar today is a pretty stabilized dollar.

QUESTION. The purchasing power hasn't gone up much yet, has it?

MR. HUMPHREY. But it hasn't gone down, as far as stabilizing is concerned. Now, I am not talking about any miracle job of taking this dollar and putting it back to the 100 cents that it was. That involves a great many changes. Certainly, if it should occur at all, it would be after a very long and very gradual period, because it would mean lower prices for everything and might involve a terrific disruption of the economy.

QUESTION. As a practical matter, can we ever put it back where it was?

MR. HUMPHREY. I wouldn't want to say that you could, nor would necessarily think that it was desirable to make the attempt. But I am absolutely convinced that it is desirable to stabilize it. The first half of the decline in your money goes the slowest. After you have passed the halfway mark, if the people haven't the courage and the determination and the vigor to stop it, the second half may go faster than the first.

QUESTION. Let's examine the cause of that. Presumably the cause of that was the serious international situation in the world, wasn't it? Nobody deliberately drove this dollar into its unsound position, did they?

MR. HUMPHREY. I don't know what you mean by "deliberately." The policy that they had been pursuing of manipulated money over this period of time—I don't think just happened. I think somebody planned it that way. They might not have known what the result was going to be, but I don't see how they could have avoided knowing what they were doing.

QUESTION. You have stopped the downward path of the dollar?

MR. HUMPHREY. That is correct.

QUESTION. And if you hadn't stopped it by reason of the things you've done, do you think it would have tended to go on and on toward less and less value? . . .

MR. HUMPHREY. As of January 1 of this year—or January 20. We will have, I think, at least a $7 billion deficit in this fiscal year that ends June 30 of this year—the 1953 fiscal year. The Truman budget provided for what they said was a $9.9 billion deficit for 1954, and they estimated not only the highest take that has ever been had in taxes, but they overestimated the highest take. We have actually taken the highest amount of money we have ever taken in taxes, and we are going to be at least a billion and a half short this year on their estimates, as near as we can figure it, and we will probably be around $1.2 billion short in the budget for fiscal year 1954.

QUESTION. Is that because they figured in the tax cut?

MR. HUMPHREY. No. It was because they overestimated the highest income that had ever been received. So that cut down in the apparent deficit that was left. The actual deficit that was left is $11.1 billion, according to their figures—

QUESTION. For the year ahead?

MR. HUMPHREY. For the '54 fiscal year. So you've got deficits of $7 billion plus $11 billion in just two years. Then they estimated deficits for every single year for the next three or four years.

Then there is $81 billion of COD deliveries which were bought in previous years with no money in the box to pay for them on delivery when they are presented, in addition to all the current expenditures of running the Government. And with proposed paper tax cuts, meanwhile, that cut the income down.

QUESTION. Authorization for that $81 billion is largely committed, too, isn't it?

MR. HUMPHREY. Well, they use many words—"authorized," "committed," "obligated," "allocated"—you can get yourself into terrible confusion. But, anyhow, it was material to be paid for later for which there was no money in the box. And, strangely enough, as I have appeared before some of these congressional committees I have had to argue for some minutes with some Congressmen on the ground that, if they "appropriated" $81 billion, why haven't we got the money. They say, "Why don't you have the money?" "Who stole it?" "Where has it gone?" I say, "There is no money in the box," and they say, "We don't understand it—we appropriated it—that means you ought to have it!"

We would like to have it, I will grant, but it isn't there because a congressional appropriation is simply an authorization to spend money but does not in any way provide the money to be spent. That can only come from more taxes or borrowing by the Government.

QUESTION. But isn't that the customary way that this thing has been done for years—you appropriate ahead and you are always getting COD's, because you can't always spend in one year what you do appropriate?

MR. HUMPHREY. There is always some pipe line and some overhang.

But when you have a period where you rush and appropriate way above your past appropriation then you build a tremendous backlog of appropriations with no cash in the box. As you work down toward a normal level, whatever that may be, you get back to where you about balance off what was the pipe line one year with what is carried over to the next, and you are about on an even keel.

QUESTION. You are going to start cutting that down?

MR. HUMPHREY. We have already started cutting down. It will come down $8 to $10 billion this year. The point is just this when you talk about spending money. Several different times when I was in business—before I became a bureaucrat—I was associated with companies that were spending a large amount of money. We tried to spend a lot of money and did spend a lot of money for great, major developments. It was a pittance compared with what we are talking about now, but it was an awful lot of real money. The hardest thing I believe there is to do in business is to spend a lot of money in a short time and get your money's worth. It's a lot harder than making it. Because when you are making money you are organized to go on in a regular way—you have your organization developed to do it.

But when you move into a big expenditure program, you haven't the organization for that particular large expenditure—that is an unusual thing—and that means that unless you are careful enough to build your organization first, project your plans first and then build your organization to fit your plans and have your organization in being and functioning with the right kind of people before you start to spend the money, you waste an awful lot of it and you don't get results. You don't get things done just by spending money. You don't say, "I want this or that—I need this or that" and just spend money and get it. . . .

We were budgeted to spend $78.5 billion. We have reduced that by $4.5 billion in four months, and we are now budgeted to spend about $74 billion. We are going to have—with no changes in the tax law—a $6.6 billion deficit if nothing else is done.

If we get the change in the tax laws that we are asking for, we will get about a billion dollars that we would otherwise miss and so reduce that to $5.6 billion. I think that we can, and should, reduce that $74 billion as we go along every month so that by the time we get to June, 1954, we will have our income and our outgo about in balance. That does not mean that we will have saved that $5.6 billion, but it does mean that we will be on a basis of bringing the expenditures and the income together over a period of time.

QUESTION. At what level of spending and income will that balance occur a year from this June?

MR. HUMPHREY. In the vicinity of $70 billion.

QUESTION. What about foreign aid?

MR. HUMPHREY. Foreign economic aid is pretty well gone—well on its way out right now.

QUESTION. Foreign military aid?

MR. HUMPHREY. Well, when you are spending for military purposes, it is for military purposes—

QUESTION. Whether it is for here or abroad—

MR. HUMPHREY. Sure. Just because you mix up your budget and call some billions Mutual Security Administration money, it is still military money, if that is what it is spent for.

QUESTION. Will a substantial dollar reduction in the budget give the economy of the country a jolt?

MR. HUMPHREY. I don't think so at all. I think what would happen is this: We have already anticipated some reductions in the $74 billion, or else we would not dare to permit this individual income tax reduction to go in January 1. We have been criticized. I have been criticized for taking the position that we ought to put in a tax reduction in January before our budget is balanced. I don't think that's correct.

I don't think we ought to wait to get our budget completely in balance before we anticipate the release of some of the money that we are expecting to save for the people themselves to spend for their own purposes. I think we have to take a gamble, that we can make some of the savings we think we can. We have to take a chance and release to the people for their own expenditures some of the money that we've been spending for them and not wait until we get it all in the bank before we give any of it to them.

We are betting on ourselves, that we can make some reductions ahead of time and give the money to the people before we've demonstrated that we are going to perform.

QUESTION. Your objective isn't a slower-operating economy, then?

MR. HUMPHREY. Indeed, not. We don't want a slower-operating economy. We want a full-operating economy from now on in America! Not only that—we want an expanding economy in America. The American people don't want simply to maintain their standard of living—they want to improve it. Every man, woman and child in America wants a better standard of living. We want to work for that and have a country that will let everyone have just that.

QUESTION. How far is the Administration willing to go to encourage that?

MR. HUMPHREY. All out to do it, and I think we are on the way to doing it. I think these sound moves that we are making are the way to establish that and maintain it.

QUESTION. Suppose things turn down. How far then is the Administration willing to go?

MR. HUMPHREY. Well, I don't think you will ever get a completely stabilized economy. Now, by "things turning down," if you are talking about another 1932, I don't think the Government will stop at anything to prevent it. We ought not to permit that to occur in America again, if it can possibly be avoided. Whatever is necessary must be done. . . .

I don't believe depressions are inevitable, and I'm not going to believe it until we've tried everything there is to stop it. I believe if we have the guts and the courage to do the things we ought to do that we won't run into that sort of thing. In a small way it goes back to what we are trying to do this minute.

QUESTION. What is appropriate for a government to do in a real downturn, Mr. Secretary, assuming one starts?

MR. HUMPHREY. There are all sorts of things you can do. You can ease up on your credit structure, you can encourage further expansion, you can promote public works—there are a good number of things you can do that will make it more attractive to have people start to move forward on their own.

QUESTION. You wouldn't advocate "leaf raking" and "made" work?

MR. HUMPHREY. I certainly would not. I don't think it is required and I don't think it is sound policy.

QUESTION. What about really needed public works? Do you think the Federal Government should get into that?

MR. HUMPHREY. It all depends on what the situation is and how much fear may have been spread through the county and how much trouble you may be in. What you need are stimulants sufficient to get the people to start themselves moving.

I believe fundamentally that the success of America is all wrapped up in and almost completely dependent upon the efforts of 160 million people, each one of them trying to get himself to be a little better off. It is the accumulated effect of all those people working in their own ways, and each with his own ambitions for himself and his family to be a little better off, to do a little more, to have his children a little bit better off than he was, and so on. It's that spirit, and almost all of the 160 million of us have that spirit. I suppose there are a few that don't, but the great majority do.

If you don't interfere with them and you give them the best opportunity that you possibly can to do the things they want to do to exercise that initiative and carry forward that ambition, that's what makes this country go.

QUESTION. What allowance are you making for the improvement of economic conditions in other countries which will permit them in turn to take a larger share of the burden of defense in the world?

MR. HUMPHREY. Well, that improvement is going on all along and I think also that a number of these foreign countries have got to look over their own situations in pretty much the same way we are. I was tremendously impressed when I first came down here with the troop of people who came in from abroad and everyone telling exactly the same story, and their story was our story. They were going broke by overspending for defense. All of us were in the same boat trying to overdo defense spending. I don't know whether they were justified in overdoing it, or whether they were getting value for their money or whether they weren't. But I'm pretty sure we weren't.

QUESTION. What can you tell us about the general philosophy or theory of tax reform? There has been some discussion about the administrative provisions of the tax laws, and equities in taxation, and so on. Have you formulated any plans yet?

MR. HUMPHREY. No. It is too early to go into that, at this time. What we are doing is this: The Ways & Means Committee is already studying it, the business organizations are studying it, we ourselves are studying it. Recently newspapers have entirely overplayed everything that we have said or contemplated with respect to the sales tax.

The facts about the sales tax are just these: It is exactly what I have said—nothing is ruled out. We are going to have to raise a good deal of money over a long period of time. I don't think we are going to get back to the low budgets, the really low budgets, for a long time. There are just too many changes that have to take place in the world to antici-pate anything of that kind before you can drop clear back.

So I think we might just as well make our plans to raise a substantial amount of money over an extended period. If something happens that that can be avoided, that will be wonderful, but we had better pre-pare for it.

Now under these circumstances I think we have to give very careful consideration to the means of raising the money which will leave active and available the strongest forces of initiative and encouragement to a high level of activity in this country—for individuals and for busi-ness. Because, after all, the only way you get any of this tax money is by high activity, high productivity of all the people of this country and the businesses in it.

So I think we should attempt to recast our tax system to whatever extent we possibly can to encourage that, and still raise a lot of money that we probably are going to need. That means that, instead of just making little adjustments here and there, by moving rates around, we ought to take a complete look at every possible means of raising reve-nue—how much revenue will it raise—what effect will it have on the economy and on the people if we adopt it? To what extent is it feasible, to what extent is it not feasible? After we have that study we will try to come up with a program that will do the best job and still maintain the greatest incentives to a high level of activity.

QUESTION. You've been criticized for offering rates that were too high, yet you offered a 3¼ per cent bond, which was the highest I think in 19 years, and promptly it fell below par. Then you came along with a 2⅝ per cent certificate and it was not too successful. How do you account for that? Your rates are way up, and yet your issues are not all that might have been expected—

MR. HUMPHREY. In the first place, you've said something I want to take exception to. You said the rates are way up. They are up over what they were during a period of the greatest manipulation of fictitious money rates and credits that the world has ever seen, extending over a very long period, beginning with debasing our currency by eliminat-ing the gold dollar. It started from there and has been going on ever since.

Now during that period we have seen this depreciation of our currency, we've seen this tremendous increase in our debt and the cost of everything we've bought. A distinguished man was in my office the other day and he said in his opinion we've got $150 billion of debt that we ought not to have. Well, I don't know whether that is right or wrong, but I am sure that we have a lot of debt that we ought not to have, that we've paid a lot too much for a lot of things because of the policy that we pursued in the manipulation of our money to try to save a fraction of a per cent of interest.

Our interest rates are not high by any reasonable standard of interest rates. These changes in interest rates began before we came in. I wish we could take credit for it, but we can't. The worst of the manipulation was stopped nearly two years ago, when the Treasury and the Federal Reserve came to an accord and the Federal Reserve backed out of the open-market transactions.

Now the market has begun to operate with money just like it does with any other commodity—money is a commodity just like anything else, and it fluctuates with supply and demand. We have been running in this past year into a very substantial demand for money and the Treasury, since we've been here, has deliberately contributed to the demand in a very modest way—relatively, from our point of view, but in a big way from the market point of view. In other words, $1 billion of American money is still a lot of money.

We have been very cautious in entering that market, with the big demand from municipalities and States and cities and utilities and railroads and businesses, and have attempted to enter the market in a way that would not put up interest rates. You don't need to guess very much of what your money market is, because every day there are tradings in the securities and you can tell just about what your interest rate is today. All you've got to do is take the newspaper and look at it, and you can tell pretty much what your interest rate is.

Of course, in figuring the rate on these new 2⅝ per cent certificates, we had to compete with outstanding securities selling at a discount. Buyers of such securities get part of their return as a capital gain with a lower tax rate. For a comparison, you figure the net yield after taxes. Some people who did not figure carefully thought we were overgenerous when we really were right on the market. The results proved it.

The same was true of the new 3¼ bonds compared with the outstanding shorter-term 2½s.

So in both cases, we put our securities out at just about what the current market was, as near as we could figure it. And while they were higher rates than we have previously paid during the manipulated period, nevertheless they were just about the current rates at the time, as determined by a wide market of transactions. I think most people feel that what we did on the bonds was to go to 3¼ in order to put the rate up, but we didn't at all.

We took a billion dollars of new money out of the market. That had an effect, and always will have an effect. Our demands were added to the other demands that were coming in, the other demands that were made upon insurance companies and banks and other investors.

QUESTION. You don't think it was the fact that you paid 3¼, but the fact that you went into the market at all?

MR. HUMPHREY. Yes, we did it with the thought that it was a proper move for us to make under all the circumstances. We wanted to begin to move this debt back. We had to have about $3 billion of new money. We wanted to get about half of it in long-term money. We wanted to get about half of it in short-term loans—we were playing both ends against the middle to a certain extent—the shorter-term money, largely from business corporations, we felt would be paid off partly from tax collections.

And so we took both courses to help to stabilize the economy and not upset the economy. If we took it all in short-term money it would be inflationary. If we took it all in long-term, it is deflationary. And we thought we could in this way give the best stabilization.

Now as it turned out, I think on our interest rate we just about hit it on the nose. We had some free riders who were trying for a profit. They didn't make it and got disappointed and sold out or are selling out and that puts a little pressure on our bonds.

QUESTION. Do you think that is why the 3¼ per cent bonds fell below par?

MR. HUMPHREY. I think the reaction of the banks in raising their rates had an effect on it too. There also continued to be a very heavy demand for money, a heavy volume of new issues. I think a combination of circumstances was to blame. As the market becomes adjusted to the new level I personally think that these bonds will sell at a premium.

QUESTION. What impact will this have on the international dollar—

your policy here of sound money? What do you expect it to do? I noticed the Canadian dollar and ours are coming out about even now—

MR. HUMPHREY. We heard that the other day for the first time in two years the American dollar was the top dollar in the world.

QUESTION. Where?

MR. HUMPHREY. Every place.

QUESTION. To what do you attribute that?

MR. HUMPHREY. Hard money. We are getting stabilized and it is recognized.

QUESTION. What effect will that have on the opportunity of other countries to buy from us—at stable prices?

MR. HUMPHREY. Stabilization of any currency, particularly of your prime currency, is the greatest thing you can have. If we can have a hard dollar that really is a sound dollar, it will do more to stabilize— will be a great asset to stabilizing—the whole world conditions as convertibility of their currencies gradually becomes possible.

QUESTION. Will it make tariffs less necessary?

MR. HUMPHREY. I don't believe it has too much to do with that. But you've got to have a yardstick somewhere. And a firm sound dollar is a fine yardstick.

QUESTION. They can adjust their currencies around that?

MR. HUMPHREY. Yes. Somebody has to say, "That's 36 inches." And then everybody else measures according to 36 inches. If 36 inches can be 40 inches today and 24 inches tomorrow, you have a terrible time adjusting.

QUESTION. You've been here now four or five months—do you see any possibility of really establishing business principles in Government?

MR. HUMPHREY. I have found that Government and business are quite different things. A lot of the principles that apply in business just don't apply in Government—and I am beginning to understand they just can't apply in Government in a lot of cases. On the other hand, by that I don't mean to condone any inefficiencies or waste or things of that kind. . . .

Business heads up some place—if it doesn't head up with one man at the top, it at least heads up with a few men, your board of directors, and you get a final decision and that's it. You have an automatic check-up every three months. Over a period of two or three years you either do well or you're out. There isn't any guesswork about it. Nobody needs to guess whether you're good in business or not—you either are or you aren't, because over a short period there is an automatic check on every businessman through the quarterly and annual reports that are made showing the results of his business.

In Government there is no check that I know of—it's a matter of opinion. There is no check on your activities, except as to what people believe.

Ultimately I think the people find out what's good for them and what isn't. But sometimes, as long as you've got a full pocketbook, you can do a lot of things that really aren't good for the people and they don't find it out for quite a long while. There is no quick checkup, like there is in business.

The issue of "what you do first"

*Remarks by Secretary Humphrey on Man of the Week
television panel in Washington. Alfred Friendly,*
Washington Post; *William H. Lawrence,* The New York
Times; *John O'Brien,* Philadelphia Inquirer, *and others.*

June 21, 1953

MR. FRIENDLY. Mr. Humphrey, looking at the business situation, would you say the present situation is inflationary or deflationary?

SEC. HUMPHREY. Mr. Friendly, I don't think we are going up or down at the present time. We are on a very high plateau.

MR. LAWRENCE. Will you or will you not get your extension of the excess profits tax by June 30, nine days away?

SEC. HUMPHREY. Mr. Lawrence, I think we will get our extension of the excess profits tax. I think the President's program will carry.

MR. O'BRIEN. Now, President Eisenhower conferred over the weekend with Representative Daniel Reed of New York, head of the House Ways & Means Committee, which up to now has declined to okay the President's tax program. Can you tell us whether or not this meeting brought us any nearer to getting the tax program through Congress?

SEC. HUMPHREY. I wasn't at the meeting, Mr. O'Brien, and I think anything that is to be said with respect to what was done or said at the meeting should be said by one of those who were present. I think we will get our bill before Congress and I think the bill will be passed.

MR. O'BRIEN. Does this depend entirely on persuading Mr. Reed to support the President's program, or does the Administration have the means to get its tax program through Congress with or without Mr. Reed's consent?

SEC. HUMPHREY. It doesn't necessarily depend upon persuading Mr. Reed, but that is the way I hope it will be. Mr. Reed has a very definite opinion about this. He has studied it a long time, and he has a definite opinion about the way this thing should be done. I have the very highest respect for Mr. Reed and his opinion. I, however, have an entirely different opinion than Mr. Reed. The President has. In America when two people have strong opinions that vary from each other, the proper and usual way of doing it is for each to advocate his own position, not to recede from his own position, but to put the question to a vote and when the vote is taken to let the majority decide. I think that is the proper way for this to be done. I think the time will come and the proper procedure will be that Mr. Reed, who is a very fine man, who has very fine thoughts and who is determined in his position, will put his position just as firmly as he can, will advocate his position, and the matter will be put to a vote and Congress will decide the issue between us and that will settle it.

MR. LAWRENCE. What about the Senate? They have had no hearings.

SEC. HUMPHREY. I doubt that additional hearings will be required. The House hearings were full and complete, as you know. They have heard a lot of witnesses, and it isn't a complicated issue after all. The issue is quite plain. It is simply a matter of what you are going to do first. Are you going to balance your budget or attempt to get your expenses in hand so you can begin to balance your budget? Are you going to do that first, or are you going to cut taxes regardless of the deficit involved? We have a $5.6 billion deficit if the President's program is carried through to start with. That means during the ensuing twelve months, the fiscal year running from June to June, that we have to reduce that sufficiently to have—and I hope we will have—our budget, incoming and outgoing, balanced in June a year from now.

Now, if Mr. Reed's bill is passed, Bill No. 1, which provides for an income tax reduction and a dropping of the excess profits tax both as of the first day of July, then we have an $8 billion deficit. It is impossible to balance an $8 billion deficit out within the ensuing 12 months. . . .

MR. LAWRENCE. If you face a $5 billion deficit, how can you contemplate a tax cut in January?

SEC. HUMPHREY. The reason we can do it is this, Mr. Lawrence. We had been in about four months when we came in with these revisions of the budget. We are able to contemplate reductions and effect reductions of about $4.5 billion in this relatively short time. With a whole year to go, twelve months, and knowing more about the situation—all of the departments, not just the Treasury, but all of the departments, knowing what they are doing every single day—it doesn't seem out of reason today that we ought to be able within the twelve months to make a reduction of $3, $4, $5 billion. We were able to make approximately that same amount, $4.5 billion, in four months.

MR. FRIENDLY. Even on the reduction in the budget you made so far, criticism has arisen that you actually made it for the purpose of balancing the budget so taxes could be reduced instead of considering what the nation had to have, particularly in defense. . . .

SEC. HUMPHREY. Mr. Friendly, that is one of the problems we have since Government has been in business. Here we are, if you please, one side of Congress being attacked because we cut too much and the Defense Department is in a hassle down there because they think they were cut too much. At the other end, I am in difficulty with Dan Reed, whom I respect highly, because we didn't cut enough. . . .

The fact is that we did not make these cuts for the purpose of trying to balance the budget, that is, a tax reduction; I mean, in an improper manner. What we did was to start out to take all of the various expenses of the various departments and go through them to see what could be done, to see where cuts could be made within the limits of safety, within the limits of carrying on the services that the Government has to render; and we kept adding them up until we came to a balance. . . .

MR. LAWRENCE. Congressman Reed is much concerned about the Administration jeopardizing itself because he says you promised a tax reduction and you have got to deliver. Do you think the Administration is placing itself in jeopardy by not reducing taxes right away?

Sec. Humphrey. That is where we differ entirely from Congressman Reed. It is a matter of when we do it. It is a matter of what is of first importance. It is my opinion that to balance the budget and get the economy away from this inflationary spiral, and get on a sounder, more permanent basis, is the thing that people want first. Perhaps you noticed the Gallup Poll that was published this morning. Approximately 60 per cent of all the people thought a balanced budget should come ahead of a tax reduction, and when it came to those who were the actual voters, it was three or four to one that thought a balanced budget should come ahead of a tax reduction. . . .

Congressman Reed says in the days of Andrew Mellon he reduced taxes three times and each time he got in more money. He says if we reduce taxes now, we will get not less money but more money. The difference is this. Andrew Mellon reduced taxes in the Twenties. 1924 was a very, very bad year. I remember that very well. We were in bad shape. Production was low and everything was bad. From 1924 we went to 1925 and 1926 and 1927 and 1928, until the peak in 1929, each year higher and better than before. Naturally, reductions could be made and a greater volume of business produced more cash income for the Government.

Now where are we? We have the highest volume of business that this country has ever known. We have the lowest unemployment that this country has ever known; there are less than 1.5 million people out of jobs today in America. We have never seen such good times in this country, taking the level as a whole, as in the last three or four months. We are right at the very top. There isn't any place up from here the way there was in 1924. . . .

I think we have a healthy condition on a very high level, and I think we can have some minor adjustments that move it a little down here and up here, and I think that will go on and can go on if we keep sound and if we don't go back to this inflationary business that we have been in.

Mr. Friendly. You said, Mr. Secretary, so high up that there was no place to go from here?

Sec. Humphrey. I am talking about Dan Reed and I are in a controversy and our controversy is $2.5 billion in six months; that's all. I want $2.5 billion in the till to help pay our bills for the next six months. . . .

🖢 The Gallup Poll referred to by the Secretary was an important factor in the outcome of the battle on the floors of Congress.

"Good money means good times"

Remarks by Secretary Humphrey on Reporters'
Roundup television panel in Washington.
John D. Morris, The New York Times; *Arthur*
L. Moore, Business Week, *and Marquis W. Childs,*
United Features Syndicate.

June 22, 1953

Mr. Morris. Secretary Humphrey, what is the reason for your optimism that the Ways & Means Committee will report out a bill extending the excess profits tax?

Sec. Humphrey. My reason for optimism is I think it is such a natural American tradition to put controversial issues to a vote. I have the very highest regard for Chairman Dan Reed of the Ways & Means Committee. He is a hard fighter. He is a man who has trained football teams and taken the gaff that goes with it. He believes very firmly in his position. We, on the other hand, believe very firmly in ours. Neither one of us knows which side is right or how it will work out in the end; and we never will, because one side will be carried forward and the other always wonder what would have happened if they had been chosen. When you have a controversy, where you have people seriously believing in different and opposing views, the American way is to put those views to a vote, to let each side explain his own position to the limit of his ability, and then let the vote decide it; and I believe that is what will and should happen in this case.

Mr. Morris. But you still have Mr. Reed to contend with, regardless of what you think is the fair thing to do, Mr. Secretary. Could you tell us perhaps what methods might be used to get around him or the committee?

Sec. Humphrey. I hope that no methods will ever be used to get around Mr. Reed. Mr. Reed is a fair-minded, fine man, and I think he will put this matter to a vote of his own volition when the proper time comes.

Mr. Childs. Secretary Humphrey, I believe this tax expires on June 30, and you have just got six legislative days to go before that deadline. Do you still hope that, even after the deadline passes, you could have the tax continued?

Sec. Humphrey. Well, Mr. Childs, the fact is that the deadline means that the law as now drawn would expire at that time. But the present law requires the tax to be computed over a 12-month period, so that June 30 is not the date when the computation stops. The computation will carry on over a twelve-month period, and I think the law could be extended at almost any time after that and still be perfectly legal and in no way upset the calculation of the tax as contemplated. . . .

Mr. Moore. Secretary Humphrey, suppose we get it past Dan Reed, as we have been talking about here. Would your proposition carry in the committee, first of all, and then what do you think would happen to it in Congress if it came to a vote?

Sec. Humphrey. Well, all I can do is to guess from the expressions that we have heard. I am thoroughly convinced, in the first place, from the editorials and from the words that we hear, and as recently confirmed by the polls, that the people of America are strongly behind the President's position that the first job is to balance the budget and have a sound economy, to have sound money, to get our financial house in order. That is number one. Taxes, in all the polls and all the votes everywhere, are second. I believe the Ways & Means Committee and Congress will reflect the same feeling.

Mr. Morris. Well, that reminds me, Mr. Secretary, that when the President asked for the extension of the excess profits tax, he had four or five other tax propositions that he wanted Congress to consider. He wanted the regular corporate rate extended; he wanted some excise taxes extended beyond April 1; he wanted a rise in the social security tax postponed; and he suggested he had a very broad study of the whole tax structure under way. We don't hear much about any of those any more. Have they been forgotten in this fight over the excess profits tax?

SEC. HUMPHREY. No, they have not been forgotten, but in a way they are secondary because of the timing. The changes in those other taxes do not take effect until next year. The only thing that there is any immediate pressure on is the excess profits tax.

MR. CHILDS. On this problem, Secretary Humphrey, of getting the bill out of committee, are you appealing to the Democrats to help you, or what steps are you taking about the Democratic minority?

SEC. HUMPHREY. Mr. Childs, we will appeal to anybody and everybody to try to get this carried out because we believe it not only is the will of the people, before election, today—but we believe that it is essential that we get our economic house in order and this is the first step.

MR. CHILDS. I noticed the Gallup Poll the other day said, I believe, 55 per cent was in favor of keeping the excess profits tax. Do you think they polled the people in Dan Reed's district? Have you any way of knowing?

SEC. HUMPHREY. I don't know where they got the people from, but you are a little off on your figures. It was 59 and a fraction per cent of all of the people, but of those voting it was nearly four to one in the Gallup Poll in favor of not reducing the tax prior to balancing of the budget. . . .

MR. MORRIS. Mr. Secretary, you have spoken frequently, as you did just now, of preserving the soundness of the dollar. I take it that the way you plan to do it is to keep the Government from spending any more money than is necessary over what it takes in. Is that correct?

SEC. HUMPHREY. Our ambition is to not spend any more money, period, than it takes in. Now, we haven't yet reached that point. We haven't had time to get these expensive programs that have been under way in hand. As you know, we are in difficulty at one end of Congress— the armed services are—because they say we have cut too much. I am in difficulty at the other end of Congress because they say we haven't cut enough. But our ambition and our objective is going to be to get ourselves in balance, to have our income equal to our outgo. . . .

MR. CHILDS. What you are saying, Mr. Secretary, is that the balanced budget comes before any kind of tax cuts; isn't that right?

SEC. HUMPHREY. Not necessarily an accomplished balanced budget, Mr. Moore, as you can see, but a sufficiently near approach to a balance so that we have a right to feel that we can accomplish it by the time the tax cut becomes effective. We want to precede the balance by the tax cut; but we must feel that we have our expenses sufficiently in hand so that we can see we are on the right road and we are going to accomplish our purpose.

. . . Mr. Childs. I wanted to ask you about two aspects. The first is in connection with the stand by the United States Chamber of Commerce against the Administration's position and the National Association of Manufacturers refusing to alter their previous stand against the excess profits tax. These men are the owners of industry. How do you explain their stand in opposition to, as you would say, a balanced budget?

Sec. Humphrey. I can't answer for the Chamber of Commerce. As I understand it from the reports I received, their vote was extremely close on the reconsideration. You see, what happened, Mr. Childs, was that both of these organizations took votes before they knew what the Administration program was; after they found out what the Administration program was, they took new votes to see how they stood. The Chamber of Commerce, as I understand it, had a very close vote, almost fifty-fifty. The NAM, however, voted 84 to 46 in favor of the Administration's program, and the only reason in the world that the NAM opposed the program was that they lacked a couple of votes of a two-thirds rule which they had to have to reverse a previous policy. They were almost two to one in favor of the Administration's program when it came to the real vote.

Mr. Childs. The second aspect of this question is that there has been some political criticism that you put the new interest rate at 3¾ per cent, thereby making money perhaps too sound or too tight.

Sec. Humphrey. Well, in the first place we believe in sound money, hard money. Now, that doesn't mean money hard to get; that means good money. And good money means good times. You can't have good times; you can't have a sound economy without good money. You can't have free trade and a big volume of trade unless you have sound money so that people know how to count on their money and how to make their plans.

Now, we do not make the interest rates. The interest rates are made every day in the open market. You can look in the newspaper every day and see the trading in bonds, and the interest rate goes up and down by the trading. The interest rate is made in a free market, which is what we now have. In a free market the interest rate is made by the people who have bonds to sell and by the people who want to buy bonds, and between them those are bought and sold on the market and the interest rate is fixed daily. Now, when we come to put out an issue of bonds, we don't fix the rate; we just adopt the rate that is current at the time. Of course, we couldn't sell the bonds for less. If there are other bonds available that pay a certain rate of interest, we can't sell ours for less. So we just follow the market and put our bonds out as the market goes.

MODERATOR. Here are three prize-winning questions from our listeners. From P. J. O'Connor of Norwich, Connecticut: "Is it true that your decision to boost the interest rates on mortgages and Government bonds was a windfall for the bankers and the moneyed people, but tough for the average American?"

SEC. HUMPHREY. We haven't the exact figures, but we have enough to indicate pretty clearly that there are more lenders than there are borrowers in America. Now, lenders in many cases don't realize that they are lenders. They are depositors in savings banks; they are people with insurance policies; they are people that have pensions; they are people who have put a little aside. All those people are lenders; all those people gain, and there are millions of them that gain when the interest rates move up a little bit. The borrowers, of course, have to pay the difference.

MODERATOR. From Thomas B. Allen of Los Angeles, California: "Do you favor a retail sales tax at the consumer level as a means of increasing federal income and balancing the budget?"

SEC. HUMPHREY. I do not at this time. What we are doing is studying all methods of taxation to see what are the proper ways and the best ways that have the least harmful effects on the economy to raise the large amounts of money that we have to raise, and in making that study we are studying every form of taxation that is known.

MODERATOR. From O. W. Erickson of Scandia, Minnesota: "Does the Eisenhower Administration have an emergency program ready to deal with an economic depression if one should develop?"

SEC. HUMPHREY. Such a program is being worked on by a group that encompasses all the branches of the Government. Not that we feel that there is anything around the corner, not that we feel it is required, but just in the ordinary course of business procedure, we are looking for the places where large volume of business can come from as time goes on. Business is always changing; you are always readjusting. Some groups are moving up; some groups are moving down. We don't want all groups to move down at one time, nor do we want them all to move up at one time, because that means a big boom and a bust. We have today both groups moving sideways, some moving up, some down, and we are looking forward to see what things can be done in the future that will come in to take the place of anything that drops off as we go forward.

🖋 The bond issue discussion was prompted by the Treasury's issue of a 30-year issue paying 3¼ per cent interest, the first long-term federal bond issue in many years. The argument for the issue was in the main two-fold: Resumption of issuing longer-term bonds would greatly add the huge debt management and, all the federal controls on prices, quotas, and wages having been removed, the Government was tempted to affect the business interest rates upward to counter any wave of price and wage raising that would have serious inflationary effects. The bond issue acted in this service as estimated; the controls disappeared without inflation results.

Ally of the Federal Reserve

Statement by Secretary Humphrey from the
Treasury Department.

June 24, 1953

The Federal Reserve Board acted on its own responsibility but after full consultation with the Treasury.

Its action is an orderly continuation of the standing policy of providing the reserves needed for seasonal demands of business and finance and for necessary Treasury financing.

The action is entirely consistent with the policy of restraint of inflation without too drastic credit restrictions.

Just don't let'er
blow up, boys!

Fitzpatrick in
The St. Louis
Post-Dispatch,
1956

🔰 Some critics of the Federal Reserve Board in Congress had spoken up when the board reduced banks' reserve requirements, in some ways a credit-loosening action, and the Secretary thus came to the board's defense.

"We had to pick up the tab"

Statement by Secretary Humphrey from the
Treasury Department related to the Government's
fiscal status at the end of the fiscal year 1953.

July 19, 1953

... We have been forced to pick up the tab for the biggest deficit in history outside of two world wars, even though income was higher than in any previous year in history.

While receiving its highest income of more than $65 billion, the Government, under the spending plans and programs of the past, spent more than this income by $9.389 billion in the fiscal year just ended.

Although the receipts were the highest in history, they fell $3.5 billion below the estimates made by the previous Administration in January....

Current levels of profits and national income give assurance that receipts for the year 1954 will be above those in 1953. Corporate profits in the first quarter of this calendar year are now estimated at an annual rate of about $3 billion above last year's total. Likewise, national income in the first three months of 1953 is estimated at an annual rate of about $305 billion—an all time high and $14.5 billion above the 1952 level.

We see no reason yet to change the estimate of total revenue of $68.5 billion for fiscal year 1954 contained in the President's May 20 message....

Problem of the debt limit

*The July 1, 1953, national deficit and the number of bills
coming due largely incident to the Korean War prompted
President Eisenhower on July 30 to ask Congress in a special
message to raise the permissive national debt limit from
$275 billion to $290 billion. Following the message,
Secretary Humphrey and Budget Director Joseph Dodge
held an impromptu briefing of the press at the press
auditorium of the White House.*

July 30, 1953

SEC. HUMPHREY. . . . The debt is now about $272.5 billion, of which
$272 billion is subject to the legal ceiling. This leaves $3 billion for
additional necessary borrowing, and we have about $8.5 billion in cash
on hand, or a total of about $11.5 billion in cash and borrowing au-
thority.

Expenditures between now and the end of this year are expected to
exceed receipts by $7.3 billion, leaving slightly more than $4 billion to
meet unexpected contingencies, provide any leeway for monthly fluctuations in disbursements, and allow for errors in the advance estimates
of income and outgo.

This is not a big enough cushion for sound operation of the Government. The very minimum sound cushion requirement would be at
least $6 billion. It is our belief that you can't run this Government with
this level of expenditures on less than a $6 billion cash amount, be-
cause you are spending at the rate of about $6 billion a month; and
that means that you only have on hand at the beginning of a month about
the same number of dollars that you are going to spend in that month.

In other words, you are running on about a 30-day basis, and that is
very much closer than a business can run, and it is about as close as
it is humanly possible to run the Government and not run into periods
where you can't pay your bills.

QUESTION. What will you do if Congress refuses to raise the debt
limit?

SEC. HUMPHREY. We will just run out of money and we can't pay our bills, and that is all there is to it; it is that simple. . . . Frankly, I think that if this country didn't pay its bills, if we didn't pay our payrolls, if veterans' payments weren't paid, if goods were delivered and not paid for—if we had to call up somebody and say, "Don't ship something, because we can't pay for it," I think it would just cause a near panic. . . . I think bumping our head up against the ceiling all the time is a very bad thing, and a very bad thing from the point of view of the sale of our securities. . . .

"Because somebody saved"

Speech by Secretary Humphrey to the dinner of the
Governors' Conference at the Olympic Hotel, Seattle.

August 4, 1953

Because somebody saved, America grew productive, prosperous and powerful.

Who are the savers in this country and who borrows the money? Why do they save? What stimulates saving and what deters it? Who benefits from saving and why is it so important?

Strangely enough, there are more savers in this country than there are borrowers of money (excluding, of course, the Government itself), so that actually there are more people who receive higher interest than there are those who pay it.

At once you say, "I doubt that statement," and I think I know the reason why. Obviously a man who has bought furniture, household appliances or an automobile on credit payments is frequently reminded when each payment becomes due that he owes that money and must pay both the principal and the interest. The same is true of the man with a mortgage on his house or farm, or any other borrowers of money.

But the saver in many cases has not so direct a contact, and oftentimes does not realize how directly he is affected.

Of course, a man who owns a mortgage and receives interest and payments on it—and there are millions of them—or a landlord who receives rent, or a depositor in a savings bank or a share holder in a building and loan association, or any one of a number of others who have direct obligations owed to them realizes just as effectively as do the debtors what a higher interest rate can mean to him.

But there are millions of other Americans—all those millions who carry any kind of insurance and millions who are looking forward to pensions or retirement payments or other forms of future receipts, patients in hospitals, beneficiaries of charitable organizations and all endowed institutions—who do not realize how directly a higher interest rate benefits them. But it does so just the same.

Millions and millions of our people receive interest in one form or another. More than 45 million families and 122 million individuals have investments such as life insurance, savings accounts, E Bonds, annuities and pensions, publicly owned stocks, Government bonds, privately held stocks, real estate mortgages, and corporate bonds.

When a higher interest rate is paid, it does not go just to a few bankers, as some of our senators and others who have commented on this subject would lead you to believe, but it goes to benefit directly and to encourage the savings of millions and millions of others.

Why do people save? What stimulates them to do so, and what deters them from it? There are many stimulants to saving stemming from the sterling qualities of self-reliance and protection of one's own future and that of one's family, which is such a strong American characteristic. These include the desire to own your own home or farm, hoping some day to be your own boss, to go into business for yourself, to have a little nest egg laid away for a rainy day, saving for an education, and many, many other reasons—too many to enumerate. Perhaps the most direct stimulant to saving is the return from earnings on the money, whether it comes directly or through extra benefits on insurance, pensions or in other forms.

Of even greater significance is the soundness and honesty of the money that is saved. Unless the people can believe in the continued honesty of their dollar, if they fear that over a few years it will greatly depreciate or even disappear in value, no other incentive to saving is of much avail. Fair interest and honest money, the value of which can be depended upon over the years, combine to form the greatest incentives and the essential requirements which induce people to save.

Savings have made America. Because somebody saved, we have jobs, we have all kinds of things for better living. We have food, transportation and everything that each of us has each day, not only for daily necessities and comforts, but for livelihood itself.

Did you ever stop to think why Americans have a higher standard of living than others in the world? Why American productivity is greater than the productivity of any other nation? Why we are so powerful and strong? Just by themselves an American's two hands are no stronger, no better, not much more effective than those of the citizen of any other nation. Why is it then that American hands can do so much more than any other hands in all this world? The real reason is the fact that somebody saved.

Because somebody saved there were funds available which attracted expert management to invent, design and build efficient machinery, factories, mills, explore for and develop mines and oil wells, provide transportation, and power plants, which through management and organization put tools, equipment and tremendous power into every pair of hands in this country backed up by thousands of dollars of investment, to multiply by tens, twenties and hundreds the strength, the ability and the effectiveness of those American hands as compared with any other hands elsewhere.

Because we can create more, we have more, and that is why we have the highest standard of living on earth and stand in the earth's most powerful position. Because somebody saved, Americans have jobs today. Because somebody saved, Americans have and are what they are today.

A skilled mechanic who, in his spare time, decides to build a new kitchen on his house with the help of a neighbor or a friend, takes great pride when this job is finished and thinks he did it himself— but how much help did he get because others had previously saved? He worked with common tools, but the head of his hammer, his nails, chisel, plane and saw required great steel mills before he could have them.

The lumber that he used required logging operations and saw mills; his floor coverings and walls required building material operations; the paint came from chemical plants; the icebox, stove, washing machine and fixtures meant copper mines, iron ore and coal mines, steel and brass plants and manufacturing operations, and many of the materials came long distances in ships, over railroads or in trucks, which in turn required more steel, more metals, and more plants; and so it goes.

That single kitchen which that man thought he built by himself required millions and millions of dollars of savings and the employment of thousands of people who, unseen by him, lent a helping hand that made his kitchen possible.

There is no one in America who is not better off than he otherwise would be because somebody saved, even though he may not yet have done so himself. That is why fair interest rates and sound, honest money are of benefit to every man, woman and child in this land. That is why any manipulation or restriction that unduly depresses a fair rate of interest, or that tends to depreciate the value of the American dollar, is directly to the disadvantage and threatens the very existence of life in America today.

Do not let anyone fool you into thinking that no one benefits from fair interest rates but some banker. Do not let anyone fool you into believing that running Government deficits, increasing inflation, and depreciating the value of our money is not directly harmful to every citizen.

When nobody has any money to help to put tools and power into American hands, they will again be on the road to becoming no better than the hands of the savage.

Not only the prosperity in this country, not only the creation of more jobs, but the military security of this country as well as the economic security are all inextricably tied into stimulating and not deterring the simple fact that somebody saves.

I should like to emphasize again that this Administration does not have, and never has had, a "hard money" policy as our critics sometimes charge, meaning as they say hard-to-get money and hard times. The goal of this Administration is honest money; we mean money that will buy as much next week, next month and next year as it will buy today. . . .

Americans by tradition expect honesty in all things. This Administration is determined to put an end to further decline in the value of our money and provide again an honest dollar. . . .

The Treasury's main role in this business of keeping honest money lies in its handling of the public debt. That debt is now over $272 billion, and the manner in which refinancing and the placement of new issues is handled can effect the entire nation's well-being. The Treasury is trying to make the debt sounder by gradually extending the length of its maturities. Now nearly three-quarters of the debt matures within less than five years.

In April we took a first step in trying to convert some of this into sounder and less inflationary issues by putting out a 30-year bond at an interest rate of 3¼ per cent. That rate was higher than the coupon rate for previous issues but it reflected the going rate at the time of issue as fixed by the current daily market purchases and sales at the time the bonds were sold. Gradually and at opportune times, further long-term issues will be sold, but care will always be exercised not to press the market unduly in competition with other state, municipal and private financing.

An honest dollar means a lot to you governors. Just compare in your minds what it cost a few years ago to build a two-lane concrete highway; or a schoolhouse or improvements of any kind with the costs of today. And a similar story goes down the line of all state, county and municipal expenses. The lack of good, honest money or the presence of inflation has caused large increases in the amounts of money you have to raise to do the things that you have to do.

On the national scale, it cost the states about 50 per cent more to operate in 1953 than in 1946.... We are glad to find that your pension and retirement funds are so interested in the purchase of Government securities. Your financial people have found that there is no better place to put short-term funds than in our Treasury bills, certificates and notes.

We had an interesting and successful meeting with a number of state fiscal officers at the Treasury in May of this year. State and local governments own more than $11 billion of United States Government securities at the present time. That is almost twice as much as they held at the end of the war, and 20 times as much as they held before the war began....

It is sometimes said that the Federal Government has come into some traditionally state activities because of the failure of other levels of government to provide services which citizens demanded. It is the philosophy of this Administration that at all levels of government we must try to develop more the traits of individual responsibility, saving, enterprise and initiative—the traits which have made this nation great.

The thrift and savings of our forefathers laid the foundations upon which all that we now have has been built. We have incurred tremendous debts but they are not overpowering if intelligently and carefully managed.... Let us always remember how much all that we have in our life every day was created by the self-reliance, industry and initiative of millions of Americans—and because somebody saved.

For the $290 billion debt limit

Interview with Secretary Humphrey published by
U. S. News & World Report.

August 7, 1953

QUESTION. Would you care to comment on Senator Byrd's contention that there is no need to raise the debt limit because the Treasury can draw on that $9 billion cash balance which he says you have on hand?

SEC. HUMPHREY. The difference between Senator Byrd's thought and our thought relates very largely to the amount of cash that you have on hand to do business.... It is our experience and our belief that you can't run this Government with this level of expenditures on less than about a $6 billion cash amount, because you are spending at the rate of about $6 billion a month and that means that you only have on hand at the beginning of a month about the same number of dollars you are going to spend during that month. In other words, you are running on about a 30-day basis, and that is very much closer than a business can run, and it is about as close as it is humanly possible to run the Government and not run into periods where you can't pay your bills....

QUESTION. At what point, Mr. Secretary, did you realize that you might have to make this request?

SEC. HUMPHREY. I think the President spoke about it first in May. ...This has been a perfectly obvious thing, that at some point this would have to occur. Now, the reason it was put off until this particular time is because we wanted to get the estimates as nearly as we could to what the appropriations for this year were going to be. You see what it is; it is really a very simple matter when you get right down to it. Congress decides how much money is to be appropriated and

"I always run into
this same Byrd. . . ."

Jim Berryman in
The Washington Star,
1955

to be spent. They authorize certain things to be done. When they authorize the different departments to do things, they appropriate the money for them to spend and they tell them to go ahead and do it, just as they have—there is no blame attached to this at all. Congress ordered all this material bought and said that when it came they would pay for it, and they authorized the payment.

At the time it was bought, they authorized that it should be paid for. The only thing they didn't do was supply the money at that time. The Congress authorizes how much money will be spent. When you find out how much money Congress has authorized to be spent, then the executive department goes ahead and does the business to spend it.

Now, the money, the cash, to pay those bills when they come due, or to pay the current salaries and the various things and expenses of Government comes from just two places. One, it comes from the authority of Congress for the taxes or customs duties or income of the Government, and if the appropriations for expenditures made by the Congress are more than the taxes and customs that are authorized by the laws of Congress, then you have a deficit. Now, when you have a deficit, there is no place to get your money except to borrow to make up the deficit. That is the position we are in, and that is the position we were in last year and we are in at the moment with respect to this year. . . .

QUESTION. Mr. Secretary, you do not consider the debt limit sacrosanct, do you? You can raise it?

SEC. HUMPHREY. Very frankly, a debt limit is a secondary consideration. . . . It must be, because, when you decide what your expenditures are going to be, when you decide what your income is going to be, you have to borrow the difference in money. There is no other place to get it from, and if you have a debt limit which prevents you from borrowing the money it simply means that you cannot carry out the orders that Congress has given you. . . .

I think that what we ought to do is to get a limit which will permit us to operate over the next two or three years, as far as we can see, in a reasonable way, rather than going through this every few minutes and I think bumping our head up against a ceiling all the time is a very bad thing; and is a very bad thing from the point of view of the sale of our securities. . . .

Congress, however, adjourned in August without the Senate voting on the legislation to raise the debt limit.

"No retreat" from honest-money policy

Interview with Secretary Humphrey published in Newsweek.

August 10, 1953

QUESTION. Do you think a business recession is likely to follow the Korean truce?

SEC. HUMPHREY. Not in the slightest. America grew great in peace and there is no reason why we will not grow even greater as world conditions improve and as we have to spend less of our national income for implements of war. All the reports that we get indicate that business this year is operating at a new high level.

QUESTION. What steps could be taken to cushion a recession if one should develop?

SEC. HUMPHREY. There are certain things such as hospitals, schools, and highways which need to be built or improved. There are also many private business expansion plans which are being temporarily held up due to heavy demand for credit. These could be pulled out if the present high level of business activity tends to ease off.... With business at the present high level, I think some private projects might well be postponed until both credit and materials are easier. This would not only help to spread activity, but make it easier for the businesses to get the capital they need without the Government taking inflationary measures.

QUESTION. The Eisenhower Administration has been criticized for its so-called "hard money" policy. What is your answer?

SEC. HUMPHREY. This Administration does not have and has never had a hard-money policy, in the sense that our critics have attributed that policy to us, and gone on to suggest that hard money means hard-to-get money and eventually hard times. What we do have is not a hard-money policy but an "honest money" policy. By honest money, I mean money that will buy as much next week, next month, and next year as it will buy today.... We have not retreated and will not retreat from our policy of trying to achieve honest money for the American public. That must be accomplished through co-operation of several branches of the Government. The Federal Reserve System, of course, is the primary agency for money and credit control and this Administration has assured the Federal Reserve System that we are going to give minimum interference while it goes about its operation providing necessary credit and at the same time helping maintain honest money. In the Treasury, we are working toward honest money by handling the debt so as to avoid inflationary pressures. We do this by gradually getting the debt into longer-term issues and also getting the debt into the hands of private investors instead of the banks where it is inflationary, because it makes more credit available....

QUESTION. Are you still optimistic about balancing the budget in the fiscal year beginning July 1, 1954?

SEC. HUMPHREY. I have said and I still say that our hope is to have spending and income at a rate of balance by July, 1954. As every day and each week go by, we will have to keep looking at our spending programs to see where savings can be made. These programs cannot be changed overnight because they have been built up over a long period of years; however, we can keep working at them to reduce expenditures, get our money's worth, and continually work toward our objective of balancing our expenses and our income.

Turning point

Statement by Secretary Humphrey in a news
conference at the Treasury Department.

August 27, 1953

We have good news today. I am proud to announce that present estimates indicate that the Government spending for the fiscal year 1954 will be $2 billion less than the forecasts for the spending as recently as last May.

These substantial savings were made possible by economies urged on the heads of all Government departments and agencies by President Eisenhower when the last fiscal year ended on June 30. The expected deficit and the national debt both will reflect these sharp savings.

These economies exceed my own hopes for our fiscal situation. However, as we work up toward an eventual balance of the budget, I would warn you that such things as unexpected developments abroad, heavier requests for domestic agricultural loans than estimated, and other unforeseen demands might well upset the progress that has been made.

For the first time since 1948, new obligational authority is substantially less than the estimated annual budget expenditures. Thus the build-up of accumulated commitments for which cash will have to be paid from the income of future years will start declining. Therefore, the lower level of new obligational authority promises lower expenditures not only in 1954 but also in future years. New obligational authority lower than the year's expenditures and receipts is the essential turning point toward a balanced budget. . . .

"Some progress for the honest dollar"

Remarks by Secretary Humphrey before a luncheon of the National Press Club in Washington.

September 16, 1953

Inasmuch as the main recent Treasury news was made by the $2 billion planned cut in fiscal 1954 spending and the very successful Treasury refinancing, I am today without fresh, hard news to announce. So I will ask myself a few of the questions which seem to be in people's minds about our operations these days and try to answer them with something of the philosophy of what we are doing.

QUESTION. What about the debt limit?

Just before the Congress adjourned, the House of Representatives by a large majority passed but the Senate Finance Committee refused to approve our request for an increase in the debt limit from $275 to $290 billion. We thought then and think now that the increase was a proper request in the best interests of orderly fiscal management to provide adequate elasticity in handling our finances.

The Government is spending about $6 billion a month. If our balances fall below this, it means that we must operate on less than a 30 days' cash basis. With the amount of debt we have maturing, the financing requirements to cover the estimated budget deficit, the unequal receipts of income because of the Mills Plan, and the possibility of large unexpected requirements for cash outlays in so many directions, it seems most imprudent to us not to have adequate elasticity to meet whatever our financial requirements may be.

The problem concerns not economy but the fiscal management of the Government. We pledged that we will continue to work for increased economies in government, whether or not we have the debt-limit ceiling we requested.

However, as I said immediately following the Senate committee's decision, we will bow to their judgment and we will try in every way that we can to operate within the restrictions of the present limit. The total amount of September tax collections should be known within

"... and MY price has
gone up, too!"

Berryman in
The Washington
Star, 1953

the next two weeks. If our income is up to estimates and there are no unexpected expenditures, the chances are that we may be able to get by without going over the present debt limit and so not need a special session of Congress. . . .

QUESTION. Will proposed tax cuts go through?

Some people have suggested that we shouldn't allow tax cuts to become effective January 1 unless we have a balanced budget. I do not know what we will have clearly in sight, when the next Congress convenes. But the progress we are making toward a balance is sufficient so that I do feel sincerely that the President's program of letting the excess profits tax die as well as making effective the reduction in personal income taxes on January 1 should be allowed to go through on schedule.

There is nothing in our present estimates of spending and income which would tend to change our recommendation in this matter. We are continuing to make progress toward balancing the budget and we are going to keep right on trying in every reasonable way to do so.

It is not an impossibility to balance the cash budget before the year is over, or at least to get into a current balance by that time.

In the tax field in general, Treasury people are working diligently with congressional counterparts in studying the whole tax structure to help in every way we can the Ways & Means Committee in preparing a tax reform bill which may be considered by the next session of Congress.... This new tax bill will propose revision of our present tax laws and regulations which will remove many inequities and injustices.

QUESTION. Why does the Government have to pay more interest on Government bonds?

Over any extended period, interest rates will respond to the supply and demand for money. They are currently determined daily by widespread purchases and sales of securities in the financial markets. If a bond pays a fixed rate of interest, then the rate of interest which a purchaser of it will receive on his investment will depend upon the price he pays to buy it. If he pays par, he gets the fixed rate, but if he pays more or less than par, then the fixed rate will be equivalent to a lesser or greater rate on the amount of money he has paid to acquire it.

When Government bonds are sold by the Treasury either to refinance a maturing issue or to borrow new money, the rate of interest they bear must reflect the rates then currently being determined by the purchase and sale of other outstanding Government securities on the open market.

If a too much higher rate is put on the new bond, it favors the buyer as against the Government and will further depress the price of other issues.

If too low a rate is paid on the new bond, buyers won't buy them but purchase other securities which give a better return....

QUESTION. What is it this Administration is trying to do about money?

This question has been asked in discussions about "hard money," "sound money," higher interest rates, the prices of Government securities, etc. Information on all of these matters is due all Americans, and it is my purpose to keep trying to provide that information.

What we are trying to do is to make the money of America honest and sound so that it will better serve the well-being of the American people.

I think most of us do not realize until we stop to think about it what it takes to make a job in America today. First it takes savings. Who are these people who save? They are almost everybody in America. They are the Americans who have savings accounts; who are buying insurance; who are paying on pension plans for decent old age, and many, many more. Banks and insurance companies are simply the instruments through which those savings of millions are funneled into the channels of trade and investment.

Because all these people save, there is money available for investment. This investment enables the development of not only our national resources but also the scientists, managers, and all the people who co-operate in the production of machinery, the people who explore for new mines and oil wells, the people who build factories and equip them with tools, the farmers who produce so much more with modern farm equipment, the power plants, and the transportation so that the two hands of an American can produce twenty to a hundred times as much as those two hands could do without these great developments that savings have made possible.

There is an investment of $17,000 for every man working in a steel plant today. This means that there are $17,000 worth of plant and tools which put power in his hands. . . .

Fair rates of interest and fair earnings on money saved and sound honest money are essential for saving. No one will save money that earns little or nothing or that he thinks will grow less and less valuable or may become worthless. . . . We know that good money means good times.

QUESTION. What are we doing to try to provide honest money?

We are working at it in three main areas.

The first area has to do with the budget and deficit financing. When a government spends more than it takes in, it has to borrow to pay its bills, just as a family or a business does. When the Government borrows from the banks, it creates more credit, increases the money supply, and thus can help cause inflation. Inflation means that the dollar is worth less. Honest money means the absence of inflation and a more constant, assured value of the dollar.

The second area has to do with the proper activities of the Federal Reserve System. In the past, under Treasury domination the Federal Reserve has contributed substantially to inflation by artificial manipulation of the value of government bonds, which added substantially to the supply of currency and thus aided inflation. Freed from arbitrary control, it can contribute greatly to stability of the value of the dollar.

The third area is in the management of our too huge national debt. The well-being of the nation is substantially affected by the manner in which we refinance and place new issues in this $275 billion problem. We are trying to make it less inflationary by gradually extending the length of the maturities of the issues and placing more of it in the hands of investors and non-bank holders. Nearly three-quarters of the debt matures in less than five years. That is too high a percentage for the safety of an honest dollar.

QUESTION. How are we doing in getting honest money?

I think we are making some progress. There are indications that the 13-year decline in the purchasing power of the dollar at last has been halted. The dollar which is worth only a little over 50 cents today was worth 100 cents some 13 to 15 years ago. The value of the consumer's dollar for all items has changed less than half a cent in the past six months as compared with a decline of nearly 20 cents in the past six years. While six months is of course a short time in which to gauge a trend, it does indicate that for the moment at least the dollar has become better stabilized.

In the budget field, some real progress is being made. Estimated expenditures for the current year have been reduced by nearly $6.5 billion under the estimates we found upon entering office. Eighty-one billion dollars of COD orders previously placed will come due in the next one, two or three years and must be paid for. These past obligations make it impossible to wipe out deficit financing overnight, but these forward obligations will be reduced by about $9 billion according to present estimates. . . .

Recent revelations that the Russians may have gone beyond the atomic bomb in the field of nuclear weapons is additional sobering evidence that our course in being careful as we review our defense machine is a most proper one. The stakes are too high to chance being only second best.

This does not mean that we cannot continue every day to more efficiently plan our programs to get the most for the money we spend. . . . We must make sure that what we have is the most possible in intelligent planning and organization to provide that balance and efficiency of forces which will give the best defense at the minimum of cost to the economy of our nation....

The Federal Reserve has been assured by this Administration that it will have the prime responsibility for maintaining a proper money supply and conditions of bank credit free of artificial restraints.

The third area important to honest money is debt management. We have been asked if we have abandoned our goal to try to get more of this debt into long-term issues. We have not abandoned this goal in any sense. We took a first step back in April by putting out a 30-year bond. The rate of 3¼ per cent was higher than the rate on previous issues, but it reflected the going rate as fixed by the current daily market purchases and sales of outstanding Government securities current at that time. Within the past few days we have had a most gratifying response to a proposal to elect between a one-year and a 3½-year maturity in refinancing a large issue that came due. Holders of more than $3 billion of the total issue elected to take the longer term security.

All in all, we have made some progress in this effort for an honest dollar. It will take a lot more time and a lot more work to make further progress, but we intend to keep at it....

The "three pillars" of sound money

Speech by Secretary Humphrey to the American Bankers Association at Constitution Hall, Washington.

September 22, 1953

The decision of the American Bankers Association to hold this year's convention here in Washington, was made at your sessions three years ago. Many things can happen in three years and many things have happened. A new Republican Administration is here and I as Secretary of the Treasury wish you a warm welcome. You have done and are doing a magnificent work in assisting the Treasury particularly in the distribution of savings bonds. Nothing is more important in the

Treasury's plans and few things are of greater significance in our whole economy. We thank you and rely upon your further intensified efforts.

Since you as bankers are concerned intimately every day with the money problems of this nation, I am going to take the liberty this morning of talking for a few moments about what this Administration is trying to do to achieve sound money. I say sound, not hard but honest money.

Sound money is based upon three principal pillars—a proper budget policy, a properly functioning Federal Reserve System, and proper debt management. This Administration is working constantly to strengthen all three pillars. Our goal in each of these areas is clear. If we have not achieved our goal overnight, it is not only because of the size of the job itself but also because we realize that our economy is a very sensitive mechanism and we must proceed carefully, but always steadily, toward the goal we seek. Too drastic and precipitous action might react badly in many ways. We must approach our objective cautiously but resolutely and always press toward it.

The first pillar—and one which we have already made substantial progress in strengthening—is the budget pillar. As you gentlemen well know, deficit financing—that is, spending more than you take in—means more and more borrowing and debts which in times of high employment and incomes lead to inflationary pressures and unsound money. When a government spends more than it takes in, it has to borrow to pay its bills. When a government borrows from the banks, it creates more credit, increases the money supply, and thus helps cause inflation. This is what we are trying to check.

The midyear review of the 1954 fiscal budget showed some real progress being made in getting the budget in hand. Estimated expenditures have been reduced by nearly $6.5 billion under the spending estimates this Administration found upon taking office in January. In addition, income was overestimated by more than a billion dollars. So that the prospective deficit has really been cut from over $11 billion to less than $4 billion.

Eighty-one billion dollars of COD orders which were placed by the Government from one to three years ago will come due in the next year or two and must be paid for. These inherited obligations make it impossible to balance the budget overnight, but even these forward obligations will be cut this year by more than $9 billion, according to present planning.

As our midyear budget review showed, we have turned the corner in attempting to get our Government's finances in hand. For the first time in the past few years we are planning to spend less this year than in the year before. The sharply rising curve in federal spending has now turned downward.

This is a very encouraging development. If we can reach a current balance in our cash income and cash expenditures by the end of this fiscal year, it will be much better than we had dared to hope for six months or so ago.

The budget review we announced a month ago also is a turning point because, for the first time since 1948, we have total appropriations which are less than estimated receipts for the year. This points to future reductions in both spending and taxation.

For this encouraging start, the Administration is deeply indebted to the Congress and to the various departments and agencies of government for their wholehearted co-operation. Unless some unexpected event arises which substantially changes the need for money, we believe that we are finally on our way toward getting the budget under control.

Of course, this is all based upon estimates—estimates which we hope are realized—but this business of estimating how much the Government is going to take in and pay out has a great many pitfalls.

Estimating a year ahead in a business this size is more than risky and a small per cent of error in our huge figures can mean the difference of a great deal of money.

For instance, over 70 per cent of our expenditures are for national security programs, and even a relatively small estimating error can mean hundreds of millions of dollars. For these programs alone we are spending about a billion dollars a week. There are other programs, too, where the relative margin of error is even greater than it is for the military, although there may not be so many dollars involved.

Take the Commodity Credit Corporation for example. In order to figure its net outlays in advance you have to not only estimate the size of the various crops but also just how the farm price support program is going to work out in the year ahead and, even more important, how much of it will be handled by the banks instead of the Treasury.

In the last fiscal year (1953) the budget estimate was about $800 million for Commodity Credit but when the year closed it actually turned out to be about $1 billion more. That is just one illustration. There are many, many others.

Every banker knows that the matter of estimating budget expenditures is further complicated by the necessity for estimating the distribution of those expenditures from month to month—and even day by day in some instances—and preparing to have sufficient funds on hand to be able to meet current requirements. You all appreciate that that is why we cannot run our cash balances too low—a point we made in the debt limit discussion. It is sometimes hard to realize that if our cash runs down too much, a few days of unexpected heavy expenditures, or an unpredictable shift of a few days in tax receipts, might easily force the Treasury to do borrowing at a time when conditions in the money market were not propitious or in amounts that might substantially exceed our estimated borrowings.

Every banker knows that some real elasticity in such circumstances is only prudent management. That was the basis for our request for raising the debt limit. We were not seeking to remove any limitation on or deterrent to greater spending. We have demonstrated, we hope, to everyone our insistent interest in and demand for economy and getting our money's worth, but because we are responsible for the Government's fiscal policies we must have the elasticity required to plan them in the best way.

The operation of the Mills Plan, with which you are all familiar, requires the payment of 90 per cent of the corporate tax money in the first half of the next calendar year. In accordance with the practices established by our predecessors when the plan was first inaugurated, tax anticipation notes in the amount of several billion dollars must be issued in the last half of the calendar year, when only 10 per cent of corporate taxes are received, against the 90 per cent to be received in the following spring. This makes a temporary increase in the Government debt a practical necessity for a short period even though a cash balance in the annual expenditure is achieved; and under present laws there is no way to avoid it.

The great and really important reason, however, why it is most difficult to cut expenditures radically and bring both a balanced budget and a tax reduction into quick being at the same time relates to our national security. Without due consideration for it, the rapid reduction of expenses would be comparatively easy. But with the real possibility of an atomic Pearl Harbor hanging directly over our heads, and with the knowledge of the Russian capability to produce an even more potent weapon, national security is a matter of first concern.

I do not mean that hope of reduction in expenditures and taxes must be abandoned. Quite the contrary. But the necessity for caution and planning and assurance that reductions are justified before they are made is paramount. A balance between our military and our economic security must be achieved. The ability, the ingenuity, the management, planning and experience of all Americans, under the present able leadership of our Defense Department, I am sure will devise and provide means of accomplishing stronger defense for less money as time goes on. We cannot move as rapidly as we would like, but our course is plain, our objective is definite, and we will achieve it with only the time necessary to be sure of the safety of our actions as we move toward it.

The second pillar of sound money is a properly functioning Federal Reserve System. This is another way of saying effective monetary policy. The balance between the money and credit supply and the actual flow of goods in commerce is best maintained by letting the price of money rise and fall with the demand for money. At the same time our Federal Reserve System can and should use its powers to keep the market for credit orderly and to avoid excesses in either direction, to avoid either inflation or deflation.

In the years preceding the March 1951 accord, the Federal Reserve System, under Treasury domination, contributed substantially to inflation by artificial manipulation of the value of government securities. During and after World War II, the Federal Reserve System lost much of its independence. It was used by the Treasury to raise unprecedented amounts of money, and during the war this requirement completely overshadowed monetary policy. As long as the war was on and Government controls kept wages and prices pretty well in line, there wasn't so much trouble. But when in 1946 direct controls were removed without also concurrently releasing the Federal Reserve, the excesses of the war years brought inflation and hardship to millions of Americans.

From 1946 to 1951, the Federal Reserve was a prisoner of the Treasury policy in handling the national debt. Instead of allowing the natural increases in interest rates, the Federal Reserve focused major attention on making sure that the Treasury could handle the debt at low rates. This was not in the best interests of the country as a whole. It resulted in the absence of effective monetary policy until the accord of March 1951.

As you gentlemen well know, the March 1951 accord partly restored effective monetary policy to its rightful place in our economy. It laid the groundwork for the policy which the present Administration is pledged to continue.

I should also note that the Federal Reserve System has no "hard" money policy. It is a good money policy. It is free to allow the demand for money to have its normal and natural effect and to supply funds to keep pace with normal growth. It believes as we do that good money makes good times.

The third and final pillar is proper debt management. As of the moment our debt is more than $273 billion—which is a terrific amount of debt. The manner in which this debt is handled—that is, maturing issues refinanced and new issues placed—has a very substantial bearing upon the well-being of our nation's economy.

Nearly three-quarters of this debt matures within less than five years or is redeemable at the holder's option. One of the things we are trying to do is to extend that average maturity gradually.

We took a first step in this direction back in April by putting out a 30-year bond at 3¼ per cent. That rate was higher than the rate for previous issues, but it reflected the going rate at the time of the issue as determined by the daily current market purchases and sales of outstanding Government securities. Earlier this month we had an encouraging response to a proposal which allowed a choice between one and 3½-year maturities in refinancing an issue of $7.9 billion. About $3 billion of the total exchanged was voluntarily placed in the longer term security.

It is our firm intention to offer more intermediate and long-term issues at opportune times in the future. We will use care, of course, not to press the market in competition with state, municipal and private financing which is at a peak of demand at the present time.

Too rapid movement on our part at this time in crowding into this market and increasing the already enormous demand for longer term funds might very well still further unduly press up on the interest rates for all loans and even deny many other governmental and private borrowers an opportunity to obtain the necessary funds.

It is also our goal to move at opportune times a portion of the debt out of the banks into the hands of private investors.

Randolph Burgess, who is known to most of you and who is the Treasury's chief officer in this matter of debt management, will talk to you in more detail and more scientifically, I am sure, tomorrow about this very important subject. Before I leave it, however, I wish to make known to you my very great appreciation for the work that Mr. Burgess is doing not only for the Treasury but for the whole country in his very intelligent, patient and wise counsel in this very difficult matter of handling our public debt.

Now I want to say just a word about the current outlook. My crystal ball is no bigger or brighter than yours. Indeed the composite knowledge from so many localities represented in this room is far superior to anything we know. We are most anxious to learn from you. The decline in the stock market is heralded by some as a sure sign of disaster. I cannot believe that that is so. It may well be that, as the fear of inflation declines, some switching is taking place from stocks to bonds or cash which the holders have not dared to make during the past period of growing inflation. It may also be that there is some fear of declining earnings as certain supplies more nearly approach demand and goods become available. That is nothing to shiver about. In our great and growing economy, some adjustment is constantly going on. Wherever adjustment is required, let's face it with confidence and get at it.

I do not believe in blind faith. If trouble is possible, just the opposite is indicated. Keep your eyes open. Seek out the soft spot and see what can be done about it. For over two years now, from quarter to quarter businessmen have been expecting and predicting some downturn. It has not materialized in many lines because Government and private spending has been increasing faster than new productive capacity came in.

Government spending now appears to be on the road to reduction. That is what the American people want and demand. But in spite of all we can do and all the savings we can make, a relatively small reduction is the most that we can hope to accomplish—quickly. That means that there will still be a tremendous amount of money to be currently pumped into the economy. And furthermore it is the definite policy of this Administration, through tax reductions, to return to the people for them to spend for themselves all the real savings in Government spending which can be reasonably anticipated.

As I promised at the time, the excess profits tax will expire on December 31st, and there will be no request for renewal. At the same time an average of 10 per cent reduction in individual income taxes is scheduled to go into effect, and it will become effective. Many further adjustments in taxes are now under consideration by the Ways & Means Committee and the Treasury for submission to the next Congress.

The great additions to producing capacity in several lines which have been stimulated by Government action over the past few years are now becoming available. The volume of goods we can now produce is far greater than ever before. Lower levels of operation in some lines will develop more material than we have ever had, and it may well be that in some cases this output may be all that the country needs for a while.

But does this mean catastrophe? Our volume of production and employment can be higher than ever and we may still have some capacity in reserve. High volume but good supply—that means competition, efficiency and more value for the consumer's dollar. Surely we have not deteriorated in this country so that all we can see is calamity if the day of allocations and the order-taker is passing and we again have to develop a salesman.

It cannot be that Americans can fear a free competitive economy. That is what we have thrived on. That is how we grew great. The necessity for a little more active selling never hurt anyone. A little more quality, a little more value for the customer has given us the best merchandise in the world. A little more production from the same amount of human effort through organization, management, ingenuity and invention, labor power and tools has given us higher and higher standards of living.

Surely we are not fearful that we cannot do it again. It is the American way. Bankers, too, can do their part. You too can and should look forward with confidence. Your service can be improved. You can do that little extra for your customer to help him do his share. And if we all do all we should, America will march forward on sounder ground than we have had under our feet for some time.

I can assure you that this Government is dedicated to the maintenance of a high level of employment and production, and it will pursue policies to foster that end. . . .

The achievement of sound money is one of the most important charges placed upon this Administration. It is important because sound money lies at the very base of our national existence. Sound money is fundamental for saving and the creation of jobs.

Because Americans have saved, we have developed our national resources. We have the scientists, the managers, and all the people who make possible the production of complicated machinery, the people who build and work in factories, the farmers who have put modern equipment to such great use, the technicians, mechanics and workmen who have made our great power plants and transportation systems possible. All these things and the employment they provide would not have been possible if the savings of the people had not been available to finance them.

Then why have these millions of people saved and what must we do so that they will keep on saving? Sound money is an essential to keep people saving money. Without assurance in the worth of their money in the future, as well as the ability to obtain a fair rate of income on it when it is saved, people are either going to save less or not at all. No one will save if he fears that the money he saves will be worth less and less as time goes on or may even become worthless entirely. . . .

Our national security is also involved. Sound money is of the utmost importance to it. Without sound money and without the sound economy that sound money produces, the great productive power of America will deteriorate, and it is America's productive power when mobilized that has won two wars and now provides the greatest deterrent to aggression throughout the entire world. Sound money is the basis for both our economic and our military security. Sound money is essential for the future of America.

A prosperous nation—which means continuing high levels of employment and production—can only be assured by sound money, for prosperity that is not solidly based on sound money is illusory, fleeting and sure to end in disaster. We shall continue to press resolutely toward our goal of high employment and sustained prosperity.

◢ This proved to be one of the Secretary's most important speeches for a number of reasons. It was his first to the bankers of the country, and delivered at a time when the stock market was wavering over the results of the truce in Korea and the end of large war production; and the first in which he undertook to state his faith in the Federal Reserve Board's independence and the longer-term government financing he had just introduced. The speech had a tonic effect on the bankers.

A nation "much freer of interference"

*Speech by Secretary Humphrey to the 100th
Anniversary Dinner of the New York Clearing
House Association at Hotel Pierre, New York.*

October 5, 1953

This dinner tonight marking the 100th Anniversary of the founding of the New York Clearing House is really an anniversary of free enterprise at its best. It took leadership to establish the New York Clearing House in 1853. It took courage, foresight and character.

In America today we need to practice the principles which motivated the men who founded the Clearing House. We need the leadership and the courage to try new things in America even more today than we did a hundred years ago. If we have that leadership we can go forward to more and better things than we have ever known.

The founding of the New York Clearing House is an especially good example of what free leadership can do, . . . because New York is still the heart of the money market of America and so exerts a powerful influence on the economic life of the country. You men in this room tonight have a position of leadership and with it great responsibility. That is why I am impelled tonight to suggest to you that, as leaders in this money center of the nation, you would do well as you think of your future plans to recall how well the leadership and enterprise of a hundred years ago have paid off to the betterment of every one in this great nation.

Here in New York are many of my personal friends, either in business or in the great New York banks. The Federal Reserve Bank in New York is of inestimable value to the Treasury in supplying valued information and counsel as well as the huge volume of its operations as our fiscal agent. The fact is that the financial officers of your Government in Washington get a great deal from New York City, which is in the best interests of all the people of the nation. . . .

The founding of the Clearing House as a more progressive method of handling banking transactions between individual banking institutions was a vital factor in speeding the development of all lines of the American economy. Today your Clearing House is the largest of more than 230 in the United States, and your operations involve the keeping of figures in the trillions of dollars. Your daily clearings average $1.8 billion. You have survived and grown under some serious strains, like the panic of 1857 and the crash of 1929. For this growth and for your many achievements I congratulate you on your 100th birthday. Yours is a fine heritage. . . .

The nation today is a nation which is much freer of interference from Washington than it has been in many years. Soon after the new Administration took office in January, almost all remaining controls were lifted on the calculated risk that the American economy and its leaders, if given the opportunity, could operate without going to excesses. There has been no runaway inflation. There have been adjustments here and there, as there always will be in any free conomy. But as of the moment we have relatively stable purchasing power in the hands of all Americans.

In this connection, the announcements of record highs in the cost of living from month to month seem to me improperly emphasized. It is of course true that when the cost of living rises one-tenth of one per cent, a new high record may be set. The important thing, however, is that in the past year the cost of living has increased only six-tenths of one per cent. This is in contrast with the situation from 1946 to 1951 when the cost of living went up more than 30 per cent, or an average of 6 per cent a year. Rather than accentuating the new high which the fractional increase has established, the emphasis should be just reversed. The relatively small increase of less than one per cent in the past year is evidence of stability.

It will take the continued intelligent cooperation of all the leaders of America's business and money markets, working with the Government, to help maintain stability of the purchasing power of Americans. It will take even more leadership and enlightened action to make sure that free enterprise makes the adjustments which are bound to occur in a free economy from time to time without letting them snowball into more than being individual adjustments.

The stock market is not a sure barometer. The fact that earnings decline as supplies in some lines more nearly approach demand means only that competition becomes more keen and it is nothing to shiver about. With the proper leadership in the business of America and in the heart of the money market of America here in New York City, we can face these adjustments and go on about our business with confidence.

This great nation of ours, now free from controls, can continue to avoid inflation without going into recession and resulting large-scale unemployment. There is no excuse to do so—and I firmly believe we will not do so.

An important factor is that Government spending is being reduced. That is what we all want and insist upon. But, in spite of all that we can do and all the savings that can be made, only a relatively small reduction can be made in Government spending rapidly. It follows that large amounts of money will be put back into the economy by defense spending for some time to come. It is just as important that the savings that we are making in Government spending will be returned to the people through tax reductions so that the people can spend for themselves what the Government up till now has been spending for them.

This Administration is committed to see the excess profits tax expiration and the 10 per cent individual income tax cut go into effect as scheduled on January 1st of 1954.... The President's tax program when announced in May included the extension of the 52 per cent corporate rate and excise taxes at the present schedules beyond their automatic expiration date of March 31, 1954. The Administration's requests that these two levels of taxation be continued still stand. Any readjustments in either of these tax schedules will only be recommended as a part of the general tax revision program which is now being studied by the Treasury and the Ways & Means Committee to propose a new tax law to the Congress next January.

As leaders of the United States money market, you gentlemen have a great responsibility in seeing that free enterprise, now given its chance, continues to function. With less government regulation, less props, and without price and wage controls, free competitive enterprise is really free to both compete and enterprise. It can only really function well if it does enterprise. In the past twenty years it has been easy to become used to a sort of Santa Claus paternalism which was supposed to take care of us if we got into trouble or were afraid we were going to get into trouble. It will now take more leadership and more vigorous enterprise to solve any troubles or fears of troubles without looking to or coming to the government for aid.

It will also take greater daring and ingenuity by free enterprise to solve the problems and adjustments which may develop from time to time. But they must and can be solved to produce greater and finer developments throughout the land, with resulting higher employment and better standards of living for all, and do it better than all the paternalism in the world from government could ever obtain. . . .

As leaders in the money market, you must be ready to keep that market virile, active and strong on both the buying and selling sides. You must be ready to take the rap as well as to reap the gain of fluctuations in the market. If you are not, then all we have been saying about wanting to return to free enterprise and all we have been criticizing in regulation and restraint has been just conversation.

If we really believe in free enterprise—and I think we all really do—then we must really "enterprise." The money market must act and think in broad constructive terms and try to think ahead to encourage and continually maintain a high level of activity.

I am going to take the liberty of making some suggestions as to certain areas in which I think perhaps you leaders of American finance and business can help free enterprise to work; and perhaps, too, you can suggest ways in which we can be more helpful.

(1) One is in the Government securities market. Free markets never stand still. The fluctuations provide opportunities for enterprise, for making money by buying and selling in an active market. This operation in itself provides a measure of stability which is beneficial to all.

We think we detect occasionally a tendency, carried over from the days of Government price pegging, for the market to stand aside waiting to see what the Treasury or the Federal Reserve System will do. There is nothing as you well know that is really very mysterious about the policies of these two agencies. They are well described in the report on the Reserve System which the Clearing House itself has published, and we and the System have been frank about our policies. One of the best things the New York money market can do is to assure a broad and vigorous market in Government securities. This market is vitally important because its behavior is watched and magnified throughout the country and the world. . . .

(2) The market for new issues needs study to see whether ways can be found to spread out financing and lessen the risk of congestion and indigestion such as occurred earlier this year. Most people do not realize that $7 billion of new issues, exclusive of United States Government issues, were placed in the market the first six months of this year—probably the largest amount in history.

No one wants to increase the rules or regulations, or establish a capital issues committee in time of peace. But a further study of this problem might suggest some further freely operating mechanism for the better handling of prospective issues. There may be something the Treasury, the SEC, or the Reserve System should do.

(3) We told Senator Homer Capehart's committee that we believe the government must look very seriously at further use of government funds abroad to aid the financing of competitive enterprises there. Many people and groups of people are studying this whole field, and we feel certain that it should be this Administration's objective to increase the role of private participation in foreign investment. This being the case, you as money and business leaders might well be prepared to take a fresh look at this field. If foreign trade and foreign industry are to be developed, it more and more should be the money of free enterprise which is to do the development. We know of all the difficulties and all the sad experiences in the past. But we also believe that ways can be found for private enterprise to venture profitably beyond our own borders. . . .

(4) Finally, we wonder if the banking and investment houses of America might not have more people who are detached from the routine operations of the business who could be constantly watching

such things as I have mentioned to make sure that the right things are first thought of and then done at the right time. It is just as important for the money market to have its research and planning people as for other large industries in America to have their research and planning staffs. At least I recommend that more of it be considered as paying possible dividends both for the future of free enterprise and the welfare of the nation. . . .

In all of these things you have been most helpful. We have talked many times about how this Administration is trying to obtain honest money for the citizens of America. We are doing it through what we call the three pillars of honest money—a proper budget policy, a properly functioning Federal Reserve System, and proper debt management. The details of those three pillars are well known to most of you here tonight. We are making some real progress on each of those pillars. We are making enough progress so that we feel there can be less and less government entering into your affairs as time goes on. As this comes true, there will be more and more free enterprise in addition to that large measure which has already been returned to you. It is my hope—in fact, it is my firm belief—that with active, intelligent, alert leadership on the part of the market of New York and the business leaders of America, free enterprise based on sound money and sound fiscal policies will move on to more and better things, to new avenues of employment, and higher standards of living for all Americans.

The "middle way"

Speech by Secretary Humphrey to a dinner of the
Union League Club of Philadelphia.

October 30, 1953

Every American wants peace.

We are living in a time—not of peace—but of peril.

In the world today the physical security that this nation once enjoyed by reason of geography and our two broad oceans has now been jeopardized by the long-range bomber and the awful destructive power of atomic weapons.

Continuing discoveries in the field of science can of course be used either for good or evil. But because these discoveries are also known to others in this world who may have different objectives, we cannot be sure that they will be used only for good always.

We must realize that in this time in which we are living there does exist the possibility of sudden and mass destruction, the swift wiping out of whole cities and populations.

These terrible forces must somehow be brought to the service and the good of the world's people rather than their destruction. This can be done only as a result of a just and durable peace throughout the world.

Our search for this lasting peace cannot succeed on hope alone. We cannot ignore the factual conditions that exist in the world as they may affect our own nation.

This quest for peace is complicated by the inheritance, which this Administration fell heir to ten short months ago, not only of conditions among nations but of conditions affecting the daily lives of each of us here at home.

This inheritance involves matters of foreign relations and the military, as well as financial and economic conditions here in our own country. They are all entwined. I will speak tonight principally of our financial and economic inheritance and programs but, as you will see, they are deeply woven into both foreign policy and defense.

It is sometimes hard to realize how closely the world today is knit together; how foreign policy affects military plans and how together they actually determine the course of our economy right here at home.

What we do about what may happen in some foreign land may well determine the number and type of jobs which people here in Philadelphia will have tomorrow. What happens in the Valley of the Nile or in Pakistan or on the plains of Turkey may have a real bearing upon the welfare of our farmers in Kansas and Iowa.

Our foreign policy and our military policy can very largely fix the shape and size of our financial commitments and economic policies. The one and only complete answer to real freedom in America is true, lasting and durable peace throughout the world. For only in peace —in real peace—can this nation and the other peoples of the world go on to the better things which the economies of nations at peace can produce.

Our financial inheritance, which complicates all our efforts, includes several areas I would like to discuss tonight.

First, there is the problem of our huge public debt. When the bonds are issued that have just been sold, it will almost reach $275 billion. The manner in which it has been handled—maturing issues refinanced and new issues placed—in the past twenty years presents a financial inheritance to stagger the stoutest of hearts.

Nearly three-quarters of this debt matures within less than five years or is redeemable at the holder's option. Too large a proportion is in the hands of banks. We are trying to work our way out of this inherited problem by doing two things which will make this public debt less dangerous to the value of money and to the nation's economy: We are trying to extend the maturity of the debt by placing longer term issues. We are trying to move more of the debt away from the banks and into the hands of private investors.

We cannot move on both fronts always at the same time. We cannot move too rapidly to dislocate the sensitive balance of our economy and we must always be guided by current market conditions. But our goal is clear and we are constantly working toward it.

Second, there is the problem of the debt limit. This is another financial inheritance which is causing concern. After passage by a large majority of the House, the Senate Finance Committee last August refused to approve the Administration's request to raise the statutory debt ceiling.

We said then—and we say now—that a higher debt limit will enable the Government to better handle its fiscal affairs. It does not in any sense mean that we are not working vigorously for economy. We have demonstrated that we have accomplished reductions in spending as rapidly as we can safely do so.

The existing law requires the payment of the bulk of corporation taxes in the first half of the calendar year. When this law was first enacted a few years ago it substantially increased government receipts in the first half of that calendar year, which was the last half of the fiscal year, and served to substantially reduce a budget deficit at that time.

The practice was then inaugurated—and there is no way to correct it now—of issuing tax anticipation notes in the fall when tax collections are low, against anticipated receipts in the spring when tax collections are high. The result means that now Government borrowing goes up in the fall and comes down in the spring, which automatically forces temporarily increased borrowing for at least a six-month period.

This fixed inheritance, which there is no way to correct under present conditions, means that, in spite of all we can do, the present debt limit is too restrictive.... By careful handling, and barring any unexpected demand for large additional sums of money, it now appears that we will barely get through the present period and until the Congress returns in January without exceeding the ceiling.

Third, there is the inheritance of what I like to call the COD orders. This is one of the most troublesome—and least understood—legacies this Administration inherited. When the new Administration assumed office, it found on the Government's books some $80 billion of orders placed by the former Administration from one to three years previously for goods which will be delivered during this year, next year, and even the year after that—and which must be paid for when received.

These orders are in general too far committed to reduce or cancel and must be met with payments in cash for which no provision was previously made.... Payment for these large COD orders, for which no money was provided, is a major factor in our present problem of raising cash. It is an important factor in the twin problem of the debt limit. This large COD inheritance is also, of course, a major reason why it is impossible to balance the budget quickly.

A fourth financial inheritance is the habit of extravagance in government in many places. Some government agencies are of course well run and perform unquestionably essential functions, but there are others which have acquired habits of extravagance which must be curtailed. We are continually probing to see if each activity is really necessary for the good of the American people or if it is merely a self-perpetuating expenditure.... There is also often extravagance and waste which can and should be eliminated even in the case of indispensable functions.

This Administration is trying—and succeeding slowly—in generating a new spirit of dollar consciousness on the part of all governmental personnel, both civilian and military. We believe that all governmental agencies must remember that every cent they spend comes not from some unknown pool of wealth but is taken from the toil and the savings of American citizens. . . .

Fifth is the financial inheritance of an almost staggering tax problem. The inherited obligations that I have cited and current operations of the Government can be paid for only with taxes—or borrowing. If we are to get our financial operations under control, they must be met with taxes rather than additional deficit financing to the greatest possible extent. Therefore, our inheritance in the field of taxation is a vital area requiring most careful future planning. . . .

Excessive planned deficits were implicit in our inheritance. There was a deficit of over $9 billion in the year we came in. There was a planned deficit budgeted for us when we arrived of $9.9 billion for our first year in office. This soon increased to $11.5 billion through overestimating income. Fortunately, we have been able, by untiring efforts of every branch of the Government, to cut this deficit to a present estimate of less than $4 billion. Because of this reduction, and only because of it, we have been justified in reducing some of the most burdensome taxation. The excess profits tax will expire on December 31 and will not be renewed. Personal income taxes will be reduced by approximately 10 per cent at the same time. . . .

Our entire tax system, however, is being revamped so as to reduce inherited obstacles to growth and incentive and correct unfair provisions and inequalities. This program is the joint undertaking of the Treasury and the Ways & Means and other Congressional committees. There are many desirable changes which should be made. We hope to accomplish some of them. But loss of revenue can only be limited in amount, and each proposal must be carefully evaluated. We cannot afford as much reduction as we all would like immediately, but our ambition is to establish a pattern of reduction on which a modest start can promptly be made with provision for future additional reductions in taxes as rapidly as reductions in expenditures indicate that they are possible. . . .

In the word peace, are all our dreams and all our fears. Danger to peace is danger to all. The prayer for peace is the prayer for America. No government can proclaim it, no congress can enact it, no group of nations can declare it.

Peace for America demands these things:

First: A defense of the nation strong enough to impress upon any would-be aggressor the folly of attack.

Second: An economy strong enough not only to sustain such a defense but also to allow Americans to enjoy the fruits of their own toil and genius.

Military defense ... begins with a readiness to spend and to sacrifice whatever is necessary—and I repeat, whatever is necessary—for a logical, ordered and balanced defense program.

But this is only the beginning. What must be sought is this: The finding of the ideal middle way between extremes which—on the one side—would stupidly cheat our defenses to save money, and—on the other side—would amass weapons and strength with an abandon that would wreck our economy—and hence our nation—without a gun ever being fired.

This is not merely economic sense. This is military sense, and, best of all, it's common sense.

We live in an age witnessing a revolution in the technique of arms and armies, and in the creation and production of all weapons for defense.

In such an age, there is one certain way to invite disaster: To commit a nation's whole resources and productive machine today to the abundant production of weapons that may be obsolete tomorrow.

In such an age, there is only one way to avoid disaster: To be ready for the danger of today—while continuing to develop industrial power that can be swiftly directed to meet a newer and different danger tomorrow.

This, I repeat, is a middle way. It has its analogy in our foreign policy—where we steadfastly seek a course that is firm, prudent, and bold, without ever being belligerent.

Such a defense does more than take account of the needs of our economy. It depends upon our whole economy—for the greatest strength, not only for ourselves but for the whole free world, is nothing other than the power and potential of American mass production.

This truth is known throughout the world. It is known to our enemies—for their greatest hope lies in an American depression. It is known to our friends—for their greatest fear is such a dread event.

How has your present Government applied this knowledge?

(1) We have placed our faith firmly in the genius of American

initiative and enterprise—and we have showed that faith by removing from our economic life, needless stifling controls.

(2) We have set the course of the Federal Government firmly toward the soonest possible balancing of the budget—as an indispensable battle in any serious war against inflation.

(3) We have redirected the monetary policy and the management of the public debt so as to give the American people their first hope in a decade of having sound, honest American dollars to spend and to save.

(4) We have committed ourselves to achieving, within limits dictated by essential defense needs, those reductions in taxes which are indispensable to the vigor of our economic life....

The search for this peace, however, goes far beyond immediate demands of military defense and a prosperous economy. This search is impelled by full awareness that this world ultimately must find a way to ease the burden of arms and of fears that now weigh upon men of all nations. Knowing all this, we stay strong in arms today—we keep our economy geared to meet any emergency—we weigh every military and economic decision—all in the fervent hope of soon being able to use our strength to serve the needs rather than the fears of all mankind.

Results in one year

Speech by Secretary Humphrey to the
Investment Bankers Association of America
at Hollywood Beach Hotel, Hollywood, Florida.

December 1, 1953

...What is this Administration's record of progress in the eleven months it has been working toward the accomplishment of our objectives?

First: We are on our way toward getting the budget of the Federal Government under control. It is no easy task, and cannot be too rapidly accomplished.

The major reason why it is extremely difficult to balance this budget as rapidly as we would like is that about 70 per cent of all the money we spend in Government is for security—that is, for our military, our foreign operations and atomic energy programs. About half of the remaining amount is made up of fixed charges, interest and obligations fixed by law. This leaves only 12 to 15 per cent for the cost of all of the rest of Government.

Government spending ballooned during the past few years in the security area. We cannot swing a broadax in cutting these expenses if by so doing it affects the security of our country. Rapid reductions in security expenditures can be made only by eliminating extravagance, and, second, by getting more defense for less money.

Extravagance in some military operations has been frequently apparent. This can and must be eliminated. But this is a relatively small saving, and can only be eliminated over some little period of time. A new spirit of dollar-consciousness in the minds of both civilian and military personnel will become more and more effective as time goes on.

Big reductions in security spending can only come from perfecting a new and more effective defense program which costs less money. This too takes time and tremendous planning, work and effort. . . .

We have not abandoned effort or hope for an early balanced budget. But the inheritance which we found of tremendous spending obligations for present and future years make this goal of budget balance one that cannot be achieved as rapidly as we all might wish. Only by continuous detailed work and effort can we get nearer and nearer to it and eventually accomplish our objective.

Our dollar has depreciated half of its worth in less than fifteen years. This is fast depreciation. But, more important, history shows that the early stage of currency depreciation and inflation always is slower than the latter part. It is high time expenditures must be controlled.

We had a $9 billion deficit for the fiscal year ending five months after this Administration took office. If we had accepted the $11 billion deficit that the past Administration planned for this fiscal year we now are in; and if we do not reduce the deficits that would surely result from the planning of the previous Administration for the years ahead, the results would be disastrous.

The solution of this dilemma means finding and maintaining that delicate balance between security from attack from abroad and a strong economy here at home. . . . Indeed, we must do more than plan our defense on a crisis-to-crisis basis. We must do more than plan on the basis of a short and all-out effort for a limited period of time. We must plan our defense and the ability to sustain it for the long pull, for an indefinite number of years, not knowing when, if ever, the critical moment may appear.

Second: We can and we must spend whatever we have to spend to defend ourselves. But we know that our defense must be measured not by its cost, but by its wisdom.

Third: This Administration is doing two things to make our nearly $275 billion debt less inflationary and less dangerous to the value of money and our economy.

We are extending the maturity of the debt by placing longer term issues whenever conditions permit, and as rapidly as possible we are moving more of the debt away from the banks and into the hands of long-term investors.

We cannot always move on both fronts at the same time. We must be careful not to dislocate the sensitive balance of our economy, but our goal is clear and we are working toward it.

We have but a single objective in plans for our debt management. We have never changed that objective. We are seeking sound, honest American money. We will continue to seek it in our handling of this too huge debt, as well as in all other fiscal and economic policies which have a bearing upon the value of that dollar.

But we must approach it with care and caution and must adjust our operations to always respond to changing market conditions. Halting inflationary pressures is like stopping an automobile going down an icy hill. If you slam on the brake, you spin around and smash into a telephone pole. As you well know if properly done, you alternately apply the brake a little, then release it a little, and feel your way, bringing pressure gradually until you finally come to a stop.

In February, owners of $9 billion maturing certificates were given the chance to exchange their holdings for a bond of six-years maturity instead of the usual one-year certificate. In April, the Treasury offered a 30-year bond, the first marketable long-term bond since 1945. In September a three and one-half year note was offered, and in October a new cash offering of eight-year bonds was made. In December $1.75 billion of five-year bonds were issued.

The net result of our debt management so far in 1953 has been to finance a huge inherited deficit with little or no increase in bank holdings of Government securities, and so without any increase in inflationary pressures due to that cause. Ownership of Government securities by investors outside the banks, in fact, increased by $4 billion the first nine months of this year, while holdings of commercial and Federal Reserve banks dropped a half billion dollars.

Fourth: The Administration is determined to halt further cheapening of the dollar. This has been accomplished at least temporarily. There has been a change of only one-half of one cent in the purchasing power of the dollar during the past year. This is real proof of gaining stability.

Fifth: Taxes are being reduced by this Administration. The tax reductions which will go into effect on December 31 would not have been possible except for the reductions in spending which this Administration has been able to achieve since last January.

Let there be no misunderstanding about this simple fact. The elimination of the excess profits tax and the 10 per cent cut in personal income taxes on January 1 are possible only because this Administration was able to cut government spending by billions of dollars in its first few months in office.

Additional tax reductions are desired by every one and are necessary for the continued growth of our economy. This nation cannot long endure as a land of opportunity under the restrictive taxes which we inherited. But taxes can be further reduced only as expenditures are further reduced. And expenditures can be reduced only as consistent with maintaining a defense adequate to meet the dangers which confront us.

The entire tax system is being revised to remove inherited obstacles to growth and incentive, under a joint undertaking of the Treasury and the proper committees of the Congress. We cannot afford as much reduction as we would all like immediately, but we can set a pattern of reduction on which a modest start will promptly be made, with provision for additional further reductions as rapidly as reductions in expenditures—consistent with security—indicate that they are justified.

Sixth: Needless and stifling controls were lifted almost as soon as we assumed office. They had failed to keep down the cost of living. They were curbing initiative and enterprise. The ending of controls was a calculated risk. But runaway inflation did not result, as our critics had gloomily predicted. . . .

Korea, the Seventh: Shooting and bloodshed in Korea are ended, at least for the time being, and the tension in the homes throughout America is lessened. In its place our every effort is at work to fashion a lasting, sound and equitable peace, and substitute reconstruction for destruction in that war-torn land. It is our fervent hope that out of it may come a permanent and constructive settlement.

Our accomplishments are real. They are a good start toward substantial progress, have yet far to go, but are far enough already to give us pride in the past few months of effort and real hope for greater things to come.

If only real peace can result in Korea to dissipate anxiety for our sons, it will help to relieve our financial pressures and may even be a first step toward accomplishing the real and lasting peace so craved throughout the world. May Divine Providence guide us ever toward peace and give us the strength, the wisdom and the courage to realistically face facts as we see them and act vigorously with fear or favor for none.

📧 Some partisan criticism in Congress and a mild dulling of business in the first half of 1954 prompted Secretary Humphrey to make several low-key "reassurance" speeches during the spring and fall. He had hardly finished them when, in the autumn, business indices began to rise which pointed in the direction of the considerable boom year of 1955.

Toward higher living standards

Interview with Secretary Humphrey published in Newsweek.

January 4, 1954

QUESTION. On the whole, do you look for a prosperous level of business activity in 1954?

SEC. HUMPHREY. I look for a continued high level of activity in 1954. This does not mean that there may not be adjustments in some particular lines, but there is every reason why the total economic activity should continue very high.

QUESTION. With defense spending going down, do you agree with some observers that economic adjustments could degenerate into a depression?

SEC. HUMPHREY. Neither American business nor American labor needs war to be prosperous. Our population is increasing—by thousands of newborn each day. The needs and wants of Americans are increasing just as swiftly. And our capacity to meet these needs—as we stand on the threshold of an atomic age for the good of mankind, we hope, instead of for evil—is beyond the imagination of most of us.

As the threat of aggression recedes, our huge expenditures for defense can decline. But this doesn't mean that we are headed for a depression.

In our growing economy, adjustments are constantly going on. Wherever these adjustments are required, let's face them with confidence and correct them: Keep our eyes open; seek out the soft spots and see what can be done about them.

QUESTION. Do you think these current readjustments are healthy?

SEC. HUMPHREY. Yes, they are. The volume of goods we can now produce is far greater than ever before. Lower percentage levels of operation in some lines will develop more material than we have ever had, and it may well be that in some cases this output may be all that the country needs for a while. But this doesn't mean catastrophe. High volume but good supply means competition, efficiency, and more value for the consumer's dollar. Surely we haven't reached the point in this country where all we can see is calamity if the day of allocations and the order-taker is passing.

A little more production, a little more selling, a little more effort and ingenuity have given us higher and higher standards of living. Surely we are not afraid that we can't do it again.

This Administration is dedicated to the maintenance of a high level of employment and production.

This American economy—healthy, vital, daring—is our first line of defense for freedom itself. For a fact that cannot be too often repeated is this: America's greatest defense against any enemy is the power and potential of American mass production.

QUESTION. Will the budget be balanced?

SEC. HUMPHREY. As I have said many times, we are making good progress toward getting Federal spending under control. As I have also said, it is slow work because we cannot use a broadax where security is concerned. But this does not mean that we will not keep working every day and every week toward cutting expenses and eliminating waste. We are still hopeful of reaching a balance in the cash budget in 1954. The budget estimates for 1955 will be presented the latter part of January. We shall have to wait until then to see what the outlook is for fiscal 1955.

QUESTION. Some critics fear that our security may be jeopardized by this desire to balance the budget. Is there any such danger?

SEC. HUMPHREY. Not as far as I am concerned. We must—and will—spend what we have to spend to defend ourselves. But we must have a fluid, continually modern defense. And we must plan to keep a strong economy to support it—for the long pull.

QUESTION. Do you expect to make a start soon on a substantial tax-cutting program in keeping with the Administration's announced goal for stimulating incentive?

SEC. HUMPHREY. As of January 1, 1954, the savings in spending made by the new Administration in its first eleven months in office make it possible for tax cuts totaling $5 billion a year to go into effect. Those tax cuts could not have become effective if the present Administration had not cut spending by some $6.5 billion in this fiscal year. The President's programs to be announced in January will show that this Administration is making real progress in stimulating incentive by tax reductions and reform.

✉ Background of the interview: Speeches by Senators Paul H. Douglas (Illinois) and Wayne Morse (Oregon) declaring the symptoms of a depression had appeared.

"We have reduced spending over $12 billion"

Statement by Secretary Humphrey at a news conference on the President's budget at the Treasury Department.

January 20, 1954

As the Director of the Budget has told you, we have reduced anticipated Government spending by over $12 billion since just a year ago.

The deficit of over $9 billion for the last year of our predecessors will be less than $4 billion in the current year and less than $3 billion in the year for which this new budget—our first—is made. That is a tremendous reduction both in dollars and in percentage in any business anywhere.

And in addition to all this, over $5 billion has been cut from the tax bill for the public.

Our dollar has been stable in value for months. Our debts are increasing only by approximately the amount of the bonds we put in the trust funds. We are not having to increase short-term borrowing for additional money from the banks, with all its inflationary implications.

Controls are forgotten. Money and credit are plentiful. A new foreign policy is crystallizing. A new defense program is here, and its first economies are included in this budget. Defense spending is still high but on the way to continual, moderate, orderly reduction, with more security for less expense.

The first tax cuts have just become effective within the last few days, and the recommendations for the complete revision of the tax laws are included in this budget. Over $5 billion of tax savings are now being left with American consumers to increase their purchasing power in this year, and more will be released as rapidly as additional savings in Government expenses are in sight.

The proposed revision of the tax system represents much cooperative work by the House Ways & Means Committee, its staff and the Treasury Department. The 25 specific items listed in the President's message are very important for the future of all Americans.

The revision accomplishes two principal objectives:

(1) It will make the tax burden fairer for millions of individual taxpayers by removing most of the more serious tax inequities and tax complications.

(2) It will encourage small business, stimulate production and create bigger payrolls and more and better jobs by reducing restraints and by encouraging initiative and investment.

The revisions, which will benefit millions of individuals, include those giving better tax treatment for working children, for child care expenses, for doctors' bills and for annuities, as well as simplified procedures for filing returns.

The proposal for partial relief from double taxation of dividends will be a stimulant to investment for the purchase of new and improved machinery, plants and equipment to make jobs and improve earnings.

The exemption from taxation of the first $50 in 1954 and the first $100 in 1955 and later years will be a real benefit and encouragement to smaller investors.

This start toward relief from the double taxation of dividends will be helpful to the whole economy by making equity financing—that is, buying of shares of stock instead of bonds in an enterprise—more attractive. This will counter the trend of recent years toward too much dependence on borrowed money for working capital and expansion. Any enterprise which is too heavily in debt is not able to develop as well or as quickly as it could if not so burdened. It is also in a less favorable position in more highly competitive times. So, the double taxation of dividends proposal encourages greater economic growth and steadier, better employment.

The proposal for liberalization of the tax treatment of depreciation also will aid economic growth and be especially helpful for small business. The proposed revision will allow more discretion in how investments will be written down without increasing the total deductions.

At present the deductions are usually written off uniformly and often, especially in the early years, are below actual depreciation. This discourages long-range investment on which the risk cannot be clearly foreseen. It also makes it more difficult for financing, particularly for small business.

The proposal to allow more discretion will help the manufacturer in buying new machinery and the storekeeper in expanding his store. It will help the farmer get new machinery. It will stimulate building, revamping and modernization of plants and equipment and spur on the whole machine tool industry to greater production.

Nothing can so add to our national strength and the preparedness as modernization of the whole industrial plant in America and nothing will make more sure more jobs at which millions of people can earn high wages by producing more and better goods.

These revisions, as they help our economy expand, will also result in more personal income to be spent by taxpayers for their own account and in their own way and so will provide more money for the purchase of these better goods and services.

I have mentioned only a few of the many revision items which contribute to the growing healthy economy so important to all of us as well as give proper help to the millions of individuals involved.

I have said many times in recent months when talking about this revision program that we cannot afford as much reduction in tax as we would all like immediately, but that we will set a pattern of reduction on which a start can be made. The President is proposing today much more than a start. He is proposing a completely new framework for the tax system. The revision proposal definitely puts us on the road to fairer tax returns for millions with more incentive for a continually expanding economy, with all that that means for future employment and higher standards of living for all Americans.

The budget situation does not permit further reductions in the Government's income at this time. We are therefore requesting that the proposed cut in corporation taxes be deferred for one year and that the excises scheduled for reduction on April 1 be continued. Any adjustments that may be considered in other excise taxes should only be such as to maintain the total amount of money we are now receiving from this source.

However, you must always remember that as rapidly as further reductions in Government expenditures are in sight we are determined to make further reductions in taxation. In that way more people can have more money left after taxes to spend, to save or to invest in their own way for the purposes which they think best for themselves instead of having the Government taxing and spending it for them.

"Jobs more important than tax cuts"

Speech by Secretary Humphrey before the American Society of Newspaper Editors at the Statler Hotel, Washington.

April 15, 1954

Just about a year ago I had the pleasure of appearing before you. If you will remember there was then great concern as to whether or not a hoped for peace in Korea would quickly bring on a depression. . . . We all were grateful that the fighting in Korea soon ended and 1953 was the biggest and the best year in American history.

Then we had only plans for reduction of Government expenditures and only hopes of tax reductions to follow.

And now a year later, with actual accomplishments in both fields where then we had but plans and hopes, many people have again been concerned with fears of depression and the prophets of gloom have been loud in their dire predictions.

It is easy to be misled about how "good or bad" business really is in this country, after all the loose talking that has been done. It would be especially unfortunate if the editors of the great newspapers of this country should not have the proper perspective on the state of our economy.

Let us remember such things as these:

Average employment in the first three months of this year was 60 million people—the highest number of people employed during that period of the year in any year of our history except for the first three months of last year immediately following President Eisenhower's election.

Construction contracts awarded in March of this year were 13 per cent higher than a year ago.

Total personal income is running higher than it was a year ago.

There are some other indicators which are down, and we recognize that unemployment is up over a year ago. Moreover we fully realize that each individual who is out of a job has a serious personal problem, and this Administration is greatly concerned to see that everyone who wants work can have employment.

But basically our present economic condition is a result of necessary inventory adjustments plus a transition from war time to peace time spending by the Government. As we cut Government spending, we must return to the people in tax cuts—as we are now doing—the billions of dollars of Government money saved so that it can then be put to making new jobs for the people who previously got their income from Government spending.

We are transferring this money back to the people by tax cuts which, when the tax revision bill is passed, will mean total tax cuts effective this year of $7.4 billion—the largest single dollar tax cut in any year in the nation's history.

When our tax program is fully effective, every single taxpayer in this country will have received some tax cut and benefit in this year. . . .

The fact that employment continues at the very high level of 60 million people at work shows that this transition to making things for living instead of for killing is being made remarkably well. I am confident of the future, and that we are not now headed for a depression.

Some people, fearing further downward trends, ask when the Government is going to get "in" and do something about it. The fact is that the Government is always "in." There are so many things that the Government does—or does not do—that have a very real bearing on the state of the economy.

There are many things that the Government has already done; things recommended which are now before the Congress; and things which the Administration has proposed either for the future or for action by executive agencies, all of which have and will help strengthen our economy.

First, in things already done, we should look at an area of Government action very close to us at Treasury—the area of flexible debt management and monetary policy.

The Federal Reserve Board—with its responsibility for monetary policy—reduced reserve requirements of member banks substantially as early as last June to make sure that there would be no bar to the proper volume of bank credit necessary to a growing economy. The Federal Reserve has purchased short-term Government securities in the market, to increase bank reserves, for a considerable period. The rate at which bankers can borrow from the Federal Reserve was reduced in February and again just day before yesterday a further reduction was approved.

Treasury debt management also has been a positive factor and Government interest rates have fallen to the lowest point in many years. Last July the Treasury had to pay 2½ per cent for a eight-month loan. In February we paid the same rate for a loan running almost eight years. And our last one-year money borrowing was at 1⅝ per cent. Ninety-day bills cost close to 2½ per cent last June; now they are down to 1 per cent.

In the current economic environment the Treasury has purposely done its financing in a way that would not interfere with the availability of long-term investment funds to corporations, state and local governments, and for mortgages to home owners. We want to be sure that plant and equipment, home building, and other construction all have ample available funds. The fact that construction thus far this year is running so high demonstrates how effective these policies are.

We have the Small Business Administration to ease the proper handling of credit in this particular and vital part of our economy.

Perhaps the biggest way that the Government is continually "in" the economy is in this matter of taxes. We have noted that tax cuts effected this year will total $7.4 billion, the largest total dollar tax cut in history. This saving of such huge amounts of money for peacetime use should have a tremendously beneficial effect in stimulating the economy.

Some of the other things recommended by the Administration and now before Congress which will have considerable bearing upon the economy are as follows:

The President has asked legislation to broaden the base and benefits of old age insurance. This legislation is currently before the House Ways & Means Committee.

In the housing bill, which is currently before the Senate, are two Administration proposals affecting the building of homes. We have asked that the Government be allowed to change the terms of governmentally insured loans and mortgages as circumstances require. We have asked that a secondary home mortgage market be established, and active steps are being taken to accomplish it.

The Administration has taken important action in reclamation matters.

The Administration has supported a bill which will help the wool growers of the West.

The Administration has urged that the highway construction program be increased, and a record sum has already been voted by the House and Senate.

The Administration is recommending a positive program for flexible price supports for the American farmer. The President's program is being actively considered by both the House and the Senate.

The Administration has taken specific actions within the executive departments and with other governmental bodies to do things that will help strengthen our economy.

We have recommended legislation to improve unemployment insurance and the Administration has asked the governors of the various states to study the possibility of making payment scales more realistic.

A committee for state, local, and federal planning has been appointed and is now at work.

The President has asked the Office of Defense Mobilization to redirect its stockpiling program, which will help distressed mining areas.

The Administration is going ahead with improved planning of its public works programs which can be available for any emergency.

Last, but far from least, the tax revision bill now before the Senate Finance Committee will upon enactment have a tremendously helpful effect upon the economy. While it is basically a long-overdue tax reform bill, it can help greatly the current economic transition. There are many business projects around the country which are being held up pending final decision on this revision bill. It is imperative that the earliest possible action should be taken. When the bill is enacted, these new or expanding businesses can go ahead with their plans, which will result in the creation of thousands of jobs and the vital expansion of our economy.

But the success of our economy depends, not upon a single government act or edict, but upon all the people trying to do a little more for themselves, trying to better themselves and their loved ones. Government can only help provide a fertile field in which the 161 million Americans can work. The tax revision bill will help provide a more fertile field by giving further relief to millions of taxpayers and stimulating the incentive and the enterprise which we need to create more and better jobs.

Jobs are more important than tax cuts. Jobs are what America lives on. The entire fiscal policy of the Government is designed and operated to promote more and better jobs, which more efficiently create the better cheaper goods, and the expansion of industry that makes for the ever improving standard of living we all want in America.

"The trend . . . has been halted"

Remarks by Secretary Humphrey at an award
for Distinguished Public Service by the National
Farm-City Conference at the Town Hall, New York.

May 25, 1954

The American economy is the key economy in the world. It is vital to the security and well-being of our millions of citizens. And, every other nation is vitally affected by its strength or weakness.

As long as our economy is sound and growing, there will be more and better jobs for our people and better living for all. And as long as the American economy is sound, growing and prosperous, our allies are helped. Together, we can not only protect ourselves against aggression but, from a position of strength, can work to achieve real peace in the world.

If our economy should be weak and faltering, so as to cause loss of general confidence, we would be in danger of having large numbers of people out of work, less production, and so lowered standards of living all around. But we would not suffer alone. Our allies would also suffer. The strength of the whole free world would be threatened.

To maintain this vital strength of our nation, we must have economical and efficient operation of our own Government. For the way in which our Government conducts its affairs sets the patterns for the nation's whole economy.

In 17 of the past 20 years, this Government has engaged in deficit financing—spending more than its income. This course for a government, as for a family, can only lead to eventual disaster. The resulting depreciation of our currency has already seriously hurt millions of Americans. Continued cheapening of the dollar might finally result in the collapse of our entire economic system. . . .

This Administration, when it took office in January, 1953, pledged its efforts to institute sound money policies. We pledged ourselves to reduce Government expenditures and to strive toward attaining a balanced budget as rapidly as proper regard for our security would permit.

The trend toward continually growing deficit financing and all its evils has been halted.

The deficit for fiscal 1953 was almost $9.5 billion. The budget this Administration found when it assumed office presented an estimated deficit of nearly $10 billion. But because of overestimates of revenue, this deficit would actually have been more than $11 billion.

The Eisenhower Administration has cut requested appropriations by more than $12 billion, and expenditures in this fiscal year have been reduced by about $7 billion. This will give us an estimated budget deficit in our first full year of operation of less than $4 billion. In the coming year, fiscal 1955, we have further cut planned expenditures by more than an additional $5 billion.

Our plans, of course, can badly miscarry if adverse serious developments occur elsewhere in the world, resulting in a revision of our future foreign undertakings.

We must and will always spend whatever is needed for our security; that is our first concern.

But the worth of our defense must be measured not by its cost but by its wisdom.

And, barring major unexpected future international developments, we must provide adequately for our security for the long pull and still continue to strive to make further savings in addition to those already made.

The cornerstone of our whole program is our firm belief that a

Waiting at the church.

Canfield in *The Newark Evening News*, 1954

sound economy is an absolute prerequisite to a strong defense over any extended period. It is the balance needed for maximum development of both that we must maintain.

I am honored to accept this tribute in behalf of this Administration, which is dedicated to obtain more economy and efficiency in government. I am honored to receive this award with such distinguished and effective workers for economy and efficiency in government as former President Hoover and Senator Byrd, who have made such conspicuous contributions to its accomplishment over such a long period of years.

The achievements for which these awards are presented are vital. They are vital because they go to the very heart of the maintenance of a strong and healthy economy in this nation which is not only the foundation for better jobs and better living for all our people but actually is the free world's first line of defense.

"The American people are very wise"

Article by Secretary Humphrey in United States
Coast Guard Magazine.

June, 1954

I firmly believe that the American people are very wise—wiser than many of our politicians believe. Given the facts, in most cases the majority of the American people will react soundly and in the best long-run interests of the nation. That is why so many of you can help us so much by taking back to your home cities and towns the facts about what we are trying to do and help others to understand what we are trying to do, and so you will be providing a most valuable service for the whole nation.

As was once so well said: "Never underestimate the intelligence of the American people and never overestimate their knowledge of the facts."

When I say that people are wise, I am not merely engaging in rhetoric. Convincing proof is the mail which comes to us. I recently contributed an article for a national magazine on what our current tax program is about. I put it in as simple, direct language as I knew how. Let me read you a comment from a housewife in Pennsylvania:

"I have just finished reading your article about the new tax bill. It succeeded in convincing me that a reduction in income taxes at this time would be poor policy. As a housewife, I admit that I do a lot of complaining about the large part of my husband's paycheck being withheld for income taxes. When I first heard about the Government's plans to lower various other taxes but keep the same level of income taxes, I groaned. So when I began reading your article, I had a chip on my shoulder. Now, however, I understand and approve your point of view."

A retired Queens County, New York, man wrote: "Your piece showed clearly the honest approach to the right policy of paying your way as you go ahead. As you say, it should be the same for Government as for the individual."

And the dean of a small private college in the South wrote: "Year after year, we have seen our modest savings shrink in value until upon retirement they will purchase only half of what will be needed to live on in these days of inflated prices. Surely I must speak for millions of white collar workers on a fixed salary who have no union or political group to work for them. Please do not give up the battle for the sound dollar."

Those letters were written by people who are honestly voicing their feelings. They are encouraging because they are convincing me that the American people, given the facts, are wise—a lot wiser than demagogic politicians think.

This Administration has been and is still working toward two main great goals:

(1) We must and will provide the military strength best designed to promote our own security and real peace in the world.

(2) We must and will maintain the sound economy and productive power which is the basis for that military strength and leadership for peace. It is in connection with this second goal—a sound economy— that the Treasury is particularly concerned. . . .

"And we did get expenses down"

Statement by Secretary Humphrey from
the Treasury Department.

September 14, 1954

The mid-year review of the estimates in the 1955 budget shows an estimated deficit for this fiscal year of about $4.7 billion. About two-thirds of the increase over our January estimate was caused by greater reduction of excise taxes by the Congress than we either recommended or estimated at the beginning of the year.

I want to make it clear that this is an interim estimate and one that we shall work every day, every week, and every month to reduce. You will recall that a year ago we presented an interim report on the prospective figures for 1954. We said then that we hoped to better them by the end of the fiscal year. We actually cut spending by nearly $4

billion between our August estimate and our fiscal 1954 year-end figures
Receipts also were down by more than $3 billion, partly due to tax
reductions. The deficit was reduced from $3.8 billion to $3 billion.

We said a year ago that we were going to keep working to get both
spending and the deficit down. We did get them down. We are going
to try to do it again this year. We shall keep working continuously
during the rest of this fiscal year to better the estimates we are presenting today.

Getting spending "under better control"

Article by Secretary Humphrey in The New York
Herald-Tribune *under the title "The Fiscal
Gains of Twenty Months."*

October 7, 1954

I have been in business for nearly forty years. I have been in Government for only twenty months.

As a businessman looking at government from the inside, I believe
that the Eisenhower Administration has been making real gains in correcting some errors we found in the operations of the fiscal and tax
affairs of the Government.

In business, the quarterly reports of a company currently show pretty
much whether it is doing well or not. While we don't have anything
quite comparable in government, those of us who have come into
government from business can see quite clearly that the steps taken
so far by the Eisenhower Administration have been for the good of
all Americans by turning us away from waste, away from bigger and
bigger deficit spending, and bigger and bigger tax loads, toward a promising new era of development for our nation.

The Eisenhower Administration is trying to help strengthen the
economy and to make more and better jobs. We know that we must
continually have more jobs for the good of all citizens in our growing
population. And we must have them to provide for the security of
our nation.

Let's look at some of the things which have been done to help the economy grow stronger and make more jobs by correcting fiscal and economic errors which we found when we came into the Government twenty months ago.

We found a deficit for the fiscal year 1953 of almost $9.5 billion, about which the new Administration could do little at such a late date. And for fiscal year 1954, the prior Administration had charted a deficit of nearly $10 billion. The Eisenhower Administration reduced the 1954 deficit to $3 billion and turned the trend away from bigger and bigger deficit financing by cutting planned spending $7 billion in that one year alone. We will keep working every day, every week, and every month to make every possible saving which is not detrimental to the needs of our national security or stability in the economy.

By getting federal spending under better control, we have been able to cut down on the intolerable burden of taxes which the American people have borne for so long. In the present calendar year, taxes have been cut by $7.4 billion—the largest dollar tax cut in the history of the country. We have also put into effect a tax revision law which not only removes hardships from millions of taxpayers, but will help the economy expand and so create more and better jobs by removing restraints to initiative and free endeavor.

By reductions in spending, and also by better handling of our too-huge national debt, we have helped to check inflation. Inflation had caused cruel hardship to millions of citizens as the value of their savings dropped from 100 cents to 52 cents between 1939 and 1953. In marked contrast, the fiscal program of the Eisenhower Administration has been largely responsible for the fact that the value of the dollar has changed less than one-half of one cent in the past twenty months.

Such inflation-producing policies had to be reversed by the Eisenhower Administration so that a free economy might once again progress toward greater productivity, higher standards of living, and more and better jobs.

In many other ways the Eisenhower Administration has reversed the trend toward a Federal "super-state." Shackling federal controls over prices and wages were speedily removed. We started to turn back to the people the many enterprises which had unnecessarily come under Government control. We sold the costly Inland Waterways Corporation. We are liquidating the RFC. We are selling the Government's synthetic rubber plants. We are getting the military out of business activities which private firms can do for less cost. And these are only a few specific instances of the many moves that are under way.

As a businessman now in government, I sincerely feel that a start toward a businesslike performance has been made in twenty short months.

We haven't yet balanced the budget. But we have come two-thirds of the way toward it, which is a good start, and we will keep continuously working at it. We are moving a few steps at a time and, by tax reductions, getting money back into the hands of the people for them to spend for themselves as they deem best rather than having the Government taxing and spending it for them.

The longer-term debt

Speech by Secretary Humphrey to the American Bankers Association at Haddon Hall, Atlantic City.

October 19, 1954

All Americans can welcome the fact that this nation is making the shift from high to lower Government spending without more strain on the economy.

Hundreds of thousands of our people have successfully changed from making things for killing to making things for living. This has involved temporary hardships in some individual cases but this great shift is being made without a great economic upheaval.

Industrial activity and total employment have held remarkably well throughout recent months. The fourth quarter of this year is already even brighter both industrially and commercially.

The number of unemployed is currently decreasing. We have had more people working during this year than in any other year in the nation's peacetime history. Unemployment is a matter of the greatest concern to every one in this Administration. We are working and planning in every way to reach the day when every man looking for work can find a job. We have shaped our entire economic program in the way best calculated to bring that happy day at the earliest possible time.

This nation has not always been able to make the transition from war to peacetime spending without major economic upsets. American history shows that we have had severe economic adjustments following all great wars. This was true after the War of 1812, the Civil War, and World War I.

As you all know, one of the causes of postwar depressions is the fact that, when our nation goes to war, it postpones for the time being the production of all sorts of peacetime goods. Once war ends, we turn to satisfying the backlog demands which built up while the war was on.

It is wholly human, even if unwise, for such reconstruction booms to be overdone and for speculative credit structures to come into being. Soon the nation finds itself with surpluses instead of shortages and an inventory readjustment is required. . . .

Study of past depressions makes clear some of the things that ought to be done. It also makes clear some of the things that ought not to be done. Many of the things in both categories concern monetary policy, with which you as bankers are intimately familiar.

So that, if the record tells us anything, it says that the most dangerous thing is to permit the erection of a great collapsible structure of speculative credit. When such structures finally topple, they set off a spiral of liquidation which can quickly descend into widespread depression throughout the economy.

We should note that there is all the difference in the world between the systematic and orderly liquidation of inventories that have simply become too large and liquidation forced by fear for loans that are in danger of going "under water." History records dramatically the "race for liquidity" and the disaster that it caused in the early 1930's. . . .

There are other lessons from the past which were applied to our economic situation over the past year and a half. It was clear that the Government's policies during all the 1930's were wrong and worked badly. They were designed to solve unemployment; yet there were still 9 million unemployed in 1939. These unemployed only got back to work after war broke out in Europe. I know of no one who thinks that war is the right way to cure unemployment.

Jobs are created—and only honestly created in our free competitive price economy—by people using their money to expand existing businesses or start new businesses in the hope of making a profit. If any government policy is such as to make a profit unlikely or very difficult, people simply aren't going to launch the new ventures from which new jobs grow. New ventures are discouraged by Government controls of materials, labor, or prices or by uncertainty of labor and other costs or by the threat or actual practice of Government competing with private enterprise.

Limitations on incentives or freedom of legitimate activity in any way have a deadening effect. This Administration's fiscal policies are shaped about the reduction of Government spending as an absolute requirement for the reduction of incentive-destroying taxation. The reduction of Government spending and lower taxes will help to avoid the inflation which destroys confidence and ultimately any nation's economy.

The handout principle of deficits and resulting debts of the 1930's was a temporary expedient that assisted nothing fundamental. It actually deterred individual risk-taking in competition with the free money that was being passed around, and finally became a means of destroying the soundness of the dollar.

A primary responsibility of government must, of course, be to relieve human suffering and destitution which cannot be taken care of by the individuals themselves when overtaken by adversity. But this must be done in the proper ways which this Administration has already improved and enlarged.

We seek the multiplication of production and income, not simply a new division of a stagnant pool.

Most of you are well familiar by now with the major accomplishments of this Administration during the past twenty months. You know how spending and spending programs have been cut by billions of dollars. You know how taxes have been cut by the largest amount in any year in the nation's history. You know how waste and extravagance have been stopped in many areas of Government. You know how these and other policies have been successful in creating a remarkably constant value of the dollar during the past year and a half while the cost of ordinary living has shown a slight decline.

You know what efforts we have been making to reconstruct the debt. I would like to give you today an analysis of what we have done in the past twenty months, which shows that we have made steady, if not spectacular, progress in this vital field.

President Eisenhower, in his first State of the Union Message in February, 1953, said, in his discussion of fiscal policy, that "too great a part of the national debt comes due in too short a time." The President said that the Treasury would undertake at suitable times a program of extending part of the debt over longer periods and gradually placing greater amounts in the hands of longer term investors.

Our determination to do this at suitable times was based, of course, on the knowledge that too much short-term debt is inflationary. Handling of the debt by previous administrations had contributed substantially to the inflation which robbed the dollar of almost half of its purchasing power from 1939 to January 1953.

Every month the debt gets closer to maturity simply as a result of the passage of time. Like the Red Queen, we have to run fast just to stand still. Our immediate job has been to stop the debt from getting shorter—and then to start lengthening it gradually. This we have done during the last twenty months.

In nine of the eleven major financings of the last twenty months, the debt was lengthened by offering investors securities other than one-year certificates. This is quite a contrast to the twenty months prior to January 1953, when on only two occasions out of 13 was longer term debt offered.

The major debt lengthening in the last twenty months has been a reduction in the amount of very short-term debt. The amount of marketable debt maturing in less than one year was cut down by over $11 billion.

The amount of marketable debt running more than five years was increased by about $8.5 billion.

We have made progress, too, in placing greater amounts of the debt in the hands of longer term individual savers, largely as a result of the highest level of E and H Savings Bond sales since World War II. Individual investors altogether hold more than $66 billion of Government securities at the present time.

We are continuing to work to further the objective of reconstructing the debt, but we will continue to operate with extreme care because, as you so well know, our economy is a sensitive mechanism that can be seriously upset by hasty or ill-considered action. . . .

The Government must borrow the money it needs so as not to interfere with the needs of other governmental units or private enterprise for any money they may need. The Government should not borrow large amounts of long-term money at times when it would seriously interfere with the supply of that money to finance the building of schools, hospitals, or highways by local or state governments or the expansion of power plants or building of new factories or other industrial enterprises by private business.

What we are trying to do at this particular time is to have the Government borrow its money in such a way as to avoid the possibility of interfering with the expansion of our economy and the making of more and better jobs.

Every program that the Eisenhower Administration undertakes, every problem that we inherited, we look at with one thought in mind: Is it necessary for the good of most of our people? ... There is nothing to fear about the long future of this economy or this nation. If we keep doing the things we ought to do and this Administration can continue to put its sound fiscal and economic policies into effect, the years ahead will see greater prosperity and more jobs for more people making more, new, better and cheaper things for better, fuller living for us all, than any of us have ever dreamed.

The higher bond interest "worked"

Statement and testimony by Secretary Humphrey
before the Sub-Committee on Economic Stabilization
of the Joint Committee on the Economic Report.
Senator Ralph Flanders of Vermont, chairman.

December 7, 1954

... At the outset and before considering in detail the activities of the Treasury during the past two years, I want to make a few general comments on the direction of our entire fiscal program as well as the principles guiding us in the management of the public debt.

The Administration's budgetary and tax policies, along with its debt management policies, have all been designed to promote high employment, rising production, and a stable dollar.

We have in fact been following the policies advocated by your predecessor subcommittees that—as stated in the Douglas report of January, 1950, in language reaffirmed in the Patman report of June, 1952—"appropriate, vigorous, and co-ordinated monetary, credit, and fiscal policies" should "constitute the Government's primary and principal method" of promoting the purposes of the Employment Act, and further, their recommendation "that federal fiscal policies be such as not only to avoid aggravating economic instability but also to make a positive and important contribution to stabilization, at the same time promoting equity and incentives in taxation and economy in expenditures."

Government spending programs have been cut by billions of dollars. Waste and extravagance have been eliminated in many areas. Economy in Government and efforts to get the federal budget under even better control are continuing without letup. These efforts are of great importance to the future of our country and are fundamental in the Administration's honest money program.

Major tax reductions and comprehensive tax revisions, along with the ending of price and wage controls, are removing barriers to economic growth and restoring individual initiative and enterprise. Savings in Government spending which have been returned to the people in the form of tax cuts are helping sustain the economy, increase employment and production.

Progress is being made toward getting our huge public debt in better shape, so that its maturities can be handled more easily and debt operations will not stimulate either inflation or deflation. Treasury financings have been designed to tie in with action taken by the Federal Reserve System to keep the supply of money and credit in line with the needs of the country.

The principles we have been following in the management of the large public debt are not new. They are, likewise, principles that have been laid down by your predecessor subcommittees after extensive study and careful consideration of the fundamental role they can play in effective monetary policy.

The first principle is that monetary and debt management policies should be flexible. To be effective, they must lean against inflation as well as deflation. As put by the Douglas subcommittee and reaffirmed by the Patman subcommittee: "Timely flexibility toward easy credit at some times and credit restriction at other times is an essential characteristic of a monetary policy that will promote economic stability rather than instability."

The second principle is that Treasury debt management operations should be consistent with current monetary and credit control policies of the Federal Reserve. This means close co-operation at all times between the Federal Reserve and the Treasury. As Representative Patman's subcommittee reported in 1952: "Neither the problems of monetary policy nor those of debt management can be solved in isolation from the other. We recommend that the Treasury and the Federal Reserve should continue to endeavor to find by mutual discussion the solutions most in the public interest for their common problems. . . ."

The answers which we have already submitted to your Subcommittee's questions detail the actions we have taken in co-operation with the Federal Reserve during the past two years in carrying out these principles. They show the manner in which our debt operations have been designed to complement monetary action taken by the Federal Reserve to promote economic stability, first by helping to restrain inflation and then later by helping to avoid deflation.

The record has not always been as impressive. As you know, at the time of the earlier congressional hearings on monetary policy and debt management, the economy had been under strong inflationary pressures. Monetary policy had been largely ineffectual in helping to control inflation because of the previous Administration's policy of selling mostly short-term securities and using the powers of the Federal Reserve System to hold down interest rates artificially. A fundamental conclusion of both of your predecessor subcommittees was that such action was not in the best interest of the nation. This was their considered judgment in language used by the Douglas subcommittee and reaffirmed by the Patman subcommittee: ". . . we believe that the advantages of avoiding inflation are so great and that a restrictive monetary policy can contribute so much to this end that the freedom of the Federal Reserve to restrict credit and raise interest rates for general stabilization purposes should be restored even if the cost should prove to be a significant increase in service charges on the Federal debt and a greater inconvenience to the Treasury in its sale of securities for new financing and refunding purposes."

This Administration has followed these principles because we believe them to be fundamental principles of good government. We believe the record of the past two years has indicated their effectiveness in giving us honest money and laying a firm foundation for the sound growth and prosperity of our country.

Cross-examination of Secretary Humphrey

REP. WRIGHT PATMAN (Texas). . . . This committee is aware of what seems to be a "hard money" or a "dearer money" policy pursued by the Treasury, and will appreciate your opinion or your explanations. It seems to us it began with the higher interest rates set by the Treasury on its long-term bond issue of May, 1953, which certainly was "dearer money" and in my opinion turned out to be a mistake.

SEC. HUMPHREY. . . . It was not a mistake; and it was a move toward "honest money." I have made a lot of mistakes in life, and probably I will make a lot more, but this was not one of them. This was fiscal policy that served a purpose and if I'd had it to do over I would do it again. . . . You must always remember that the bonds were put forth to pay the price required by the bond market. . . .

The policy worked; it halted an inflation which at the moment seemed to us a highly potential threat. It saved the people a great deal of money. It stabilized the market and it halted the depreciation of the dollar. . . .

REP. PATMAN. . . . That 3¼ per cent on the bonds provided the banks—all the big investors—with a tremendous windfall, something like 15 per cent. It was a case where the little fellow was left out. All the interest rates went up and the war veterans and the small home builders suffered as a result. . . .

SEC. HUMPHREY. . . . The bonds were on the market for weeks. There was no discrimination. Any one who wanted them could buy them.

REP. PATMAN. . . . The next thing to happen was that the Veterans Administration and the Federal Housing Administration raised their interest rates to 4½ per cent, just three days before the Federal Reserve decided to ease the situation by cutting their rates. . . . You must have known the Reserve System was going to do this. Why didn't you warn FHA not to raise its rates?

Sec. Humphrey. . . . That law was not doing the veterans any good at that time. They found they were not going to get loans at the lower interest rates.

Rep. Patman. It looks to me like an increase of interest rates for the benefit of the banks' profits at the expense of the veterans.

Sec. Humphrey. Actually, it gave the veterans a benefit. It brought about a great housing boom after months of stagnation. . . .

Senator Paul Douglas (Illinois). I question the wisdom of that decision of the Treasury to jump to a long-term rate of 3¼ per cent, in one swoop, from 2¾ per cent. . . . Just why did you fix that rate?

Sec. Humphrey. The interest rate, Senator Douglas, is actually not fixed by the Treasury. The public fixes the rate. And we price our issues at what appears to us to be the going rate in the market.

Senator Douglas. Oh, I can't accept that, quite. You know you help to fix the rates. When the Treasury sets a 3¼ rate, all the other rates of interest tend to follow you. You know you determine the interest rates. . . . Why did you choose this higher rate?

Sec. Humphrey. If you will recall, the Administration was about to remove the last Government controls, the economic and price controls set by the last Administration. If you also will remember, we inherited a deficit of $9.5 billion from you. We were very much afraid of a runaway price spiral with the controls removed. . . .

The Chairman. What you really faced was this: Inflation had been checked before you came into office. Controls were to be removed, and you wanted to maintain stability, you wanted to keep the existing price situation.

Sec. Humphrey. That's exactly right, Senator, and it worked.

Senator Douglas. I hadn't intended to bring that up, but now that you have and say "It worked," I will add that it only worked to halt production and bring on a recession. . . .

The Chairman. It halted production of things which flowed into inventories and so posed a problem. We had to get that situation cleared up. If we had not, we would have been in for a very bad time. . . .

Sec. Humphrey. I wouldn't say that we had a recession, exactly; if it was, it was a very temporary thing. . . . Certainly the economy is on the way up again. Our latest figures at the Treasury show very substantial upturns in the leadership industries, such as steel and automobiles. . . . I want to assure this committee that, from the start of this Administration, all policies on the budget, on taxes, and on debt management have been designed to promote high employment, rising production, and a stable dollar. . . .

The way to check inflation

Article by Secretary Humphrey in Nation's Business
Magazine under the title "Our Continuing Policy."

January, 1955

Halting inflation has been one of the great accomplishments of the Eisenhower Administration.

One of our most important objectives for 1955 is to prevent any reappearance of inflation.

The narrow swing of the consumers price index in 1954—as in 1953— is solid proof that the long decline prior to 1953 in the purchasing power of the dollar has, for the time being at least, been ended. A dollar earned and saved in January, 1953, will buy just about the same dollar's worth of food or clothing today that it would then.

This is vitally important to every individual, every business—in brief, to everybody's pocketbook.

The rising prices of a period of inflation spell losses just as real as when a pickpocket rifles a wallet. Inflation hurts everyone.

It hurts especially those who endeavor to lay away a portion of their earnings for their own or their children's future, and find later that inflation has sapped the value of their savings.

A stable dollar benefits everyone. To the individual it affords a greater sense of security in the value of such basic things as savings bonds, savings accounts, insurance policies, and all the other recognized forms of savings.

It relieves the whole business field of the uncertainties which inevitably accompany the rising prices of inflation and inflationary trends. It enables business people to buy and sell and produce more confidently and **more** intelligently.

The world runs on confidence, and there is no greater destroyer of confidence than an unsound currency.

The checking of inflation was accomplished through the sound money policies which the Administration inaugurated in 1953 and continued in 1954. The way to keep inflation in check is to keep doing the things which in the past two years have been so successful in halting inflation.

Our methods have been simple. We are getting the fiscal affairs of the Government under control.

We are cutting deficit financing.

We are slowly but surely improving the structure of the public debt.

The Federal Reserve system is exercising proper monetary control without interference.

All these things have served the purpose of helping keep the nation's supply of money and credit in line with the actual needs of a growing economy, and avoiding excesses.

There have been other important steps, of course, to stimulate prosperity.

Controls which hobbled the economy were discarded. Defense spending is being used only to buy defense—not to support unsound economic practices.

Taxes have been cut, and the structure of the tax system greatly improved.

Recognizing that the economy must provide not only the men and the weapons needed for defense but also an even higher standard of living as well as the social services which our people want and need, we have lifted our economic sights to bring these goals in range.

The economy for which we are working will provide a dependable flow of new and improved products and new, better-paying jobs for a steadily increasing population. It will be a firmly footed economy, directed away from blind alleys and in step with the times.

Sticking to the program which for two years now has worked so well means supporting courageously the leadership which developed that program. I think that the advantages of such a course to the American people are very plain.

Ours has become a nation of small to medium savers—of "haves" rather than "have-nots."

Our national income this year will be about $300 billion, which after

It used to be
a very bad crossing!

Dowling in
*The New York
Herald Tribune,*
1955

allowance for price changes is six times the national income of 1900.

National production for the year will probably exceed $355 billion, which—again after allowance for price rises—is six times the national output of 1900.

The national output per capita is three times that of 1900—with our population more than doubled. Our per capita income, after price adjustments, is three times the 1900 figure. In terms of today's prices, 55 out of every 100 American families now earn more than $4,000 a year, compared with ten out of every 100 families early in the century.

If we act with determination to forestall any further inflation threats, our possessions will remain secure.

Wage and salary earners will receive the full fair share of their earnings.

Savers who lay away a dollar for a rainy day will still have a dollar when need for it arises.

Insurance payments and pension payments will not have shrunk cruelly in purchasing power below the expectations of the recipients.

A particularly important consideration is that our industrial and commercial system depends heavily for investment money on the great aggregate of the small savings of our people. Little savings, passing through the hands of savings banks, building and loan associations, insurance companies, investment trusts, pension funds, and various other agencies, become big investments in plants and equipment. Such investments in 1954 have reached nearly $27 billion. Here is the indispensable source of the new jobs we must have in our fast-growing country, and the source of tomorrow's necessary increase in productivity. It is vastly important that the savings available for such investment be protected with the greatest care from inflation's eroding effects.

To continue our program is absolutely essential if we want to go on bettering our economic state.

Inflation dead—keep it dead

Article by Secretary Humphrey in the Washington Post and Times-Herald *under the title "Keep Inflation Dead, Goal of Humphrey."*

January 2, 1955

There is one matter with which this Administration has been concerned—and will continue to be concerned in 1955—which affects the daily life of every individual and every business in the country. This is the matter of inflation.

The halting of inflation has been one of the great accomplishments of the Eisenhower Administration.

Keeping it checked will be one of our most important objectives in the year 1955.

The world runs on confidence, and there is no greater destroyer of confidence than an unsound currency. That is why the checking of inflation has such high priority in this Administration.

In the nearly two years starting in January, 1953, the long decline in the purchasing power of the dollar was, for the time being at least, ended. A dollar saved in January, 1953, will buy just about the same dollar's worth of food or clothing today as it would two years ago.

That is why the checking of inflation means so much to the pocketbook of every person in America.

When prices are rising, the loss to millions of individuals is just as real as a pickpocket rifling a wallet. It is especially harmful to those who try to lay away a portion of their earnings for their own or their children's future, only to find at a later date that inflation has stolen a portion of their savings.

With inflation checked, individuals have a greater sense of security. The nation's whole economy is relieved of the uncertainties which accompany inflation. There is more confidence everywhere.

We have checked inflation in the past two years by following sound money policies. We hope to keep it checked in the years ahead by continuing to do the things which have been so successful in halting inflation in the past two years.

What are some of those sound money policies? We are getting the fiscal affairs of our Government under better control. We are cutting deficit financing. We are improving the structure of the public debt. And the Federal Reserve System is exercising its proper monetary control without interference.

All these things have helped keep the nation's supply of money and credit in line with the actual needs of a growing economy. This control of inflation, which we must continue in the year ahead, is of vital importance because it means so much to all American people. This is so because this nation has become one of small-to-medium savers, of "haves" rather than "have-nots."

In terms of today's prices, 55 out of every 100 American families now earn more than $4,000 a year, compared with ten out of every 100 families who earned $4,000 in today's buying power at the turn of the century.

Another important consideration is that our economy today depends for its investment money on the total of the small savings of our people. These savings passed through savings banks, building and loan associations, insurance companies, investment trusts, and pension funds, become big investments in plants and equipment—investments which this past year reached nearly $37 billion. Here in this investment of small savings is the indispensable source of the new jobs we must have in our growing country. Here is the source of tomorrow's necessary increase in what we can produce. It is vitally important that the savings available for such investment be protected with the greatest care from the theft of inflation. We must continue this program of keeping inflation in check, then, as an absolute essential to continued betterment of our economic life.

The news that gets no headlines

Speech by Secretary Humphrey on the award of the 1954 William Penn Medal by the Chamber of Commerce of Greater Philadelphia at the Bellevue-Stratford Hotel, Philadelphia.

February 16, 1955

... As Secretary of the Treasury, I am doubly indebted both to the Chamber of Commerce and to this community for the splendid support we have always enjoyed from your business people and your citizens in the wide distribution of United States Savings Bonds. These are not only the soundest of investments but they are one of the most ideal means of promoting the savings of the people, which are essential to the continued progress and security of our country.

I am deeply honored to receive the 1954 William Penn Award of the Chamber of Commerce of Greater Philadelphia. It is a great privilege for me to receive this honor as a member of President Eisenhower's Administration.

I am going to talk to you tonight not as Secretary of the Treasury, not as a Cabinet officer, or even as a businessman who is now a bureaucrat. I will talk rather as a friend and fellow-citizen and a taxpayer who shares with you the responsibility of good government, of keeping America the land of opportunity—the land where the economy of today must build for the economy of tomorrow by its wisdom, its soundness, and its farsightedness. We must build a world with more and better opportunities for our children and our children's children and not a world that will take opportunity away from them. . . .

I am going to talk to you not of headlines, controversy, and crises, but of the quiet, undramatic, progressive developments that are going on all around us in America. There have been no headlines to tell you that more than 60 million Americans are working at jobs of their own choosing—jobs that they are free to leave or change if and whenever they so desire.

There are no headlines to tell you that about 55 per cent of the 47 millions of families in America own their own homes, that Americans have savings of $80 billion in life insurance policies; almost $50 billion in United States Savings Bonds; and $25 billion in retirement pension funds.

There are no headlines to remind you that stringent wartime Government controls no longer hamper or restrict the individual or the businessman. And there are no headlines to herald the stirring return of confidence of Americans in their Government, in each other, and in our ability and strength to do whatever may be required of us in any emergency. . . .

It has been a dedicated goal of the Eisenhower Administration to keep alive and vigorous the priceless principles of free, competitive enterprise and initiative. But we must do more than keep them alive and vigorous. We must keep them growing and always developing the new things and the better ways of doing things which have made this nation great.

What has been done in encouraging initiative and enterprise has not been sensational or dramatic. But it has been important to every American in his daily life. It is important to the standard of living of every American worker and his loved ones. And it is vitally important to the defense of all Americans against any possible enemy attack, for the power and strength of American industrial capacity is the very foundation of our security.

It is often true that "good news" is "no news" to attract public attention in the daily news outlets of press, radio, and television. Yet the quiet, undramatic, progressive developments that are going on in America—without making sensational news—are important for the present and future of our people.

I have no quarrel with what makes news. I make these observations only as a reason for talking a little tonight about . . . important things which are worth mentioning because they do not draw the attention that controversy and violence do.

The undramatic but steady and healthy progress which has been going on in this country has increased the confidence of all Americans in the possibilities of our future. This increasing confidence is the most important stimulant to the development of the strength of our nation's economy, with the careful and quiet assistance of an administration which knows that government can do relatively little except to help to properly set a stage upon which free, vigorous Americans can perform.

Our nation has made the transition from a wartime high to a lower level of Government spending without a major economic upset. This transition was helped substantially by heavy tax cuts and other moves stimulating confidence.

While there is still high tension in many places, there is no armed warfare between major powers at any point on the globe as of this moment. There is peace—uneasy as it is—as far as American fighting men are concerned. War in Korea has halted. War in Indo-China has ceased.

The present improved relationships in many places throughout the world have been achieved by ceaseless and dedicated pursuit of solutions for the vexing and serious widespread international problems. It is a treacherous path. Bold risks must sometimes be taken, but success to date is high proof of the competence and wisdom of the policies which have been adopted in wrestling with this problem of preserving the peace and making it more secure.

Inflation has been stopped. In the past two years the value of the dollar has changed only one-fifth of one cent. This compares with a drop in the value of the dollar from 100 cents in 1939 to only 52 cents in January, 1953. All departments and many people in government have been working hard for, and insisting upon getting, our federal spending under control. Deficits—which lead to more borrowing and so to inflation—have been cut substantially.

The Federal Reserve System has acted promptly, courageously, and wisely to adopt monetary and credit policies which have met the needs of the economy while walking the fine line between deflation and inflation. And the Treasury has done its bit in halting inflation—and avoiding deflation—by doing its borrowing so as to be as careful as possible concerning its effect upon the constructive course of the economy.

Boy, oh boy!
A pair of thrillers!

Alexander in
The Philadelphia Bulletin,
1954

This is well illustrated by the issue and highly successful placement only a few days ago of nearly $2 billion in 40-year 3 per cent bonds. They are the longest bonds that have been sold by the Government since an issue to help pay for the Panama Canal in 1911.

There is nothing academic about the importance of keeping inflation locked out. The value of earnings and savings can be protected in no other way. Just realize that 55 out of every 100 families in America now earn more than $4,000 a year as compared with only 10 out of 100 earning $4,000 a year early in the century in terms of today's prices. And recall the millions of owners of their homes, accounts in savings banks, savings bonds, insurance policies, and pensions, of which I spoke just a moment ago. Because this nation has quietly become a nation of "haves" rather than "have-nots," inflation must stay checked to protect the earnings and savings of millions.

We had a cash balance between money collected from the public and money paid out by the Government last year. Although we will not have a cash balance this year, we are estimating a small surplus in the fiscal year ahead. . . . The inflationary effect of deficit financing has been almost wholly eliminated now that most of the increase in debt is being financed by securities issued to government trust funds rather than borrowing from the public.

In fiscal 1956, spending will be almost $12 billion less than in 1953. We have not yet balanced the budget. We could have done so in 1954, but a big tax cut was more stimulating to a growing economy and we believe that it was better for the people to have more of their own money left with them to spend, as they thought best, rather than to have the Government spending it for them.

We have cut the deficit from more than $9 billion in fiscal 1953 to what we estimate will be less than $2.5 billion in 1956. We are still a year and a half away from the end of that period, and we have every hope of cutting this deficit even further if some development elsewhere in the world does not upset our plans.

There is nothing in the Formosa situation or elsewhere in the world which up to this moment has altered our budget program for reduced expenditures in the year to come. And reduced expenditures we make do *not* mean reduced defenses.

As the President has said, the United States is in a stronger position to defend itself against aggression than it was two years ago. The Defense Department has developed a better balanced, more mobile and flexible and effective defense establishment at lower cost to the taxpayers.

Progress has been made in reducing waste and extravagance. Obsolete equipment and supplies are being eliminated. There is much left to be done, but much has already been accomplished. We have a far better balanced program. We are making progress in real unification in the armed services, so that competition between them is less likely to duplicate efforts and expenditures that squander both tax money and our national resources. Greater unity adds strength to our defense position. . . .

The President's decisions on our defense forces are recognition of the fact that in this age of almost unbelievable developments in science and production techniques, we cannot have a static defense committed to old-fashioned strategy and weapons. Real security for our nation over an extended period must also rest upon sound and growing economy. . . .

The role which the Government can play in the economic affairs of the nation should be limited. Government manipulation is the antithesis of a free America, and encroachment by government in restricting the freedom of its citizens should be limited to doing, as Lincoln said, "for a community of people whatever they need to have done, but cannot do at all, or cannot so well do for themselves—in their separate and individual capacities. In all that the people can individually do for themselves, government ought not to interfere."

The future of free America lies in the initiative, the resourcefulness, the tenacity, daring, and courage of 160 million Americans, each free to choose how best he can promote his own interest and the interest and future of his loved ones in whatever way he can best devise only so long as he does not interfere with the rights of others.

It is the cumulative power of this great effort which has made America great in the past and which I am convinced will drive us ahead in the future at an accelerated pace in excess of anything we have ever known before. You and I as citizens must participate in this great drive toward a better America. . . .

The Secretary quizzes himself

Speech by Secretary Humphrey to the National Canners Association at the Conrad Hilton Hotel, Chicago.

February 19, 1955

. . . I am greatly impressed with something I have just heard about your association. I am told that your financial statement for the past year shows that you have operated with a budget that is balanced. To one who has the ambition to do likewise but is beset with all the problems of the Secretary of the Treasury of the United States, that is something I note with great envy. . . .

We live in an age of change, devoted to the use of new techniques. Now, as I am not an orator but at heart, and by experience, just a businessman like yourselves, to whom deeds mean more than words, I am going to choose a new technique in speaking to you this morning, the technique of the presently popular radio-television quiz show. By using questions which I am constantly being asked by Government officials, newsmen, members of Congress, and people like yourselves, I will try to inform you by my answers of our problems, our accomplishments, and our hopes.

Gentlemen: The stage is set. The clock is marking off the seconds. The kleig lights are on. The moderator is in his place. We are on the air and are ready for the first question.

QUESTION. Mr. Secretary, please tell us—has the Administration abandoned its program of trying to balance the budget?

The answer to that is absolutely no. We are working, and with a reasonable amount of success, toward a balanced budget. The record shows that progress has been good, even though we have not reached the goal. The Government's deficits have been cut substantially since we came into office. The deficit in fiscal 1953 was almost $9.5 billion. We could do very little about this in five short months as actual spending plans were committed beyond recall. However, the Eisenhower Administration did cut the deficit in the next fiscal year, fiscal 1954, down to $3.1 billion—or two-thirds of the way toward a balanced budget. It is true that the deficit in the present fiscal year (fiscal 1955) looks like $4.5 billion, but the new budget for fiscal 1956 again cuts the deficit to $2.4 billion. Both the present deficit and the deficit for the next fiscal year may be less than now estimated if revenue holds up and if we are able to cut spending further. . . .

QUESTION. Why haven't we cut Government spending faster?

The Government can only reduce its expenses by putting people out of work, either directly or indirectly. This sounds harsh, but the fact is that the Government spends most of its money for only two things: (1) the employment of people working directly for the Government, or (2) the purchase of goods which are made by people who will be out of work if the orders for the goods are cancelled. Under these circumstances, it would not be prudent to cut Government spending too fast, even if it were possible to do so. Of course the most important reason is that in these perilous times our first obligation to the nation is to adequately provide for our security. But there is another very important consideration that must be prominently kept in mind.

We must constantly have in mind in making these reductions the

Three years late
already!

Orr in
The Chicago Tribune,
1955

necessity of creating new employment to absorb those who will thus
be out of work. There must be a great transition—moving people
from working for the Government, either directly or indirectly, into
jobs working for the production of goods for the general public.

We have gone through two years of this transition with reasonable
success. . . .

QUESTION. Why has this Administration cut so much from the
defense budget?

Sixty-five per cent of our latest budget goes for major national
security programs. This amounts to about $40.5 billion a year. Of the
remaining $21.9 billion, $14.8 billion or 24 per cent of the total budget
goes for payment of interest on the debt and other charges fixed by
law. That leaves only $7.1 billion, or 11 per cent, of the total budget
for other so-called civilian agencies of Government. So, it simply
follows that if any large cuts in spending are to be made, they must
largely come—but carefully and wisely made—from the heavy total
for defense.

Now, when we talk about "cutting" expense, let's always remember
that does not mean cutting our effective defense. Let's recall how
much stronger we are today than we were when Korea began in June

of 1950. At the outbreak of Korea, our armed forces had less than 1.5 million men, equipped almost wholly with material of World War II manufacture. We now have 3,100,000 men in service, and our present target for 1956 is an armed strength of 2,860,000 men, or almost double the number of June, 1950.

By the end of fiscal 1956, we will have an Air Force of 131 wings and 975,000 men as compared with 48 wings and only 411,000 men when the Korean fighting began. The Navy and Marines will be second to none (with 857,000 men). And the Army will be 80 per cent above June, 1950, in manpower (1,027,000 as compared with less than 593,000); but of even greater importance is the fact that because of advances in the science of warfare, each Army division will have 80 per cent more firepower than a division of World War II.

To support these forces, we will spend an estimated $34 billion— almost three times what we were spending when Korea broke out. So the total in both personnel and money going into our defense forces today is comparatively substantially increased.

QUESTION. Have we cut too much from our security?

No! The reductions that we have made in spending for defense have not reduced our armed strength. As the President has said, we are increasing it; this nation is in a stronger position to defend itself today than it was two years ago.

We have a more flexible and better balanced defense establishment tailored to meet the requirements of future warfare and at lower cost to the taxpayers. Nothing that has happened in Formosa or elsewhere in the world up to this very day has changed our budget plans for lower spending in the year to come. I say this while emphasizing one basic fact: We can and will spend whatever we need to spend for our security. But this Administration is operating in the firm knowledge that real security comes not from merely spending billions of dollars but rather from spending them wisely.

What we are doing is shifting some of the emphasis from men to machines, from the old concept of slugging it out with masses of men to being ready to beat the enemy with mobility, technological know-how and the most modern superiority of weapons and equipment.

QUESTION. Can't we cut spending and balance the budget by just eliminating all foreign aid?

That is a program which is often suggested but is neither simple nor wise to carry out, if you stop and think about it. It is better to put military equipment in the hands of our friends overseas so that they can help to defend themselves if the need comes. . . . Total expenditures for mutual security, including both military assistance and economic support, are estimated at $4.7 billion for fiscal 1956, including the provisions for a program in Asia. This compares with mutual security spending of $4.3 billion in the present fiscal year.

The total cost included in this program for economic assistance alone is $1,025 million in fiscal 1956 as compared with $1,075 million in the present fiscal year. The total estimated expenditures in 1956, not including obligations for the future, for all Asian economic assistance will be about $585 million as compared with about $500 million to be spent for economic aid in Asia in the present fiscal year. So, while the estimated over the actual spending for economic aid increases slightly in Asia, the overall foreign economic aid program is still decreasing. . . .

While significant accomplishments have been realized through foreign aid which are in the mutual interest of the United States and other free countries, history has sadly proved that large grant programs not only burden the American taxpayer but do not always produce either stronger or more friendly allies. The entire program is under intensive, continuing review, to be sure that in the future both military and economic assistance may be properly balanced as operating parts of our foreign relations and defense programs.

QUESTION. In view of the big reductions in expenditures that have been made could the budget have been balanced?

Yes! If we had not accompanied the heavy cuts we made in spending with substantial tax cuts, we would have balanced the budget. But we had to consider the proper balance in our sensitive economy. We knew that heavy cuts in Government spending meant putting people out of work. We believe that we should cut taxes sharply and so give more people added money to spend for themselves to help create jobs for those who previously got their pay checks directly from the Government or from Government purchases.

We cut taxes in calendar year 1954 by a total of $7.4 billion—the largest single dollar tax cut in history. We did this to help make possible the easier and quicker transition in jobs from high Government spending to lower Government spending. The fact that the economic downturn was so quickly checked and that we are now proceeding upwards on a broad front is proof that the policy of cutting taxes as we cut spending is a sound policy. The fact that consumer spending in the past year was the highest that it has ever been is also good evidence of how the tax cuts help to make the successful economic transition.

QUESTION. Will there be further tax cuts?

Not this year, if the Administration's recommendations are accepted by the Congress. The President has proposed that the corporate rate of 52 per cent, as well as excise taxes which would go down on April 1, be continued for one full year. We are asking this because we think the current status of the economy will take it and because further tax reduction would lead to too heavy deficit financing and a possible revival of dangerous inflationary pressures.

This does not mean that taxes must not be cut further. They are still too high for the long run and must come down. As the President has said, we certainly hope that we can be planning additional tax reductions a year from now.

QUESTION. If you are going to cut taxes further next year, how can you ever balance the budget? . . .

As I have said, we have not abandoned the goal of balancing the budget, and neither have we stopped cutting taxes. We can and will do both. We will keep trying to cut Government spending further. At the same time, our expanding economy can provide greater tax income even at lower tax rates because it is on a broader base. As this country continues to grow, there is no reason why we can't have both a balanced budget and lower tax rates provided only that world conditions continue to improve.

Let's notice here the difference between the administrative and the cash budgets. As long as the Government is not taking out of the economy more than it spends, the Government is not increasing the money supply and thus being inflationary. So when we have a balance in the cash budget (which includes the receipts of the trust funds such as social security) we have eliminated that particular inflationary pressure. We did have a cash balance between money collected from the public and money paid out by the Government last year, although we will not quite have a cash balance this year. We estimate a small cash surplus in fiscal 1956. So that the inflationary effect of deficit financing will have been almost eliminated during the entire period this Administration has been in financial control.

QUESTION. Why do you have to raise the debt limit if you are really cutting spending as you claim?

When we came into office, there was $8 billion between the amount of the then-existing debt and the $275 billion debt ceiling. Now, in the very first year, the previous budget which we inherited turned out with a deficit of $9.5 billion. Actually there was little we could do beyond carrying out the spending that had already been planned and paying the bills that were presented. We had no leeway under the debt limit as we entered our first full fiscal year, 1954, so we asked the Congress for an increase, as a matter of prudence. As things came out in fiscal 1954, we cut the prior Administration's $11 billion estimated deficit (after an overestimate of revenue is figured in) to $3 billion—a cut of $8 billion. But even then we still had this $3 billion deficit that had to be put on top of the $9 billion deficit that we inherited from the preceding year. These two things, plus the wide seasonal variations in collection of corporate income taxes, made some elasticity in the debt limit absolutely essential.

Congress recognized this and last year authorized a $6 billion temporary increase in the limit on the condition that the debt would go back to the $275 billion limit at the end of this fiscal year.

This year we estimate a $4.5 billion deficit, which we hope we may cut a little, as I have said. And in fiscal 1956 we are estimating a smaller deficit of $2.5 billion or less. But regardless of the size of the deficit and the reductions we are making, each deficit pushes up our debt still further, and so involves the problem of what to do about the debt limit. It will be with us acutely again this June. . . .

QUESTION. Is the Government improving its debt structure?

Yes. The enormous debt is too heavy in short-term maturities. These can be inflationary as well as the source of trouble and possibly real danger to our whole economy under certain circumstances with so many short maturities. We are making progress slowly in lengthening the average maturities, and we must move slowly so as not to upset our sensitive economy.

The 40-year 3 per cent bonds just issued have been a real step forward. The issue was a great success. It has lengthened the average maturity of our whole marketable debt from four years and two months to four years and nine months. It is the longest government bond issued since 1911 when some 50-year bonds were issued to help finance the Panama Canal. This issue, like all our financing operations, had to be rightly timed for market conditions which were appropriate to be sure that we did not interfere with other financing requirements and so affect the economic situation in an unfavorable way.

QUESTION. Will there be more long-term issues?

Yes. It is our firm goal to continue to lengthen the maturities of the debt as rapidly as appropriate conditions permit. . . .

QUESTION. Have we permanently stopped inflation?

That depends upon the courageous and tenacious will of the great majority of the American people to do so. The lure of inflation is something that is never permanently killed. It beckons like a siren to enticing evil ways. Unless continuously watchful resistance is always exerted, the weak may fall for its false promises of ease to riches and be led down the primrose path to their ruin. It means the destruction of savings, which make investment possible, which in turn makes jobs. . . .

Our record of the past two years has been good. The value of the dollar has changed less than one-fifth of one cent between January 1953 and today. This compares with a loss of 48 cents in the value of the dollar from 1939 to the time when this Administration took office.

Inflation will stay checked only if we continue to actively resist the things which bring inflation about. Government must continue to cut down deficit financing and to handle its debt in a proper way. . . .

QUESTION. Isn't a little inflation a good thing?

No, it is not, and such thinking is very dangerous. I know there are millions of Americans who are earning more dollars today than they did 20 years ago. That's good. In many cases there is a real improvement in that they have better homes, automobiles, and so forth. But the fact that this increase in dollar income has been accompanied by less value of the dollar must be considered. In addition, the large numbers of persons on fixed incomes and persons who have put aside savings for retirement and old age have been cruelly hurt by inflation taking away 48 cents of each dollar they saved 15 years ago.

Fortunately, inflation has now been stopped. As economists of the American Federation of Labor put it recently, according to press reports: "Unionized labor fared better in 1954 on the wage front than in any other postwar year. Higher hourly wages and stable living costs had given most workers their greatest postwar gain in purchasing power. This was true even though the average pay rise of 5 to 9¢ per hour was modest in comparison with increases in previous years. Last year the wage earner got the full benefit of a fatter pay envelope. In other years, inflation gobbled up much of his gain. . . ."

QUESTION. What is the prospect for more jobs in this country?

The prospect for jobs is very closely related to what I have just been talking about. Probably the most important thing in promoting a high level of employment and business activity is confidence— people's confidence in our Government, confidence in each other, and confidence in the future.

If the great bulk of the American people are reasonably confident of the future they will expand their activities, invoke new initiative and try new ways of doing things. As they continue to find their confidence justified, they will not only save money but will invest their savings. This will provide the funds to produce the tools and power for the new plants, new equipment and new and better ways of making more things. . . .

QUESTION. What is the economic outlook today?

The economic downturn of last year is behind us. In general, the economy is now moving upward on a broad front. There are some lines and areas which are still depressed. Unsolved problems still remain on which we are diligently working. Unemployment in January was 3,300,000, an increase of 500,000 over the previous month and an increase of 200,000 over January a year ago. But, as concrete evidence of the economy's upward movement, employment in January was 60,200,000, or 400,000 higher than in January a year ago. The economy never moves in a smooth straight line, up or down, but as long as our broad movement is upward we are moving in the right direction. If Government, business, labor, farmers and all our citizens remain both confident and reasonable in their demands upon the whole economy, we should be able to maintain this upward trend, and supply the rightful demands of an ever-growing population.

"Credit restraint: equally necessary"

Article by Secretary Humphrey in Fortune *Magazine
under the title "The Future: Sound as a Dollar."*

April, 1955

It is easy to be too conservative when we think about the kind of world we will be living in 25 years from now. If we project recent trends, we are likely to picture 1980 merely as a "souped-up" version of 1955. This can be misleading. For the really significant features of 1980 are likely to be the unpredictable contrasts with the present rather than the similarities. If we picture ourselves back in 1930 trying to form an idea of the world of 1955, we can readily see how a conservative approach would have led us astray. Who, 25 years ago, could possibly have predicted the vast changes that have taken place in the world's political and economic structures; who could have foreseen the fantastic developments in electronics, antibiotics, or atomic energy?

I have always been skeptical about flat economic predictions; our economy is a sensitive and complex mechanism and any one of a thousand factors can affect its behavior. So I would like to base this look at the coming quarter-century on certain assumptions. There are, after all, some factors in the outlook that seem reasonably predictable even though they can't be projected exactly—the growth of population, the quickening rate of technological development, the rise in productivity and employment, the steady improvement in living standards. Assuming these basic trends, we should give them every encouragement in the years ahead. We must aim not just to maintain but to accelerate the favorable trends of the present. We can't possibly control all the factors bearing on the future, but we can work toward helping the world of 1980 become the kind of world we would like to see.

A goal that may overshadow all others in importance to our nation is the maintenance of confidence—living, enthusiastic confidence both for today and for the future. It must be shared by everyone—businessmen, workers, investors, and consumers alike. It must be contagious confidence and it must also be practical and justifiable. With such confidence, our nation can move to new heights of production and services, create new and better jobs, and constantly push ahead on a sound basis to an ever finer future.

The confidence displayed last year by American citizens was a main reason the economic readjustment was not more serious. Consumers ignored the gloomy predictions of some economic forecasters and went on to spend more money than ever before. Investors kept making risk capital available. Businessmen went boldly ahead with development and expansion plans. They put large sums in plant, equipment, and research with the firm objective of improving their competitive positions in future years.

All of this helped to create new jobs, to raise incomes, and to advance the nation's productive capacity. It enabled the economy to meet the needs of our growing population and was an eloquent demonstration of the life-giving role confidence can play in a free-enterprise economy.

How can this essential confidence be maintained and strengthened during the next 25 years? We shall have to keep working at it all the time. What is required most of all, I believe, is that people develop assurance on the following five major points. They must be convinced:

(1) That their Government is working fervently—and successfully—for the blessings of lasting peace.

(2) That the management of Government is in the hands of men of integrity and high moral purpose.

(3) That the value of the dollar, with which all transactions are made, will be preserved.

(4) That the dynamics of a free competitive economy will be stimulated by Government encouragement of private enterprise.

(5) That future business declines can and will be held within moderate limits.

I would like to discuss the prospects for the coming quarter-century largely in terms of these basic objectives.

The present high degree of national confidence derives in large part, of course, from the belief that business readjustments now can be kept within tolerably narrow limits, and that, in the future, serious recessions can be avoided. Certainly, events of the past six months have given people new faith in the ability of the Government to help moderate economic fluctuations. The fear of a severe recession that was prevalent a year ago has disappeared, and for this the Government's monetary and fiscal policies can take partial credit. Will the next 25 years justify the belief that economic adjustments can be kept within reasonable bounds? I happen to believe that if we continue to pursue flexible and sensible financial policies the current optimism may prove to be warranted.

One major lesson concerning recessions is still too little understood, however. We have learned that when business begins to slacken—as a result of excessive inventory accumulation, overbuying by consumers, or for any other reason—an easy credit policy is helpful. The lesson that still needs learning is that credit restraint is equally necessary during periods of expansion, when the seeds of future trouble are sown.

If we are to reach 1980 with our confidence undiminished, and with the economy continuing to operate at highest efficiency, restraints on credit may be needed just as often as easing of credit. This is something to be expected, to live with, and to take into account in making business plans. In this way the Government can help diminish the maladjustments and excesses responsible for serious recessions.

A major factor in the maintenance of national confidence is people's confidence in what the dollar is worth. During the decade prior to 1953, the severe decline in the purchasing power of the dollar robbed people of nearly half the value of their savings. This inflation has been brought to a virtual halt, and during the past two years consumers' prices have remained practically unchanged.

We must make sure that the inflationary trends do not reappear. We must work to ensure that the dollar of 1980 will buy at least as much food and clothing as the dollar will buy today—preferably and properly more. If that is done, all will share the benefits of increased productivity, and the saver who puts away a dollar for his retirement, to buy a house, to educate his children, for an emergency, or for any other purpose, will still have a dollar that is worth a dollar when he needs it.

This goal of a sound dollar has gained tremendously in importance during the past half-century. This nation, since 1900, has gone through an economic transformation that far exceeds any other in the long history of man's efforts to achieve a better life. The U.S. today is a nation made up, overwhelmingly, of small-to-medium savers and investors. It is a nation of "haves" rather than a nation of "have-nots."

Since the turn of the century real income per man, woman, and child in the United States has tripled. And the lower and middle income groups have received the greatest share of this increased income. Early in the century, only ten out of every 100 American families earned as much as $4,000 a year in terms of today's prices; now 55 do. Most families now have enough money not only to live adequately, but to save besides. That is the basic economic development that has enabled this country to reach fantastic heights of material prosperity as compared with the rest of the world.

The flow of small savings into an ever-broadening investment stream during the past fifty years has been truly remarkable. Ownership by individuals in life-insurance policies has increased from under $2 billion in 1900 to more than $80 billion today. Small investors' holdings of United States Savings Bonds now total nearly $50 billion. More than 10 per cent of all families today own stock in American corporations. Whereas in 1900 individuals had liquid savings amounting to less than $10 billion, now such savings total more than $225 billion.

You can see from these few examples what has been happening to the individual and the family in our wonderland economy. The "average" man in America has acquired a financial stake in the future such as no other "average" citizen anywhere ever had before. We need a completely new set of standards in thinking about ourselves and in defining the "general interest." This nation's economy has grown right over, and left in the dust, both socialism and communism.

We all want the great beneficial development of the past half-century continued in the next quarter-century—and in many quarter-centuries beyond that. But the progress won't be continued unless we follow national policies that allow the healthy advance of the day-to-day process of "betterment from the bottom up." By this I mean not only policies that will safeguard individual savings against the corroding effect of inflation but also policies that will encourage investment in job-creating plant and equipment, and in rising production and employment, and so prosperity for an ever-growing population.

Renewing the debt limit extension

*Statement and testimony by Secretary Humphrey
before the House Ways & Means Committee.
Representative Jere Cooper of Tennessee, presiding.*

June 24, 1955

I am here today to ask your approval for a year's extension of the $6 billion temporary increase in the public debt limit. Last August the Congress authorized a temporary increase in the limit from $275 billion to $281 billion in order to give the Treasury needed elasticity in handling its seasonal borrowing problems during the year. It provided, however, that the limit would go back to $275 billion on June 30, 1955.

We have lived within those limits. The $281 billion temporary limit permitted us to do the necessary borrowing to meet the Government's bills during seasonally low tax-collection periods. Moreover, we expect to end up on June 30 with the debt around $273.5 billion.

We have lived within the limits, but the basic problems are still with us. They are, in fact, even more acute this year than last. The debt stood at $270.8 billion on June 30, 1954. On June 30 this year, it is expected to be almost $3 billion higher. Thus, the Treasury will have even less elbow room to handle its seasonal borrowing needs in the months ahead under a $281 billion temporary limit than it did last year. Even more crucial will be the problem of getting the debt back to $275 billion by the close of the 1956 fiscal year.

This goal can be accomplished only with the full co-operation of the Congress in giving the most careful consideration to all budget expenditures and rejecting all requests for appropriations that are not absolutely necessary for fully adequate security for the nation and proper services required for the people. Added expenditures or reductions in income will require further lifting of this proposed debt limit.

Nevertheless, we are currently asking for no more of an increase in the debt limit, either temporary or permanent, than the Congress authorized last year. It will be a tight squeeze but we will try to live within it.

We are setting ourselves this very difficult task for very important reasons.

In the first place, having to keep the debt within the $275 billion limit by the end of the year on June 30, 1956, may be helpful to all of us in redoubling our efforts for even greater economy in Government.

It is also important in a situation like the present that the Federal Government itself set an example of economy and prudence. We believe at this time of great prosperity that all of us—Government, business, and individuals alike—should exercise self-restraint in the use of public or private credit and the accumulation of debt.

Today, Americans are enjoying new peaks of prosperity—of employment, production, and income—setting new records all along the line. Only a year ago there was reduced activity and false prophets were predicting that we were heading into a depression. These swings in economic activity should remind us of the need for wisdom and restraint as well as courage in both private and public affairs.

High productivity, more and better jobs, and increasingly higher standards of living for the great mass of all our people can continue if we face the future with confidence tempered with prudence.

These, then, are our goals. It is our firm intention to attempt to live under the present debt limit with this temporary extension. It is also our firm intention to have any temporary increase in debt back to the present limit of $275 billion by the end of the year on June 30, 1956. We want to do next year just what we have successfully done this year, even though it will be harder. If conditions change so that this becomes impossible, we will promptly advise the Congress. But with our present promising business and international outlook, we hope and believe we will succeed.

Cross-examination of Secretary Humphrey

REP. FRANK M. KARSTEN (Missouri). Mr. Secretary, in the third paragraph of your statement, you say: ". . . but the basic problems are still with us." What about that "bold, new, dynamic program" that we have heard so much about? Has that had any application to the Treasury Department? . . .

SEC. HUMPHREY. The basic debt problem is still with us.

MR. KARSTEN. Then has there been any change since you have taken over the Treasury in the basic problem? It is still there; is that correct?

SEC. HUMPHREY. As long as the Congress votes more money to spend than it votes to collect in taxes, the basic problems of the debt limit are going to be with us. And the Congress last year, and the Congress this year, is voting more money to spend than it is voting to collect. As long as that goes on, we will be in trouble on the debt limit.

MR. KARSTEN. When was the last decrease in the national debt?

SEC. HUMPHREY. The last decrease in the national debt was when taxes were increased by the Government beyond the expenditures that were projected soon after the beginning of the Korean War. I can't remember the Congress, but it was early in the Korean War. And when the war scare came on, the Congress voted very substantial increases in taxes, expecting to spend money in preparation for the war. And they did not get the money spent as rapidly as they had planned, and therefore the money came in faster than it went out, and the difference was used to reduce the debt.

MR. KARSTEN. Your requests have always been to increase the national debt ceiling?

SEC. HUMPHREY. They have been two, and they have been made for the purpose of meeting the swings due to the bills that had previously been passed relating to the collection of taxes, in which taxes are collected unevenly during the course of the year.

MR. KARSTEN. Are we moving toward a reduced national debt? . . .

SEC. HUMPHREY. I don't know why you ask that. I have just stated our debt has gone up $3 billion in a year.

MR. KARSTEN. In other words, we are not moving toward a reduced national debt. Is that correct?

SEC. HUMPHREY. I think your question is self-evident, if you read what I said. . . .

MR. KARSTEN. What was the national debt when your Administration took over, Mr. Secretary?

SEC. HUMPHREY. About $267 billion.

MR. KARSTEN. Well, what is it today, Mr. Secretary, after two and one-half years of your Administration?

SEC. HUMPHREY. We estimate it will be $273,500 million.

MR. KARSTEN. What do you estimate for the end of this current fiscal year, 1956?

SEC. HUMPHREY. Under $275 billion.

MR. KARSTEN. The figures would certainly indicate that we are moving toward an increased national debt. . . .

REP. RICHARD M. SIMPSON (Pennsylvania). This committee will probably give a unanimous vote to report this bill out. It will probably pass the Congress by very substantial votes. I am sure we expect that, because there is a responsibility that rests on this committee and on the Congress to provide that dollars are available to pay any bills that we create. It borders on irresponsibility, in my opinion, if the Congress accepts a bill like this and then does not live within its limits.

Would you care to comment on that?

SEC. HUMPHREY. Well, Mr. Simpson, the Congress fixes the amount of appropriations for expenditures. The Congress fixes the amount of income for the Government. If the income fixed by the Congress is less than the expenditures fixed by the Congress, there is nothing for the Administration to do but to borrow the money. And when we borrow the money, we increase the debt. Now, if the Congress does not authorize an increase in the debt limit so that we can issue legally proper certificates of debt or indications of debt, evidences of debt, bonds or bills or certificates, or whatever they may be, we cannot sell those certificates, we cannot get the money, and we just cannot pay the bills. . . .

MR. SIMPSON. If the committee proceeds to report out and the Congress to adopt a bill spending some $2 billion more than anticipated by your budget, will that in any way affect this debt limitation?

SEC. HUMPHREY. Mr. Simpson, I would like to point out to this committee, and I hope that this committee can take the opportunity to point it out to every member of the Congress, that we have now reached a point in the relation of our debt to the debt limit where there is absolutely no room for this Congress to either reduce income or to increase expenditures, without concurrently increasing the debt limit, unless they want us to stop paying bills. And if we stop paying bills, as you all know, the credit of the country is jeopardized.

MR. KARSTEN. Mr. Secretary, as a matter of fact, would the social security changes we make in any way affect the national debt?

SEC. HUMPHREY. The social security changes will very definitely change the national debt if the funds provided for social security are not sufficient to cover the obligations to be incurred by social security.

Mr. KARSTEN. As a trustee of the fund, is it in such a condition now that it is unable to meet its obligations, could you tell us?

SEC. HUMPHREY. Well, obligations are obligations, both current and prospective, and where you have trust funds you have to provide not only for current expenditures, but you have to provide for the obligations as they accrue.

Mr. KARSTEN. Is it able to meet its current obligations, Mr. Secretary?

SEC. HUMPHREY. It can meet current obligations. I think it is very questionable that the fund is sufficient to meet its full obligations as they are incurred.

Mr. KARSTEN. But actually, changes in the social security law to date have not affected the national debt, have they?

SEC. HUMPHREY. Not yet.

Mr. SIMPSON. Any further liberalization on the part of social security will increase the obligations on the fund?

SEC. HUMPHREY. That is correct.

Mr. SIMPSON. And unless new money is brought in to meet those obligations, it will eventually provide a charge on the Treasury?

SEC. HUMPHREY. The fund will be unable to meet its obligations, and if obligations are increased, the fund's collections should be increased. And it should be done concurrently. . . .

Mr. KARSTEN. Now, to come to the classic question, I am going to ask you here in open session: Are you for or against further liberalization of the Social Security Act as we have contemplated it?

SEC. HUMPHREY. The Social Security Act is not up for discussion here, so far as I am concerned. I am here testifying on the debt limit. I am not prepared on social security. . . .

REP. WILBUR D. MILLS (Arkansas). Mr. Chairman, rather than leave the record so that it could be susceptible of misunderstanding by anyone who might be following the questions and answers:

Mr. Secretary, with respect to the relationship of social security to the public debt, is it not a fact that the social security program could not affect the public debt at any time unless Congress in the future provides for payments to be made out of the general funds of the Treasury? There is no such authority at the present time in law.

SEC. HUMPHREY. I think that is right, Mr. Mills.

Mr. SIMPSON. If this committee or this Congress increases benefits under social security over and beyond what the dollars collected would justify, the payment will have to come out of the Treasury, which would increase the debt, under that circumstance, in the absence of new taxes to meet the obligation. Is that right?

SEC. HUMPHREY. Mr. Simpson, I think you are both right. I think that Mr. Mills is technically correct. It would take an appropriation of the Congress to do it. On the other hand, I think you are correct in stating that under such circumstances there is very little doubt that the Congress would see that its promises were made good. . . .

REP. ROBERT W. KEAN (New Jersey). When you, Mr. Secretary, in the Treasury Department, get actual figures on what some certain situation would do, do you rely entirely on one actuary from the department—how good he may be—or do you also try to get information from outside sources, from qualified experts in the field, to check your figures?

SEC. HUMPHREY. We do, Mr. Kean. Actuarial computations, as you know, are subject to all sorts of interpretations. And what we try to do is to get the most experienced people we can in actuarial matters to give us the benefit of their advice.

MR. KEAN. The reason I am asking that question is that insofar as social security is concerned the committee has before it the very important question of disability insurance, which involves very difficult actuarial problems.

SEC. HUMPHREY. It is very, very complicated.

MR. KEAN. The majority on the committee seem to be relying on the figures of a very excellent actuary, whom I have a great deal of confidence in, from the social-security department; but the Democrats have refused and turned down my motion to invite the actuaries of insurance companies to testify as to the possible cost of the program.

MR. KARSTEN. The Secretary has refused to comment on the social-security measure.

SEC. HUMPHREY. I think anybody, Mr. Kean, who has had experience, with actuarial matters, knows you want the very best advice you can possibly get in trying to estimate your accrued liabilities. . . .

REP. NOAH M. MASON (Illinois). Mr. Secretary, as a result of the revised tax bill that we passed last year, are there not more millions coming into the Treasury now than there were a year ago, as a result of that revision say, this June 15 as compared with last June 15? . . .

SEC. HUMPHREY. Well, Mr. Mason, I do not have the figures right at hand, but I can answer it in this way. The improvement in the country in income is such that individual income is now at the highest peak at which it has ever been in this country. We are estimating that individual taxes will be higher. On the other hand, corporate income that we receive now is based on earnings of a year ago, when earnings were lower, and on top of that, we have come to the end of the Mills Plan, when we do not get that additional money brought forward. And that is reducing the corporate income tax that is received this year. So our individual income-tax receipts are going up, and our corporate income receipts are down. . . .

MR. MASON. Mr. Secretary, as you very well know, I have had a bill before Congress to tax the untaxed, which it has been variously estimated would bring in approximately a billion or more in taxes from those who are not now paying. Would that not be kind of a nice little nest egg to bring into the Treasury if we could pass that bill now?

SEC. HUMPHREY. Mr. Mason, I can only say that we would welcome a billion dollars with a floral wreath. . . .

MR. MASON. Now, this national debt that has been increased since the present Administration has been in: But has not most of that increase in the national debt been the result of obligations that were inherited by this present Administration, that have caused these expenditures above our income and have resulted in this increased national debt?

SEC. HUMPHREY. Mr. Mason, I think that I would like to state as nearly as I can just the facts, without regard to responsibilities as to parties. But the fact is that we assumed, when we came in—we found around $80 billion of unspent balances. That has been very substantially reduced. Those balances were there, and a great deal of that money had been obligated. Not all of it. We canceled some of it. But a great deal had been obligated. And of course, as those obligations had to be paid out of the Treasury, it meant that we had more money going out than we had coming in. And until those incurred obligations were behind us and we got back in balance, there was nothing you could do but to have the debt go up.

REP. THOMAS B. CURTIS (Missouri). Mr. Secretary, I want to direct your attention to this amendment to the debt limitation, the extension for one year, which of course is a temporary proposition. . . . I think you would agree that we cannot just raise tax rates just to meet revenues, just to meet our expenditures, because we also have to consider what the economic effect of raising those rates would be.

SEC. HUMPHREY. That is right.

MR. CURTIS. I believe we are in an era of very high tax rates. Some of us, myself at any rate, believe that we are beyond the point of diminishing returns, and that actually we have been hurting and undermining our economy with this high-tax rate.

Now, if we had not passed this tax revision bill last year and some of these tax cut bills, I would suggest that we would not have the healthy economy that we have right now.

SEC. HUMPHREY. I do not think there is any question about it, Mr. Curtis. We would not.

MR. CURTIS. And of course, as you say, in trying to preserve this healthy economy, with this tax revision and tax cutting that we have done, in order to make it healthy you have cut expenditures in order to accomplish the tax cuts.

SEC. HUMPHREY. That is right.

MR. CURTIS. I wonder if that is your general philosophy, that we still are in an era of tax rates that are perhaps unhealthy or detrimental to a healthy economy.

SEC. HUMPHREY. Well, Mr. Curtis, I think nobody can say just what straw breaks the camel's back. But I think you can say very definitely, or at least I believe, that our present tax rates are too high for the development of the most desirable expanding economy of this country, for the greatest development of our incentive system in this country. And I think that just as rapidly as reductions in our expenditures can be made to justify additional tax cuts, the additional tax cuts should be made. On the other hand, I do not think that additional tax cuts should be made unless concurrently you see in sight and in view means and ways of accomplishing reductions which will provide the money that the tax cuts are going to be paid with. . . .

MR. CURTIS. And of course, if we can keep a healthy economy, we can continue to lessen the ratio of the federal debt to the gross national product, which is, I again suggest, the more important thing, rather than the actual dollar sign on the federal debt.

SEC. HUMPHREY. They are both important, but it is certainly extremely desirable that we maintain a healthy economy. Because if our economy suffers, our income will suffer tremendously with it.…

MR. CURTIS. Is there anticipation that the executive department, the Bureau of the Budget, will present to Congress next year a balanced budget?

SEC. HUMPHREY. We do not have our figures yet, Mr. Curtis. Definitely our estimate to date is that our 1956 budget will show a deficit of about $2.5 billion. Now, we will make a semiannual revision of those figures in August. We start with July, and the figures usually become available about the middle of August. Just how that revision will look is very difficult to see now.…

Also, we must always keep in mind, as Mr. Mills pointed out, that we have this extremely important matter of security. And as long as the world situation is as it is, the largest part of the budget goes for security. And in that case, we must protect security, and on the other hand, we must get more for our money. Our objective must be to get more security for less money in that field. Our objective all along the line must be to get better performance for our money, to come nearer getting our dollar's worth.

Now, whether with the duties prescribed by the Congress, the laws prescribed by Congress of things to be done by the people, we can get enough out of waste, we can get enough in better performance, better management, better controls to balance the budget, I am not prepared to say. That is our objective. We have been working at it ever since we came here. We hope to get the job done. I do not know how or when we will, but that is what we are trying to do.

MR. CURTIS. Do you actually think there is a real possibility that you might have a balanced budget? I mean an offer of one.

SEC. HUMPHREY. Mr. Curtis, I did not work at anything in my life that I did not think there was a possibility of getting it done.…

REP. ANTONI N. SADLAK (Connecticut). I have no questions, Mr. Secretary, but I would like to commend the forthright statement and the straightforward answers that you have always given in appearances before this committee. What has seemed like a wave of resignations in other agencies which we have read about in the paper, I hope does not get to the office of the Secretary of the Treasury, because of the wonderful experience he has had in the job which he holds.

SEC. HUMPHREY. Thank you. I appreciate that.

Mr. Karsten. Mr. Secretary, earlier in your testimony you expressed doubt that the social security system would be able to take care of its accrued obligations and liabilities in the future. Were you suggesting then that the system may be actuarially unsound?

Sec. Humphrey. You mean at the present time?

Mr. Karsten. No; from the standpoint of the future, under existing law.

Sec. Humphrey. Yes, under the present provisions of collection and disbursement.

Mr. Karsten. I do want to read into the record at this point, Mr. Chairman, a statement from the President's tax recommendations relating to social security. This is the President's message dated May 20, 1953, in which the President said:

"The increase in the old-age insurance tax from 1½ to 2 per cent on both employees and employers, now scheduled to go into effect next January 1, should be postponed until January 1, 1955.

"The old-age and survivors trust fund has now reached almost $18 billion. Receipts at present tax rates are currently well in excess of expenditures. The further addition to the fund which would flow from the projected tax increase is not required.

"From now on, the old-age tax and trust accounts, while maintaining the contributory principle, should be handled more nearly on a pay-as-you-go basis.

"The postponement of the tax increase will reduce the impending tax burden on every covered employee and employer. It will not influence the administrative budget, but it will involve an increase in the cash deficit."

Evidently, Mr. Chairman, the President is of the opinion that the system is sound, or he would not have made such a recommendation in his tax message. And I think that should be in the record.

Sec. Humphrey. I think you don't want to talk just quite so fast. "Sound" and "actuarially sound" are two very different things. The President pointed out not that it was necessarily actuarially sound, but that it had reached a point where they could consider some division between a complete actuarial computation and some carryover for the future. And I just do not know. As we said here a moment ago, talking to Mr. Simpson and Mr. Kean, actuarial computations are very difficult. You have to take into account the various premises, and the slightest change in some of those premises will give you a very different answer. So you have a lot of problems to face in that connection. And I think that what you have to do, if you want to be on the safe side, is that you have to be very careful that you have a complete and thorough actuarial analysis of where you stand. . . .

MR. KARSTEN. I think that we should be very careful in what we say about this fund. If it is actuarially unsound, would you not say that it would be extremely unwise to postpone tax increases of this kind?

SEC. HUMPHREY. Not necessarily; no. You could have a fund that did not fulfill a theoretical actuarial computation, that still was a sound fund, on the basis of contributions and expected distributions; and you might not want to carry it too far. . . .

THE CHAIRMAN. . . . You will recall, I am sure, that in the Social Security Act of 1950 a provision was included which repealed a prior provision of law authorizing the taking of funds out of the Treasury to supplement funds in the trust fund of social security. . . . If the time should come when funds would be needed to supplement the trust fund to pay benefits, it would require authorization of Congress before any funds could be taken out of the Treasury to be used in that trust fund.

SEC. HUMPHREY. I think that is correct, Mr. Cooper. . . .

MR. SIMPSON. I want to be sure I get the correct statement, Mr. Secretary. My understanding is that if this committee and the Congress passed a bill increasing social-security benefits, at a cost of $2 billion or more, and failed to provide money to meet the obligations so created—that at some time if there will not be money available to pay the claims under the law to the individual who seeks social-security payments, so far as the law is concerned today, that individual would not get his or her social security.

SEC. HUMPHREY. That is my understanding of the technical aspect of the law.

MR. MILLS. Now, the only way any imbalance could be offset would be to immediately impose an additional tax at the time we create the obligation, to impose an additional tax at a subsequent time to meet a previous obligation, or for Congress to pass legislation which would authorize taking money out of the general funds of the Treasury to meet that obligation.

SEC. HUMPHREY. I believe that is right.

REP. HAL HOLMES (Washington). In order to bring this back down to the point we are discussing, it is absolutely necessary, is it not, Mr. Secretary, to give you some leeway here to try to help correlate—which you cannot reduce to a constant flow—the income versus the outgo of the Treasury of the United States?

SEC. HUMPHREY. That is exactly right. . . .

MR. HOLMES. And with any fiscal problem of the magnitude of that of the United States Government, it is still the amount of income versus outgo that you have to have, just the same as the individual does in relation to his business.

SEC. HUMPHREY. Just the same as your own, exactly, except that there are a lot more zeros on ours. I will just say this, Mr. Holmes, in that connection: There is no business I know of or have ever seen that is operating on as close a margin as we are trying to operate the Government. It is the closest margin I have ever seen attempted to be operated. And I do not think a business could do it. . . .

THE CHAIRMAN. With respect to the social security matter, Mr. Secretary, I would like to state that I do not know of anybody on the committee that is advocating that the social security trust fund not be kept in as actuarially sound a position as we can make it. As the author of the bill to be considered by this committee, certainly my purpose is and has been throughout all the years since the inception of the program that the social security trust fund be kept as actuarially sound as we can make it.

REP. EUGENE J. MCCARTHY (Minnesota). Mr. Secretary, last year, with a national debt of $271.3 billion you came before us and asked for an increase from this committee to $290 billion in authority. This year with a debt of $274 billion you ask for only $281 billion.

In your statement you indicate that you would really like to have a little more room for operation. Would you care to indicate how much more room you would really like to have?

SEC. HUMPHREY. Well, I think that when I came before this committee when we were discussing this matter before, we were talking not about a temporary, but about a permanent change in the debt limit. And we were talking about an appropriate limitation within which this Government could be operated on a proper and suitable basis, on a permanent change.

Now, as we went along in those discussions, we got into the Senate, and the Senate was adamant against a permanent change, and they proposed a temporary change to see what could be done on a temporary basis.

When the matter came up for consideration this year, I still believe that the request I originally made of this committee is the proper request to make if you are going to do it on a permanent basis. And I do not think it permits any leeway that we should not have. If we were here asking for a permanent change, I think I would make exactly the same request that I made then, and I think that the figures, and all, would substantiate it as justified.

Now, in thinking about it this year, we decided, after talking to your chairman and after talking with the chairman of the Senate Finance Committee, that, rather than get into the seriously complicated and controversial question we raised last year, we again adopt a temporary basis rather than a permanent basis. And I was willing and glad to do that, this year. . . . I think the pressures on everybody that this extremely tight situation involves are a good thing to have temporarily and for another year.

At the end of that time, as to whether we want to then say, "We can now see far enough ahead," or "We now ought to get on to a permanent basis," I am not crossing that bridge now, as I said to one of the gentlemen down here.

Mr. McCarthy. Mr. Secretary, does that mean that if you were to project your judgment two or three years into the future you would anticipate that the national debt will rise close to $290 billion?

Sec. Humphrey. Well, I don't know. But if we were going to go on a permanent basis, I think that any prudent financial management with as big a debt to finance and refinance as often as we have to should have a lot of elasticity.

You see, gentlemen, I don't think that we realize, and I think we keep forgetting, how much we owe. Nobody in the history of the world ever owed the money that we owe. I think that we tend to think that money grows on trees and that all that is necessary is for the Government or anybody else to just say, "We want another billion or two billion dollars." This money has to come out of the pockets of the people. And you have got to have a government and a situation in hand where the people are willing to take these securities. And we have to tap every possible market. We have to get into every possible field to do this.

Now, this money just doesn't automatically flow in here. This is a financial transaction. This is a financial problem that has got to be met. And this Government cannot get money, just the same as a business cannot get money, because the money has to come from the people. And you have to have reasons and securities and setups that are going to induce the people to buy them. You cannot go and take money away from people, here. These are voluntary purchases that people make. And you have to have your financial house in order and your setup in order so that you can finance in a proper way and at the proper time and in the proper amounts. And you cannot do that with limitations that just bind you into a tight spot. . . .

MR. McCARTHY. I have one other question, Mr. Secretary, with regard to the matter of obligations incurred by the previous Administration which this Administration had to carry. You indicated, I think, to a large extent that these were military obligations which arose in connection with the Korean War. . . . You were able to rescind some of them. Some of them, you had to assume.

The Administration spokesmen have on occasions indicated they were having trouble with the debt and with balancing the budget because of these obligations. Has the Administration ever published any list or made any record of which of these obligations they would like to repudiate or rescind?

SEC. HUMPHREY. Well, as I recall it, I think there were about $10 billion of prospective obligations that were involved. . . .

MR. McCARTHY. Which would probably have been rescinded by any administration with the situation that pertained.

SEC. HUMPHREY. I don't know what somebody else would have done. I know what we did.

MR. McCARTHY. There is no indication that obligations would have been carried out, such as for the procurement of ammunition?

SEC. HUMPHREY. They were voted and ordered, and whether they would have been carried out I am not prepared to say.

REP. HALE BOGGS (Louisiana). In connection with that line of questioning, Mr. Secretary, I believe about $40 billion, if not more, were rescinded after VJ Day in 1945. Do you know what that figure was? . . .

Sec. Humphrey. I do not know the amount, but I know there were a lot of rescissions at the end of the war.

Mr. Boggs. Does this limitation have any effect on how much your money is costing you? ... What are your obligations costing you now?

Mr. W. Randolph Burgess (Under Secretary for Monetary Affairs). Around 1.42 per cent, as I remember the figures. It fluctuates from week to week.

Mr. Boggs. Is that substantially what it has been all along?

Mr. Burgess. Well, it is a little less now than it was a few months ago. It fluctuates, depending upon what the conditions are in the money market.

Mr. Boggs. Now, in connection with the national debt, are you having any difficulty financing the debt?

Sec. Humphrey. Indeed you do. You have to do an awful lot of planning to know what you can sell and when you can sell it. Indeed, that is what we spend most of our time at. And we work our heads off. And I want to tell you that the response of the American people to the sale of savings bonds is one of the greatest things that there is. Individuals have $50 billion, approximately, in savings bonds, which is a great thing. ...

Mr. Boggs. The American people have full confidence in the obligations of the American Government, do they not?

Sec. Humphrey. Well, they have responded very well since the dollar has been stabilized. When the dollar was depreciating so rapidly, we were greatly concerned about them, but as the dollar has been stabilized and the cost of living has been stabilized and the people are getting more confidence in the strength of their money, the savings bonds have been picking up quite substantially.

Mr. Boggs. Well, now, Mr. Secretary, you do not know of any time, really, do you, when there was any very great difficulty in financing the obligations of the Government?

Sec. Humphrey. I think it is difficult every day; yes.

Mr. Boggs. Well, do you think it is less difficult or more difficult than it has been?

Sec. Humphrey. I think it is less difficult now. I think that as people are having more confidence in investment, which they are, this confidence of people having the ability to put their money out and get their money back at relatively the same values has instilled a lot of confidence and has made all sorts of investment opportunity better, in fact, I know it has. There is no question about it. It is just a matter of record and history. . . .

MR. BOGGS. Well, I think that people do have complete confidence in their Government, and I am very glad to know that they are keeping it. Do you think if we continue this temporary sort of thing we will have to keep on doing this, that we will have to do this again next year? . . .

SEC. HUMPHREY. I don't know, Mr. Boggs. We will probably have to do something. Now, what it will be desirable to do next year, I just would not want to guess. The reason I ask it on a temporary basis is because I do not think this is the best time to try to guess permanently. . . .

🔖 Secretary Humphrey's views on social security fund management were obtained here coincidentally because one other matter before the Ways & Means Committee at this time was a proposal to extend social-security benefits. . . . The debt limit again was increased by Congress to $281 billion, for one year.

A 3 per cent cut will balance the budget

Statement and answers by Secretary Humphrey
with Director of the Budget Roland Hughes
at a news conference at the Executive Offices.

August 25, 1955

SEC. HUMPHREY. The anticipated deficit for the fiscal year 1956, originally estimated at $2.4 billion last January, has been reduced in this midyear review to $1.7 billion, the lowest deficit estimate in five fiscal years.

A reduction of less than 3 per cent in expenditures as presently estimated would balance the budget. Now, this summary: 1952, a deficit of $4 billion; 1953, a deficit of $9.4 billion. The budget document for 1953, $9.9 billion; the actual for 1954, $3.1 billion; 1955, $4.2 billion; the estimate for 1956, $1.7 billion.

In times like the present, with the highest employment and the most jobs ever in the history of this country, the highest personal disposable income, and records in profits, wages, earnings, and production, if there is ever a time when our budget should be balanced, it is now.

Under these circumstances, it does seem that enough more unnecessary expenditures can be found so that with care and close planning by all departments in Government a reduction of only 3 per cent in expenditures can properly be made while continuing to strengthen our military security and without lessening in any appreciable degree the proper standards of service which should be rendered to the public.

Every effort will be made by everyone in Government service to accomplish this result. Public support of these efforts and understanding throughout the nation will also be required to keep all programs on a basis of real need and to resist the constant and unremitting pressures for expanding various programs beyond necessary requirements. . . .

Everybody knows that no family can continually live largely beyond its means. It is worse for a government to do so. History shows how continued heavy deficits contribute to inflation, with rapidly rising costs of living and cheapening of the money, finally resulting in the destruction of all values and disaster not only for the Government but for its people as well.

High productivity, more and better jobs, and increasingly higher standards of living for all our people can continue to benefit all Americans if we handle our affairs with confidence, tempered with common sense, and seize this opportunity to achieve the goal towards which our efforts always have been directed—to have the Government live within its means.

Barring some unforeseen development, we think that we should, and that we can, balance the budget this year. . . .

ROLAND HUGHES (Director of the Budget). The appropriations, which are the starting point of the spending of the money, as you see, have come down very drastically, as would be expected, and have been brought since we have been running the budget in this Administration below both expenditures and receipts, which is a very important point to watch, because, if your appropriations are below expenditures, then at least, as far as the current actions of the Government are concerned, you are going to run in the right direction.

You are going to bring it down closer to a balance, and the same thing, of course, if receipts are below appropriations or above appropriations, why, then, you are at the same time not appropriating all the money that you are receiving, and you are gaining ground toward achieving a balanced budget at lower levels.

This brings up another point which is of great importance in connection with these things and some times overlooked in the actual budget figures, and that is the unexpended balances carried forward.

At this time, when the Administration came in, it was about $80 billion. That is a COD hanging over which must be paid for when it is delivered and funds must be provided to meet it, in addition to the new appropriations which the Congress makes.

Therefore, when we reach the point that $80 billion is more than the total year's expenditure, we are skating on thinner ice than we should.

Now it is down to about $50 billion. . . . We hope to continue to make more progress along that line.

The other factor which has been discussed at various times is the receipts and payments to the public and that. . . . is perhaps the direct inflationary and deflationary impact of the Government operations as nearly as they can be measured.

This, as you can see from the book, will be balanced for the first time in the last four years, as the expenditure and income estimates show, and that is a good sign to continuance of what we have been accomplishing in the last two and a half years, of avoiding inflation with the damage it does to the value of the dollar and everyone's spending, the cost of living, and also deflation, which is also a threat if you cut down expenditures and operations of the Government.

The cost of living has been steady during the last two and a half years, and this indicates a steady progress as far as this year's estimates are concerned. . . .

FRANK O'BRIEN, JR. (Associated Press). Mr. Secretary, will you be able to ask Congress to cut taxes next winter?

SEC. HUMPHREY. Frank, it is entirely too early to make any estimate of that kind. I have said a great many times that I would not favor a further tax reduction until I saw where the money was coming from.

On the other hand, I have also said many, many times that we think these taxes are too high, that we think it is for the benefit of all of the people and for the benefit of a strengthening economy that the taxes be reduced just as rapidly as it is possible to do so.

We have said that we do not believe that we have to wait until we have the money on hand, but that when we can look forward to see, with some assurance, that it will eventually be true that we can save enough money or have enough additional income so that we know where the money will be coming from that we can release to the people in taxes, that we will then favor tax reduction to be coincident with the saving that we anticipate can be made.

Mr. O'Brien. By that you mean that you have to be able to see that your expenditures are going to go below your income, in other words, a little better than the balanced budget is coming up before you feel that you can protect that?

Sec. Humphrey. Well, if we are able to balance the budget this year, we will have to have one of two things happen. It will probably be a combination of both. There will have to be a reduction of up toward 3 per cent, not to exceed 3 per cent, in expenditures, and there will have to be whatever the expenditures are not reduced by the amount of 3 per cent, any difference in that, any lessened amount than that, will have to be covered by increased income; and if either of those things occur to the extent of about 3 per cent, or if a combination of the two occurs, to about that extent we will have a balanced budget this year.

Now, then, as we go along and as we can see that that is going to be accomplished, I have said this morning, I believe we should and I believe we can accomplish that.... If we can look further and see that that same trend is going on and that through the operation of these two sources, of either increased income or decreased expenditures or a combination of the two, there is going to be some additional money that will be available, looking into the future, then I will be for a reduction of taxes to the amount that we can see is available to distribute when, if, and as we obtain it.

Mr. O'Brien. Do you think you will be able to see that far ahead by January, sir?

Sec. Humphrey. I don't know. We will see further in January than we can see now. We see, as you recognize from this document, we see, I think, quite clearly, better today than we did when this document was prepared six or eight months ago....

RODNEY CROWTHER (*Baltimore Sun*). Mr. Secretary, first, have you sent instructions to the various departments to further reduce their budgets by 3 per cent?

SEC. HUMPHREY. The answer to that is no.

DIR. HUGHES. We don't operate on the basis of a flat percentage cut. Anything that we do, as in the past, will be a selective consideration of each item.

SEC. HUMPHREY. What we have done is to ask every department of this Government and everybody in it who is responsible for spending any money to recognize how near we are to accomplishing a balanced budget and to review his situation in the greatest detail to see if there isn't some way that he can so improve his efficiency and improve his operations that, without the sacrifice of service in the other departments of Government, and with continuingly growing strength in the Defense Department, we can still get more for our money sufficiently so that we can balance this budget.

MR. CROWTHER. My other question, in January we had quite a hassle here about $1.75 billion of unallocated cuts that you were going to make. On page twelve of this document, you say you have made $750 million of those in the Defense Department, and you still have $1 billion to make. Is the 3 per cent in addition to the $1 billion?

DIR. HUGHES. The 3 per cent is on the basis of the figures in this document, which include defense expenditure at $34 billion.

FELIX COTTON (International News Service). From what you have said, Mr. Secretary, I gather that you are placing the balanced budget as the first goal, ahead of the next tax cut?

SEC. HUMPHREY. That is correct, at this time.

MR. COTTON. Obligational authority is now $61.8 billion and expenditure is $63.8 billion. Does that indicate that we are getting down to a level where, while this present international situation continues, that an expenditure level of something around $61.8 billion or somewhere near that will be expected from now on?

SEC. HUMPHREY. Well, what it means is this, that as conditions remain constant—that is, I am talking about world conditions—what it means is that the easiest reductions were the earliest reductions, and as you make reductions and get down, it is harder to—and as you grow more efficient and as you grow better balanced, it keeps getting harder and harder to save money and still get all the results.

Now, that can still go on, however, and all you have got to do is take any ordinary operation—I don't care what it is. Nobody ever, if they are really running their business in the right way, is satisfied with what they are doing. You always have got some room for improvement, and if you keep at the job, you always can find some place to improve. But it gets harder all the time.

MR. COTTON. Now, your tax estimates are based, as I understand it, on income levels, personal income levels, and corporation profit estimates. Could you say, now, in view of the fact that you have revised your taxes upward $2.1 billion, what level of income, personal income, and what level of corporation profits these new estimates are based upon?

SEC. HUMPHREY. Yes. Let me see if we can't develop that for you in just one minute. It is the breakdown of $62.1 billion total; is that right?

MR. COTTON. Well, the individual income level on national income, I suppose, is based on a national personal income estimate.

SEC. HUMPHREY. That is right: Individual income tax that we estimate we will collect that goes into the $62.1 billion total of receipts for us is $32.8 billion. That is based on $300 billion of personal income. The corporation income taxes are estimated at $19.2 billion, and that is based on $40.6 billion. Now, that is somewhat less. The actual—the figures—I will take back the word "actual," because I want to explain that—the figures, preliminary figures, the Government figures for personal income are estimated at $300.3 billion for the second quarter; $293.6 billion for the first quarter. The corporate figures are estimated at $40.9 billion for the first quarter and $42.5 billion for the second quarter. From that you will see that the figures we have used on which we are basing our tax collections are somewhat less than these preliminary figures that have been presented. The reason is this: With the personal figures, you will see that we are right on the button for the second quarter, and that assumes that, if that is to be the average for the year, that the deficit against that bogey for the first quarter will have to be made up in subsequent quarters. For the corporate tax, we are right on the button for the first quarter and below for the second quarter. We have found that these preliminary corporate figures are very often widely revised when we get through with the fourth quarter, that estimates of corporate profits are carried on by companies through, and corporate earnings are carried on through the year, and when you come to the fourth quarter, that is when all the adjustments are made and the write-offs and the extra depreciations and the various things that have to be done, or less carry-backs and all the things there are that enter into the final computation of a corporate tax are usually adjusted in the fourth quarter, and, until we get that, we find—even 18 months later, we have gone back and we find—that the figures of 18 months ago have to be quite widely revised.

So we are using a figure we think is the best, a reasonably conservative but yet as near the actual fact that we believe will be finished.

MRS. MAY CRAIG (Maine Papers). Mr. Secretary, as I understand it, if you get the budget firmly balanced, you will recommend reducing taxes. Do you ever plan to start reducing the national debt?

SEC. HUMPHREY. Well, Mrs. Craig, I have answered that several times before, and I think that what I have said previously, maybe a year or two ago, is exactly the thing that I will say again, the thing I believe.

I don't believe that any substantial reduction in the Government debt can practically be made until the time comes when there is a different situation in the world and a different requirement for our expenditures for defense.

As long as we are spending these huge sums for our defense and as long as that is required, I think the level of taxation, the burden of taxes on the people of the country, on the economy of the country, is about as high as it can properly be. I have said many times I think it is too high. I have said it a few minutes ago, and I want to repeat it. I think our taxes are too high for the best interests of our country, and I think they should be gradually reduced within our ability to do the things we have to do and should do and still do it, so that I don't think that we should increase taxes, if you please, or hold taxes higher than we have to when we are at this very high level, anyway, to reduce this debt. But I do think that just as soon as we are able to make a substantial reduction in this big field of defense expenditure, when that happy day arrives, then I think we can and properly should begin to make some reductions in the debt.

DONALD H. SHANNON (Los Angeles *Times*). Mr. Secretary, on that 3 per cent that you hope to save this year, that you were talking about

Finally got the genie
back in the jar!

Dowling in
*The New York
Herald Tribune,*
1956

earlier, did you say that you anticipate or hope to do it voluntarily on
the part of the individual agencies of the Government? Aren't you
going to help them any at all?

Dir. Hughes. I can answer that one, George.

Sec. Humphrey. Rollie is the boy with the bull whip.

Dir. Hughes. We are in constant touch with the heads of the departments and the top people, and they are working in turn with their
people in the Government to find the proper ways to selectively and
efficiently reduce the—again the 3 per cent—and that is not being left
just to chance for somebody to bring it up and say, "Here is $5." But
at the same time, we have to remember that any effective job of this
nature has to come from the people who spend the money in the
departments, and we can stimulate and we can point out things that
can be done, but when you try to do it just by saying, "Cut this 2 per
cent, or cut this 1 per cent," you don't get the results you get when

it is a teamwork operation.... We have found tremendous cooperation among the people in the Administration who are just as anxious to accomplish this result as we are.

RICHARD E. MOONEY (United Press). Mr. Hughes, you said in connection with the cash budget that payments to and receipts from the public, that the surplus or deficit there has inflationary or deflationary effect. If the administrative budget is balanced, the cash budget will come out with a surplus of $2 billion-plus, I guess.... Isn't a surplus of $2 billion a deflationary influence?

DIR. HUGHES. Of course, but there are—

SEC. HUMPHREY. The answer is, that is the tendency.

MR. O'BRIEN. The document here said that the cash surplus is going to be $300 million if you carry out this program here.

SEC. HUMPHREY. That is, if we have the $1.7 billion, Frank.

MR. O'BRIEN. In January when you were forecasting a $2.4 billion deficit, there was nearly a $600 million cash surplus predicted, was there not?

DIR. HUGHES. Well, as we pointed out, that is working closer together constantly—because of the effect of the trust fund operations.

MR. O'BRIEN. Because they are spending more; is that it?

DIR. HUGHES. Yes, and there isn't the same accumulation that there has been in the past years. In some cases there are changes in law, more people coming in, and the way the whole operation is moving in that direction are bringing them closer together.

MR. O'BRIEN. Is it mainly because of higher spending by the trust funds?

DIR. HUGHES. Yes, that is the principal factor.

SEC. HUMPHREY. The time will come, you know, and may well come, when it will be the other way, when instead of having cash in, we will have actually cash out. That may occur.

MILBURN PETTY (*Oil Daily*). At Chicago recently the Governors' Conference pointed out that the total collection of taxes on highway users ran to $2.5 billion a year, and made the point that that was sufficient to finance any reasonable highway program. I was wondering if you had any comment or observation on their position.

SEC. HUMPHREY. If you don't mind, gentlemen, let us stick to the budget, rather than some of these extraneous matters, because we have got a lot of people who want to ask questions strictly about the budget.

MR. PETTY. I beg your pardon, sir, but that does affect the budget if Congress should vote that tax.

SEC. HUMPHREY. Yes. But they haven't voted that yet, and I was very much opposed to their doing that. That gets into quite a different field. If you don't mind, let us just stick to the budget for a few minutes.

J. A. O'LEARY (*Washington Star*). Mr. Secretary, on page seven, where you say that a balanced budget is in sight, you add that "still further progress would justify lower taxes." Does that mean that you actually want to see a surplus on hand above the balance?

SEC. HUMPHREY. No. What that means is what I explained a minute ago, that we want to be able to see down the road that we are going to have some money with which to pay the taxes that we are going to release down the road.

MR. O'LEARY. But it would not have to be on hand.

SEC. HUMPHREY. It doesn't need to be on hand today. And the best proof of that is what we did the last time. We looked down the road. We saw savings in expenditures coming up. We couldn't do it within a year, but we could see that we could save $6 billion or $7 billion down the road. So we gave tax cuts of $7.4 billion that took effect down the road, and with one hand reasonably washed the other.

MR. MOONEY. While you are on those figures, sir, could you give us the actual income from corporate taxes for 1955?

SEC. HUMPHREY. Yes. 1955 corporate taxes were $18.3 billion. I think I will volunteer something here, ladies and gentlemen, because it might lead to some confusion in your thinking if somebody didn't think to ask. I would like to just explain why that increase that you have brought up is not greater. In other words, corporation taxes actually in 1955 were $18.3 billion. Our current estimate is $19.2 billion. That is approximately $1 billion of increase, with substantially higher corporate earnings. Now, the reason why that isn't more is this: We estimate that the increase in profit, in taxes on profits, on corporate profits, will go up $2.8 billion, but there are offsetting deductions to come off that, the largest of which is the end of the Mills Plan, which is about $1.5 billion. Then there is about a half billion dollars of tag ends of other taxes that are holding the decrease in profits of the previous term, and there is still a little excess profits tax coming in which is below the estimate, so that instead of having a $1 billion increase in corporate tax that we are estimating, we are actually estimating a $2.8 billion increase in corporate tax, but that is eaten up, $1.5 billion of it is eaten up by the termination of the Mills Plan, which used to throw money from one quarter to another. Do you see what I mean?

Ross F. MARK (Reuters). Mr. Secretary, can you tell me when the last time the budget was balanced? is the first question. The second is, would you describe this budget as having restrictive trends?

SEC. HUMPHREY. The last time it was balanced? Rollie, can you tell me?

DIR. HUGHES. About 1951.

SEC. HUMPHREY. I will tell you when it was. It was when we were getting ready for the Korean War, and we put the taxes up in anticipation of big expenditures, and then didn't make the expenditures, so the money came in faster than it went out, and we happened to have a balanced budget for a period.

MR. MARK. Sir, would you say this budget is restrictive in character? The national income seems to be expanding, and expanding industry, and the budget expenditure seems to be going down.

SEC. HUMPHREY. But what of it? I mean, there isn't anything wrong, is there, if you have got more income coming in and yet you are doing a better job on your expenditures?

JOHN T. NORMAN (Fairchild Papers). Following on Frank's question, you are ready to say now you want some tax relief of specific types, is that the idea, but you don't want to commit yourself to general tax relief?

SEC. HUMPHREY. No. That was a hangover of a previous request made long ago in connection wtih the foreign trade problem, and it does involve some taxes. It is a relatively minor matter, and it is part of an old program that is simply going along. . . .

TOM HUGHES (*U. S. News & World Report*). Is there included in that estimate the amount of money that the corporations are required to return on the tax benefits they received on 1954, under the two sections of the Internal Revenue Code that were repealed?

SEC. HUMPHREY. They never got any. There never were any tax benefits. It was just that it was threatened. We found out the mistake in plenty of time to correct it before anybody got anything out of it.

Nobody ever got a nickel out of that. We repealed it before they even filed their returns.

PETER EDSON (NEA). Mr. Secretary, are there any tax provisions expiring next year? ...

SEC. HUMPHREY. The corporation and the excises both go off on April 1, but our figures here are based on the existing law being continued. There might be some discrepancy there if they were not.

MR. COTTON. Mr. Secretary, you want the taxes to continue which expire April 1, both the corporation and the excises?

SEC. HUMPHREY. Well, I am going to cross that bridge when we get there. We will cross that bridge when we get there. ...

MR. O'BRIEN. Mr. Hughes, could I come back to an earlier question about the Defense Department, that $1.75 billion? You say now that you have already got the $750 million of that saving. Are you $750 million ahead, because that was a saving that was going to be made in fiscal 1956?

DIR. HUGHES. No. That was calculated on, and it was a question of identifying it.

MR. O'BRIEN. The further savings in expenditures which would have to be made to balance the budget, does that include the $1 billion, still unidentified savings?

DIR. HUGHES. No. The $1 billion has already been included in arriving at the net estimate of expenditures for the Defense Department of $34 billion.

MR. O'BRIEN. So any further savings would have to be in excess of that extra $1 billion?

DIR. HUGHES. And the 3 per cent is after using that as the base of calculation.

M. STEWART HENSLEY (United Press). Did the action of Congress this year help to bring this figure down, to get down to $1.7 billion, or did it make it a little harder?

SEC. HUMPHREY. I think by and large, Rollie, that the work of the Appropriations Committees was good all the way through.

DIR. HUGHES. They held it down all the way through. The proposals were bad. ... Some of the bills even passed in one House were bad, but the actual appropriations in total weren't too bad. Some of the things that we asked for didn't get passed, and some of the things that we didn't ask for got passed. But when you added up the totals, it was not unfavorable.

MR. HENSLEY. Does this mean that—your remark is not exactly enthusiastic—does this mean that what they actually appropriated will result in slightly larger expenditures? . . .

SEC. HUMPHREY. No, I don't think so. I think they contributed to the reduction.

◪ This 3 per cent announcement shortly had interesting repercussions, as will be seen.

Memo to a future President

Statement by Secretary Humphrey at the
Treasury Department.

September 29, 1955

I am in full accord with the program outlined in Secretary Wilson's letter to Senator Johnson.

A reduction in expenditures which would require an alteration of that program was never in contemplation. However, as Secretary Wilson says, "our purpose is to carry out our military program with maximum economy and efficiency" and to reduce waste and eliminate extravagance which "some people who resist such economies call cuts."

The hope has been and still is that savings can be made by continually exercising the greatest care in scrutinizing all expenditures and by increased efficiency in administration, while at the same time increasing effective military strength.

As I said just a month ago, our hope of balancing the budget lies in the combination of two things: First, the possibility of increasing Government revenue. Second, the continual day-after-day and everyday effort of everyone in Government to eliminate every expenditure which properly can be saved. At the same time, we will continue to strengthen our military security and maintain proper standards of service to the public by all departments in the Government.

🖾 Early in 1955, the President had presented a military defense budget estimate of $35.75 billion for the fiscal year ending July 1, 1956. When Secretary Humphrey in August said the 1956 budget could be balanced if every Government department cut its estimated spending 3 per cent, Secretary of Defense Wilson subscribed to a $34.5 billion re-estimate for his department.

After published reports that this meant an army cutback of 80,000 personnel and a half billion reduction in aircraft development spending—circulated by several generals—Senator Lyndon B. Johnson, head of the Senate Committee on Preparedness, demanded of Secretary Wilson whether any overtones of reduction of national security had been precipitated by budgetary moves. Secretary Wilson promptly wrote the Senator that the department budget of $34.5 billion would be adequate for maximum security and said the department was in no sense any victim of Secretary Humphrey's economy drive.

As it came out July 1, 1956, the surplus of this first budget balance was somewhat greater than the 1956 reduction in defense spending.

"Who wants to go back?"

Speech by Secretary Humphrey to a Republican Dinner at Convention Hall, Philadelphia.

October 4, 1955

The whole country rejoices to know that the word from Denver continues to be good. The shock that the country, in fact, the whole world, suffered with the news of the President's illness is decreasing as the critical days are passing and improvement continues.

Never before in the history of the country have the hopes of so many millions of its people been centered in one man, and they all rejoice as the days of favorable progress keep passing by.

What the future holds, no one can foretell. It is idle to speculate until the good progress has continued for a much longer time. In the

If they want to add
the finishing touch!

Parrish in
The Chicago Tribune,
1955

meantime, we are thankful for each day's improvement and have good reason to hope that it will continue unabated as time goes on until a full and complete recovery has been made.

Surmounting the first shock of anxiety, the Government has continued to function in an effective, normal way, carrying out the President's policies which were definitely defined and well established, and well known in detail to us all. We have been trained as a team, and we will continue to function without interruption in the programs previously adopted until the President is fully recovered and able to return.

The whole country has responded in a similar manner and while it gains assurance as the good news continues, it is settling down to facing everyday problems in a normal way.

On a bright afternoon just two months short of three years ago today, I boarded by helicopter the heavy cruiser Helena off Wake Island in the mid-Pacific. Already aboard were President-elect Eisenhower, just returned from Korea, and several other appointees to the new Cabinet. Mr. Eisenhower had just finished one of the missions which he had laid out in his campaign for the presidency. He had been to Korea to see for himself what, if anything, should or could be done about bringing an end to death and suffering in the war of stalemate that was dragging on and on and taking the lives of American boys month after month. . . .

The most pressing problem, of course, was Korea, where 33,000 American boys were killed and nearly 104,000 wounded, and where there was no end to war in sight.

The war in Indo-China had been going for six years and there were no plans to bring it to an end.

Although we were spending record amounts for our defense and for foreign aid, we found as we tried to be strong everywhere at once that we were diffusing our efforts to such an extent that we weren't really strong enough anywhere to be as effective as we should be.

President Eisenhower on the Helena then was as determined as he is today, that "mankind longs for freedom from war and from rumors of war," and that working toward peace must be the primary goal of the new Administration. . . .

In January of 1953, President Eisenhower and his new Administration went promptly to work to correct abuses and restore freedom to the people.

A constructive program was designed to bring about peace in Korea, and in July the armistice in Korea was achieved, to end the killing and wounding of our American youth as well as to bring welcome relief from worry and heartbreak to thousands of families back home. . . .

Do you want to go back?

There remained the greater problem of establishing better relations throughout the world. We sought to establish relations which might eventually lead to peace—a just and honorable peace for all nations. To keep strong meanwhile was prerequisite to everything else. Plans and programs for ourselves and our allies have progressed far since then, with such developments as an armistice in Indo-China, improved foreign relations in many other directions and finally the Geneva conference, which holds high hope for further progress.

We determined early in 1953 to adopt a fiscal program which would help to make more jobs and better living for every citizen. This program involved the restoration of freedom in many fields.

In my very first public statement after taking office, I said on February 8, 1953, that we were determined to work toward the following goals:

(1) That we have a sound and stable dollar—not one of declining value.

(2) That we do not spend more than we earn.

(3) That we pay a little down on our debts from time to time instead of rapidly borrowing more.

(4) That we keep our credit good by properly handling the debts which we already have.

(5) That slowly but surely and definitely we reduce the too heavy burden of taxes which, hidden in the cost of everything we buy, are now stifling initiative and increasing the cost of living.

(6) That we maintain free markets in America in which the great American consumer can buy what he needs when he wants it and choose for himself what he will buy at prices he is willing to pay.

(7) That producers are free to strive to produce more, better and cheaper products, to compete for the consumer's favor in buying their particular products in competition with all others.

(8) That we protect the savings of the old, their insurance and their pensions.

(9) And, above all, that we preserve for the young the great symbol of America, the opportunity to advance and improve themselves to the limit of their own abilities and their own hard work and endeavors. . . .

In the spring of 1953, as the prospects for a Korean armistice appeared brighter, fear was voiced by some that the coming of peace and the reductions in Government spending which our program of economy was producing might lead to an upset in business and a depression. In April, 1953, my first speech as a member of the Eisenhower Cabinet began with these words: "There is no reason to fear peace. We are not headed for a depression."

We did get peace. And we did not have a depression. It was in peace that America grew great and accumulated the homes, industries, farms, and mines that saw us through two wars. It was wars that brought us debt and taxes and inflation. There was no reason why we should fear peace, even though there might have to be adjustments in the economy as there were swings in Government spending.

In only about six months we had obtained freedom from war in Korea. We had obtained freedom from controls on the private lives and businesses of our citizens. Does anyone want to go back?

In the spring of 1954 prophets of doom and gloom proclaimed that our economy was in a bad way. These prophets loudly predicted that the economy was headed for serious trouble unless the Executive Branch should greatly increase deficit spending and embark on large public-works expenditures to "stimulate the economy." They advocated that Washington should again start telling the nation in detail what to do. They advocated less, rather than more, freedom for the people of the country.

The Administration resisted the pressures to move in and try to run the economy from Washington. We retained the new freedoms which we had won, with confidence in our position. We had made tremendous savings in Government expenditures over the past two years by big reductions in both Government employees and purchasing.... One reason it was certain that the private economy would make the jobs to hire people previously employed by the Government or by the Government's spending was the tax program.

Tax cuts put into effect in 1954 totaled $7.4 billion—the largest total dollar tax cut in any year in history. This tax cut left this huge sum in the hands of all of the people to buy the goods which they wanted to buy rather than in paying it in taxes. Returning this huge sum to the people to spend for themselves was certain to result in the creation of more and better jobs for the people who used to make their living from Government spending.

The tax revision bill enacted by the Congress in 1954 had a very beneficial effect all through the economy. Many business projects which had been planned but were awaiting a more propitious time for development were immediately put into effect once this tax revision bill became law.... New or expanding businesses were encouraged in many ways to go ahead with their plans, which resulted in the creation of thousands of jobs and the vital expansion of our economy.

Millions of individuals were assisted by these great tax cuts. Every single taxpayer in this country received a tax saving, and millions of cases of hardship existing under the previous laws were corrected so that individuals were encouraged to expand their purchases and all their activities. The great bulk of all the money went to individuals....

Prosperity in America cannot be had just by stimulating consumption, desirable as that certainly is. Unemployment in the heavy industries can be just as real a problem. To solve this, the people must buy the production of heavy industries. This means more investment because it is the investors who buy the heavy goods. That is what makes the jobs in the heavy goods industries of America, and that is what creates new plants and new tools and new jobs for the ever-growing work force of this expanding country. That is what the tax revision bill helped to accomplish. . . .

The cost of living which had doubled during the preceding fifteen years has increased less than one per cent in the past three years. The dollar has been stable and is the most prized currency in all the world. Pensions and savings have been protected. Investment is encouraged and we at long last are on the way to a balanced budget for the Government.

It is this course of Government conduct, so carefully planned and so rigidly adhered to, that inspires the great confidence of the people and which has brought us so far from the predictions of doom and gloom into the greatest volume of business and highest employment of people in the long history of this country. . . .

Most importantly, there is no longer a feast-or-famine program of defense. In its place, the new program is for a planned and well-developed mobile, constantly up-to-date defense maintained at the most economical cost which can be sustained for the long pull over an indefinite number of years for our protection. Today, at less cost, we have an armed strength more efficient and better organized than ever before. We have the great advantage of guidance from the foremost military leader in this world and under President Eisenhower's great leadership, the defense of America is today stronger in peacetime than at any previous moment in our history.

Who wants to go back? . . .

📢 An exuberant newspaper editorial on the Philadelphia speech declared: "Secretary Humphrey asks the real $64 question—who wants to go back?"

"We have seen that day dawn"

Article by Secretary Humphrey in the
Washington Post and Times-Herald *under the title*
"Future Promising, Humphrey Writes."

January 4, 1956

The future is promising—if we pull together. For three years we have been shaping this Government's economic policies into the policies required for a strong and forward-looking nation, its economy firmly rooted and self-supporting; an economy that will pump a continuous flow into the day-to-day American evolution of self-betterment; an economy that will constantly generate new and better-paying jobs for an ever-growing population.

At the same time our economy must provide an ever-higher standard of living, plus the social services the people want and need as well as the men and the weapons we must have for our defense.

All hands in our nation—labor unions and employers, the rich and the poor, both major parties, the farmer and the city man, the woman at home and the man at his job—all have a part in making our new productive way of life.

This peaceful evolution has resulted in a tremendous upheaval of this nation's whole economy that has really created a different kind of nation, a unique nation of "haves" that needs an up-to-date way of thinking about itself and up-to-date policies in keeping with its strength and growth potential.

We have curbed inflation, avoided deflation, and encouraged initiative and expansion which have developed into the greatest period of prosperity that our fast-growing, now unhobbled, economy has ever known.

Barring unforeseen developments, we will have a balanced federal budget in the present fiscal year. The anticipated deficit of the Government for fiscal 1956 was $1.7 billion at the time of the midyear review last July. If present estimates are realized, we will have a balanced budget for this fiscal year ending June 30, 1956.

Our prosperity didn't just happen. It was brought about by the confidence of the American people in the Eisenhower Administration and

"Wait a while—
I think I have it!"

Fischetti for
the NEA Service,
1956

the favorable climate which has been created for 166 million free Americans to exercise their own initiatives and endeavors to the full limit of their abilities to improve and better the lives of their loved ones and themselves.

The Administration's program promised a new, a better day. Not for any particular segment of the population but for all the people. We have seen that day dawn. It is just the beginning if we can continue to achieve national unity and improve the lot of the farmer, about the only large segment of our population still suffering from the overhanging effects of past unrealistic Government programs.

We have the greatest productive machine the world has ever seen. It is expanding rapidly. From the apparently unfailing spring we call research flows a stream of new ideas and new products, resulting in new opportunities and new wealth for every one.

We have set new records in almost every way in which good times can be judged and measured. Employment last summer reached 65.5 million for the first time in history. Unemployment declined in October to 2.1 million. The dollar has been stable for three years. Wage earners have been getting real increases instead of the "cost of living" wage increases of the previous several years.

If all Americans—workers, producers, businessmen, consumers, and investors—all go ahead and work and buy and build and improve with confidence tempered with prudence, this nation will continue to be even more a nation of "haves" enjoying new peaks of prosperity in business, production, and wages and constantly higher standards of living—for all the people.

⚓ The Secretary put the first outright harbinger herein that the budget at last was balanced.

A "very small surplus sighted"

Statement by Secretary Humphrey at the
Treasury Department.

January 14, 1956

Ever since we took office, one of the most important objectives of the Eisenhower Administration has been to balance the budget. Today that ambition has come true.

Budgets, of course, are only estimates. When you are working with figures as large as Government figures of income and expense, differences between estimates and actual performance can easily arise.

The fiscal year 1956 does not end until next June 30, when the final figures will be known. But we are able today, for the first time, to present the most carefully prepared estimates of budget receipts and expenditures, showing an approximate balance—in fact, a very small surplus, for that year.

Balancing this budget is not simply a bookkeeping exercise or a businessman's fetish. It is the very keystone of financial responsibility.

In a home, in a business, or in this great Government, no one can continually spend more than he earns and not have it result in disaster. With the enormous debt our Government now has, it becomes of even greater importance.

"Bring me
the black ink!"

Berryman in
The Washington Star,
1956

The great prosperity which is so nearly universal throughout this country today is largely inspired by this Administration's continuing accomplishments toward the realization of sound government finances.

Your job, your increased earnings, the stability in your cost of living are all involved.

There is much more to be done, but we have passed a great milestone today when we can honestly present estimates for a balanced budget for both 1956 and 1957—two years in succession—which is eloquent evidence of real progress.

We must all work together to make them come true and to continue to enjoy the benefits which only sound financial management can provide.

📧 The budget balance was "real" by late January, and was proudly announced. Statistics on the two consecutive budget balances are relevant here. 1955–6: receipts, $68.1 billion; expenditures, $66.4 billion; surplus, $1.7 billion. 1956–7: receipts, $69.8 billion; expenditures, $69.1 billion; surplus, $700 million.

The cost of government rises

*Remarks by Secretary Humphrey on Meet the
Press television panel in Washington. Ned Brooks,
moderator.*

January 22, 1956

SEC. HUMPHREY.... Unless we reduce costs, a great deal more than we have, or unless we get more revenues, from sources not now in sight, there will be no tax cut this year. Not as we stand now.

NED BROOKS. What would you think the prospects would be for a tax cut if there were a surplus of say $3 billion to $4 billion?

SEC. HUMPHREY. I would favor a tax cut in such an event. The President said he wanted some money applied to reduction of debt; he wanted at least a modest payment made on the debt. I think that is proper and right. On the other hand, I think, and I have said many, many times, that our tax structure in this country is now so high that we ought to bring our tax structure down as rapidly as we can afford to do so, and I think with the figures you mentioned there would be room to do some of both. . . .

. . . The cost of government has gone up, actually. This budget is up in almost every department, not much in most of them. The big amounts are in the defense budget—I think the defense program should satisfy even the most ardent enthusiast of excessive military spending—and the farm payment for crops. But all of the departments, almost in every item, have had some small advance so that while our costs of government now are about $10 billion less than they were when we first came in and about $14 billion less than was projected at the time for the ensuing years, we still are up nearly $4 billion from where we were at our low point in our estimate for the future. . . .

"Enjoying plenty—in peace"

Statement by Secretary Humphrey before the Joint Committee on the Economic Report.

February 3, 1956

. . . The United States today is enjoying plenty—in peace. Americans have broken all records in the numbers of people with jobs, the high wages they are receiving, and in the production of goods and services for the people to enjoy. They are benefiting from this high prosperity while reasonably resisting pressures toward inflation.

Whether this high prosperity will continue without involving the excesses of either inflation or deflation depends in very large part upon what 167 million Americans do.

Continued high activity in our economy depends not so much upon Government as upon the efforts of all the people, all in their own ways trying to do a little more for themselves and their loved ones. It is the sum total of all these individual efforts that makes our system so superior to anything ever known in this world before. That is what makes free America.

This Government has helped in several specific ways to provide a more fertile field in which free Americans can work to better themselves.

Total Government spending is now $10 billion below that of three years ago, and $14 billion below what had been previously planned.

We, at long last, have proposed a balanced budget, the surest index to thrifty management in a home, in a business, or in the Federal Government.

We have made the largest dollar tax cut of any year in the history of this country. This tax reduction of nearly $7.5 billion was a strong assist in the transition from a wartime to a peacetime economy.

And the long trend of inflation that dropped the value of the dollar from 100 cents in 1939 to 52 cents 13 years later has been halted, with no significant loss in the buying power of the dollar now for over three full years. . . .

If all Americans—workers, farmers and other producers, businessmen, consumers and investors—all go ahead and work, and buy, and build, and improve with confidence tempered with prudence, this nation will continue to enjoy new peaks of prosperity in business production, and wages, and constantly higher standards of living—for all the people.

The surplus pledged to reduce the debt

Statement by Secretary Humphrey before the
House Ways & Means Committee.

June 19, 1956

I am appearing before you to ask for a temporary increase in the public debt limit from $275 billion to $278 billion for the fiscal year 1957. Because of our improved fiscal position, we are following the suggestion that the temporary increase granted by Congress for two years past be cut in half.

We succeeded in living within the $281 billion limit set a year ago, but by a narrow margin. On several days, we were within $100 million of the debt ceiling, and, at times, our operating cash balance was less than enough to cover ten days' expenditures. This is closer than is prudent in handling the Government's huge operations efficiently.

However, I am in full sympathy with the desire of the Congress to keep a limit on Government spending.

We hope to finish this fiscal year with a budget surplus of about $1.8 billion and the debt under $273 billion. We still face, however, a heavy seasonal swing in receipts, which means borrowing in the first half of the fiscal year for repayment from heavy tax receipts in the second half.

This swing is gradually being reduced by the shift in time of payment of corporation taxes, provided by 1954 legislation.

Taking these facts into account, I believe we can operate under a $278 billion ceiling, though it will take careful management. If this becomes impossible, we shall advise the Congress promptly.

Our success in living within this ceiling will depend on great restraint by both the Congress and the Administration in expenditures.

On the basis of present estimates, there is no leeway for any reduction in tax rates. The program calls for applying any surplus to debt reduction in accordance with the recommendations made by the President.

I hope that this year we are setting a precedent which may be faithfully followed year after year, and that from now on we will so handle our financial affairs that we can make each year a modest payment in reduction of our huge indebtedness as a matter of standard practice.

This program is one more step in maintaining fiscal soundness and ensuring the integrity of our money, so that our people can count upon its value and go forward with all their undertakings with full confidence. This is the basis of continuing and growing prosperity and constantly more and better jobs. . . .

◀ The Secretary well knew the $278 billion debt limit figure in the mind of Senator Harry F. Byrd, chairman of the Senate Finance Committee—it was the lowest debt limit figure for which Secretary Humphrey had asked, and the Treasury would shortly report a triumphant $1.7 surplus at the fiscal year's end, which would make it difficult not to ask for a lowering of the debt limit from the previous year's $281 billion.

Price of money as the regulator

Speech by Secretary Humphrey before
the Economic Club in Detroit.

October 8, 1956

. . . Today a very high percentage of all the people in the United States are employed and the goods of the United States are being largely consumed. Materials are in most cases in full demand and in some cases there are even shortages. Except for a few scattered soft spots the situation by and large is one of great prosperity straining the nation's resources.

When as now widespread confidence in the future is so high that we seek to go further and faster than that, what happens? We start drawing either man power or scarce materials away from each other.

That is what is going on today. If you don't think it is, do what

I did the other day. Take the Sunday editions of half a dozen major city newspapers across the country—including Detroit. Throw away all the pages except those pages which have to do with advertising by various concerns to hire people and in these half a dozen papers these pages will be several inches thick. Pretty nearly everybody in business is advertising in some paper to employ some man for some company, other than the one he is now working for.

The same thing is going on with many materials.

There has to be some governor, some restriction, in this situation. Otherwise the price of materials and goods keeps going on up without producing any more goods, and we all must pay more for the same.

If this big demand for money is used to expand sales and plant and capacity and activity when expansion means only hiring more people and trying to get more goods than there are, then the price of goods and services will rise with no corresponding increase in either goods or productivity.

But if the price of money rises, then it will tend to keep the demands for expansion in line with supply of our resources.

And it is easier to contract the price of money when it has served its purpose than to contract the price of goods and services. You don't contract what you pay for goods and services and materials without some very serious hardships resulting. But you can contract the price of money without hurting people. That is why it is the best economic governor. It protects jobs, prices, and wages while it works.

We don't want to go the "easy money" road, the old familiar road to inflation. We don't want to go up only to come down. We want to let natural corrections and restraints operate freely. The Government is not putting up the price of money. It is the accumulated demands of people and business that is doing it.

As more and more people want to expand and use more money to do so, the demand for money increases and the price rises. Now, if the Federal Reserve Board neither arbitrarily increases the supply nor arbitrarily holds down the price, interest rates naturally rise. As they rise and money costs more, some people refrain from so much expansion and the demand for money decreases. As supply again catches up with demand, the price again begins to decline and the pressure on the cost of living is reduced without an excessive advance hurting all the people.

There are other sources of pressure that must also be taken into

A neat trick if
he can make it fit!

Marcus in
The New York Times,
1954

account. The Government of the United States collects and spends so much money that it has a tremendous effect on the economy. In this Administration we have reduced our expenditures about $8 billion. At the same time we cut taxes nearly the same amount as the money we saved. In cutting taxes we gave back to the public to spend for themselves as they thought best the money we saved in Government spending. This helped to make jobs in private industry for those whose livelihood had formerly depended on Government spending. They helped to produce more goods for all the people to buy, whereas when those Government employes were working for the Government they didn't produce any goods that the rest of the people could purchase.

Today we are spending in the neighborhood of $40 billion for military goods and services. That $40 billion is money that goes out in wages and for goods that turn into wages. It makes that much spending power in the country. Yet there isn't anybody involved in that whole $40 billion who makes goods that a consumer can buy. Consumers don't buy tanks or bombers.

Defense spending is necessary, and we will continue to spend on defense every penny and every billion we need to spend to provide the nation with security. But the economic significance is that the Government in its own fiscal policy is putting a great pressure on the market for goods by putting that much money into this spending stream and not putting added goods out for the people to buy.

That brings us to the next point, the Government's policy with respect to debt and savings. When interest rates are kept down arbitrarily, not only is the incentive to save money reduced but the fear of inflation helps to create a lack of capital—a lack from which the whole world is suffering.

We are short in this country and in the whole world of capital—which means savings.

We have been through a period of years when there was little incentive to save. In the first place, the interest rate was held so low that there was very little return. There was no natural incentive. In the second place, as the value of the dollar declined and as inflationary pressures took hold, people were afraid to save a dollar because it was constantly declining in value. . . . So the lack of incentive resulting from low interest and the fear of inflation took away the reason to save; and as it went on it actually did keep people from saving. On top of all this, some of our public leaders then scoffed at saving as outmoded and old-fashioned, and urged spending and more spending, regardless of more debt or adequate income.

Saving money and thereby creating capital is no mystery. It simply means that some one must deny himself the desire or pleasure of spending some part of his pay check rather than save it.

Part of his income he can properly spend but part of it must be laid away for the future, if (1) there is sufficient incentive to do so because of a fair return in interest or dividend and (2) if he feels safe in the continuing value of his savings. Most all Americans are saving something today through purchase of insurance, payments for pensions, the purchase of Government bonds, or in a savings account, or in the many ways to do so.

As interest rates rise, all those savers benefit. But if inflation sets in and the dollar declines, they are all robbed of part of their savings. Inflation is the great thief. The young, the old, the sick, the small saver—all those least able to protect themselves—are the helpless prey of wicked inflation. It must be held in check. . . .

There can be some differences of opinion as to the timing and the degree with which this process of using the price of money as our economic regulator takes place. But the process is a sound, right step in the direction of sound money, a sound economy, and continuing to have the people of this country working at more and better jobs at higher pay and ever higher standards of living, for all the people.

🔖 A national financial columnist gave Secretary Humphrey credit for considerable courage in defending and explaining the Federal Reserve Board's current raise of the interest rate, raising "the price of money"; the Eisenhower campaign for re-election was in full swing and many Republican leaders were urging "easier money" to boom the good times further. "It took courage," said the columnist, J. A. Livingston of Philadelphia, "to say in Detroit that credit must be rationed."

"A depression...that will curl your hair"

Remarks by Secretary Humphrey concerning
the President's 1958 Budget at a press conference
at the Treasury Department—
accompanied by Under Secretary W. Randolph
Burgess, Dan Throop Smith, deputy to the Secretary,
and Nils A. Lennartson, assistant to the Secretary.

January 15, 1957

MR. LENNARTSON. Everything distributed and said here is for use with the budget message at noon Wednesday.

SEC. HUMPHREY. I think perhaps the best thing to do is to start by reading a statement. . . . In support of the President's budget message for the fiscal year 1958, which has just been presented to the Congress, there are several recommendations which I want particularly to emphasize.

The President has often said that the basic fiscal problem confronting this Government is how to meet the necessary costs of an adequate defense and other governmental activities and, at the same time, furnish the incentives necessary to a thriving, growing, and reasonably stable economy. Failure in either direction could well mean the gradual loss of our freedom and of our way of life.

During the past few years the greatest strides in history have been taken in the development of modern lethal weapons which can literally destroy great cities and whole areas of population. The methods are completely new. They are extremely costly. They are shared to some degree by two great powers with wholly different ideologies.

In this state of affairs, we must remain both militarily and economically strong. To do so, the extremely high cost of the new weapons demands that we be highly selective and quick to abandon the expense of obsolete methods and equipment.

No one can say exactly how much we can continue to spend for defense and all other governmental services without seriously weakening our economy. While military manpower and equipment protect our lives and our land, they make virtually no addition to the permanent wealth of the nation—to new plants and machinery, new mines, new farms, new homes, or to new jobs for peacetime living.

The billions of dollars spent annually by the Government for military equipment and manpower go into the spending stream but are not matched by an increase in the production of peacetime goods, so that heavy pressure is put on the price of goods which all the people must buy. This imbalance makes it more difficult to keep the cost of living within bounds. Monetary measures alone may not be sufficient for this task unless the Federal Government makes reductions in it manpower and in its purchases which will help to increase the production of additional peacetime goods and so help to hold down prices. Moreover, the funds so released will then be available to build up the capital needed to help create the new jobs, to build the new schools and the countless other improvements required in this growing country of ours.

Our reduction in Government expenditures three years ago made possible the greatest tax cut in history, and stimulated the surge of national confidence which has created the prosperity of the past two years, the greatest we have ever known.

These reductions in Government spending also helped to give greater stability to the cost of living than we ever had in a period of such prosperity. The cost of living has recently moved up somewhat in spite of monetary measures to restrain it. Governmental expenditures and the number of Government employees are now increasing. This trend should promptly be stopped.

This Administration has a record of gratifying achievements in economical and efficient management of the Federal Government. The civilian working force of the Government has been reduced by over 234,000 persons during the past four years; the accounting and management procedures of Government have been vastly improved; over 400 federal enterprises competing with business have been abolished; surplus real estate worth $366 million has been sold and turned back to local tax rolls. These are but a few specific illustrations of our progress. We all must work together to widen and enlarge these accomplishments.

Long hours of painstaking and conscientious work have gone into the preparation of the budget for the fiscal year 1958. All departments of Government should be commended for the efforts they have made.

The President in his State of the Union Message has just said: "Through the next four years, I shall continue to insist that the executive departments and agencies of Government search out additional ways to save money and manpower. I urge that the Congress be equally watchful in this matter."

To accomplish these essential objectives we should now all go to work, not simply to keep within the limits of this budget, but to make actual and substantial reductions through improved efficiency of our operations during the period of the next 18 months which this budget covers. To make this possible, every department of Government must with vigor and determination modernize and streamline their services. The management of every service must be conducted with the possibilities of economy always in mind.

The President has said that the Federal Government alone cannot successfully combat inflation without the earnest co-operation of all individuals and groups of our citizens. As emphasized in the State of the Union Message, business leaders and labor leaders, through their wage and price policies, must make their full, constructive contribution. All other groups must also contribute to the common effort.

(1) We must seek the full co-operation of the public generally in limiting its demands upon the Federal Government for only essential federal functions, especially at this time when the economy is operating at such a high level. Requests should be avoided for services or assist-

Speaking of Reds!

Reg Manning,
McNaught Syndicate,
1954

ance which properly can be supplied by States or local communities or by the citizens themselves.

(2) We must request the support of the Congress to restrict the appropriation of public money to amounts within those recommended in the budget which may be required to carry out the necessary federal functions.

(3) We must require every department and agency of the Government to take vigorous measures, without harm to either security or service to the public, to see that actual expenditures are kept well within the present budgeted figures between now and the end of the next fiscal year and, as the President has said, "search out additional ways to save money and manpower."

(4) We must plan for the 1959 budget, giving urgent attention to making further reductions both in Government employment and in expenditures where these savings will not lessen our security or the quality of the necessary services rendered to the public.

If this program is adopted and resolutely followed, we can, a year hence, give consideration not only to some further payment on the public debt but also to further tax reductions. This, of course, must be conditioned upon continuation of our present prosperity. Just when and how a tax reduction should be made can be determined only when it is known how well these conditions have been fulfilled. In any event, any such tax cuts must provide relief so that every *individual* taxpayer may have some benefits. In the meantime, and until this is accomplished, we must continue to oppose any revision of the tax laws which results in any substantial loss of Government income.

This program will provide more effective control of our spending. It will become a desirable restraint on inflationary pressures through release to the private economy of added manpower and money which, in turn, can open the way to lower taxes, with a sharper spur to incentive and greater opportunity, and production of more and better jobs.

You have heard a good deal of talk about whether or not we are just continually going to go up and up and up and that is my answer to that talk.

QUESTION. Mr. Secretary, on page two you say "governmental expenditures and the number of Government employees are now increasing; this trend should promptly be stopped." Who do you blame for this increase?

SEC. HUMPHREY. Everybody.

QUESTION. The Administration?

SEC. HUMPHREY. Everybody. Congress enacts laws that start with the public. The public, various groups of the public—and it is getting so more and more—keep turning to the Federal Government for everything in the world to be taken care of. Whenever anybody gets into a little bit of trouble he immediately runs to Washington and asks for something to be done about it.

The pressure is put on Congress to enact laws to help them. Congress enacts some laws to help them and the Executive when the laws go in has to support the laws and work with the laws and that adds to the payrolls and it adds to the employment and it adds to the cost of government and that adds to the taxes. It is just everybody—

QUESTION. Are you criticizing the Administration for this?

SEC. HUMPHREY. I criticize everybody from the public right straight through to myself. We have not been firm enough. We have to be firmer than we have been and we have to get our expenses in better control than they now are.

QUESTION. Mr. Secretary, in your statement you speak of cutting back expenditures next year, you hope, and we all remember how you complained over the past four years that it was very hard to cut expenditures because of the immense carry-over of unexpended funds. How do you figure that you can cut expenditures next year when your unexpended balances are once again going up?

SEC. HUMPHREY. They only went up a little and they have been substantially reduced. In this budget you will notice they are held down to about the same amount. The appropriations are right close to the estimated expenditures. . . .

QUESTION. Do you support those parts of the current budget which propose increased expenditures?

SEC. HUMPHREY. I think this budget as now drawn has been prepared with the very greatest care and I think it is the best that we can possibly do right now. Now my whole point is this: That it is 18 months before we get through living under this budget and I think there are a lot of economies and a lot of savings that we ought to be able to make if we pay strict attention to our business and work at them hard enough during the 18 months. I don't think there is anything in sight at the moment that can be done better than is now proposed in this budget but I think we ought to improve it as time goes on.

QUESTION. Mr. Secretary, you say on page two that the expenditures are now going up and must be promptly stopped, yet the four budgets this Administration has had beginning with the low of $64.6 billion have gone up every year. You're now $7 billion up.

SEC. HUMPHREY. We made—let's see, 3 years ago—a very substantial reduction in our expenditures. . . . The thing has been creeping up ever since.

QUESTION. You are up $7 billion?

SEC. HUMPHREY. That's right, $7.2 billion.

QUESTION. Do you really think it will go down at any time?

SEC. HUMPHREY. I think it must.

QUESTION. Why didn't it this time?

SEC. HUMPHREY. It just kept creeping up on us. It did it for the reasons I gave. Everybody from the public all the way through have just been looking to the Federal Government for more and more and more and we have not controlled it. . . .

QUESTION. Mr. Secretary, on page M-68, it tells about your increase in interest rates. There is a $100 million increase in interest. You can't stop a thing like that.

The statement reads: "As a result, the average rate the Treasury pays on outstanding interest-bearing public debt has risen in the past 12 months from 2.49 per cent to 2.67 per cent." Will they not increase?

SEC. HUMPHREY. I don't know whether they will increase or decrease. That will depend on what the demands are. There again reductions of federal expenditures would have a wholesome effect in supplying additional capital which would be available for use in peacetime industry and living and for peacetime goods, and the production of goods would tend to reduce the price of goods and would tend to reduce the demand for money and would tend to reduce the cost of interest. Interest would come down. . . .

QUESTION. What I am asking is, will that rate increase as you do your refinancing?

SEC. HUMPHREY. It will all depend on market conditions. And as I just got through saying, if we can reduce our Government expenditures, it will help to tend to bring those interest rates down and we will have our money for less interest instead of more.

QUESTION. The point a lot of people are interested in is whether you are going to raise the rates on your E Bonds?

QUESTION. You have already said you were.

SEC. HUMPHREY. No, we never have said it.

QUESTION. Because you are getting more E Bonds cashed in than you can sell. Isn't that a serious problem?

SEC. HUMPHREY. Very little difference. . . . That has no part in the budget. We will have a permanent and definite decision and statement before very long on E Bonds.

QUESTION. To clarify this particular point, you say the average rate has risen to 2.67. Of course, you have a decline in the public debt, whereas your total debt interest charges are going up. That increase in the total interest charges is based on what assumption as to an average interest rate in the 1958 fiscal year?

SEC. HUMPHREY. You mean this estimate here. I presume that is based on approximately the present rate.

QUESTION. Mr. Brundage told us that he thinks we have got about to the peak of the tight money market. Do you share that judgment?

SEC. HUMPHREY. I wouldn't undertake to say. I think it depends on a great many conditions and again I get right back to what I said a minute ago. It depends a good deal on how much the Government itself spends, how much the Government takes out of the economy. And it is taking a great deal out of the economy today. My own feeling is that we are taking more out than we can continue to do over a long period of time. I think the present trend must be reversed. I think our present taxes, the trend in our present taxes, the amount of our present taxes, are too high. I think they have to come down. Over a period of time, the only way they can come down is by spending less money, and having a greater margin between income and outgo.

QUESTION. Where would you cut?

SEC. HUMPHREY. I think there are a lot of places in this budget that can be cut.

QUESTION. Name three.

SEC. HUMPHREY. I think—well, I don't believe I will do that. We have been all over this with the greatest care and I don't believe it is up to me to start now to point the finger at people to make cuts, but I think a lot of people will make some cuts. I think we will do so in the Treasury.

QUESTION. Don't you think that is an executive problem—must not leadership come from the executive branch for cuts in the budget?

SEC. HUMPHREY. That's right.

QUESTION. The Administration proposes the budget. They make the proposals. If there are to be cuts must they not necessarily come right from the White House?

SEC. HUMPHREY. You just heard me read it. I read you a statement that said cuts ought to be made.

QUESTION. But they didn't do it.

QUESTION. The small business proposal, the President's Message is rather vague on it. I wonder if you can make it more specific as to what tax recommendations you are making with regard to that?

SEC. HUMPHREY. So far as the Treasury is concerned, we are saying just as I said in this statement: "Until the time comes when a general overhauling of our taxes can be made and reductions can be made, we are opposing any changes that will substantially reduce the Government's income."

QUESTION. In the Cabinet Committee's recommendations, one was for a change in the corporate tax rate which would help small business. Are you opposed to that particular recommendation this year?

SEC. HUMPHREY. I am opposed to that this year. . . . There are a large number of suggestions for reductions in taxes that are going to be brought before this Congress . . . by Congress and by various people.

The Congressmen themselves are going to be bringing lots of things up. A lot of people are here in Washington now, complaining about various taxes and asking for reductions. Just at the moment it is particularly confined to the excises. But there will be more and more coming and there are three or four committees of Congress who are making reports or will make reports. So far as the Treasury is concerned, we object to any reduction, any law, any change in the tax laws which will mean a substantial loss of revenue.

QUESTION. Would you favor, sir, the suspension entirely of the five year write-off, the so-called fast tax write-off?

SEC. HUMPHREY. I don't think it should be entirely eliminated. It is reduced now as you know to a very small amount and it is confined now by order to only, I think, 15 or 16 classifications, out of something over 200 previously, that apply directly to the defense effort.

Now, I think perhaps it is well to leave it for those few particular things that are directly and importantly and in a large degree strictly defense. Does that answer your question?

QUESTION. Yes, sir, if you give me a definition of defense. You use a very narrow definition, sir. You are not talking about any wide category of defense support?

SEC. HUMPHREY. That's right. I am talking about direct defense.

QUESTION. Like steel?

SEC. HUMPHREY. Not at all. Any industry like steel where a relatively small amount of the total production goes into direct defense and the great growth is in the normal economy, I am opposed to having any rapid amortization. . . . That does not apply necessarily to the consideration that is being given all along to the previous adjustments of depreciation and the proper depreciation schedules. We are talking about rapid amortization.

QUESTION. Mr. Secretary, on the receipts side what estimates are you making for calendar year 1957 on personal income and profits?

SEC. HUMPHREY. Well, we are estimating personal income for calendar 1956 at $325.5 billion. I don't know why I put in .5; it came out that way. That is the estimate for last calendar year's personal income and I will give you the figure for the next calendar year personal income, and those are the figures on which we base the estimates of income with respect to fiscal years. Last year it is $325.5 billion. We are estimating $340 billion for calendar 1957.

Corporate profits have been estimated at $43 billion for calendar 1956 and $44 billion for calendar 1957.

QUESTION. Mr. Humphrey, a year ago with reference to depletion allowances on oil, you said "Proper depletion is a very proper deduction and a very desirable one from the whole point of our economy." Do you regard, sir, the rate of 27½ per cent in oil a proper rate?

SEC. HUMPHREY. I don't know whether it is proper or not. That figure was arrived at after long hearings and a great deal of discussion on the subject and all sorts of evidence and proof and the Congress finally picked out that figure. That was done before we came here. . . . In the way the thing has worked out, our reserves of oil, our new development of oil in this country, which is continually more expensive, both searching for it and getting it after it is discovered, has just about kept pace over the past half dozen years or more with the consumption so that from a practical point of view it looks as though this thing was about working out practically. . . .

QUESTION. You commented in the past on the size of the budget surplus. You thought that would properly be necessary before you could consider a tax cut, and I think one time the figure of $2 billion was mentioned—$2 to $3 billion.

SEC. HUMPHREY. I said I thought two was too small. There is no magic in that at all. We are figuring on getting about $37 to $38 billion from individual taxpayers, you know. If you talk about a 10 per cent cut in individual taxes that is $4 billion. There is no magic in it. There would be no cut in corporate taxes in that amount. It all depends on what you are going to do. I think about all you can say is, as to the amount required before you make a general tax revision, is that you should have enough money to make a reasonable, respectable tax reduction. I don't think you would want to make a one per cent tax reduction and get all the confusion that would follow.

QUESTION. Would you say at the present income levels that something like $3 billion would be a minimum?

SEC. HUMPHREY. $3 to $5 billion.

QUESTION. Mr. Secretary, the tone of what you are saying here today might be taken as encouragement for Congress to go ahead and cut this budget quite a lot. Do you want to encourage that sentiment or not?

SEC. HUMPHREY. Dick, that is a hard question to answer. If the Congress in further study, after hearing the expressions of the Executive Department on what they believe it is necessary to do, if the Congress can find ways to cut, and still do a proper job with respect to our security and with respect to the proper services to the public, I would be very glad to see it. It is possible there are some things we still are doing that were necessary some years ago that we are still continuing that we might find ways of eliminating.

I think that in all of these things we don't want to stand still, we want to go ahead and continue to do new things and continue to meet changing conditions.

On the other hand, I think we have to be very selective and I think that you just can't do everything. As a matter of fact it isn't a bit different than it is in your own home. You can't have everything you want and what you want to do is to pick out the things that the present situation demands the most and then in order to be able to afford them you have to eliminate some of the things that maybe you did before that now you can get along without.

QUESTION. That would be a pretty good political story, wouldn't it, Mr. Secretary, if a Democratic Congress cut a Republican President's budget?

SEC. HUMPHREY. To be perfectly frank I am only thinking of the good of the country. I am not thinking of the political angle—what we want is to have a good country and that is what I am interested in.

QUESTION. Could you tell us a little something about why this strong call for economy comes from you rather than from the President himself and the budget? Has this been a result of consultation? Is this your view or are you speaking for the Administration or the President?

SEC. HUMPHREY. I am speaking for the Treasury Department largely. We are responsible for the federal finances. I am trying to give as good a picture as I can of what is required for what I believe is the strongest financial position for this country. Referring to the previous question I am thinking of ourselves as citizens and not as voters. . . .

QUESTION. The tone of your statement this morning makes it sound as though you had pressed in the Administration's councils for some sharp spending cuts and would have been overruled. Would that be an unfair inference?

SEC. HUMPHREY. Yes, that is unfair. I have pressed for less spending right along. There is no division or difficulty in the Administration at all on this subject. This is a thing that we all are in accord on. This budget was made up with the very greatest care and a great deal of time spent on it and this is apparently the best we can do at the present time.

But I just believe that over 18 months we ought to keep doing better.

QUESTION. Are you for instance for that federal aid to education program? That is a $1.4 billion outlay. That is what you are talking about as far as taking money in the local communities and giving it right back.

SEC. HUMPHREY. I don't believe I can get into these specific things. If you do, you get into a maze of problems...

QUESTION. You put a lot of contingencies on your tax reduction but you do say a year hence we can give consideration. What information do you have that all of these conditions you laid down in the matter will be met in the next year?

SEC. HUMPHREY. I say if you do it in the year then you can give it consideration.

QUESTION. Does it mean anything?

SEC. HUMPHREY. I don't know. We did it once before. We made some very substantial reductions once before....We ought to set our sights for that and ought to try to accomplish it. If we do accomplish it, then we are in a position for a tax cut. If we make no progress whatever, then there is no tax cut next year.

QUESTION. No consideration?

SEC. HUMPHREY. How are you going to? You have nothing to pay it with.

QUESTION. You did it before without a balanced budget....

SEC. HUMPHREY. It was right on the line and coming down. I have said always that you don't have to wait until you have the money in your hand; you have to have your trend of expenditures going down and be able to estimate ahead to see that it's coming down, and have some real firm basis for seeing that it is coming; the last time we did have a firm basis because it came true.

QUESTION. Aren't you really paying now for the tax cut you gave then?

SEC. HUMPHREY. No. Why would you say that?

QUESTION. Well, your budget is going up.

SEC. HUMPHREY. But we balanced the budget on the last tax cut. The budget was balanced right the following year after the last tax cut.

QUESTION. But you emptied the pipelines on defense.

SEC. HUMPHREY. No, we didn't do anything on the pipelines on defense.

QUESTION. Yes, you did. They testified they did. . . . Has not the tax cut been offset by taking more money away from the taxpayers the succeeding three years?

SEC. HUMPHREY. I don't think you can offset it. We have taken more money out of more taxpayers who had bigger incomes. If the tax cut had not been made, we would have taken still more money out of them. We have taken less out of every taxpayer during these three years than we would have taken if it hadn't been for the tax cut. . . .

QUESTION. Mr. Secretary, you say that a tax reduction must be conditioned upon the continuation of our present prosperity. Does that mean that the Administration will not cut taxes so that it can add to purchasing power to offset a recession or to prevent a threatened recession?

SEC. HUMPHREY. I will contest a tax cut out of deficits as long as I am able. I will not approve, myself, of a tax cut out of deficit. I think it would start a downward spiral that would be serious. I don't believe in this idea that you can cut taxes out of deficits, and then build up from that.

QUESTION. Then you don't believe in compensatory spending?

SEC. HUMPHREY. What do you mean by that?

QUESTION. Increasing the level of Government spending during a period in which business generally is declining and therefore, presumably tax receipts will be declining.

SEC. HUMPHREY. No, I don't think so, Joe. I don't think you can spend yourself rich. I think we went all through that for a good many years, and we kept spending and spending and spending, and we still didn't help our employment or help our total position.

QUESTION. Mr. Secretary, perhaps the answer is to put more of the Government's operations under trust funds like the highway program.

SEC. HUMPHREY. Well, I don't think that is necessarily so. The reason for the trust fund is, I think, a very good one.

QUESTION. Your budget would look better today if highway was in the budget.

SEC. HUMPHREY. That is right. Why fool the people? . . .

QUESTION. Mr. Secretary, would you resign if the Administration embarked upon the deficit program you have just described?

SEC. HUMPHREY. I think I would. . . .

QUESTION. In the increased spending in this budget, can you make any estimate as to how much is inflation and include in that inflation the increase in interest rate?

SEC. HUMPHREY. Well, that is pretty hard. You mean inflation for how long a period? . . . In the last four years the general change in the price level has been comparatively little. Even up to this minute, it is only two or three per cent. So I would think that up to date comparatively little is due to depreciation of the dollar. It has to be that. If the dollar has only, over the four years—the depreciation of the dollar is measured in your price levels of various commodities—and if all balanced out, it has only moved a cent or two or three in that area, it couldn't be anything different than that.

QUESTION. You don't regard the increase in interest rate as an inflationary factor?

SEC. HUMPHREY. Yes, I do, but the increase in interest rate is relatively small. . . .

QUESTION. Will the Eisenhower Administration put more pressure on Congress to eliminate the Post Office deficit than they have in the past?

SEC. HUMPHREY. They are going to put all they can. I hope it is more.

QUESTION. Could you tell us what is contemplated in that legislation—five cents for first class—

SEC. HUMPHREY. The detail of it, I can't. The objective is to make the Post Office a pay-as-you-go.

QUESTION. They didn't put much pressure on last time.

SEC. HUMPHREY. They thought they did. They worked awfully hard at it. I don't believe I would tell Art Summerfield that. . . .

QUESTION. Mr. Secretary, a few minutes ago you were asked a few questions about your own reactions to taxes and budget policy in the event that we faced a depression.

SEC. HUMPHREY. Let me interrupt to make perfectly plain that on small business, I am not opposed to help for small business, but I am opposed to that particular proposal this particular year.

QUESTION. What other ones would you be for this particular year?

SEC. HUMPHREY. I am opposed to any reduction for anybody in a way that substantially reduces our revenues. . . .

QUESTION. Which of those recommendations to give help to small business with a minimum loss of revenue could be approved by the Treasury?

SEC. HUMPHREY. There is one recommendation that costs very little. There is another that costs $20 million and another that costs $30 to $40 million.

If the Congress is going to adopt one and only one tax cut for anybody, and they pick out a $20 or $30 million item, I can say for these proposals that the committee has given them very good and careful consideration, that they are good proposals, and that they are worthy of consideration and worthy of help, and if they are only going to give one of $20 or $30 million or something of that kind, I would be glad to see them have some one of these. . . .

I think we all want—and you all want—to think as citizens. Now, what goes on is this: Our tax laws are so very high, the amounts that we take from everybody are so very high, that there is hardly anybody in this country or any group in this country that cannot come down here and show that they are hurt by the taxes they pay. It hurts almost everybody in this country and almost any group can come in and make an awfully good case for tax relief. What has been going on—and it still goes on—is this—and it is perfectly natural that it should.

Groups come down here and make a showing that they are badly hurt by these taxes and they ask for tax relief and, if that group is sufficiently powerful and has a sufficiently powerful backing and makes a sufficient effort, the Congress has given them some consideration. From a little tax law this thick, we have one that is as thick as this, because all sorts of gadgets and relief of various kinds have been granted to various sets of people instead of having overall relief granted.

Of course, there are a few strictly unfair things that creep into the law occasionally that need to be straightened out, but if we can stop making all these little adjustments all around, except the very unfair ones, and save our money until we can make a reduction all down the line, everybody gets the benefit of that, and the pressure on everybody is taken off. And I believe that instead of this group and this group and this group, each one being favored here and there all over the place, what we need in America is to have this whole tax structure come down, and when our whole tax structure comes down, everybody will be better off....

If you take the opposite side of that and if you go on just giving little groups here and there and everywhere special consideration and bringing them down, the first thing you know, you are going to have to raise the rates on the poor fellows who are left, and they are going to have to pay higher rates, because we have to have so many dollars to run the business with.

Every time you give a special group some relief, you are just putting that much burden on everybody else, and I think it is high time we quit burdening everybody else for special people and we should try to get everybody down all at one time....

QUESTION. Just how do you do it, sir?

SEC. HUMPHREY. It all depends on what is the matter.

QUESTION. Would you let them starve?

SEC. HUMPHREY. No, I wouldn't let them starve, no, sir. Or sell apples on the corner.

QUESTION. Suppose there was a decline, a considerable decline in plant and equipment expenditures of corporations, would you not advocate a speed-up, let us say, in Government expenditures on construction, in order to countervail that?

SEC. HUMPHREY. I don't think so, no. Of course, you would have to know where it was and why it was, and all that. I think you just can't sit and speculate without knowing all the conditions. I will put it this way; we didn't do it the last time, did we? Pressure was brought on us to do it. We didn't do it, and it worked....

QUESTION. Mr. Secretary, Senator Russell said yesterday he would not consent to grants for Middle East economic aid. Would you consent to an economic program in the Middle East that created a deficit?

SEC. HUMPHREY. That is a very difficult and hypothetical question. I myself really do not know. Our whole program, as you know, is under consideration by Members of Congress, and the committees, and all I think I am going to say is that I am going to be extremely interested to see what the recommendations are and how they work out. There are a good many things that we have done in the past that I personally do not approve of and that I hope will be terminated.

On the other hand, I would certainly not urge the complete elimination of any activity of that kind.

QUESTION. Mr. Secretary, isn't nearly all the talk here today about cutting spending and cutting taxes largely academic, as long as the world situation remains what it is? ... I find that the lion's share of the increased expenditures, $2.6 billion of it, is for mutual security and defense. Is there any hope anywhere in the world situation that you can do any cutting in defense spending in the next few years?

SEC. HUMPHREY. I think there is; yes. I do. I think there is some hope you can reduce expenditures all along the line. I would certainly deplore the day that we thought we couldn't ever reduce expenditures of this terrific amount, the terrific tax take we are taking out of this country. If we don't over a long period of time, I will predict that you will have a depression that will curl your hair, because we are just taking too much money out of this economy that we need to make the jobs that you have to have as time goes on.

QUESTION. Could we have the stenotypist read that back to us? That is a good quote.

QUESTION. The President says he will make recommendations on the waiver clause in the British loan. Are you in favor of postponement as against cancellation of the interest payment due on December 31?

SEC. HUMPHREY. I am in favor of an adjustment in that document that will carry out the spirit of the document. I would feel just as I would if I had any business arrangement with anybody, that conditions had changed so that some of the wording was no longer applicable. The spirit is perfectly plain that some relief should be available....

QUESTION. Would the spirit include paying the interest some day, if not now, rather than cancelling it?

SEC. HUMPHREY. There are a lot of ways to work it out, and we haven't come to an agreement as to how it should be done. The general spirit of it should be carried out....

..... A DEPRESSION THAT
WILL CURL YOUR HAIR.
— SEC. HUMPHREY

"Whose hair, George?"

Fitzpatrick in
*The St. Louis
Post-Dispatch,*
1957

✍ Secretary Humphrey's most famous of all press conferences (and his longest)—all because of a colorful phrase, "...a depression that will curl your hair..." which he uttered in the last minute and a half of an hour-long session with more than 100 news men as to his thoughts in connection with the Administration's new budget.

The phrase was immediately garbled in popular communication, which excitement frequently causes to happen. The first impression the public got was that the Secretary of the Treasury was foreseeing an eventual depression of major proportions. Quoted not in its exact context, the phrase set cartoonists and editorial writers to ringing the alarm bells for several days, in the conviction that (1) Secretary Humphrey had predicted depression as the end result of big Government spending, or (2) depression as result of the collapse of business under the current tax burden.

Actually as is reported in exactness here, the Secretary was conjuring up a record depression as the classic fate of a Republic which resigned itself to spending so much of its income permanently on massive defense outlays—the resignation of the people to such permanent burden being the psychological key to the remark.

It was several days before the first commentator, David Lawrence, set the record of the remark exactly in print; and a number of newspapers and magazines followed in correcting the popular misapprehension. On the other hand, the grim tone of the remark was deliberate on Secretary Humphrey's part; he did not know, nor thought any one knew, at exactly what point an economic burden of great weight would cause general collapse, but he did know that mass acceptance of huge military and foreign aid subsidy as being "for good" would hasten the time.

The furor over the phrase robbed the press conference of attention to its prime importance of Secretary Humphrey's acceptance of the 1958–59 budget as "the best we can do now" without accepting that it should not be further studied for important spending reductions. He did not mince many words as to his qualms over the increase in the budget, after years in which decreases in Government spending had been made to prove the balance of the budget a possible performance.

"I blame everybody, including myself"

Remarks by Secretary Humphrey on Meet the Press
television panel in Washington. Ned Brooks,
moderator; Marquis Childs, St. Louis Post-Dispatch;
Edwin Dale, The New York Times; Martin Hayden,
Detroit News; and Richard Wilson, Cowles Publications.

January 27, 1957

MR. BROOKS. And welcome once again to Meet the Press. Our guest is the Secretary of the Treasury, Mr. George Humphrey. His concern over the rising cost of government has developed into one of the big news stories here in Washington. In discussing the new $72 billion federal budget Secretary Humphrey used a phrase that has been widely quoted. He said unless a way is found to reduce the spending in the future we will have a depression that will "make your hair curl." Mr. Humphrey's strongly worded warning against big spending provided the central theme for President Eisenhower's recent news conference. Since the beginning of the Eisenhower Administration, Mr. Humphrey has been one of the President's closest advisers. . . . Mr. Lawrence

Spivak is not with us today; he will be back next week.—Now Mr. Secretary, if you're ready, we'll start the questions with Mr. Childs.

MR. CHILDS. Mr. Secretary, the President said at his press conference that he would use any Constitutional means to cure a depression, whereas, you said that you would resign, probably, if there were a tax cut in the face of deficit spending. Doesn't this open up a pretty wide difference between you and the President?

SEC. HUMPHREY. No, I don't think so, Mr. Childs. I think that we both have the same objective. We both would do anything that we thought would be effective to prevent a depression. The only question is what and when various things are effective.

MR. CHILDS. Do you reject the theory of so many of the professional economists that you must use government spending when business falls off? Do you think that's an unsound theory?

SEC. HUMPHREY. It all depends upon what happens to income at the same time. I think that the time, the real time, to prevent a depression is before it starts. The old adage of "an ounce of prevention is worth a pound of cure" is a very good thing to remember.

MR. CHILDS. Would it be fair to say that your disagreement is with the Council of Economic Advisers, and perhaps with Gabriel Hauge, the President's economic right hand in the White House, because they suggest, or at least the President suggested in his economic report, that there would have to be very flexible policies in relation to economy?

SEC. HUMPHREY. I don't think that necessarily there's any disagreement anywhere. Flexible policies can be used, but, as I say, the various things that you would and might do should be used at various times. I think when you attempt to answer hypothetical questions and haven't all the facts before you it's very difficult to pick out the timing of when one method would be appropriate or another would be appropriate.

MR. CHILDS. But, you don't anticipate this hair-curling depression anyway, do you?

SEC. HUMPHREY. I don't anticipate it, and I think, Mr. Childs, there's no reason we should have it if we do the proper things as we go along. My warning was a warning that things might happen at some future time, if we didn't do the things that we should do as we go along—the principal one of which is to reduce our spending at the present time.

MR. HAYDEN. The Eisenhower Administration has now been in for four years. Now of course you coupled your hair-curling expression with the other comment that you thought this record peacetime budget was probably the best that could be conceived at this time. Well, after the four years you've been working at it, what is going to happen next year and the year after that is going to give you a chance to make a material reduction?

SEC. HUMPHREY. I think and I hope that maybe it will happen this year. My whole point on this thing is this: That we have worked hard for several months to prepare a budget, which is, the consensus says, as good an estimate . . . as we can now make of what we propose to do over the following 18 months. Now the thing I am urging is that we do not just accept that estimate and say, That's all over, we'll just go ahead and spend that amount and do no further work on it. The thing I'm urging and the thing I'm trying to impress on people is the necessity of working all of that 18 months, the ensuing 18 months, days, nights, holidays, and Sundays, to reduce those expenditures as we go along.

I can't see why we shouldn't make some progress in doing it. It doesn't seem to me that we need necessarily just to say we accept those estimates and forget it. I think we ought to work at it, and I believe that if we work intelligently and hard enough we will make some progress and that there should be some room to make some reductions.

MR. HAYDEN. Mr. Secretary, you've been working hard for four years and I'm sure intelligently, but, thinking back into history, the business community, of which you were then a member, used to say in Franklin Roosevelt's day that he was spending us to ruin. I looked up the figures and in 1941, the last year before the war, even though defense was on, Roosevelt's Administration was taking $59.28 in taxes per citizen. The Eisenhower Administration last year took $461.64; that's getting way beyond the Roosevelt ruin. How do you tie it together?

SEC. HUMPHREY. You have a great many factors that happened in between, you see. In the first place, your dollar is only half as much as it was then. In the last end of the Truman Administration, the dollar depreciated very, very rapidly, as you'll remember. That accounts for a good deal of it. Another important point is that, since that time, you've had a very great increase in your population, and an increase in productivity, and our total annual product is much greater now than it was then. Now all of those things have to be taken into consideration in comparing the two periods.

MR. WILSON. I believe when you first came into office you felt quite certain that it would be possible to reduce federal spending to about $60 billion a year.

SEC. HUMPHREY. That's what I hoped.

MR. WILSON. Now it's up to $72 billion and probably actually nearer $100 billion and that's at least 20 per cent higher than when you came into office. What happened to all those dreams about a so-called sound economy?

SEC. HUMPHREY. I don't know where you get your 20 per cent. The budget we found when we came here exceeded $70 billion; now we've cut that budget in a period of about 18 months by nearly $10 billion. The budget has crept back on us; various new devices, various new things have arisen to increase expenditures pretty well along the line. We haven't felt that sufficient cuts could be made, we haven't seen—been able to work out—places where sufficient cuts could be made to offset those increases as we've gone in. I have the hope, Mr. Wilson—I believe that we are spending too much money; I believe we're taking too much out of this economy over a long period of time. I'm not concerned, as I said to Mr. Childs, about a depression, an immediate depression; that isn't the point. The point is that if we continue to take as much money out of this economy as we have been taking, as we are now taking, I don't believe we are going to have the capital to supply the necessary tools, the machinery, and all of the things that are required to make the jobs that we need for our growing population.

MR. WILSON. Yes, sir, but the other day you placed your main emphasis, in a statement you issued, on a reduction in individual income taxes.

SEC. HUMPHREY. If we can reduce taxes, yes.

MR. WILSON. The accumulation of capital is impeded by high corporate taxes; is that right?

SEC. HUMPHREY. By high corporate taxes and by high individual taxes.

MR. WILSON. Why by high individual taxes?

SEC. HUMPHREY. Well, the individuals have less money to save and invest—the great amount of our investment that's used to buy tools;

to make plants; to provide transportation; to do all the things that are required; to provide the jobs for our increasing population, young men and women. There are a million and a half of them a year almost coming in and wanting new jobs; that means a lot of new expenditure and new capital. Most of that capital comes from the savings of the people.

Mr. Wilson. You said you wanted to reduce taxes a year hence, as I recall.

Sec. Humphrey. That's what I hoped. If we could make a sufficient reduction now in the expenditures, then we would be in a position to reduce taxes a year from now.

Mr. Wilson I thought your main concern was inflation. Wouldn't reducing taxes be inflationary?

Sec. Humphrey. I think reducing our expenditures is the greatest brake on inflation we could possibly have, and the reason I think it is simply this: If we reduce expenditures, it means that the Government—and I'm talking about Government expenditures—the Government will employ less people and will buy fewer goods. If the Government buys fewer goods and if it employs less people, it means that those people are released to make more goods for things that the people can buy. In other words, we will release people from making guns, and planes, and various things, and doing various things, in the Government that the people can't buy, to go into industry and make things that the people can buy.

Now, as more goods are available, you will stabilize your prices. The greatest thing that can happen to the stabilization of prices and of costs of goods is to have more people working at it to make more goods, to have more goods available. That relieves the pressure on prices, and that will prevent inflation.

Mr. Dale. I'd like to return for a moment, Mr. Secretary, to this possible recession or depression problem. First, would you concede that there ever could be a time when deliberate budget deficits would be a good weapon to fight a depression with?

Sec. Humphrey. It's very hard to say, to answer a hypothetical question like that and have it accurate. I can say this: I think it is hard for me to see just the circumstances that would prevail when you'd want to do that. Now this is the reason, Mr. Dale: The Government is spending about one dollar when at the same time the people of this country are spending eight or ten dollars. Now when you're in a declining volume of business, when you're in what we refer to as a depression, the real cause of that is lack of confidence in the people; the people become fearful. They do not buy; they curtail their own expenditures. The thing that will end that is to restore confidence. Now, if the Government in such a situation does something that will injure confidence, it will just compound the difficulties. What the Government must do is do something that will restore confidence. If the Government by increasing its deficit by one dollar so scares people that the people withdraw from some of their expansion, they can shut off eight or ten dollars for every dollar that the Government spends. I think that in most cases you find that confidence would be more shaken by a deliberate big deficit spending than you would by having the Government do more constructive things and restore confidence so that the people themselves would begin to spend.

MR. DALE. Then further on, to your prediction of a depression that would curl your hair if the tax burden on the people could not be reduced at some time: How do you account for the fact that, with the given level of high taxes, last year saw an all time record by a big margin in capital investment and new creation of jobs in the face of present taxes?

SEC. HUMPHREY. I personally think that you have to take things over a little period of time.

MR. DALE. They've been rising every year now for three or four.

SEC. HUMPHREY. Well, what happened? Let's just go back and review this for a minute. We came in, and we had a budget of some $70-odd billion, and there was a great feeling throughout the country that we were spending too much money. We, by various means and a lot of hard work—the same kind of hard work I want to see us indulge in again—cut that budget and we reduced those expenditures by about $10 billion. We then gave a tax cut, a $7 billion tax cut, which was the biggest tax cut in history. The combination of what we did and the feeling that the people got restored a confidence in the people, built a confidence in the people, and we've been going on up on that confidence ever since.

MR. BROOKS. Mr. Secretary, you mentioned a moment ago the rising number of employes in the Government. A lot of people seem to be able to understand why the cost of goods has gone up but they find it harder to understand why the Government has to keep adding to its payroll and number of employes. Could you explain that?

SEC. HUMPHREY. I find it pretty hard to understand myself. Of course there's always the alibi that we have a growing population and that with a growing population we have to render greater service; we must continually go up. But the thing that makes America is that we get more production per man, than we do more per hour per man, all of the time, and if we can do that in industry I don't know why we can't and shouldn't do so in government.

MR. BROOKS. We have about 2.5 million employes or somewhere around that number; would you care to suggest any number you think might be cut off that 2.5 million?

SEC. HUMPHREY. I can't specifically go through the Government and state to you just where I think people should be cut off. I will tell you this: So far as the Treasury is concerned, we have teams that are out studying every function that we have; we are finding places every day where we're reducing forces and where we're making progress, and we're going to make some reduction in the Treasury budget.

MR. CHILDS. I noticed in the papers today that you proposed that all foreign economic aid should be on the basis of repayable loans. Wouldn't that keep economic aid away from the countries of south-eastern Asia where it is most needed for building their economies and resisting communism?

SEC. HUMPHREY. You know, I'm often quite interested to read in the paper what I do think. Sometimes it's quite a novel experience. This particular thing you refer to is this: When the Fairless Committee was appointed to study the foreign aid situation,—as you recall, we have the Fairless Committee and Congressional committees and all— I was the first witness to testify before that committee, and they rather experimented with me. When I finished testifying, they asked me if I would just put my ideas in a letter and send it to the chairman. I did that, and the letter that I sent went to Mr. Fairless. Now that's my letter to Mr. Fairless. Mr. Fairless is the head of this committee that is studying the subject. The letter in some way, some part of the letter, leaked. The whole letter has not been published, and until Mr. Fairless releases the letter, I don't think that I want to discuss it. I don't think it's proper for me to do so.

Mr. Childs. You wouldn't care to say how you feel about repayable loans in terms of economic aid?

Sec. Humphrey. I will just say I read the piece in the paper with great interest, and it isn't accurate.

Mr. Hayden. Getting back to the inflation question, Mr. Secretary, both you and the President have more or less indirectly laid it on business and labor as the ones who must now take the ball on controlling inflation, calling on them to moderate their pay demands in the case of the unions and to minimize their profits, you might say, in case of business. Now isn't it basic in our system that business is entitled to the profits that the market will provide and that labor is entitled to anything it can negotiate in fair negotiation with management?

Sec. Humphrey. Over a long-term period. I don't think that anyone feels that it's good business—I don't think any business feels that it's good business—to just look at things from a short-run point of view. You try to look at things over a long period and to run your business for the best interests over that long period. Now I don't think that it is up to just management and labor; I think that this involves everybody. One of the reasons I'm glad to be on this program today is because I think that all the public in America is interested in this thing. I think it's greatly to their advantage to try to help us to reduce these expenditures, and the public can be of great assistance in this matter. These things, these requests for expenditures, all arise with the public in the first place. It's public pressure for this service or that service, or this help or that help, that starts these things. That has a reaction on the Congress, because the public is demanding things, and the Congress goes forward with programs and plans that cost money. The Executive can't do it all; the Congress can't do it all; the public can't do it all. But all together, if we all turn in and if we all desire to get these expenses down, I think we can make some progress doing so. I think we want to start with the public and then go to the Congress and go to the Executive and have the Executive carry it through.

Mr. Wilson. Well, Mr. Secretary, that's very persuasive, what you just said, but aren't you actually just about making a one-man campaign on this subject? I've heard it said in a Cabinet meeting the other day there was a showing of hands on an indication of what the sentiment was and that you and the President were the only ones who thought this budget was too high. Is that about right?

SEC. HUMPHREY. I don't recall that incident; that's another one of those interesting things that you hear about afterwards. I will say this, contrary to the newspaper stories that I've read that the President and I are at odds on this matter, the President—I've never seen any man work harder or more intently to reduce this budget, to bring this budget into proper shape than the President himself—the President and I are just as much in accord as we can possibly be in trying to do this thing that we think is for the benefit of all of the American people, if it can be accomplished.

MR. WILSON. You've appeared before the House Appropriations Committee, and you've been talking on this line for several weeks; what is the outlook for actually bringing this figure down within a more reasonable range?

SEC. HUMPHREY. I think it's a hard job. I don't expect any miracles. I don't believe you can have any miracles, but if you don't try, I'm sure you won't get it done. You say that most people are in favor of this big spending; I don't think so. I think when you go out through the country you'll find hundreds and hundreds and hundreds of people who are as concerned as I am about this, and those are the people I want to incite into action and get them to help in their communities to lessen the pressures on the Congress to do things that cost money.

MR. WILSON. I was only referring to people in the Administration when I said that most people in the Administration appeared to be in favor of this.

SEC. HUMPHREY. I think if you took the Cabinet and went right straight through you would find almost unanimous belief that we have to do more than we have done, that we have to improve our situation in reducing expenditures.

MR. WILSON. Are you getting a big public response? Are a lot of people coming in to support you on this?

SEC. HUMPHREY. There is a large public response.

MR. DALE. Mr. Secretary, you blame the public for this and the pressures arising. Don't you blame the Russians?

SEC. HUMPHREY. . . . I can hardly say I blame the Russians. The fact that the Russians are there—

MR. DALE. A threat.

SEC. HUMPHREY. And are a threat and a continuing and a great threat is, of course, one of the big elements in this.

MR. DALE. You have spoken frequently about working every day to reduce this between now and the 18 months when it's all over with, but the last three years, if I'm not mistaken, turned out to be higher, not lower, than the original figure. If that is not the case, at least two of the three.

SEC. HUMPHREY. I think that is more accurate. I think in two of three that is correct. We just didn't do as well as I think we should, that's all; and because we haven't done as well, it's no reason we shouldn't try and try our best and keep trying to do better.

MR. HAYDEN. Mr. Secretary, as a businessman four or five years ago you used to be a very bitter critic of Government financial officers. After four years, have you got a little more sympathy for your predecessors?

SEC. HUMPHREY. I think I've seen a lot of things that I hadn't seen before.

MR. WILSON. Mr. Secretary, if this—

SEC. HUMPHREY. Just to finish your question, I'm critical of myself. I don't blame just the public. I don't blame just the Congress. I blame everybody, including myself. I think we all ought to do a better job.

"We have not been too successful"

*Cross-examination of Secretary Humphrey
(in part) before the Joint Economic Committee.
Representative Wright Patman of Texas, chairman.*

February 4, 1957

SEC. HUMPHREY. . . . Whether we suffer a disastrous inflation depends on the self-restraint, courage and the determination of the people themselves. . . . We ought to be able to reduce Government spending. We have not been too successful. . . . If the pressures are to be continually for more and more spending, the Congress responds, and the Executive must respond, too. . . .

SENATOR RALPH FLANDERS (Vermont).... Since you advocate less Government spending in times of inflation, would you then advocate an increase in federal expenditures during periods of deflation?

SEC. HUMPHREY. I think I would. I would if such increases were kept in reasonable bounds; as long as they did not injure the confidence of the public, the business population. ...

REP. WILBUR D. MILLS (Arkansas). In what ways, as it occurs to you, could we cut taxes and still provide enough revenues to meet fiscal 1957–58 and the expected 1958–59 spending figures?

SEC. HUMPHREY. The only way would be by an increase in income rapid enough. Even if today's good times continue, I think we will have to reduce Government spending, along with increased income to pay for any tax cut. ... I firmly believe—I can't prove it, only time will tell—that if we retain our present high tax rates over a sufficiently long period of time we won't be able to maintain the activities necessary to provide jobs for our people. ...

REP. MILLS. As fast as we gain revenues from increased business activities, the spending goes up, too.

SEC. HUMPHREY. That's exactly what disturbs me. ... If the Government had held expenses level over the past three years, we would have money for tax reductions, with the increase in our receipts. But that may be too late now, and holding expenses to the level will not be enough. ... To warrant any tax cut, spending will have to be reduced. ... You would need a surplus of at least $3 billion, probably nearer $5 billion, to give you the margin for any tax reduction. ...

There are no recommendations for general or structural revisions in tax policies at this time. As you know, a sub-committee of the Ways & Means Committee is now at work considering various ways of making minor technical improvements in the tax law; we hope these changes can be made in the near future because they will improve the law technically and remove some loopholes. But they will have no significant revenue effects; they are not major changes. ...

My chief concern has been to avoid any new special relief provisions for any particular group of taxpayers. They would not only further complicate an already complex law, but they might involve finally so much revenue loss as to postpone indefinitely the time when it will be possible to have general relief for all taxpayers. ...

THE CHAIRMAN. We are interested to know whether the Treasury has any recommendations on fiscal or monetary policy if during this year we have a decrease of the inflationary pressures. . . .

SEC. HUMPHREY. Well, I don't like to anticipate what any agency has to do in hypothetical circumstances. Whenever inflationary pressures do abate, there will of course be an easing in the monetary situation. . . . Any tightness in the monetary situation during an inflationary period arises because of an excess of demand for funds over the supply of savings. A reduction in inflationary pressures will operate in the direction of restoring the balance, with a consequent monetary easing. . . . The pressures are on prices, even with the restraints that can be imposed. Right now, the American economy is very closely balanced; there are certain things that are developing—certain places where an adjustment is taking place. That is a good way to have it. . . . I don't think the level of interest rates unduly high; I think 3 per cent money is pretty reasonably priced money. . . .

THE CHAIRMAN. Don't you think the way the debt in this country is rapidly climbing is alarming? . . .

SEC. HUMPHREY. No, that doesn't frighten me so much, but I do think our debts have been going up pretty high and pretty fast.

THE CHAIRMAN. I should of course ask you whether it isn't true that debt is necessary to expansion, in the capitalist system.

SEC. HUMPHREY. It's desirable, naturally, to have some debts. But it's undesirable to have too many.

Looking to a third balanced budget

Statement by Secretary Humphrey before the House Ways & Means Committee.

February 6, 1957

. . . This legislation would extend for one year the existing excise rates on liquor, tobacco and automobiles and the tax rate on corporate income. If this legislation were not adopted, the tax rates would drop on April 1.

The full year effect of the one-year rate extensions would be slightly more than $3 billion. $2.2 billion of this comes from the corporation income tax; $231 million from various alcohol taxes; $185 million from the tax on cigarettes; and $436 million from the tax on automobiles and automobile parts and accessories.

Of the total of more than $3 billion, we estimate that $186 million will be collected in the current fiscal year; $2 billion, $166 million in the fiscal year 1958; and virtually all of the rest in the fiscal year 1959.

The President made his recommendation for these rate extensions in his Budget Message.

The estimated surplus for the fiscal year 1958 is less than the revenue which will be received during that year from the legislation which is now before you. Therefore, if these rates are not extended, we would have a deficit in 1958. After we have two years of balanced budgets as a result of the combined hard work of the Congress and the Administration, it would be inexcusable to slip back into deficit financing for next year. We must have the revenue that a continuation of existing tax rates would provide.

As I have said many times, the present rates are too high and will in the long run seriously hamper our economic growth. I believe that the most important tax change that could be made to promote steady economic development would be to reduce the rates for all taxpayers when our fiscal situation permits. My chief concern now is to avoid any new special relief provisions for particular groups of taxpayers. Such relief provisions not only would complicate a law that is already too complicated, but they also, in the aggregate, can involve so much revenue loss as to postpone indefinitely the time when it will be possible to have general relief for all taxpayers. . . .

No "threat of dangerous inflation—now"

Taped interview with Secretary Humphrey in
U. S. News & World Report.

February 8, 1957

QUESTION. Mr. Humphrey, now that you've been in Government several years—and you've been in business a good many years—have you any thoughts as to how the Government keeps its finances compared to how a private businessman keeps them? After all, the businessman seems to think he has to have a surplus and pay debts, but the Government doesn't, and the average fellow wonders how Uncle Sam—

SEC. HUMPHREY. Wait a minute, wait a minute. Don't say that. Don't say the Government doesn't. There are people who think the Government doesn't, but that isn't the fact.

This Government believes—and the President believes it very strongly—that we do have to keep our financial house in order and that we do have to make some payment on our debts as well as work toward getting our taxes down.

QUESTION. If you were running the Federal Government as a private business, what would you do that you don't do now?

SEC. HUMPHREY. The problem in the Government is the length of time that it takes to get things done and the number of people you have to see, and convince. What it means is that a government is a series of compromises. Business is certainly very, very much less a compromise—there is some, but very much less. . . .

QUESTION. If the object is to take in more money than you spend, or as much, then carry that parallel further—has the Government an obligation to spend the money wisely?

SEC. HUMPHREY. I should say it has.

QUESTION. Why does it spend money on things which private business would never spend it for?

SEC. HUMPHREY. That isn't quite a right parallel. The functions of a government are not limited to the same functions as business. On the other hand, the other side of your coin is that I think the Government should be just as careful to get its money's worth in the spending of its money as a business should.

Now, it may spend money for things a business wouldn't spend money for—properly—there are a lot of functions that a business doesn't properly have. But the way it should do it—it should get its money's worth in exactly the same way, and there should be no more laxity in the way a government handles its affairs than there is in the way a business does.

Your problem is always to do the best job for the most people. Now, the difficulty is to know whether it's really for the most people or whether an organized minority through political pressures is securing special advantages for itself.

QUESTION. And you can't charge always for your services the way a business can. You charge through taxes, but not for a particular service?

SEC. HUMPHREY. That's right. But there are some things that can pay for themselves, and I think that we can and should go somewhat further in "user" taxes than we do. But, again, it's more difficult because somehow people have the idea that there's a great well here that you can get money out of that costs nobody anything. . . .

QUESTION. Can't Government make money by creating debt?

SEC. HUMPHREY. No, only to this extent: Money is a facility to aid in the total exchange of services and goods. That's all. We live in barter age; business is a barter. But you do it with little piece of paper called money because it's easier. Instead of having to say that you'll work for a television company for a month in order to have a new television set, you work at your regular job for one month and take a little slip of paper and give it to the television company. The Government through sound financial policies can help make these slips of paper a stable standard to measure your work against these expenditures.

QUESTION. But the Government can make those little slips of paper, which an individual can't—

SEC. HUMPHREY. The Government can also destroy them. Printing-press money which loses its value doesn't do the job.

QUESTION. But a lot of people feel it can, and that causes inflation at times, doesn't it?

SEC. HUMPHREY. It's one of the pressures. They feel that all you have to do is turn up the printing presses and you have more money, but you can't do that. You can have any standard you want. You can have ten little pieces of paper that represent your work and that represent a television set or you can have a thousand of them. But actually what you've got are just little pieces of paper of whatever number that represent the value of your work as compared to the value of a television set. If you keep decreasing the value of the money it is finally disastrous.

QUESTION. Looking into the future—you've been in Washington now long enough to feel these different factors—do you think we're going to survive from an economic viewpoint in the next several years in America?

SEC. HUMPHREY. Oh, certainly.

QUESTION. Do you think we're going to be fiscally sound?

SEC. HUMPHREY. I think we ought to be. There's no reason why we shouldn't that I know of.

QUESTION. Do you see any dangers on the horizon?

SEC. HUMPHREY. Yes. There's the danger from outside. A perfectly terrific instrument of death has been developed within a very short period of time, just in the early development stages, probably, and only known over a very limited period of time, and it's shared or it's in the hands of two great groups of people with different ideologies. That poses a threat.

Our greatest periods of peace have been when there was a balance of power in the world, so that nations were a little cautious before they took a final step, not knowing just exactly where the real balance or the real power was. There may be a better balance if there are several rather than if there are only two.

QUESTION. Does that put a greater burden on us, as you see it?

SEC. HUMPHREY. It puts a different burden on us—a different kind of burden. And that's one of the reasons why I am extremely hopeful that they will make progress in Europe in the integration of Europe because there is the nucleus for a great power.

QUESTION. You're speaking of economic power, aren't you?

SEC. HUMPHREY. Economic—every kind. There are 250 or 300 million people living on the Continent outside the Iron Curtain. They live in a good climate, they have tremendous natural resources, they have a good country, they're intelligent, hard-working people.

QUESTION. Does that imply that we can be of help in stimulating and perhaps in actually assisting in such an objective financially?

SEC. HUMPHREY. If you're talking about another Marshall Plan or something of that kind, no. I don't think so.

QUESTION. How could it be done, then, financially?

SEC. HUMPHREY. Let's get right down to cases. I think we've rendered much help to them recently. We have helped Britain maintain her monetary unit, the pound. Half the currency that people do international business with in the world is the pound; half the world's foreign commerce is done in pounds—

QUESTION. More than dollars?

SEC. HUMPHREY. I would think that, possibly, total dollar transactions might be more in total value than total transactions in pounds because our own internal value of trade is so great. But outside the United States, pounds are used more than dollars in many places in the world.

We want a strong pound; we want a good pound because a good medium of exchange means good business.

QUESTION. Did we save the pound recently?

SEC. HUMPHREY. We helped to strengthen the pound, within the last couple of months. The economy of Western Europe has changed in the past few years—it's changing rapidly and going more and more all the time from a coal economy to an oil economy. No industrial economy can survive without cheap fuel. It's basic; cheap fuel is basic to any industrial economy.

Britain and Western Europe grew up on cheap coal. Their cheap coal is getting more expensive for various reasons. Right at their door is the greatest pool of cheap oil in the whole world, and the only thing that stands between them and it is transportation.

QUESTION. But won't transportation be threatened if the Russians get control of that area?

SEC. HUMPHREY. It's one of the great problems. I think that the Middle East is one of the most important spots in the world to the life of Western Europe.

QUESTION. Then do you think the new Eisenhower proposal comes at the right time?

SEC. HUMPHREY. I think it comes at exactly the right time, and I think it's absolutely essential. I think that it will help to provide the basis for restoring normal trade which will assure to the Arab countries their great markets and to Western Europe this necessary ingredient to their economic life.

QUESTION. We can't leave the Canal, then, under the control of a dictator?

SEC. HUMPHREY. Some mutually satisfactory arrangement must be worked out and there is good reason to think it will be. There is every reason on all sides to do so because it is advantageous to everyone to have it done.

QUESTION. Why is that?

SEC. HUMPHREY. The great market for this oil is in the Western world. To realize its value it must be moved to market. Satisfactory transportation is essential. This volume of business is just a matter of a comparatively few years. With this rapidity of growth, satisfactory transportation under normal conditions must be provided and the Canal is a desirable route. The more it can be used, the more profitable it can be. . . .

QUESTION. Mr. Hopkins, president of the General Dynamics Corporation, has the idea of a crash program for atomic energy in Western Europe as a substitute for the Suez Canal. Do you think this is a feasible idea?

SEC. HUMPHREY. I have to be pretty careful what I say about the possibilities of commercial atomic energy because the developments in it are so rapid that, unless you're right up to the minute, you hardly know. But I have never seen any program anywhere yet of really cheap power out of atomic energy. Now, maybe it will come.

I'm talking about atomic energy competing with really cheap power, which is cheap coal and oil. Up to date, it seems unlikely soon. But it may be, you see—it develops so rapidly.

QUESTION. Will capital aid be needed for the Middle East countries?

SEC. HUMPHREY. I think that we can help—and very properly help by various methods. I think we have a lot of institutions—and both public and private, that are in good position to help and have a lot of ways to help, and I think what we need in this world—more than any other thing—to develop the worldwide stability of government that welcomes investment of capital.

Now, there are not many places in the world where you can afford to invest money over a period of years and not fear that the investment will be made unattractive before many years are up. That isn't a very healthy atmosphere to attract investment....

QUESTION. You commented on our helping to save the pound. You might explain how—

SEC. HUMPHREY. Saving the pound is too broad a way to put it. We helped to stabilize it. When this situation was at its worst, the demands on the pound were mounting.

QUESTION. Like a run on a bank?

SEC. HUMPHREY. It was something like that.

Just what you have to do to correct it is to re-establish confidence. The way to do that is to let everyone know that the situation is sound and can meet any demands.

First thing the Export-Import Bank arranged a loan and the International Monetary Fund made credit available, and we said we would go in and ask Congress for a revision of the loan agreement, and so on. This all helped to re-establish confidence and a run was avoided.

QUESTION. Turning to the domestic picture, a great deal of the money is spent for armaments, which is not productive—destructive expenditure—

SEC. HUMPHREY. Pretty nearly all of armament is nonproductive.

QUESTION. And that creates an imbalance; but how does that affect the cost of living?

SEC. HUMPHREY. It is perfectly simple. We're spending for national security about, let's call it nearly $50 billion, for round figures. It isn't quite that, but it's approaching it.

Now, that includes all of our security items. We have about a $400 billion gross economy. Fifty billion dollars is about an eighth of that. That means—very roughly—that about one man in eight is working on security, and seven men are working on production of peacetime goods.

Now, what's going on is that seven men, then, are producing goods for living in America and eight men are getting payroll checks, so there are eight buyers for seven pieces of goods, and you just can't help but have a pressure on prices. That's a crude illustration, and omits some factors like taxes, and so on, yet it illustrates the point. What seven people make, eight people want to buy and you can't help but have pressure on prices when you have eight buyers for the production of seven people.

QUESTION. What's the answer?

Sec. Humphrey. The answer is for the Government to spend less money.

Question. And to reduce manpower engaged in armament particularly?

Sec. Humphrey. Well, it's almost all manpower because all the money that we spend is manpower one way or another. It gets back to manpower. The Government hires people directly and it buys goods. Because it buys goods, other people hire men and put the men to work to make those goods, so that practically every dollar the Government spends hires men either directly or indirectly.

I've said the only way the Government can save money is by putting people directly and indirectly out of Government jobs so they can go into other jobs. That's a rough way to put it, but it's a fact. The only way we can save any money in the Government is to move people either directly or indirectly out of unproductive places into jobs making things for peacetime and productive living. . . .

Question. Mr. Humphrey, you made a remark the other day: "We'll have a depression that will curl your hair—"

Sec. Humphrey. What I said was that if we did not begin a better control of our expenditures and reduce Government spending and taxes, then, over a sufficient period of time, the Government would be taking so much money that should be going into power, farms, factories and tools that we would not have enough jobs to keep our growing population well employed and that would make a depression.

Question. How does Government spending affect this?

Sec. Humphrey. We have eight men now, seven of them producing goods for consumption or contributing to capital, and the eighth man is working hard every day, getting full pay for it, and producing something that is only good for war and rapidly becomes obsolete and worthless. In other words, a B-52, a guided missile, an armored tank— all of these various things are obsolete in a comparatively short time.

You can't eat them; you can't use them; they aren't tools to make any new jobs for anybody; they don't help living at all, except to protect our lives in the meantime. . . .

Question. Where does the "depression" come from, then?

Sec. Humphrey. A depression will come, if over a period of time, we keep on spending nearly $50 billion a year in preparation for war which contributes comparatively little to new capital and making future new jobs. Now, there are a million and a half persons, mostly boys and girls coming of age, wanting new jobs every year. In ten years, $50 billion a year is $500 billion—far more than our total Government debt. As a matter of fact, in the ten years since World War II, we've spent for security more than our whole debt.

QUESTION. And unproductively?

SEC. HUMPHREY. There is comparatively little of that money which was spent for preparedness for war that is going to make tools to make a new job for another fellow to work at next year or in future years from now. That money didn't do much of anything to build up the country for peacetime living and new future jobs.

QUESTION. It means more employment now, doesn't it? People say it gives us good times rather than a depression—

SEC. HUMPHREY. Temporarily, perhaps; and that is because you have this extra fellow employed making tanks and guns becoming obsolete, but your capital assets are not increased by his efforts. Your necessity for capital for peacetime purposes keeps going up and you are not putting the capital into new mines, factories, farms and equipment to make more new jobs for these boys that are coming along.

QUESTION. Mr. Secretary, if the defense spending is necessary, though, isn't there a temporary answer to be found in collecting more taxes?

SEC. HUMPHREY. That might help to hold down prices but I don't think it does a bit of good in accumulating capital. If you collect more taxes and reduce debt, it helps hold down prices. That's why we must keep our budget in order.

QUESTION. If you could encourage people to save more, wouldn't it also work in the same direction?

SEC. HUMPHREY. We've got to save, because it's the people's savings that are the machine tools which create the new jobs.

QUESTION. Are you doing all that you could to encourage people to save?

SEC. HUMPHREY. Well, that's a very difficult question. I think that the increase in interest rates helps people to save. It encourages them to save, unless we have inflation which loses their principal. In other words, the way to encourage a man to save is to pay him more rent for his money, unless at the same time he fears for the safety of his principal. We must try to balance out so that the people feel they're getting a little more return for their money and, therefore, will make a little more effort to save it instead of spend it, and they must also feel sure that they will get their principal back. . . .

QUESTION. How near are we to dangerous inflation in this country, and are we making progress toward it, or have we got to do some very drastic things yet to prevent a dangerous inflation?

SEC. HUMPHREY. No, I don't think we're threatened with a dangerous inflation now. I think that such an inflation as we face at the moment is relatively small. But this is the time to protect—to prevent anything more. Right at the moment our monetary measures are not being fully supplemented with our measures. In other words, we have our monetary measures, which are reflected in interest rates, and so on, which are in a downward pressure and over a period are quite effective.

But, on the other hand, our fiscal measures, as I have pointed out, are tending in the opposite direction. We are spending—putting more money into the spending pressure without putting more goods in. We are putting downward pressure on prices with the left hand, and we're putting upward pressure on prices with the right hand.

If this could all be run just exactly as it should, we would reduce our manpower in armament and Government, and curb Government spending to some extent, and put more people to making goods that the people can buy. With more goods, the pressure would be less on prices and they would be more stable. But there are many other things also to be considered. There are some Russians over there that you've got to think about.

QUESTION. Could you be specific, Mr. Secretary, about some of the things that Government does that you think it shouldn't do? You said there were activities that you don't approve of.

SEC. HUMPHREY. Well, I think we're spending too much money now, for one thing. . . .

QUESTION. Do you feel that the local people should do more financing of their own projects?

SEC. HUMPHREY. I do. I think that in this country we must basically insist that the Federal Government's activities be more restricted and that we do not try to solve every local problem by running to Washington.

QUESTION. In the 1930's we had a big dispute over the State of Kansas, which had a terrible relief problem. It was almost busted, and the State couldn't raise any money—

SEC. HUMPHREY. We're not talking about emergencies. Emergencies come along in all sorts of ways and part of the function of the Government is to relieve emergencies, but it should be limited for the emergency purpose and for that purpose alone.

QUESTION. Well, now there are a good many localities that are having trouble borrowing at any interest price that they think they can pay. Is this an emergency?

SEC. HUMPHREY. In the first place, a good deal of that is in the hands of their own voters. Because the only emergency they've got is that they have a constitution, or a State law, that limits the amount of money they can borrow or of interest they can pay, and they can change it themselves if the people there want to change it. In the great majority of states, I think, where they say they can't borrow, it's because the voters won't give them the power to borrow. That's their own problem.

QUESTION. Is the Government giving any study to the proposal that's been made to guarantee the bonds of those areas, simply to give them a good credit standing?

SEC. HUMPHREY. Not that I know of, and I certainly would look at it with a fishy eye. You know, when I was a boy my father told me, "You can put your name on the front of your own check but don't ever get your name on the back of someone else's note.". . .

QUESTION. It's sometimes assumed and implied—mostly in political speeches—that the Treasury feels that a certain amount of money should be spent because it's a percentage of the budget, and that military security is influenced by how much money you've got. What is your answer to that?

SEC. HUMPHREY. No, I don't think that how much money you spend has a thing to do with whether you get full value for it or whether you don't.

QUESTION. No, I mean safety—

SEC. HUMPHREY. You mean, you just ought to spend it, regardless?

QUESTION. No, the theory on Capitol Hill is that you in the Treasury say to the military, "Now here's all the money you have. Do the best you can with that amount of money—you're not going to get any more." And, when the military man says, "Well, but we won't be secure with that," you say, "Well, you'll have to abide by it—that's all the money we've got"—

Sec. Humphrey. The Treasury does not make these decisions. It's not done arbitrarily. It's balanced judgment after exhaustive consideration of all the facts. The person who makes the final budget recommendation as to the total amount of money that can be spent is a wise man, the President. He makes it with the best of knowledge. . . . And the final review is by the Congress.

Question. Mr. Secretary, are the national-security programs responsible for most of the increase in the budget that has taken place in the last couple of years?

Sec. Humphrey. I am sorry to say, they are not. From our lowest point up to this budget, we've gone up $7.2 billion in spending—$2.6 billion of that is in the security and $4.5 billion is in the rest of the Government, spread around in various places.

Question. Why did you have to increase the other nondefense—

Sec. Humphrey. Well, I asked a lot of people that.

From our low point, which was three years ago, we have gone up $7.2 billion in our expenses. Our income has gone up over $13 billion in that same period. Now, that $13 billion has gone in this way: Three years ago we had a $4.2 billion deficit—we now have an estimated $1.7 billion surplus for fiscal 1957—that's $6 billion. Our expenses have gone up $7.2 billion and that totals $13.2. That $13.2 billion is taken from all you taxpayers, and that's what has happened to it.

It is obvious to ask—if we were safe three years ago, and if we were doing a fairly good job of Government three years ago—why are we spending any more money today than we spent three years ago? Why aren't we back where we were? And, if we were, we would have a $9 billion surplus this year. We could do a lot with a $9 billion surplus; why couldn't we pay down some debts and give a tax reduction? . . .

Question. If we do certain things and reduce spending, will there be some consideration of a tax reduction a year from now?

Sec. Humphrey. That's right.

Question. Are you hopeful about that?

Sec. Humphrey. I think that it ought to be done. I think we ought to have tax cuts before too long.

Question. Does that mean taking that budget that is just now going to Congress and pruning it?

Sec. Humphrey. Yes.

Now, let me be perfectly clear on it. We've spent an awful lot of time on this budget. It's not that I'm critical of this particular budget. Today I don't know how we can further reduce these figures.

But, the last of this money won't be spent for 18 months and I think, instead of saying, "Well, here's the budget, boys, now we're through with that one—now let's just go ahead and spend the money and see how we come out"—I think, instead of figuring that the budget is the end, it should be just the beginning. This is the beginning of the 18 months and we ought to try to save more every single day during that 18 months. If, in 18 months, we can't improve on what we know today, we had better get somebody else for our jobs.

QUESTION. Do you feel the dollar is sound?

SEC. HUMPHREY. Yes. You'll have some little fluctuation—we have a little too much, I think, just lately. The pressures on prices are a little too much, just for the reasons I say.

QUESTION. Does that mean that you don't feel that the money's been too tight, and interest rates have been allowed to go up too fast?

SEC. HUMPHREY. Not now. I thought, at the time, that we were moving a little too fast when we started moving. I thought we moved in a little too early.

If you want to start a run on tomato catsup, all you have to do is to publish in the newspaper that some official of the Government is going to limit the amount of tomato catsup you can have, beginning on Friday. And there will be a rush to get tomato catsup. What we did, I think, was perhaps to move a little too fast on higher money, and people went into the market to get money on the ground that they say, "We'd better get in quick...."

QUESTION. Is it desirable, Mr. Secretary, to effect a very substantial reduction in the national debt when we can?

SEC. HUMPHREY. I'd like nothing better. But I don't believe it's practical to think of a big reduction in the debt until the time comes and I believe it will some day—when we'll have some kind of satisfactory disarmament arrangement.

I think the whole world is spending too much on armaments.

We will all be smart enough in the world someday to have some kind of an inspection system—some kind of satisfactory system which will cut this expense. . . .

☙ The "hair curling" press conference prompted this interview, in which the Secretary restated the background of his remark and developed further his belief that international agreement was the primary route by which to seek not merely American but world relief from the armament burden. Also in the background of events were the Suez "crisis" of late 1956 and the companion threat on the stability of the British sterling, about which the Secretary furnished both news and views.

Only 12 per cent
of budget "expendable"

*Speech by Secretary Humphrey at
the Masonic Temple in Detroit.*

March 6, 1957

. . . Under the Eisenhower Administration, the position of the Federal Government has been so improved that it is now living currently within its income. We had a budget surplus last year. We will have another budget surplus this year. And we have proposed still another balanced budget for 1958. This is the first time we have had a real prospect of three balanced budgets in succession for more than 25 years.

It is the size of this budget, even though balanced, that concerns us.

No man has worked harder than President Eisenhower to bring about a lower total of budget expenditures. This is equally true of all others in responsible positions in this Administration who have given long hours of painstaking work in the budget's preparation.

The fact is that the budget as we presented it to the Congress in January is the best that we could propose at the time, even though it provides for increasing Government spending.

It is important that the public understand fully just how the functions of Government are divided in connection with budget making and the authority for expenditures.

The law establishing this procedure specifies that "The President shall transmit to Congress during the first fifteen days of each session, the budget . . ." which "shall set forth . . . [the] proposed functions and activities of Government; . . . [the] estimated expenditures and the proposed appropriations necessary in his judgment for the support of the Government for the ensuing fiscal year . . . [as well as the] estimated receipts of the Government. . . ."

But the final decision is the decision of the Congress. Its responsibility is established by the Constitution which provides that "no money shall be drawn from the Treasury, but in Consequence of Appropriations made by Law. . . ." So that the Congress makes the final determination not only of how much the Federal Government may spend, but for what purposes all expenditures may be made.

It should, therefore, be clear that when the Executive asks the Congress, as we have done, to help to search out ways in which spending can be properly cut below what the Executive has proposed that we are acting only in strict conformity with constitutional processes in the way our Government is established.

It is also important to bear in mind where the money goes that the Federal Government spends.

By far the largest amount—63 per cent of the total—is for security. That includes the amounts in the various programs which it is estimated we need to protect ourselves against aggression.

The second largest category of Federal spending is for programs fixed by various laws passed by the Congress. These programs, such as veterans benefits, agricultural price support and soil bank payments, grants to states for welfare payments and the like plus interest on the Federal debt total about 25 per cent of Federal spending.

In these programs, after Congress passes the laws, the Executive has little opportunity to exercise any discretion, but merely administers the program and writes and distributes the checks which the various laws direct.

This leaves but 12 per cent of Federal spending in which there is some elasticity in the opportunity to save money.

It therefore becomes quite obvious that, while some savings can always be made by ferreting out waste, extravagance, and duplication, the really substantial reductions in Government spending can come only from changes in programs. These programs now in effect by decision of the Congress can be changed only by new decisions of the Congress. The executive branch must, of course, work closely with the Congress to arrive at the best judgments as to what the various programs must provide for.

That is exactly what the Eisenhower Administration is currently doing with the Congress in this campaign which has received so much public notice recently searching to find out ways and means of reconsidering existing programs so as to make substantial reductions in Government spending without either impairing our security or the necessary services to be rendered to the public.

The President in his State of the Union message said that he would insist that the Executive Department, in the next four years "search out additional ways to save money and manpower." There are 16 months remaining before spending under the proposed budget will be completed. We are working and will keep working on a day and night basis to find additional ways and places to save money so that we may come out with a lower spending figure at the end of the budget year.

There is reason to be optimistic about the prospects for success in this effort as everyone is cooperating with vigor and sincerity. We have asked the Congress to co-operate with us to this end and it is doing so in its actions on the appropriation bills. We are confident that some specific and substantial reductions can become possible if the people of this country continue their insistence that Federal spending *be* brought under better control.

Whose job is it to cut Federal spending? It is everybody's job. It needs the active support—not just the approval—of the public.

Basically, it is the job of the American people for it is with the people—at the thousands of crossroads over the Nation—that the pressures for spending begin. A group of people who want some assistance or who get into trouble of some kind, turn to the Federal Government for help on the mistaken theory that money from the Federal Government does not cost anybody anything.

The pressures applied are well known and are visible in Washington everyday. If some federal activity is to be discontinued because it is no longer really needed, the townspeople in the community where federal spending is to be curtailed will organize a campaign with their chamber of commerce to continue the spending within their

locality. They will take up the matter with their Congressional delegations and the branch of Government which is trying to curtail the
unnecessary spending comes under heavy criticism from them. It is
these pressures for continuation of present programs or the beginning
of new programs, for local groups or in many localities throughout
the country, which, added together, result in the terrific sums of money
the Federal Government is spending today.

We need a campaign of public education so that the public will
better understand the facts of life about federal spending. They must
realize that there is no bottomless well of unlimited money in Washington. The only Government money that any person can get must
come from the taxes he pays whether the payment is by check from
Washington or from the city or county treasurer or the town select-
men. . . .

The public must understand better that local spending for local
needs is more efficient and that federal programs for local needs should
be curtailed. Public projects locally determined and locally financed
are likely to be more efficiently administered than any project which
is put into effect and supervised by some distant agency. A town
meeting is less likely to spend its tax money on some unnecessary programs than an agency in Washington a thousand miles away where
a growing bureaucracy is entrenching itself. . . .

Finally, the people must be awakened to the true meaning of freedom. If the people of America are to have the benefits of freedom
they must also bear the obligations of freedom. The Federal Government cannot absorb the obligations of the people and still permit
the people to have and cherish the freedoms which have made this
country great. The feeling is growing in this country that regardless
of how careless you are of your own obligations and activities, if you
get into trouble somehow or other the Government will take care of
you and bail you out. If the people for themselves abdicate all self
controls, they can only have, in time, complete Government control.

As our economy produces more it does not mean that the Government must spend *more*, continually increasing the paternalism of Government. Just the opposite is true. The more we have the better
able more of us should be to do for ourselves and be less and less
dependent upon the Government.

High spending for our security will be required for some time. But that is all the more reason why our expenditures in many other ways must be curtailed and postponed until security becomes less costly and we are better able to afford more expense for some of the other things we might like to do. . . .

▰ The Secretary, after reflecting on the national reception of his remarks at his January 15 press conference, decided he had not made clear enough to the country that the enlarged budget was, in his opinion, the best and most rational job the Administration could present at the time—however he might hope that subsequent events would permit it, before the end of fiscal 1958, to be cut. To make clear this reflection, he took to the platform at an opportunity offered in Detroit, and the portion of his speech here subsequently appeared in *U. S. News & World Report* (March 22) as an article by him entitled "Why the Budget Is So Big—and How 'The People' Can Cut It."

The president cuts the budget

Remarks by Secretary Humphrey to the National Industrial Conference Board in New York.

April 18, 1957

. . . The President's letter of April 18 to Speaker Rayburn puts into proper perspective the problems about the budget which have been the subject of discussion since the budget was sent to Congress in January.

At that time, the President requested a further painstaking review of the budget by the Bureau of the Budget and by all the departments and agencies of the Government. This has now been prepared and discloses the feasibility of postponing certain appropriation requests which can be made without serious damage to the program.

The President, however, stated that actual spending in the coming fiscal year cannot be cut by multi-billion dollar amounts without danger to the national safety or interest, or the modification of some of the existing programs now authorized or required by law. I urge every

Baby sitter

Seibel in
The Richmond
Times-Dispatch,
1957

citizen to earnestly consider and support the President's direct and simple analysis of the principles involved in our budget problems.

The President's position not only guards the nation against ill-considered or dangerous slashing of the budget but it also points the way to well-considered steps toward holding future Federal spending down. Controlling the upward march of total Government spending is of greatest importance to us all.

There is nothing new about this approach or the principles that guide it. They are the same principles that have guided this Administration for the past four years. We have been constantly vigilant to continually make every effort to live within our means and to get a dollar's worth for every dollar that we spend.

We have continually striven to avoid waste and extravagance and to adequately balance the necessary costs of our national safety with the equally necessary maintenance of a strong and vigorous economy. We have sought to stabilize the costs of living and foster more and better jobs, to protect the Government's, as well as the people's, high income.

It is perseverance in this continuing effort that has brought us now to the prospect of three balanced budgets in succession for the first time in 25 years. But we have also been ever minded of our position of leadership in the world and the obligation we must necessarily bear in that regard to protect our national security.

The everlasting search for possible reductions and the drive to make them real will necessarily continue in the future as it has in the past. With the help of the Congress and the public, and the persisting efforts of the Administration toward a proper balancing of our fiscal affairs and full performance of our national obligations will continue.

The proven principles set forth in the President's letter well serve both our national security and the people's best interest. They deserve the full support of every American.

◪ President Eisenhower's letter to Speaker Rayburn was in reply to a House Resolution (190) that "the public interest" demanded "a sub-stantial reduction in the 1958 budget." (The House was controlled by a Democratic majority.) The President made two important statements. He "solemnly advised" the House not to cut appreciably the defense-security items in the budget at risk of "endangering the world's peace" and asserted that a "multi-billion" reduction would be "at the expense of national safety and interest." Then, from results of the Bureau of the Budget study he had ordered earlier in the year, he tendered a total of $1.342 billion postponements and adjustments, made up from the following revisions: $500 million in estimate of military assistance of the Mutual Security Program; $200 million in the spending authority of military public works; $50 million in special assistance functions of the Federal National Mortgage Association; $254 million in Soil Bank spending authority; $25 million in college housing spending authority; $13 million in the Army Engineers Corps budget; and $300 million in contingent spending authority.

The President then proposed ten pieces of legislation by Congress to produce more income and to relieve the expenditures of administering programs required by Congressional enactment independent of the Adminis-tration.

The President's suggestions brought the 1958 budget closer to an esti-mated balance, but whether it would have been was never to be determined. The first Russian "sputniks" later in 1957 produced a reaction in the United States which resulted in unanticipated expenditure for space flight, explora-tion, and invention. The 1958 final deficit was the outcome. This hap-pened after Secretary Humphrey's departure from his Treasury service.

"Proper use" of economic freedom

Speech by Secretary Humphrey to a dinner of Iowa
Republican leaders in Des Moines. In this his last
public speech as Secretary, Mr. Humphrey outlined
further than at any other appearance his
personal philosophy of true freedom, American style,
and indicated he still had hopes that
the 1958 budget could be brought into balance.

May 7, 1957

I want tonight to place in somewhat broader perspective than usual some of the things that concern us daily—such as our constant concern for prudent government; for government limited to activities that are truly necessary; for a solvent budget; and for the soundness of our money.

These thing are not ends in themselves. They are, rather means toward something far more important. They protect our economic freedom.

It is economic freedom that gives our daily economic activities direction, and gives meaning to our economic concerns. It is this special quality that has made our economy the richest and strongest economy known to man. . . .

We must never neglect our economic freedom, our freedom to make our own individual economic decisions, to choose for ourselves how we shall spend and save what we have earned.

We have seen lately the pitiful defrauding of the Russian people by the all-powerful ruling group in Russia who coolly announced that they were defaulting on payment of the Russian people's savings bonds. We do not wish our Government to become so overpowering that it could compel our people, as in Russia, to buy savings bonds and then repudiate their payment when due. A government with authority to force savings can later abscond with these savings. The one excess follows the other.

I do not think any American wants things to be like that in this country. But, I repeat, we too can lose our economic freedom if we do not understand it well enough to insist upon it and protect it as we should.

We must understand that there is nothing except security from attack that we can get from government half so precious as our freedom to work, to earn, to save and to spend as we please—our freedom to choose for ourselves freely what we will do and how and when we will do it.

We can give this all away gradually and almost without realizing it for the sake of obtaining too much government service or insisting upon subsidies, or excessive government spending or by demanding special tax concessions, or tolerating harmful tax rates, or by a discriminatory tax system. These things add up to false economic security. We can lose far more than we can gain when we make it a habit to ask the government to do for us the things we can and should do for ourselves, as individuals, as businesses, or as states and communities.

We are inclined to think that we have a "right" to economic freedom just as we assert for ourselves the "right" to free speech, freedom of worship, freedom of assembly, and the great freedom of being governed only by consent.

We are quick to assert our political rights, and we are quick to defend them. That is as it should be, for, unless we are as quick to defend them as we are to assert them, we should certainly and swiftly lose these rights, for they are not really "rights": They are, in fact, privileges we must earn and protect all over again each day.

We can earn our freedom by accepting corresponding responsibility—individual, local responsibility—for their proper use. Responsibility is an inseparable duty that goes with every liberty. Never for a moment can we forget that our freedoms must be earned, every day and every hour. We must never forget that only by facing up to the responsible use of those freedoms can we defend our claim to them as rights. . . .

Our history would indicate that this is a lesson we have learned pretty well in our political life. But we must continue to place our economic democracy on an equal plane with our political democracy if we wish to preserve our economic freedoms. Regard for economic freedom is one of the most important developments that has taken place in this nation. Nothing could be more important at this juncture in our history. . . .

We must accept personal responsibility for the proper use of our economic freedom, and for the proper functioning of the system economic freedom has brought forth. If we fail in this, then we will lose it—little by little at first—but each bit that is lost may never be regained. In the end government dictation will take it all over.

At the heart of economic freedom is the right to earn, and the right to hold as our own private property the things and the savings that we get from our earnings. From this flows the right to choose where and how we shall work, as an individual working for himself or starting a business or going into some job as an employee, or working at a profession, with the right to profit individually from our individual efforts, and to keep and use the products of those efforts. But this freedom must always be limited by the requirement that in using it for the benefit of ourselves we must always so limit its use that we do not interfere with the equal rights of others. And the Government should properly protect this equality of freedom.

It is the most obvious thing in the world that this economic freedom is a fragile thing, dependent upon consent and understanding, and needing to be constantly nurtured by sound and responsible judgment in its day-to-day use. No collection of people in Washington, no government, that is can do this job. It is the job of all the people of the United States.

No government can keep our money sound if the people of the United States shrug off their responsibility to live within their means, as individuals, as families, as businesses, as states, as communities, and as a nation.

How shall we preserve the right to earn, and to use our earnings, if we allow inflation to destroy the value of what we earn? Or if we call upon the Government to do so much spending that the resulting taxes take our earnings away from us?

And how shall we preserve the right to free enterprise if we fall into the habit of asking the Government to do an ever increasing part of the enterprising which we should be carrying on privately or through our state or local organizations? . . .

But we can preserve our individual freedom and our free enterprise if we look our responsibilities full in the face, if we assess the costs of the things we want, and decide if the price of more and more Government intervention with its higher and higher taxes and with correspondingly less and less individual freedom of choice and activity is a price that we are willing to pay.

All too often, we think only of what we want to *get* from Government intervention in our private affairs and all too seldom do we consider the *price* in loss of freedom that is involved.

Make no mistake about it, nothing is free. We pay and pay for every bit of it. There is no great well of unlimited wealth in Washington, or in any other seat of government, that can be tapped for extra Government services or responsibility without cost to anyone. Every cent that any government ever has comes out of the pockets of the people. Moreover, we get back only part of what we pay, because the cost of bigger and bigger government takes more and more of our money for expensive supervision. . . .

The size of government, the limit of its activities, and the price you pay in taxes is purely up to the people. The cost all comes out of the people, and we want to be very sure that the benefits are worth it. You pay not only in money in taxes, but also always in some limitation and some loss of your previous individual freedom whenever and to the extent that government takes over.

Let us look tonight in this context at where we *are* and where we can go from here. This is, of course, of great concern to you as leaders in Iowa of the Republican party now directing the Executive Branch of our Government. For it is the Republican Eisenhower Administration in the past four and one-half years which has been most successful in keeping our nation's economy in a healthy, free and growing condition. And it is the Republican Party that can best continue to do so.

Where do we stand now? We are the strongest nation on earth. We have the greatest prosperity ever enjoyed by any nation. The overwhelming majority of our people now have the highest standard of living ever achieved by man—in peace and in freedom.

What is the outlook? There is every reason why we should continue to be the strongest, most prosperous nation, with the best supplied people, on earth.

But—it is always possible for us to dissipate our strength by unwise actions. The basic natural laws have not been—and never will be—repealed. . . .

Under the Eisenhower Administration, the position of the Federal Government has been so improved that it is now living currently within its income. We had a budget surplus last year. We will have another budget surplus this year. And we have proposed still another balanced budget for 1958. This is the first time we have had a real prospect of three balanced budgets in succession for more than 25 years.

No man has worked harder than President Eisenhower to bring about a lower total of budget expenditures. This is equally true of all others in responsible positions in this Administration. . . . The budget as we presented it to the Congress in January is the best that we could propose at the time, even though it provides for increasing Government spending. . . .

At the time he presented the budget in January, the President requested a further painstaking review of it by the Bureau of the Budget and by all the departments and agencies of Government. This has been prepared and discloses the feasibility of postponing certain appropriation requests which can be made without serious damage to the program.

The President, however, pointed out that *actual* spending in the coming fiscal year cannot be cut with a broadax by multi-billion dollar amounts without danger to the national safety or interest, or the modification of some of the existing programs now authorized or required by law. I urge every citizen to earnestly consider and support the President's direct and simple analysis of the principles involved in our budget problems.

The President's position not only guards the nation against ill-considered or dangerous slashing of the budget, but it also points the way to well-considered steps toward holding future Federal spending down. Controlling the upward march of total Government spending is of greatest importance to us all. . . .

The everlasting search for possible reductions and the drive to make them real will necessarily continue in the future as it has in the past. With the help of the Congress, and the public, and the persisting efforts of the Administration, progress toward a proper balancing of our fiscal affairs and full performance of our national obligations will continue. . . .

The President has said that he would insist that the Executive Department, in the next four years, "search out additional ways to save money and manpower." There are 14 months remaining before spending under the proposed budget will be completed. We are working and will keep working on a day and night basis to find additional ways and places to save money so that we may come out with a lower spending figure at the end of the budget year, but without sacrifice of essential programs. There is reason to be optimistic about the prospects for success in this effort; every one is co-operating with vigor and sincerity and the people of this country are continuing their insistence that Federal spending *be* brought under the best possible control.

Basically it is the job of the American people, for it is with the people—at the thousands of crossroads over the nation—that the pressures for spending begin. A group of people who want some assistance or who get into trouble of some kind, turn to the Federal Government for help on the mistaken theory that money from the Federal Government does not cost anybody anything. . . . If some federal activity is to be discontinued because it is no longer really needed, the townspeople in the community where federal spending is to be curtailed will organize a campaign with their chamber of commerce to continue the spending within their locality. They will take up the matter with their Congressional delegates, and the branch of Government which is trying to curtail the unnecessary spending comes under heavy criticism for them.

It is these pressures which, added together, result in the large sums of money the Federal Government is spending today. . . . There is a general feeling in many localities that "we must get our share" of any federal program or "we will be cheated out of our rightful share of the money that the Government is spending. . . ."

The public must understand better that public projects locally determined and locally financed are likely to be more efficiently administered than any project which is put into effect and supervised by some distant agency. A town meeting is less likely to spend its tax money on some unnecessary programs than an agency in Washington a thousand miles away.

As our economy produces more, it does not mean that the Federal Government must spend *more*, continually increasing the paternalism of Government. Just the opposite is true. The more we have, the better able more of us should be to do for ourselves and be less and less dependent upon the Government.

High spending for our security is necessary and will be required for some time. That is all the more reason why our expenditures in many other ways should be curtailed and postponed until security becomes less costly and we are better able to afford more expense for some of the other things we might like to do.

We must remain strong economically, for our greatest strength lies in our strong economy and the might of our great industrial machine.

This is a further reason why we should take great care about non-defense spending while our security costs remain so high.

The billions we pay for military items and personnel exert substantial inflationary pressures in competition for the use of men and materials. The money goes into the spending stream but is not matched by production of goods which create future capital for the country or goods that the people can currently buy. Monetary measures are helping to restrict these inflationary pressures, but reductions in non-defense federal spending would contribute greatly to the release of manpower and materials for increased production of peacetime goods and so help to keep prices from rising. . . .

We must continue to pursue with vigor and determination the Eisenhower policies which have guided us so well in the past and which have the widespread active support of our citizens. We must have the unselfish support of all groups who are willing to lessen their demands upon the Federal Government in the interests of preserving our full freedom of choice, which has made us the most prosperous people on earth.

We are Americans first. We are Republicans next, but we are absolutely certain that the Republican principles of the past four years have given us all more, better, and sounder conditions than we have known for years and that the best thing for all America is to have them continued. . . .

Looking back at four years' gains

*Statement by Secretary Humphrey before the
Subcommittee on Fiscal Policy of the Joint
Economic Committee.*

June 14, 1957

. . . I want to repeat my conviction that although present tax rates are too high and the present heavy tax burden will, in the long-run, seriously hamper necessary economic growth, no general tax reduction should be considered at the present time.

The most effective tax cut that can be made to promote healthy economic development is a reduction which will bring benefit to all taxpayers—*when* our fiscal situation permits. By this, I mean when we can see ahead a sufficient surplus of income over outgo to pay for such a tax reduction. We should and will keep working vigorously for the day in the not too distant future when we can see such a surplus. Such a surplus does not exist at the present time.

In this connection we must keep a close watch of our budget position and make certain that Government spending is conducted as efficiently as is humanly possible. There is nothing new in this goal. We must continue to follow the principles that have guided this Administration for the past four years. We must make every effort to live within our means and to get a dollar's worth for every dollar that we spend.

In watching our budget we must constantly guard against ill-considered, or dangerous, or so-called meat-axe slashing of the budget.

As the President said in his April 18 letter to the Speaker of the House of Representatives, *actual spending* in the coming fiscal year cannot be cut by multi-billion dollar amounts without danger of the national safety or interest or the modification of some of the existing programs heretofore authorized by the Congress. It is not the size of any particular budget which is our paramount concern. It is control of the upward march of total Government spending which is of greatest importance to all of us on a long-run basis.

The biggest budget problem, as I see it, is one of seeking out long-term savings. The problem of how much and for what we should spend in the fiscal year 1959—which will not end until two years from now—is already upon us. What we must continue to do vigilantly is to keep up not only the everlasting search for possible reductions but the drive to make them real. We must do this while being ever mindful of our position of leadership in the world and the obligations which we must necessarily bear in that regard to protect our national security.

We must balance the necessary costs of our national responsibilities with the equally necessary maintenance of a strong and vigorous economy.

The Administration's fiscal record is a good one. The budget in effect when we took office in 1953 produced a $9.4 billion deficit, and the budget proposed by the prior Administration for fiscal year 1954 called for a $9.9 billion deficit. Our Administration, with the help of the Congress, cut spending, reducing the projected deficit for 1954 by two-thirds, or to a final minus figure of $3.1 billion.

But for the largest tax cut in history (a $7.4 billion cut in 1954) the budget would have been balanced in 1955. A balanced budget was delayed for one year because it was then apparent that the savings we then had in prospect would be sufficient before the end of the next year not only to cover the amount of the tax cut but to give us a balanced budget at the same time.

By fiscal 1956 we had eliminated deficits and had a balanced budget with a surplus of $1.6 billion. We will have a surplus in the fiscal year ending this month and the budget proposed for fiscal 1958 also is balanced. This means that we have in prospect a balanced budget for three consecutive years for the first time in more than 25 years.

Federal spending was reduced from the rate of $74.3 billion in the inherited budget of 1953 to $67.8 billion in 1954 and $64.6 billion in 1955. Spending moved up to $66.5 billion in 1956, to an estimated $68.9 billion in the January budget for the present fiscal year, and to a proposed $71.8 billion for 1958. Even with the recent increases the budget for the current fiscal year is $5.4 billion below the budget we inherited in 1953 and is 16 per cent of our gross national product as compared with 21 per cent taken by federal spending in 1953.

If we are successful in properly controlling the size and spending of Government, we can look forward to a continuing period of high prosperity for our country. A major ingredient in this high prosperity is the confidence of the American people—confidence in themselves, in each other and, of fundamental importance, confidence in their Government.

The greatest hope for major reductions in Government spending lies in a better world situation. Some day the nations of the world must arrive at some better and insured form of understanding which will make it possible to reduce the large amounts of money and energy and resources now going into making things for killing. I confidently believe that such a better day will come....

No federal pay increases in sight

Statement by Secretary Humphrey before the
House Committee on Post Office and Civil Service.

June 24, 1957

I appreciate the opportunity to appear before this Committee and to express the views of the Treasury Department on the pending bills for general increases in pay rates established under the Postal Pay Act.

The new schedule of pay rates for postal employees which is included in the proposed legislation would, I am told, add more than a billion dollars a year to postal service costs. It would triple the size of postal deficits and require substantial additional increases in postal rates, if the postal service is to be put on a pay-as-you-go basis as it should be.

It is reasonable to assume that an increase of pay rates for postal employees would be followed promptly by similar demands for increases for other federal employees and in military pay rates. Demands might also follow for increases in pension payments to retired employees. Thus we face in this legislation potential increases in federal expenditures of several billions of dollars per year.

I fully recognize and pay tribute to the devoted and competent service of our postal employees and of our hundreds of thousands of federal employees in other departments. We have many people who serve their government at tremendous personal sacrifice. Over the past four years this Administration has taken positive steps to improve the attractiveness of federal service through employee pay raises and many other fringe benefits. We are also studying ways and means of adjusting the types and levels of federal pay to attract the best personnel possible into Government service.

The financial program of the Administration for fiscal year 1958 does not include pay increases. Enactment of the legislation which we are here discussing would require an increase in the tax burden or, as an alternative, the very real possibility that the budget for fiscal 1958 would not be in balance.

For two years now the Government has been operating within the framework of a balanced budget with small budget surpluses. A balanced budget and further surplus has been proposed by the President for the coming fiscal year. Keeping the federal budget under control however is not something we can accomplish by giving lip service to our objectives.

I have many times discussed the problems of inflation with which all of us are constantly threatened, and have pointed out the ways in which the Government is working in the fiscal and monetary areas to hold down the inflationary pressures operating in our high level economy. One of the important ways in which our Federal Government promotes price stability and sound long-term growth and prosperity for our Nation is through balanced Federal budgets, and substantial pay increases now would not only destroy the chance for a balanced budget but would be inflationary and a step toward higher costs of living for everyone.

An increase in Government cost of these dimensions means just one of two things:

(1) Either an increase instead of a decrease in federal taxes for all the taxpayers of America; or

(2) An unbalanced budget with inflationary pressures substantially increased and higher costs of living for every one in this country, including in either the tax increase or the cost of living increase all of the members of the Post Office Department, along with all other Americans.

The final conclusions

In his final days in Washington, the Secretary underwent the most sustained examination by Congressional questioners of all his four and a half years. This was 14 days of statement and testimony June 18, 19, 20, 21, 25, 26, and 27 and July 1, 2, 8, 9, 10, 11, and 12 before the Senate Committee on Finance.

The committee had been directed by resolution to study the fiscal and monetary policies of the Administration in their effects on the financial condition of the country. The exact occasion for this study had been a somewhat confused matter in Congress, but a rise in 1957 of prices—the

"Ever think of pleading the Fifth Amendment?"

Berryman in *The Washington Star,* 1957

first in four years—a rise in interest rates, Secretary Humphrey's open nervousness about Government spending levels, and his resignation late in May to return to a critical situation in matters in his business empire all helped to produce the inquiry.

Two fairly historic records came out of this marathon of hearings. Secretary Humphrey set a new record for continuous testimony by a Cabinet officer (he testified a few hours longer than had Secretary of the Army Stevens in 1953 before Senator Joseph McCarthy's committee). And he produced a prepared statement on fiscal policy and business conditions which was not only the longest of his career but may be the longest report ever made by any Secretary of the Treasury.

Perhaps because this was his farewell appearance, there was an occasional attempt in the committee to twit him about the current price rise and softening of the dollar which he had so valiantly protected up to that time. Some attempts were made by senators to refer him to his earlier public statements hailing stabilization of the dollar; and some questions referred to his announced beliefs that the tax level was too high to be borne forever. There was discussion of Federal Reserve policies over which he had no authority, in connection with "easier money" prejudices of some senators. The Secretary remained serenely ready to talk as long as the committee wished, and adjournment finally came not at his but the chairman's request. Later in the year, the Senate Finance Committee accepted practically all of Secretary Humphrey's dicta in its report, and a majority found no reason to disagree with credit or fiscal management activities of the Treasury.

In this considerable report, Secretary Humphrey voiced his faith and beliefs in the superior national powers of free American society and enterprise, his record of adherence to these in his office, and their results in current national prosperity, investment, and confidence. This was the most all-encompassing statement he was ever to make about his job and his service. It appears here with three minor abridgements: A recital of the original Eisenhower campaign promises, a collection of subtitles used by the Secretary reiteratively to introduce and conclude his points, and a number of statistical charts with which he illustrated them.

A steward's summary of his service

*Statement by Secretary Humphrey before the
Senate Committee on Finance, Investigation of
the Financial Condition of the United States.
Senator Harry F. Byrd, chairman.*

June 18, 1957

...Broadly speaking, your study relates to the financial condition of the United States.... It seems appropriate that I provide a statement as to the problems we have faced, the goals we have set, and the record of our accomplishments in the past four years.

This is a record of a prospering America with new high levels of employment, rising income, and increasing purchasing power. It is a record of more and better jobs, more homes, more cars, more leisure, and more recreation. It is a record of unequaled prosperity with both the blessings and the problems of such a period.

Last year an average of 65 million of our people were gainfully employed, an increase of 3.7 million in only four years. During the same four years, unemployment has averaged only 3.8 per cent of the civilian labor force compared to 4.1 per cent during 1949 through 1952, and 15 per cent from 1937 until the beginning of World War II.

The present low level of unemployment has been achieved although the civilian labor force has increased from 63 million in 1952 to 68 million today. For the first five months of this year, unemployment has averaged about 3.7 per cent.

During this period, average annual family income, after Federal income taxes, has increased from less than $4,600 to an estimated $5,200, an increase of about 12 per cent, even after eliminating the effect of price changes.

In 1956 the average family purchased 12 per cent more goods and services, in real terms, than in 1952.

Almost 5 million families have moved into new homes since 1952. Almost 30 million families own their own homes today, an increase of 13 per cent in only four years.

The number of homes with electric refrigerators has increased from 38 million to 45½ million, accounting for 96 per cent of all wired homes. In only four years, the number of homes with food freezers has increased from five million to 8½ million; the number with clothes dryers (either electric or gas) from 1½ to 5½ million, and the number with television sets from 21 million to 38½ million. The number of families owning automobiles has increased from 31 million to 37 million.

This growing prosperity has extended to nearly all segments of our society except the farmer. The postwar adjustment in farm income has only recently been reversed, with a small increase last year for the first time in several years. . . .

The record of the past four years is one of great enhancement in personal financial security. The number of life insurance policies increased from 219 million four years ago to an estimated 265 million in 1956, an increase of 21 per cent, and the number of persons covered by hospital insurance increased from 91 million to 112 million, or 23 per cent.

Time deposits in banks and share accounts in savings and loan associations increased from $79 billion to about $112 billion, or 41 per cent, and the estimated number of shareholders in American industry increased from 6½ million to more than 8½ million people.

There has been a 19 per cent increase in the amount of time Americans took for their vacations—85 per cent with pay. . . .

Now, this great increase in the income, the living standard, the recreation, and security of our people has been achieved at a time when there has been a substantial contraction in defense expenditures.

Our free economy has again demonstrated its ability to absorb the reductions in Government expenditures not by contracting, but by expanding employment and the living standards of our people.

The record of the past four years has been one of unequaled investment. The nation has devoted a vast amount of its resources to improving and enlarging its productive capacity.

Businesses have spent an all-time high of $152 billion on new plant and equipment, compared with $123 billion in the preceding four years. This record volume of capital outlays has provided a dramatic answer to those who would contend that our economy would run down without the artificial stimulus of chronic deficit spending and the backlog of private demands deferred by the war.

Total public construction in 1956 was $13.4 billion, 23 per cent above 1952 levels, and educational construction outlays during this same period increased 56 per cent, from $1.6 billion in 1952 to $2.5 billion in 1956.

The increased confidence of our people and of our business concerns, that they will be free to determine their own course—free from unnecessary regulation or harassment—greater confidence in the stability of our Government and the wider distribution of purchasing power, have encouraged our consumers, our homeowners, our business concerns, and our communities, to plan for the future, and to buy the automobile, or the home, to build the factory or the schoolhouse, that a brighter future justifies.

Thus the record of the past four prosperous years has been characterized by the many blessings of widely shared prosperity—but it has also been beset by one of the problems of prosperity.

The tremendous outlays to expand our public and private facilities have required financing, and this has inevitably given rise to a heavy demand for borrowings. With growing confidence on the part of lenders as well as borrowers, there has been a rapid increase in the volume of both long- and short-term credit.

Almost all of this increase has come from savings and not from an increase of money supply in the banks. Nevertheless, there has been, and is, the ever-present threat of rising prices.

The monetary policies of the Federal Reserve and the fiscal policies of this Administration have been designed to encourage the growth of the supply of goods (as the foregoing figures indicate), but not to encourage excessive credit expansion.

The cost of living has risen an average of only six-tenths of 1 per cent per year for the past four years, as compared with an average increase at the rate of about 7 per cent per year for the preceding 13 years.

In short, the rise in prices during this Administration has been at only one-tenth the average annual rate of the preceding 13 years. Even this rise is more than I like to see, but it is a record of far better price stability than in many years.

Nevertheless, prices have been rising a little faster for the past 12 months, and the threat of renewed inflation, which had been so severe from 1946 to 1952, is perhaps our most serious domestic economic problem.

The greater increase in demand for credit than in the supply thereof has inevitably brought about higher interest rates. . . .

It is a record of encouraging savings and investment in increased productive capacity, of encouraging an adequate volume of credit, but of not encouraging that excess of credit which, in a period of high employment, could only penalize our people by bidding up prices without increasing production.

It is essentially a record of flexible and quickly adjusting fiscal and monetary policy designed to continue the sound improvement in levels of living, widely shared, which is the wonder and ambition of all the rest of the world.

It is a most significant record, important to us all, because the monetary activities of the Federal Reserve System and the fiscal activities of the Treasury affect the wages, the standard of living, and the savings.

It is above all a record of the renewal of widespread confidence of the people in the preservation of their individual freedom of choice, in their jobs, in their right to the enjoyment of the fruits of their own initiative and endeavor, and in the security of their savings. It is a record of renewed confidence in the security of our country.

Feeling as I do that there should be the widest possible public interest in this subject, and feeling such a deep pride in what this Administration has done and is doing, I welcome this opportunity to speak to your committee and, through you, to the more than 171 million Americans whom the Congress represents. . . .

In discussing fiscal, monetary, and credit policies, as I am doing today, I do not want to give the impression that they alone can prevent inflation and assure economic wealth. They are, however, a subject of the present inquiry and I shall concentrate my attention on them.

Certainly if they are not sound, there is little chance for sound money and sound long-term economic growth.

As a preface to our present policies, let us review the situation as it existed when we came into office. We came in in 1953.

You will recall the tremendous changes that had occurred in the period before 1953. In ten of the thirteen fiscal years from 1939 through 1952, the Government operated at a deficit, as it had in the preceding nine years.

Largely as a result of World War II, the federal debt increased in only 13 years from $47.5 billion at the end of 1939, to $267.5 billion at the end of 1952. Those are figures that to me are simply astounding. It is attributable to a war period, but a debt going from $47.5 billion to $267.5 billion, in only 13 years.

The interest charge on this indebtedness had grown from an annual rate of $1.25 billion per year in December of 1939, to $6.25 billion in December of 1952, an average increase in interest cost of almost $400 million per year.

In 13 years, annual federal taxes had increased from a little less than $5 billion in 1939, to almost $65 billion in 1952. This amounted to an increase in the average tax burden of each American citizen from $36 in 1939, to $413 in 1952.

When this Administration came to office in January of 1953, we faced:

(1) A federal debt equal to 89 per cent of our annual national income.

(2) Budget expenditures of $74.3 billion for fiscal 1953, and proposed budget expenditures, a prepared and then existing budget, of $77.9 billion for 1954.

(3) A budget deficit of $9.4 billion for 1953, and a planned deficit of $9.9 billion, almost $10 billion, for 1954.

(4) A continuing spiral of inflation which had reduced the purchasing power of the dollar from 100 cents in 1939 to 77 cents by 1945, and down to 52 cents by 1952.

In appraising these conditions and the course to pursue, we were influenced by a recognition of the overpowering importance of preventing other devastating postwar inflation which, prior to 1953, the Government was attempting to control by inadequate means. . . .

The first objective was to reduce the planned deficits and then balance the budget. To what extent have we accomplished this goal?

(1) We first reduced and then entirely eliminated planned deficits.

The budget in effect when we took office in 1953 produced a $9.4 billion deficit, and the budget proposed for the fiscal year 1954 called for a $9.9 billion deficit. Our Administration immediately went to work, with the help of Congress, to reduce the planned deficit for fiscal 1954, and indeed the final deficit ($3.1 billion) was only one-third of that anticipated by the prior administration.

Without the largest tax cut in our nation's history, the budget would have been balanced in 1955. However, in view of the transition resulting from the reduction in military spending, and anticipated further reductions in spending which in fact materialized concurrently with our action, we were able to pass some of the savings from our reduced expenditures back to the people, even though this meant another year's delay in achieving a balanced budget. Fiscal 1955 was, however, the last year of deficits.

(2) We have balanced the budget.

By fiscal 1956, we had entirely eliminated deficits, balanced the budget, and completed the year with a surplus of $1.6 billion.

The 1957 budget will result in another surplus, and the budget proposed by the President for 1958 provides for a third successive surplus for the first time in 25 years.

(3) We have reduced federal expenditures.

Federal expenditures were reduced from $74.3 billion in the inherited budget of 1953, to $67.8 billion in 1954, and down to $64.6 billion in 1955. As a result of additional programs authorized by the Congress, substantial pay increases, and the need for increasingly expensive military equipment, expenditures increased slightly in the past year to $66.5 billion, with further increases anticipated to $68.9 billion for 1957 and $71.8 billion for 1958.

The 1957 budget is nearly $5.5 billion below the budget we inherited in 1953, and is but 16 per cent of our current gross national product now as compared to 21 per cent in 1953.

The second objective was to meet the huge costs of our defense.

Major national security expenditures have been reduced from $50.4 billion in 1953, to $46.9 billion in 1954, to an estimated $41.0 billion in 1957, with a proposed $43.3 billion in 1958.

This reduction has been achieved despite the fact that, though not at war, we are still engaged in a titanic contest which requires not only the expense of preparedness, but extremely expensive research and development. . . .

We have met these huge costs with a balanced budget and with a reduced tax burden. We have provided the necessary large amounts of expensive and revolutionary new equipment needed for our national safety, greatly expanded our productive facilities, and at the same time enabled far more capital and labor to be directed toward building more cars, more houses, more of all of the good things our people need and want.

Our third objective was to properly handle the burden of our inheritance of debt and obligations.

As you have invited the Under Secretary, Mr. Burgess, to meet with you, I have asked him to report to you in detail on our handling of the debt.

In preface to his remarks, I might say that the management of $275 billion of debt is not a simple assignment under any circumstances. The Federal Reserve's proper withdrawal from the pegging of the Government bond market, which withdrawal was the most effective single action taken in the battle against inflation, has made it more difficult to manage debt operations than it was when a fixed rate was assured.

Had such a policy continued, however, the resulting inflation would eventually have produced even greater complications for debt management than we have experienced under a system whereby interest rates are determined by the forces of the market.

In January, 1953, when this Administration took office, the average rate on all Government interest-bearing issues outstanding was 2.35 per cent. The total net computed interest cost at an annual rate at that time was $6.2 billion.

Four years later the average rate on all Government issues outstanding was 2.67 per cent, or an increase of about .3 per cent. The total net annual computed interest cost, as of December 31, 1956, was $7.3 billion, of which $0.9 billion is due to increased interest rates, and $0.2 billion is due to an increase in the debt incurred to pay obligations inherited from previous commitments.

This increase in interest rates results from the free market influences of supply and demand in a period of unparalleled prosperity. It is a continuation of a rise that has been going on for the past ten years under the growing pressure of borrowing demands.

In this little table the computed interest rate is shown:

Computed interest rate on the public debt

	PER CENT
December 1946	2.06
December 1952	2.35
December 1956	2.67
May 1957	2.75

So that the rate has increased over the ten-year period from 2.06 to 2.75, or a little less than .75 per cent.

For the entire period from December, 1946, through May, 1957, there was an increase of .69 per cent in the computed interest rate on the public debt. Of that increase, .29 occurred prior to this Administration, and .41 occurred during this Administration, right up to now.

During the past four years there has been no increase in public debt interest cost in relation to national income. The interest cost was 2.1 per cent of national income in December, 1952, and was exactly the same percentage in December, 1956, for the increase in interest cost has only kept pace with the increase in national income.

Furthermore, the $1 billion increase in interest paid reflects increased earnings received by the investors who own the securities.

Now, who are those investors?

Of the $7 billion of interest paid on the public debt during calendar year 1956, $1.4 billion represented the payment of interest to social-security funds and other Government investment accounts.

About $0.6 billion of public debt interest was received by the Federal Reserve banks, and 90 per cent of that comes back to the Treasury as surplus earnings.

Commercial banks received approximately $1.4 billion of such interest last year. About $0.6 billion went to other financial institutions—mostly insurance companies and savings banks; about $0.5 billion to corporations, about $0.4 billion to State and local governments, and about $0.4 billion to nonprofit institutions, foreign accounts, and so forth.

The remainder, of about $1.8 billion—the largest single segment of the interest on the public debt—went to individuals, either in the form of cash payments or accumulated interest to the 40 million holders of savings bonds. Millions of Americans are benefiting from these higher interest rates.

At the risk of oversimplification, let me condense the story of inflation to about a dozen lines.

Almost all of our employable labor force is employed—and at higher wages than they have ever received before. Our people are buying virtually all that they are producing, but they want to buy more, both more consumer goods and more productive facilities.

Being confident of the future, they desire to borrow to buy more. The lenders are lending more than ever before, but still not as much as the public would like.

However, with most resources fully utilized, additional bank credit would not put any more people to work—it would merely provide additional demand in excess of the supply of both labor and goods. Such a demand in excess of supply would cause a rise in prices if it were fed by excessive bank credit expansion.

A rise in price hurts every housewife, everyone on a pension, every person with a fixed or lagging income, every saver. It robs labor of much of its gain in wages. This rise in prices has been a principal cause of the farmers' difficulties, because while income per farm remained fairly static during the last ten years, the farmer has had to pay higher prices. As a consequence, he has been particularly hurt by the inflation which, to a lesser extent, injures every single one of us.

There are two ways to check this rise in prices: (1) increase the supply of goods, and (2) slow the expansion in the number of dollars bidding for the goods.

We have utilized both methods. The Administration in many ways has encouraged an increase in productive facilities which is the only way to increase the supply of goods. The Federal Reserve and the Administration have taken action to restrain a too rapid growth in the number of borrowed dollars available to bid up the price of the limited supply of goods and services.

I would like to take a moment to identify the respective roles played, on the one hand by the Treasury, which influences fiscal policy—through its recommendations on tax and budget policy as well as its management of the public debt—and on the other hand by the Federal Reserve, which is responsible for monetary policy—through its influence on the cost and availability of money and credit.

A mere statement of the respective functions demonstrates the major role of the Federal Reserve in the effort to stop inflation. The Federal Reserve has the authority and the tools to take monetary and credit action. We do not.

The Treasury cannot determine the level of interest rates, but must pay the rates determined by market forces. The Federal Reserve can influence the levels of market rates, although there are definite limits to its power to maintain any fixed level of rates, as is shown by history.

I do not point this out to shift any responsibility from the Treasury. On the contrary, we approve wholeheartedly the course which the Federal Reserve has followed, and have admiration for the courage and decisiveness with which the board has acted.

As you will recall, throughout the decade prior to 1951, the Federal Reserve followed a policy of supporting the market for United States Government securities at or above par. This was done to enable the Government to sell, at a low interest cost, the great volume of securities which was necessary to finance World War II.

It accomplished that purpose, but it created cruel inflationary conditions which required the sale of more bonds and increased debt to pay the resulting higher costs of the war.

In artificially holding interest rates at low levels, the Federal Reserve made credit cheap, not only for the Government, but for all borrowers. By maintaining a market which enabled the banks to liquidate their

Government bonds at any time at par or better, it encouraged a continuance of the war-born expansion of excessive bank credit.

This cheap and plentiful credit was an important cause of the wartime inflation which, despite wartime restrictions of direct controls and rationing, robbed the dollar of 23 cents of its purchasing power between 1939 and 1945.

At the end of World War II there was an acute shortage of goods. There was, however, a pent-up demand, a demand made effective by both a large amount of liquid assets accumulated during the war and a rapid increase in private credit.

The war-born policy of the Federal Reserve, mistakenly continued into peacetime under Treasury insistence, enabled the supply of credit to rise too rapidly, with the result that this credit-backed demand for goods exceeded the supply of goods.

While interest rates were held at artificially low levels, prices continued their serious rise, at an average annual rate of over 7 per cent from 1945 to 1951, and in those six years the dollar lost another 23½ cents of its purchasing power.

The dollar at 77 cents in 1945 depreciated to only 53.5 cents in 1951.

It was becoming clear to increasing numbers of observers that the unwise credit stimulus provided by the Federal Reserve should be withdrawn. Such a withdrawal could be achieved only by paying the lesser penalty of an increase in the interest rates to be paid.

It was clear that if the Federal Reserve ceased purchasing Government securities at par, natural market forces, reflecting increasing demand for credit, would result in the higher interest rates which the Federal Reserve purchase policy had so far postponed.

During this postwar period the Federal Reserve made several modest moves toward freer short-term markets but was held back by the Treasury. After a most thorough review of the relative advantages and disadvantages of such a change, the Subcommittee on Monetary, Credit and Fiscal Policies, known as the Douglas subcommittee, concluded in 1950 that,

"As a long-run matter, we favor interest rates as low as they can be without inducing inflation, for low interest rates stimulate capital investment. But we believe that the advantages of avoiding inflation are so great and that a restrictive monetary policy can contribute so much to this end that the freedom of the Federal Reserve to restrict credit and raise interest rates for general stabilization purposes should be restored even if the cost should prove to be a significant increase in service charges on the Federal debt and a greater inconvenience to the Treasury in its sale of securities for new financing and refunding purposes."

Partly as a result of that review and report, the Administration then in office and the Federal Reserve, by an agreement referred to as the "accord," changed the prior policy, and the Federal Reserve began to withdraw its support of the market for Government bonds in March of 1951.

While this was a step in the right direction, it was not a complete step. On a number of occasions during 1951 and 1952, the Treasury still relied on Federal Reserve purchases to keep new issues from sinking in the market.

Let me pause in this chronology to remind you of the facts about that change in policy. It was put into effect by an independent agency, the Federal Reserve. It was urged by many of the best informed Members of Congress.

It occurred during the preceding Administration—21 months before this Administration took office.

This new policy of the Federal Reserve was not so much anti-inflationary as it was a tempering of what formerly had been positively inflationary action. The Federal Reserve began to reduce the amount of credit it had been artificially creating. It freed natural market forces.

As an incidental result of the reduction in the volume of artificial credit generated by the Federal Reserve, the supply of credit grew somewhat more slowly than the demand for credit. As a consequence interest rates began to rise, and the market prices of bonds went down.

Though the full force of this change in the Federal Reserve policy was not immediately effective, almost a quarter of the increase in the computed interest rate on the public debt—from 2.22 per cent at the time of the Federal Reserve-Treasury accord in 1951, to 2.75 per cent in May, 1957—almost a quarter of that occurred in the 21 months prior to the time this Administration took office.

As a result, banks and insurance companies, which had such large blocks of Government securities, were more hesitant to sell them at a 3- or 4-point loss in order to make a loan. This caused them to make fewer loans than they would have made had the earlier policy been continued.

Although by the accord of March, 1951, the Administration then in office had reluctantly agreed to the right of the Federal Reserve to take such monetary action, that Administration itself continued to rely on direct controls on wages, prices, and rents.

In addition, after the short-lived budget surplus of 1951, increasing Government spending, and renewed deficits in 1952, largely as a result of the Korean conflict, encouraged a further depreciation in the dollar to 52.3 cents.

If inflation was to be effectively checked, the Federal Reserve's new policy had to be supported more vigorously and supplemented with parallel fiscal policies.

In 1952, General Eisenhower campaigned for the Presidency in part on the ground that further inflation must be prevented, and advocated, "A Federal Reserve System exercising its functions in the money and credit system without pressure for political purposes from the Treasury or the White House."

We have conducted our affairs so as not to interfere with the Federal Reserve's monetary policies. We have lived up to that promise that the President made. To do so, however, has subjected the Treasury to certain burdens, just as it has other borrowers. Not to do so would have created much more serious burdens for all of us.

Although new financing was less expensive and easier in 1954, it has again become more costly. With a very high percentage of bank and insurance company assets now in loans, these institutions are not clamoring for long-term—or even intermediate-term—Government securities.

We must, therefore, at present, sell mostly shorter-term securities, which are attractive because of their high liquidity. I do not say this to complain, but to acknowledge an obvious fact.

We will meet these difficulties and solve them as we have in the past, continuing our flexible policy, postponing debt extension when we must, achieving it whenever we can.

There is a strong demand for short maturities. Our bill auctions each week are always well oversubscribed. The Treasury faces no crisis. Our securities are the most highly regarded in the world.

But in a free market, we must compete for funds. That means the factors of supply and demand determine the rates we must pay. Rates may decline or they may go higher. I would be disappointed to see them go higher, but if that is the price we must pay to prevent growth of excessive credit and consequent inflation, it will well justify the price.

Planned deficits have been eliminated. Federal deficits necessitate increased federal borrowing. More federal borrowing, to the extent it comes from the banks, means the creation of additional bank credit. This tends to create more spendable dollars than there are goods to buy.

As your chairman, Senator Byrd, so clearly pointed out in his remarks to the Senate on August 13, 1954: "Deficit spending is perhaps the greatest single factor in the cheapening of the value of the money."

In ending deficits, we have eliminated this very inflationary pressure.

We reduced the public debt in fiscal 1956 as a result of our budget surplus of $1.6 billion. Another budget surplus is being applied to the debt this year, and we expect to do it again in 1958. Reduction of the public debt is one of the best ways to fight inflation.

Government expenditures have been reduced. Government expenditures are inflationary, particularly when the economy is at a high level of output and employment. Taxes divert to Government spending some funds which, in the hands of the taxpayer, would have gone into savings.

Furthermore, some Government expenditures go into payrolls to produce goods and services—especially military equipment and military services—which neither contribute to the nation's capital account nor become available for private consumption.

Yet this additional purchasing power competes for the existing supply of both goods and services.

By reducing Government expenditures, we have released more workers and materials directly to private industry where they could add further to the supply of goods and services needed to meet our heavy demands for plant and equipment, and greatly increase the supply of homes, cars, television sets, and other consumer products necessary for our rising standard of living. Reduced Government expenditures have been an anti-inflationary influence.

We have reduced the floating debt. The amount of marketable public debt maturing within a year, plus demand obligations (other than E and H Savings Bonds) in the hands of the public—securities which in many ways are close to cash—has been reduced by $25 billion from the high point in 1953.

We have also shifted some of the debt away from the banks. Since increases in bank loans represent additional spendable money, they tend to be more inflationary than loans that grow out of a transfer of existing savings. As a consequence, one of the Treasury's long-range debt management objectives has been to reduce bank holdings of Government securities to a reasonable minimum.

To this end we have, in the past four years, reduced the amount of Government securities held by the banks by $4 billion. This has been achieved in part by paying off some securities and in part by designating the terms of new issues—such as tax anticipation bills and certificates— to be particularly attractive to non-bank investors.

We have stimulated increased savings. Greater confidence in the future, higher rates of interest, and increasing confidence in the stability of the dollar, have all encouraged our people to save more, both in dollars and in relation to disposable income.

As one means of encouraging savings and combating inflation, we have emphasized the continued sale of Series E and H Savings Bonds. The amount of these small-saver bonds outstanding has increased from $35.3 billion to $41.4 billion during the past four years.... The past four years have been characterized by greater price stability than any other four-year period since 1939. But inflation is not stopped. It is only slowed down.

Indeed, there has been a disturbing renewal of pressures in the last 12 months, during which the dollar has lost almost 2 cents in purchasing power. This most recent decline in purchasing power is disturbing. It reinforces our conviction that we must continue the vigorous pursuit of our present policies. We should certainly not abandon them.

While over the past four years it has been necessary to follow generally anti-inflationary fiscal and monetary policies, we have had changes in the economy which have required us to moderate them on occasion, and we may encounter other circumstances which may require some relaxation at some times in the future. . . .

Our Administration had been in office only a few months when the coincidence of the full effect of the Federal Reserve's new policy, and the curtailment of defense spending, temporarily changed the problem.

We were, at that time, more concerned with preventing a decline in employment and production than with a rise in prices. Taxes were reduced, and the Administration relaxed down-payment and maturity terms on FHA- and VA-guaranteed housing loans.

At the same time, Federal Reserve policy also eased, making funds more readily available. The decline was stopped and a sound economic expansion got underway with renewed public confidence in the courage of the Administration and the flexibility of its policies.

By 1955 economic activity was again vigorous and the problem was one of inflationary pressures—which have continued—and easy bank credit expansion was no longer encouraged.

In view of the breadth of the subject of your inquiry, it is appropriate that we consider what might have been some available alternatives to the general monetary and credit policy.

Some of these alternatives are:

(1) Direct controls prohibiting or limiting certain types of credit.
(2) Compulsory saving.
(3) Physical controls on prices and wages—plus, perhaps, rationing and allocation of materials and labor.
(4) Higher taxes and large governmental surpluses to be applied on the bank-held debt.
(5) Greater individual savings and voluntary effort at restraint.
(6) A reversion to the pre-1951 policy of Federal Reserve purchase of Government securities at or above par—and consequent encouragement of severe inflation.

The use of any of the first three alternatives in peacetime would have been inequitable, impractical, and inconsistent with our traditions of freedom.

The fourth alternative would have required the imposition of additional taxes on top of our present heavy load, and would not have been acceptable.

The fifth, which the President emphasized in his State of the Union Message just a few months ago—namely, voluntary efforts—can help immeasurably, but can be achieved only if other policies are effective.

Thus, as a practical matter, the real choice is between the anti-inflationary course which we have pursued, and a new round of inflation.

Those who, in a period such as this, urge an abandonment of our anti-inflationary policies, those who urge either deficit financing or a policy of artificially creating more spendable dollars are, whether unwittingly or by intention, inflationists. . . .

The fifth goal was to work toward the earliest possible reduction of the tax burden.

The Eisenhower Administration and the Congress, working together, have already made possible the greatest single tax cut in history. In 1954 we brought about a tax cut that has provided them with annual savings of about $7.5 billion.

As the President pointed out in his letter of April 18, 1957, to the Speaker of the House, this tax cut has already saved our people almost $25 billion in taxes.

More than 60 per cent of that reduction went to individuals. Every taxpayer benefited....

We relieved the public of the burden of controls. When this Administration took office in 1953, the country was still handicapped with controls over prices and wages, and the use of certain materials. We promptly terminated these controls.

We have reduced Government activities which compete with private business. During the past four years, some 500 federal enterprises competing with business have been abolished. We have disposed of the Government-owned synthetic rubber producing facilities and the Government-owned tin smelter to private enterprise; and the Reconstruction Finance Corporation is now in the process of liquidation. Surplus real estate, worth $366 million, has been sold and turned back to local tax rolls.

We have created a more favorable climate for enterprise. We have moved vigorously to prevent monopolies. The number of antitrust prosecutions has been materially increased and the number of convictions, guilty pleas, and consent decrees obtained in the past four years has been more than 40 per cent higher than in the preceding four years.

The number of prosecutions under Section 7 of the Clayton Act, as amended in 1950, has increased from only one in the two years, 1951 and 1952, to 29 during this Administration.

We have encouraged small business.... In the past four years, small business has benefited materially from tax law changes—the expiration of the excess profits tax law, the reduction in personal income tax rates in 1954, and the extensive revision of the Internal Revenue Code.

To aid small firms which are unable to obtain adequate credit from normal sources, President Eisenhower signed the Small Business Administration Act on July 30, 1953. That act created the Small Business Administration, and authorized a revolving fund of $275 million to provide needed loans to small business concerns.

Subsequently, the Administration supported increases in the SBA funds to $375 million in 1956, and to $455 million in 1957. The Administration now has a bill pending to increase this to $600 million, and to make the SBA a permanent organization.

Each year the SBA has made a larger number of loans, with over $125 million in the last ten months, and currently is making loans to about 60 per cent of the applicants whose files have been reviewed.

We have encouraged trade with other countries. This Administration has effected measures which have aided the increase in our total foreign trade in 1956 by 22 per cent (exports 25 per cent) over 1952.

In addition, the Treasury, with the cooperation of your committee, has put into effect a number of customs simplification acts which have reduced the complexities attendant on the movement of goods into the United States. We have also provided greater certainty in our Administration of the tariff laws. . . .

During the past four years, 500,000 new business corporations were formed in the United States. Of course, not all succeeded. A free economy is not a riskless economy. During that period, 44,000 enterprises— noncorporate as well as corporate—failed, but that is lower in relation to the number of new corporations formed than during the preceding four years—34,000 failures and 355,000 new incorporations.

We have encouraged savings. The importance of savings as the anti-inflationary source of financing is so great that I would like to make these points:

There are many people who benefit from higher interest just as there are many who find it an additional cost.

You and I hear complaints today about the increased cost of money. We know it is nowhere as important as the increased cost of labor, but we also know that higher labor cost is a two-sided coin, it is a two-way street. Someone pays more—but someone receives more.

Now, the same is true of interest. . . . We have a further stake in a higher interest return on our money. We are owners of millions of share accounts in savings and loan associations, time deposits in banks, and mutual life insurance policies.

Many of us belong to a pension system.

Some critics allege that higher interest rates benefit only the bankers. That is nonsense. Earnings of insured commercial banks as a return on average capital accounts in 1956 were 7.82 per cent . . . substantially less than the average earnings of all manufacturing companies which averaged 12.3 per cent. In 1952, bank earnings of 8.1 per cent compared with manufacturing earnings of 10.3 per cent....

The higher interest rates paid in the past few years have encouraged greater savings. During the four years of the Eisenhower Administration, our people saved more, both in terms of dollars ($75 billion of personal savings compared to $56.5 billion in the preceding four years), and in relation to disposable income, 7.1 per cent as compared to 6.4 per cent....

Increased capital investment—more tools, more factories, more equipment—is necessary to provide the jobs with the high wage levels which are paid in this country today. It is the principal means by which we can raise our living standards.

To the extent such increases in capital investment are provided by excessive bank credit expansion, they are inflationary. To the extent they are financed out of savings, they are not....

In the past four years, we have moved to an unparalleled prosperity. More people are living better than ever before. It is this prosperity, in turn, which creates heavy demands for money and requires some anti-inflationary restraint....

This Administration has successfully encouraged saving, enterprise, and production. This is a demonstrable and desirable accomplishment. With such means as it has had at its disposal, the Administration has attempted to arrest inflation and has been largely successful.

I note, however, that there have been some complaints that the monetary and fiscal policies have been too severe and have affected certain segments of the economy unfairly....

Let me review again what the Administration has done to fight inflation. We have reduced the Government debt. We have reduced Government expenditures. We have balanced the budget. We have reduced the floating debt. We have moved some of the debt out of the hands of the banks and put more of it into the hands of individual citizens.

The reduction in Government expenditures has perhaps injured those corporations which might have received orders had the Government spent more money. The entire course of action, having been anti-inflationary, may have injured those few who might have benefited, at the expense of the rest of our citizens, from runaway inflation.

But, except for these few, the good of the overwhelming majority of our people was best served by the course we have followed.

We have also endorsed the independence of the Federal Reserve and conducted our affairs in such a way as to avoid interference with its anti-inflationary monetary policy....

The Federal Reserve's program is one of allowing the natural market forces to operate, while adjusting credit availability to meet the needs of normal seasonal activities and sustainable economic growth.

The Federal Reserve has ceased its earlier policy of creating additional bank credit, except to the extent needed to meet the basic requirements of a healthy economy.

Some current discussions of Federal Reserve policy proceed on the mistaken assumption that the Federal Reserve has reduced the amount of credit below an amount previously available.

Nothing could be further from the truth. Credit—the aggregate of new savings and new bank credit—has expanded substantially in the past four years, and at a rate fully equal to the need, to sustain a very high use of both services and materials.

There is more credit outstanding today than ever before—$146.5 billion more than in 1952. I am going to read that again: There is more credit outstanding today than ever before—$146.5 billion more than in 1952.

Mortgage credit has gone up $49 billion, consumer credit $14 billion. This is over a period of four years we are now talking about, over the period of 1952 to 1956, through December of 1956. Mortgage credit has gone up $49 billion; consumer credit $14 billion; and "Other," $8.5 billion, or a total of $72 billion.

Corporate has gone up $46.4 billion; state and local governments nearly $19 billion, for a total of $137 billion.

Now then, the Federal Government has gone up during that same period $9.3 billion, making a total, if you add it all up, of $146.5 billion which occurred during the four-year period.

As important as the fact of the increase in credit, is the source of this increase.

Non-bank credit over the four years which came about through savings during that period, nearly $136 billion; bank credit, less than $11 billion—for a total of $146.5 billion.

In 1956 alone, total debt—other than Federal Government—increased

$37.5 billion. Of this increase, $17.5 billion was individual debt, $15.5 billion corporate, and $4.5 billion state and local government debt.

The increase in total credit in the past four years has been greater than in either of the two preceding four-year periods. But a most important fact to note is that 93 per cent of this increase has come from savings and only 7 per cent from an expansion in the money supply.

Of the $146.5 billion increase, $135.8 billion has come from existing funds of non-bank investors—which amount may be called "savings"—and only $10.7 billion from bank credit expansion, or increased money supply—new and additional spendable dollars.

The total increase has been adequate for our most healthy economic expansion in many years. The growth in the money supply, at the rate of only 2 per cent per year, has prevented any objectionable bank credit inflation.

The secret of success in providing adequate funds for proper expansion without inflation is to encourage savings as the principal source. That we have done.

Total loans have increased substantially in the past four years—indeed more than in either of the two preceding four-year periods.

This increase has been primarily in private credit—credit to buy homes, cars, consumer goods—rather than tanks or guns.

This increase has come much more from savings and less from bank credit expansion than in prior years—hence it has been much less inflationary.

The Federal Reserve policy of not encouraging more rapid bank credit expansion has been based on the premise that further expansion of bank credit would merely have enabled more would-be buyers to bid up the price of the limited supply of goods and services.

This policy has been necessary and in the best interests of the great majority of our people. But despite the substantial credit expansion that has taken place, since there has been less new credit created than the demand therefor, there has been some disappointment, and in some cases, real hardship.

It is said that the unavailability of unlimited credit has been particularly burdensome on the housing industry, on small business, and on state and municipal projects. As these areas are very important to all of us, perhaps we should briefly review them.

It is charged that we have impeded the flow of credit to housing. During the past 25 years, far from restricting credit to housing, the Government has greatly increased the volume of credit available to this industry—over what it would be in a normal free market—by stepping in and guaranteeing the payment of millions of homeowners' mortgages.

This has helped to provide many Americans with homes which they otherwise could not afford. On the whole, this has been a good program, but we must recognize that it has introduced certain artificialities into the free market for the purpose of diverting credit from other uses into home mortgages—credit that wouldn't be available to housing without these Government guaranties.

Has this Administration restricted the terms on new housing loans? We have not—we have relaxed them. We have lowered the minimum down payment on FHA loans, and we have permitted 30-year loans in place of the former 25-year maximum. We have materially liberalized FHA mortgage terms on existing homes.

In addition, FNMA special-assistance programs have been innovated since 1952 to provide mortgage support for relocation, redevelopment, and rehabilitation housing under Sections 220 and 221 of the National Housing Act, for housing for the elderly, and for Capehart military housing.

The voluntary home mortgage credit program, started in 1954, has helped obtain home financing for veterans and others in small and remote communities, and for minority group members.

Purchases of mortgages by FNMA in the secondary mortgage market, during the last 12 months, have totaled nearly a billion dollars, an amount surpassed only in calendar year 1950.

Furthermore, in 1950, all of those funds were provided by the Treasury; under the sounder participating programs as Congress has now revised it, the funds largely come from private sources.

According to preliminary figures, in May of this year there were 96,000 private non-farm housing starts. This is a second consecutive monthly increase on a seasonally adjusted basis, and brings the annual rate of new housing starts in May up to 990,000.

While this is somewhat below the annual rate of 1,146,000 starts in May a year ago, and even further below the 1,398,000 rate in May, 1955, it is still a substantial volume of housing.

There are undoubtedly many contributing causes to this decline. For the past few years, home construction has been running ahead of new family formation, with a consequent reduction in the backlog of young families needing a home.

Building costs have risen substantially in the past ten years. The price of land has also risen, as have state and local taxes, which are an element of cost. As the aggregate of these costs result in substantial increases in the price of a home, the number of potential purchasers is reduced.

This cost increase has been accentuated by the host of new labor-saving appliances and luxury equipment which our people feel are now necessary in a home. There has been actual overbuilding in some localities and a diminishing supply of desirable building sites in others.

All of these factors have had an adverse effect on new home construction, but the unavailability of unlimited mortgage credit is also a major factor, and it falls most heavily on those who heretofore have been able to obtain mortgage credit only through Government assistance.

The number of new homes financed through conventional mortgages (based entirely on the credit of the borrower and the amount of his equity) has not declined. Indeed the number of such housing starts so financed in the first five months of this year (269,400) was slightly higher than the number so financed in the first five months of last year.

It is the Government-guaranteed mortgages which are finding the less receptive market. The number so financed in the first five months of this year (114,200) was 42 per cent less than the number financed in the first five months last year. This decline is due to the lower interest rate which such guaranteed loans bear.

The increase in the maximum rate on FHA loans from 4½ per cent to 5 per cent has given such financing renewed strength, but the lack of congressional authorization of an increase in the rate on VA-guaranteed mortgages has made it increasingly difficult for a veteran to obtain such a loan.

The significance of rate limitations is indicated by the most recent figures. Housing starts financed by conventional mortgages increased from 63,900 in April to 69,000 in May—which compares with 64,500 in May, 1956.

Housing starts under the FHA program increased from 12,100 in April, to 15,000 in May—as compared with 19,700 in May, 1956.

Housing starts under VA inspection declined from 13,500 in April, to 12,000 in May—compared with 26,600 in May, 1956.

Thus it appears that there is only a relatively limited supply of mortgage credit available for the small down payment, extended terms, and 4½ per cent interest rate on VA guaranteed loans.

There is a substantial volume of mortgage money available for FHA insured mortgages at the 5 per cent rate, although there is some insistence on higher down payments than the minimum permitted under FHA terms. There appears to be sufficient mortgage credit available to finance those borrowers who can make an adequate down payment and pay the going rate of interest.

This is the result of a free money market. It undoubtedly has caused many young families to postpone the purchase of a new home. Their disappointment, and that of the builder, is understandable.

Yet how much better off would they have been if a more than adequate supply of credit had brought about increased prices, not only of their home but of all the other articles which they desire?

I am sure that there have been some small business firms which have been unable to obtain all of the credit that they would have liked at the rates they would like to pay. I believe this has been true in every year through history, and it has been true for each of the past four years, but this does not mean that there has been any reduction in the dollars of credit extended small business in the past four years. Quite the contrary. Both the number and amount of loans made to small business have been increasing substantially.

In this connection, we must remember that the great majority of our banks are themselves quite small, and the size of the loans they can make is limited by law. Of the 13,101 insured commercial banks in the United States, 10,853 have deposits of less than $10 million each and, in general, cannot make loans above $100,000.

That is almost 11,000, out of the 13,000, that are small banks.

Total loans of banks in this category increased by almost $2.1 billion during the past four years, an increase of 19 per cent. Virtually all of their loans are to farmers, homeowners, consumers, and small business firms.

Another 1,802 banks generally can make loans up to $500,000, but most of their loans would actually be in amounts of less than $100,000. Total loans of banks in this category increased by $4.4 billion during the past four years, an increase of 44 per cent.

The remaining 446 banks do indeed represent almost two-thirds of the nation's deposits, and are of great importance to the economy. They are the primary source of bank credit to larger business firms, but even they make many loans to small business.

A survey made of a representative group of 78 such large banks indicated that in the year from September 1, 1955, to August 31, 1956, their small business loans—for amounts of under $100,000—had increased by $228 million, or 14 per cent; and that the number of such loans had increased by 5 per cent.

Within this group there was more of an increase, both in numbers and dollar amount, in the loans under $50,000 than in those between $50,000 and $100,000.

While it is true that total business loans of banks increased somewhat more rapidly than those loans for amounts under $100,000, this is a pattern which would be expected in such a period of rapid economic expansion, for the cyclical heavy goods industries naturally tend to require a larger volume of credit in such a period.

At all times the established, successful firm is more able to obtain necessary credit than is the new, unproven or unsuccessful company, and this is particularly true of a period of credit stringency. Not all firms have obtained all of the credit they have wanted. Yet, in the aggregate, they have obtained more than ever before.

In addition to the increased amount of bank credit received by small business during the past four years, there has also been a sizable volume of book credit extended by larger firms to smaller firms—distributors, merchants, and suppliers.

I do not mean to minimize the disappointment, inconvenience, and in many cases real hardship, that some businesses have experienced because of their inability to obtain as much credit as they would have liked.

Indeed, this is a matter of deep interest to the Administration which, as you know, has supported the creation of the Small Business Administration, the enactment of improved tax laws, and the granting of exemptions from certain Securities and Exchange Commission regulations. In addition, we have made vigorous efforts to see that more defense work is subcontracted to smaller firms.

Let's look at states and municipalities. In the past four years, a quarter of a million new schoolrooms have been built for our youngsters. Total public construction in 1956 was 23 per cent above 1952 levels, and educational construction was up 56 per cent.

During 1956 alone, new borrowing by states and municipalities totaled $5.4 billion; and during the last nine months for which figures are now available, more elementary and secondary school bonds were sold than in any nine-month period in our history.

State and municipal financing has increased by $18.8 billion in the past four years. This is more than it has ever increased in any other four-year period, and compares with only $11.5 billion during the period 1948–52.

These figures do not demonstrate any extraordinary burden on state and municipal financing from lack of available credit. Undoubtedly, local governments have been unable to obtain all of the funds they would have wished, but they have built more and they have financed more than in any other four-year period.

The Federal Reserve's monetary policy for the past four years has been, and is, one of discouraging the growth of credit at quite as rapid a rate as would-be borrowers desire. As a consequence, some individuals, some home purchasers, some small businesses, and some municipalities, and other categories of our citizens, have felt some pinch as a result of limited credit. But—in the past four years, small loans to business have increased substantially.

In the past four years, $57.5 billion has been spent for housing—as much as had been spent in the preceding six years.

In the past four years, $16.7 billion has been spent for new highway construction—more than had been spent in the preceding 11 years.

In the past four years, $8.8 billion has been spent for school construction—more than had been spent in the preceding 20 years.

This is not the record of extreme credit stringency. Any freer credit would have further inflated prices.

Let's look at the rise in interest rates. The Federal Reserve's abandonment of its pegging of prices in the bond market has prevented an unlimited growth in credit. It was intended to, and did, slow the rate of growth of bank credit.

It also has resulted in some increase in interest rates. It is alleged by some that this increase in interest rates has brought about a severe increase in the burden of taxes and in the prices we pay for manufactured goods, or utility services; that it has materially increased farmers' costs, or the price of a home.

Higher interest—although the result of a lesser supply of credit than the demand therefor, a condition which prevents far greater inflationary increases in other costs—is itself an element of general costs and in some cases may be reflected in higher prices.

However, interest payments are such a small fraction of the total cost of business operations, that a rise in the rate does not represent much of an increase in total cost.

What is the interest burden on the taxpayer?

Total budget expenditures for fiscal 1957 are estimated at $68.9 billion. Of this, $7.2 billion, or 10.4 per cent, represents interest expenditures. The per capita cost of all expenditures of the Federal Government for this fiscal year is $406; for interest alone, the per capita cost is $42.40.

In 1952, interest on the public debt was $37.57 per capita. Thus the increase in interest on the public debt during the past four years amounts to less than $5 per person.

Now, what is the effect on the price of manufactured goods?

In 1946, gross sales of all manufacturers amounted to $132 billion. Manufacturers had net interest expense in that year of about $154 million, equal to one-eighth of 1 per cent of total sales.

In 1952, interest expense had increased to about one-fourth of 1 per cent; and on the basis of limited information now available, it appears that the 1956 ratio will be about one-third of 1 per cent. Thus, interest costs are only one-third of 1 per cent of the average sales price of manufactured goods.

Of the cost of an article selling for $100, about 33 cents represents interest, with no more than 10 cents of that representing an increase since 1952.

Furthermore, the increase in this minor item of interest costs reflects an increase in the amount of debt as well as an increase in interest rates.

The relative unimportance of interest as a part of total costs is reflected in the fact that during the same ten-year period, prices of goods that consumers buy rose 27½ per cent, or $27.50 on a $100 item (due to labor and other costs), compared to the 20-cent increase due to higher interest.

The far greater significance of the increase in labor and other costs is reflected quite clearly in the price of consumers' services which have risen 43½ per cent during the same ten years.

It is apparent from these figures that even with increased interest rates and increased indebtedness, the burden of interest costs on manufacturers in reference to their total costs is very slight. The effect of higher interest on the sales price of goods is hardly significant.

This is even more apparent when we compare the increased costs of the last year. Prices of goods bought by consumers (which reflect material, labor, interest, and profit) have risen 1.3 per cent. The price of consumers' services (which reflect primarily labor costs) has gone up 2.3 per cent.

It has been suggested that higher interest rates lead to substantial increases in public utility rates. . . . However, the latest figures available indicate that the net interest expense of public utilities is still less than four per cent of gross revenue—the same proportion as in 1952. Even for electric utilities, where average interest cost on long-term debt now exceeds 5 per cent of gross revenue, the relative cost of interest has risen very slowly.

The estimated average of 5.2 per cent for both 1955 and 1956 compares with 4.8 per cent in 1952 and 5.0 per cent for 1946. In other words, 5.2 in the last 2 years; 5.0 per cent in 1946.

Difficult as the farmer's position has been, it is not the result of interest rates. The Department of Agriculture estimates that only about 5 per cent of farmers' cost are for interest.

Interest rates on farm loans outstanding in insured commercial banks on June 30, 1956, averaged 6.1 per cent. This was four-tenths of a percentage point higher than the average rate reported in a similar survey made in 1947; less than one-half of 1 per cent difference since 1947.

This four-tenths of 1 per cent increase in rate would be less than one-half of 1 per cent of his total costs, or 5 cents on a sale of $10 worth of farm products.

The effect of higher interest rates in relation to the decline in private non-farm housing starts from 465,000 units in the first five months of last year to 384,000 for the same period this year, has been grossly exaggerated.

Housing is perhaps the most dramatic example of the effect of rising costs. Hourly wage rates in building construction have risen 21 per cent in the past four years. In the manufacture of some products, the increased cost due to hourly labor rates has been offset by greater efficiency. Through use of additional capital goods—tools—the productivity per man-hour has been increased enough so that the total cost has been kept fairly stable. This is true of most of our home appliances.

However, in those fields in which mechanization is not practicable or in which restrictive practices or legal requirements have prohibited maximum efficiency, the cost of the finished product has risen in close relation to the increase in hourly labor rates. There is no better example of this than housing.

Many home purchasers consider only the size of the required monthly payment—not the number thereof or the elements that make it up. To them, interest is of no significance. To the more sophisticated purchaser who inquires as to the component elements in his mortgage payments, increased interest rates are small in relation to increased labor and material costs. . . .

While interest is an element in the cost of mortgaged homes, the increase in interest rates has not been the major factor in delaying home construction. Mortgage interest rates were higher in 1955 than in any prior recent year; yet new non-farm housing starts were the second highest in history, at more than 1,300,000.

Almost 5 million new dwelling units have been built in the past four years. Less than 3.5 million new households have been formed in that period, so that 1.5 million units have gone to satisfy prior shortages and to cover houses abandoned or razed to make way for new construction. The proportion of married couples without their own household has declined 21 per cent since 1952.

A strong desire continues to exist for better housing, but it is hindered from becoming an effective demand by today's inflated prices. To attempt to force an acceleration in home construction today by making more credit available for housing would add further to the already increased building costs.

This would not only be inflationary, it would encourage uneconomic practices and curtail the new construction that we might otherwise expect in years to come.

The foregoing review of the effects of this Administration's fiscal policies indicates that the supply of credit has not been reduced. The supply of credit has merely been prevented from expanding as rapidly as the demand therefor.

This slowing of the rate of growth of credit has inconvenienced those who have found credit unavailable, and imposed a higher charge on those who have borrowed. These results are hardly welcomed for their own sake, but they are the price we have to pay for the price stability that we have achieved in the past four years.

This has been a far greater stability in prices and in the purchasing power of the dollar than we have enjoyed for two decades. Faced with this choice between the inconvenience of limited credit and the robbery of renewed inflation, our people would certainly choose the course which we have pursued for the past four years. . . .

We have not achieved perfection by a long way. We have been unable to fully accomplish some of our debt-management objectives. We have perhaps checked, but not entirely stopped, inflationary pressures.

In the process, some of our citizens, some of our municipalities, and some of our businesses have been unable to obtain all of the credit they would have liked.

We have had a large measure of success in encouraging the initiative of our citizens, but not every business has prospered as much as it might, nor every citizen had all of the comforts he would enjoy.

I acknowledge imperfections in our accomplishments, but I entertain no doubt as to the propriety of our goals or the wisdom of our policies. To aid you in your consideration of the alternative courses, and to help you measure their promises against the actual results of the past four years, let me remind you of some of our achievements.

When we took office in 1953, the federal debt was equal to 89 per cent of our national income—in December, 1956, it was 79 per cent, as compared with 89.

For the fiscal year 1953, budget expenditures were $74.3 billion; and, for the year 1957, they are estimated at $68.9 billion, and $71.8 billion for 1958.

For the fiscal year 1953, the budget resulted in a deficit of $9.4 billion—for 1957, it will result in a surplus.

From 1939 through 1952, the cost of living increased an average of 7 per cent a year—for the past four years, the average increase has been only six-tenths of 1 per cent.

In the past four years, civilian employment has risen 6 per cent, average weekly earnings of production workers in manufacturing have risen 18 per cent and, after allowance for the 2.4 per cent increase in consumer prices which occurred between 1952 and 1956, the gain in workers' earnings, after taxes, amounted to about $10 per week, or more than 15 per cent in real purchasing power gained during the period.

Personal income of individuals has risen every year, from $272 billion in 1952 to $325 billion in 1956, a gain of 20 per cent, and an estimated $340 billion for 1957.

Labor income has not only risen in dollars; it has increased from 67.2 per cent of national income in 1952 to 69.8 per cent in 1956, while corporate profits declined from 12.7 per cent of national income to 11.9 per cent.

Striking achievements have been made in housing. The 5 million dwelling units that were constructed exceeded the number built in any previous four-year period, and substantially enlarged the housing stock available to the American people. . . . A growing proportion of our homes were owner occupied—60 per cent in 1956, as compared with 55 per cent in 1950.

This is a gratifying record of the improvement in the level of living that can be achieved only through a vigorous, competitive, free-market economic system which offers both individual freedom of choice and the stimulation of initiative through personal incentive.

In particular, it shows the capacity of such a system to bring about confidence and daring in enterprise and widespread participation in the benefits of economic expansion. This is a sharp contrast to the artificial restrictions, interferences, and controls of a paternalistic bureaucracy.

The past four years have demonstrated the ability of the nation's private economy to expand, to provide an increasing number of better jobs at better pay, and to raise levels of living. . . .

Because the problems are continually changing in a dynamic economy, policies aimed at promoting stable growth must be flexible. This fact was well illustrated in the past four years of the Eisenhower Administration. Our problems have shifted from those of a controlled, wartime economy to those of a rapidly widening prosperity. We have been able to encourage this prosperity.

Through the flexibility of monetary and fiscal policies, the Government has been able to adjust to the rapid changes in our economy. We have moved forward toward our goals and demonstrated the great

The curl he left behind.

Warren in
The Cincinnati Enquirer,
June 30, 1957

capacity of a free economy to correct imbalance and to maintain growth with a high degree of stability.

We have accommodated the reduction in wartime Government spending, accompanied by record-breaking tax reduction, and offset a threatened decline in employment and business activity in 1953–54.

We have encouraged an expansion of enterprise to new high levels, and, through expenditure and debt reductions as well as debt management, we have slowed the growth of inflationary credit.

We have encouraged a rapidly rising economy which has brought more wealth, more purchasing power, more comfort, more jobs, more homes, more luxuries, more leisure, more education, and more security to our people than they have ever enjoyed before.

Gentlemen, I take great pride in making this report.

Marathon on the stand

*Cross-examination (in part) of Secretary Humphrey
before the Senate Committee on Finance.
Senator Harry F. Byrd, chairman.*

June 19 to July 12, 1957

... THE CHAIRMAN. Do you regard Government spending as inflationary?

SEC. HUMPHREY. I do.

THE CHAIRMAN. Has anything been done by the Administration to reduce that Government spending?

SEC. HUMPHREY. Well, Mr. Chairman, I do not want to get into an argument that sounds political. I want to make it and keep it factual in every way that I can.... I just want to say this: That there is nobody—I have worked with a lot of people in my life, in a lot of ventures of various kinds, and I have never seen anybody more concerned, more thoughtful, who puts in more time and effort than the President of the United States on this budget, and who is more concerned about increasing Government expenditures.

Now, how you balance the services that the people ought to have, that the people demand, how you balance what Congress may do with respect to certain programs where they exceed the requests, how you balance what you ask for, how you balance what is needed for our security against a threatened attack, a threatened enemy, and it is real, and the terrible expenditures that are required continually for the security to save our lives, and how you balance all those things out with an expenditure level for the whole Government that will help to reduce and confine inflationary pressures and still, at the same time, maintain us between inflation and deflation—because that is where we want to try to be, where you are just balanced and can turn either way, that is the happiest situation that America could be in—and how you balance that and maintain it is an extremely difficult thing.

Now, in my experience, I have never seen anybody more dedicated, more honestly attempting to arrive at a proper balance of those factors than the President of the United States, nor anybody who works harder at it.

THE CHAIRMAN. Do you think it is the duty of the President of the United States to yield to all requests for federal expenditures?

SEC. HUMPHREY. No, I do not.

THE CHAIRMAN. You mentioned the fact these programs are being demanded by the public. You say the public have not changed their minds. I do not agree with that.

I have been over the country a good deal, and people have changed their minds. That is reflected by what Congress has done to appropriations.

SEC. HUMPHREY. Well, I of course recognize, Mr. Chairman, just as you do, that there is a great wave of public protest against Government spending. But I still believe you are wrong, to a degree at least, in the extent to which that Government spending protest has reached to the person who is after something for himself....

THE CHAIRMAN. How many letters did you get when you made that statement on the budget about "curling the hair?" How many approving letters did you get?

SEC. HUMPHREY. I got a great many. . . .

THE CHAIRMAN. We have increased borrowing in the last four years by $200 billion—that is the corporations, individuals, and Government. Now, that money is circulating in the economy of the country. Has that borrowing been inflationary?

SEC. HUMPHREY. I think probably it has....

THE CHAIRMAN. Is reduction in taxes inflationary?

SEC. HUMPHREY. I think perhaps temporarily, under certain conditions, it might be. In one of the most important cases of the Supreme Court they enunciated long ago the doctrine that the power to tax is the power to destroy.

I believe that, and I believe that the excessive use of the power to tax can destroy the American system, if it is carried to a sufficient excess; that it will so limit and so decrease the natural pressures that we rely upon to stimulate individual incentive, individual activity and individual endeavor, that you can first change and then perhaps ultimately and finally destroy our system of government.

THE CHAIRMAN. Well, then, you regard the reduction of taxes when they are too high as not inflationary?

SEC. HUMPHREY. I think our taxes now are too high. I think we are taking too much.

Again, these things are never just for the moment. Their effects are extended, they are over a period. But the effect sometimes comes suddenly and very unexpectedly. And I think our taxes are too high, and we should move in every way that we can, and as rapidly as we can and still perform our other obligations, and reduce these taxes.

THE CHAIRMAN. But it should be done only when there is a balanced budget and a surplus in the Treasury?

SEC. HUMPHREY. That is my belief.

THE CHAIRMAN. How much Treasury surplus do you think you should have, to justify a reduction of the taxes?

SEC. HUMPHREY. That, again, is not a fixed amount, it is not a definite thing you can pin right down. We are collecting, in round figures, $70 billion. A 10 per cent reduction of all taxation would be $7 billion. Five would be 3½. I think that to make a suitable and a proper tax reduction, it would take several billion dollars.

THE CHAIRMAN. Would you favor a percentagewise tax reduction, or some other kind?

SEC. HUMPHREY. Well, there again, Mr. Chairman, I have been asked many times to state exactly what to do. I do not think any man can intelligently state exactly what he would do until he knows the amount that would be available for disbursing.

Now, whether it would be advisable to reduce or increase excise taxes simultaneously with a reduction or an increase in income taxes, or how you would apportion it, I think depends very largely upon how much money you have and very largely upon conditions existing at the time a reduction is made.

THE CHAIRMAN. Let us take the imaginary figure of $5 billion. If you had $5 billion, would you pay any part of that on the public debt?

SEC. HUMPHREY. That again would depend very largely on the times that you were in. If you were in a period of very high prosperity and all, your inclination would be to use more of it in debt reduction than in tax reduction.

If you were in a different period of time, you might favor more tax reduction and less debt reduction. It would depend upon the pressures that were on the economy at the time you were confronted with the movement.

THE CHAIRMAN. Eliminate the debt reduction, and if you had $5 billion that could be used for tax reduction, what are your views as to how a $5 billion tax reduction should be made?

SEC. HUMPHREY. I would try to do it in two ways: I would try to do it in ways that would cover the broadest list of people. I would try to cover, if possible, every single taxpayer in some way. And I would try to keep in mind the things that would best serve to stimulate the growth and development of the country.

And between the two, I would try to figure out the most advantageous tax reduction.

[Secretary Humphrey later submitted the following for the record.]

The Secretary of the Treasury
Washington, July 12, 1957

Hon. Harry Flood Byrd
Chairman, Committee on Finance

Dear Mr. Chairman:

I am glad to give you the following answers to the questions you asked of me when you summarized what you regard as "the dangers of our fiscal situation."

I share some of your concern, but, I think, perhaps not to the same extent. I do not believe that great difficulties are inevitable. The good sense of the American people in the conduct of their own affairs supported by appropriate action by the Administration and the Congress, can minimize, if not entirely avoid, most of the difficulties you fear, but this will not be easy. It will take careful thought and analysis and persistent and courageous effort by all concerned.

More specifically:

(1) I hope very much that there will be no necessity for increasing the debt limit, even temporarily. As you know, we have worked very closely with you for the past three years on narrower margins than were previously thought possible in order to preserve this debt limit and still permit the Government to function. I believe in the debt limit. It is a wholesome deterrent to undue spending and it would be unfortunate if it had to be increased permanently, barring, of course, some unforeseen change in worldwide conditions.

(2) I agree with you that a further increase in taxes is not only undesirable but I do not think it could be accomplished and accepted by the public unless some very unusual and unforeseen conditions would justify it. In fact, I will go further and again repeat what I have said so many times before: I believe our present taxes are far too high and must

be reduced in successive reductions over a period of time whenever an excess of receipts over disbursements becomes available in sufficient amount to justify a decrease in taxes, which should then be made concurrently with the accrual of the excess. I think our fiscal policy should be so fashioned that this will result.

(3) I hope that the fear of inflation will continue to concern us because inflationary pressures are incident to prosperity. Just a little continuous inflation, which is often urged, is neither inevitable nor desirable. The happiest situation for the people of this country is to have our economy so balanced between inflation and deflation, with both in such good control, that neither predominantly develops. This is best accomplished by relying principally upon the good sense, the industry, and the great care with which the American people are capable of looking after their own affairs, aided by proper Governmental monetary and fiscal policies. It will, however, require courageous action, promptly taken, probably against criticism, but which, in the end, will prove its worth in better times and better living for our whole nation.

(4) I cannot agree with you that we have no reserves. The United States has a real reserve of credit. Our governmental credit is not unlimited, but as long as we have a Government in power which not only believes in, but practices, sound monetary and fiscal policies, controls its expenditures, and is wise in its operations, the Government of the United States has ample credit and the people will have sufficient confidence in it to meet its needs for financing for whatever it properly may require.

Finally, I do not think it particularly significant to consider what might happen if we returned to the level of governmental receipts in fiscal 1955 which reflect national income levels of 1954. Our population is growing; our individual earnings are increasing; our whole economy has been expanding, and, I hope, will continue to do so. We have had a substantial growth in both population and in income since 1954 as well as in the number of income producers and people employed. If we were to reduce our total governmental income now to the dollar amounts of 1955, it would involve much higher unemployment and deeper cutbacks in production than occurred in 1954 because of this growth in the meantime.

I do, however, share your belief which is based on history that the economy will not grow continuously and uninterruptedly. We will have periods when buying will not be as extensive, confidence will not be as great, and jobs will not be as plentiful nor the income of the people or of the Government as large as at other times. Just when conditions may develop that will effect such changes, it is impossible for anyone to forecast. How much conditions might change, what might be the immediate causes, and how they should best be met can be told only as the conditions unfold and the problems are presented. . . .

George M. Humphrey
Secretary of the Treasury

[The budget balancing record of the Government since 1929 was asked for and submitted by Senator Byrd]

Budget receipts and expenditures
[In millions]

Fiscal year	Budget receipts	Budget expenditures	Surplus or deficit (−)	Fiscal year	Budget receipts	Budget expenditures	Surplus or deficit (−)
1929	$4,033	$3,299	$734	1944	$43,635	$95,059	−$51,423
1930	4,178	3,440	738	1945	44,475	98,416	−53,941
1931	3,116	3,577	−462	1946	39,771	60,448	−20,676
1932	1,924	4,659	−2,736	1947	39,786	39,032	754
1933	2,021	4,623	−2,602	1948	41,488	33,069	8,419
1934	3,064	6,694	−3,630	1949	37,696	39,507	−1,811
1935	3,730	6,521	−2,791	1950	36,495	39,617	−3,122
1936	4,069	8,493	−4,425	1951	47,568	44,058	3,510
1937	4,979	7,756	−2,777	1952	61,391	65,408	−4,017
1938	5,615	6,792	−1,177	1953	64,825	74,274	−9,449
1939	4,996	8,858	−3,862	1954	64,655	67,772	−3,117
1940	5,144	9,062	−3,918	1955	60,390	64,570	−4,180
1941	7,103	13,262	−6,159	1956	68,165	66,540	1,626
1942	12,555	34,046	−21,490	1957	70,628	68,900	1,728
1943	21,987	79,407	−57,420	1958	73,620	71,807	1,813

. . . SENATOR ROBERT S. KERR (Oklahoma). In your testimony you have developed a puzzle in my mind. . . . You said, "As the cost of money rises, there is more incentive to save that money and to put it out at rent." You also said, "Now as you stimulate the savings, of course that generates more money for use in the development of the country, in the building of equipment and machines, and increasing the productive power of the people. . . ." Yet, you told the chairman, ". . . There is a deterrent effect that rises from an increase in the cost of interest, in that people are deterred from taking on obligations that require that additional payment. They do not expand so rapidly or they do not expand inventories quite so rapidly, or they become more cautious. . . ." As I understand it, you are saying that increasing interest rates discourages investment so as not to create inflation.

SEC. HUMPHREY. That is right. Now as between the two . . . it is perfectly simple.

SENATOR KERR. Increasing interest rates encourages savings to make it possible for more expansion, and at the same time, when you increase them, you discourage investment and deter expansion.

SEC. HUMPHREY. And between encouraging the savings and discouraging the expenditures you finally bring them to balance. You operate from both ends and come to a balance. That is exactly where you want to be, and produce some stability. . . .

SENATOR JOHN J. WILLIAMS (Delaware). Mr. Secretary, who actually gets hurt worse as a result of inflation or devaluation of our currency in the country, what classes of people get hurt worst?

SEC. HUMPHREY. The person who is hurt the worst, Senator, I believe, is the individual citizen who is a relatively small saver, who is not a speculator, who is not conversant with and active in financial markets, but who is just a good common citizen of America, and the respected right kind of a citizen of America who is trying to save to protect himself and his family with some nest egg for the future for the purpose of sending children to school or to cover sickness or getting ahead, promoting his own position, and who is unable to and not qualified, and does not want to, study financial markets and/or be in and out of markets and all that sort of thing. He is the fellow who really gets hurt in inflation.

SENATOR WILLIAMS. It could be said that the man who can really afford it the least gets hurt the most?

SEC. HUMPHREY. That is exactly right.

SENATOR WILLIAMS. Is it not also true that in the history of all these instances where we have had wild inflation that the extremely wealthy of the country involved are usually the ones who come out the best in that their investments are usually in fixed assets?

SEC. HUMPHREY. The fellow who comes out the best is the speculator.

SENATOR WILLIAMS. Yes.

SEC. HUMPHREY. The next are the fellows who have advice and help in the handling of their affairs, and who are people of larger affairs; the people who really get hurt are the people who are just going along about their own business doing the right kind of a job and being the fine citizens of the country.

SENATOR WILLIAMS. And whose security is pretty much tied up either in life insurance, pension account, social security, or retirement systems of some type?

SEC. HUMPHREY. That is right.

SENATOR WILLIAMS. You made the suggestion in your opening statement before the committee here, or in reply to one of the questions, I forget which, that inflation grows in a degree proportionate to the prosperity of the country.

SEC. HUMPHREY. I think I said the inflationary pressures grow. . . . The more prosperous you are, Senator, the more watchful you have got to be to see you do not succumb to those pressures.

SENATOR WILLIAMS. Is it possible for a country to have wild inflation in a period of depression or a recession? . . .

SEC. HUMPHREY. It is perfectly conceivable that, having succumbed to the pressures of inflation in a period of prosperity, and started the printing of money, that that might be continued clear on through a depression, and keep going on and on and on until you had the whole economy completely destroyed. . . .

SENATOR GEORGE A. SMATHERS (Florida). Mr. Secretary, what have you specifically done to unhitch inflation from prosperity in the past year?

SEC. HUMPHREY. Well, I think that the monetary policies pursued by the Federal Reserve Board have been beneficial, and will be more beneficial, as time goes on. There is always a lag in these things. They never correspond exactly in timing. What you do today has an effect tomorrow or some time hence, and I think the policies pursued by the Federal Reserve Board in general, with which we have been in accord, have been and will be helpful in restraining the inflationary pressures.

SENATOR SMATHERS. Well, it is an admitted fact, is it not, that the purchasing power of the dollar has decreased by 2 cents in the past year or 18 months.

SEC. HUMPHREY. Two cents in the last year.

SENATOR SMATHERS. That the Consumer Price Index has gone up 3.9 points, I believe it is, in the last year.

Now, is it your opinion that these policies which you have instituted may begin to be felt, possibly not this year, but maybe next year?

SEC. HUMPHREY. Well, I would not say that. I think perhaps they are being felt all along, and that they have had a restraining influence, that the Consumer Price Index might have gone further up without those pressures.

In fact, I feel quite sure that they would. But the full effect, I think, will be delayed somewhat as we go along. It takes time for these things to begin to operate fully.

SENATOR SMATHERS. Do you think that if you had acted sooner, or instituted any new policies or different policies than those which you have instituted, you might have been able to stop the inflation which resulted this past year?

SEC. HUMPHREY. Well, Senator, it is always hard to say. This economic machine of ours is a delicately balanced affair, and I think after most events you can look back and think perhaps you could have done a little better.

On the other hand, if you had begun earlier or had exerted greater pressures, which might have been done, it might have had repercussions which would have been worse than the present situation we are now having. You see, you do not want to go so far that you turn the whole thing about.

I think the illustration I used the first year I was here is about as good an illustration as I can give in the handling of the economy and the care with which it must be done, that is, the Government's participation in it. I likened it at that time to driving a truck down an icy hill. You are going too fast and you do not know what will happen when you get to the bottom of that hill. You try to slow down to make a turn at the bottom of the hill, and you just have to apply the brakes and gradually bring yourself down.

If you slam the brakes on, you will spin around and wind up around a telephone pole. You just have to do it very carefully. . . .

SENATOR SMATHERS. Using that same illustration, however, do you see anything in the statistics of last year to indicate that the brakes you applied are slowing down this inflationary trend?

SEC. HUMPHREY. I think I do. I said something about that the other day. I think, as I said to Senator Kerr, that the short supply situation has been ameliorated, particularly in the heavier lines, and I think there is some evidence that this whole thing is slowing somewhat. . . .

SENATOR SMATHERS. You have been questioned a great deal about the increasing cost of interest rates on Government bonds, and I think in answer to Senator Kerr's question, you stated something to the effect that if we had to refinance our Government debt at the present rate of interest, that it would cost us an additional, I think it was, $2 or $3 billion, was it not? . . .

SEC. HUMPHREY. I think that was it, right in that area somewhere.

SENATOR SMATHERS. Now the question which occurs to me is this: You would like to avoid that, and certainly all of us would. Have you given any thought to the fact that cities and counties and states, and authorities created by those agencies can issue bonds which are tax free? Do you think there would be any advantage if the Government decided to once again make Government bonds tax free?

SEC. HUMPHREY. We have been through that many times, Senator, and I have always been opposed to it. And I am opposed to it for this reason: As it is now, we get back 30 or 40 per cent of this cost, so that while it would cost us, say, $2 billion, the actual cost itself, we collect back quite a bit of it through taxes.

Now, the reason I am opposed to making them tax free, which would automatically tend to make the interest rates lower and probably leave us in about the same position, because by getting back these hundreds of millions we are taking a good big slice out of the $2 billion we pay out, anyhow. The way we are doing it, I think that is the fairest way of doing it, because if we made them tax free, the man who pays a 20 per cent tax would only get 20 cents off; the man who pays a 90 per cent tax would get 90 cents off. And I do not think it is fair to discriminate between the buyers of our bonds in that way. I think so long as we have this steeply graduated tax system, that the thing to do is pay the interest and take it away in taxes on a graduated basis rather than to charge the little man the same amount we do the big man. . . .

SENATOR SMATHERS. Would you say that this trend toward concentration of more assets in the larger firms poses a threat to what you have described as our free-enterprise system? Do you think this is a bad trend, or sort of a dangerous trend?

SEC. HUMPHREY. I really do not know, Senator, and I do not know that I can get it, quite, from this table.

SENATOR SMATHERS. Well, if you do not follow this table, I think that Mr. Mayo and you gentlemen know that there has been a greater and greater increase in the assets of the very large corporations, and I think there has been a consequent—

SEC. HUMPHREY. I think that is right. I think what is going on is that, as we are making bigger and bigger things and more expensive things, and turning out larger volumes, that we are requiring, in order to make costs reasonable, larger machinery and larger investment, larger machine tools, and all the things that we use; we require much more power than we used to use.

For a man to earn the kind of wages he gets today, he has to have more power, and he has to have bigger machines, and more of them. And I think that our whole trend is toward bigger and more expensive things, more mechanical, electronic, and all sorts of devices, in order to multiply a man's earning power.

Of course, that is what makes this country; it is the ability to increase an individual's productivity. If you can supplement that with investment, with power, with all these new machines and larger machines, and more powerful machines, and electronic devices, and all of the things we have, that makes that man more productive, and, as he becomes more productive, it permits the making of goods that would cost less; it makes better goods, and it means that the man can earn more money. And I think that is part of this whole great program that is going on in America.

SENATOR SMATHERS. With respect to this matter of industrial production which we talked about just a few minutes ago, I understood you to say that while you expected capacity to be getting bigger in the immediate future, you did not indicate whether you thought that production would continue to decline and level off or would increase. . . .

SEC. HUMPHREY. I suppose that is going to be selective in various industries. There are some industries where I think this adjustment is taking place, and we are always adjusting, you know, we are never static; we are always adjusting someplace, and as this adjustment is operating, I think you will find that production will be increasing in certain lines, and maybe decreasing in others.

SENATOR SMATHERS. On page 16 of the *Economic Indicators*, it shows that in December, 1956, total industrial production was at a figure of 147; that in January, February, March, April, May, it declined until in May it indicated 143, total industrial production, which would indicate that the trend as far as production and business activity, is down.

SEC. HUMPHREY. Some leveling off.

SENATOR SMATHERS. You feel that that trend will continue for some time?

SEC. HUMPHREY. Well, I do not know whether it will continue. If the adjustment just rolls on in that sort of way, I think it probably would be a very salutary thing. It would help us all along the line. . . .

SENATOR SMATHERS. It is your opinion that that would create unemployment and things of that nature?

SEC. HUMPHREY. Not if it is just a little. Not if it just levels off and we have just a continuing adjustment, first here and then there.

SENATOR SMATHERS. Do you think that that would result in less operation at plant capacity in many of the firms?

SEC. HUMPHREY. In some lines, there would be a little, and in others not. It is again, as I say, it will be an adjustment, and that, you see, Senator, is the happiest thing that can happen to this country, because if we let these excesses grow, if you let demand go and excesses do reach a point where the whole thing lets go at once, that is when we have a lot of trouble.

Now, if it can just happen a piece here and a piece there, readjust here and readjust there, a piece at a time, that is when we have our best times in America. . . .

SENATOR GEORGE W. MALONE (Nevada). What kind of a money system are we using now? How would you describe it?

SEC. HUMPHREY. I do not know just what you mean.

SENATOR MALONE. Well, suppose someone just asked you, as they ask me all the time. It has been some time since you have been out there, but you are going back, I understand, so you had better look this up. . . . Is it a "managed currency," for example?

SEC. HUMPHREY. Well, I do not know, exactly.

SENATOR MALONE. What I am driving at is whether we are running it on a principle of sound money or is it being managed by somebody or a board or commission? What is behind the currency, or how do you regulate the value of the currency?

SEC. HUMPHREY. Well, I do not know just how to answer you, Senator.

"There goes my
strong right arm!"

Russell in
The Los Angeles Times,
1957

SENATOR MALONE. In your own way; put a little horse sense in the
thing. We do not want any of these pat answers.

SEC. HUMPHREY. Under your Federal Reserve Act, the issuing of
money is under the control of the Board, and so are the limitations
on credit. . . . I really think, if you want to get into that sort of thing,
you are far better off to ask it of Bill Martin.

SENATOR MALONE. No. He is too smart. I assure you, I did not
mean that to be funny. I would not know Mr. Martin if he walked
through the door, and I have been here 11 years. I know you, I knew
you the second day you were here. You are easier to get acquainted
with, and you have not yet elevated yourself above ordinary mortals.

You say he controls the monetary system?

SEC. HUMPHREY. No; I do not think he controls it.

SENATOR MALONE. Who does?

SEC. HUMPHREY. Well, you really have got to get out the Federal
Reserve Act and read the powers they have.

SENATOR MALONE. Did you ever read it?

SEC. HUMPHREY. I have read it.

SENATOR MALONE. I have tried to, but you are in the business. Now
tell me about how it is done. Is it a managed currency?

SEC. HUMPHREY. There are some ways of expanding and contracting credit ... that are reflected in the currency; yes. ...

SENATOR MALONE. What happens to a man who saved his money and worked hard to put it away in the bank, and deprived himself, his wife and children of things they really wanted in order to save, what happens to that fellow when the dollar is worth 48 cents instead of the 100 cents when he put it away, Mr. Secretary?

SEC. HUMPHREY. Well, it just means that his savings will buy that much less than they would have bought.

SENATOR MALONE. Less than half. They gave him back a dollar out of the savings account in the bank, but they did not give him the purchasing power by 52 per cent.

SEC. HUMPHREY. That is exactly right. That is what happens when you get these uncontrolled inflations.

SENATOR MALONE. Is that what we have had, uncontrolled inflation?

SEC. HUMPHREY. It wasn't too well controlled for a number of years. The last four years it has been very moderate.

SENATOR MALONE. Well, the table you are going to give me will show that, will it not?

The table at the top of page 344 was subsequently submitted.

SENATOR MALONE. The Government makes 38½ cents on every ounce of silver used for money. In other words, when you stamp a silver dollar—and I always carry a couple of them—

SEC. HUMPHREY. I have one of them, too. I will match you.

SENATOR MALONE. My whole point is, after all the argument about this business, and to keep the record straight, that the price of silver by law is $1.29 when it is used for money, just as gold is worth $35 an ounce when it is used for money.

SEC. HUMPHREY. That is right.

SENATOR MALONE. Of course, we do not use it for money now. It is just a theatrical term as far as American citizens are concerned.

SEC. HUMPHREY. You have got one extra dollar, anyway. [They matched dollars and Malone won.] ...

SENATOR WALLACE F. BENNETT (Utah). The point I want to get at today, you related equity financing to the financing through retained earnings.

SEC. HUMPHREY. Yes.

Consumer prices and the purchasing power of the dollar, 1913 to date

	Consumer Prices (1947–49 =100)	Purchasing power of the dollar			Consumer prices (1947–49 =100)	Purchasing power of the dollar	
		1934=$1	1939=$1			1934=$1	1939=$1
Calendar year averages:							
1913	42.3	$1.351	$1.404	1937	61.4	$0.932	$0.967
1914	42.9	1.333	1.385	1938	60.3	.949	.985
1915	43.4	1.318	1.368	1939	59.4	.963	1.000
1916	46.6	1.227	1.274	1940	59.9	.955	.992
1917	54.8	1.044	1.083	1941	62.9	.909	.944
1918	64.3	.890	.924	1942	69.7	.820	.852
1919	74.0	.773	.803	1943	74.0	.773	.803
1920	85.7	.668	.693	1944	75.2	.760	.790
1921	76.4	.749	.778	1945	76.9	.744	.772
1922	71.6	.799	.830	1946	83.4	.686	.712
1923	72.9	.785	.815	1947	95.5	.599	.622
1924	73.1	.782	.812	1948	102.8	.556	.578
1925	75.0	.763	.792	1949	101.8	.562	.583
1926	75.6	.756	.786	1950	102.8	.556	.578
1927	74.2	.771	.801	1951	111.0	.515	.535
1928	73.3	.781	.810	1952	113.5	.504	.523
1929	73.3	.781	.810	1953	114.4	.500	.519
1930	71.4	.801	.832	1954	114.8	.498	.517
1931	65.0	.880	.914	1955	114.5	.500	.519
1932	58.4	.979	1.017	1956	116.2	.492	.511
1933	55.3	1.034	1.074	Months:			
1934	57.2	1.000	1.038	May 1956	115.4	.496	.515
1935	58.7	.975	1.012	May 1957	119.6	.478	.497
1936	59.3	.964	1.002				

Source: Department of Labor and derived computations.

SENATOR BENNETT. I would like for a second, with your help, to relate financing through the issuance of debt securities, mortgages, debentures, to financing through retained earnings.

After all, do they not come back to the same fundamental source of money? If I were to go out to seek a source or sources from which

I could borrow a million dollars, one of the first questions I would have to answer is, "Is your earnings position good enough to give us an assurance that this money will be paid back when it is due?"

And does that not mean, then, that when you borrow money, you simply create a difference in the time pattern when that money must come out of earnings?

SEC. HUMPHREY. Well, very broadly. But the second question he will ask is, "How much money have you got in your business?" And, I do not care what your earnings are, if you do not have any money in your business, you probably will not get the loan.

SENATOR BENNETT. Is it fair to say, Mr. Secretary, that in the end, all expansion, whether in an individual's own inventory of household or other fixtures and supplies, or in an industry's inventory of facilities and goods, must be financed out of the earnings of the company, over the long pull?

SEC. HUMPHREY. I do not believe so, not necessarily.

Let us say again that you and I are going into business, and let us say that—I think you can get these things awfully complicated. . . . We are going to start in business, and we will not start on quite as big a scale as you are on, as you started on, but let us say that we need, you and I have an idea, we starting out in business, and let us say we figure that with $25,000 we can get ourselves started.

I have a little money and you have a little money, and we go around and we get Senator Williams and Senator Frear and Senator Flanders all to come along with us. They put in a little money, and out of it we raise $25,000, and we issue some stock with that. That is equity. We do not owe anybody. They cannot ask us to pay it back, we do not have to pay it back and never intend to pay it back.

That money is in the business, and we intend it shall stay in the business as long as we will stay in business. The only way anybody will ever get it back is if we liquidate the business.

But we expect to get some return, we expect the business to earn something and pay us some dividends on it.

Let us say we are successful, and we go along and get started, and let us say we do pay ourselves some dividends so that we are all getting a modest return on our money. But our business is growing and developing, and we get the Senators together and we say, "Now, this year we have earned $4."

Let us just say, for sake of argument, that we have $25,000 invested in equipment, and that we sell $25,000 worth of goods in a year.

I will make it $100,000, just to make it even. Just to make it easy, let us say we have $100,000 invested in equipment and plant, and we sell $100,000 worth of goods in a year. And the goods, our labor and our materials and all the rest of it, cost us $92,000; we sold it for $100,000 and we have $8,000 left.

That is not an inordinate profit, it is a reasonable profit on a turn-over. The first thing we have to do is to pay $5 or to pay $4 and a few cents, of each hundred dollars of that to the Secretary of the Treasury, he gets the first bite, and that leaves us with $4, in round figures.

Now, our business is growing, we want to expand a little, we want to buy some new machinery, and so we get together and we say, "Last year we paid $2 in dividends, but we want to spend a little money this year, a little extra money this year, and what we would like to do would be to cut down this dividend, and we will only pay $1 in dividend, and that will leave us $3 that we can use of this $100 to help pay for this new equipment."

But that is not enough. That does not buy enough. We all say we do not think we want to put in any more stock equity in the company; we will put in our earnings, $3 of earnings, instead of getting them in dividends, but we would like $1 in dividends or something for the money that is in there.

But the rest of it, we do not want to put in. You go to the bank, Senator, and see what you can do. You go to the bank, and the first question the bank asks you is what you said, "What are your earnings?"

And the second question he asks you is the question I said, "How much money have you got in your business?" And if you have that amount of money in your business, and if you have that kind of earnings, and you want to borrow a reasonable amount of money that is a safe loan against that—$25,000, $50,000, some number of dollars of that kind, against what you have got in—you will get your loan.

If you want to borrow a million dollars on that basis—he will turn you down. He will say, "You have got neither the earnings nor the equity," or if you had some exceptional earnings with that equity, he will say you cannot have it anyhow, because he must feel sure.

He is lending other people's money, the bank's money does not belong to him. It belongs to thousands of other people, and he has to be cautious to see that it is loaned, first, to make a return on it but, above all, to be sure he gets paid back, so that he will have that money paid back to him. . . .

Now, you can get awfully complicated reading about these things in books, but when you do it, it is a perfectly simple, obvious transaction.

SENATOR BENNETT. You feel, then, that—

SEC. HUMPHREY. Now, that is all equity, the $3 we put in is just the same, and it goes in alongside of the original money we put in.

Now, that money is never going to get back to us. We do not expect to draw it out. We expect to get earnings on it; but not the money back.

But the money we get from the banker we have to pay back, or if we sell bonds. . . .

SENATOR ALBERT GORE (Tennessee). . . . In view of this statement by former President [Hoover] that the raising of interest rates had no effect at all to stop the boom, or check the speculation in corporate issues, I wonder if you would be willing to indicate whether you think the higher interest rates imposed for the past four years have had an appreciable effect in that regard.

SEC. HUMPHREY. As I have said, Senator, a number of times, both in this hearing and previously, I do not believe that there is any single system or any pat way or easy way of controlling the whole economy from Washington.

I do not believe, and I think everybody must recognize, based on the experience that we all went through, that you read from the situation in 1929, that interest rates alone or Federal Reserve Board action alone can prevent a reaction if excesses have occurred in the economy of so great a nature that they, in turn, will force revisions through economic laws.

I think, as I have said yesterday and as I have said many times before, that we can in Government lean against the wind, the Government can attempt to discourage on the upside and encourage on the downside, and I think its efforts can be helpful, within limits.

I do not think they can be conclusive. I do not think any one of the things that can be done is particularly effective unless it is joined in with others. I think that a sound financial position—a sound fiscal policy—must follow along.

I think control of Government spending is a very important element of this whole situation. I think the fact that we are spending so much money now for our security, that we are putting so much money into payrolls for the manufacture and production of goods which make no contribution whatever to the permanent capital of the country—and I am thinking of armaments and I am thinking of bombs, I am thinking of guided missiles, I am thinking of long-range bombing airplanes. We are putting billions of dollars into those things and into research for the further production or the improved production of those things, all of which goes into payrolls, goes into the spending stream, goes into the power of people to buy, and produces no goods whatever for the people to buy with the money that goes into that spending stream.

Now, I think that that situation, in and of itself, is a great inflationary pressure. It is going on in other countries of the world, and for pretty much the same reasons.

I believe that by leaning against the wind, by attempting to restrain excessive optimism at proper times, and to discourage excessive pessimism at other times, we can moderate swings. I hope we can do so, and by Government financing and better control, and continually improving Government control of expenditures, and ultimately a lessening of Government expenditures by substantial amounts, by some way or other in this world working out a more secure system so that so much of the world's effort is not directed to the production of goods which do not contribute to the living of the people, the armaments that I speak of, so that so much effort is not dissipated in that form but can be turned into the making of machine tools and the building of factories and the making of goods that people can enjoy currently, add to the capital of the country or to the living of the people. As that goes on I think we have, if we are wise and careful, and if we are flexible and do not get rigid in our positions, I think we have an opportunity to at least ameliorate swings, and I hope avoid any serious swings. . . .

SENATOR GORE. It was only yesterday that you told Senator Anderson that taxation, in your opinion, should be for one purpose, and I believe one purpose only, that of raising revenue.

This would indicate that in 1954 you had a different purpose in mind.

Continuing the quote: "Largely because of tax restrictions, the trend in recent years has been sharply away from equity financing toward borrowing. This is the wrong way for America's economy to finance its expansion."

Now, that comes to the point I asked you a few moments ago: To what extent you thought it was proper for corporations in a quasi-monopoly supply position to finance expansion from prices and profit increases, price and profit inflation, rather than from equity financing.

In 1954 you said this was the wrong way for America's economy to finance its expansion. Is that your view today?

SEC. HUMPHREY. Well, now, you have asked two questions, and let me answer them one at a time.

The first question you asked, if I had a different view four years ago about taxation than I had yesterday when I was talking to Senator Anderson—

SENATOR GORE. That was not a question. That was a statement. You may treat it as a question.

SEC. HUMPHREY. I want to correct it, because it is a misstatement.

SENATOR GORE. Why?

SEC. HUMPHREY. It is not correct. I have had exactly that same view, and if you will look back into many of my speeches at that time, you will find exactly the statement I made yesterday, I made at that time.

The reason that I favored at that time, and still favor, a reduction in the double taxation of dividends is because, as I said to Senator Anderson yesterday, I believe that in raising the amount of money we have to have to pay our bills, it should be as fairly distributed as possible, and I think it is unfair to tax double the dividends that are earned by corporations. I think it is a double taxation on the same money.

We limit it to a limited number of people, and those are the people who are stockholders in corporations.

Therefore, I advocated and recommended, and I still advocate and recommend, that double taxation be eliminated.

SENATOR WILLIAM E. JENNER (Indiana). Is it desirable to retain the present plan of giving the Federal Government a monopoly of all investment funds of the social-security system, particularly when Government is taking the money as received and spending it for general Government expenses? Do not those who have contributed this money have a right to put their money where it will bring the highest safe return?

SEC. HUMPHREY. Well, I think I can only answer that question, or best answer that question in this way: I have said this before; when I first came down here, I was talking to a business friend, who said to me, "The people pay money into these funds. You collect money from them and take it from funds or pensions for social security and so forth. I am told that what you do is that, the minute that money gets in there, you take that money all out and spend it for your general purposes, and you just stick an IOU in the box and that all you have got in the box there, in the fund, are a lot of your IOU's...."

And I said, "Yes, that is true."

"Well," he said, "that is stealing, is it not? You are just about stealing, are you not?"

And I said again, "No, I do not think we are." I said, "Your company has a pension fund, has it not?"

He said, "Yes, it has."

"Well," I said, "you try to protect that the best you can, do you not?"

And he said, "Yes, I do."

I said, "What have you got it invested in?"

He said, "We have got our pension fund invested in Government bonds."

I said, "So have we."

Senator Jenner. But it is still an IOU; is it not?

Sec. Humphrey. It is still an IOU.

Senator Jenner. It has to be paid.

Sec. Humphrey. That is right.

Senator Jenner. Would it not have good political and economic effects if the Government had to bid for social insurance trust funds by putting its fiscal house in order, and offering competitive rates, rather than having a monopoly in these funds by law?

Sec. Humphrey. Somebody has to determine what this money is put in. And, very frankly, in spite of all that we have heard and all the questions—and they are all proper questions and proper matters of concern—I think a promise to pay of the United States Government is the best investment in the world, the most secure, the safest investment.

The Chairman. It has been my privilege, Mr. Secretary, to serve with you closely during your five years of service as Secretary of the Treasury. We have had our differences and some have been rather sharp, but I have a great admiration for your ability and your high patriotism, and this close association with you has been a great privilege.

I regret that you are leaving the public service, and wish you much contentment and happiness in whatever work you may undertake.

The committee wishes to note that you have testified on 14 days since the hearings were started on June 18, and that your interrogation has covered nearly 1,500 pages.

The chairman has not checked the record, but your examination must be among the most exhaustive. I am advised unofficially the former Secretary of the Army Stevens also was on the witness stand 14 days, in an examination of some television fame earlier in this Administration. . . .

I am proud of the manner in which these complex and difficult matters have been brought before you, the committee, and the public.

Fourteen members of the committee have examined you on all aspects of the problem, and I believe they have exhausted your official and personal knowledge of the situation confronting us. . . .

As chairman of the Senate Finance Committee, I am glad to have the opportunity to make this statement today, because this is perhaps your last appearance before the committee as Secretary of the Treasury.

It is possible the committee will want your counsel as times goes on, and, if so, I know you will be glad to appear whenever requested.

So I bid you good day, but not goodby.

SEC. HUMPHREY. Mr. Chairman, I would be entirely out of character if I did not say that I was very glad that this examination is terminated, at least for the present. And, of course, I will make myself available in the future, probably not in the capacity in which I am now here, as long as this committee is active and wants anything that I can contribute.

I should like to say this: This has been a long hearing, and it was an exhausting hearing; but while it was exhausting of your physical resources, it was also, as you pointed out, exhausting the subject.

And I agree with you that there is no subject, no subject, that is as important to the American people as the subject you were discussing, which is, in its broadest aspects, the fiscal and monetary policies of this Government, and what is required.

And you are blazing new trails. We are going to blaze new trails in the future. There never has been any country in the history of the world which has owed so much money as we have. The effect of this debt, the effect of our obligations, the effect of the degree of taxation to which we have been submitting ourselves, are things that nobody knows where they will land or how they can best be handled.

So that, whether I am here or whether I am not here—and I just want to say in that context that, while I again would be out of character if I did not say that I am looking forward to the things that I am going to do when I leave here, these four and one-half years have been the most rewarding and the most interesting years of my life. Any association with you, Mr. Chairman, and with the members of this committee, with whom we have worked just as closely and, I think, just as agreeably, I think, as it would be possible to do, is one of the very fine things that has happened to me in Washington. I am glad to have been able to seek the counsel and have the benefit of the advice that you and your associates have given me.

Now, I hope that this investigation will continue and, despite its length and despite all the things which have been said about it, I just want to compliment you and the members of this committee on the fact that, brushing aside the little things, the objective of this investigation has been to try to probe into these extremely difficult things that we do not any of us know exactly how they are going to work, and to try to decide how best really to do it, what is best for America. . . .

TAXATION

◤ This collection of Secretary Humphrey's speeches and statements is intended to set forth his philosophies and observations as to taxation rather than the timetable of 1953 postponement of tax reduction and 1954 reduction of taxes in which he took a prominent part; the detail of his tax operations is principally reported in Fiscal Policy and the Sound Dollar, with which it is inseparably mingled.

Let it be noted here, then, that under the President's leadership he succeeded in halting Congress in 1953 from midyear cancellation of the excess profits tax and in postponing Congress' intended midyear ten per cent tax reduction of ten per cent until 1954 for individuals and for corporations until 1955, pending a year's Congress-Treasury revision of the entire tax structure. By 1955 actual tax reduction by the Eisenhower Administration totaled $7.4 billion, "the largest dollar tax cut in the history of this or any other country."

During his service, three Congresses produced various tax proposals piecemeal. The Secretary induced the first to wait on the overall tax revision of 1954 and in general stood off the next two when proposing departure from the principles of the 1954 revision. He departed feeling that the tax burden was too heavy on the nation and that he ought to have done more to bring the burden into fiscal safety.

"How much reduction in expense"

Remarks by Secretary Humphrey before the American Society of Newspaper Editors in Washington. The Secretary appeared in a panel discussion; Under Secretary W. Randolph Burgess and Assistant Secretary Marion B. Folsom also took part. The panel was devoted to questions from the floor.

April 16, 1953

MARSHALL FIELD, JR. (*Chicago Sun-Times*). If we were to be threatened with a recession, would you favor a tax reduction, Mr. Secretary, in spite of the fact that the budget is not balanced?

SEC. HUMPHREY. I think we have to have tax reduction. I think our taxes are too high. I think we have got to bring them down, but I also think our expenses are too high and we have got to bring them down. I think we can do both and should do both.

LLOYD M. FELMLY (Newark, N.J., *Evening News*). . . . Have you given any real thought to the question of putting gold back into circulation?

SEC. HUMPHREY. The answer is no. . . .

J. N. HEISKELL (Little Rock, Ark., *Gazette*). Was the Roosevelt Administration justified in taking us off the gold standard?

SEC. HUMPHREY. Maybe we should say we are too young to remember that. . . .

WARREN BOOTH (*Detroit News*). When you mention the figure of $2 billion as a loss of revenue coming from the demise of the excess profits tax. . . . I have in mind income taxes on individuals which would retrieve, I think, a very large per cent of the revenue lost. . . . It seems to me all businesses should shoulder the burden of supplying the necessary revenue to come from corporations. I was wondering whether the Treasury Department had any thought as to how they would save themselves whole; would they suggest the upping of the basic rates on all business or all corporations? . . .

MR. FOLSOM. We are not in a position to comment on that until we see the budget figures.

SEC. HUMPHREY. I will just say a word about that. We do not believe in reaching decisions until we know the facts that we have come to reach them on. Now, until we know how near we are going to come to balancing the budget, what our deficit is, and what we are facing, we are not making any decisions with respect to what position we are going to take in connection with the reduction of taxes.

That will depend entirely upon how much reduction in expenses we can get, how nearly we can come to balancing the budget. When we know the facts that we have to face, when we know how much money we have to spend, then we will determine what we have to do about getting the money in to spend.

ROBERT KENNEDY (*Chicago Sun-Times*). Will the Secretary comment on the theory some people have that tax reduction is actually a revenue producer for the Government?

SEC. HUMPHREY. That of course is very largely a matter of timing. We believe that, to a very large extent, the kind of taxes and the manner in which they are levied, can make a great deal of difference in the amount of dollars that you get in. We believe it is perfectly possible to have a tax system and rates that will be self-defeating, that will curtail the actual amount of taxes that you can get in; and that, over a period, will kill initiative and destroy the incentive that makes for income for the people, which will in turn reduce the taxes.

Neither one of those things happens all of a sudden. If you reduce rates you do not immediately get the return back in. It takes some time for both to work out but certainly the height of the tax rates and the manner of distribution, the base of your system, can have a great deal to do with the total amount of money you can get in over a period and still have an effective, flourishing economy.

"We will interpret the laws without bias"

Remarks by Secretary Humphrey to the White House Conference of State Governors in Washington.

May 5, 1953

Two weeks ago I said publicly in a speech at New York that I did not believe that we are headed for a depression. I meant it then, and I can only repeat here now to you governors that I firmly believe we are not headed for a depression.

Some people have been talking as though they were afraid of what peace might bring. They fear what might happen to our economy if Government spending for defense is reduced. They seem to think that a free economy devoted just to peace would lead to a depression. Readjustments take place in any active economy, and will take place whether we have an armistice, a real peace, or continue to develop a proper and balanced posture of defense. But a depression need not occur if we American citizens—and that includes you leaders of state governments as well as the Federal Government people here in Washington—have the courage to avoid the excesses of speculative boom as well as the courage to deal with readjustments as they occur. . . .

We have now turned from unhealthy policies followed during the past 20 years, which induced inflation, depreciated our currency, and threatened to exhaust our credit. During that time our dollar has gone to 50 cents, and the manipulation of interest rates on billions of dollars of short-term indebtedness was created became awfully close to printing money. We find ourselves with more than $264 billion in total indebtedness, with more than $175 billion maturing in less than five years.

Last Thursday President Eisenhower pointed out that we have inherited a carry-over of $81 billion in outstanding obligations and unsatisfied authorizations, which will have to be paid for from revenues in 1954 and future years. As the President pointed out, this situation has occurred because of the lack of balance between the military logic and the economic logic. It is our purpose to try to bring our military and economic requirements into joint and sensible relationship.

This legacy that we have inherited includes a tax rate structure so high that it is adding greatly to the cost of living as well as threatening to destroy the incentive to work and save. However difficult the problem may seem, it is one which I am confident that we can solve, given proper courage and forebearance on the part of all Americans. . . .

As governors of our great states and territories, you are all as aware as we are here of the public clamor for reductions in taxes. There is no question in my mind but that present taxation is far too high and must come down. It is simply a matter of the timing when taxes can be reduced as we are able to get our spending under control.

In addition to simply reducing taxes so that our citizens can have to spend in their own way what the Government has been spending for them, we are also concerned with revising our tax system's patchwork and often unfair structure. This long-range study of the entire tax structure was directed by the President in his State of the Union Message, so as to "impose the least possible obstacle to the dynamic growth of the country." In this study we are taking up such things as the proper balance between individual income taxes, corporation income taxes, and excise taxes. We are also going into the question of depreciation allowances. Undersecretary of the Treasury Folsom is devising some proposed fundamental changes in tax allowances for depreciation, which we think will encourage people to go ahead and make more capital investments. We are inclined to feel that the desire to write off a large part of the cost of new heavy machinery in its early years is a perfectly legitimate one in view of the risks involved in long-term capital investment. As greater discretion is allowed in this field, it will be of advantage to the whole economy, which will benefit in greater industrial activity and consequent higher employment, wages, and standards of living.

In this long-range tax structure review, we are working closely with the interested Congressional committees and hope to have some results ready sometime in 1954.

The administration of tax collection, as carried out by our Bureau of Internal Revenue, is a matter in which we at Treasury also have great interest. The Bureau of Internal Revenue in recent years came under a cloud of improper actions by some of its personnel. Under the energetic leadership of Commissioner Andrews, the Bureau in the first three months of the new Administration has shown substantial improvement, and I feel that as the months go by it will regain its rightful stature of integrity and efficiency for the American public. . . .

We feel that it is our job to collect only the taxes that have been imposed by the Congress. I feel that we should commend both the employee who finds overpayment and the employee who finds underpayment. . . . We will interpret the laws without bias. We will not penalize any particular activity because it is out of line with a philosophy.

An example of this is the provision which allows income earned abroad by any one who is out of the country for 17 out of 18 months to be exempted from U. S. taxation. As enacted the law allowed very high salaried people to get a net income several times as high if they stayed abroad as they would have received if they had done their work at home. It was suggested that Treasury solve the problem by interpreting the law so as not to apply in cases we disapproved of. The Treasury informed the Congress, however, that the better course was to change the law rather than get around it by arbitrary rulings.

I have mentioned the tremendous public debt which this Government faces. It has been the objective of this Administration not only to reduce this debt but to convert it into longer-term securities, which will tend to be less inflationary than the short-term securities in the hands of banks have proven to be over the past twenty years.

Last month the Treasury successfully sold its first issue of long-term marketable bonds since 1945. This was slightly more than a $1 billion offer of 3¼ per cent bonds. This offering was well taken by non-bank buyers, and we have reduced by this extent inflationary financing through the banks.

There has been, I notice, some uninformed criticism of our higher interest rate, which I might try to explain in a moment. The bond was sold at the going market rate without any help from the Federal Reserve System. The results show that we were not overgenerous in the rate, in view of the large demand for money at this time.

The market for money is tight, and the sale of our long-term issue has made it a little tighter. If that should lead to the postponement of some projects by business or government units, it would be a good thing. Today we have full employment and high production. It makes sense to stretch out some projects into later years.

This bond issue was a part of our campaign to preserve a sound dollar for the American people and to help avoid inflation or deflation. . . .

We believe in the American way of life and a free-market economy. This is what has made America great. It has withstood wars and political manipulations and all sorts of experiments. It will overcome all the problems of today.

As I said a couple of weeks ago, peace is what we all want. It is nothing to fear, nor is there any reason for depression. As long as we maintain the soundness of our money, attain that nice balance between security from aggression and economic strength at home, eliminate waste, and handle our fiscal affairs with wisdom, we can look forward to the future with real hope.

Not for a U. S. sales tax

Statement by Secretary Humphrey at the Treasury Department.

September 30, 1953

The Treasury has advised the President that its studies indicate that the general retail sales tax is in such widespread use by states and other governmental taxing authorities that the Administration should take the position that this field should not be invaded by the Federal Government.

The Treasury's studies on the wide range of other tax reforms and methods of taxation will continue, in collaboration with Congressional committees and their staffs.

☛ After a summer of work with the Ways & Means Committee on the 1954 tax revision-reform bill, the Secretary had met with the "sales tax" inquiry from various Congress members and some protests from the many states employing the sales tax as a chief revenue support. This settled the matter.

The Administration "is reducing taxes"

Article by Secretary Humphrey in Nation's Business *under the title "More Tax Cuts Are Essential."*

January, 1954

This Administration has worked toward two great goals during its first year in office.

In the first place, this nation must—and will—provide the military posture best designed for its own protection and to promote peace in the world.

Second, this nation must—and will—maintain the sound economy and productive power which are prerequisites for that military strength and leadership for peace.

This Administration is sincerely committed to—and working strenuously toward—both these vital goals.

Only through peace—real, lasting peace—can the forces for possible destruction of great cities and peoples be brought into use for the service and good of mankind. While seeking this real peace, we must be militarily strong. And to be militarily strong, we must maintain the healthy productive economy which, after all, underlies and provides the very basis for any strong defense.

During the first year of the Eisenhower Administration our aim has been to establish sound, honest money as a primary basis for a healthy economy. We must have sound money not only for the protection of millions of Americans who work and save. We must have it so that all the virtues of thrift, enterprise and initiative, which have made this nation great, will continue not only to live but to develop further.

We believe that the sound, honest dollar is the foundation of economic strength in America.

This administration fell heir to heavy burdens of fiscal and economic policies. These include:

(1) The huge public debt.

(2) The restrictive debt limit.

(3) $81 billion in COD orders.

(4) Extravagance in government.

(5) The staggering tax burden.

(6) A rigidly controlled economy.

(7) On top of it all, a war of stalemate, not only taking the lives of American boys in Korea but putting additional financial burdens upon our people.

The fiscal and economic objectives which President Eisenhower set forth in his State of the Union Message two weeks after assuming office were:

(1) To reduce the planned deficits of the previous Administration and then, at the earliest possible time, balance the budget by reducing federal expenditures to the very minimum within the limits of safety.

(2) To meet the huge costs of our defense.

(3) To manage properly the burden of our inheritance of debt and obligations.

(4) To check the menace of inflation.

(5) To work toward the earliest possible reduction of the tax burden, remove inequalities, cover omissions and reconstruct the tax laws to lessen their restrictive effect upon the vigorous growth of our economy.

(6) To remove the strait jacket of wage, price, and other controls and directives which then held the country hidebound and to make constructive plans to encourage the initiative of free citizens.

The first year's operation of this Administration shows substantial progress toward the accomplishment of these objectives.

The first step toward reducing deficits and balancing the budget was a tremendous effort by both the committees of Congress and the

Administration to get previously planned spending under control. Little could be done about expenditures in fiscal 1953, which was all programmed and more than half gone. But a thorough review of all future military and civilian programs was immediately undertaken. No program was too large to be challenged, no operation too small to be thoroughly examined.

Conditions were worse than we expected. Corrections have not developed as rapidly as we had hoped. But progress has been made. By August, 1953, previously planned expenditures for fiscal 1954 had been cut by more than $6 billion under the January estimate of the outgoing Administration. This, plus $800 million of income gained from the six-month extension of the excess profits tax, resulted, according to present estimates, in cutting a prospective deficit from more than $11 billion to less than $4 billion.

This is a real saving. The taxpayers of America will have these billions of dollars to spend for themselves instead of having to let the government spend them. As for the costs of defense, this Administration is determined to develop a proper posture of balanced defense, which will provide not only for our security today but for tomorrow and thereafter for as long as may be required until we find the way to real and lasting peace. We can and must spend whatever we have to spend to defend ourselves.

We also know, however, that the real defense of America will not result simply from spending huge amounts of money. We know that any program for defense must be measured not by its cost but by its wisdom and that, to be effective, it must be fluid and continuously modernized as time goes on.

In debt management this Administration is doing two things which will make the nearly $275 billion debt less inflationary and less dangerous to the value of money and to the nation's economy.

First, at every appropriate time we are extending the maturity of the debt by issuing longer-term securities. Second, we are moving more of the debt away from the banks and into the hands of long-term investors.

We cannot always move on both fronts at the same time. We must be careful not to dislocate the sensitive balance of our economy and we must always be guided by current market conditions. But our goal is clear and we are working toward it.

In February, owners of $9 billion of maturing certificates were given the chance to exchange their holdings for a bond of six years' maturity instead of the usual one-year certificate. In April the Treasury offered a 30-year bond—the first marketable long-term bond since 1945. In September, a 3½ year note was offered; in October, a new cash offering of eight-year bonds was made; and in December, $1.75 billion of five-year bonds were issued.

The net result of our debt management in 1953 has been to finance a huge inherited deficit with little or no increase in bank holdings of Government securities, and hence with no increase in inflationary pressures due to that cause. In helping to spread the debt, we are also encouraging the widest possible ownership of savings bonds. We note with pride that the sales of Series E and H Savings Bonds in 1953 were higher than in any year since 1946.

Our policy is fixed and determined. It is flexible only in its execution. Our progress under it realistically recognizes and adjusts to the changing conditions in which we operate, but we have made no change in either policy or objective. Our goal has been and will continue to be sound, honest money for a healthy economy—for the military and economic security of this country. . . .

This Administration is reducing taxes. Because we have reduced expenses and only because we have made these reductions in spending, the excess profits tax expired December 31 and individual income taxes went down an average of ten per cent at the same time. Let no one be deceived. No tax reduction whenever planned could be justified otherwise.

Additional tax reduction is desired by all and is essential to the continued growth of our economy. Stability of the dollar affords protection to those older citizens who have earned and saved, but this nation, as the land of opportunity for the young—eager for work and ambitious to better themselves—cannot long endure as such under the restrictive taxes which we inherited. They must be further reduced.

But taxes can be further reduced only as expenditures are further reduced. And expenditures can be reduced only as consistent with maintaining a defense adequate to meet the dangers which confront us. . . . We cannot afford as much reduction as we would all like immediately. But we will set a pattern of reduction on which a modest start will promptly be made, with provision for future reductions in taxes as rapidly as reductions in expenditures, consistent with security, indicate that they are justified. . . .

¥ The joint Senate-House Congressional Committee on the Economic Report came into existence early in the Eisenhower Administration along with the President's Economic Report on the Nation and for four years the Secretary was its principal witness-and-advisor following each Economic Report. The background for this testimony in 1954 was the business transition period after ending of the Korean hostilities, in which business nationally was somewhat but not seriously duller. Secretary Humphrey chose to encourage the committee about the future of business because of the new Treasury Department's tax and cost reduction policies, and subsequently was borne out by the rise of business indices late in 1954 and the arrival of the 1955–6 boom.

The basis of the tax program

Statement by Secretary Humphrey before the Joint Committee on the Economic Report.

February 2, 1954

. . . I subscribe to the conclusion of the report to the effect that this nation can make the transition to a period of less costly military preparedness without serious interruption in our economic growth. . . . As you gentlemen well know, this Administration in the past 12 months has cut more than $12 billion in anticipated Government spending. This reduction in proposed spending made possible the tax cuts on January 1. These cuts are now leaving with the taxpayer over $5 billion a year which formerly was spent by the Government. We are cutting taxes even though we have not arrived at a budget balance.

There is a very good reason for this. We must always anticipate the reduction of Government expenditures and begin to transfer billions of dollars which the Government will not be spending back to the taxpayers so that there will not be any sudden dislocation. . . .

It is important to notice that we expect to almost reach a cash balance this year—and a small cash surplus in fiscal 1955. We are eliminating the necessity for cash deficit financing from the public, which is inflationary. . . .

In addition to the $5 billion tax cuts of January 1, we are recommending a general revision of the tax system. It will do two principal things:

(1) It will make the tax burden fairer for millions of individuals by removing the more serious tax inequities and complications.

(2) It will stimulate production and create bigger payrolls and more and better jobs by reducing restraints and by encouraging initiative and investment.

Millions of Americans will benefit from better tax treatment for working children, child care expenses, for doctors' bills, for annuities, and from easier procedures in filing returns.

And these same millions will benefit even more from such revisions as liberalization of the tax treatment of depreciation and partial relief from double taxation of dividends. Everyone will benefit because the economy will benefit with the resulting creation of more jobs with better tools and machinery to produce higher payrolls and cheaper, better things for public consumption. . . .

In this connection the proposal for some relief from the double taxation of dividends may not be well understood. Under present law, earnings of a corporation are taxed twice—once as corporation income and again as individual income when they are paid out in dividends to the millions of shareholders in American industry. This has restricted the market for shares of stock in companies which want to expand and has forced them to borrow money instead of selling shares in their future. In the past ten years better than 75 per cent of private-industry financing has been done by going in debt instead of selling shares.

What does this mean? It means simply that we have enterprise heavily in debt so that it doesn't develop as well or as quickly as it would without heavy debts hanging over it. Should business turn down, a company in heavy debt is, of course, easily drawn into trouble.

Better prospects for enabling companies to get shareholder financing—instead of going into debt—thus means better prospects for all Americans who work, for increasingly better jobs come more surely out of companies that are moving forward and expanding.

There has also been some misunderstanding about what we are proposing in depreciation. Depreciation is really the wrong word. Buildings and machinery not only wear out but they become old fashioned and neither the workman using them nor the business owning them can do as well either in earning wages or in decreasing costs as more modern, up-to-date equipment would make possible. Depreciation is simply the method by which the original cost of a building or piece of machinery is recovered over the years during which it is being used up and worn out.

At the moment these deductions must usually be spread out evenly over the years for tax purposes. But if the cost of a piece of machinery has not been written off by the time it should be replaced with the better machinery, there is less inclination to buy a new piece of machinery that will do the job better and cheaper than keeping the old machinery still in use. Our proposal to let more depreciation be taken in early years does not increase the total that may be taken as tax deduction by one cent. It simply recognizes the facts and allows more of the deduction in earlier years. Doing so helps our economy to stay modern and up to date, and so to grow and expand faster. . . .

Nothing can so add to our national strength and preparedness as modernization of the whole industrial plant in America, and nothing will make more sure more jobs at which millions of people can earn high wages by producing more and better goods at less cost. . . .

Additional tax cuts for all the taxpayers will of course benefit them. But, until more reductions in Government expenditures are in sight, further cuts in taxes will only add to the deficit. However, as rapidly as reduced expenditures can be seen, further tax reductions will promptly be made. . . .

As long as Americans know there is adequate chance to gain, they will save and invent. They will try new things that will bring forward new business, growing business, more jobs, better jobs, and higher and better standards of living. In the past decade, the growth of American industry was stimulated by debt and war and inflation. With these unwanted pressures fading, we need to again make initiative and enterprise more compelling if our economy is to continue to grow.

That growth, stimulated by tax relief and reduction to almost every taxpayer in the nation, is the basic purpose of our tax program. . . .

Cross-examination of Secretary Humphrey

REP. WRIGHT PATMAN (Texas).... Do you consider that the national debt will ever be paid, Mr. Humphrey?

SEC. HUMPHREY. Well, "ever" is just about as bad as "never." That is a long, long time.

REP. PATMAN. Do you anticipate in the next four years ever making any payments on the national debt?

SEC. HUMPHREY. My feeling about payments on the national debt is just this: There is only one way that you can pay down on the national debt, and that is to tax the people more money than you are spending. And when you tax the people more money than you are spending, the surplus that is left should be used to reduce the debt. And it is the only way that it can be done.

Now, as long as we are required to maintain the very heavy military expenditures that we are under for our security, as long as we are forced to spend these tremendous sums for that purpose, and we have to tax the people to get that out of them, I do not think that it is wise to tax the people more than that very great amount in order to pay down on the debt. I think we had better be content not to do so.

REP. PATMAN. The answer to my question, then, is that in the next four years you do not see any payments?

SEC. HUMPHREY. No, that is not the answer. I do not know when we are going to have some sort of peaceful arrangement. I do not anticipate it within four years, because I do not anticipate that the world is going to come to peace within that time. But the time will come sometime. It has got to come in the world sometime, when these armaments, these expenditures for armaments throughout the entire world will be suspended and will be reduced. The world cannot take it, in my opinion, on the basis of which it is now going on, for an extended period of time. Some day that has got to stop. When that stops, when our expenditures for armaments, those tremendous expenditures, can be radically reduced, we can then, I believe, reduce our income slower than we can reduce our expenditures, and we will have some surplus to begin to pay down on the debt. . . .

REP. PATMAN. But is it not a fact, Mr. Humphrey, that our economy is now geared to the point that any reduction in national debt would be deflationary? In other words, our economy is geared to debt. Without debt, there is no money. Our money is based upon debt. And if we are to pay off our national debt, it would be paralyzing to the economy. . . .

Sec. Humphrey. Well, I will put it this way, Mr. Patman: I do not expect to be in this office when the debt is fully paid. . . .

Senator J. William Fulbright (Arkansas). . . . It seems to me that your statement and that of the President have heavy emphasis upon taxes designed to increase production. I thought as a layman—and these matters are relative, of course—that our greatest problem now, for some time, is rather underconsumption. Now . . . I am conscious of great surpluses in agriculture, and more recently in automobiles. There seems to be an adequate, in fact, overly adequate—in fact, greatly excessive—supply of these commodities that people can purchase, or at least are willing to purchase. But when it comes to taxes, I would like to feel that maybe an increase in exemptions—that is, individual exemptions—in order to generate the greater purchasing power directly in the hands of people. . . .

My only view is that we ought at this particular time to give a greater purchasing power into the hands of the consumers rather than to encourage greater production. Is there anything to that argument?

Sec. Humphrey. Our tax program does both. In some of the provisions, notably the depreciation provision and things of that kind, those are stimulated things. In addition to that, we are cutting off about $5 billion—well, it will be between $5 billion and $6 billion—of money that is going back to the people, cash money that is going back into industry and to the people, that was collected and spent by the Government last year. Now that cash money goes to people who will have the money to spend this year for themselves that they did not have last year. . . .

Senator Paul H. Douglas (Illinois). . . . In your tax program . . . you outline some 24 proposals. Now, how much in the aggregate will this come to in terms of tax reduction?

Sec. Humphrey. About $1.5 billion this [fiscal] year [ending June 30, 1954]; $1.3 billion to $1.5 billion, somewhere in there.

Senator Douglas. When the rebate on dividend payments fully comes, the 15 per cent, how much will that amount to?

SEC. HUMPHREY. As I recall it, it starts out between $200 million and $300 million.

SENATOR DOUGLAS. Yes. But I mean the total.

SEC. HUMPHREY. That is the total. And then over the four years, it runs up until it gets to $1 billion, somewhere, $1.2 billion, to—

SENATOR DOUGLAS. And at the end of the fourth year, what will be the total cash reductions contemplated in your program as a whole?

SEC. HUMPHREY. . . . You see, it all depends on volume of activity, and everything else.

SENATOR DOUGLAS. I know. But what would be the general figure? Say $3 billion?

SEC. HUMPHREY. In that neighborhood; $3 billion to $4 billion. Maybe $4 billion.

You see, you have to take each one of these things and estimate what the volume is in order to gauge it, so that your question is an almost impossible one to answer.

SENATOR DOUGLAS. . . . How much of this $2.5 billion is given to the lower-income groups in the first three or four years of your tax proposals, and how much is given to investment and those receiving incomes from investments in the later portion of your tax proposal?

SEC. HUMPHREY. I am afraid you are asking a question that we will have to make a lot of assumptions on to try to answer, because these things all depend. For instance, if corporate dividends decline, the amount of the tax relief on dividends will be very largely reduced, so that you have to make all sorts of assumptions on what things are going to be four years from now.

SENATOR DOUGLAS. I know. But I am willing to take your assumptions. Now, here is the point: You put up at the head of your program a number of various proposals of children earning over $600, that they are not to be deducted, and there could be split incomes for heads of families in terms of dependents, that the expense of baby-sitters will be a proper deduction for working mothers, and extra allowance for medical expenses, and so on. Those are very excellent. But how much do those come to in comparison with the allowance for accelerated depreciation and the dividend factor? The dividend factor, you say, ultimately comes to $1.2 billion. How much do you estimate on the amortization? How much reduction in its income will that be in the first three or four years?

SEC. HUMPHREY. You see, you start right out, Senator, with something in excess of $3 billion that is handed back to the taxpayers right off by the tax reductions.

SENATOR DOUGLAS. But remember this, Mr. Secretary, that in the lower-income groups that is canceled by the increase in the Social Security tax.

SEC. HUMPHREY. That is only at the very lowest level, and that is because—

SENATOR DOUGLAS. The break-even—

SEC. HUMPHREY. Now, please let me answer when you ask a question. . . . It is only in the very lowest bracket that that is an offset, and that is for the purchase of something that is of value to the man who buys it.

SENATOR DOUGLAS. . . . Do you know the precise points where they balance? According to my figures for a single man, the increase in Social Security will offset the reduction in income tax at approximately $900 a year, $872, and a man and wife at approximately $1,800 a year, a man and wife and two children at $3,550. Now . . . this reduction in the income tax which you turned to, and which as a matter of fact was put into effect by a Democratic Congress, was offset for these groups by the increased Social Security, so that the full gain of this income tax reduction goes for those above these break-even points which I have given.

SEC. HUMPHREY. The tax reductions that have been made are very much in favor of the lower brackets. The scale of rates went for the largest reductions in the lower avenues. . . .

They are in the lower brackets all the way through in the larger amounts. As the brackets increase, the tax reductions get down to very small amounts, and at the top it is a very small amount. Now, in addition to that, the Social Security payment—this Administration recommended that that should not be made, that that should be withheld, until the time came when it was desired to substantially increase the benefits of Social Security, and a program was presented for substantially increased benefits. Because of the substantially increased benefits that were provided or that were suggested and proposed, the payments to provide those increased benefits—the recommendation to withhold them was withdrawn, and they were permitted to proceed. So the reason those are being paid is because the man who pays them is buying prospectively a lot more than he ever had before, and is buying something of value for the dollar that he pays, which has nothing to do with his tax reduction.

SENATOR DOUGLAS. Mr. Secretary, if I may continue with this previous course of reasoning, is it not true that the first four or five decreases which you proposed in your program would net to those in the lower-income groups a return of approximately $200 million, but that the reduction coming from accelerated depreciation and rebate of taxes against taxes, a rebate of dividends against taxes and not against incomes, that that will net something in the order of $2 billion, ultimately, primarily for those in the upper-income groups, who are the owners of industry?

SEC. HUMPHREY. . . . But we start out by giving back to the tax-payers something in excess of $3 billion. That is to individuals. Now, then, in addition to that, the $1.2 billion, $1.3 billion, or $1.4, or whatever it is, that this revision gives, is split about 50–50 between relief provisions and incentive provisions.

SENATOR DOUGLAS. I think this is something of an overstatement, and I say this respectfully, that even for the first year, when the rebate on dividends is predicated against taxes for the subsequent years, with the increase from 5 to 10 to 15 . . . that will be close to $700 million more and, of course, the overwhelming proportion of dividends are received by those in the upper-income group?

SEC. HUMPHREY. I do not believe I will agree to that. Dividends more and more are being received by the people who own pensions, who have insurance, of all sorts. It is the great mass of the American people that are getting the great ownership in American industry today, and it is coming through pension funds and through insurance funds and things of that kind that are drawing tremendously and are going into equity securities.

SENATOR DOUGLAS. It is the poor people who receive the dividends?

SEC. HUMPHREY. Oh, yes, indeed. They get dividends through their pension funds and through their insurance.

SENATOR DOUGLAS. Do they receive the major portion of the dividends?

SEC. HUMPHREY. . . . I don't know how you divide it.

REP. RICHARD M. SIMPSON (Pennsylvania). Is it not a fact that the people who will benefit under the changes contemplated with respect to the so-called double taxation of dividends are the individuals who own stock in the nation's enterprises?

Sec. Humphrey. That is right.

Rep. Simpson. Well, studies that have been before the Committee on Ways & Means indicate that . . . 64 per cent of the corporate stock of the nation is owned by people having incomes of less than $6,000 per year. The Committee . . . was amazed to discover that.

Rep. Patman. That is not so.

Senator Fulbright. . . . To go back to my original question—and I grant that there is no absolute dividing line—but I was under the impression that as far as plant, the investment in equipment was concerned, we are pretty well equipped. . . . During these last few years, there has been an enormous investment in plant, which . . . would lead me to emphasize the increase in the exemptions rather than the depreciation as of this time. Granted that these change from time to time, but under present conditions, accepting your own statement, which I do with full credibility, with regard to plant investment, it does not seem to me you would get a very immediate reaction from giving still further depreciation privileges when you just stated that it has been overdone during the past few years, and that, as of the present, what you said yourself would lead me to believe that the emphasis should be put on the consumption. In other words, the increase, we will say, from $600 to $700, which I understand you refused to recommend, or you rejected as an intelligent thing to do as of the moment—

Sec. Humphrey. . . . What has happened, Mr. Fulbright, is this, that with these expedited depreciations, we have had a large expenditure in many lines, particularly those lines which have to do with war-making materials. . . . Those new facilities have the advantage of the very latest designs and latest models, and you have thereby created quite a discrepancy between the cost of production with those new facilities and with the other facilities, so that you have, just contrary to your thinking, caused a great stimulation to people who want to bring their other facilities, and who, to be competitive, must bring their older facilities up to these newer standards. So you have in this country some brand new plants that have been built in quite large numbers.

You have a lot of much older plants, and for those much older plants to continue to give the employment that they are giving to be competitive and to keep people at work, those old plants have to be rehabilitated and brought up to the standards of the new plants so that the entire production can proceed; otherwise you are having part of your industry at a great discrepancy with other parts.

SENATOR FULBRIGHT. But that is against the background of over-production, it seems to me, and that is where I leave you.

SEC. HUMPHREY. Mr. Fulbright, the goose that lays the golden egg is production.... If you haven't got a pay roll, you haven't got con-sumers. Pay rolls are what make consumers. Pay rolls are the things that get the money out to the people, and you stop the pay rolls, and you stop the consumption automatically. . . .

REP. RICHARD BOLLING (Missouri). Mr. Secretary, how do you characterize the present economic situation?

SEC. HUMPHREY. . . . By and large, whether you use the word "recession" or whether you use "rolling adjustment," or what is the proper term, I do not know. It is idle to say that employment is as high as it was six months ago. It is not. It is idle to say that buying is at exactly the same level. It is not. But the buying is only down so far; the retail buying is only down a very little. There has been a definite accumulation of inventories. We know that. In many cases already those inventories, those excessive inventories, are beginning to be taken away. Now, the reason I use "rolling adjustment" is this. There are some industries that are operating at exactly the same level they did a year ago. There are others that are down a little. There are others that are down more. And they are in different places and different geographical locations.

Now, if this adjustment takes place, as it appears to be doing, with readjustment in one industry at one time and another industry at another time and one place at one time and another place at another time, then we haven't anything that is very disturbing. If that does not occur, and if it becomes an across-the-board difficulty all the way across the board, then it becomes more disturbing. . . .

Now . . . which way it will go, I do not know, and I am sure nobody else knows.

REP. JESSE P. WOLCOTT (Michigan). Did we not have a right to expect that when we stopped inflation, we might have an adjustment period?

SEC. HUMPHREY. I think, Mr. Chairman, it was inevitable. You cannot swing from one side to another and not have some readjustment.

REP. WOLCOTT. What is happening now is no more than we have had a right to expect, and which we should have expected?

SEC. HUMPHREY. If it is no more than we have now, I think it will be a very fine situation.

REP. BOLLING. If, however, we had a second-best year this year and continued at that same level for a considerable period of time, we could, by population increase, go on and work ourselves into very substantial difficulties.

SEC. HUMPHREY. I think the American economy must be an expanding economy. I think it is bound to be. I think with the spirit of the American people, unless the Government does something to interfere terribly or make some terribly bad mistake, it seems to me that over a period of 10 or 15 or 20 years we are just bound to move ahead. . . .

REP. GEORGE H. BENDER (Ohio). . . . . Is it not a fact that the condition that you are faced with now is something that you did not create as a member of this Administration, or this Administration did not create? Rather, you inherited it?

SEC. HUMPHREY. Mr. Bender, we inherited an enormous debt. We inherited a tremendous amount of what I have always referred to as COD orders, or orders that had been placed for the delivery of goods with no money in the cash drawer to pay for them. We inherited a lot of complications. We inherited a thing that is almost forgotten. We inherited an economy that was completely governed by restrictions—wage restrictions, price restrictions, a complete set of controls over everything that was done. Of course, some of those things are things that could be changed very rapidly, and some of the things are things that you cannot change rapidly. As I have said many times, you cannot change the course of 20 years in 20 days—or 20 months, as far as that is concerned. So that there is a lot of inheritance that is involved in our present situation.

SENATOR JOHN J. SPARKMAN (Alabama). . . . . What about the corporation tax? If I read the newspapers right, there seems to be a very strong feeling that the corporation tax ought to be lowered to 50 per cent.

SEC. HUMPHREY. Well, if it is, Mr. Sparkman, I have not heard of it. I have seen no objection from authoritative sources to the continuance of that. . . .

SENATOR SPARKMAN. Now, Mr. Secretary, I was interested in the statement you made about bringing the budget close to a cash balance this year, and I rejoice in your approach to that. I hope you are able to accomplish it. But I have been looking over some of these statistics, and so often we speak about the possibility of a cash balance this year that I think a great many people are thinking that we have never had one in the past. And I have noticed that, during the seven years since the end of the war, we have had a cash balance five times. That is correct, is it not?

SEC. HUMPHREY. I have not the figures, but I do not doubt it. . . .

SENATOR SPARKMAN. In the calendar year of 1946, there was $42 million surplus; in the calendar year 1947, it was $5.666 million; calendar year 1948, it was $8.027 billion; calendar year 1950, it was $45 million; calendar year 1951, it was $1.244 billion. Then in the 1952 calendar year, we went back by $1.641 billion; and then last year we had $6.2 billion. . . . Mr. Secretary, one other thing. We had virtually no controls in January, 1953.

SEC. HUMPHREY. I recall, Senator, one thing that was a little out of control and that was our spending.

SENATOR SPARKMAN. Yes.

SEC. HUMPHREY. But, outside of that it seems to me that business and activities of the public were under all sorts of controls in January.

SENATOR SPARKMAN. Of course, we are still facing a big deficit, but I did not want to bring that up.

Sincerely, I am quite sure that a fair checking of the records would show—and I think most of the members of this Joint Committee are on the two Banking and Currency committees, and they well realize that inflation had been brought well under control, and, as it was brought under control, the controls on our economy went off. Lots of people continued to talk about them when they actually were not there.

SEC. HUMPHREY. Why, Senator, we had—I forget, now—6,700 people, or something, here in Washington at that time administering controls on prices and wages and allocations, and everything that you could think of.

SENATOR SPARKMAN. Yes. But two years before, we had written into the law a requirement for decontrol, and they were being decontrolled as fast as we could, and practically all controls were off in January, 1953.

SEC. HUMPHREY. I think you had better look at the record on that.

SENATOR DOUGLAS. In order that the statistics may partially catch up with the statements, I should like to put into the record two pages from a study by the Brookings Institution entitled "Share Ownership in the United States," dealing with the statements that have been made, that in the main it is the low-income groups which own the stocks of the country.

This study shows that the estimated total number of share owners in the country was 6,490,000, or only 4.2 per cent of the population, and 4,750,000 families, or 9.5 per cent of the population owned shares. . . .

REP. WOLCOTT. When were the studies made?

SENATOR DOUGLAS. 1952. And now I would like to state it by income groups and by families. Families with less than $2,000 in incomes, it was found that only 2.2 per cent of these families owned shares. Families of $2,000 to $3,000, 3.6 per cent owned shares. Families of $3,000 to $4,000, 4.6 per cent owned shares. Families of $4,000 to $5,000, 7.4 per cent owned shares. Families $5,000 to $10,000, 19.8 per cent owned shares. Families $10,000 and over 55.1 per cent owned shares, indicating that the percentage of stock ownership is, one would believe, infinitely higher in the larger-income groups than in the lower-income groups.

REP. PATMAN. . . . Now, on the pension plan—I assume that you have charge of the Social Security Fund, about $18 billion, do you not, Mr. Secretary? Now, none of that is invested in securities except United States Government securities, is it?

SEC. HUMPHREY. That is right. That is the federal.

REP. PATMAN. Therefore, they could not—

SEC. HUMPHREY. Oh, but there are millions and millions of dollars of other plans.

REP. PATMAN. Do you know the average amounts of assets of those other plans?

SEC. HUMPHREY. No, I cannot tell you. But, between pension plans and insurance companies, we are getting into the billions of dollars, and it is growing tremendously. . . .

Opposing "blanket exemptions"

Statement by Secretary Humphrey at the Treasury
Department. An "interim report" on the progress
and performance of the 1954 tax structure
revision was called for early in 1954 when
the first "piecemeal" Congressional proposals for
individual tax reductions and exemptions appeared.

February 25, 1954

The Administration's tax program has not been changed.

We must pay the bill for the cost of our national security. This cost is coming down but is still very high, and is the reason why taxes must continue to remain relatively high until Government spending can be further reduced with safety.

Tax cuts will release more than $6.5 billion to the people this year. This has already been partly accomplished, by reduction of over $3 billion in individual taxes effective January 1, 1954, and by elimination of the universally condemned excess profits tax of almost $2 billion.

The Ways & Means Committee, co-operating with the Treasury staff, has been working continuously on the Administration's program to select the most effective ways to promote the prosperity of all the people. The proposed changes in the tax system will result in further reductions that will amount to something more than an additional $1.5 billion. This work, after weeks of hearings and months of study, is almost completed and will be ready for final Congressional decision soon.

About two-thirds of the additional relief will go directly to millions of individual taxpayers suffering from special hardships and unfair taxes. About one-third of the total amount will benefit all individuals by strengthening incentives; by making more jobs; by increasing the efficiency of our farms, mines and factories; and by increasing the demand for their products.

This total tax reduction of more than $6.5 billion can be accomplished, we believe, substantially within the limits of the President's proposed budget.

We have said time and again that we are determined to continue to make tax reductions from time to time and to return tax money to the people, for them to spend for themselves rather than have the Government spend it for them, just as rapidly as further reductions are justified. We believe in carrying out this vital task in a way that will bring permanent benefit to all our people and our country. But we will vigorously oppose blanket increases in exemptions that will throw us back into substantial deficit financing which cannot be justified at the present time and which we have been working so hard to overcome.

When the Ways & Means Committee's proposed bill is presented in detail, millions of taxpayers will find in it correction of many of the tax hardships and abuses from which they have suffered in the past. The release of this huge amount of money for the people to have this year, when the whole program is adopted, will be stimulating to the economy and will be within the limits of sound financial management which is essential to further progress for the nation's welfare.

"To spend for themselves"

*Speech by Secretary Humphrey to the League of
Republican Women of the District of Columbia at
the Mayflower Hotel, Washington. The Secretary
could take his case to the people, on occasion,
as when he disclosed the cost of the piecemeal
Congressional proposals for individual exemptions.*

March 1, 1954

The Eisenhower Administration, in its first year in office, has been working toward the accomplishment of two great goals. They are:

That we have military strength sufficient not only to defend ourselves but also to help bring real peace to all the world.

And that we maintain an economy of such strength and productive power that it can continuously support that military requirement.

In both defense and foreign relations the Administration has made great progress in the past twelve months. We have taken substantial steps toward shaping a posture of defense which will provide reasonable security from attack from abroad and at the same time be within the limits of our economy to support for the long pull if necessary. We are reshaping our defense so that it is not on a crisis-to-crisis basis. We are reshaping it so that it will be fluid and continually modernized and progressively stronger and stronger and still be within the limits of our economy to support for an indefinite number of years, not knowing when, if ever, the critical moment may appear. . . .

During the past year the shooting war in Korea has ended. This, of course, has been not only a thankful thing for all Americans who had loved ones involved in it, but provides less drain on the financial requirements of the Government.

This, with the reductions which are being made as a result of the "new look" in defense and the greater emphasis on the use and effectiveness of new weapons, has permitted substantial reductions in the expenditures required in the coming year. However, the costs are still high and about seventy cents out of every dollar of tax money collected from the people still is being spent for our collective security. Added to this is also the continuing costs which we must now bear for the expenditures made in past wars which were not paid for as the money was spent but which was then borrowed and now is a continuing charge against us and burden upon future generations.

Enough of this deficit spending has already been done and we must see to it that we in turn avoid more and more deficit financing and keep our present taxes sufficiently high to pay-as-we-go currently to the greatest possible extent. In that way we will not pass more and more debts on to already overburdened future generations which our children and grandchildren will have to pay for us.

We are now passing through a period of transition. . . .

I feel today, as the President said in transmitting the economic report in January, that there is much that justifies confidence in the accomplishment of this transition with a minimum of difficulty.

A main reason for my confidence in the future is the Administration's tax program. Changes which have already been put into effect and others which have been recommended to be made in the tax structure contribute greatly to our confidence in the creation of new jobs for better, fuller, peaceful living to replace the declining jobs for making instruments of death.

In the past 12 months this Administration has cut more than $12 billion from anticipated current and future Government spending. This reduction in proposed spending made possible the tax cuts on January 1. These cuts are now leaving with the taxpayers more than $5 billion a year which formerly was spent by the Government. Further changes in the tax system being worked out between the Treasury and the Ways & Means Committee over recent months will, when enacted, provide further reductions that will amount to something more than an additional $1.5 billion.

Thus more than $6.5 billion will be released to the people by tax cuts this year. This is a tremendous sum of money which is being left in the pocketbooks and transferred to the purchasing power of millions of Americans. . . .

About two-thirds of the $1.5 billion relief from this tax revision bill will go directly to millions of individual taxpayers suffering from special hardships and unfair taxes. About one-third will benefit all individuals by strengthening incentives, by making more jobs, by increasing the efficiency of our farms, mines and factories, and by increasing the demand for the products of fuller and better peaceful living. . . .

We have said time and again that we are determined to continue to make tax reductions from time to time and to return tax money to the people, for them to spend for themselves rather than have the Government spend it for them, just as rapidly as further reductions are justified. We believe in carrying out this vital task in a way that will bring permanent benefit to all our people and our country. But we will vigorously oppose blanket increases in exemptions that will throw us back into substantial deficit financing which cannot be justified at the present time and which we have been working so hard to overcome.

When considering just what blanket increases in exemptions would do, we must note exactly what the revenue losses would be. The key fact is that for each $100 increase in exemptions above the present $600 per person there is a loss in revenue to the Government of $2.5 billion a year. So that an increase this year to $800 in personal exemption, as has been suggested, would result in an additional deficit of $5 billion in complete reversal of all that we have done toward sound financial management of the Government's affairs.

I do not believe that the American public wants its Government to reverse itself, to shirk its current responsibilities and to pass on to future generations, our children and our grandchildren, the costs that we ourselves should currently bear. . . .

"No magic source of free money"

Article by Secretary Humphrey in Life *Magazine under the title "How New Tax Bill Can Promote Prosperity."*

March 15, 1954

While I was working in my office the other day a businessman called me up from California. A large manufacturer, he had just come out of a meeting with his board of directors. "I want to know," he said "whether or not the tax revision bill will be passed by the Congress. Can you give me any assurance that it will?" Naturally I could only say that I didn't know, but that I felt strongly that it should be.

When I asked him why, he said, "Our business has been slowing up. My company wants to spend several million dollars in a big sales campaign to get things moving again. If we are sure the new tax program will pass, the board of directors will approve the expense. If not, I doubt that I can talk them into it."

We get many such calls. In fact every day somebody telephones to ask the question, "Will we get that tax revision?" A widow called. She had a small savings acount which she wanted to invest if she could only be sure that she would be relieved of double taxation on the small investment she already had. The other day a food processor flew in from the Midwest to see us. His firm had developed a new product and he brought along a sample for me to taste. "We have tested this stuff in every way," he said. "We know we can produce it and we are ready to build a brand new plant and hire several thousand people to make it and market it. But under present tax depreciation provisions, the risk would be too great."

The interest of these people and thousands of others in similar dilemmas show what is at stake in the decision on taxes now before the Congress. In my opinion our tax program is a key to whether or not this country stays strong and growing. This program will breathe into American industry a new incentive that will create more and better jobs, more and better products and above all will bring our money affairs to a level of sanity.

We have worked for more than a year on this program. President Eisenhower stressed the importance of tax revision in his first State of the Union message. The House Ways & Means Committee, under the direction of Chairman Daniel A. Reed, and the Joint Committee on Internal Revenue Taxation began working together early in 1953. Last summer the Ways & Means Committee held some 50 days of hearings and heard testimony from more than 1,000 witnesses. Recommendations for changes were prepared and fully considered. That work has now been completed. The finished bill is being reported this week to the House of Representatives. It is a good joint product of the Congress and the Administration working together.

The philosophy behind this program is precisely opposite from the philosophy that motivated the financial conduct of the Government of the Thirties and Forties. During this period the Government repeatedly resorted to deficit financing. This simply means living beyond your income, and it is just as damaging to a government as to a family. Suppose a father and mother called their children together and said, "Now look, kids, we are going to spend a lot of money this year. Instead of spending only what we can afford, we are going to spend *more* than we can afford and we are going to borrow the rest. The borrowed money won't come due until we are dead and gone. Your children and your children's children will have to pay it off."

That's what the nation was doing. We were borrowing in this generation and putting the burden of raising taxes to pay off the loan on to the next. We have been mortgaging our children's future; we have been getting a free ride on the young people. If the old folks want to saddle the young folks with this extra future tax load, and if the young folks want to take it, that might look—momentarily—like an easy way out of the problem. But I don't want it that way myself. I want to pay my own share. To pay our own share we have to pay as we go and, like the American family, pursue the fundamental economic law of living within our income.

The first step in this direction, after *fully* providing for the costs of our national security, is to reduce the cost of Government. There are two ways to do this: (1) drop people from whom the taxpayers are not getting full money's worth or whose jobs are not necessary, (2) stop buying things for which the Government is not getting full value or which it can get along without. We have already made big strides in this direction. Our budget for the coming fiscal year shows a reduction of more than $12 billion from the spending plans of the last Administration. Though we will not be able to balance the budget in the coming fiscal year, our budget's deficit of $2.9 billion is $6.5 billion less than the $9.4 billion deficit of the last fiscal year of the previous Administration.

These governmental savings, of course, cut down the number of jobs paid for with government money. This creates serious problems for each person affected. So new jobs in private enterprise must be created as rapidly as possible for those released by the cuts in what the Government spends.

A lot of men and women have been employed making military equipment. Now many of those people can be transferred to making the things that can be used in peaceful pursuits. It is this transfer which the country is now going through and which necessarily creates some temporary unemployment. Some people have called it a recession. It really is a transition during which the billions of dollars' worth of spending by the Government is transferred to spending by the millions of private individuals whose taxes have been cut.

It means transferring men from jobs making things for killing to jobs making things for living.

There are many good signs that the transition—difficult as it is—is being accomplished without generally serious trouble.

The new tax program will help to ease the transfer.

Let's consider the average family with savings to invest. The rate of individuals' savings in this country is running at record peacetime levels—$18 billion last year. If invested, those savings can be a big source for providing more and more jobs through creating new farms and factories and other places to work. Under the present tax laws, investment in ownership shares of American enterprise is taxed twice. This is the only case of double taxation in America. It penalizes investment in common stock which is so vital to raising money for new ventures. Our new program begins to cut down this double levy and so helps create more jobs.

About two thirds of the tax reductions from our new proposals will go directly to millions of individual taxpayers suffering from special hardships and unfair provisions. There will be larger deductions for medical expenses and special deductions for working widows for the cost of baby sitters. Heads of families will receive benefits so that the death of a husband or wife will not bring a sharp increase in taxes at a time of great personal distress. Parents will be able to claim a child as a dependent even if the child makes over $600 a year in helping to earn his own living or working his way through college. Fairer consideration will be given income from pensions, and there will be a tax exemption up to $100 a week of amounts received as sickness and accident benefits.

Farmers' soil conservation expenses will be given more liberal tax treatment. Farmers will be able to write off depreciation on their equipment faster and so be in position to buy new and better farm implements and tools.

The tax problems that these provisions are intended to answer have brought a lot of people to my office. One was a policeman's widow who represented a private group pension plan for widows of policemen and firemen. Under the present tax law, her group is meagerly treated compared to the tax advantages of those who fall under social security. She rightly thinks her group should get a better break, and if the Congress puts our program into law, it will.

We believe that further tax reduction should be made just as soon as further cuts in Government spending are in sight. Taxes should go down by the reduction of rates along the line so that all taxpayers are fairly treated.

It would be unrealistic to say that our tax programs will be adopted by the Congress without opposition and without the danger of undermining compromises. Indeed, in recent weeks a strong pressure has been felt to substitute for this program a lush cut in individual income taxes. An argument is brewing around a proposal to raise individual income tax exemptions from $600 to $800 this year and to $1,000 next year. There are three things wrong with this idea of cutting taxes now by increasing the exemptions:

(1) A $1,000 exemption would mean that about 15 million people

now filing tax returns would be exempt from paying any income tax at all. That would be a mistake. All Americans ought to make some contribution to their Government, in relation, of course, to what they can afford. Every American wants to pay his share. He doesn't want to pass his fair share of the load off to some other fellow. As a matter of fact, he can't. If he does, the load will become too heavy to bear for the other taxpayers with average incomes, and the unbalanced structure will all come crashing down.

(2) Putting more money into the hands of consumers by raising tax exemptions is not the best way to stimulate the basic propelling force that makes jobs. Jobs make payrolls and payrolls make the money that makes for higher standards of living and pays the taxes as well.

(3) The proposal of the opposition is more than the budget can stand. It would cost us nearly $5 billion of lost revenue this year and nearly $8 billion next year. We are just beginning to get the recurrent deficits of the past years under control. This would be the worst possible time for us to turn around and head back in the opposite direction. We would lose the confidence of all the people in the financial stability that we have gained, and confidence is vital to an expanding, growing economy. Many people forget, too, that we have already handed back more than $5 billion of tax money for this year to the people to spend as they choose. This was done by ending the excess profits tax and cutting Government spending to make possible the 10 per cent income tax reduction of January 1.

Moreover, the rest of our tax program will bring the total tax money handed back to the people this year to more than $7 billion, by far the greatest step in many years toward lightening the tax burden of the individual citizen. Those who would have us go further into debt by excessive and supposedly politically expedient tax cuts are really telling the American people: "Never mind. You won't have to pay the bill. You can get out of your obligation." To be taken in by such a false philosophy at a time when we are not in war or in a real emergency would be a tragic mistake.

There is no magic source of free, unlimited money. All that the Government spends must finally be paid by taxes collected from the people. If taxes paid this year are less than we spend this year, the excess has to be borrowed. Whatever is borrowed has to be repaid later by the collection of taxes to repay it. All that we spend this year, over and above the taxes we pay this year, will just be added to the taxes we will have to pay in a later year. We can shirk our responsibility today and not pay our share, but only by passing it along to be paid a little later. Those who die in the meantime will be ahead, if that is any comfort to them, but their share will be added to the burdens of their children and grandchildren.

This tax program is a vital part of the entire program of this Administration as proposed by President Eisenhower in his State of the Union and other messages. It is designed to make America more secure, both from without and from within, and a better, safer, more really prosperous country for us all to live in.

Reform of "double taxation"

Letter by Secretary Humphrey to Speaker Joseph W. Martin, Jr., of the House of Representatives.

March 17, 1954

My dear Speaker Martin:

The House of Representatives is now debating the tax revision bill granting relief to millions of taxpayers as well as the extending of the 52 per cent rate on corporations. I want to re-emphasize some of my thoughts as to the vital importance of this bill. I feel as strongly as I can that it is in the long-run interests of the American people that this bill be enacted substantially in its present form.

This program has been developed by the House Ways & Means Committee, under Chairman Daniel A. Reed, working with the Administration after months of study, hearings and careful analysis.

There is a substantial amount of misinformation circulating about one proposal in the revision bill. This is the proposal to reduce by a modest amount or percentage the existing double taxation on dividend income.

This is not something new. Both major political parties have for almost 20 years recognized the unfairness of double taxation of dividends.

(1) President Roosevelt recognized the inequity of double taxation of dividends in his tax message of March, 1936.

(2) The House Committee on Postwar Policy and Planning recommended consideration of the elimination of double taxation in its reports of both 1944 and 1946. This committee, under Democratic chairmanship and composed of ten Democrats, including Congressman Cooper, the ranking Democrat on the present committee, and eight Republicans, said that "consideration should be given to the elimination of the present double taxation of dividend income" and that this tax reform "would not only correct an inequity in the present tax structure but also provide an important stimulus to risk capital."

(3) The Committee for Economic Development, in its November, 1947, tax report, described double taxation of dividends as "gross inequity," and pointed out that its existence encourages business financing by borrowing rather than the issue of securities, which "increases the vulnerability of the economy to serious deflation and unemployment."

(4) The minority report of the House Ways & Means Committee in 1948—a minority which then included many of the present Democratic members of the Ways & Means Committee—supported relief from double taxation of dividends. Their report suggested a comprehensive revision of the entire federal tax system and listed "such important matters as the double taxation of dividends" as among "needed amendments."

(5) Organizations ranging from the American Farm Bureau Federation to the Investors League and the American Retail Federation have opposed double taxation of dividends in hearings before the Congress from 1947 to the present.

As President Eisenhower told the nation Monday night, the relief provisions for double taxation of dividends "will be important to all of us, whether our savings are large or small."

There are 6.5 million stockholders among the 47 million people now on the federal income tax rolls, so the number of taxpayers who will benefit from the removal of this inequity is large, both in numbers and in percentage.

But the most important thing is what encouraging incentive to invest means to the future of our economy. Somebody has to provide between eight and ten thousand dollars to provide the tools and facilities to give one American a job. As tax inequities discourage people from investing their savings, there is just that much less money to provide those tools and facilities.

Investment makes jobs. It keeps millions of workers now engaged in heavy industry at work at their present jobs and it creates new jobs with the tools which heavy industry makes. To encourage investment is in the best interests of *all* Americans and not a selfish shortsighted advantage to a few.

This well balanced tax program is the cornerstone of the entire program of this Administration as proposed by President Eisenhower in his State of the Union and other messages. It is designed to make America more secure, both from without and from within, and a better, safer, more really prosperous country for us all to live in.

I am sure that every Congressman in voting on this vital bill will be guided by his highest sense of the national interest.

Sincerely,

G. M. HUMPHREY
Secretary of the Treasury

"Good sense" put tax bill over

Remarks by Secretary Humphrey on Youth Wants to Know television panel in Washington. Stephen McCormick, moderator, and ten teenage interviewers under the Public Relations Division of the National American Legion.

March 28, 1954

JIM HOLMES. Mr. Secretary, you said to have real prosperity, we must have jobs, or have the jobs filled. President Eisenhower has said that this rolling readjustment we are now in is necessary and is healthy for the country and yet, there are over 3 million people out of jobs. Are we going to have real prosperity that way?

SEC. HUMPHREY. Jim, there are about that many people out of work today. On the other hand, there are over 60 million people working in America today. There never were that many people working in America until 1951. The year 1951 was the first time we had over 60 million people at work and we had them at work in 1952, and last year, in 1953, and we still have more than 60 million people at work in America today. That is a great many people at work, and in this transition period, we have to—boys and girls, if we are going to lower taxes—and I think we must, in America, lower taxes—there is only one sound way in which you can lower taxes, and that is to cut down on Government spending. Nothing else is sound. All you are doing is postponing the time. Any time you make a tax cut that is more than a reduction in spending, then you are making a false cut, because you have to borrow to make that difference, and that is simply having us—we older ones—put the burden of paying that bill on you young people. You will have to pay it or your children will have to pay it if we don't pay it currently.

MR. HOLMES. Mr. Humphrey, you say we have a large working force, now. But isn't our production up or shouldn't it be up to take care of these other people? The 3 million people who are out of jobs can't purchase as much as they could if they were employed, and if they were employed, wouldn't our production be able to take care of them?

SEC. HUMPHREY. That is right, Jim, and, of course, for the man who is out of a job, it is just as bad for him as though everybody else in the country was out of a job. He is in a tough spot when he is out of a job. It should be and it is the ambition of this Administration to have just as many people working as can possibly be kept working all the time. But you must remember that when you are talking in such large figures, that there are people who are changing jobs from time to time. You can't have everybody in the country working every day. There are some transition periods and we are now in a transition, as I explained a minute ago, when there are not as many people working as we would wish to have working. We want everybody working, but you just can't have them all the time. We want this transition effected as soon as we can, and the purpose of this tax bill and the reason it has the provisions in it that we have in it, is to try to minimize just as far as possible the unemployment in this country and to try to make the transition just as fast and as easy as we can. . . .

LOIS ALLEN. Mr. Secretary, I would like to know why Mr. Dodge

[Joseph M. Dodge, Director of the Budget] resigned. When he went, he was supposed to balance the budget. Does that mean that the budget cannot be balanced?

SEC. HUMPHREY. It does not. It means that when you undertake a job as big as balancing the budget and swinging this over from a big deficit—the biggest deficit we ever had, two years ago—down to a balanced budget, it can't be done all at once. We have to do it a piece at a time and Mr. Dodge has made a perfectly wonderful contribution toward the balancing of the budget of this country and toward straightening out our accounts. You see, Mr. Dodge had a wonderful experience. He helped straighten out the finances in Japan. He helped straighten out the finances in Germany. More than that, he is an excellent banker and he is a very fine man in every respect. So with all that experience and then with his own great ability, he was a very unusual man to help with this job. He came in, not to take the job for the life of the Administration, but he came in with the express purpose of helping to get organized and helping to get set up, and he did that. He had planned to leave before this, but he wanted to get this budget in hand and get it set, which he has done, and now he is going back to his own job, which I think is a very proper thing for him to do, although I am going to miss him very, very much indeed.

LOIS ALLEN. Will the budget ever be balanced?

SEC. HUMPHREY. I think it will, yes; I don't know whether we can do it next year or the year after but we are getting nearer all the time, you know. It has come down a great deal in these two years and we are very much nearer to being in balance—well, you know, two years ago, the last Democratic year, there was a $9.5 billion deficit. Last year it was around $4 billion and this year we hope it will be $3 billion unless we get too far out of line in making too big tax cuts. . . .

HAPPY O'CONNOR. Mr. Secretary, I would like to know, since $600 no longer buys what it used to, shouldn't personal income tax exemptions be raised?

SEC. HUMPHREY. I don't think so. I think the way to reduce taxes— if you are going to reduce taxes, you should do it in rates and not by exemptions. The rates have alarmingly increased and that is what makes the taxes high. So what ought to happen is that the rates come down and that will reduce the taxes, rather than by changing the exemptions.

CLARINDA JACKSON. What do you think of Representative Rayburn's prediction of a $2.5 billion income tax reduction?

SEC. HUMPHREY. I don't believe we are going to have it. I think that it is the wrong thing to do, at this time. That would put us right back into a very large deficit and I think that is the wrong time and the wrong method, as I have just finished saying, of reducing taxes, to reduce exemptions, now. I think what we need in America are jobs. We need places to work and people working and I think it is much more important for people to have wages, salaries and jobs than it is to have a change in the exemption in the tax laws and I think that would interfere with it. . . .

MARIE ANDREW. I would like to know, would the Administration compromise on Senator George's bill to increase the exemption up to $1,000?

SEC. HUMPHREY. No, they will not. That is not the thing to do at this time. You want to remember that $7 billion which is being released, which is the entire tax program, is being released to the people, and it is a tremendous lot of money that is being handed back. All along the line. Every single taxpayer in America is getting some tax relief under this bill.

RONALD NUTTLE. I would like to know what kind of pressure was used on the Republican Congressmen to make them support your tax bill.

SEC. HUMPHREY. Just good sense, Ronald. I believe so firmly in this, I believe it is right and I believe you can demonstrate it to anybody who will stop and think about it. I think just good common sense is what persuaded the great majority of the Republicans to vote in the way they did.

QUESTION. Could part of the reason that the Administration is opposed to Senator George's bill be that the people affected by that bill will not be of voting age? . . .

SEC. HUMPHREY. I am afraid you are confused in what the bill does. You are just confused in what happened. Senator George's proposal is that the exemption of all taxpayers be increased. The fact is that if the exemption is increased and if we run into a substantial deficit, then the deficit will have to be passed on. We'll borrow that, and it will have to be paid by you boys and girls at a later time. But it doesn't just relate to people earning less than $800. . . .

A tax system grows "like Topsy"

Speech by Secretary Humphrey to the
Republican Women's Centennial Conference
at the Statler Hotel, Washington.

April 7, 1954

I am glad to have the opportunity to speak to more than 1,000 ladies from every state in the Union, Puerto Rico, and Hawaii who are attending this Republican Women's Centennial Conference this morning. I appreciate the importance of having women understand what we are trying to do. I also appreciate the importance of women and the effective influence they can have upon decisions because I, like most male Americans, am a married man with a wife upon whom I depend a very great deal....

I firmly believe that the American people are very wise, wiser than many of our politicians believe. Given the facts, in most cases, the majority of the American people will react soundly and in the best long-run interests of the nation. That is why so many of you here today can help us so much by taking back to your home cities and towns the facts about what we are trying to do and help others to understand what we are trying to do, and so you will be providing a most valuable service for the whole nation....

This Administration has been and is still working toward two main great goals:

(1) We must—and will—provide the military strength best designed to promote our own security and real peace in the world.... (2) We must—and will—maintain the sound economy and productive power which is the basis for that military strength and leadership for peace.

Most Americans—the average wise Americans that I have already mentioned—pretty well realize by now that this Administration has cut spending and has cut taxes.

We have cut the spending program which was in effect (or had been prepared by the prior Administration) when we arrived by $12 million. Of this saving, $7 billion is being made this year.

Tax cuts which will be effective this year will amount to the largest total dollar tax cut ever made in any year in the history of our country. This total will be $7.4 billion. . . .

About two-thirds or nearly $5 billion of the taxes cut go directly to individuals. The remaining one-third goes to increase production and make more and better jobs, cheaper and better goods, and increased standards of living for all the people.

On January 1, individual income taxes were cut by over $3 billion. The expiration of the excess profits tax meant an additional tax cut of nearly $2 billion. On March 31 the President signed into law the excise tax bill, which resulted in a further reduction of nearly $1 billion. And now the very important tax revision bill, which has been passed by the House and is before the Senate, will result in further reductions of $1.4 billion. . . .

The whole tax level is still too high and restrictive of full opportunity in America, but there are two good reasons why we cannot cut Government spending too quickly:

(1) We must remember that 70 cents out of each tax dollar goes for our security. We must spend all that is required for that purpose, and no one wants unwisely to cut this field and endanger our security. Further savings in security expenditures will continue to be made, but only after most careful consideration and with the assurance that we will maintain an adequate posture of defense and actually get more security for less money.

(2) We cannot drop down too rapidly from such a very high level of Government spending without seriously dislocating our economy— producing shut-downs and unemployment. . . . Many of the people who have been making weapons of war for the Government for killing must now, in this period of transition, get jobs making things for people for better living.

The Administration's tax program is designed to help make this transition as quickly and as smoothly as possible. The tax measure currently before the Congress is well timed to do much to help this transition of people from defense work to peacetime work. This is the so-called general tax revision bill, recently passed by the House of Representatives and now under consideration before the Senate Finance Committee.

It is primarily a reform bill, not a reduction bill. Please keep this in mind when you hear political arguments against the bill in favor of some wholesale tax cut which certain leaders of the minority party propose as an alternative. It is a long-overdue reform program which can help greatly in the current economic transition.

It cuts taxes to millions of individuals primarily to help straighten out a tax system which has grown like Topsy with little rhyme or reason. And at the very same time it increases taxes on corporations by about an equal amount. It has been called a business bill and criticized for favoring business, whereas the real fact is that the increase in taxes on corporations is almost as much as all the reductions provided individuals and business combined.

It helps millions upon millions of taxpayers who have been plagued by unjust and unfair hardships over many, many years. Most important of all, it will help our economy grow, help new businesses to start, old businesses to modernize, and so help make more and better jobs, bigger payrolls and better living for every one—and speed the transition from Government jobs to jobs in industry for the people.

Some 1.3 million taxpayers will benefit by a change which allows a child to be continued as a dependent even if he earns more than $600 a year. This will protect from the loss of exemption parents whose children are helping to meet their own expenses while going through school.

Some 1.5 million retired people, other than those on already tax free Social Security and Railroad Retirement will get a 20 per cent tax credit on income up to $1,200. This covers such people as retired policemen and firemen and their widows. This will cover retirement income of interest, dividends and rents, as well as pensions and annuities for people over 65.

Some 800,000 widows and widowers with dependent children or other single close dependent relatives will be allowed the tax benefit of splitting their income. At present when one parent dies the tax rate on the single head of the household is increased, an obviously unfair thing.

Some 8.5 million people will be able to deduct medical expenses of 3 per cent or more of their income as compared with the requirement that medical expenses must be 5 per cent or more of income. Also the ceiling on medical expenses will be doubled to $2,500 per person and $10,000 per family.

Some 300,000 working widows, widowers, or mothers whose husbands are incapacitated will get a tax deduction of up to $600 for the care of their young children.

Some 500,000 farmers will benefit from more liberal allowance for soil conservation expenses.

Some 6.5 million of the 47 million taxpayers will benefit from partial relief from double taxation of dividends. Recipients of small amounts of dividends will be fully exempt from tax on such income. The tax on larger amounts of dividends will be reduced through a credit of 5 per cent in 1954 and 10 per cent thereafter.

Some 9.6 million individuals—farmers, small businessmen, etc.—as well as 600,000 corporations—will benefit from the proposal to give more liberal allowance for depreciation while it helps to modernize the entire industrial plant of the nation. . . .

This tax program reduces in our tax structure those barriers which seriously limit the chance for a man to better himself by saving a little money and making a small investment. It lessens the provisions in the tax law which make it look risky for businessmen to expand and try new ventures because of present tax restrictions.

The so-called "business" provisions in the bill, such as relief from double taxation of dividends and more flexible provisions for taking depreciation, are not really for business alone; they are for the growth and expansion of the economy of America—for more and better jobs and better living.

During the depression of the Thirties we never had less than 7.5 million men out of work—in spite of the WPA's—until the beginning of the World War II. This definitely demonstrated that there cannot be real prosperity in America by stimulating consumption alone. There are millions of men in this country who work in heavy industry. No matter how full the consumption industries operate or how much consumers are stimulated to spend by tax revision or otherwise, there cannot be prosperity unless the millions of men in heavy industry also have purchasers for their products. And those purchasers are investors. So for full employment for all, both consumers and investors must buy and a balanced tax program to assist toward that end is required.

This is why an increase in exemptions is not in the best interests of the country or of the workers of America. Fat tax reductions are of small value if there is no job. The balanced provisions of the Administration's tax revision bill will contribute far more to the creation of jobs, payrolls and prosperity than any increase of exemptions.

Moreover, an increase in exemptions as proposed by some would increase the prospective deficit by $2.5 billion for the first $100 of exemption increase and by $4.5 billion for an increased exemption of $200 which would take 7.5 million taxpayers entirely off the tax rolls. This could only mean that the remaining taxpayers would eventually have to take on and pay for the share of all those let out in addition to their share of the taxes they otherwise would pay.

Not only would all the remaining taxpayers so increased think this was unfair to them but the great majority of the ones released should and want to pay their own fair share. They only want to be sure that their share is fair and that the Government gets its money's worth for what it economically spends for the benefit of all.

The greatly increased deficits which the increase in exemptions would involve would directly contribute to further inflation with further decline in the value of the dollar. Expenses would tend to rise and the savings in taxes soon would be lost in increased cost of living with no offsetting gain. We would be headed back toward the old merry-go-round of inflation and all that we have worked so hard to correct would be jeopardized.

On the contrary, the Administration's tax program—and particularly the tax revision bill, about which you will be hearing and reading a great deal—can be a major factor in helping the economy grow and expand and so not only guarantee those who want to work a job but guarantee that as the days go by the jobs will be better jobs and provide more and better things for living for our ever-growing population. . . .

✒ This was the Secretary's first public preview of the tax reform and reduction bill of 1954. Almost all of the provisions he discusses were passed into law. The tax reform did not repeal the "double taxation" of which he spoke, but created small exemptions recognizing it.

Against 25 per cent income tax ceiling

Letter by Secretary Humphrey to the Sub-committee
of the Senate Judiciary Committee. Senator William
Langer, chairman.

April 27, 1954

... The proposal before your Sub-committee to place a 25 per cent ceiling on income tax rates and to repeal federal gift and estate taxes will cost this Government $13.3 billion in annual receipts. While a redistribution of federal tax burdens may be desired by many of our citizens, it is highly important that any such alteration be undertaken in a manner which does not disrupt the financing of the Government....

At best this proposed amendment would keep the Government's finances in a precarious position; and it is possible that it could precipitate a very large deficit....

The tax cut and the worker

Speech by Secretary Humphrey to the CIO
Full Employment Conference at the Washington
Hotel, Washington.

May 11, 1954

Needless to say, it is a great pleasure for me to be here with you today. I received the invitation and I promptly wrote Walter Reuther that I would be just delighted to come. I didn't know at the time that my good namesake, Hubert Humphrey, was going to be here on the platform with me.

Whether one platform can hold two Humphreys or not, I don't know.... I think we may have had from time to time slightly different ideas about things. Nevertheless, we are for one thing. We are for America. We want what is good for America.

The objective is perfectly clear. There are sometimes various ways to reach that objective. But that is the one thing that we all want in this country, and that is the great thing about this country. That is what we all want and what we are all striving to attain. . . .

I want to talk just for a minute to you about the matter of taxes and jobs. I say "taxes and jobs." It should always be reversed. It is jobs first always in America.

Now, what is it that makes jobs? You can't have taxes unless you have jobs. Unless there are jobs in America, unless America is well employed, the taxes just disappear. We can't operate unless we have jobs that pay the taxes with which to run the Government.

Now, what is it that makes jobs? Jobs don't grow on trees. Jobs are created by someone; they are made by someone. They are made and produced almost out of thin air, you might say, in the first instance.

The first thing you have to have to make a job is an idea or an invention. Go back to when I was a kid. When I was a kid, I remember very well when I saw the first automobile. It came in a parade with Hi Henry's Minstrels, and it was a Stanley Steamer, and the whole town turned out to see that automobile. It was only a year or two after that that there were a few Buicks being made over in Jackson, Michigan. They went busted, and they brought the Buick plant over to Durant, which was a buggy-manufacturing plant in Flint. Somebody had the idea that they could make a product which could be sold, which eventually has been built and built in America until we have all the thousands of jobs that are now in the automobile industry.

A few years ago, who ever heard of a radio? And even fewer years ago, who ever heard of television? Somebody invented something; they got an idea for a product that they thought they could sell to the people, and then they went ahead to make it.

What is the next step in the making of a job? The next step in the making of a job is that somebody buys the tools, creates the plant and buys the tools to start, usually in a relatively small way. But they begin to take this invention, this idea, this product that can be sold, and they have to start to make it. Nobody can sell you a television set until somebody has made one. They have to start to make it, and, after they start to make it, they start to sell it.

Now, why is it that we have developed this system in America whereby we can have the high wages that we have? There is simply one reason. Nobody over any extended period of time can get more than he can earn. The thing that has made high wages possible—and higher wages coming as we go on through the years—in America is that individual productivity is being increased in America.

Your hands are better than mine, but my hands or your hands are no better than the hands of a savage when it comes to producing things just with your hands. The reason your hands can produce ten, twenty, thirty, forty, a hundred times more than a savage's hands can produce is that we have developed this system of organization, the system of putting power and tools into your hands. By the power of those tools in your hands you can create many, many times what the savage's hands can create; and because you can create it, you can earn it. Because you can earn it, you can have it. That is because we have developed this great system of organization and creation by the giving of tools....

Now, what is it we are trying to do? I think everybody in this country wants lower taxes. I am sure myself that we must have lower taxes in America if America is to be the land of opportunity for the young man. America has been known as the land of opportunity for the young man. We want to keep it that way; we want to keep it the land of opportunity for the young man. That means that we cannot take so much money from all the people in America and put that money into big government as we have been doing. We have to decrease that expenditure.

Now, as we decrease that expenditure, how do we get taxes down and really get them down? Why is it that we don't like deficits? Why is it that we don't like running up huge deficits and borrowing additional money?

The only way in the world that you can reduce taxes, and really reduce taxes, is to cut Government expenditures. If you don't cut Government expenditures, you may think you reduce taxes but you really only partly reduce them and partly postpone the time of payment. Whatever money is spent by the Government has to be paid by somebody, and it has to be paid at some time by somebody, and the only way it can be paid is by the collection of taxes.

Now, if we run deficits, if we do not collect taxes currently for as much as we are spending currently—we have to pay the bills as they come in; there is no magic that we in the Treasury Department have, no wand that we can wave. When the Government spends money, the bills come in and we have to pay those bills. Now, if we don't collect enough money in taxes to pay the bills with, what do we have to do? We have to do exactly what you have to do.

America is nothing but 160 million people in one great big family, and all the fancy talk about finances and fiscal policies and all the big words people use don't amount to anything. The rules that govern your family govern the American family. If we don't collect enough taxes currently, which is our pay check, we have to borrow the rest. . . .

We then can pay our bills currently, but who is going to pay for what we borrow? The only way we can pay for what we borrow is more taxes. So all we have done when we have reduced taxes more than we reduce expenditures is to postpone the time to when that final tax is going to be paid. That means that I, an old man, pass the buck to you, a young man. That means that if we borrow and keep borrowing and running deficits, all we are doing is burdening the young men of America who are coming along, passing it on to your children and their children.

I don't think that is the kind of thing we ought to do in this country. I think if we are going to keep America as the land of opportunity for the young, which we older people inherited, it is our duty, as nearly as we possibly can, to pass on that opportunity for the young people of this country and not keep saddling them with more and more debt. Today just the interest on our debt is more than the whole Government debt was when I was a young man. We pay every year in interest more dollars on money that we have borrowed than the whole debt was when I was a kid—and when I was fairly old, at that.

When we talk about balancing a budget, all we are saying is that we are trying to collect enough now to pay the bills that we owe now, and that we are not trying to pass the buck for paying some of our bills on to some of these younger people. So we are striving for a balanced budget.

Why haven't we got a balanced budget? There are two great reasons. The number one reason always is the matter of security of our country. Now, we do a lot of thinking. We all get absorbed in our own thoughts; we all get absorbed in our own activities. But don't forget for a minute that this world is today a boiling caldron. We never know when it may break out, where it may break out, or in what way. The safest thing we can do for America is to have strength. We must keep America militarily strong, and to be militarily strong we must keep it economically strong. We must keep our business going; we must keep our jobs going and all those things to support it. But we must keep militarily strong, with the world in its present state of affairs.

As long as we are faced with that, we can't just cut off all the money we would like to cut off. We have to spend a lot of money for security of this country. We have to be sure that what we do will enable your old friend, Charlie Wilson, to get us more security for less money and greater efficiency.

I have just told you that the only real way to cut taxes, which is what we are trying to do, is to cut expenditures. Now, even eliminating the question of security, why can't we go further more rapidly? Well, let's just think about this. This is pretty tough, ladies and gentlemen; it is pretty tough to say it this way, but we might just as well not kid ourselves. We might just as well face facts. There are only two ways that the Government can save much money, can reduce its expenses in large amounts.

The great bulk of the money that America spends goes for two things. It either goes for hiring people to work directly for the Government or it goes for buying goods of various kinds that the Government buys. Now, when we say we are going to save money, that means we have to hire fewer people directly. That means that temporarily the people that we don't hire are out of a job. We have got to be buying less goods and materials that we have been buying. When we don't buy those goods, that means that those people who have been making those goods have got to be out of a job. . . .

This coming year we are planning on saving about $7 billion. That is a lot of money; it is a big cut in expenditures. That has got to come out of money that otherwise would go to wages or salaries to people that the Government hires or wages and salaries to people making those goods. If we stop that, we have people temporarily out of jobs.

To try to avoid a situation of having large unemployment because the Government is stopping spending that money, we give the $7.4 billion back to the people of America in tax reduction. It goes out to the people so that the people will have that $7.4 billion to spend directly, for them to spend themselves rather than to have the Government spend it for them. That means that the people of this country will spend that $7.4 billion; and the man who was making a cannon or a gun or ammunition for killing somebody, will get a job making something for better living for somebody. Instead of that cannon or ammunition, he will be making a television set or an automobile or a radio or a refrigerator or something for better living for people. And the money that we save on the Government's side we turn around and hand back to the people for the people to have on their side, and in that way we want to make this transition to eliminate as rapidly as possible any resulting unemployment and facilitate the change-over from one job to another as rapidly as we can.

You can't have prosperity in America, ladies and gentlemen, just by having stimulation of consumption goods. Now, I will prove that to you in just a minute. All you have to do—and nobody can know it better than you people—all you have to do is think of the millions of men and women in America who are working not in consumption industries but in heavy industries. Your president stated today to you that unemployment was still increasing somewhat. Where? In the heavy industries. The total volume of spending in America has only dropped off about 3 per cent; the total volume of consumer goods in America has only dropped off about 3 per cent. The place where employment has dropped the most and where it still is dropping, he said today, is in the heavy lines.

Now, you can stimulate consumers till the cows come home and you can buy all the consumer goods you can, but you will not put these fellows back to work in the heavy lines of industry. You have to also stimulate them. . . .

You have to get industry to buy new machinery so that the heavy machine tool builder can keep his men at work. You have to get industry stimulated to get more power plants built so that you have more power. You have to stimulate the expansion of all business in America—the development of America—all those things that go on in America, in order to have everybody employed all along the line, both consumers and producers of heavy materials.

And you have to do it for another reason. Stop and think about this for a minute. Nobody in America wants to stand still. People say we want to maintain our scale of living. I think that is baloney. We want to increase our scale of living. I want to live better; you want to live better. You want your children to live better. You want your children to have more opportunity than you had. You want this thing to move forward.

Now, how can you do that? You can only do it in one sound way, and that is to be able to produce more. The only way you can keep having more, having the standard of living going up, is to produce more, to produce better, cheaper things for people to have.

Now, we are having an expanding population in America. We have got a lot of people coming along every year in America. It won't do just to have 60 million people working in America. That is a lot of people working in America today. There are over 60 million people working in America today. That is more people than have ever worked in America in any year of America's history except a year ago today. So this is the second highest employment we have ever had in this country that is going on right now, but it won't do to have that five years from now or three years or some other years from now, because you are going to have more people in America, and that 60 million has to go to 65 million and it has to go to 70 million and keep going up.

How can you keep it going up? It is only by creating jobs, by putting power and tools in the hands of Americans so they can earn the high wages that we pay, and so that with that power and with those tools we can produce and compete with anybody in the world, which is where we are today.

We are in competition with the world—we have to be there—and the only way to outproduce the world is by more power, more tools, more invention, more organization of things that we have.

Now, that is our program, ladies and gentlemen. That is why we are handling ourselves the way we are. That is the basis on which we are operating, and I think it is sound for America.

DAVID MCDONALD (President of United Steel Workers). Mr. Secretary, I am sure that you understand that we are all most appreciative of the fact that you took time out from your very busy day to come here and speak with us. Mr. Secretary, if I may, since you are leaving, I would just like to call your attention to one fact. That is that the 1946 Full Employment Act is still in operation, and we are hoping that the Administration will take immediate steps to implement it, because we do have almost 5 million unemployed.

🖾 Walter Reuther, CIO president, wrote the Secretary his thanks for the speech.

How the 1954 tax revision moved

Speech by Secretary Humphrey to the Tax Institute
of the School of Law, University of Texas, Austin, Tex.

October 1, 1954

... The tax revision law—or the Internal Revenue Code of 1954—is one of the most important of our time because it sets a trend that will lead to greater economic progress for the country as well as bring relief to millions of individuals who have suffered specific hardships under the old tax code.

As you people well know, this is the first time in some 75 years that there has been a major revision of the whole federal tax structure. In addition to reducing restraints on business and removing hardships on individuals, this revision has attempted to make the tax laws more simple and certain and also to close loopholes under which some persons could have avoided their fair share of the tax burden.

The provisions in the law which remove hardships from individuals provide direct benefits which our citizens will note as they come to pay their income taxes next spring. Incidentally, they also will notice the benefits of the rest of the Administration's tax program, which in this calendar year has made effective tax cuts totaling $7.4 billion—the largest dollar tax cut in the history of this or any other country. But from the new Internal Revenue Code specifically, tax pressures will be eased where they have hurt millions of taxpayers severely in bygone years.

Among those who will benefit are working mothers; parents of children who are helping to pay their way through school; retired policemen, firemen, teachers, and their widows; families with heavy medical expenses; farmers who want to buy new equipment; people with sick and accident policies; taxpayers with non-relative dependents; farmers doing soil and water conservation; and many, many others. . . .

Helpful as these direct benefits are, they can in no way compare in my mind with the indirect benefits which will flow from the tax revision law. By removing restraints, this new law will release new energies throughout our economy. These energies work quietly but steadily to create new enterprises, more and better jobs, new productive efficiencies, larger payrolls, and rising standards of living for all the 160 million people of this nation.

The tax structure that we found on coming to Washington had grown up haphazardly and illogically. In the past 20 years, most of the changes in the tax laws were put into effect under the pressure of crisis of war or depression. The Congress reached for income where it could find it. In the process of imposing new taxes to meet new emergencies, stifling burdens were placed upon those very parts of the nation which provide for progress.

When this Administration came in office, we were told that getting a major tax revision bill adopted early in our Administration was simply impossible. But President Eisenhower himself had become deeply convinced of the need of tax reform. Also, President Eisenhower has a very deep suspicion about the word "impossible." Very soon after taking office, he instructed the Treasury to proceed with the basic job of recommending tax revision, and he always helped when the going was tough. Last March, in a nation-wide television broadcast, he described his tax proposals as "the cornerstone" of the Administration's entire effort. . . .

In the Treasury proper, the work of producing tax revision recommendations was headed by Under Secretary Marion Folsom, a man of wide experience in business and tax matters, who brought to work with him two other outstanding tax authorities—Dan Throop Smith, Professor of Finance at Harvard; and Kenneth Gemmill, a Philadelphia tax attorney.

Tax revision was also lucky in the leadership on Capitol Hill. Russell Train, the able Clerk of the House Ways & Means Committee, told you on Wednesday of this week of the progress of the tax revision bill through the Congress. As most of you know, a most vital force back of the drive to get tax reform was Chairman Dan Reed of the Ways & Means Committee, an ardent and courageous leader in the tax field. In the Senate, likewise, tax revision came under the wise handling of Eugene Millikin, chairman of the Senate Finance Committee.

Both the House and the Senate committees, of course, had superb technical assistance from the staff headed by Colin F. Stam, a Government tax man who has been giving expert guidance in this field since the 1920s.

As you gentlemen well know, the tax reform law was a result of very intensive study and hearings conducted for almost a year and a half. More than 5,000 pages of testimony were taken, and hundreds and hundreds of witnesses were listened to. Then their suggestions were gone over by teams of experts from both the Congressional and the Treasury-Internal Revenue staffs.

Throughout all of this, we tried to keep focused on one basic premise: Are we changing the law so as to help the economy to grow and so create more and better jobs and better living for every one?

In addition, of course, we tried to see if we couldn't put more certainty into the law. Economic progress and clarity do have a real connection. As you gentlemen also know, many of our tax laws have been vague and ambiguous. This meant that an individual considering a new venture could not figure for sure just what his tax liability would be. Likewise, because of vagueness, the tax liability might be changed, subject to the personal judgment of a tax official. We feel that more certainty is going to permit hundreds of new ideas to be put into actual business practice.

Most significant are substantive changes which we have made in the Internal Revenue Code designed to restore more of the normal incentives to business and individual progress. Probably the most controversial of these has been the provision which partially eases the double taxation of dividend income. Despite the political heat which has been kindled by the opposition on this point, it is my sincere opinion that the whole country will benefit from this provision.

Risk capital has made possible the phenomenal growth of our nation, and dividends are the incentives which make people take risks with their capital. Without this risk capital we never could have developed the wilderness as we have done. We couldn't have developed the mines, drilled for the oil, built the factories, and done all the things which over the years have led to more and better jobs and higher wages.

During the New Deal of the mid-thirties the provision for double taxation of dividend income crept into the tax law. Thus the citizen who provided risk capital was tapped twice for taxes. The company earnings bore the full brunt of the corporate income tax, and when what was left reached the individual as dividends, it was subject to the full personal income tax.

Without thinking of the personal injustice of this, let's take a quick look at the effect on the economy. It takes a good deal of money to make a job. A recent survey of 100 of the largest manufacturing corporations in the United States showed an average of nearly $15,000 of risk capital back of each job. In the development of most of our natural resources it can be much more.

So, more of our business capital has come from borrowing rather than from sale of stock. Companies which are heavy with bonded debt have to move more slowly and carefully than a company which is financed with risk capital, and in times of economic decline companies with a heavy debt burden are less likely to keep their heads above water.

Another most noteworthy change is the provision which provides more flexible allowance for depreciation. Some 600,000 corporations and nearly 10 million individuals, especially farmers and small businessmen, will benefit from this. But the greatest long-term benefit will be to the whole nation by the stimulation of plant expansion, the buying of more efficient machinery, all-around modernization—and so cheaper products and more and better jobs.

While tax experts talk about "depreciation," I like to think of it more as amortization. Under the new law, a man pays the same total tax but he can get his equipment paid for more quickly. Then he is in a position to look about for something newer and better and the quicker write-off helps him to finance his new purchase of better, more modern equipment. In other words, the impulse is forward. This is certainly in the best interests of all Americans.

In many other ways the new tax revision law encourages enterprise to go ahead. By removing barriers, it permits greater rewards for successful inventions and for those who develop them. It provides more liberal treatment for research and development expenditures to create new, better and cheaper products for everyone to enjoy. It gives more leeway to small companies which want to retain earnings for future expansion, which would create new jobs and better things for better living. This removal of barriers to incentive pervades the whole new law, even down to such things as encouraging youngsters who forward their own education by outside work.

The tax reform law does one other thing, it helps the security of our nation against any potential aggressor. It does this by helping the modernization of our industrial base, upon which all our military strength ultimately rests. This is particularly true in this day when new weapons and techniques are developed with amazing speed. We have no way of knowing what the decisive weapons may be a few years from now. But we have to make sure that our industrial strength is modern and ready to keep abreast.

The tax revision law is not perfect. In spite of all the care, we know that as time goes by we are bound to discover errors and better ways of doing things. There are also additional items in the code which must be the subject of further study before we can come forward with recommendations.

I would be the first to admit that there is much left to be done in the whole tax field. Our tax rates are too high. But they must remain relatively high as long as so much of our income has to go for the protection of our nation against a possible enemy. We will, however, continue to pass on to the taxpayer promptly the benefits of any spending reductions which can be achieved while always giving first priority to our national security.

There has been a good deal of nonsense and misinformation in recent weeks falsely suggesting that the Administration's tax program might not be in the best interest of all of our citizens. Such nonsense seems to increase in inaccuracy the closer we get to November.

I would like to explain why this program is in the best interest of every American:

First, every taxpayer in America has benefited directly from the tax cuts totaling $7.4 billion—the largest dollar tax cut in any year in the nation's history—and possible only because of cuts in spending made by this Administration.

Second, 62 cents of each dollar of the $7.4 billion goes to individuals—and almost 25 cents of each dollar to taxpayers with income of less than $5,000 a year. This leaves 38 cents of each dollar tax cut going to corporations.

Third, there is nothing un-American about helping the economy make more and better jobs, which is what our whole tax program is doing. What is important is that this Administration's tax program has and will continue to help bridge the transition from high to lower Government spending by helping the economy make new jobs.

American citizens are likely to understand that a program which helps make jobs is a program they should support. Despite the erroneous arithmetic of our critics, the average American, who is a very intelligent person, is likely to realize that more jobs and better jobs are more important to him and his family than any amount of political oratory and promises. This is the philosophy that this Administration has operated on. It is the philosophy back of the tax revision law and our whole tax program. It is the philosophy which we must continue to follow to help promote ever-increasing prosperity for all....

The story of the 1954 tax revision

Article by Secretary Humphrey in The Saturday Evening Post *under the title "What the New Tax Law Does for You."*

October 2, 1954

Last summer Congress passed, and President Eisenhower signed, a law with the unexciting title of Internal Revenue Code of 1954. In the weary heat of August people may not have paid much attention to this 929-page piece of legislation. Yet this law is one of the most important of our time, for it sets a trend that will affect the prosperity of every one of us; it clears the way toward greater economic progress for the entire country.

This new law is nothing less than a major revision of our entire federal tax structure—the first such overhaul in more than seventy-five years. Its purposes are to remove many hardships on individuals; to reduce restraints on the kind of enterprise which creates new business and new jobs; to close loopholes; and—so far as possible—to make the tax laws more simple, clear and certain.

The benefits of the new law are of two kinds—direct and indirect. Direct benefits will be felt by many millions of citizens when they come to figure their income taxes next spring. The tax burden will still be heavy. In spite of the fact that the Administration's economies have this year made possible tax cuts of more than $7 billion, the largest of any year in our history, the tax weight will be a strain on us all so long as nearly 70 per cent of our federal revenues must go to maintain America's security in a world threatened by communist aggression. Nevertheless, millions of taxpayers will find that the revised law eases the tax pressure where it hurts the most. Working mothers, people retired on a modest income, families with heavy medical expenses, parents of youngsters who are working to help pay their way through school or college, farmers who want to buy new equipment or improve their land—these are examples of individuals who will find the tax bite less painful.

Incidentally, we of the Treasury and the Internal Revenue are making every effort to acquaint the taxpayer with his rights under the new law. Instructions are being drawn more carefully than ever before; and for those taxpayers who are still puzzled—for even the clearest tax law is frequently hard reading—a large staff of Internal Revenue men is being specially trained to give advice on the new rules. If in doubt, don't hesitate to go to the nearest Internal Revenue office for help with your tax return.

These direct benefits I have referred to are important, especially to taxpayers living on a close budget. But in the longer view they are not nearly so important, in my opinion, as the indirect benefits which will flow from the tax revision. By removing restraints this new law will release new energies throughout our economic system, working quietly but steadily to create new enterprises, more and better jobs, new productive efficiencies, larger pay rolls and a healthily rising standard of living for all the 160 million people of America.

It is these indirect but broadly dynamic benefits of the new law which I would like chiefly to talk about here. But first I had better say something about the background of the new law; of the really prodigious efforts required to write and enact it; and of the general philosophy on which it is based.

The enormous federal tax structure, we found on coming to Washington, was not built according to a logical long-range plan. It grew up haphazardly and piecemeal. Especially during the last twenty years, most of the great changes in the revenue laws were improvised under the pressure of one crisis after another—of the Depression, of World War II, of the Korean War. Legislators reached for revenue where they could find it, and ideas of tax reform were deferred.

Furthermore, in the process of piling taxes on taxes to meet emergencies, shackling burdens were often placed on those very parts of the body politic which provide the momentum for progress. Uncle

Sam, in fact, had got himself into a fix something like that of a camper who is routed out at night to escape an approaching forest fire. In his hurry he grabs up his equipment every which way. Some he piles on his back; some he hitches on his belt; some he ropes around his neck; some he even stuffs into the tops of his boots. At first he bears this strange load pretty well. Under the stimulus of danger and excitement he plunges along briskly until he reaches a point of relative safety.

Then he realizes that the stuff in his boots hurts his legs and feet. The lopsided load on his back makes it hard to walk straight. The burden on his neck has produced a crick which prevents a clear view of the trail ahead. If he is going to make the long march back to civilization, he sees that he must rearrange his entire load. If he is a good woodsman, he will get it so repacked and balanced that he finds it easier to walk forward than to stand still.

In the simplest terms, that is the main purpose of the tax-revision bill: To rearrange the tax burden to make it easier for the economy to push forward.

For years our economy was spurred onward by the feverish stimulations of war and inflation, thus overriding or concealing the many restrictive, deadening, stifling features of our tax system. Thoughtful men have long predicted that such restrictions would rise to plague us as the artificial stimulants were withdrawn. For ten years congressional committees, Democrats as well as Republicans, have urged comprehensive revision of our cumbersome tax structure so as to free normal incentives to business progress. As long ago as 1947 the Committee for Economic Development, in a farsighted tax study, recommended many of the objectives which now have been achieved.

From then on, the demands for tax revision grew to a chorus throughout the nation. Taxpayer organizations, bar associations, farm groups, labor unions, the American Institute of Accountants, small businessmen, bankers, economists—all these and many more passed resolutions, appointed study committees and turned out enough learned reports to fill a good-sized library shelf. Among the hundreds of recommendations there was a remarkably wide area of agreement. But still, nothing happened. Tax revision had, like the weather, become something which everybody talked about, but nobody seemed to be able to do anything about.

The reason was this: Tax revision is easy in theory; in practice it is a task of formidable complexity. Changing the federal tax structure was like a vast game of jackstraws or pick-up-sticks. Each time you moved one tax stick, you were in danger of toppling down whole sections of the crazy edifice. I have been told a hundred times that a thorough tax-revision bill was just plain "impossible." As for enacting such a bill during the brief two-year span of one Congress—even practical men of an optimistic turn smiled in disbelief.

President Eisenhower was deeply convinced of the need of tax reform, and he had an ingrained skepticism about that word "impossible." Immediately upon taking office he gave tax revision his steady, firm, sanguine support. He could always be counted on for a push when the going was rough. Last March in a nation-wide radio and telecast, he rightly and boldly described his tax proposals as "the cornerstone" of the Administration's entire effort. To say that, with the fate of the legislation still in doubt, took courage.

The time and other factors were favorable. When the President first urged tax revision, the Korean War was drawing toward a close, permitting calmer appraisals. The new regime in the Treasury was in complete sympathy with the President's objectives. I had been fortunate in getting as my Undersecretary Marion B. Folsom, a man not only of wide experience in business, finance, economics and taxation, but with a background of earlier work with congressional committees. We were able to obtain the services, as the work got under way, of Dan Throop Smith, professor of finance at Harvard School of Business Administration, who has specialized for many years in the effects of taxation on business activity; and of Kenneth W. Gemmill, a brilliant Philadelphia tax lawyer. Both these men worked at their long tasks with great energy and devotion.

It was also fortunate that the leadership of the tax committees on Capitol Hill was in good hands. Chairman Daniel A. Reed, of the House Ways & Means Committee—long an ardent champion of tax reform—carried the bill through the House with a skill and will and drive which confounded the pessimists. In the Senate the bill came under the wise scrutiny of Eugene Millikin, chairman of the Finance Committee. Under his leadership his committee smoothed out some rough spots which had slipped into the bill.

I should also pay tribute to the work of other committee members in both houses, including some Democrats, but maybe the latter, with elections coming up, would rather not have compliments from a Republican Cabinet member. And certainly I must mention the tremendous job done by the technical staff which advises both House and Senate on tax matters. This staff is headed by Colin F. Stam, a dedicated Government career man who, ever since the 1920's, has given expert and impartial guidance to Republican and Democratic legislators alike.

Altogether, what with luck and good management combined, we had a pretty fine lot of men to carry out the colossal job of tax revision. And we needed them, every step of the way.

The mechanics of legislation are usually tedious, but there were features in the building of this great tax revision which I think will interest everybody. For one thing, the public itself participated to an unprecedented extent. What did the people who pay the taxes think was wrong with the laws? To find this out, Chairman Reed had detailed questionnaires sent to groups and individuals throughout the country. More than 15,000 replies were received. They came not only from organizations, large and small, but from individual businessmen, farmers, housewives and professional men. Most of them were specific, well-reasoned and constructive. Taken together, they touched on almost every aspect of the tax system. The suggestions were sorted, analyzed and condensed into a report of 150 closely printed pages—a comprehensive digest of taxpayer opinion.

The public was heard from further, and at length, during the hearings of the House and Senate committees, which took a total of more than 5,000 printed pages of testimony. The Internal Revenue Code of 1954 might well carry the subhead: "Co-Author, John Q. Public."

Another remarkable feature of this bill was the co-operation between the Executive and Legislative branches. Without that, the revision would indeed have been "impossible." The experts of the Treasury and Internal Revenue on the one hand, and of the congressional committees and staff on the other, worked together on a scale, and with a harmonious efficiency, never before achieved in this field, I am told.

For example, in tackling the jumbled mass of the old laws, we first had to break them down and sort them into some fifty fairly logical categories. Then these were assigned to special work teams.

Each of these teams, consisting of four to sixteen men, was drawn from both the congressional and Treasury-Revenue staffs. They included tax draftsmen, administrators, lawyers and economists. Thus each revision had the study not only of the men who drafted it but of the men who could write the regulations to accompany the law, collect the taxes under it, interpret and enforce it in the courts, and estimate its effect on the general economy.

This last consideration brings us to the heart of the matter. Throughout this revision, all of us kept our eye on this question: Is the new law so drawn that it will permit our economy to grow—new businesses to start, old businesses to expand, all businesses to modernize, and so facilitate the creation of more and better jobs and better living for everyone?

As part of this, we strove all along the way to make the law more clear and certain. At first glance, tax clarity and economic progress may seem to have little connection. Actually they are closely related. The old tax laws, for all their vast bulk, had many gaps—wide areas of vagueness and ambiguity. Consequently the man planning a new venture often could not calculate what new tax liabilities would develop from it. Where the law was unclear, the type and amount of the tax might be fixed at the discretion of a tax administrator.

That is why we have tried, so far as possible, to replace fallible official "discretion" with the clear, written words of the law. Encouraged by the new certainty, we are sure countless thousands of promising ideas for new and expanded business enterprises will be brought out of storage, dusted off and put to work.

Even more significant are the multitude of substantive changes in the law directed toward restoring normal incentives to business and individual progress. I will touch on only a few of them here. One of the most controversial, yet I believe one of the most salutary, is the provision partially easing the unfair and shortsighted double taxation of dividend income. In my opinion, the whole country would benefit by reducing this burden still further, but at least Congress has made a good beginning.

Dividends are the incentives which provide risk capital. It was risk capital, primarily, which made possible the phenomenal growth of America. Without it, we could not have pushed the railroads out through the wilderness, opened up the vast fertility of the Western lands, dug the mines, raised the cities, built and improved the factories, creating along the way ever more jobs and higher wages.

Then, in the mid-1930's, there crept into the tax laws, in confusion attending an experiment with an undistributed-profits tax, full double taxation on dividend income. Now the useful citizen who supplied the risk capital had run the tax gantlet twice. First, his share of the company earnings took the full whack of the corporate income tax; next, when the residue reached him as dividends, he had to pay on it the full personal-income tax. . . .

Let's for the moment forget about the personal injustices of this, and look at the effects on the economy. It takes large sums of money to create jobs. A recent survey shows that for 100 of the largest manufacturing corporations in the United States the cost of providing plant and equipment for one job is about $8,000 in the auto-and-parts industry, $12,300 in iron and steel, $20,000 in chemicals, $41,000 in petroleum products; the average for all manufacturing industry is nearly $15,000 of capital per job. (National City Bank Monthly Letter, July, 1954.)

The double taxation of dividend income has made it increasingly difficult to attract risk capital to create these jobs. Consequently most funds from outside the business have come from borrowing rather than from the sale of stock. In recent years more than three-quarters of industry financing has been through bonds.

This is not the best way for America's economy to finance its expansion. Bonds of course have their proper place, but when a company gets top-heavy with bonded or other debt, it has to watch its fixed charges the way an invalid watches his blood pressure. It moves timidly instead of boldly. It nervously slows down when the going is rough. It shrinks from the uncertainty involved in promising new ventures. In other words, it loses the very spirit which has made this country great. That is why I am so glad to see some reduction in the double taxation of risk capital. Modest as it is, it will halt a dangerous trend and set us back on the road of vigorous advance.

Incidentally, this provision is especially favorable to the small stockholder. The first $50 of dividend income is now entirely free from personal income tax. On dividends above that sum a tax credit of 4 per cent is now allowed. Already about 7 million, most of them of modest means, own shares of stock. I hope the tax revision will encourage an even wider public participation in the growth of American industry.

One of the most noteworthy changes made by the new law and one long overdue is that which permits more liberal and flexible tax allowances for depreciation. It will benefit some 600,000 corporations and nearly 10 million individuals, particularly farmers and small businessmen. But the greatest long-term benefit will be to the entire nation through the stimulation of plant expansion, more efficient machinery, all around modernization—and so cheaper products and more and better jobs. . . .

Under the new law faster write-offs of the cost of new equipment are permitted in the years immediately following its acquisition. Under the straight-line method, for example, on a new $10,000 machine with an estimated useful life of ten years, the taxpayer could charge off $1,000 a year during each of the ten years. Under the new law, using the "double rate declining balance," he can charge off $2,000 the first year, $1,600 the second, $1,280 the third, $1,024 the fourth, and $819 the fifth. Thus in one-half of the machine's life he can charge off $6,723 or more than two-thirds of its cost. . . .

Tax theorists range all over the lot in their predictions of how the new depreciation rules will affect the federal revenues. Some, defenders of the old system, say the new one will cost the Treasury vast sums over the next two decades. Others calculate that the Treasury will lose for the first few years, then make it up in the next few. My own belief is that the new rules will so increase productive activity and vitality that revenues may well increase from the very first year. . . .

This comprehensive tax revision has one further important advantage, generally overlooked by the commentators. That is the tendency of the new law toward the modernization of the industrial base upon which all military strength ultimately rests. In recent years new weapons have developed and changed with a speed never before dreamed of in history. Most of today's super-ultra-modern weapons may soon be obsolete. Not even the wisest scientists or military leaders can predict what will be the decisive weapons of even five, ten, or twenty years hence. But this we do know: Whatever inventions may be ahead, their value will depend on industry's ability to fabricate them quickly, skillfully, and in quantity. Insofar as this new law contributes to industrial strength and modernization, it will make America safer in a dangerous world. . . .

Even if the new law were perfect, our tax troubles would not be over. Tax rates are high, and must remain so, as long as defense needs call for expenditures on anything like the present scale. We will continue to follow the policy of passing on to the taxpayer promptly the benefits of any expenditure reductions which can be achieved without endangering national security. We have tried meantime to revise the details of the law so that the hardships and restraints which this severe burden of taxation necessarily imposes are reduced to a minimum.

Taxes at best are a wearisome, burdensome, complicated business. Few of us can achieve the philosophy of Mr. Justice Holmes, who paid his tax bill with the cheerful comment, "With taxes, I buy civilization." But I think we can agree on the close relationship between the tax structure and national progress. . . .

Taxes and more jobs

Remarks by Secretary Humphrey interviewed by
a panel at the New York Herald-Tribune
Annual Forum in New York City.
Interviewers: Murray D. Lincoln, president of
the Farm Bureau Insurance Companies;
Robert S. Byfield, New York investment counsellor;
and Henry R. Luce, editor-in-chief of Time, Life,
and Fortune *magazines.*

October 21, 1954

Mr. Lincoln. Mr. Humphrey, according to the Joint Committee on Internal Revenue, the quick tax write-off for corporations and the dividend tax credit for stockholders, both enacted this last year, may save the big taxpayers as much as $19 billion during the next 18 years. Now compare this to the fact that the proposal to raise personal exemptions on individual taxes by only $100 was slapped down. Now, does the Treasury contemplate equalizing tax relief by proposing action to increase exemption for the millions of low-income people so that the vast majority may get a taste of the benefits now being given largely to the big taxpayers?

SEC. HUMPHREY. Well now, Mr. Lincoln, I'm delighted to have an opportunity to answer a Democrat face to face on that subject. Because you know there's been a lot of nonsense going around about this tax program and the tax bill. It's been misrepresented in many ways.

What I'd like to do, Mr. Lincoln, if I can, is to just differentiate for just a minute between the tax bill that you referred to and the tax program. Now the reason I want to do that is just this. The tax bill is only one part of the tax program that's effective this year. And the tax bill involves only about one-quarter of the total amount of money that was given back to the people in tax cuts this year.

Now, the total tax program released to the people this year was $7.4 billion. That's the most money that ever was cut in taxes in any year in this country or any other country at any one time.

That program is divided into several parts. The first part of that program is the cut that was made effective on the first day of January of this year of about $3 billion, all made in personal income rates. Every individual who pays taxes got a cut, amounting in the gross to about $3 billion. Effective January 1 of this year there was a cut of about 10 or 12 per cent in the lower brackets graduated down to about 2 per cent in the upper brackets. And every single taxpayer participated in that tax cut.

The second thing that happened was this. The excess profits tax expired this year and was not renewed. You will recall we did renew that for a part of the preceding year.

MR. LINCOLN. That helped the corporations mostly, didn't it?

SEC. HUMPHREY. Now, that excess profits tax involved about $1.8 billion, only about half of what the preceding cut that I just referred to involved. The excess profits tax, everybody, Democrats, Republicans and all, agreed was wrong and ought to be eliminated. It was almost a universal approval.

The next thing that happened was this. On April 1, excise taxes amounting to about $1.1 billion were cut. Those excise taxes were largely on things of relatively low price, that the general public bought and paid for. They paid the tax in the price that they paid for articles that they bought. And that $1.1 billion was released very largely to individuals making purchases of low-priced commodities.

Now we come to the tax bill which you speak of, which cut about $1.4 billion. Now that tax bill of about $1.4 billion was divided very roughly in half. More than $700 million went to individuals and less than $700 million went to corporations or to business firms of one kind or another. The money that went to individuals in that cut was for the purpose of relieving hardships for millions of people in various ways.

There were all sorts of hardships that had grown into our tax pattern and I won't try to detail them one at a time. You've all seen them. But those were things that were unfair, unjust, improper charges that had been made against people.

Now as to the business end—this is where the most debate has taken place, and that's why I want to refer to it by itself. That's divided largely into two things. First, the cut in the tax on dividends—the double-taxation of dividends—and second, the depreciation allowances.

I'll take the dividend cut first. What we have to have in America are jobs. More important than a tax cut to a man, is a job. If a man hasn't got a job and he hasn't got pay coming in, it doesn't make much difference to him whether he's got a tax cut or not. Now, how do you get a job?

In America today we can't pay the high wages that we pay, we can't pay the amount of money that people get to maintain the present standard of living, unless a man is furnished with tools, with equipment, with power in his hands, to do his job. Every job in this country has to have a substantial investment back of it in order that the man can earn what he's paid, and if he doesn't earn it, he can't be paid it.

MR. LINCOLN. Isn't that the trickle-down theory?

SEC. HUMPHREY. No, that isn't the trickle-down theory, that's building from the bottom up. If you don't build at the bottom, if the man at the bottom doesn't have a job and pay, there isn't any top to it. If we have a firm foundation we have to have jobs in this country. We've got an ever-growing population and they all have to have jobs and more jobs and better jobs every year.

Now the way you get that job is by somebody buying and paying for those tools, and if somebody doesn't furnish those tools, that man can't have that job and earn those wages and have that standard of living. So we have to induce people, by giving them a chance to make a profit on their investment, to save their money and put their money into tools so that people can have these jobs and earn these wages.

This double-taxation crept in during the New Deal days. It never was intended, it's been objected to by both Democrats and Republicans, but nobody ever had the nerve to go ahead and get it done before; and it should have been done long, long ago.

I'll talk just a minute about depreciation. The thing we need in America more than anything else is a modern machine, a modern plant, modern equipment. We need it for our security first. . . . We don't know what kind of weapons the next war will be fought with. We don't know what kind of weapons we need for our defense. If we've got a great industrial machine in America—which we have today, and it's modern—we'll make whatever is required for that purpose.

Depreciation is simply getting your money back and getting it back quicker in order to buy new and better machines and make more jobs, not only for those who build the new machines but for those who use the better machines when they get them.

Mr. Lincoln. Well, thank you, Mr. Humphrey, for your answers, but I sure would like to have about 15 minutes to argue with them.

Mr. Byfield. Madame Chairman, I'd like to ask Secretary Humphrey a question that I don't think any Democrat would dare. In the past year, or year-and-a-half, wholesale prices have practically stayed on a straight line, and I'd like to ask the Secretary how the monetary policy of the Administration, together of course with the Federal Reserve Board, has accomplished this. And on that subject, Mr. Leon Keyserling, the Chairman of the President's Council of Economic Advisers under the Truman Administration, recently made the following amazing statement. He said, "We need to continue and improve an easy money and liberal credit policy because hard money promotes hard times." Now, Mr. Secretary, in view of that, would you spell out for us the relationship of sound money to human welfare?

Sec. Humphrey. I'll be delighted to, Mr. Byfield, as best I can. Inflation is a thief in the night. Inflation is this Administration's Public Enemy No. 1, and we're going to stop inflation if we can. For the present, we have stopped it. We have it arrested. The value of a dollar from 1939 until the time we came in office, fifteen short years, was cut in half. It depreciated in its volume just one-half in the short time of 15 years. During the time we've been there, which is nearly two years now, the value of a dollar has changed less than one-half of one per cent, so that the value of a dollar now has been stabilized and we are going to in every way do everything we can to keep it stabilized.

When we first came into office—and most people forget this, because we think we live in a free country—when we came into office, if you'll stop and think for just a moment, you'll realize that we had complete controls all over this economy. We had wage controls, we had price controls, we had coupons, you had all sorts of bureaus and bureaucracies in Washington that were telling the people what they could and couldn't do all over the country.

The first question that came up was, can we release these controls, can we free this country? On one side, a group of people said that if we do we'll have a runaway inflation and the prices will run away and we'll have a terribly serious time.

Facing that, we decided that the thing to do was to free the economy; to take the controls off and to let the economy seek its natural level. At that time we put out some long-term bonds, if you will recall. Those long-term bonds assisted in stabilizing the interest rates, and the interest rates at that time—because the demand for money was high—were at fairly high levels.

That signal went all over this country that prevented and deterred people from accumulating inventory—from rushing in to accumulate inventory. The result was that when we took the controls off the prices didn't move. Only one price, the price of copper, moved up 3 or 4 cents, and that moved down 3 or 4 cents in a matter of about six weeks, and all the other prices remained where they were, or were stabilized, or gradually slightly declined.

As that occurred, and as the prices declined, or stabilized, then money, the demand for money, because it wasn't used for a speculative inventory, became more plentiful, and as money became more plentiful, the interest rates began to decline. Money is like other commodities you have—when it's scarce you pay more for it, when it's plentiful you pay less for it. So as there was more money, and it wasn't in such demand, the price for it went down and kept going down and is down now to a relatively low level. It's now about at the lowest level it has been at any time in the last few years. And the dollar during that period has remained constant.

Mr. Luce. Mr. Secretary, I'm sure that we all agree on the vital importance of maintaining in this country a sound economy, an expanding economy, and your name, sir, is connected with this great effort in the most distinguished manner. I should like to ask you about the importance of this country's helping to bring about an economic advance throughout the whole free world. May I put my question by quoting a few lines from a speech made in this city a few days ago by Ambassador Aldrich to a group of American businessmen:

"As a nation devoted to the ideal of free, competitive enterprise, we have a natural leaning toward a world in which trade is conducted on a multi-lateral basis, a world in which there is a minimum of government interference, and into which currencies are freely convertible. We all know that these conditions will not be created unless the United States is prepared to take a hand in bringing them about. If we do not move in the direction of a more liberal trade policy, there is every likelihood that we will move backward into the morass of greater restrictions, new bi-lateralism and lower volumes of trade. Such a development could endanger our whole economy. . . ."

Sec. Humphrey. I think a high level of employment, a high level of activity in business in every respect in America, and the maintenance of that is the most important thing to be done economically in the whole world. The whole world reflects conditions in this country. The whole world is affected by conditions in this country if there's any particular movement in them, any substantial movement in them, and not only that, but psychologically, the American economy— America, the land of opportunity, America the land of progress, of opportunity for the young and progress and development, America as a beacon light in this world of freedom of what can be accomplished under freedom—is the greatest thing we can have from a psychological point of view. So that I think that nothing should be done that will in any way detract from high productivity, high employment in this country.

Now there are things that can be done without in any way harming our own economy. As a matter of fact, over the past 15 years there have been very substantial reductions in the tariffs. The reciprocal trade acts have been in effect for 15 or 16 years.

If you'll just stop and think back for a moment, we never have had a trial of these lower tariffs that have been put into effect during the last 15 years. Our tariffs during the last 15 years on most things have been reduced to about a third of what they were 15 years ago. As a matter of fact, 55 per cent of all the goods that come into this country come in entirely free. Of the 45 per cent that come in that have some tariff burden on them, the average of the whole 45 per cent is only 12 per cent of the value of that 45 per cent—so that our tariffs are very low. That 12 per cent was 30-odd per cent, 33 or 34 per cent, only 15 years ago.

During that 15 years, we've either been in war, or Europe—or competitive countries that will make the goods in competition with us—has been flat on its back, so that we have had no competition from abroad to speak of for that 15 years, during the time we've had this tremendous reduction in rates.

We're now beginning to get that competition for the first time, and just what effect that competition will have, nobody can tell. . . .

I think what we have to do, and what we should do is to take these tariffs as they are now, to see what happens as the goods come in, and when, as in some cases that have occurred in the past, we find that goods are coming in to the detriment of employment in America, to the detriment of American industry and to the detriment of American productivity, then the peril-point provisions should be used and we should find a level which will balance that off, so that our economy here will still function and still be strong.

We can do that, I think, and still increase our volume of trade, and still increase our volume of exports, and increase trade all through the world.

Now, as to convertibility, of course you can't have full trade without convertibility.

The difference in the past two years is just remarkable in what's happened in Europe, as you well know. In Europe, Holland, Germany, Belgium, Switzerland, all those countries, have de facto convertibility right now. They're not waiting for any further action. You can transfer those currencies into dollars or into any other currencies at face value.

The big currency in the world, and half the world's business is done on it, is the pound. The convertibility of the pound, the release of restrictions by England to permit trade, to permit our trade to go there—

and, mind you, they have many more restrictions against us than we have against them right now—and the removal of those restrictions and the making of their pound convertible into dollars, is a matter for them to determine as to when they can go ahead with it.

Now many people—just bear this in mind—many people think of convertibility as something that when you say we're going to go convertible you've done your job. That's just the first day. It's after you say you're going to go convertible that you've got to keep being ready to stand there and pass out your dollars and other currencies and exchange them for pounds, and keep doing it day after day and year after year.

And until the United Kingdom is satisfied that they can take that, I don't think we should push them. I think we should help them, but I don't think we should push them. I think they should do it in their own good time.

Against a $20 exemption

Statement by Secretary Humphrey before the Senate Finance Committee.

February 28, 1955

Your committee has before it this morning a $20 tax cut which was suddenly sprung on the Ways & Means Committee and hurriedly passed through the House of Representatives last week by a scant margin of only five votes with only a limited hearing and no time for thoughtful consideration.

I strongly urge the Senate Finance Committee to reject this proposal as completely contrary to the public interest.

President Eisenhower asked the Congress to continue responsible financial management of the Government's affairs by extension of (1) the corporate income tax rate at 52 per cent and (2) the excise taxes on tobacco, liquor, etc., both of which otherwise would go down automatically on April 1. These two extensions will give the Government $2.8 billion in revenue and will help to continue the progress toward lower deficit financing and a balanced budget.

The $20 proposal has been hastily tacked on as an amendment to this sound bill. This proposal would give every taxpayer a reduction of $20 for himself, his wife, and each dependent. It would take about 5 million taxpayers completely off the federal income tax rolls. And it would lose about $2.3 billion of revenue in a full year.

Now, why is this $20 proposal contrary to the public interest? It means reversing the successful trend of the Administration during the past two years in cutting deficits and working toward a balanced budget. The budget deficit for fiscal year '53 was almost $9.5 billion and a deficit projected for fiscal year '54 was nearly $10 billion.

We cut planned spending in fiscal year 1954 by more than $10 billion. We cut the deficit in fiscal 1954 by more than $6 billion and so moved two-thirds of the way toward a balanced budget. With these spending cuts firmly in sight, we cut taxes by $7.4 billion—the largest single tax cut in history.

This Administration advocates further tax cuts but only at such times as we can see them justified by further cuts in spending and increased revenues from economic growth that broadens the tax base.

Both the President's Budget Message and his economic report expressed hope for a tax reduction next year, but only if expressly justified by spending cuts and increased income from economic growth.

To vote a $20 tax cut now—before we know we can afford it next year—and without any indication of where the money is coming from is nothing but an irresponsible gesture. It is based only on hopes as yet entirely unrealized which may well turn out to mean heading back into heavy deficit financing, with all the inflationary dangers that such borrowing means for the American people.

There has been some misleading talk about justifying the $20 proposal on the ground that the "little folks" have been entirely neglected. Let's look at the record. The $7.4 billion tax cuts last year included an income-tax cut for every taxpayer in America. The cut averaged about 10 per cent for all the lower income taxpayers but was scaled down to only about 2 per cent for the highest bracket incomes. These reductions applied to every single taxpayer in the nation.

Excise taxes were cut by a billion dollars on goods of everyday use. And millions upon millions of Americans got tax reductions in relief provisions for retired people, widows, working parents, and the sick or hospitalized. These reductions were predominantly in the low-income group.

But even more important is the fact that this Administration has been slowly getting the Government's financial affairs under control to help the economy expand and so make constantly more and better jobs.

A job is more important than a tax cut.

This proposed tax cut is entirely unjustified by firm evidence at this time. If it is paid out of borrowed money requiring additional deficit financing, which is all that is in sight at this moment, it can start us right back on the reckless road of inflation with all its cruel thievery.

Inflation, rampant for several years, has been checked. The cost of living has not increased now for over two years as compared with the fact that it almost doubled in the 15 previous years. This has been worth billions of dollars to millions of Americans.

This checking of inflation has protected not only the full purchasing value of peoples' current earnings but has insured the full worth of their savings in savings accounts, insurance policies, pension funds, etc., with which they are trying to provide for their own and their loved ones' futures.

And let us always remember that it is not the rich who need protection against inflation. It is the little folks who suffer the most when inflation takes hold in a land.

I hope the committee will vote out a bill excluding the $20 tax cut proposal.

🖙 Early in 1955, one of the piecemeal tax cut provisions was tacked to an Administration tax renewal bill and passed the House of Representatives. This statement about it to the Senate committee in charge was about as stern in words as Secretary Humphrey ever spoke. The proposed further exemption died in the Senate.

Correction of some tax errors

Statement by Secretary Humphrey before the
Senate Finance Committee.

May 11, 1955

I am here today to urge the repeal of Sections 452 and 462 of the Internal Revenue Code of 1954.

The original objective of these two sections, which cover prepaid income and reserves for estimated expenses, was simply to conform tax accounting with business accounting. It was never intended that these provisions would result in any substantial loss of revenue or result in windfalls to taxpayers. A review of the consideration of this subject by this committee will confirm the impression held at the time by lawyers, accountants, and businessmen that the basic motive for these provisions was simplification of tax accounting procedures, and not radical tax reductions.

This tax law became effective on August 16, 1954. During the fall, as the knowledge of its provisions increased, there began to be rumors that these particular provisions might not work as originally intended. Before the end of the year, studies by the Treasury staff, working with the staff of your committee, were undertaken to see if the threatened situation could properly and effectively be cured by regulation. Proposed regulations were issued on January 22.

However, until the time came when these provisions began to be put into actual practice by taxpayers preparing their income tax returns and the thirty days expired for protests against the proposed regulations, there was not much reliable information available.

It then developed that there is a sharp difference of opinion between taxpayers and the Government as to the scope of these sections. The tentative regulations issued by the Treasury on January 22, in order to carry out the provisions of the law, have come under strong attack as being too restrictive in limiting the intended application of the sections.

Taxpayers have already served notice that they intend to litigate this restriction. Should they be successful in the courts, the revenue loss under the law might be far in excess of anything contemplated by the Congress. As soon as the checks were sufficiently conclusive to satisfy the staff that the original objective might not be carried out and that the situation could not be adequately corrected by regulation, they reported their findings and we promptly called the matter to the attention of the Congress.

The original estimate for several so-called bookkeeping items, of which Sections 452 and 462 were the principal revenue items, was $47 million. The limited check that we have made around the country indicates that the loss would be substantially greater than the original estimates. How much greater it might be we cannot now say because we simply do not have the information as to what the bulk of taxpayers concerned might claim should these provisions remain in the law. And with the litigation that would surely be involved in many cases should the provisions remain, we might not have final figures on the loss for years to come.

Repeal of these two provisions will reinstate the legal rights of every one just as they were under the old law prior to last August and protect the Government from revenue loss which was never intended by the Congress.

The objective of trying to conform tax accounting with business accounting is still a sound one. In trying to do this, however, a serious mistake was made in not sufficiently limiting the application of the provisions and restricting the revenue impact of the changes as enacted. That is why repeal is required rather than amendment, so as to be sure that in any new approach to the original objective the revenue is adequately protected.

We have studied many proposals to correct the situation by amendment of the sections rather than repeal, but we have found no proposal which we can be sure will accomplish the original objective without giving some taxpayers an unintended advantage or producing very involved technical problems creating uncertainty and litigation.

The Treasury Department is firmly opposed to any tax legislation which gives any American an unfair advantage over another taxpayer. We will always recommend prompt action be taken to correct any situation which can result in windfalls to any taxpayer. To firmly follow out our policy of being as fair and just to all taxpayers as is humanly possible, I am urging outright repeal of the two sections which would have resulted in some taxpayers getting a break over others.

As the Chairman knows, I sent the Chairman of the House Ways & Means Committee last week a letter stating that none of the other approximately 70 suggestions for perfecting the Internal Revenue Code of 1954 require immediate legislation. With this the Chairman of the House Ways & Means Committee agreed in a letter which was made public last Friday along with my letter to him. All of the suggestions considered by the staffs of the Joint Committee on Internal Revenue Taxation, the Ways & Means Committee, and the Treasury are wholly noncontroversial. More than half are clerical errors, such as misprints, misspelling, bad punctuation, and like errata with no legal significance. Other suggestions pertain to items on which the Treasury could issue better regulations if somewhat more precise statutory language were adopted. The revenue effect of the suggestions is insignificant, if indeed they have any over-all revenue effect.

📑 The Secretary made haste to plug a loophole which suddenly had appeared in the reform tax revision legislation. The Congress plugged it.

Defense industry tax "write-offs"

*Statement by Secretary Humphrey before the House
Government Operations Committee, Sub-Committee
on Legal and Monetary Affairs.*

July 18, 1955

I welcome this opportunity to appear before you and to express the point of view of the Treasury Department on the provisions in our tax laws which allow accelerated amortization for income tax purposes of the cost of certain "emergency facilities."

I want to make it clear that I am not urging repeal. Final decisions on the scope of the program should not be made until the studies now being made by the Defense Mobilization Board have been completed. I wish at this time simply to make certain suggestions which I believe should be carefully considered in any study of the matter.

The "crash" defense program which was initiated in connection with the Korean War has been substantially completed.

Emergency amortization served a useful purpose during the early phases of rebuilding and expanding defense plant capacity to meet that emergency. However, the accelerated tax write-off is an artificial stimulus of a dangerous type. Its indefinite continuance involves the very real danger that interests receiving the benefits of it come to rely upon it to the detriment of others who are not so favored. A defense mobilization program on a substantial scale may be essential for years to come. Expansion of our defense facilities should be an integral part of our broad, orderly, long-range, natural economic growth. Our basic defense capacity cannot soundly be separated from the broad base of productive capacity in general on which our nation relies for its economic strength. Artificial stimulants may well become artificial controls. Because this is not of universal application but is bestowed only upon some who especially qualify as against others who do not, it could become a hindrance to sound, balanced, vigorous growth of our whole free economy. It is not the American way.

Moreover, I think it important to remember, in any consideration of the problem, that several recent changes in the tax laws have substantially altered the tax picture which existed when accelerated amortization of emergency facilities was first adopted. Then we had an excess profits tax which took up to 82 per cent of the profits from corporate business, and thereby tended to discourage large expenditures for new plant facilities. That tax was repealed as of January 1, 1954. The new liberalized depreciation methods under the 1954 Internal Revenue Code now permit faster capital recovery by all taxpayers equally and meet the basic needs of the whole economy. This reduces the need for singling out particular taxpayers or particular facilities for more favorable treatment than others receive.

A highly selective program may well have merit if it is strictly limited to very special cases—where there is present and pressing need for goods that would be a "must" in time of war and which cannot be met by present facilities and where Government contribution is necessary to meet those goals. I suggest, however, that the broader the program—the more it extends into areas other than the direct production of goods that are directly needed for war—the more difficult it becomes to administer wisely, without essentially arbitrary or discriminatory results.

Indeed, the very existence of such a program may lead some taxpayers to construct facilities deliberately colored to meet supposed defense need. The tax benefits often could more than absorb the waste and extra expense to the taxpayer—but it hardly would be good for the economy. . . .

You will note that the estimated revenue loss this fiscal year will be $880 million. With our budget not in balance, this figure gives us serious concern. Extension of the program well may stand in the way of future more general tax reductions for all taxpayers which would be of important assistance to all business and to our continued economic growth and expansion.

Finally, I should like to speak very frankly about this use of the tax laws to further special programs and accomplish purposes other than simply the collecting of taxes. The power to tax is the power to destroy, and revenue laws should be used only to equitably raise revenue, not for other indirect purposes. It is dangerous to use the tax laws for social purposes, to favor one citizen or group of citizens over others, to exercise economic controls, or to indirectly subsidize any segment of our economy.

If, in the wisdom of the Congress, such subsidies or assistance to special communities or for special purposes are desired, then appropriations should be made for the purpose which can be submitted to the Congress through regular channels where the amounts will be well known and where the Congress specifically can vote in favor of or in opposition to special treatment for any group. Under this program of tax reduction in special cases, our net revenues can be reduced and our deficits increased without formal action or appropriations by the Congress. This use of the tax laws, where the stimulants are applied by men, not by law, is appropriate only in an emergency or under special conditions under rigid restrictions when usual procedures are inadequate for our protection.

Rapid amortization unquestionably was of real assistance in expediting preparation for the war and still can be useful if limited strictly and exclusively to that end. It induced the investment of large sums of private means for production that was made available under private management far better and far quicker than otherwise would have been obtained. It kept the investment of public funds to a minimum and it left no great burden of public properties to be disposed of when their war purposes had been served.

The Office of Defense Mobilization has recently requested the agencies that make recommendations to it such as the Departments of Commerce and Interior and the Defense Transport Administration, to review all existing expansion goals with the following points in mind:

(1) Evaluate goals on the basis of defense need. The need for additional expansion shall be quantitatively measured in terms of wartime supply and requirements.

(2) Expansion goals shall be based upon shortages which, in the judgment of the delegate agency, will not be overcome without the incentive of tax amortization.

When the Defense Mobilization Board has completed its review of the program in the light of these criteria, and made its recommendations to the Director of Defense Mobilization, it is expected that the program for the future will be on a proper basis.

This is not critical of the past. Nor is it thought best to abandon the practice entirely. But its usefulness in the future will be greatest for the good of the nation as a whole if from now on it is used only sparingly and very rigidly and strictly confined to direct war-requirements applications.

◄ The continuing problem of defense production "write-offs" had begun to arouse some controversy in Congress. The Administration attempted to cure the inequity by gradual reduction of "write-off" certifications where possible, but the principle as stated by the Secretary remains not entirely solved.

About fast write-offs

Statement by Secretary Humphrey on rapid
amortization of emergency facilities before
the Senate Committee on Finance. Senator
Harry F. Byrd, chairman.

May 7, 1957

. . . I strongly support the general purpose of this proposed legislation to limit emergency amortization to strictly defense items.

In July, 1955, I first expressed publicly before this very committee my growing concern about the emergency amortization program before a subcommittee of the House Committee on Government Operations. I stated that while emergency amortization may have served a useful purpose during the Korean emergency, it was an artificial stimulus of a dangerous type.

From November, 1950, to March 20, 1957, almost 22,000 certificates were issued under the five-year amortization program. The total cost of these projects was almost $39 billion. Almost $23 billion, or about 60 per cent, was made eligible for the five-year write-off.

Some degree of defense mobilization on a substantial scale may be essential for years to come. But expansion of our major productive facilities should be an integral part of our long-range, natural economic growth. Our basic defense capacity, except for a few very special items, cannot be separated from the broad base of our productive capacity.

Artificial stimulants may well become artificial controls. Because rapid amortization is not applied universally, it could create a competitive imbalance in the sound, vigorous growth of our free economy. It is not the American way.

The revenue lag from certificates issued through 1956 probably exceeds $5 billion during these early years which will be recovered in the years after 1960. But the interest cost to the Government, over the entire period of lag in tax collections, will be roughly $3 billion.

The effects of a broadly applied amortization program go far be-

yond the effects on Government revenue. First, there is the stimulating effect which can temporarily add to inflation, with the possibility of a lag later. Then when rapid write-offs are permitted for
facilities which will be largely used to supply eventual regular civilian
demand, there inevitably will be dislocations and unfair advantages
between whole industries—and individual companies within an industry. . . .

Much of the total has been of this type. For example, over 14 per
cent of the total amortizable cost of facilities through December 28,
1955, was granted to utilities and sanitary services; over 16 per cent
more went to railroads; and about 20 per cent went to primary metal
industries. Other whole industries had none.

There are many industries where some percentage of production
would be required in the event of war; but where without war our increased population and productivity will require their continued expansion. These are in sharp contrast to limited-purpose defense
facilities such as shell loading or specialized aircraft or armament plants.

Five-year amortization may be an alternative to direct Government
construction and ownership of limited-purpose facilities since private
capital is not likely to go into them. But this is far different than
giving rapid write-off to selected industries for general-purpose plants
or equipment in an expanding economy.

There is no fair or logical end to such a program. The margin of
excess capacity in such industries at any time will regularly be absorbed by growing civilian demand and have to be regularly reestablished in later years. There would be continuing costs and revenue lags
and the creation of new competitive problems. . . .

Our high productivity of labor is possible only because of tremendous capital investment—over $10,000 per man in general manufac-
turing, and over $50,000 in several industries.

Getting funds for the construction of new plants or facilities is a
continuing serious problem. High tax rates make it harder to save
from current income. They also lessen the incentive and discourage
the productive and perhaps risky use of savings.

It is essential to reduce tax rates as rapidly as can be done soundly.
But tax reduction for favored groups only postpones the day when
general tax reduction can be enjoyed by all the people.

The program, cut back by the executive branch of the Government, now applies only and strictly to limited direct-defense items. I have consistently advocated this and feel sure that the present limitations should be continued.

S. 1795 is in line with this Administration's policy in granting emergency amortization certificates. Subject to some possible changes in language consistent with its objectives to be worked out by the technicians, I am glad to support this legislation.

Cross-examination of Secretary Humphrey

THE CHAIRMAN. Mr. Secretary, as you remember, I wrote to Mr. Arthur Flemming, the Director of the Office of Defense Mobilization, on October 22, 1956, expressing the hope that the policy of granting these rapid write-off certificates could be deferred until Congress could act.

In the meantime, as you remember, the staff on the Joint Committee on Internal Revenue Taxation made a very exhaustive investigation, a copy of which was sent you, I think. It was made a Senate document.

Mr. Flemming replied: "It was determined that no final decision would be made on the policy to be followed until the matter has been discussed at the Cabinet level. After this discussion has taken place, a decision will be made and announced on the policy to be followed and on the relationship of the decision to the request for new steel expansion goals."

I received no further communication from Mr. Flemming. In fact, I was under the impression that this was to be deferred until Congress could act.

He sent me at that time, last October, a list of pending applications which totaled, I think, about $4 billion. Do you recall whether the Cabinet considered this matter and what action was taken?

SEC. HUMPHREY. I don't, Senator, but I do very distinctly recall that these goals were reduced from a large number down to 20 or 30, I guess 30 or 40 to start with and then down to 20 or so, and then finally down to—I don't recall exactly, but I'll say it was—12 or 13, something of that kind, and they were gradually closed off over this period from when we first started talking about this, which was—I had had that date right here—July, 1955.

From July, 1955 on, we just kept pushing these down by Executive order and by action in the ODM, eliminating goals where these were available until we got them down to a very small number.

I think that is where they were when you had your letter from Mr. Flemming. I assume that what you have in mind is this last authorization that was issued just a few days ago, and frankly I read about this myself for the first time in the newspaper. . . .

THE CHAIRMAN. I received no further communication from him, and I was under the impression that only those very directly connected with the defense program would be approved, and I was shocked when I was told and saw in the newspaper that the Idaho Power Company had been granted a rapid amortization of $65 million.

SEC. HUMPHREY. You are entirely correct in your general understanding. That was the understanding and that was the basis on which they were operating.

On this particular thing, Mr. Gray had some special circumstances that he can explain to you.

As I say, I read it for the first time in the newspaper.

THE CHAIRMAN. It seems to me there is no justification whatever for a power utility to get a rapid tax depreciation. They are guaranteed profits and, secondly, in this instance the construction had already started. It had been going on for six months and, therefore, they were able to go ahead without the understanding that they would get a rapid depreciation write-off.

SEC. HUMPHREY. He has it very definitely in mind, and I think it would probably be better for him to give you the explanation himself than for me to try to do it.

THE CHAIRMAN. Mr. Gray came to see me and we had quite a long talk, and I won't quote him now because I think in fairness to him he should be permitted to testify.

I am also somewhat concerned by the fact that since the peace was declared in 1953 6,000 certificates of necessity were issued covering investments of $18 billion and tax write-offs of $7 billion.

That is since the end of the Korean War.

SEC. HUMPHREY. Mr. Chairman, as I have indicated in my statement, this went right along until July of 1955. In July of 1955 we began shutting it down very rapidly. That was when the change in policy was first adopted and it took hold very rapidly from then on.

SENATOR MARTIN. I haven't any questions to ask, Mr. Chairman. I am fully in accord with what you have stated and the statement of the Secretary. I was surprised that the cost in interest would be $3 billion.

SEC. HUMPHREY. I was surprised myself, Senator. We have had it gone over very carefully and I think it is a reasonably accurate estimate, a reasonably illustrative estimate, I will put it that way.

It has to be estimated you know. You can't measure it exactly. But it is reasonably illustrative, it is not deceptive, of what is involved.

THE CHAIRMAN. Have you got a breakdown, Mr. Secretary, on the interest involved in the 6,000 certificates, the tax write-offs of $7 billion? . . . The total interest, as I understand your statement, $3 billion included all of it.

SEC. HUMPHREY. That is correct.

THE CHAIRMAN. 6,000 of the 22,000 were tax write-offs after the end of the Korean War?

SEC. HUMPHREY. We have no breakdown on it.

THE CHAIRMAN. Could you furnish the committee with an estimate?

SEC. HUMPHREY. I don't know that it would be possible. What happens, you have these things in process, and if you take filing date you would have one thing, if you take process dates you would have another thing. . . .

THE CHAIRMAN. If you take the report of the Joint Committee on Internal Revenue taxation staff, it was $7 billion. That was the amount of write-offs. You can figure it on that basis. I don't mean to go into each individual item but just a rough figure.

If this report is correct, and the staff is usually correct, the write-offs covered investment of $13 billion and the tax write-offs were $7 billion. That is after the end of the Korean War.

SEC. HUMPHREY. That is right. I think you might get at it probably reasonably accurately by taking relative amounts in the percentage of the interest but we will check and see what we can do.

THE CHAIRMAN. What are the total write-offs, $23 billion?

SEC. HUMPHREY. Total costs were $39 billion, almost $23 billion of which, 60 per cent, is what was deferred. We would have to check to see if the ones you refer to had about the same percentage. If they had the same percentage of amortization, then you could, I think, get very close and it would be fairly illustrative to take the same proportion of the total.

THE CHAIRMAN. I only want a rough figure and not to deal with each individual item, but this $23 billion, I assume, compares to the $7 billion referred to in the report?

SEC. HUMPHREY. That would be it.

THE CHAIRMAN. Which would indicate about one-third of the write-offs occurred after the war ended. I am more concerned about that than I am on those write-offs that occurred during time of war. If that is correct then, one-third of the $3 billion loss on interest would come on those projects that were given write-offs after the war ended.

SEC. HUMPHREY. We will check that to see how close it is, but I think you will find that isn't unduly out of line. . . .

SENATOR J. ALLEN FREAR, JR. (Delaware). Mr. Secretary, in the third paragraph of your statement, 22,000 certificates were issued and 60 per cent were made eligible. Do you mean after a certificate has been issued, they really are not subject to the rapid amortization, only 60 per cent of them?

SEC. HUMPHREY. No. What you do, Senator, is this: If I have a project that costs me a thousand dollars, then they can give me rapid amortization on some portion of that.

SENATOR FREAR. It is 60 per cent of the project.

SEC. HUMPHREY. And they would say $600 of that thousand is subject to rapid amortization and the $400 takes the regular rate. . . . Their practice was to vary the percentage that was subject to rapid amortization by the degree of necessity and various other things they took into account, and they might go as high as 90 per cent or they might get down to 50 per cent.

SENATOR CLINTON P. ANDERSON (New Mexico). Do I understand that you are not familiar with the defense so-called of the Hells Canyon rapid amortization that is to be made by Mr. Gray?

SEC. HUMPHREY. That is correct.

SENATOR ANDERSON. Could you apply the general principles of your statement to the general principles behind that defense? For example, you say in your statement: "Our basic defense capacity, except for a few very special items, cannot be separated from the broad base of our productive capacity."

There would be no reason why we shouldn't just separate the Hells Canyon situation from that of the Snake River generally; is there?

Is there anything in the vicinity of the Snake River that makes it especially adapted to separate and split off from the rest of our general economy?

SEC. HUMPHREY. Senator, it is a little difficult to discuss that. As the chairman says, in fairness to Mr. Gray, he really ought to make his own explanation of how it came about.

I will say this in answer to your question: That, except for special circumstances with respect to it, it would not be available at the present time under our general policy. . . .

You and I might have some different ideas as to how the original act should have been enacted perhaps, but nevertheless it was the law. It did aid very materially in the development of the defense of this country, and it was applied very broadly. We are talking now about the detail. We are not talking about whether there was a law or not. There was a law. We are talking now about the detail of fair operation under it. . . .

SENATOR ANDERSON. But last year we went this far in the holding of hearings in the Senate alone to consider the Hells Canyon Bill, and time after time we tried to find out if the proponents of the private utility dams, a series of them, were going to come in and claim amortization on them. Surely that was not part of the program.

But just as soon as the final decision got written by the Federal Power Commission, then it is learned, you remember, that they were going to be for amortization all the time and Mr. Gray granted it without a word.

These had no connection with defense, had no connection so far as I can tell with the need of the company to get the amortization before they could go ahead, because they went ahead in haste to make sure that the Congress didn't pass that high Hells Canyon Bill.

Furthermore, there is available in the Snake River some 12 million kilowatts of energy and they are going to take six or eight hundred thousand of them and put them into their dam whereas the high Hells Canyon Dam would have taken a million kilowatts.

The difference between four or five hundred thousand and a million kilowatts of current isn't very great. There is 10 or 11 million kilowatts still left so there was no possibility of connecting this thing to defense.

SEC. HUMPHREY. You see the difficulty is that when you have a program going on, you have great difficulty in curtailing it fairly because you already have certificates and you are upsetting competitive conditions and that is one of my principal objections to the whole program, that it causes dislocations and unfairness as between competitors depending on the dates when applications are made and when building is done.

Senator Anderson. I have been trying to find Mr. Gray's statement. We will have it undoubtedly when he gets here. . . . He points out undoubtedly that there was no justification for a Hells Canyon tax write-off except that somebody else got it. I don't know his exact words.

Sec. Humphrey. Even that, Senator, in fairness in the administration of a program is something that is right to take into account.

Senator Anderson. Why?

Sec. Humphrey. That is one of the basic reasons why I object to this program. It is a program that applies to some and not to all, and I think that is one of the difficulties with it.

Senator Anderson. As a general program just because one utility had gotten an unfair and bad write-off, is there any reason why another utility should get the write-off?

Sec. Humphrey. Wait a minute, I don't think it is quite right to say that it is unfair and bad. This was a law that was passed and a great deal of development was done under it. I think that you will have to talk that part of it over with Mr. Gray because as I say, I read about it in the newspaper.

Senator Anderson. You know of no Cabinet decision to continue them, in view of the letter to the chairman?

Sec. Humphrey. This particular item was not discussed at a Cabinet meeting, no. . . . Let me say this, Senator: I again am not familiar with the detail of this particular thing, but under this law as passed, and in the way this law was administered right from the beginning, if there was a locality where there was a power shortage that was required for the production of materials that contributed to our defense effort, it was very proper in the early days that that should have amortization, and a great deal of it was granted.

As a matter of fact, I have the figure right here. A substantial percentage of the total was for exactly that kind of thing, and it was granted right straight along. Fourteen per cent of the total was for exactly this sort of thing.

SENATOR ANDERSON. Fourteen per cent of utilities, was it not?

SEC. HUMPHREY. Yes; that is utilities. That is to supply power, and this is a utility to supply power.

SENATOR ANDERSON. The Secretary of the Interior, for whom I have very great respect as I have for you, as you well know, just issued a statement talking about the fact that the utilities were going to need $90 million in some period in the future to modernize their plants.

I am wondering if they are going to get an amortization bill for all of that?

SEC. HUMPHREY. They are not if I can help it. . . .

> *Secretary Humphrey on May 13 wrote this further*
> *statement of position to Chairman Byrd, which was*
> *put into the record of the committee hearing:*

MY DEAR MR. CHAIRMAN: This is in reply to your request for a report on your bill, S. 1795. This would impose a strict statutory limitation on the use of five-year amortization certificates. Future certifications would be confined to facilities to produce new defense items or components of new defense items or to provide research, development, or experimental services during the emergency periods for Department of Defense or the Atomic Energy Commission, as a part of the national defense program. Such a limitation is, in principle, consistent with the limitations imposed under present Administrative policy.

The Treasury Department favors a statutory limitation which would restrict amortization certificates to strict defense purposes. Widespread use of amortization certificates is very costly in terms of revenue during the period when they are effective. Their availability and use in other than strict defense applications will result in dislocation and unfair advantages both as between whole industries and as between individual companies within an industry.

The use of five-year amortization for some part of the cost of general purpose plants or equipment to stimulate earlier construction of capacity is neither fair nor logical. The margin of excess capacity, deemed to be needed for defense purposes at any one time, will regularly be absorbed by civilian demands in a growing economy and would have to be regularly reestablished in later years. There would be continuing revenue lags and continuing creation of new competitive problems.

Subject to possible technical changes consistent with the bill's objectives, the Treasury Department strongly supports the general purpose of S. 1795 to limit emergency amortization to strictly defense items.

The Director, Bureau of the Budget, has advised the Treasury Department that there is no objection to the presentation of this report.

Sincerely yours,

G. M. HUMPHREY
Secretary of the Treasury.

INTERNATIONAL

POLICY

Prospects for "sound financing" better

Remarks by Secretary Humphrey at the Eighth Annual Meeting of the Bank and the Fund (World Bank and International Monetary Fund), Washington.

September 9, 1953

At the outset, may I express my firm personal belief in the objectives of the Fund and Bank? These objectives can be stated very simply.

The Fund envisages the establishment and maintenance of currencies in which people can have confidence and will be willing to hold as a matter of free choice, currencies that can serve as a basis for a healthy and expanding world trade with a minimum of Government interference.

The Bank is an instrument for channeling capital, primarily drawn from the private market, to supplement the savings of member countries in the development of their resources. The resources of the Bank are not a substitute for direct private investment. Through its good offices the Bank can do much to assist member countries to pattern their actions so that private capital may be attracted.

In the course of the last year most of our member countries have made great strides in the direction of sound internal finance. Prices have been relatively stable in all but a few countries. Monetary policy has been used to check inflationary strains. Governments have adopted better financial measures. One of the results has been the reduction or elimination of balance of payments deficits.

This lets us hope that the world is in a better position to move toward the Fund objectives. Under more stable conditions, the prospects for sound financing of economic development are also better.

We financial officials should resolve to continue these policies. They are essential to healthy economic expansion. We need not fear the consequences of peace. A real peace would merely permit us to use more of our resources constructively to the betterment of world conditions rather than expending them on defense measures.

The United States under its new Administration has as one of its main purposes to restore sound domestic finance in our economy. We shall pursue this end by all the necessary means. The stability of the dollar in purchasing power at home and abroad is fundamental in our view not only to our own economic welfare but to the stability of the world economy as well. We shall direct our efforts to maintaining a sound dollar.

The United States Government recognizes that its policies have an important bearing on the welfare of other countries. We in the United States realize that other countries are as anxious to pay their way as we are to stop the drain of foreign economic aid on our own economy.

My Government, as you are aware, is now engaged in a careful reexamination of its international economic policies. The President has requested, and the Congress has established pursuant to that request, a Commission to undertake this review. The Commission is composed of distinguished citizens, including representatives of both parties in the Congress. I shall not endeavor to anticipate the conclusions or recommendations of this group. I believe, however, that I can assure you that the Commission in its work will be fully mindful of the importance of our economic policies for the well-being of the rest of the world as well as the great significance which the actions of other countries have on our own economic life.

We have taken some steps already. The Congress at its last session enacted a Customs Simplification Act. As a result many obsolete provisions of our law, which have caused considerable annoyance in world trade, have been repealed. The Congress also has extended the Reciprocal Trade Agreements Act for another year. We will continue to co-operate with other countries in measures looking toward the expansion of worthwhile trade.

Keep reciprocal trade treaties

Statement by Secretary Humphrey before the House
Ways & Means Committee.

May 4, 1953

... Just over a week ago I was in Paris with Secretary Dulles, Secretary Wilson, and Mr. Stassen. In the weeks before that, in Washington, I talked with representatives of the United Kingdom, Germany, and France. There is a uniform concern in the minds of these people about the problem of achieving a balance of trade in their dollar accounts.

There is full realization on their part that United States assistance just as economic aid cannot, and should not, go on forever. To an increasing degree they are focusing their attention on ways and means of freeing their trade from restrictions and getting themselves into a position where they can stand on their own feet.

I believe we ought to encourage these efforts. I believe it is important to the United States that these countries make as much progress as possible in the direction of easing up their restrictions on trade and payments.

But the program is complex and it needs a good deal of very careful thought. It needs the kind of study which the President has proposed, before we can establish firmly the line of policy which we wish to set. Both the Executive Branch and the Congress, I am sure, will bring to that study a consciousness of the need for insuring a continuing high-level of employment and a continuing high standard of living in the United States. We will be conscious also of the need for more solidly based economies in friendly countries around the world.

A careful balancing of all of the various aspects of this problem will take some time. What should be our policy in the interim? The President has recommended an extension of the Reciprocal Trade Agreements Act in its present form. I am sure that this is a wise recommendation. Until we have soberly considered the whole problem of our foreign economic policies, it would be highly unwise to make radical changes in either direction.

I would not recommend to the Congress any hasty action which ignores the legitimate safeguarding of domestic industries, agriculture and labor standards. By exactly the same token, I would recommend against any action, at this time, to remove the stimulus to foreign exports which has been granted by the Reciprocal Trade Agreements Act. I do not believe that the United States should fall back at a time when we need the co-operation of all of the free world. What this moment requires is a measure to hold the situation open until the whole problem can be looked at. Extension of the act in its present form is, I believe, the measure required.

If this can be done, we can move forward with completely open minds towards formulating an appropriate foreign economic policy for this country. In doing that the Treasury will have a simple objective. We would like to help friendly countries, in the soundest and least expensive way possible, to stand on their own feet. We will be seeking a course of action which will reduce the burden on our taxpayers, but we will want to guard against the creation of new national problems in the form of unnecessary hardship to the industry and agriculture of this country. I believe that a judicious course of action can be worked out, and I recommend that the act be renewed in its present form to give us time to work it out.

On the foreign assistance program

Statement by Secretary Humphrey on extension of the mutual security provisions before the Senate Foreign Relations and House Foreign Affairs Committees.

May 5, 1953

You have noted from what has previously been said by the preceding witnesses that the great bulk of the money that is now being requested is to be spent for direct contributions to our security. It will be largely for military-end items, or directly contributing to our friends' and our own mutual defense.

You have also heard it said by the previous witnesses that we will get as much, or more, for our money in security in this way than by making additional direct military expenditures. It is our purpose to secure the maximum of security, wherever it may be, for the least possible expenditures of money. I believe that the assistance proposed in this legislation meets that requirement.

I think it should be rendered and that we can render it advantageously as compared with any equal expenditures elsewhere. It is understood, of course, by all concerned that as time goes on and if conditions change, proposed expenditures will be reduced or omitted wherever that can properly and suitably be done without prejudice to our security, and at all times every effort will be made to fully get our money's worth.

A good part of the money being requested in this bill will not be spent in the coming fiscal year. Its authorization enables the forward planning and contracting that is necessary when you are engaged in building a defense force. But it is planned for expenditure at a later date.

This question of continuing new obligational authority has been a matter of deep concern to the Administration. As you know, when President Eisenhower entered office he inherited the problem of $81 billion in outstanding obligations and unsatisfied authorizations to spend Government funds. The expenditures for the fiscal year 1954— the expenditures I will talk about in a few minutes—will come largely from this overhang.

If we are ever going to balance the budget and bring expenditures within the tightest possible control, we must do something about achieving a run-off of the large carry-over of unspent authorizations. We cannot continue to ask each year for substantially more money than we will actually spend in the ensuing twelve months, because that means the overhang constitutes a snowballing threat to financial stability.

Now, we have tried to do something about this problem in the bill that is before you. We are changing the direction that has been followed in the past few years. But we are not proposing to do so with unreasoning abruptness. We are trying to strike a proper balance between maintaining an adequate and continuing free world defense and creating the conditions for long-term financial stability in this country.

The way to do that, it seems to me, is to request each year less than will be spent in the next 12 months. You will note from the exhibits before you that we are beginning to put that policy into practice right now. Changing the practice of the past, we now propose that the Congress authorize new funds for foreign assistance in an amount smaller than the anticipated expenditures during the coming fiscal year.

As we do our future planning, we will have constantly before us the objective of reducing the overhang of unutilized authorizations. That is a very important objective, and I want you to know that it is not only our objective but is now our determined practice. That is why I have talked first about this problem of new obligational authority.

Now I turn to the problem of actual expenditures during fiscal year 1954. These will be large. There is no question that these expenditures and others necessary to our national security will affect the possibility of balancing the budget and the time when we can look forward to tax reductions. Because this Administration is committed to a program of sound money and of reducing taxation at the earliest possible time, I can assure you that these expenditures have been most carefully studied from the standpoint not only of their effectiveness but also from the point of view of the necessity of making them in the proposed amounts to contribute to essential security.

We are committed to the policy of constantly reviewing the necessity of making the expenditures currently during the year and will make reductions or eliminations whenever and wherever justified. Although expenditures of such magnitude will necessarily create problems, they can be handled under the sound financial principles to which we are committed.

In formulating the foreign assistance program, close attention has also been given to the desirability of fostering private investment abroad. This will not only reduce public expenditure but the Government should not undertake activities that can better be carried on by the people themselves. In this direction we will be constantly alert to utilizing the International Bank for Reconstruction and Development and the International Monetary Fund wherever possible.

To this end also, it is the policy of the Government that interest rates on any governmental loans which may be necessary shall be such as not to discourage private investment.

As we progress throughout the year we will give serious consideration to the problem of the rate of expenditures which we will lay before you next year. We will strive for proper balance between military preparedness in the United States and overseas, and maintenance of economic strength at home.

We have already laid the groundwork for establishing that balance. In the NATO meeting in Paris last month, my associates and I took steps in that direction. Our friends abroad were fully advised of this policy. As we go through the next year, we will build upon that foundation.

Meanwhile, we feel that the program which has been presented to you today is the best balance between security for our friends and ourselves and our necessity for reducing expenditures that can be appropriately managed at this time. We are looking forward to making savings wherever possible and further progress in making additional reductions in the future.

◄ The Secretary struck two new notes in giving before the Congressional foreign committees his approval of the Administration overseas aid-security program. One was that unexpended carry-overs would be canceled or reduced by underestimating requests, the other that private overseas investment would be attracted if possible. There was a forecast in the conservative character of this testimony—not long afterwards, large plans elsewhere in the Administration for a new "Marshall Plan for Asia" were quietly dropped.

Using "taxpayers' money" abroad

🖎 Secretary Humphrey brought to his post a fundamental belief that the repair of the world from the ravages of World War II depended chiefly on the energies of private enterprise rather than on any conceivable total of subsidies and grants by governments, because these energies would be so much greater, more powerful, and more skillful. His faith was stated early in his service as Secretary before a Congressionally-created special committee of members of Congress and the Government and public and private leaders.

> *Remarks by Secretary Humphrey before*
> *Senator Homer Capehart's Advisory Group on*
> *International Trade, Washington.*
>
> *September 15, 1953*

We are all indebted to Senator Capehart for bringing together such an outstanding group of businessmen, labor leaders, and farm leaders. I know that we will all benefit. The Government is indeed anxious to have the views of representative citizens' groups as to the proper course of action in our foreign economic policy....

We have recently been giving special attention to the area of foreign investment and considering what are the appropriate roles for the United States investor and the United States Government.

During the past few years American private investors have invested or reinvested abroad about a billion dollars a year net. These investments have been primarily in the dollar area. Early postwar private capital outflow was concentrated in Latin America, and Canada has taken an increasing amount in the last few years.

Petroleum investments, which bulked large at first, have declined from the 1949 peak, and in 1951 the flow of petroleum investment was substantially less than the total invested in all other industries together.

These substantial net United States private investments have exceeded by more than four times the combined annual net disbursements on loans of the International Bank and the Export-Import Bank.

During the last three years the International Bank has disbursed more than $400 million. The Export-Import Bank paid out nearly $900 million and received capital repayments of $565 million, resulting in net payments to foreign borrowers of slightly more than $300 million. What these two banks have accomplished in recent years and what they can best achieve in facilitating private investment and economic development abroad in the coming years is a subject which you gentlement will be thinking about.

In this connection we suggest that the two institutions should complement each other and overlap in their respective activities to the least possible extent. To accomplish this result it seems to us that the names of the institutions are of real significance and may be a guide to their respective fields of activity.

The International Bank for Reconstruction and Development implies loans of a capital nature of long duration and for construction and development purposes.

The Export-Import Bank implies the aid to exports and imports and to current trade by loans of much more rapid turnover and shorter duration. Indeed, the whole set-up for each institution is such that, if confined to their respective fields much more definitely than has been the practice of the past, a broader combined service can be given and competition between them practically eliminated.

Last week Senator Capehart, Senator Maybank, and some of the rest of us attended the annual meeting of the International Monetary Fund and the International Bank for Reconstruction and Development. One of the sessions was devoted to a very interesting panel discussion on the role of private international investment in underdeveloped countries. We found it very enlightening to hear the views of outstanding representatives from some of the capital exporting countries as well as from countries seeking capital such as Egypt, India, and Mexico.

There is an obvious and important role for private enterprise to play in foreign investment. In fact, I hope that a much larger and more important role lies ahead for the profitable investment of private capital and technology abroad. These discussions will be published and available to you. I recommend them to you for study.

Since the end of the war, many countries abroad have been looking to the United States for assistance in financing their economic development. In many instances foreign countries have preferred to obtain their assistance from governmental sources. This raises the very serious question of to what extent this practice should be followed in the future and how it can best be provided, to whatever extent it seems best to carry it on.

Some countries have taken only limited steps to provide the conditions under which private investment will voluntarily move abroad on the basis of normal economic considerations. More attention must be paid abroad to making investment attractive to foreign capital. The countries which have made the greatest strides in their development over the years are the countries which have provided the conditions under which private capital was most willing to invest.

The United States and Canada are two of the most conspicuous examples of countries which have in the last century moved from the state of underdeveloped countries to strong industrial countries in a position to export capital. But I remind you that our development and Canadian development was on the basis of private investment voluntarily made. Countries will be better off if their capital requirement can be met by securing private investment, which brings with it not only money but technical know-how, established trade connections, and business experience.

I cannot foretell what you gentlemen are going to suggest as proper policy for the United States Government to apply in the field of foreign investment and I am sure there will be different views. I do not wish to prejudge the conclusion which may be reached either by this advisory group or by Senator Capehart's Committee. However, as Secretary of the Treasury I do want to make clear to everyone that the Government must question both its right and its financial ability to continue to use taxpayers' money to finance investments abroad on a large scale in the development of competitive enterprise.

Our scale of taxation is already too high and to maintain a sound and honest dollar we must bring our own expenditures and revenues into balance. We must continue to examine most carefully every proposal to spend money, whether it is a proposal for spending at home or abroad. The maintenance of our credit and of a sound dollar is most important for foreign countries as well as it is for us here at home.

Prosperity in the United States is essential for prosperity in the rest of the world, and it is not only our duty but it is for the best interests of everyone concerned that we keep that fact always uppermost in our minds.

The rules for foreign investment

Remarks by Secretary Humphrey in a panel discussion,
Prospects for Private International Investment,
at the ninth annual meeting of the International
Bank for Reconstruction and Development
(World Bank). Other panel members: R. A. Butler,
Chancellor of the Exchequer, United Kingdom;
Chintaman Deshmukh, Minister of Finance of India;
and Egenio Gudin, Minister of Finance of Brazil.
J. van de Kieft, chairman of the Bank Board of Governors,
and Eugene R. Black, president of the Bank, presiding.

September 28, 1954

...I have been asked to speak to you about some of the problems which face the private investor in a relatively young capital-exporting country. This does not mean I am unaware that there are two sides to this question, but merely that I am sure my colleagues from India and Brazil can present the picture as it appears to the capital-importing countries much better than I. They will be followed by the Chancellor of the Exchequer whose broad perspective is based on the United Kingdom's long experience in making investments in so many places in the world.

Before discussing the obstacles which confront the investor, I should like to say a few words about the improvements we have been witnessing abroad, and the very substantial accomplishments private investment is making despite the difficulties which still exist in some areas.

As has been said before at this conference, confidence has been increasing. Currencies have grown stronger as reserves have increased. There has been progress in removing quantitative restrictions on trade. Payments in many of the world's currencies are becoming freer as governments relax the grip of their exchange controls.

These are all marks of an improvement in the financial position of many countries of the free world.

These changes have been reflected in a profound shift in our own balance of payments. During the years 1946 through 1948, the transactions of the rest of the world with the United States resulted in our collecting $4.5 billion in gold and in dollar balances and investments from foreigners; that is, they paid us this amount to settle their accounts. In 1949, we were in approximate balance. But in the past four years, from 1950 through 1953, the reversal was pronounced, and our transactions with the rest of the world added about $7.7 billion to foreigners' assets in gold and dollars. Thus, for the postwar period as a whole, we have not drawn reserves away from the rest of the world, but, instead, have contributed to them.

This has been the end result of our trade policy, our customs reforms, our aid policy, our military expenditures, and our private and public investments abroad. In the current year the same trend is continuing, and at present rates another $1.5 billion will be available for building up foreign assets in 1954.

Durability in the balance of payments in a world subject to events changing as rapidly as those of our generation is not an easy thing to assure. But the record of the past four years is favorable.

In many countries, however, there is scarcity of investment capital and a pressing demand for funds for development.

All of us in the free world must be ever mindful of the extremely low standards of living which exist in many parts of the globe. In some countries, very low standards of living exist where natural resources are bountiful. In others, rapidly growing populations are pressing hard on existing resources, but even in these cases the absence of modern techniques of cultivation and tools of production, low standards of education, and poor conditions of health, present a challenge and offer an opportunity for improving the lot of many millions of mankind. We must keep these problems to the forefront and co-operate in every practical way to bring modern science, tools and technology to bear upon them.

But private investment is not made for philanthropic reasons. It is made for profit that is freely available to the investor on principal that is safe.

Chairman van de Kieft in his opening address called attention to the complicated economic problem of differences in wealth and savings among countries, and the flow of private capital which is needed to help allay these differences. He noted that there are "new economic and political factors" in the postwar period, which in some cases "have tended rather to slow down than to increase the flow of private capital to the regions that are most in need of development."

What he has said is quite true. Nationalistic trends resulting in laws that discriminate against investors from other lands and restrictions jeopardizing either principal or the receipt of income slow down investment from outside. Vacillating policies of governments can be warnings to prudent investors to look elsewhere.

Nevertheless, in many places private investment has been making a substantial attack on the problem of promoting development.

At the end of 1953, our private investors had approximately $23.7 billion invested in foreign lands on which we have recently been averaging earnings of approximately $1.5 billion a year, much of which came to us in the form of needed goods imported through foreign subsidiaries and branches of United States corporations.

At the same time, during the past six years, our private investors were providing to other countries about $900 million a year in newly exported private funds, net of repatriation of capital. In addition to these exports of new dollars, about $600 million a year in earnings by foreign subsidiaries of United States corporations abroad were reinvested directly without being brought home and thus do not appear in either of the two figures I have just cited. In all, new capital provided by private sources from this country has reached at least $1.5 billion a year. As I suggested on Friday this total is about three times the rate of public lending by Government agencies during the same period, net of amortization and repayments of principal on United States Government loans.

A very substantial proportion of our private investment has been made in Canada, where conditions have been particularly attractive. Nevertheless, we estimate that private investors in the United States have been placing as much as $900 million a year in the rest of the world, during the past six years, including the reinvested earnings I mentioned above. Even if we make a rough estimate and take out all investments in Canada and all investments anywhere in petroleum enterprises, we would have left about $600 million a year which has financed a wide variety of other enterprises outside of Canada. These amounts represent a very substantial supplement to local savings.

Some concern has been expressed that the rate of new private investment appeared to slacken rather sharply in 1953. Actually, this appearance was accounted for largely by security transactions and a reduction in commercial credit; direct investments by United States corporations continued at about the rate of previous years. I am happy to report that during the first half of 1954 our private investors placed $644 million in new capital abroad, even without allowing for reinvested earnings. At an annual rate this is a larger overflow than in the peak post-war year of 1950.

What about the prospects for continuance of this flow or its increase? The prime factor which will determine this is the establishment of confidence in the country seeking investments among investors abroad.

Ordinarily it takes time to build confidence. As with individuals, it is best established by a definite course of good conduct over a period of years. The old saying that "actions speak louder than words" was never more apt.

Moreover, as frequently pointed out, the progress of years in establishing confidence can be shaken overnight. But long continued good behavior is not always required. Governments change and, even more important, the thinking of the great mass of the people of a country can also change either for the better or for worse. It is the real spirit of the people that is most important. They either resent the foreigner and his operation or welcome him as a well recognized means of more rapidly improving their own lives, and so express themselves by their conduct and through their governments. That is the real flag of invitation or of warning.

Moreover, foreign capital is not so different from capital at home. It is attracted to countries where conditions are also favorable to the local investor. No country can reasonably hope to attract foreign investors if its own savings are seeking shelter abroad. Inflation or unfair treatment from popular resistance affects all investors, whatever their nationality.

It is hardly necessary to discuss in detail the familiar types of deterrents which adversely influence the investor today. It is probably enough to mention that some of the principal ones are threats or a history of confiscation or discrimination.

There are also the risks associated with exchange restrictions and multiple rate systems which are both complex and subject to considerable instability. An abrupt and sharp depreciation can seriously impair the fruits of past efforts for the foreign investor. Restrictions on transfer present a constant fear to the investor that he will find himself queueing up at the end of the line to receive permission to transfer his income into the currency he needs. In many of these areas the members of the International Monetary Fund are co-operating to provide a better basis for the flow of international capital.

Sound large-scale private investment abroad can only result from assurance of the security and the right of ready repatriation of principal and an opportunity for greater profit than at home. The private investor has a choice between his own market and opportunities in foreign countries. Where, as here, there are good possibilities open to him in his own country, every day, he will need some additional inducement to undertake the extra risks of going to foreign lands to cope with the differences in language, law and customs. He will want to be doubly sure of his business associates abroad. And he will be slow to go if he feels that his activities will be approached in a general atmosphere of criticism rather than one of warm welcome.

Of our own substantial direct private investments abroad, more than $6 billion is connected with petroleum and mining enterprises. These funds go where the resources are to be found, and when they are needed, and when the pulling power is great enough to overcome the many obstacles, both natural and man-made.

In the area of manufacturing or merchandising, such considerations are much less compelling. The economic inducements must persuade the foreign investor that his chance for profit is greater.

On the other hand there may well be more resistance from a feeling of nationalistic possession in the case of the development of natural resources than when only manufacturing or merchandising is involved. And the large size of the investment required and the length of time in which it can normally be returned is far greater for natural resources than in manufacturing or trading lines so that greater security of principal and return of profit must be assured.

But there is no way in which a country can develop faster for the rapid improvement of the lives of its own citizens than by the use of foreign capital in turning its natural resources otherwise lying dormant into jobs and homes and better living for the numbers of its people that will be so employed.

The high yields on common stocks in the United States have been a powerful attraction for the private investor. During the past year, the growth in confidence and the supply of capital for investment here has brought somewhat lower yields. This may provide some stimulus to interest in investment abroad where the assurance of security and the lure of higher profits is sufficiently attractive. Special tax consideration and other methods of stimulation can also contribute to increased interest in foreign fields.

What are the policies which attract private capital from abroad? I think they can best be summed up in a simple way: Security and the right of ready repatriation of principal and attractive return.

It is not unlike the conditions which induce two individuals to embark on a common venture. There must be mutual confidence. The private foreign investor must be really wanted and welcome not just by the Government at the time but by the people as well and for a long time because they are truly persuaded and believe that by the use of his money they can better themselves faster and further than they can alone. They must be willing and glad to pay a reasonable price for the risk involved and show by a history of fair dealing that, after the risk has been once undertaken and when success for both has been won, that they will then not go back on their bargain and through direct action or ruse or sharp practice of any kind seek to enlarge their fair share of the original basis on which the joint enterprise was begun.

If governments and laws are responsive to such a conviction of the people, their country will have little trouble in obtaining private foreign investment for any venture within their borders that can properly earn an attractive return.

I want to emphasize that we have been discussing private investment abroad as distinguished from Government programs. While much of the criteria for investment is equally applicable to both, there may well be inducements in the latter case which would go beyond those to be properly considered in the former.

For our part—that is, in the United States—surely our greatest contribution will be to maintain a high level of economic activity and income in the United States, and thus to provide a reservoir of venture capital. If we can proceed with mutual trust and confidence I am sure that, as President Black has so well said, we will through the channel of private investment as well as the efforts of the International Bank, succeed in converting a revolution of expectancy into first a practical business-like approach and then into a real revolution of achievement.

✍ The remarks of the three other panelists were quite responsive to Secretary Humphrey's opening statement.

Sir Chintaman Deshmukh welcomed the current shift in volume from government to private investment abroad because it implied "more disciplined economic management" and pointed out that in the newly liberated countries the character of investment projects had decisively changed from the "colonial" investment to those somewhat based on the new nation's program of needs. He defended India's investment controls as not onerous and as a supply of safeguard in the program investments. India, he said, would appear to satisfy largely the conditions set out in the Humphrey remarks. The more foreign investment increased, he said, the less the need became for government controls of investment. In discussion of the need for broader contacts for borrowing nations, he cited the new Commonwealth Development Corporation set up for India investment by leaders of three nations.

Minister Gudin granted that in underdeveloped and emerging countries there frequently are three "plagues," sometimes expropriations, more often inflation and nationalism, and he agreed that the underdeveloped lands need to fight these down before they can enjoy very much investment from abroad. He cited statistics for various periods of time to demonstrate that United States' private investment abroad totals considerably less than United States' income from abroad, and advised the United States Government that American investors abroad deserved more compensation than they are getting for income tax paid abroad.

Mr. Butler, in discussing Britain's long history as an investor, largely private, abroad, cited these general rules for British success in international investment: That the borrower enterprises in foreign lands respect all contracts and pledges surrounding the investment; that the investor must feel his compensation; that the investor must interest himself in long-term and not quick-turn results of investment; that the successful investor should reinvest his profits in the foreign enterprises; and that the country of the investor should adopt a broad and tolerant attitude toward imports from the lands invested in. He believed that the fullest and best use of investor capital is the greatest weapon in the hands of the free world, to keep its freedom.

Fiscal issues in Latin America

✍ Secretary Humphrey carried out a delicate diplomatic mission late in 1954, to which he was enlisted by Secretary of State Dulles. The Secretary of State had recently effected the Organization of the American States and the Inter-American Economic and Social Council as a prime cold-war defense. One result was an increase from Latin America in projects involving considerably greater United States economic assistance; and one of these which came up to Secretary Dulles was for a bank or a fund largely financed by the United States which would be available to Latin-American nations without comparable investment on their part.

When Secretary Dulles reported this request one day at the White House to the President and Secretary Humphrey (who were in the midst of their battle for national fiscal balance), he found them very reluctant to contemplate the inter-American suggestion. So he asked Secretary Humphrey to come to a meeting of inter-American finance ministers at Rio de Janeiro and explain tactfully why by United States standards this was not a good idea. The President seconded the idea after Dulles said he had promised an answer.

Some weeks later the Secretary of State told Secretary Humphrey it would be impossible for him to attend the Rio meeting because he had to be at a Southeast Pacific Organization meeting the same date. He asked Humphrey to take the chairmanship of the Rio delegation. The Treasury Secretary balked at this, and suggested Under Secretary of State Herbert Hoover, Jr., head the delegation. "I've promised only to go and make one speech," he said.

The speech was a diplomatic success; however, the United States several years later was induced to enter an inter-American fund on terms which somewhat followed the original request.

> *Speech by Secretary Humphrey to the Meeting*
> *of Ministers of Finance and Economy, Rio de Janeiro.*
>
> *November 23, 1954*

... Just before leaving Washington we discussed with President Eisenhower the views of the United States delegation on the problems we shall discuss here. He emphasized to us his deep interest in this historic meeting and asked that we convey a personal message to our colleagues here. With your kind permission I shall read it:

"I am very pleased to send greetings and best wishes to the meeting of Ministers of Finance and Economy of the American family of nations, convened in Rio de Janeiro, the capital of our great sister nation, Brazil. I am happy to send this message through our Secretary of the Treasury, Mr. Humphrey, who, as chairman of the United States delegation, speaks for our nation and will authoritatively present our policies.

"I am confident that this conference will advance still further the unique relationships which have developed among the peoples and nations of this hemisphere. As those relationships evolved and grew, the people of the United States learned to call their own attitude toward their sister nations the policy of the good neighbor. Today, the bonds which unite us as sovereign equals who are working side by side for the betterment of all of us—nations and citizens—have elevated this neighborly relationship to one of genuine partnership.

"No longer is it sufficient to maintain the mutual respect and cordiality of neighbors, useful and pleasant as that is. In the world of today, the well-being and the economic development—as well as the security—of all peace-loving nations are so closely interrelated that we must be partners. If this is true in the larger context, it is especially true among the American republics where we share the same traditions and many of the same favorable circumstances for progress.

"As the conference discusses a wide variety of measures for economic and financial co-operation in this hemisphere, and endorses those that are sound and durable, I earnestly hope that the meeting as a whole may join with the delegation of the United States in common dedication to the policy of the good partner...."

While this gathering was called in response to a resolution of the Tenth Inter-American Conference held in Caracas earlier this year, this conference is in reality the realization of a desire expressed repeatedly throughout the rise and development of the inter-American system. It is the desire to strengthen the continental economy so as to benefit all the nations that share the hemisphere....

We have come here with the same spirit of cordial solidarity with which the delegates of our nations arrived in this city of proverbial hospitality for the Third Pan American Conference. To describe it I shall borrow the eloquence of a great fellow countryman, Elihu Root, at that time Secretary of State, who said: "I bring from my country a special greeting to her elder sisters in the civilization of America . . . there is not one of all our countries that cannot benefit the others; there is not one that cannot receive benefit from the others; there is not one that will not gain by the prosperity, the peace and happiness of all."

And so it is today. Our country is part of the inter-American system; our Secretary of State, John Foster Dulles, recently affirmed that this is the cornerstone of our foreign policy.

We take our places with pride in this association of states which has established the complete equality of all members, has consecrated the principle of nonintervention, and has built a juridical system that has put an end to war among American nations.

We have bound ourselves, moreover, by pacts that stipulate that an attack on one American nation is an attack on all of them, and that any threat to the political integrity of one is a threat to all. Our presence here is a declaration that we also consider economic solidarity as part of the common defense.

None of us expects that we can at this meeting solve all of the economic problems of a hemisphere. But we can confidently expect that 21 nations, each motivated by a deep and brotherly interest in the welfare of every other, can accomplish enough here to convince us all that our efforts were richly rewarded, that our accomplishments justify our looking forward to future meetings.

We all have our own ideas as to how the economic interests of the entire continent could be promoted. We in the United States naturally subscribe to those principles that in our own country have proved effective in raising the living standards of the people and promoting the prosperity of the nation. We shall present them here with the same friendly frankness with which we are ready to listen to the opinions of other delegations. No one of us alone has the wisdom and experience necessary to solve all our problems. . . .

When we shall have finished our work here it should be possible to speak of this meeting in the same words as those used by a great American, the Baron of Rio Branco in commenting on the Third Pan American conference, when he said:

"Here concessions represent conquests of reason, amicable compromises or compensations counselled by reciprocal interests."

We would first hope for a clear definition of the economic goals toward which we shall press. We are profoundly aware that we are here not so much as representatives of political entities; instead we are here as the spokesmen for 330 million of men, women, and children whose problems, whose sufferings, and whose aspirations must constantly be present in our thoughts and in our deliberations. . . .

I believe that we are capable of putting into words here at this meeting just what it is that our people would have us accomplish, and I believe that we can adopt that definition of our goal. It seems to us that the men and women of the Americas, living as they do among our mountains, on our plains, and along our seacoasts are united and clear in their aspirations. They do not ask the impossible, but they do demand of us, who as government officials are their servants, that we promote those conditions which will give maximum assurance that everywhere in our Americas man has an opportunity to better himself, give his children even greater opportunities—and enjoy meanwhile those freedoms which we have achieved in the Americas and which are denied to so many millions elsewhere in the world.

I believe that we must face another problem in which our people are vitally interested. All of us are exposed to an insidious disease that stealthily robs us of our strength. It is the evil of inflation which makes the prices of food, of clothing, of all the necessities of life climb upward in a grim spiral which again and again snatches away the benefits of progress. . . .

Our agenda is admirably fashioned to help us appraise not only our place today on the road which has already brought us so far toward our goal, but also the measures which we can take jointly and severally to hasten our progress on that road. It is our conviction that to accomplish this purpose two basic principles should underlie all our thinking.

The first is our belief that the road which will lead most surely and most directly to the goals which we seek is that of the vigorous free enterprise system. This system in its modern form builds new industries, new enterprises, and opens new areas of development. And it does all these things without endangering those free institutions which are the very foundation of the social and human progress which we have achieved in this hemisphere.

The other is our belief that we as governments should reduce to a minimum the scope and the duration of our own intervention in the fields of commerce and industry. We best serve our people when we encourage them to produce the goods and services required for our progress, when we stimulate them to bring new regions and new resources into productive use, rather than when we compete with them or otherwise take over the functions of private enterprise. Government intervention deprives the people of the full benefits of their earnings. . . .

We shall support and defend the right of every state to define its own economic course. Our own belief in the principles I have stated derives from the fact that wherever they have been applied in the Americas and elsewhere in the world they have brought improvement in the lives of our people, improvement that can be measured in terms of lower costs, greater per capita income, higher production, improvement that is visible in new factories, industries and increased agricultural production and intensified conversion of idle and undeveloped natural resources into jobs and usable wealth. These are the marks of vigorous, expanding and self-reliant economies. These are the economic ends that we pursue.

The detailed discussion of each agenda item is the function of our committees. I would like, however, to say a word or two regarding our views on some of the more vital ones.

The first is international trade. We intend to the utmost of our ability to maintain a strong, healthy economy in the United States. This will insure a growing volume of trade with your countries at a steadily increasing level of demand. This will help sustain a high level of demand for the world's goods and so foster trade on a mutually beneficial basis. My Government is convinced that a strong, stable and expanding international trade is the best single guarantee of economic strength in our hemisphere. . . .

For your economic development you count heavily upon markets in the United States for your products. We value just as highly the strong markets which you afford for our own agricultural and manufactured exports. We hope to see our inter-American trade which has increased so greatly in recent years, further expanded, and the markets available to producers in all our countries strengthened by the gradual elimination of those artificial barriers that hinder access to them....

Our tariffs on imports from Latin America are low. Two-thirds of all our imports from this area are on the free list and tariffs on the remaining third are among the lowest in the world.

We have also made marked progress in freeing imports into the United States from unnecessary and cumbersome customs requirements....

These Congressional steps have been accompanied by an intensive management improvement program and by administrative simplification within the framework of existing law, both contributing to speedier customs action. We are continuing our efforts along these lines and plan to submit to the next Congress further legislative proposals consistent with the President's program of last March. As an example of the progress we are making, just a few weeks ago we announced a further relaxation of requirements for consular invoices—an action made possible by the 1953 Simplification Act.

The problem of international trade is closely related to that of prices. We are aware of your intense and very understandable interest in this problem as it relates to the prices for your products sold in world markets. We share that interest, not only because of the importance to you of adequate and stable prices, but also because our own producers suffer when the prices of their exports fluctuate widely.

Our experience convinces us that if we as governments follow policies which will give our producers everywhere maximum assurance that consumption of their products will enjoy a steady and healthy growth and that their access to international markets will be facilitated, then we will have gone far toward solving this basic problem of prices which so concerns us all.

The subject of financing for economic development is one of the most important which we shall consider. My Government has devoted much study to its policies in this field and within the framework of the general principles to which I have referred, has reached certain decisions of whose nature you are already aware and whose effect we believe will prove to be far reaching.

When we speak of the great need for economic development financing in this hemisphere, what we are really saying is that throughout our countries there are profitable and attractive opportunities for the establishment of productive enterprises that will provide steady employment to our people; that will provide more of the goods and services which we need for higher standards of living and that will diversify our economies.

These opportunities cannot be converted into realities without capital, technical knowledge and experience. As governments, we owe it to our people to promote those conditions which will help make available the capital and technical knowledge required.

I think that every one of us here can agree that in this field our greatest opportunity and our greatest responsibility lies in creating in our several countries those conditions which will give maximum access to the great reserves of private investment capital that are available throughout the world. The reason is obvious. The aggregate amount of private capital that is available today in your countries, in mine, and in the rest of the world is many times greater than any that we as governments could possibly provide. . . .

We all recognize that the movement of private capital cannot be forced; that private investors of all nationalities enter only where the circumstances are attractive. So numerous are the investment opportunities throughout the free world today that he who seeks investment capital must compete for it. But here again the position of Latin America is privileged and fortunate. Throughout your countries there are challenging and attractive opportunities for new investments such as are found only in young and rapidly developing economies. . . . It is easy to understand, therefore, why the American states whose governments have established those conditions which have always proven attractive to private investors everywhere in the world have experienced little difficulty in finding ample supplies of capital, both domestic and foreign.

This has been demonstrated so drastically that there can be no longer any doubt but that in this favored area of the world, where nature has done its part so well, each government can, if it will, attract a volume of private investment that will compare most favorably with that of any other area of the world.

One of the things which our governments must do to encourage free enterprise is to insure that those projects necessary for economic development, but for which private capital is not reasonably available, are adequately supported by public investment. We view this as a necessary support to an economy which relies principally upon private enterprise as supplementing and encouraging, rather than as displacing free enterprise. I am sure that each government will shoulder as much of their burden as it reasonably can, but we agree with you that substantial foreign lending will be necessary if we are to achieve our goals in this hemisphere. We shall do our part generously and loyally in meeting that need.

To that end we have reviewed the whole scope of our public lending policies and have arrived at certain changes which we consider significant.

The first relates to the United States Export-Import Bank whose activities are to be intensified and expanded. The Congress of the United States by specific legislation increased the lending authority of the bank from $4.5 billion to $5 billion, in anticipation of its increased lending activity....

Within the last few months the Export-Import Bank has authorized loans of $130 million to nations in this hemisphere and other important loans are under consideration. The loans which have been authorized will help two important Latin American cities develop municipal waterwork systems and will make possible the development of one of the world's largest copper deposits.

The Bank has made loans to finance the sale in Latin America of machine tools, of aircraft, of electric equipment, of textile equipment, and of wheat. It has facilitated the development of sulphur production. The range of its activities has been as wide and varied as the production process itself, from the extraction of basic materials to the fabrication of complex industrial products. Since its organization the Export-Import Bank has authorized loans in excess of $2.25 billion to Latin America.

Within the past few weeks, the Export-Import Bank has opened up new sources of credit for the countries of Latin America that wish to import equipment from the United States. With the assistance of lines of credit from the Export-Import Bank, United States exporters will be able to offer medium term credit on equipment of a productive nature. This program will be in addition to long-term capital and should help to accelerate the flow of trade and ease temporary credit problems.

In addition, a large New York bank announced last week that it proposes to form a multi-million dollar export financing company. The Export-Import Bank will also participate in this new venture. . . .

In the field of economic development, of course, the International Bank has a primary role to play in helping to promote the economic growth of the American republics. Most of the countries represented here were founding fathers of the International Bank. Your countries and my own participated in its establishment and we have contributed importantly to its personnel and capital. The International Bank is our common institution. It was established to carry the major burden of financing reconstruction and development loans at a governmental level. While the International Bank in the early post-war years was primarily concerned with reconstruction, it has accelerated the tempo of its operations and has, more recently, concentrated its major efforts on economic development.

The International Bank has financed a steady succession of high priority development projects in Latin America. The total now exceeds $500 million for the last five years. Its first development loan was in Latin America, and today its investment in this hemisphere is greater than in any other developing area. Its loans have been made primarily for basic facilities and public works on which further fruitful investment depends: For electric power, for transportation, and for communication facilities.

The loans of the International Bank are important not only in themselves but in their secondary effects. Electric power installations, new road and communication systems, new port facilities, all have encouraged new industries and lowered costs. . . .

In his report to the conference, Eugene Black, President of the Bank, states:

"It is my personal judgment that, given a continuance of present trends in Latin America, there is every reason to expect expanded lending activity by the Bank in that area during the period which lies ahead. The Bank has the resources to do so and it has the will to do so. The extent to which it may be able to translate its will into action depends largely on conditions within the control of the Latin American countries themselves."

At the meeting of the Board of Governors of the International Bank last September, representatives from many of the American republics strongly urged support for the establishment of an international finance corporation to encourage private investment. The subject has been under study for several years.

The matter has been given most careful consideration by the United States Government, and we are going to ask the Congress to support United States participation in such a corporation. We have in mind an institution organized as an affiliate of the International Bank, with an authorized capital of $100 million to be contributed by those members of the International Bank who wish to subscribe.

The corporation would be able to make loans without the guarantee of member governments. It would not directly provide equity financing. It would, however, be empowered to hold securities bearing interest payable only if earned, as well as debentures convertible into stock when purchased from the corporation by private investors. In that way it would operate in the area of venture capital without holding equity right of control. It would not compete with the International Bank, or the Export-Import Bank and indeed it would facilitate private investment.

If the international finance corporation is established, we shall then have three major financial institutions to help promote economic development. We shall have the Export-Import Bank that has had a long history of useful work in Latin America and whose activities are to be intensified. We shall have the International Bank, in which we are partners, to help finance basic resource development. We shall have an international finance corporation in which we would work together to assist and encourage private enterprise.

In the spirit of the resolution on private investment and taxation adopted at the Caracas conference, the United States continues to explore feasible measures to remove tax impediments to increased foreign investments. The Administration and the Congress, as well as numerous private groups in the United States, have given the matter intensive study. This has disclosed the complexity of the problems involved.

In the light of this experience, the Administration will again submit to the Congress proposals with respect to the reduction of taxation of foreign income along the general lines recommended by the President last year. We trust these proposals will find acceptance by the Congress.

We desire to complement these unilateral legislative steps with bilateral tax treaties. To that end, we are prepared to explore with individual countries the possibilities of the tax treaty as a medium for creating a more favorable tax climate for international trade and investment. For example, one of the matters which might be considered in treaty discussions is how the United States might give recognition to tax concessions made to foreign capital by the country where the investment is to be made. Under proper safeguards, we would be prepared to recommend giving credit for general foreign income taxes which are waived for an initial limited period as we now grant credit for taxes which are imposed. Such a measure as this will give maximum effectiveness to your own laws designed to encourage new enterprises. . . .

We recommend that each of us expand and further diversify our joint activities in the vital field of technical co-operation. The interchange of people under this program draws us closer together and provides a better understanding of each other's problems. Through technical co-operation we pool our accumulated experience and knowledge to utilize the human and natural resources available to us as we seek to match resources against our needs. The enormous mutual benefits already produced by our efforts in this field justify our confidence in its future expansion.

The President of my country has very rightly called us partners in this great enterprise. He has declared the policy of our Government to be that of the good partner. I know that the American states can be good partners, determined to work for the betterment of all our people.

🔊 The international investment corporation referred to by the Secretary was created by general comparative contributions and was not what the more eager promoters of the "United States money corporation" had been advocating to Secretary Dulles. One Latin-American minister was candid enough to say that what was needed was a lending agency of that degree of daring which would limit private Latin-American investment in it.

The Secretary had an amusing experience during his speech. His hearers sat around a huge oval table on which demitasse (coffee) was served; but Secretary Humphrey, rising to speak, subconsciously brushed away the waiter who offered him coffee. Later he recounted: "Toward the end of my remarks I had the strangest feeling you get once in a while that something ominous was creeping up the back of my neck. I paused long enough to hear some low whispers among the waiters back of me, and I wondered, and then tried to guess, what they were whispering about. I guessed that it was about my not having coffee—pretty conspicuous in a nation where coffee was almost life—and when I finished I turned around to the waiter group and said, 'Hey! Where is my demitasse?' One was shot in front of me, and the entire table burst into applause."

The reciprocal trade treaties

Statement by Secretary Humphrey on the Trade
Agreements Program before the House Ways & Means
Committee.

January 18, 1955

In my contacts over the past two years with foreign financial officials I have been impressed with two major principles in our economic relations.

First, the importance of keeping our own economy strong and dynamic and sound. Our policies are directed toward economic strength and growth—toward greater freedom from governmental interference and control. Our policies aim at encouraging initiative and freedom and maintaining economic progress and a high level of economic activity at relatively stable prices.

Such a condition helps international trade in both directions. A strong internal economy helps to keep us competitive and makes our goods attractive to foreign buyers. It also promotes a high level demand for imports. With high levels of business activity, the capacity of our economy to absorb imports is enormous—particularly imports of raw materials.

Maintaining the strength and value of the United States dollar is a vital part of our contribution to international monetary stability—for the United States dollar is the yardstick for all of the currencies of the free world. The free world's vigorous economic growth must rest on a sound financial basis. What is essential for our own strength at home is equally essential for the other free nations of the world.

Many countries, I am glad to say, are appreciating the importance of keeping their financial houses in order, not only to strengthen their internal economies but also to keep their foreign payments and receipts in balance. I am encouraged by the progress many of these nations have made toward more internal stability and toward convertibility of their currencies.

Convertibility will be encouraged by a balanced development of world trade; and, in turn, will contribute to such a development.

The second point which has impressed me in my contacts abroad is the concern of foreign countries with the broad direction of our commercial policy. Foreign countries do not expect us to lower our tariffs drastically. What they want to have, however, is assurance of continuity in our policies and they watch for moderate steps in the direction of our objectives.

This argues strongly for a three-year extension of the Trade Agreements Program. A three-year period is needed to provide reasonable assurance of such continuity.

The bill before you is moderate. It does not interfere with existing safeguards for our domestic producers. It does not contemplate any drastic changes which would adversely affect sizable groups of our citizens.

I would like to mention one other broad principle in connection with the bill. From the budgetary viewpoint, the President's trade program should help to reduce Government expenditures for foreign aid over a period of time. I believe it is best, where possible, for foreign countries to earn their way, rather than receive aid from the United States Treasury. This bill is a further step in that direction.

The Treasury Department is actively working on other aspects of the President's program to promote foreign trade and investment. These proposals will be submitted to the Congress shortly.

One proposed bill will continue the program of customs simplification and management improvement initiated by the Customs Simplification Acts of 1953 and 1954. Although the existing legislation in this field has brought about substantial improvements in customs procedures and has caused an appreciable decrease in backlog of uncompleted customs work, further improvements should be made.

The complex valuation provisions of the customs laws are in particular need of improvement and simplification. As a result of studies now being completed, legislative changes will be recommended to make the process of appraisal more prompt and efficient as well as more realistic and equitable from a commercial standpoint. Again, I find other countries in many instances are about as much concerned with these questions of customs as they are about the level of tariffs.

In the field of taxation, we are suggesting that consideration again be given to certain changes in the revenue laws with respect to taxation of income earned abroad. More particularly, we recommend that corporate business income from foreign subsidiaries or branches be taxed at a rate of 14 percentage points lower than the rate on corporate domestic income, and a deferral of tax on foreign branch income until it is removed from the country where earned.

We will be prepared to discuss these tax proposals in more detail with your committee at the appropriate time. These proposals are not large or costly, but we think they will encourage sound private United States investment abroad.

Another important part of the Administration's program on which the Treasury is working is the proposal for an International Finance Corporation, to be established as an affiliate of the International Bank for Reconstruction and Development. The purpose of the corporation will be to stimulate private investment in underdeveloped countries by providing venture capital through loans without government guarantees, thus filling a need which is not being met by any existing organization.

While all of these proposals are important, the keystone is the Reciprocal Trade Agreements legislation now before you. Its enactment will show that the United States is following a sound trade policy consistent with both our domestic and our international needs.

For a world investment agency

Statement by Secretary Humphrey before the
Senate Banking and Currency Committee.

June 6, 1955

President Eisenhower on May 2 recommended action by the Congress to authorize United States membership in the proposed International Finance Corporation. I am here this morning to support the President's recommendation. The IFC will be an international effort to co-operate with private capital in both the capital exporting and the capital importing countries to set up new enterprises, or in some cases expand or modernize existing enterprises, particularly in the less developed countries of the world.

In recent years there has been a great deal of discussion here and abroad about the need for more investment in such countries. They are anxious to secure capital, to build up their economic development, and to raise the standards of living of their people. This is an objective with which the United States Government has always had great sympathy. Increased capital investment will aid the growth of world trade, and thus be beneficial to us as well.

Private American investors are today placing new capital abroad and reinvesting their earnings from previous investments abroad at about twice the rate of loans made by the International Bank and the Export-Import Bank. This private investment, however, has been largely concentrated in a few lines—oil, mines, and to a lesser extent various manufacturing and merchandising enterprises.

It has been pretty heavily centered in Canada and some countries in Latin America and in the Middle East. These investments have played an important part in developing the countries involved. But a more diversified form of investment would contribute significantly to the progress of the less developed countries.

The International Finance Corporation has been proposed as one way of encouraging new foreign private investment. The IFC is to serve as a catalyst in stimulating private investment. It is not another type of government-to-government aid. Instead, by assisting private ventures on a business basis, the IFC will give concrete expression to the basic American conviction that economic development is best achieved through the growth of private enterprise.

The IFC will, we hope, generate an increased flow of private capital not merely by providing financial support but also by giving additional confidence to American and other firms that are interested in going abroad but are deterred by lack of knowledge and experience. I am convinced that there are many companies—mostly middle-sized and small firms—that will engage in overseas operations if they can get IFC participation, but which would not do so solely on their own. I also believe that the proposed clearing-house function of the IFC—

bringing investment opportunities in capital importing countries to the attention of potential investors in the more advanced countries— may prove to be a very important service.

The corporation will perform a different job from that now being done so well by the Export-Import Bank and the IBRD in financing trade and economic development. The two banks do not advance venture capital. They make loans at fixed rates of interest and agreed schedules of amortization. Before the banks make loans they must have reasonable assurance of repayment. Moreover, in the case of the International Bank the guarantee of the government of the country concerned is required for each loan. The IFC, on the other hand, will provide venture capital on flexible terms and will operate without Government guarantee.

The IFC will not compete with private capital. Its job will be to join with private partners in financing productive enterprises. These partners may be local firms or they may be foreign investors, or both. The private interests will supply the management and the bulk of the capital for each enterprise, while the corporation will furnish only the margin needed to complete the financing. Where private capital can do the whole job, the corporation will not enter into the financing at all.

When the IFC project was first talked about, investment in equities was one of the proposed methods of operations. We in the Treasury did not think it would be desirable or feasible for an international governmental corporation to invest in common stock and to take the management responsibility which stock ownership entails. The present plan has eliminated the equity investment and management feature. The Administration believes this is a great improvement and supports the project fully in its present form.

Although the corporation will not hold stock, it will advance capital in various forms appropriate to new enterprises. Its investments in some instances may take the form of obligations with set interest rates, and in others with income dependent upon the earnings of the local concern.

This may mean, sometimes, that securities will bear interest only to the extent that the local concerns earn enough to pay, and in other instances it may mean that the corporation will participate in additional earnings over and above a fixed rate. It may also take obligations which could be converted into stock when sold to private investors by the IFC. The particular form of securities will have to be tailored to the special problems of the particular investment. In all cases it will be expected that private investors will provide the major share of the capital as well as take management responsibility.

Moreover, the IFC is not intended to be an international holding company. When an enterprise gets on its feet and the corporation finds that it can advantageously sell off its investment, it will do so. It will use the proceeds for investment in new enterprises. In this way a capital of $100 million, which the governments are now asked to provide, will be turned over, we hope, many times in the course of the coming years.

The corporation will come into existence after 30 countries, with subscriptions of at least $75 million, have accepted membership. All subscriptions will be paid in full in gold or dollars. The United States subscription is slightly over $35 million. This amount has been included in the President's budget. Forty-two countries have informed the International Bank of their intention to initiate the necessary steps to become members, and 15 of these have already signed the Articles of Agreement, subject to legislative approval.

The IFC, though financially independent of the International Bank, will be affiliated with it. The Bank's Board of Directors will serve as the Board of Directors of the Corporation. The Bank's president will be the Corporation's chairman. Thus the Corporation will have the benefit of the experience and sound judgment which have distinguished the management of the Bank. Operating economy will also be assured.

The provisions of the Corporation's Articles of Agreement are based largely on the relevant provisions of the Bank's Articles. The legislation proposed for United States membership follows substantially the provisions of the Bretton Woods Agreements Act, which were worked out ten years ago in this committee.

The Corporation is not an answer to all the problems facing the private investor going abroad. Much will depend upon the attitudes of the host countries to new private investment. We hope the Corporation will be able to influence these countries to take favorable attitudes toward investors. While no governmental guarantee of its investments is desirable or will be requested, the Corporation obviously can operate in any country only if the government is favorable to its activities and to other private investments. In substance, it will operate under the same conditions as private investors do in these countries.

In the present state of international affairs, it is vital that the United States and the other capital exporting countries maintain good economic relations throughout the free world. This should be done as far as possible by the investment of private capital. While the International Finance Corporation is an experiment, it offers a worthwhile chance to increase the role of private investment. I hope that this committee will give favorable consideration to the proposed legislation.

World reports of recovery

🖎 In his only other speech outside the United States, the Secretary found no occasion for diplomatic wariness. It was at the 1955 World Bank meeting at Istanbul, Turkey, an extraordinary session because it was the first at which a huge majority of the financial officers present reported their respective countries to be having unparalleled growth and prosperity; some, as the Secretary noted, were already afraid of the inflationary possibilities of their good times. The current success of the World Bank might be said to date from this assembly in Istanbul.

Remarks by Secretary Humphrey at the closing session of the Tenth Annual Meeting of the Bank and Fund, Istanbul.

September 12, 1955

We are nearly at the end of another series of annual meetings of the Bank and Fund. On behalf of the United States delegation, I want to express our thanks not only to our hosts in this cordial country of Turkey for their extensive entertainment and attention to every detail for our pleasure, convenience, and comfort, but also to our chairmen and the officers and staffs of the two institutions for their fine programs and well-executed plans.

I particularly want to thank our fellow delegates for the great privilege we have had during these few days to exchange experiences, ideas, and future plans with so many of them. Perhaps one of the greatest services that the Bank and Fund provides lies in the opportunity that these meetings afford to do this. Here are gathered for a few days many men devoted to financial problems who carry great financial responsibilities, ready and willing to contribute their collective information as to conditions prevailing throughout the whole free world and to discuss their respective problems and proposed programs for meeting them.

In this way, not only are new thoughts developed, but the benefit of combined thinking on mutual problems is brought to the service of each of us to use wherever it may be applicable to our own affairs.

How often in these few days have we heard the question asked: "How are things in your country?"

And how often have we heard the now familiar reply: "They are very good. So good that they are causing some concern."

What a fine thing it is for the future of the free world that so many of its financial advisors can share this awareness of the dangers of the possible excesses, and the pressures toward inflation, which can accompany high prosperity and, if not controlled, can lay the foundation for reaction and the difficulties of deflation that we would all deplore.

These meetings and the privilege of this interchange of views, which membership in the Bank and Fund affords, is one which the United States greatly appreciates and highly values. It is second only to our appreciation of these periodic opportunities for the renewal of former friendships and welcoming new ones.

So goodbye for now. We are looking forward with keen anticipation to seeing you all in Washington next year.

"Confidence in the value of money"

*Remarks by Secretary Humphrey before the annual
meeting of the Governors of the International Monetary
Fund, Washington.*

September 24, 1956

. . . How to finance both needed defense and high prosperity without inflation is a prime problem that today confronts the finance ministers and the central bank governors of the free world. It is our task to balance the demands for defense, high consumption, and for further economic development against available resources.

We have to steer as best we can the difficult and often unmarked channel between the whirlpool of inflation and the rocks of deflation. . . .

The public financial officers have a very special responsibility to their peoples. It is largely concerned with inflation, the specter of good fiscal government; the cruelest form of theft, because it is theft with the greatest harm to those least able to protect themselves. Inflation results in the destruction of the value of money.

Confidence in the value of money is one of the greatest spurs to economic progress, because it is an incentive to save, and it is our people's savings over the years—large and small savings alike—which have built up our countries.

We should be proud and glad in a modest way over the success to date of the International Monetary Fund. Its newly formed International Finance Corporation is a hopeful experiment in getting private investors to join as partners in providing an enlarged flow of venture capital. . . .

Faith in UN in Suez crisis

◢ The Pennsylvania Society of New York awarded its gold medal for distinguished public service to Secretary Humphrey in 1956, and its dinner date coincided with the international flurry of excitement over the "Suez crisis," precipitated by British, French, and Israeli military invasion of Egypt for having appropriated the Suez Canal. It was fitting for the Secretary of the Treasury, in accepting the Society's award, to add some words about the American position in the "crisis."

Remarks by Secretary Humphrey to the Pennsylvania Society of New York at the Waldorf-Astoria Hotel, New York.

December 8, 1956

It seems appropriate under these circumstances and at this time to say just a word about the extremely important developments in the world during the past week.

We are now seeing the United Nations as a trusted intermediary stepping into a critical situation to promote the adjustment of differences by negotiation while a previous resort to force for that purpose is being withdrawn.

The importance of these events as a precedent cannot be exaggerated. It holds possibilities for future usefulness in the settlement of dangerous controversies by negotiation rather than force. This possibility can fire the imagination with the vision of an era of peace in the world stretching out into the future for years to come.

How effective this precedent may become depends of course upon how effective the present peaceful negotiations may be in resolving the real causes of controversy in the present situation. If, in good faith by all concerned, real progress can be made in the near future toward a fair, just, and lasting settlement to eliminate the underlying causes of this controversy, then indeed can we look forward to a brighter day for the maintenance of peace.

In the meantime, our Allies, who have now wholeheartedly accepted the principles of negotiation and withdrawn from the use of military force, are entitled to our full support toward a just settlement of their problems. We took a stand against them when their action violated the basic principles in which we believe. Just so, we must now support them in their wholehearted effort to arrive at a just and fair settlement through negotiation.

This must be equally true of our attitude toward all others involved. When they are in violation of just settlement through negotiation, we must oppose their action. We must support them so long as they are in wholehearted compliance with these basic principles.

A good deal of discussion and some plain guessing is developing in connection with the degree of financial burden on various currencies which this dislocation of the normal channels of trade will involve. Some of the estimates of the need for financial support have been greatly exaggerated. The fact is that in all probability existing institutions will be able to provide most of the assistance that may be needed.

It is too early, of course, to predict a successful outcome for all of the many facets in this confused situation. But real progress has been made under the leadership of the United Nations in the past few days, and the prospects for future progress are most encouraging.

⚑ This was the Secretary's only reference to the "Suez crisis," made at the point at which the Government and other world powers had gone to the United Nations to halt the invasion of Egypt by Great Britain, France, and Israel before it developed into a "shooting war." Back of the scenes, Secretary Humphrey had a considerable role in the events of this international incident. His serious objections, expressed to the President and the Cabinet, to the proposed loan to Dictator Nasser to build the Assouan Nile Dam and develop a hydroelectric enterprise in a desert-agriculture region helped to influence the President and the Secretary of State in deciding to withdraw from the Anglo-American loan project (although the immediate breach seems to have come when the Egyptian ambassador to the United States threatened Secretary Dulles with enlisting Russian help if the western allies delayed further).

The upshot was that Prime Minister Eden, without letting his American allies know what he was planning, precipitated the invasion when Nasser moved to seize the Suez Canal. As history records, the UN restored order and the status quo—at a considerable cost to Britain in its Suez oil route, a threatened blackout of its industrial life, and an exposure of military weakness which sharply endangered the pound sterling over the world. Prime Minister Eden shortly afterwards resigned.

Secretary Humphrey was one of the American officials who promptly organized an American oil transfer for England's help. He shortly was told by Chancellor of the Exchequer R. A. Butler of the real depth of the danger to the pound; unless Britain could find an assurance of a credit of $2 billion for support in the world exchanges, Butler confessed the possibility of an immense world-rocking run on the pound. Secretary Humphrey thereupon, with the International Monetary Fund and every other means, set out on an emergency mission to save the pound. Using all resources available at home and abroad, he arranged assurance of the necessary credit in four days, and the pound was saved. After final arrangements were completed, the Secretary left for his Thomasville plantation home for a young people's party—where Chancellor Butler called him for final word by telephone from London. The noise of the party forced the Secretary to talk via a kitchen phone extension from inside an old-style icebox whose door kept out the noise and permitted him and Butler to hear each other. As soon as the assurance of the $2 billion credit became known, the danger subsided.

PUBLIC POLICY

The security of America

Speech by Secretary Humphrey to the Detroit
Economic Club at the Sheraton-Cadillac Hotel,
Detroit.

November 9, 1953

We live today in a difficult time. The world is shadowed by the fear of war and destruction.

Freedom itself is at stake. Today America is called upon to save the freedom that we cherish. What principles should rule and guide us as we strive to save the heritage we have? We must face our task soberly, patiently, and resolutely, and we must face it with confidence.

We are sober because we can see no problem that can be solved in an easy way. We do not for an instant see Soviet aggression as some obliging kind of demon that can be disposed of by speaking a phrase or indicating a threat. We do not dream that—here in our own land—the farmer can be helped, the worker protected, the consumer relieved, or the businessman encouraged—by the golden promises of the demagogue.

We scorn panaceas. We respect the fortitude, the courage, the staying-power of the American people. We show that respect by always speaking the plain truth, as we know it.

And we are confident for precisely this same reason: We believe in the people. We believe in the ingenuity and the industry of the American as resources that no nation on earth can match. We believe in his capacity to work, to save, to invent, to sacrifice, to create, to dream good dreams—and to bring them to true life.

To do all these things, the people need but one thing once more: A government they can trust—a government worthy of that trust.

That is the kind of government to which we are pledged, which we will give.

With this state of mind, we are dedicated instantly and inevitably to achieving a certain state of the nation. What do we see to be the great and urgent tasks before us? I believe they can all be summarized in one statement: A sound economy sustaining a sturdy defense against the enemies of freedom—inspired by a political leadership that is spiritually strong and honest.

In the final sense, the health of our economy counts for much more than profits or wages. We assess it not merely in terms of gross national income, balanced budgets, equitable taxes, fair interest rates. We look to it for more than homes and cars, washing machines and television sets. We see our economy as the first line of defense for every freedom that we cherish.

No other purpose is worthy of us at this time in history, and no other purpose—material or selfish or partisan—guides this Government.

Now, what have we done to serve this purpose?

We have a more stable economy than we have had in many years— free and uncontrolled.

The alarming legacy from the past was arbitrarily ruled by needless controls. We lifted those controls. They were raised almost as quickly as the voices of mourners crying that it could never be done without wrecking the economy. You all remember that debate. Yet within a matter of weeks, the debate was as dead as the controls.

This was not done by magic or oratory. It was done by applying sound, honest financial policies, freeing natural correctives which safely guarded the whole price structure. The proof of their success is that over the period of a year—when this major overhauling of our economy was achieved—the cost of living moved less than one-half of one per cent. This was the "disaster" which our critics had prophesied.

The financial policies making this possible have had a single, simple focus and aim: To give the American people honest American money. The only thing remarkable about this policy is that many critics and a few demagogues should think it remarkable. The fact that they do is a sad commentary upon the habits of financial thinking acquired over the last twenty years.

But the people themselves are not amazed. Honesty is an old American habit. So is saving. So is individual initiative. So is industry. So is working with hands and brain. So is freedom. And two decades of financial double-talk have not changed these fundamental characteristics one single bit.

Honest money depends upon three things: Sound budget policy, a sound Federal Reserve System, and sound debt management. We have worked toward achieving all of these.

First: We are on our way toward getting the budget of the Federal Government under control as rapidly as expenditures for adequate defense permit. We concentrate on this purpose because we know that indefinite deficit financing spurs the forces of inflation and eventually cheats every family in the nation. We have cut the prospective deficit for the current fiscal year from more than $11 billion to less than $4 billion.

The next year is even more difficult. The best estimates that we now have show that, if our spending continues at the present rate, it will exceed our estimated income after termination of the excess profits tax and reduction of individual taxes effective December 31 by between $8 and $9 billion.

There are four alternatives: We can accept an $8 or $9 billion deficit in fiscal 1955. We can cut expenses. We can raise additional taxes, or we can have a combination of the three.

The answer is simple to state but terribly hard to accomplish. We must first find and then maintain that delicate balance between security from attack from abroad with a strong and vigorous economy here at home. We must balance the cost of adequate military security with the capability of a strong economy to pay the bill. And this must all be reckoned not on the basis of a short and all out effort for a limited period of time, but for the long pull not knowing when or if ever the critical moment may appear.

It means the creation of a fluid, mobile, modern, and effective system of defense, and the control of its cost, within limits which the country can long afford to maintain.

It means an aggressive dynamic economy, for that is the very foundation of any sustained military strength. It means military planning and the control of all Governmental expenditures so carefully balanced that we obtain the adequate posture of defense that we require for our security within the limit of our means.

Second: The Federal Reserve System is free to ensure effective monetary policy. For many years the Federal Reserve's supporting of Government securities at par, to preserve artificially low interest rates, invited banks and other holders of Government bonds to sell their bonds—making the debt almost like currency. This, of course, was a sure way to encourage inflation. Today, the Federal Reserve System is free to use its power to provide a supply of credit to meet the requirements of natural demand and avoid excesses leading toward either inflation or deflation.

Third: We have a program to meet the problem of debt management imposed upon us by the inheritance of a total debt of more than $273 billion of which nearly three-fourths matures within less than five years. We have offered the first long-term loan in twenty years and will continue to extend the maturities of refinancing operations whenever and to whatever extent appropriate conditions will permit.

Partisan critics have loudly deplored any increase in interest rates as if they benefited only the few and defrauded most of the people. Nothing could be further from the truth. There are more savers than borrowers in America—more people who benefit from higher interest than those who pay it. These beneficiaries are the 45 million families— the 122 million people—who have invested in savings accounts, life insurance, pensions, annuities, Government bonds, mortgages, fraternal and mutual institutions and many other forms of investment for savings.

This policy means a check in the trend of dollars that continue to buy less and less in clothes, in food, in homes. It means savings, not only to give individual families better security, health and education but also to give the nation the indispensable resources to build factories, expand mills, develop mines, drill oil wells, and erect power plants. Savings make jobs, and are essential for the high productivity of American labor and our increasingly higher and higher standards of living.

It means—in cheaper costs to state and local governments—the chance to build more of the highways, the hospitals, the schools which are the priceless monuments of a nation prosperously at peace. . . .

Neither American business nor American labor needs war to be prosperous.

Our population is increasing—by thousands of new-born each day—

at a rate of close to 15 per cent in a decade. The needs and wants of Americans are increasing no less swiftly. Every American family wants more opportunity and a better and fuller life for each succeeding generation.

And our capacity to meet these needs—as we stand on the threshold of an atomic age for the good of mankind instead of for evil—is beyond the imagination of most of us living today.

As the threat of aggression recedes, our huge expenditures for defense can decline. This does not mean that we are headed for a depression. In our great and growing economy, adjustments are constantly going on. Wherever these adjustments are required, let's face them with confidence and correct them: Keep our eyes open and not believe in blind faith; seek out the soft spot and see what can be done about it.

Government spending must be reduced. But tremendous amounts of money will still be pumped into the economy by the Government because only relatively small reductions can be made quickly. Likewise, it is the definite policy of this Administration, through tax reduction, to return to the people for them to spend for themselves all real savings in Government spending which can be reasonably anticipated. This we are doing with the expiration of the excess profits tax and the 10 per cent reduction in individual income tax which will become effective on January 1st.

The reduction of taxes is a determined purpose of this Administration. The sooner it is done, the sooner the consuming community can quicken its demands upon the productive capacity of the whole nation. And the potential increase in these demands through tax relief, as fast as our defense needs permit, is the surest stimulant to continued progress and a high level of activity.

Our volume of production and employment can be higher than ever, and we may still have some capacity in reserve. High volume but good supply means competition, efficiency, and more value for the consumer's dollar. Surely we haven't reached the point in this country so that all we can see is calamity if the day of allocations and the order taker is passing.

It cannot be that Americans fear a free competitive economy. It is in such an economy that we grew great. A little more production, a little more selling, a little more effort and ingenuity have given us higher and higher standards of living. Surely we are not fearful that we cannot do it again. . . .

This is the kind of economy we are striving to encourage: Healthy and imaginative, fortified with sound currency, confident of the prudence of its Government, and ready for the exciting challenges of tomorrow. Such an economy is equipped and alert to meet—and to live by—the simple truth that America is the world's greatest unfinished business.

I remind you again: This American economy—healthy, vital, daring— is our first line of defense for freedom itself. For a fact that cannot be too often repeated is this: America's greatest defense against any enemy is the power and potential of American mass production. . . . We know that a sick American economy would fulfill the Communist dream of conquest just as surely as disaster on the battlefield.

We live in an age witnessing a revolution in scientific and production techniques. In such an age, the surest formula for defeat would be a static defense—committed to old-fashioned strategy—served by obsolete weapons. There would be not defense but disaster in a military program that scorned the resources and problems of our economy— erecting majestic defenses and battlements for the protection of a country that was bankrupt and a people who were impoverished.

There would be not defense but disaster in so massive a program of arms production that our strength and resources might become exhausted and we would lose the capacity to continue the effort—so that tomorrow's threat would have to be met with yesterday's weapons. . . . The essential truths are simply these:

(1) We know that a healthy economy is America's surest source of strength in meeting an enemy.

(2) We know that a high level of employment and industrial activity is essential for the maintenance of such an economy.

(3) We know that no such economy could be assured without the health of honest money, economical government, and sound monetary policy.

(4) We know that a balanced but adequate defense program, fluid and imaginative, mobile and elastic, will and must be supported by whatever appropriations logic and necessity demand.

We are aware, no less, that the economic problems we must meet do not end at our shores. Our trade in the world—and the world's trade with us—are essential parts of the strength all of us need to stay free. Our own industries are vitally dependent upon raw materials from the most distant parts of the earth. Our farms as well as industry need markets abroad.

What happens in the valley of the Nile, on the plains of Turkey, or in Pakistan may affect our farms in Kansas and Iowa. What happens in Malaya or the Belgian Congo may affect our industries and our defense program. And so our defense of ourselves inevitably involves the conditions obtaining in many areas—seemingly distant and strange, yet really vital and near. . . .

But above all these matters, I venture to suggest that one challenge rises to tower over all others. We must provide that moral leadership, that steadfastness of spirit and mind, which alone can make us worthy of the high commission that history has conferred upon us.

We must care more for truth than for success. We must care more for the hopes of the people than the votes of the people.

We must always worry more about our problems than the headlines. We must scorn the glib promise, the false phrase, the shallow excuse, and the clever evasion.

Let our ambition be but one: Justice and security for America. Born of a brave past, we have nothing to fear of the future. If worthy of the present, the future will be ours.

🏴 Secretary Humphrey undertook three "messages" in this speech, to an audience which he knew and which knew him: To allay any sentiment existing among industrialists that the end of the Korean War would mean an industrial recession, to state the Administration's confidence that adequate military security could be maintained without fiscal danger, and to give his own confession of faith as to what he believed the outstanding strength of America to be. It contained the longest analysis of our security Secretary Humphrey ever made in public.

Interstate highway financing

*Statement by Secretary Humphrey before
the Sub-Committee on Public Roads
of the Senate Committee on Public Works.
Senator Albert Gore of Tennessee, presiding.*

March 22, 1955

We are all agreed on the need for an expanded highway program. The question is how best to finance it.

The plan embodied in S. 1160 of setting up a self-sustaining Government corporation to handle the expanded highway program has been carefully designed to serve the following objectives:

(1) To get the road program underway with the speed required by the rapidly growing volume of automobile traffic.

(2) To produce promptly an adequate interstate network more effectively than can be done by dependence on programs of the separate states.

(3) To tie firmly together the expenditures on roads and the income which can reasonably be drawn from the users of the roads, so that the operation is self-sustaining.

(4) To finance this road program with taxable securities rather than tax-exempt securities; this is an important objective, since the growing volume of tax-exempt securities for roads involves a serious loss of revenue to the Treasury.

(5) To hold down further increases in the mounting levels of Government obligations payable out of general revenues.

The evidence that has already been presented to your committee, I am sure, has convinced all of us of the urgent need for building highways more rapidly. To do so will result in a substantial economic gain to the American people in terms of time saving through more rapid movement of traffic, greater efficiency through more prompt delivery, the reduction of the accident toll, and lower costs on the upkeep of vehicles. These are all matters difficult to measure, but all of them are important.

In suggesting this program, the Administration has clearly in mind the advantages to the whole country of an expanded road program which will employ more people, and add to the country's rate of economic growth. Such a road program will encourage the continued development of the automobile industry and the construction industry; in fact, all our citizens will be better off as benefits of the program run through the entire economy. . . .

I would be the last man to advocate a program that simply added to our federal budget and the charge on general federal revenues. We must think in terms of cutting back the volume of federal expenditures, and I have repeatedly stated that I think this can be done and that the load of general taxes, which weighs so heavily on the economy, can be decreased over a period of years. One of the reasons I am in favor of the road program is that it does not interfere with the long-term objectives of reducing general federal expenditures and reducing general taxes.

Let me say also that no one could have a higher regard than I have for the views of Senator Byrd. I have been in agreement with him on the major principles of sound Federal Government finance. I have read with care his impressive statement last Friday before the committee. It raises important questions of principle as well as questions of administrative practice and Government accounting.

I believe the principles involved in this bill are sound. There are real earning assets here—new highways vital to the future of our nation. If the program could be paid for completely by tolls, there would be no question about its financial soundness. But "tolls" can be measured in a great many ways. You can base them on mileage traveled. You can levy a charge based on the weight of the vehicle, the number of passengers, or the number of axles. Or, you can carry that one step further and measure your tolls by consumption of motor vehicle fuel. This is a practical way of doing it.

There is no doubt in my mind that this program should be handled on as close to a pay-as-you-go basis as possible. I would not object, therefore, if the Congress sees fit to increase the federal gasoline tax in order to finance this program.

If it cannot be on a pay-as-you-go basis and borrowing is necessary, then that borrowing should not involve a pledge of the general revenues of the United States Government. It should rather rely upon specific user taxes, in the last analysis, for servicing the bonds and for their security.

Now as to details of administration and accounting—the board of directors of the highway corporation would have the authority necessary to assure flexibility in handling the program in the future. I hope your committee will examine with care questions of accounting and budgetary supervision.

It may cost somewhat more to issue the bonds through the corporation rather than by the use of public debt obligations. I think it is worth it. It provides a semiautomatic way of paying off the debt thus incurred over specific periods. If they carry a higher rate, that very fact may give them wider distribution of ownership by real investors and require less use of bank credit.

It is a wholesome thing to have debt limits set by the Congress. It provides a standard in our fiscal policy for everybody to think about and respect. It is wise for the highway program to have a debt limit, too, and one is provided for in the bill.

There is one further point on this program that is very important, and that is its inflationary potential. If the Congress and the Administration were to stop suddenly right now in their drive toward a lower level of budget expenditures, then I would say that to pile this highway program on top of it might be inflationary. As I mentioned before, however, we are firmly committed to further reducing Government expenditures and working toward a less oppressive tax system. As we succeed in cutting expenditures, a highway program like this can, I believe, be handled without inflationary effects. . . .

Cross-examination of Secretary Humphrey

SENATOR GORE. Thank you, Mr. Secretary, for your statement.

. . . On page one you refer to this as a "self-sustaining Government corporation." I do not quite understand the meaning in which you use the term "self-sustaining," since under S. 1160 the revenue to retire the bonds of this corporation would come from appropriations from the Treasury, and it is without assets or other income.

SEC. HUMPHREY. I suppose the word "liquidating" would be better than "sustaining."

SENATOR GORE. Then how would it be self-liquidating?

SEC. HUMPHREY. The pledge of the gasoline taxes to the payment of these bonds will liquidate these bonds.

SENATOR GORE. That is more than a pledge; it is an outright appropriation from the Treasury of the United States enacted by Congress.

SEC. HUMPHREY. That is the same thing, is it not? As long as you have a pledge by an appropriate authority, whatever the appropriate authority may be, of monies coming in in a sufficient amount to liquidate the obligations to be paid off, you have a self-liquidating operation.

SENATOR GORE. I do not know what you mean by "self-liquidating," Mr. Secretary. There is nothing that this corporation does that brings in any revenue to liquidate itself. It is not a self-action which would liquidate the obligations of the corporation, as I understand the bill; it is rather an act of the Congress in appropriating the money out of the Treasury of the United States. How is that self-liquidating?

SEC. HUMPHREY. This provides for the dedication of certain revenues to certain purposes, dedicated by an act of Congress. . . . I do not want to quibble about words. I don't care whether you call it self-sustaining or what you call it. The setup contains its own basis for liquidation.

SENATOR GORE. I don't want to quibble about the word either, but you have used the words "self-sustaining" and the words "self-liquidating." Frankly, I do not think that this proposed highway corporation has any earmarks of self-liquidation.

SEC. HUMPHREY. That is a difference of opinion between us. I think that if certain revenues are dedicated to a certain purpose that that purpose tends to liquidate itself. And these bonds are not to be issued in excess of the anticipated revenues to be received. . . .

SENATOR GORE. Then further down on page one you refer to holding down further increases in the mounting levels of Government obligations payable out of the general revenues. Do I understand by that that you would want to hold the expenditures on the other category of roads at the present levels?

SEC. HUMPHREY. That is correct.

SENATOR GORE. For the next 30 years.

SEC. HUMPHREY. Out of these particular revenues. . . .

SENATOR GORE. I notice you pay generous compliments to Senator

Byrd and his testimony. The committee was impressed with that testimony, too. Senator Byrd described this financing scheme as "fantastic." I wonder if you would comment on that?

SEC. HUMPHREY. He has told me that. I have talked with him a number of times about this. As I said in my statement, I have the highest regard for Senator Byrd's financial knowledge and his capacity in every way, but there are occasionally times when he and I have differed in what we think can or should be done from a practical point of view. I always hesitate to differ from Senator Byrd because of my great regard for him and his abilities. But sometimes we do, and this is one of those unfortunate cases.

SENATOR GORE. Would you mind informing the committee as to whether you had hesitation in approving this plan?

SEC. HUMPHREY. What do you mean?

SENATOR GORE. This particular plan of financing—did you hesitate in giving your approval to that?

SEC. HUMPHREY. I gave it a good deal of thought, Mr. Chairman, a good deal of thought as to what was the best way to accomplish this purpose. I think we have here an objective that is really a necessary objective to be accomplished for the good of this country, and I think that it is a very difficult thing to try to figure out what is the best way to accomplish that objective. I studied it a lot and all of our people studied it a lot to try to think in our ways how is the best way to accomplish this thing.

Of course I like to, insofar as possible, pay as you go. That is not at all times practical. There are times when it is desirable that you should not pay as you go, when you want to go a little faster than you pay. And there are times when it is perfectly proper to do that. Under what circumstances and how would you accomplish that purpose? Each case has to be decided on its merits.

I think in this particular case the probabilities are that because of the limitations on the States' ability to raise money and so forth, that it is desirable here to go somewhat faster than you pay. That rests finally in the judgment of this committee. But if you are going to go on this recognized good objective faster than you can currently pay for it, then I think this is as good a way of providing for the difference between the pay as you go and the borrowing as I know of.

SENATOR GORE. Would you recommend some other plan to meet the exigencies, the severe exigencies of school construction?

SEC. HUMPHREY. Schools are somewhat different than roads although it is possible that a plan could be developed that would be appropriate for schools on a rental basis. I think that what you have to do, if you have an asset that can, on its own, because of its own contribution to society, earn money and it is so set up that it will earn money and you measure it in such a way that money is earned by it, I think it is appropriate to take the money that it earns and dedicate that money to the payment of obligations incurred in the acquisition of the asset. The simplest illustration, of course, is a toll road.

SENATOR GORE. Mr. Secretary, in your statement, the part to which I have already referred, you say that it is your objective—by which I take it, it is the Administration's objective—to reduce expenditures and taxes. To quote exactly, from No. 5: "To hold down further increases in the mounting levels of Government obligations payable out of general revenues."

One of the things we are aware of in this committee is that you would, by S. 1160, dedicate all of the funds beyond the present level, minus $100 million for secondary, primary, and urban roads, not for just the next 30 years but for such longer time as there may be bonds outstanding.

SEC. HUMPHREY. It might be shorter, too.

SENATOR GORE. If it were enacted?

SEC. HUMPHREY. It would not ordinarily exceed 30 years. It might be shorter.

SENATOR GORE. But for such time, however long it may be, until all the bonds are retired. That would appear, from your position here, to at least doom the other category of roads to the present level of expenditure.

SEC. HUMPHREY. Not necessarily. It would doom them to the present level of expenditure provided the revenues were not increased. But if you are going to spend more money you have to raise more money.

SENATOR GORE. You advocate a lowering of all other expenditures in general revenue?

SEC. HUMPHREY. That is right.

Senator Gore. So insofar as your present position, it is to hold the expenditures for primary, urban, and secondary roads to the present levels, minus $100 million for the next 30 years or until such time as the bonds are retired?

Sec. Humphrey. Or until such time as additional revenues, earned revenues from those roads are dedicated to their payment. There is no reason why the tolls cannot be increased if it seems desirable to do so.

Senator Gore. You mean the gasoline tax?

Sec. Humphrey. That is right. Or any other method of measuring income from the roads.

Senator Gore. Mr. Secretary, do you realize that those other roads carry six-sevenths of the traffic?

Sec. Humphrey. I didn't know that that was the figure but I could well imagine that it might be.

Senator Gore. Do you not think within the next 10 years or 20 years or 30 years that those roads are going to wear out and become obsolete?

Sec. Humphrey. Oh, yes. I think that you are going to have your road problem continually with you. I think you are going to have to keep working at it. I think as you build more and more roads and get increased roads that you may be justified in having increased revenues for them. . . .

Senator Gore. Do you think the earmarking of federal funds is administratively sound?

Sec. Humphrey. I think it is the best way we can handle this particular situation.

Senator Gore. How far would you go in earmarking?

Sec. Humphrey. Only to the extent, as I have said, of earmarking earnings of an earning asset measured in as practical a measurement as you can obtain. I think that is what we have here, a practical measure of the earnings of this earning asset.

Senator Gore. Mr. Secretary, do you propose to earmark or dedicate—there is no real difference in the meaning of the two words "earmark" or "dedicate," is there?

Sec. Humphrey. Well, yes; there is to this extent: If you are going to be very technical about it, the earmark is to follow the exact coin through. In other words, you start and follow a coin through. That is not a practical way of doing it. It is much more practical to do it by dedication as you do in this particular case where you estimate the amount of the exact coins and put them into the funds and out of the fund.

SENATOR GORE. I certainly don't want to put you in the position of following a nickel all the way through the Treasury.

SEC. HUMPHREY. We don't want to be in that position. It isn't practical.

SENATOR GORE. Mr. Secretary, you speak of the earnings from an asset?

SEC. HUMPHREY. That is right.

SENATOR GORE. Here you would dedicate all of the increased earnings not from just the asset of the interstate roads but from all roads?

SEC. HUMPHREY. You have to have some sort of an arbitrary measure of those earnings. We estimated this as practical a way to segregate and estimate your earnings and dedicate those earnings to the purpose as we could find. It is very difficult.

SENATOR GORE. Then when you speak of dedicating the funds from an earning asset you refer to all of the roads of the country as that asset?

SEC. HUMPHREY. Not necessarily. On an arbitrary designation of an amount you can take a slice of a whole measured in any way you want and not care where it particularly comes from if it is a slice of the whole. But there can be a lot of other roads in the country whose earnings can be dedicated to them. States can build toll roads, there can be toll roads built all over and those tolls dedicated to the earnings of those roads. There can be other ways of measuring earnings on various roads that can be built in various places, and those earnings would be dedicated to the use of those roads and wouldn't get in here.

This is a segregation of a certain measure of certain earnings which are dedicated to a certain purpose. . . .

SENATOR STUART SYMINGTON (Missouri). Mr. Secretary, I was looking through some of the testimony by Senator Byrd. He said: "In my judgment, if Senate Bill 1160 is enacted in its present form, it will destroy sound budgetary procedure and take the longest step yet taken toward concentrating power in the Federal Government. It abolishes the state matching formula for the Interstate System which has existed since 1916."

Would you care to comment on that?

SEC. HUMPHREY. I think he exaggerates the importance of it in his mind. I think that Senator Byrd is properly very jealous of the appropriating power of the Congress. I think he is properly jealous of that. But I think that because this implies a promise of the Government that carries beyond an annual appropriation that he exaggerates the importance of that sort of a step. I think that we have had those sort of steps before without their causing unusual difficulties. I don't think this would cause unusual difficulties in that regard.

SENATOR SYMINGTON. Now the next statement that he made was: "It gives the corporation authority to draw from the Treasury at any time during the next 32 years additional amounts up to $5 billion outstanding at one time without going through any appropriation action by Congress."

Don't you think that if there are going to be additional appropriations up to $5 billion that the Congress should have the right to look at them before they are made in the future date?

SEC. HUMPHREY. I think that again is of the same kind that Senator Byrd objects to because of an appropriation other than just an annual appropriation. Really what happens, as I see it in practice is that this present Congress authorizes a payment of up to that amount, which you may say is the equivalent of a contingent appropriation. It is an appropriation which is authorized, it is an expenditure which is authorized by the current Congress that may or may not be made, and this present Congress specifies the certain conditions under which it may be paid and under which it may not be paid. So that it is not an unappropriated amount, it is an amount that has had the prior authority of Congress but not the prior annual authority.

SENATOR SYMINGTON. Going on he said: "If this bill is passed, it will not include one single dollar of the expenditures that are proposed under this legislation. Not a dollar will be included in the debt limit, although this debt, let me emphasize, is just as much a debt as any other debt that the Federal Government will contract. . . ." What are your thoughts on that?

SEC. HUMPHREY. I am not in any way interested in any trick to avoid the debt limit. I believe in the debt limit. I think it is wholesome that the people of this country have currently and constantly brought to their minds the amount of money that they owe, and as nearly as we can, the full amount of money that they owe. Frankly, I have tried to estimate how much we do owe and I haven't been able to do it. We owe so much and in so many different ways already, so many different contingent liabilities of one kind or another, that it is extremely difficult to get the total amount that we owe. This will be a very much clearer delineation of amount that we owe in this regard than many that we already have enacted.

But I think that, as I stated in my statement, debt limits are good things and that they ought to be brought out and that they ought to be paraded before the people on every occasion to let them know how much they do owe and how near they are to the limit of what, from time to time, will be regarded as the maximum that they should owe. This bill does carry a debt limit in it. This is not a direct obligation of the United States Government. It is an obligation of the Government; it is something that the Government sponsors. The Government says it will take appropriate action to see that it is repaid, and it takes appropriate action in two ways to see that it is repaid. But it is not technically within the debt limit. There are a number of other things that are not technically within the debt limit.

SENATOR SYMINGTON. You would say, would you not, that it is actually a debt of the United States?

SEC. HUMPHREY. It is an obligation. It is not a debt. It is an obligation.

SENATOR SYMINGTON. If it is an obligation shouldn't it be expressed in the debt ceiling?

SEC. HUMPHREY. I would have no objection whatever to having Congress revise the requirements of those things that will be listed under the debt ceiling of the United States. There are a number of things that do not come within the present definition. There are a number of obligations, a good many obligations, and they rise to a good deal of money, that are not within the limits that are expressed in the debt limit. But I would be perfectly content—I would be more than content—if Congress did want to revise the definition of the debt limit and really put everything we could think of in it and let the people know as much as we estimate, of what might reasonably be there. . . .

SENATOR SYMINGTON. You wouldn't say this obligation was either indefinite or contingent?

SEC. HUMPHREY. No.

SENATOR SYMINGTON. Otherwise how could you sell the bonds?

SEC. HUMPHREY. I don't think this is. I think you might well change the definition of the debt limit and put this and a number of other things in the debt limit.

SENATOR SYMINGTON. Then Senator Byrd said: "In these days when we are continuously piling up debt to be paid by our children and grandchildren, the least we can do is keep the books honest and make full disclosure of obligations we are incurring." He goes further and calls this "financial responsibility by legerdemain." That worries me a great deal. I spoke to Senator Byrd about this prior to your appearance. He feels that this is properly the most unfortunate piece of legislation that has ever come before the Congress since he has been in it, and he has been here a long time.

SEC. HUMPHREY. I know he does. I have talked to him about it. Just frankly I think that he has exaggerated the difficulties and the problems and I don't think it goes to a matter of basic honesty nor do I think it goes to a matter of trick. I don't think there is anything deceptive about this. I think it is right out in the open and everybody knows what it is and where it is and just why it is handled as it is.

I think if you want to change the strict definitions of the debt law to include this in it, that is a perfectly proper thing to do. But at the same time, as I say, if you are going to include this I would include some other things, too.

SENATOR SYMINGTON. You knew that Senator Byrd has an opinion from the chief Senate legislative counsel, stating that in his opinion the bill is illegal?

SEC. HUMPHREY. I read that. Of course, in my position I take the legal advice of the Attorney General.

SENATOR SYMINGTON. Senator Byrd said: "Camouflage it all you please, the bonds issued by this corporation will be a federal debt and a general obligation of the Government. It will be absurd for this corporation to attempt to issue bonds unless the Federal Government would guarantee them for the simple reason that the bonds would be unsalable if this corporation has no assets and has no income."

Don't you feel that these bonds are an obligation of the Federal Government?

SEC. HUMPHREY. I feel that they are an obligation and not a debt within the strict meaning of the word "debt. . . ."

SENATOR SYMINGTON. Don't you think at least that they are a contingent liability of the Federal Government?

SEC. HUMPHREY. They are more than just a contingent liability. When these bonds are put out the Government will have made a promise that these revenues will be dedicated to their use for this purpose. And it is on the basis of that Government promise that they will be sold.

SENATOR SYMINGTON. Let me read now a statement of the Secretary of Commerce before this committee: "The bonds would not legally be a contingent liability of the United States."

SEC. HUMPHREY. I think you can get into the technical meaning of the words. That is what I was trying to avoid. I doubt if under a very technical meaning of the words they are not a contingent debt. But they are based on a—

SENATOR SYMINGTON. He said they wouldn't be a direct or indirect obligation of the Government.

SEC. HUMPHREY. Again, you see, you are getting into words pretty much.

SENATOR SYMINGTON. Senator Byrd said: "I point now to a glaring inconsistency in this bill, and that is where one clause of the bill states the bonds are not guaranteed by the Federal Government, there is another provision that gives the Government the right to sell these bonds to Government trust funds. It is unthinkable to me that the Congress would authorize legislation to permit bonds not guaranteed by the Federal Government to be sold to its trust funds, such as the Social Security for which the Government is a trustee with all the responsibility that a trusteeship carries. The Social Security Fund comes, as many of the committee know, from the savings and collections from those who want at a certain age to obtain retirement benefits."

Say an elderly woman is paying money into a Social Security Fund and that the assets behind that fund are these bonds. Surely the Federal Government couldn't afford to run out on those bonds after that woman put her own money up.

SEC. HUMPHREY. I don't think the Federal Government can run

out on these bonds under any circumstances, nor will it, nor will the occasion arise to do so. They will never be issued unless they are within the limits. These bonds have to be issued subject to the approval of the Secretary of the Treasury, and as long as I am here or any other responsible Secretary is here these bonds will not be issued beyond the amounts, that the proper amount of tax will be dedicated to pay for them, and there is no reason why they should be.

SENATOR SYMINGTON. The bonds then are a debt of the United States; are they not?

SEC. HUMPHREY. That all depends on whether you are going to be technical or not. Technically they are not a debt, Senator. They are an obligation. . . . I think you are getting all mixed with a lot of words, myself, and I don't see the purpose of it. I don't think that anybody claims that these bonds, if they are put out, won't be good bonds. I think they will or I wouldn't have anything to do with putting them out. I think the Government will make a promise to dedicate sufficient funds to the payment of these bonds so they will be paid. And I think that is a good promise, and I think it is a promise that the Government can make not only in this case but has made in similar cases and can do it.

SENATOR SYMINGTON. I would like to make one comment: The debt of the United States is high.

SEC. HUMPHREY. It is; too high.

SENATOR SYMINGTON. Past administrations have been very heavily criticized for putting up the debt. As a matter of fact, the debt was under $40 billion just prior to World War II. And the reason, in my opinion, that it is where it is now, is due to two words primarily, almost entirely due to two words. One word is "Hitler" and the other word is "Stalin." That in my opinion is the reason that the debt has gone up this high.

Sometimes we have felt badly about the criticism that we have had about the height of the debt. For example, I believe the figures show that between 1946 and 1952 the Government operated at a profit of about $11.3 billion, whereas in the last two years it has operated at a substantial loss. I believe the loss has been over $11 billion. All I say is that if we have to have a high debt, regardless of any past promises made by either administration, in my opinion we should face up to the fact that if this is a debt we need to raise the debt limit. . . .

SEC. HUMPHREY. Senator, I would like to say that I don't think it would profit you or me to get into any discussion of the past. I don't think that is important. I do think there is a word you ought to add to your vocabulary when you refer to it, and I think that is "inflation." I think that had a great deal to do with the size of the debt.

As to avoiding the debt limit or providing some means of avoiding the debt limit, I have already stated that this wasn't done with that purpose. I don't think it should be done with that purpose. I think it is perfectly proper to amend the technical language of the debt limit to include this and other debts or obligations which are excluded from the debt limit under its present technical definition. I would like to see that. . . .

SENATOR SYMINGTON. One other point has come up in a discussion with the Secretary of Commerce. We had some Government corporations that were conceived primarily, I believe, by Mr. Jesse Jones, as a way to get things done. We had a lot of assistants like Mr. Jeffers and so forth in the doing of them. Not too long ago it was considered wrong to have Government corporations. A sales program was put on to get rid of these corporations. I won't say at any price, but sometimes it looks to me as if they got rid of them at a price which wasn't to the best interest of the taxpayer, with the premise that he owned part of the corporation.

After the elimination of most, if not all, of these corporations, we suddenly have a plan that has now come before us, the basis of which is a Government corporation. I wonder what your thoughts would be on that.

SEC. HUMPHREY. I don't think that the Government corporation is taboo in and of itself. I think that when you have corporations— let's take RFC, for instance, which was created for a purpose, and that purpose was satisfied and finished—that you ought to liquidate that agency and have it over with. I don't think you ought to keep a lot of obsolete things around just because you have them. . . .

SENATOR SYMINGTON. So that you have no objection to a Government corporation per se?

SEC. HUMPHREY. Not if it is properly set up; no. . . .

SENATOR FRANCIS CASE (South Dakota). Would you feel that the good faith of the Government would be committed if we made the language read, "There are hereby authorized for appropriation and payment by the Secretary of the Treasury," and so on.

SEC. HUMPHREY. I think if the purpose of a change in language here was to make it subject only to annual appropriation, with no agreement that an appropriation would be made annually, I think it would destroy the value of these bonds. In other words, I don't think anybody wants to buy a bond on the idea that maybe they will and maybe they won't be paid.

SENATOR CASE. The Chairman referred to the fact that six-sevenths of the traffic is carried on highways and roads that are not in the Interstate System. Are you familiar with the figures as to what the proceeds of the gasoline tax and the oil tax would run over the period of 32 years? ... Assuming that it is $55 billion, if you divide that by the number of years that would mean an annual revenue of about $1.8 billion a year. ... If you look at the proposal here and you propose to appropriate that which is in excess of $622 million, on the average you would be appropriating two-thirds of the revenue to the completion of the Interstate System. ... The problem that bothers me—and it bothers me in connection with the use that you make of specific user taxes—is that two-thirds of the revenues would be dedicated to the completing of the system which carries one-seventh of the traffic?

SEC. HUMPHREY. That is right.

SENATOR CASE. Then it seems to me that that destroys the validity of using this as a measuring stick for the users who are paying for the roads.

SEC. HUMPHREY. That is just a measure of part of the income of the total highways. There is lots of other income from the highways. All the toll roads are not included in the figures, and a lot of toll roads of the future are intended to be built in various ways that will not be in there. And there are State gasoline taxes and State revenues that go into highways. There is an awful lot of revenue that goes into highways on these six-sevenths that you are talking about that are not included in this particular revenue. This is just a percentage of a part of the total revenue.

SENATOR CASE. In some of the congested eastern cities it may be that the Interstate System will serve as a thoroughfare for a great deal of traffic. ...

The farmers or ranchers who live two and three hundred miles from the Interstate System don't like to pay the federal gasoline tax which is not refunded for nonhighway use. They don't like to pay that and have it dedicated to the completion of the Interstate System, which they seldom or ever use. Of course I am not a road expert by any means.

Sec. Humphrey. I know very little about it. Here is the proposition as I see it. It is a very desirable thing to have an integrated highway system, Interstate Highway System in this country. Almost any way you proceed has objections to it that can be raised by this or that interest. This is the best scheme that I have seen. . . .

Senator Case. Would you like to see this principle of dedicating user taxes to specific projects applied to the tax on spirits and liquors?

Sec. Humphrey. I don't know how—I just don't know how you quite measure the use of spirits and liquors. That is a little different.

Senator Case. Would you like to see the tax on the capital stock of corporations dedicated for the Bureau of Domestic Commerce in the Department of Commerce?

Sec. Humphrey. I don't think that they measure the use; no. I think it has to have a relationship to use. I think what we are trying to do, what we are really trying to do here, is to find some measure of some practical way of collecting money based on a measure of use.

Senator Case. I think tolls are a good, clear illustration. I think that if you were measuring the gasoline, if you were selling the gasoline to be used on a particular system of roads, and wanted to dedicate that, I think that would be a direct specific use.

Sec. Humphrey. I agree with that. That is the clearest case. If this— of course I view this in the nature of a toll. I view this in the nature of a measure of a toll. Let's say you based your toll strictly on mileage or something of that kind, which would be a little more objective measurement of toll. Let's say you did that. Do you think you would have less trouble having the people in New Jersey or the people in the District of Columbia paying tolls on roads in order to pay for roads out in Iowa than you would have this other way?

Senator Case. I don't know, but I am not proposing that.

Sec. Humphrey. I am not, either. But you are talking about objections. There are objections to all these things, as I see it. I don't think anybody can think up any scheme that somebody isn't going to object to. . . .

I think we should build the roads somewhat faster than we probably can pay for them currently. . . .

Senator Prescott Bush (Connecticut). I certainly congratulate the

Secretary on his splendid statement and answers to a lot of these very difficult questions that have been put to him.

In connection with the point that the New York area pays more in federal gasoline taxes than the State of Iowa, I suppose that is true. Certainly on a per capita basis it would be very much true. And that certainly would apply to the State of Connecticut, my own state. We have been paying more in federal gasoline taxes than we get back in federal aid, and have for a long time. . . . Despite the fact that these bonds don't have behind them the full faith and credit of the Federal Government, you believe that they are marketable and can be marketed in toto over a period of years ahead?

SEC. HUMPHREY. That is the best advice we can get.

SENATOR BUSH. Do you think they will carry a larger interest rate than the long-term Government bonds?

SEC. HUMPHREY. Yes; they will. . . .

SENATOR PATRICK McNAMARA (Michigan). I was interested, Mr. Secretary, in your statement that the automobile excise tax was not a user's tax. Every time I buy an automobile I pay approximately $100 in taxes. I am a user of an automobile. I think the tax is most unfair, unjust, and an unfair burden on the industry, so naturally you can understand that. . . . You almost advocated an increase of the federal gasoline tax to cut down the $11.5 billion we would have to pay in interest on this $21 billion total. I hope that you will get to the point where you will advocate something to eliminate that $11.5 billion out of the $21 billion that we are going to have to pay for interest.

SEC. HUMPHREY. Mind you, I am not advocating paying interest. I would like to, and I think any prudent treasurer should advocate paying as near as you can as you go. But there are times when you can't pay as you go, when it is prudent to get something ahead of the time when you can pay for it. But when you do that and when you do borrow money to get something ahead of the time when you would otherwise have it, don't say that you don't get anything. The fact is that by paying this interest you will have roads for several years when otherwise you wouldn't have them. . . .

The right way to pay for roads

☛ Secretary Humphrey repeated, to the House Sub-committee, his statement of March 22 to the Senate Sub-committee on Roads of the Senate
Public Works Committee, then added to it a further reassurance as to the
method of bond financing proposed. Both Senate and House Sub-commit-
tees undertook to rewrite the bill and inject other financing terms, but no
bill passed this session of Congress. It remained for the next session, with
still different financing methods, to pass the legislation and appropriation
that began the Interstate Highways System. (Cf. the Secretary's statement
and testimony of May 17, 1956, Senate Finance Committee.)

One point which the Congressmen raised was whether the highway bond
financing would create national debt; if it did, then the statutory debt limit
was in danger. The Administration attempted to fix a legal status for the
operation outside the national debt without fully holding the highway cost
to a pay-as-you-go operation. The eventual financing method was a compromise in which Secretary Humphrey had a significant hand; to the end
of his service, he had a standing argument with his great friend Senator
Harry Flood Byrd of Virginia, chairman of the Senate Finance Committee
and principal foe of the original financing proposal, as to whether the interstate highway expenditures were part of the national debt.

> *Statement by Secretary Humphrey before the*
> *Sub-committee on Roads of the House Committee*
> *on Public Works.*
>
> *May 16, 1955*

... I should also like to call your attention to the fact that the bill
provides that the Secretary of the Treasury is responsible for the supervision of the borrowing program and all borrowing requires his consent. In this way, the borrowing of money can be harmonized with
Government fiscal, monetary and debt management policy. Within
limits, the timing of the borrowing can be subject to control and adjusted to varying conditions in the economic life of the country. Thus,
provision is made for best keeping any possible inflationary effects of
the program under control.

There are differences of opinion, of course, as to whether the corporate device should be used. I favor it in this case as a means of accomplishing the objectives set forth above. We have gone over this legislation very carefully and there is no question in my mind of the legality of the proposed corporation or of the proposed appropriation procedure.

In my view, the new highways will be earning assets, making possible a continuation of expansion in the use of motor transportation which would otherwise be seriously handicapped by the growing inadequacy of our highway network. You already know of the savings possible from improved safety, reduced time delays, greater vehicle efficiency, and lower repair and maintenance costs.

With respect to the principle of self-liquidation, there would be no general question about this program if it had been possible to pay for these roads by direct tolls. Such a plan, however, would encounter serious difficulties, particularly in sparsely populated areas. As a result the authors of this program looked for the nearest approach to it. Tolls can be measured by mileage traveled, vehicle weight, number of passengers, or number of axles. Also tolls can be measured by consumption of motor vehicle fuel. This practical way of doing it is included in H.R. 4260.

It seems to me there are persuasive arguments for considering the financing of this critical interstate system in terms of the total picture of the use of fuel by all of the nation's motor vehicles. The highways constructed will be available for the use of all such vehicles. This is not unlike the principle used generally by the states where gasoline taxes collected on the main roads help to pay for the other roads. And the heavy federal responsibility for improving the interstate system justifies using nationwide gasoline and diesel fuel taxes to pay for these roads.

It should be noted, moreover, that primary and secondary roads would be greatly improved under H.R. 4260. Authorizations would continue at the level of the 1954 Act, the highest in history. And increased federal payments on the expensive interstate mileage would release state funds for other roads. In other words, the mere inauguration of this program would have the effect in terms of road-miles of increasing federal aid for primary and secondary roads.

The borrowing under this program should be kept to a minimum.

I would raise no objection if the Congress increased the federal gasoline and diesel fuel taxes to help pay for this program. But, if pay-as-you-go financing is not feasible, then borrowing is clearly justified by our need for these roads now. Such borrowing must be related to user revenues. This is the right way to pay for roads and it will not impose an unfair burden on the general taxpayer.

H.R. 4260 quite properly establishes a debt limit for the bonds of the Federal Highway Corporation. Congress may wish to go a step further and revise the present definition of the debt limit to include these non-guaranteed highway bonds and other similar items now outside of the debt limit. The Treasury would have no objection to such action. The issuance of bonds by the Highway Corporation would provide a project basis for planning an improved highway system and would help ensure that highway borrowing is done on a self-liquidating basis.

There is probably no one on either side of the aisle, probably no thinking person in America, who does not know that the nation needs better highways. We need them for the daily business and safety of everyone. And we need them to help our defense should this nation ever be attacked by a foreign power. This being the case, I believe that men of good will and good intentions must be able to get together on a plan for starting these better highways—not on a small scale, and not just a little amount a year—but on a major scale, and right now. Every year, every month lost in having these extra miles of better highways means loss to our economy and so less better living for our citizens. It means loss of lives through loss of the safety these better highways would bring. It means loss of the best possible transportation of our defense equipment and evacuation of our people in the event of an enemy attack. . . .

If the nuclear bomb fell, what?

🖩 The preparedness tension was such in mid-1955 that the President undertook a physical rehearsal of protective moves and actions by the Government in case of attack on the United States; and, along with the other departments, the Treasury and Federal Reserve held a three-day "Bomb Emergency" meeting and drill, principally in Washington. The results were discussed by the Secretary.

Remarks by Secretary Humphrey at a press conference
following the Government's "Bomb Alert" rehearsal,
Treasury Department.

June 16, 1955

I think that this exercise that we have been through has been extremely worthwhile. I think that it has brought to the attention of everybody first the problem—and what a colossal problem it would be if it was carried out on the scale that was represented in this exercise.

Of course, they picked a very difficult one, and a tremendous amount of damage, for the purpose of posing a problem to see what could be done to raise all these questions.

From another point of view, it is equally beneficial, I think, what it has done is to have a large number of people whose responsibility it will be to meet the probems that such an emergency would raise, it had had them for three days thinking exclusively about these problems. . . .

So far as the Treasury itself is concerned, of course the first problem for the Treasury in a thing of this kind is to supply money, to get money around—cash—so that people can have some money to use.

You have got to divide the problem into two phases, when you stop to think about it.

The first thing is the phase of extreme catastrophe that occurs, and occurs quickly, and all the difficulties that arise from that extreme catastrophe.

And then the second part of it is, as you begin to get the thing in hand, to solve the immediate and catastrophic problems and begin to get back to work again.

Big as was this proposed disaster, this is a tremendous country, with tremendous potentialities, with tremendous power. There is a lot of this country that was not damaged, even though this problem showed great damage. There is great country left, and that has to go on, and would go on. And what we have to plan is, first, to meet the catastrophe, to take care of the injured and the wounded, to try to get food to the people that are refugees, to try to find shelter for them, to try to take care of them first.

Then, after that first phase is over with, then get the economy back and get the country functioning in all that tremendous part of the country that is left and ready to go.

The first thing to do was to find out how to get money to the refugees, how to get money to the man in the street, any time, whether the town is bombed or not.

The people in that town are, in the very first days, going to be trying to help the people in the towns that were bombed; all over the country you are going to have to try and ration out the money, to ration out food, and try to keep anybody from getting an undue share more than he is entitled to; to try to prevent hoarding, and to see that everybody is helped get over his first hurdle.

After that is done, then you have to try to get the economy back functioning, so that the country goes on in the normal way.

Now that is one of the great things, as we see it in the Treasury, as we try to lay out our plans, that in this country the people are used to being on their own, using their individual initiative, they are used to thinking for themselves and acting for themselves. . . .

Provided only that there is not hoarding; provided only that somebody does not get more than his share; to prevent anything of that kind, like profiteering and hoarding, getting more than your share, taking advantage. We have very severe penalties against that, to make it practically impossible for that to be done.

But in the banking system—for instance, this morning Mr. [W. Randolph] Burgess [Undersecretary of the Treasury] sat, while I was up at the other place, with the governors of the Federal Reserve Banks, and they went all over just what you would do with the banks open and with the banks closed, and just how they would handle the matter, and how we would issue orders under the President's direction that would ration out the money during the extreme period, and then get the banks back functioning, in the hands of the banks, so that the money would be forthcoming, so that the Federal Reserve and the Treasury combined could see that cash was distributed around the country where it was required, and people would have the money to buy the necessities of life and keep going.

Then later they could meet the payrolls, start up their plants, start to pay the people that were doing the work all around the country and the various places where work has to be done.

QUESTION. Mr. Secretary, could you give us some examples of what you mean by hoarding—somebody getting more than his share?

SEC. HUMPHREY. Yes. I could illustrate it very well. Suppose a man came in, during the first period, with $50,000 in bonds and said he wanted $50,000 in cash? He would be denied. We would give the banks authority to deny that. That is an extreme example, but it illustrates what I mean.

QUESTION. What banks? There ain't no banks.

SEC. HUMPHREY. Oh, yes, there will be a great many banks open in the country.

QUESTION. Oh, you mean outside the bombed-out cities?

SEC. HUMPHREY. Oh, yes. The banks that are open all over the country. And we have currency spread all over the country. We have had that for a long time—prepared for that sort of thing. We might have to move currency from Dallas to New York, or wherever it might be, so as to have currency around and available at the places where it would have to be used.

QUESTION. Would you apply that to the withdrawing of savings accounts?

SEC. HUMPHREY. That's right. Temporarily there would be a moratorium on all sorts of legal responsibilities and all sorts of legal obligations. Due dates would be passed and would be carried forward, and nobody would be in trouble because he couldn't meet a due date during this first emergency period.

Then gradually, that moratorium would be lifted, and gradually as we got functioning again, the normal processes would begin to take effect.

QUESTION. How much money would you insist—what limit would you put on the amount of money that an individual—

SEC. HUMPHREY. I think what we would try to do, just as soon as we possibly could, would be to put up to the individual banks the responsibility for talking to the man, to find out what his necessities were; whether a big payroll would be required; if he is a man running a grocery store, what he would need to buy to restore his shelves; or an individual, how much he would need. I don't think we could have any general rule. I think it would be left largely to the various places, with very severe penalties for overdoing it—very severe penalties on the bank for permitting it, so that no bank could connive with somebody and let them get more than they should have. . . .

QUESTION. Mr. Secretary, what would an attack like this cost the country in money?

SEC. HUMPHREY. Oh, I would have no way of knowing. It would be a colossal figure. The destruction of sixty-odd cities out of those actually bombed, and the loss of time. Couldn't estimate it.

QUESTION. Economically, could we take it?

SEC. HUMPHREY. I think we could. If you look at the country and see what is left and what a tremendous country this is, what a powerful country it is. There is no question in my mind at all that we could take it. Now, I am not in any way belittling the blow. It would be a terrible blow, but I think we would recover surprisingly rapidly.

QUESTION. How long do you think it would take us to recover?

SEC. HUMPHREY. That is a matter of degree. You are not going to recover at any one time. Gradually you are going to begin, first, to absorb these people, take care of people, a little at a time, look after them. And then you are going to begin to get plans here and there in operation in different parts of the country, particularly those that weren't bombed, they will get back first and then gradually begin to rebuild.

QUESTION. It is assumed that we could carry on the war?

SEC. HUMPHREY. I don't think there is any question about it. This blow is a blow that is directed at the civilian population of this country.

QUESTION. And the industrial complexes, too.

SEC. HUMPHREY. And the industrial complexes to a certain extent, but when you add it all up, we have got a tremendous lot of industrial complex left that would go on functioning and tend to rebuild and get back.

QUESTION. Have you looked at the problem of one of these bombed cities, supposing it is all vaporized, all its reserves burned up of Continental Illinois. Do your plans go into redressing in any way the loss of that, or are there permanent records of the reserves in those banks representing the assets of its depositors and which could somehow be recreated?

SEC. HUMPHREY. Oh, yes. I think that phase of this problem is the last phase. That—the phase of redress and all that is the last thing. That is after the country gets back and functioning. The last thing you are going to think about is redress.

QUESTION. I was thinking more in terms of getting business going, which requires credit?

SEC. HUMPHREY. That's right.

QUESTION. Couldn't the Federal Government conceivably make available a line of credit to a bombed-out Chase National, say, to advance credit to its depositors?

SEC. HUMPHREY. We will get credit lines established just as rapidly as the places are rebuilt, where people can live to have it.

QUESTION. You have such plans?

SEC. HUMPHREY. Indeed, you will be doing it in places that are not bombed, where it can be taken care of. We have it set up so that we can meet payrolls, of course. In rescue forces, if you take a group of men, 5,000 men, whatever it may be, into rescue, where they are working in rescue work, we can meet those payrolls and take care of them. We are set up to handle it, but with mobile equipment, and they will be made up and they can move forward.

QUESTION. Mr. Secretary, suppose an H-bomb hit Fort Knox and completely ruined its gold supply? What then?

SEC. HUMPHREY. I don't think that would be as serious immediately as it would be if it hit Youngstown, Ohio, or Pittsburgh. . . .

QUESTION. This is a hypothetical question. People have been asked to store food in their basements. Some people are actually thinking in terms of storing money. What would be your advice?

SEC. HUMPHREY. I don't think—I think that would be foolish, myself. I think that we can get a sufficient amount of cash to put around the country so that barring a comparatively few days there will be cash available for those who are entitled to get it.

QUESTION. What will you do, put it in trucks?

Sec. Humphrey. Put it in trucks, with a military escort, and move it around from one place to another, wherever it is required.

Question. What is the emergency reserves, that is, roughly, for this purpose?

Sec. Humphrey. I don't believe I can tell you exactly what it is. But the reserve that is left, I will tell you this: The reserve that is left in places that we can get at, after the damage is inflicted, is sufficient to take care of the operation of this country for quite a period of time, without any new money being printed or made, or coined, in the mints, for quite a period of time, if we can get it moved and transported around to places where it is required.

The "middle way" for farmer support

Speech by Secretary Humphrey to the National Grange in convention at Public Music Hall, Cleveland.

November 19, 1955

The unequaled present prosperity of America, except in agriculture, is well known to us all. We have set new records in almost every way in which good times can be judged and measured. Employment reached 65.5 million for the first time in history. Unemployment has declined to 2.1 million. And at the same time there has been an Eisenhower "extra" for the benefit of all Americans. This Eisenhower extra has been created in this sound way. The fact that there has been practically no change in the cost of living since this Administration has been in office means that the wage-earners of America have now been getting real wage increases instead of the "cost of living" wage increases which had previously been the order of the day. So they have more money to spend for food, for better living, for the products of both farm and factory than ever before in history.

Who wants to go back? Now, what about more freedom for the farmer?

The other day I received a letter from a midwestern farmer's wife in which she said: "I see by the papers that you made a speech asking, 'who wants to go back?' If you talked to some of the farmers, as well as the farm machinery people, in this area you would very soon find out who wants to go back."

I have thought a great deal about what that good farm lady wrote. I sense in it all the concern and anxiety of a farm family that is experiencing the squeeze of declining selling prices and the rise in some prices of the things they buy. I think I can understand a little of the puzzlement and concern that beset her. Why shouldn't she and her family be sharing more equitably in the country's unprecedented good times?

Yet I wonder if she and her family—and the farm families of America generally—really want to go back.

The peak of farm prices was in February, 1951. That was during the war in Korea. I doubt very much that anyone wants to go back to those high prices based on war. I do not believe that this farmer's wife nor anyone else wants that with all its heartache and suffering and fear for every family. Yet substantially less than half of the decline in farm prices has occurred since the end of that war.

What she wants, and what this Administration wants for her, is to share more equally with other Americans in the abundance we as a nation are enjoying. She is proud of the work that she and her family do to help provide the food and fiber needs of our country. She feels that somehow this basic part of the economy is not in step with prospering America.

She is right. But does she want to go back to the discredited program that built up the huge price-depressing surpluses which today deny our farmers better returns for what they produce? Does she want to go back to a program from which today a majority of our farmers are reaping not benefits but injury?

Does she want to go back to a program that can only perpetuate and make worse all her present difficulties? Does she want to go down that dead-end road of Government regimentation of our independent farm folk which is the sure end result of that old program? I doubt she wants to go back to that old road.

These price-depressing surpluses operate in agriculture as they would in any other industry. Imagine the situation if a whole year's production of automobiles was in storage around the country in Government stockpiles. Or if there were millions of Government-owned radio or television sets or refrigerators in Government storage. These surpluses overhanging the markets would certainly demoralize them, and it is impossible to imagine our present prosperity in those lines under such conditions.

So, too, today our agricultural surpluses plague the path ahead to a fair break for our farmers. We must stop adding to those surpluses and we must work at cutting them down.

After Korea and subsequent cutbacks in defense spending, the industrial side of our economy went through a readjustment. Reduced production, particularly in heavy industry began in 1953 and continued during a considerable part of 1954 as the inventory of excess goods stimulated by the Korean War was being absorbed by sales in excess of production. It was during this period that the false prophets of doom and gloom cried loudest of coming depression and despair. But as the excess supplies were used up, production and employment began to pick up and the industrial side of our economy began the movement toward its present record prosperity.

America's agriculture is still in its postwar adjustment, slowed down by wartime rigid supports and ever-increasing Government surplus stockpiles which have made the process even more difficult and drawn out because of the restricted ability of agriculture to bring production into line with changing demands.

There is no easy solution, but there is only one objective that will ever wholly succeed. Production must ultimately become reasonably balanced with demand and those overhanging price-depressing, increasing surpluses must be absorbed and ultimately disposed of.

Surely continuation of the plan that got us into all this trouble is not the answer.

While we still press forward to gain our place in world markets, it is obvious that wholesale dumping indiscriminately abroad is no answer. That would be not only distressing to our foreign relations with friendly nations with whom we are joined for our common defense, but it would surely result in retaliation by other countries and price wars with the prospect of ruinous prices and competition that would greatly limit our sales. So the whole thing would be worse than useless in moving the surplus crops.

The middle way is the solution. Price supports that recognize the natural laws of supply and demand and do not try futilely to repeal them. Carefully planned restriction of production. Expanded programs of research to find new crops and new uses to aid agriculture. Cautious selling of surpluses both at home and abroad with strenuous efforts continuously made to increase consumption everywhere. All coupled with a dynamic program of soil conservation and improvement of our farm lands for future generations.

The growth of our population will be of tremendous help. Three million more mouths to feed each year will eat into both limited current production and surplus at an amazing rate as time goes on. Our increasing scale of living means that 166 million of us will all eat more and better as each year passes by. Our growing industry with its continuously increasing jobs to be filled will continue to offer good opportunities for farm boys and girls to work in industry if they choose to do so rather than raising more cotton and wheat than can be consumed.

The farmer is equally interested with all the rest of us in prosperity for industry. Its workers are his customers. The more they earn, the more of his crops they can buy. And the more industry advances in its techniques and inventions the better and more effective tools for farming will be available for him to have. We are all bound together. It is not always evenly balanced, but that is the objective we must always strive to attain.

One fact we should never forget: This transition has been helped because the industrial economy has been operating at high levels. We must keep it so. Meanwhile, we must continuously adopt and apply the most effective means to cushion the hardships and ease the strains of the transition for the people on the farms. We must do this while we continue to make progress toward our true objective of a balanced farm economy, unhampered by excessive stocks of crops which destroy the very markets they were created in false hope to help.

President Eisenhower said after his recent meeting in Denver with Secretary Benson that "no problem on the domestic front is more demanding of our understanding and best ideas" than that facing our farmers. The President's great concern is illustrated by the fact that this agricultural statement was his first personal statement on a domestic matter issued from his hospital bed in Denver.

In it the President cited the need for "new steps" to deal with the farm problem so as "to speed the time when farm production and markets are in balance at prices that return to our farmers a fair share of the national income." I can assure you that there is the fullest realization at the highest levels of the Administration not only of the tremendous importance of our farm people to the welfare of the whole nation and national policies but also of the need to help farm people share more fully in the expanding prosperity which the rest of the economy enjoys. . . .

We must go forward, building on the foundation already laid, to hasten the transition to a better day for farming and better returns for farmers. This means a many-sided program designed to cut down the surpluses, adjust production to markets, expand markets at home and abroad, and spur research into new uses of farm products.

There are two related matters to which the Administration has been giving a great deal of earnest attention recently which are of interest to you.

First, I should like to mention the Treasury's position in regard to taxation of co-operatives. We made a written suggestion to the Congress on this subject last July which I recommend you read. It has been charged by some critics that we desire to tax accumulated savings first at the corporate rate in the hands of the co-operative and later to re-tax the same savings in the hands of the patrons of co-operatives as income to the individual. This is not true. The Treasury does not favor double taxation. We are interested only in obtaining a means of taxing the income of a co-operative as income either to the co-operative or to the individual wherever the income is held but not to tax at both levels. That is only fair and proper. It is to the end only of effectively providing that single tax, such as we envisioned by the Act of Congress in 1951, that we have suggested to the Congress that action might properly be considered.

Second, I should like to touch upon the Cabinet report on transportation which I know is of interest to you because of the Grange's role in getting the Interstate Commerce Commission originally established to check transportation monopoly many years ago. The main point of the Cabinet report was that all forms of transportation be allowed more freedom to voluntarily compete so that all the American public might have the best transportation as cheaply as possible. Needed safeguards would not be relinquished as freedom increased.

I am no expert on agriculture and I am conscious of being in the presence of experts. But I am sure that Secretary Benson is a true and devoted friend of the farmer, with the wisdom and the courage to do whatever is soundly required. And I know that in his intensive scrutiny of new ideas for strengthening the present program, Ezra Benson is seeking help from every farmer and every true friend of farmers. In that search he has the full support and interest of the whole Administration. Only the best efforts and the best ideas of all of us will be good enough....

Pay-as-you-build for highways

Statement by Secretary Humphrey before the
Senate Finance Committee. Senator Harry F. Byrd,
presiding.

May 17, 1956

... Improved highway transportation is one of the great necessities of our times. A large part of our commerce and industry depends upon it. Our farms require it. The jobs of millions of men and women in this country depend upon it. The further growth of the great auto industry and all the ramifications in the use of steel, fuel, rubber, and thousands of products from hundreds of sources cannot continue to develop unless our highway transportation is developed concurrently. The Treasury is prepared to lend the fullest support to the deliberations of your committee and the Congress to the end that a highway program which all Americans need and want may be realized.

H.R. 10660 has been referred to as a pay-as-you-build program. I heartily endorse this policy of highway financing. But I want to point out to you two important respects in which the revenue features of this proposed program fall short of the actual pay-as-you build principle.

The bill as passed by the House showed an estimated balance between expenditures and tax receipts at the end of the 16-year period ending in 1972. However, after an initial three years with excess receipts over expenditures, there would be ten successive years with an excess of expenditures over receipts, with annual deficiencies of from $500 million to $800 million in most of these years. The cumulative deficiency in the trust fund would begin in the sixth year—1962, and would exceed $4,700 million by 1969. This would be made good only in the last three years (1970, 1971, 1972). Furthermore, in striking this balance under the House bill, no provision was made during these last three years for regular allocation of funds to the primary, secondary, and urban road programs and expenditures for them would be limited to the unexpended balance of prior allocations with some purely arbitrary additions until the last year when any excess over the full amount required for reimbursement of the interstate deficiency would be available for the primary, secondary, and urban programs. This would leave an estimated deficiency in this latter program of approximately $1,450 million as compared with continuing the regular allocations to this program.

For ten full years these large deficits would be a charge on the general budget. This discrepancy in timing contradicts an essential part of a real pay-as-you-build program.

The substitute authorizations for expenditures made by the Senate Public Works Committee change the total amounts and annual pattern of expenditures somewhat, but they would produce the same sort of interim deficits. You will note on the first two tables which you have received the estimates of expenditures, receipts, and the condition of the trust fund under the House bill and under the alternative expenditure program of your Senate Public Works Committee. To maintain comparability, the authorization for the primary, secondary, and urban road programs in the alternative plan have been assumed to be continued at $900 million annually beyond 1961, as actually authorized, through 1969, the period of authorization of increasing annual authorizations under the House bill, thus providing about the same total amount for this program in each bill. Also, to maintain comparability, the estimated excess of receipts over the amount needed to reimburse the deficiency in the trust fund at the end of the entire period has been allocated to the primary, secondary, and urban program, as was done under the House bill.

You will note from the two tables that there are very few discrepancies between the two bills; the discrepancies are very minor. The expenditures under the Senate program are based upon the cost of a

40,000 mile Interstate System, and this is one of the principal differences between the two bills. No provision is made in either bill for the cost of the additional 2,500 miles of interstate roads authorized in the Senate program since the routes have not even been specified. In other words, the House program is 40,000 miles, and the finances are based on that and the Senate bill provides the same finances, to all intents and purposes, but adds on this system 2,500 miles for which no money is provided at all.

If the cost of these additional miles were equal to the average costs of the 40,000 designated miles, the total costs of the Interstate System as proposed in the Senate bill would be increased by about $1.7 billion.

To eliminate the prospective deficits under either the House bill or the alternate Senate plan, I urge that the bill be amended to permit allocation of funds to be so timed that the estimated expenditures from the allocations will not exceed the estimated available amounts in the trust funds. With this change, the program could be kept from being a charge on the regular budget. It could then be made, from this standpoint, a true pay-as-you-build program and whenever annual allocations were desired which would exceed the amount of funds that would be then currently available in the trust fund, the Congress could promptly provide adequate additional taxes to cover the estimated deficit.

I am taking it for granted, gentlemen, that you all have in mind that the receipts go into a trust fund, and the expenditures for the roads are paid out of the trust fund under both bills. The system is that the taxes will be allocated to the trust fund as collected, and then the payment will be made out of the trust fund. . . . Now the second departure from a real pay-as-you-build program comes from the dedication to the highway trust fund of the existing excise taxes on tires and tubes and three-eighths of the existing 8 per cent on trucks and busses, beginning in the fiscal year 1958. The estimated annual amounts start at about $275 million and rise to almost $400 million, with a total of about $5 billion through 1972. This diversion of excise taxes which have always been regarded as part of the general revenues means that these amounts must be made up in the general budget by new taxes or by a continuation of old taxes which might otherwise be reduced. It thereby would become the equivalent of a special tax diversion in lieu of a general tax reduction for all taxpayers that might otherwise be possible.

The dedication of the existing gasoline and diesel fuel taxes is reasonable because they have come to be regarded as available for highway expenditures, and in recent years the regular highway program has been based on them. But the tire, tube, truck and bus taxes are included in our regular excise tax program and have always been considered as part of the general revenue, along with all the other manufacturer's excise taxes. Their diversion to pay for highways is not really consistent with pay-as-you-build financing, and deflects our general revenue receipts. . . .

The Treasury Department did not make any specific tax recommendations to the House Ways & Means Committee. The new taxes included in H.R. 10660 are thus neither in accord with nor contrary to any recommendations of the Treasury, but I will take this opportunity to say that we have no objection to any of the proposed new taxes.

The Treasury Department will be glad to provide such information and other assistance as we can to this committee in its consideration of highway financing. In conclusion I repeat my strong endorsement of a national highway program, financed on a real pay-as-you-build basis. And I especially commend and urge you to adopt the amendment suggested to balance annual allocations with estimated receipts to be currently available in the fund.

Now, the purpose of that recommendation and my urging you to adopt it is this, that only in that way will this quickly and adequately become a real pay-as-you-build program, because if you adopt that amendment then as the allocations are made you would see immediately where the deficits in the funds are going to come, and that you want to allocate more than the fund will have money to provide and pay for, and therefore, the matter will be immediately raised for Congressional consideration as to the imposition as to whatever additional taxes are required to keep the fund solvent currently all during the period, and you will not run into these big deficits that appear as the bill is now drawn. . . .

There is another matter, in connection with the Gore Bill as substituted for the House bill that I think should be brought to your attention. In the House bill there were 40,000 miles of road laid out of a certain design and the financing and allocation was provided to build those roads as shown on a map. Now, in the Senate bill the allocation is proposed on a different basis. It is proposed on the basis of population and finances and so forth, rather than on this program. It is perfectly obvious that if, through a change in the allocations, it results in the adoption of a different road program, that your finances are going to be entirely out of kilter. And that, of course, would be the fact.

So that the allocations in the Gore Bill should be changed to correspond with the program as adopted in the House bill or else we will have to make up a whole new financial program, because the program, the financial program, is tied to the road program as defined in the House bill, not as defined in the Gore Bill. . . .

As I said, Mr. Chairman, you have to take this clause, this whole clause of declaration of policy. "It is hereby declared to be the policy of the Congress that if it hereafter appears:

"(1) That the total receipts of the trust fund (exclusive of advances under subsection (d) will be less than the total expenditures from such fund) exclusive of repayments of such advances; or

"(2) That the distribution of the tax burden among the various classes of persons using the federal-aid highways or otherwise deriving benefit from such highways is not equitable—"
that then the Congress shall enact legislation in order to bring about the balance between the two.

Only in that way can you have a pay-as-you-go tax program.

Cross-examination of Secretary Humphrey

THE CHAIRMAN. It seems to me that that indicates that Congress shall enact legislation to bring about a balance of total receipts and total expenditures.

SEC. HUMPHREY. That is what they say here. But, you see, the difficulty—the reason why this isn't a pay-as-you-go bill because this is, as I tried to point out in my statement they have proposed a bill which, if we eliminate the question Senator Kerr raised of the taking of certain funds which are now going into general revenues, just eliminate that for a minute, then the taxes as proposed in the House bill will provide, according to these estimates, the total number of dollars that will be expended under the House road-building program.

But the difficulty is, it is that it doesn't do it annually and that you run ahead for about three or four years and then you run behind until you run up to a $5 billion deficit, or almost, $4.7 billion deficit in one year before you begin to catch up in the latter years.

So that you do not have a balanced program continuously.

What I am suggesting is that this would be amended to provide that the funds—either you wouldn't spend the money faster than you get it into the fund, or if you wanted to spend it faster, you would provide for getting more money in there faster so that the fund would be continually balanced.

THE CHAIRMAN. I understood from your statement that at the end of 1969 there would be a total deficit of $4.7 billion of expenditures over receipts.

SEC. HUMPHREY. That is an accumulated deficit that arises from the fact, as I say, that you allocate your expenditures faster than you get in your money, and if you allocate your expenditures faster than you get your money in for all these years, then you have no allocations in the last three years, and the money comes in to pay up the deficit; that is the way it is estimated. . . .

SENATOR EDWARD MARTIN (Pennsylvania). As I understand it, Mr. Chairman, we have got a construction period of 13 years and a financial period of 16.

SEC. HUMPHREY. That is right and in the meantime, you are running a deficit that has got to come out of the current Treasury to the tune of nearly $5 billion. And in addition to that, as Senator Kerr points out, you have taken another $5 billion that we now are using for general revenues and allocated them to this trust fund. So that the general revenues will be headed for a cumulative effect of $10 billion in this process. . . .

SENATOR JOHN J. WILLIAMS (Delaware). How would they pay for them? Would the Treasury be obligated to put the money in this trust fund to make up the deficit?

SEC. HUMPHREY. I know of no other place it could come from. . . . Frankly, I think that is a lawyer's question. The bill clearly contemplates it. Now, whether it carries the legal authority or not—

SENATOR ROBERT S. KERR (Oklahoma). If you read to page 71, line

18, to section (d), you find provision made there for such sums as have not been taken care of by the appropriations provided for between line 3 on page 69 and including line 17 on page 71, if you would read that, sir.

SEC. HUMPHREY (reading). "There are hereby authorized to be appropriated to the trust fund, as repayable advances, such additional funds as may be required to make the expenditures referred to in subsection (f)." That is the clear intent.

SENATOR KERR. That is an authorization, and would have to be implemented by an actual appropriation by the Congress. . . .

SENATOR MARTIN. This is just an authorization, like Congress authorizes the construction of a bridge across a river, then it takes an appropriation by the Congress in addition.

SEC. HUMPHREY. Frankly, gentlemen, you are getting into an awful hole on that basis, because the contract has practically been let.

THE CHAIRMAN. Your proposal is to limit the expenditures to the actual receipts?

SEC. HUMPHREY. If you adopt the suggestion I make there is no question about it at all.

THE CHAIRMAN. Suppose there is an obligation, you wouldn't limit the obligations?

SEC. HUMPHREY. I would limit the obligations they make to the amount of money available.

THE CHAIRMAN. But it would seem to me the obligations would have to be made two years or a year in advance.

SEC. HUMPHREY. I think that would be the procedure; it would be to come to you ahead of time and say, "Here is an allocation that we have to make, we are going to be a billion dollars short,"—or $500 million short or whatever it may be—"we require more money in the fund to make this allocation in the next three years." And in the light of that you can make such additional appropriations as will be required to meet it. I think there is a lot of sense in that, for this reason. When you undertake to estimate how much travel there is going to be, how many automobiles there are going to be, and how many people are going to use them, and how much gasoline is going to be used, and tires used, and all that, for 16 years, you are going out on a long, long limb, and I wouldn't be prepared to say that these figures were anywhere near right. They are just as right as we can make them, but 16 years is a long time and a lot of things happen. . . .

THE CHAIRMAN. Just one more question. It is not clear to me—on page 71, for example, you seem to take a certain per cent of the taxes and put the revenue in the trust fund. You take 100 per cent of the taxes on diesel fuel and special motor fuels and 20 per cent of the tax under section 4061, the tax on trucks, busses and so forth, and 37½ per cent of the tax on tires. What was that?

SEC. HUMPHREY. Well, these lesser percentages are the difference between the existing excise taxes and the estimated figure they might go to, and they maintain the existing tax right straight through and take the difference and put it in this form.

THE CHAIRMAN. In other words, revenue from existing taxes continues to go to the general fund?

SEC. HUMPHREY. That is right.

THE CHAIRMAN. I understood that you surrendered $300 million of existing taxes to this trust fund; is that correct?

SEC. HUMPHREY. Well, I was defeated, let's put it that way. . . . To be perfectly frank about it, I surrendered, for the reason I just stated, these taxes. But I only surrendered on the ground that they would include the amendment that I suggested, that was the basis of it, that I think these estimates may be too much, they may be little. And it seems to me that rather than try to judge ten years ahead of today what you ought to have, that if they approximated, as they did here, that then it would be incumbent upon them not to spend the money, or to get the additional money, that would be fairer for everybody concerned, to get the additional money rather than try to forecast ten or fifteen years ahead.

THE CHAIRMAN. How much of the present taxes now being collected and now going into that general fund will go into the trust fund?

SEC. HUMPHREY. $5 billion.

THE CHAIRMAN. A 16-year period?

SEC. HUMPHREY. That is correct. . . .

SENATOR EUGENE D. MILLIKIN (Colorado). We have additional provisions in the Senate bill to lengthen the mileage. You pointed out in your earlier testimony that that made some complications. What is your suggested amendment to overcome these complications?

SEC. HUMPHREY. I think this amendment that I have already suggested would take care of that, because it would mean by adding that amount of additional road that your deficits would just accumulate that much faster, that is all, and therefore automatically you would come to a deficit sooner, and of a little larger amount that you would have to provide some new tax for as it came along, if you see what I mean. . . .

THE CHAIRMAN. The general fund is losing the excess only on the gasoline and diesel fuel taxes?

SEC. HUMPHREY. That is right.

THE CHAIRMAN. The income has been in excess of expenditures on roads?

SEC. HUMPHREY. That is correct. We lose that. In fact, with the increased expenditures, the continually increasing expenditures for highways and matching funds, that was a "gone goose" anyway so far as the Treasury was concerned. We weren't going to get much more of that under any circumstances. . . . But the other $5 billion, that is all money that otherwise we would expect to have.

SENATOR KERR. What do you think is the significance of the language on page 68 of the bill, the portion read to you by the chairman at line 13: "It is hereby declared to be the policy of the Congress that it hereafter appears that the total receipts of the trust fund will be less than the total expenditures of such trust fund, Congress shall enact such legislation to bring about a balance of total receipts and total expenditures," such equitable distribution as the case may be.

SEC. HUMPHREY. I think the significance, Senator, is that this is designed to be a pay-for-itself legislation.

SENATOR KERR. Doesn't that in reality declare the policy to be that Congress will enact whatever legislation is necessary to bring about a balance between receipts and expenditures?

SEC. HUMPHREY. That is what it is. But that is over 16 years. Now, the thing I am suggesting is that it should be annually, you see.

SENATOR KERR. Does it say that?

SEC. HUMPHREY. No, that is the way I read it, it is the total expenditures and total receipts. And that is, as I take it, 16 years. Now, if it is annual, then it is exactly what I want. But I would just like to have it with no question about it at all. . . .

SENATOR KERR. Now, you have said, Mr. Secretary, that the bill before us would create a deficit of $5 billion at a certain point in the program.

SEC. HUMPHREY. If carried out.

SENATOR KERR. And what I am calling to your attention is that, in my judgment, your statement is in error for the very simple reason that there is no specific authorization or appropriation here that would produce that result.

SEC. HUMPHREY. Well, as I say, I won't take any—I can't question the technicality of whether it takes another act or whether it doesn't.

SENATOR KERR. You don't have the slightest doubt about what it does, do you?

SEC. HUMPHREY. The intention of this bill is that these things will be done in this way, and they will lead to these results that I have given you.

SENATOR KERR. Is that binding on any future Congress?

SEC. HUMPHREY. I don't know that anything is binding. I think any future Congress can repeal the whole thing if they wanted.

SENATOR KERR. But is that binding on any future Congress?

SEC. HUMPHREY. I don't know of any law that any Congress can pass that will hold the next one if they want to void it. . . . If Congress is expressing an intent that is going to take a lot of money out of the Treasury, I want to come up here and see that intent is qualified so that they don't intend to do it.

SENATOR KERR. If this Congress expresses a policy that it hopes will be carried out, you want it then to do something which you have just said it can't do, and that is to fix it so a future Congress would be compelled to provide the money if it carried out the intent.

SEC. HUMPHREY. No, I didn't say that, Senator, at all. I said that they could not make appropriations that would exceed the fund, that is all. I don't want them to be authorized to be making allocations that will exceed the money they have got to pay for it.

SENATOR WALLACE F. BENNETT (Vermont). Mr. Chairman, may I refer my colleague from Oklahoma to section 108, which is on page 12, the House section of the bill, which contains specific authorizations for the Interstate System through the year 1969.

SENATOR KERR. The Senator is eminently correct. But the authorizations for the Interstate System for the 13 years, plus the specific authorizations for the primary, urban, and secondary systems through either of the two years in the House, or the five years in the Senate bill, will not create the deficit indicated by the Secretary. . . . They are not self-reenacting, and in order to be the intent, as the Secretary suggested, they will have to be as the result of future authorizations by the Congress. . . .

SEC. HUMPHREY. Let me just put it this way, Senator. If you build these roads you are going to run a deficit, and you want to have the money to pay for them currently.

SENATOR KERR. The Secretary is probably correct. I have a great respect for his ability to see in the future. It probably is greater than that of the Senator from Oklahoma. But neither of them is infallible.

SEC. HUMPHREY. And that is why I would like it fixed so that if we are not infallible we will get the money before we spend it.

SENATOR WILLIAMS. And, if I understand your suggestion, sir, it is that, while you recognize that this Congress cannot bind future Congresses, that to the extent that we bind a future Congress to appropriate the money, you want us to bind the future Congress to raise the money; is that correct?

SEC. HUMPHREY. That is exactly correct, Senator; that you have the same intent both ways. That you intend to collect the money to pay for your spending.

SENATOR KERR. The bill before us a year ago would have involved the issuance of $25 or $30 billion in bonds, wouldn't it?

SEC. HUMPHREY. Something like that.

THE CHAIRMAN. Twenty-one.

SEC. HUMPHREY. Twenty-one, was it?

SENATOR KERR. It would have involved a continuing deficit of $20 billion in the Treasury.

SEC. HUMPHREY. Just frankly, now, if you want to discuss that, I would suggest that I read it and come back. When that was killed a year ago I forgot it, and it is gone, as far as I am concerned. If you want me to say this is a better bill than that, I will say it gladly, this is a better bill than that. But I still don't think it is good enough. . . .

SENATOR RUSSELL B. LONG (Louisiana). We have provided a lot of tax reductions in the last several years—you have recommended them, and I have voted for them. I have always felt that we ought to do something for some people that were left out. It seemed to me that about as many people were left out as were helped—

SEC. HUMPHREY. That is one of the reasons, Senator, why I think you would feel a little squeamish about this, because what you are doing is taking $5 million and putting it here to keep you from giving $5 million to the very people you are talking about. . . .

SENATOR LONG. The question that is in my mind is whether we should increase these taxes on highway users when the highways users are already paying enough taxes to pay for all the highways. In other words, if we would just go ahead and earmark the taxes on automobiles in addition to the taxes that we are earmarking on gasoline, and let all the user taxes, all the excise taxes on highway users, go to the highways, we would have enough money for this program.

SEC. HUMPHREY. I haven't made the calculation, but I am sure you could divert enough from the funds we are now collecting to the trust fund, so that the trust fund would be intact; that is just a matter of picking out what would do it, and that is a matter of arithmetic.

But if you divert those funds to it, then you have got to make up the deficit in other funds. In other words, if you move it from here to here, your deficit, instead of being here, is over here—it is just that simple.

SENATOR LONG. I can suggest to you taxes I believe your staff is well familiar with—excise taxes on highway users that would more than pay for this program. You would get a billion dollars from your gasoline tax, as it stands today. As I understand it, you get about a billion dollars from your excise tax on automobiles.

There is about $500 million, if I recall correctly, involved in your tax on tires, tubes, diesel fuels, and automobile accessories. That runs up to a total of roughly $2,900 million. That is all you need for this program.

As far as money is concerned, there is no year immediately facing us when you are going to need more than $2.5 billion, so far as making the users pay for the highways, they are already paying for the highways. The question is whether you want those users to help us balance the budget.

SEC. HUMPHREY. If you want to move those taxes over for this purpose, if you make that suggestion, then you will also have to make the suggestion contemporaneously as to what new taxes we put on to make up—to fill the hole you have just dug for us. . . .

SENATOR LONG. The time you get through refinancing these bonds, it is going to be a lot more than $14,800 million. That is where you can save some money.

SEC. HUMPHREY. If you will buy the bonds at the lower rate, we will be glad to sell them to you.

SENATOR LONG. If you will ask the Federal Reserve to engage in some open operations to buy the bonds when the bankers hold them back on you, I don't think you will have any difficulty selling them. As I recall, you had a great deal of difficulty with that interest rate before the Federal Reserve started to go back into the open market.

SEC. HUMPHREY. Mr. Long, I think this hardly the right place to discuss the policy that your party pursued for a great number of years, and finally found to your satisfaction that it wouldn't work, so you abandoned it about a year and a half before we got here.

SENATOR LONG. Once the Truman Administration undertook to let these interest rates go on up—you sure went them one better, I will have to give you credit for that. . . . Are you really in sympathy with this last increase in interest rate that the Federal Reserve Board has passed on?

SEC. HUMPHREY. That is a long story. I don't know whether you want to take the time to go into it in detail at this meeting or not. I would be glad to do it. . . . Under the law, the Federal Reserve Board is an independent agency. There is a great school of thought in the world, based on long experience, that central banks should be independent of current administrative processes, that it works better for the finances of the country over a long period of time.

Because of that, Senator Glass proposed in the original Federal Reserve Act that there be an independence in action of the Board, and it has obtained ever since, and it is still the law.

Now, I believe that a close cooperation, and an interchange of ideas and thoughts, as between the different departments of the Government, the different branches of the Government, is a very desirable thing, in order that, when a department is independent—and most of them are independent in certain fields—that before they take independent action they should have the benefit of consultation with the other departments of the Government and the varying views of the other people.

Fortunately, the present members of the Federal Reserve Board have that same feeling. The result is that, since we have been here, we had a period, as you will well recall, before we came, when the Federal Reserve Board and the Treasury were at outs, and there was such a battle that it finally got to the White House for decision, and it disturbed a lot of conditions.

We have attempted not to have that happen again, because it isn't good for the country.

So that, we have been very careful, and we both believe that we should consult with each other and have the benefit of each other's views in all the actions that either of us take that will affect the economy.

We visit right along, Martin comes over for lunch every Monday to the Treasury, I go to the Federal Reserve Board quite frequently, and one of us, either Randolph Burgess or I, go over there every week, and we meet several times between.

Now, in looking ahead, and in trying to gage what economic conditions are going to be, and what the demands of the economy for money and credit are going to be, and what the demands for people and employment are going to be, to keep jobs going, to keep plenty of jobs, as many jobs as we can have, and to keep things on an even keel as well as we can, and to keep prices from running away and getting into an inflationary period which robs the people of their money, we meet together and discuss all sorts of things that bear on those conditions in the future.

Now, Senator Kerr has just brought out how difficult it is for anybody to gage the future, and in these discussions that we have, we very often differ in our views as to the weight to be given to certain inflationary forces or certain deflationary forces or acts here or acts later.

What we do—what we try to do is, we give them the very best estimates we can make of the effective weights and the time of the events in the future, the pressures that will be forthcoming in a few weeks, months, a year hence, inflationary pressures or deflationary pressures, so that we can have our views in their minds when they come to take their action. And they, in turn, give us the benefits of their views.

SENATOR LONG. All I wanted to know was whether you agree with their decisions or not, is what I really wanted to know.

SEC. HUMPHREY. I felt this last time; if it had been my responsibility,

I would not have made this last move—all the others, but this last one might have been postponed, and natural conditions might have taken care of it. Whether I am right or wrong, I don't know.

SENATOR LONG. It places the situation in this perspective. The Federal Reserve is created by an act of Congress. The members of that Board are appointed by the President; they are confirmed by the Senate; and their responsibility is to carry out congressional directives.

They have certain policy decisions to make, but I regard it as the responsibility of the President, and also the responsibility of the Congress, to see how the Federal Reserve Board administers the power delegated to it by the Congress. . . .

Now, here are policies being adopted by the Federal Reserve Board, which look to me like they mean about an increase of one-half of 1 per cent in the national debt. By the time you get through refinancing these things, they jump up to $1.5 billion, with an increase in the cost of the Federal debt.

With the responsibility you have indicated of wanting to have a balanced budget—

SEC. HUMPHREY. Of course, it will take you 40 years to get that.

SENATOR LONG. To get that, you would have to have a few 30-year bond issues, but I believe most of them are shorter.

SEC. HUMPHREY. Yes.

SENATOR LONG. It wouldn't take too long to run it up to a billion or $2 billion; in my tabulations, it is already up to $14 million. And it seems to be just like a dog trying to chase its tail, to raise the gasoline tax and try to balance the budget, when the Federal Reserve Board raises interest rates, and it is going to cost a lot more than these taxes will bring out.

SEC. HUMPHREY. I think one phase of this you left out of your consideration. You are raising some very broad and very sweeping questions here.

If—I say "if," because I don't know—but if inflationary pressures were such that without this action of the Federal Reserve Board we would have moved into a pricing inflation, and we moved further into it, it would be only a very short time, a very small move in a general level of prices, that would wipe out many times the amount you are talking about in the cost of operation of the Government, in the cost of building the roads, and the cost of living of all the people.

Now, I think it is a whole lot more important to have in mind the cost of living of all the people, and the price levels in this country. We have been extremely fortunate. We have gone through three years here, nearly four, of an extremely steady price level, the longest period ever in the history of this country of price stability.

Now, that means more to a 160 million people than any little quarter of a per cent in the interest rate. And if one helps to accomplish the other, if that is the effect, then you are repaid many, many times. . . .

SENATOR WILLIAMS. Mr. Secretary, you stated that under your Administration the cost of living has been stable for the longest period of time. Now, in this preceding year, just immediately prior to this Administration, when we had this low interest rate that the Senator from Louisiana is boasting about, what happened to the cost of living during those years? Do you have those statistics?

SEC. HUMPHREY. The dollar went from 100 to 50 cents.

SENATOR WILLIAMS. In other words, it was cut to half?

SEC. HUMPHREY. Yes.

SENATOR WILLIAMS. What would that amount to in dollars and cents to the American people?

SEC. HUMPHREY. Hundreds of millions of dollars.

That is one of the principal reasons why we have got this terrific debt—there was no reason to have this debt, except that we ran the price of everything we bought so high by blacking the dollar out. It would have been very much less if the advice of your chairman and a lot of others had been followed.

SENATOR LONG. Do you think that high interest rates would have prevented—if you changed two or three times the interest rate during the war, do you think that would have prevented the cost of living from going up?

SEC. HUMPHREY. Senator Long, there is no proof of a pudding like the eating. I saw what happened under the policy that you adopted, I have seen what happened under the policy that we have adopted. And so, as far as I am concerned, I would rather have the results that we have had in the last three years. . . .

✍ One of the most significant of the Secretary's statements, close to the end of the cross-examination, is his defense of the independence of the

Federal Reserve System and Board—a matter he was quizzed about by a number of Democratic members of Congress on frequent random occasions. Independence of the Government in the "Fed's" fixing of interest rates and use of the curb of higher interest rates to hold down inflation and help stabilize the dollar were most important principles to Secretary Humphrey. This is the most extended statement he made on the Federal Reserve relationship.

Item veto for the President

Statement by Secretary Humphrey before the House Judiciary Committee.

May 27, 1957

I appreciate this opportunity to appear before you to testify on H. J. Res. 47, introduced by Congressman Kenneth B. Keating. This resolution proposes an amendment to the Constitution by which Congress would be authorized to give the President the power to veto individual items of appropriation bills.

A problem of major concern to the Congress and this Administration at present is that of keeping federal expenditures under control and of seeing to it that the dollars spent by the Federal Government are well spent. I believe that this proposal which you have under consideration would help materially in this effort. ...

Under the Constitution the President has the responsibility for recommending appropriations to Congress and the Congress makes its decisions on an item-by-item basis. But the President is unable to deal on an item-by-item basis with appropriation bills voted by the Congress. The President at present can disapprove only entire appropriations bills which, in most cases would risk interfering seriously with general Government functions. The item veto would not give the President any additional affirmative power. He could only hold up an item long enough to focus attention upon it; long enough to give the House and Senate time to reconsider it, and to override his veto if desired.

This item veto proposal is not a new one. Such a grant of power would be no innovation in the American political system. The item veto first appeared in the Constitution of the Confederate States in 1861. Shortly thereafter, Georgia and Texas included this power in their constitutions. Indeed, since that time many of the older states and, with a single exception, every new state admitted to the Union have granted their governors this power. At present, forty states have constitutional provisions permitting the governor to veto items in appropriation bills. The latest to be added to this list was Tennessee, which amended its constitution in 1953 to provide for the item veto.

The experience of the states with the item veto indicates that it has been an effective tool for economy and that the power has been judiciously used. A poll of governors as to the working of the item veto in their states, as reported in hearings before the Senate Committee on the Judiciary in May, 1954, on legislation proposing the item veto, indicated that they considered the item veto a desirable feature of state government.

With the exception of two governors who expressed no opinion, every single one of the 30 governors (or former governors) who responded to the questionnaire answered that the item veto was desirable and reported savings resulting from use of the power. They also indicated that there was no agitation in their States for repealing the item veto. The model state constitution of the National Municipal League contains an item veto provision. . . .

Presidents of both parties, starting with President Grant, and including Presidents Hayes, Arthur, Wilson, Franklin D. Roosevelt, and Eisenhower have endorsed the item veto. . . .

Proposals to confer upon the President the right to veto items in appropriations bills have been introduced in nearly every Congress since 1876. While action has not been taken in the past on the proposals, the need for the item veto in appropriations bills has increased as our budget has become more complex. . . . I strongly recommend adoption of an effective item veto provision for the Federal Government.

❧ Congresses to date have continued to deny the President the item veto authority.

GOVERNMENT AND BUSINESS

Business gets better

Statement by Secretary Humphrey at the Treasury Department.

November 1, 1954

Reports of improving business and employment are multiplying.

A recent survey by the Department of Commerce indicates that orders placed with manufacturers exceeded their shipments during September. The rise in orders continued in October according to a survey just released by the National Association of Purchasing Agents. This is in line with the reports of increases in employment that keep flowing into the Department of Commerce and the Department of Labor from all over the country.

Additional encouraging news comes from the Department of Economics of the McGraw-Hill Publishing Company. I have just been informed that preliminary results of its nation-wide survey of prospective plant and equipment expenditures indicates that spending on industrial and commercial facilities during 1955 will be above this quarter's level.

All of this and other evidence indicates that employment, incomes, and trade in 1955 will be at even higher levels than in 1954, the best peacetime year in history.

◄ After a year in which business had been only moderately good, prosperity indices in November, 1954, began moving up to point of exemplary good times in 1955. With the tax reduction and tax revision now law, the Secretary allowed himself a modest public gesture.

The way the people "grow" their country

Speech by Secretary Humphrey to the Savings Bond Awards Dinner of the Investment Bankers Association, New York Chapter, at the Waldorf-Astoria Hotel.

October 21, 1954

The subject of savings bonds spotlights something that has been going on in this country—quietly, but with great force and effect— that I want to talk about with you tonight.

It is an often neglected fact that within the last half century this nation has gone through an economic evolution that makes pale any other in the long history of man's efforts to achieve a better life.

The result is—and the public's huge investment in savings bonds underscores it—that this nation is today a nation made up of small to medium savers and investors.

This means that today this is a nation of "haves," and not a nation of "have-nots." ... We in this Administration have hitched our wagon to this rising star of a "have" nation to make sure of its continued rise —to keep making "have-nots" into "haves."

We are admirers of, and believers in, what has been this uniquely American growth and progress. But on coming into office we found that this great day-to-day American evolution from the bottom up was in danger. It had not even been properly recognized by economic policy makers of the past two decades. They were too busy fighting the frightening ghosts of a "have-not" nation that had even then ceased to exist.

We found the economy blown up with the hot air of inflation, to a point where there was real danger that it might burst, letting us all down with a crash that would have maimed us as a nation, and dropped the free world's defenses invitingly low.

We found the economy's growth hampered and hobbled by a tangle of successive layers of regulations, controls, subsidies and taxes imposed in past emergencies. The economy was being twisted into the shape of things past, when it should have been reaching freely for its rightful future. We found defense spending being used partly to buy defense, and partly as a crutch to support an unsound economy.

In other words, we found an economy going stale, out of step with the times and out of step with the nation it had to serve, an economy fearful of the ghosts of bygone crises, living precariously on the treacherous dodges of inflation, subsidy, and excessive crash-and-crisis Government spending.

We have been reshaping this Government's economic policies into the policies required for a strong and forward-looking nation, its economy firmly footed and self-supporting; an economy that will pump a continuous new flow of nourishment into the day-to-day American evolution of self-betterment; an economy that will constantly generate new and better paying jobs for an ever-growing population. At the same time our economy must provide an ever-higher standard of living, plus the social services the people want and need, as well as the men and the weapons the nation must have for its defense. . . .

All hands in our nation—labor unions and the employer, the rich and the poor, both major parties, the farmer and the city man, the woman at home and the man at his job—all have had a part in making our new productive way of life. . . .

Our total national production of goods and services this year will come to about $355 billion. That is 17 times as much as our national output in 1900. When you make allowance for price rises since the turn of the century, today's national production is still six times what it was in 1900. Our population has more than doubled since 1900, but our national output per capita—production per man, woman and child in the nation—is three times what it was then.

Our national income this year will be about $300 billion. After allowance again for price changes, this is six times what it was in 1900. And our income per man, woman and child in the whole population is, like production, three times as big as in 1900.

Here is the important thing about that income change since 1900: The lower and middle income groups have received the greatest share of our increased income. Early in the century, only 10 out of every 100 American families earned as much as $4,000 a year, in terms of today's prices. Now 55 out of every 100 families earn more than $4,000 a year. Those with inadequate incomes for a decent living are becoming fewer and fewer, and more and more of them are becoming "haves"— people who have enough money not only to live adequately, but to save besides.

That is the basic economic development in this country which we are trying most fervently to keep going.

Let's see just how widespread and important this flow of purchasing power to the broad base of our economy has been and will continue to be.

One of the most common methods of saving is the purchase of insurance. At the turn of the century, people in this country had taken out 14 million life insurance policies. Today, with the population only slightly more than doubled, and with many people owning several policies, the number of life insurance policies has increased nearly 18 times, to 250 million.

Ownership of individuals in their life insurance has increased from under $2 billion in 1900 to $80 billion today.

Small investors' holdings in the United States Savings Bonds, total the huge amount of nearly $50 billion. No such investment existed in 1900.

Nearly 10 per cent of all American families today own stock in American corporations. At the turn of the century, this was just getting under way.

In 1900 individuals had liquid savings of all types amounting to less than $10 billion. Now such savings of individuals in this country total more than $225 billion.

Last year alone, Americans bought equipment for themselves and their homes of approximately $30 billion. This included things unknown to the homeowner of 1900, like 8 million radios, 7 million television sets, nearly 4 million refrigerators, about 3.5 million washing machines, and a million air conditioners. These are mass investments in a better life only a nation of "haves" could make.

About 25 million families own their own homes today, compared with 7 million homeowners half a century ago, while population has only a little more than doubled in that time. About 55 per cent of our families now live in homes of their own. Nearly all the others want to. . . .

Labor unions to which many American workmen pay dues, are also investors. Not so many years ago, union treasuries were low. Today many of them bulge with huge sums. They own banks and buildings, bonds and stocks, and investments of many kinds.

Today nearly 15 million Americans have more than $25 billion invested in pension and retirement trust funds. This represents an investment of more than $1,500 per worker. These retirement plans were practically unknown in 1900.

You can see we need a completely new set of standards in thinking about ourselves. We are a nation of "haves," not of "have-nots." This nation's economy has grown right over, and has left behind in the dust, both socialism and communism.

The consequence of this brilliant human achievement in our nation is that the basic interests of the man in the bungalow are today the same as the basic interests of the man in the penthouse.

Business long ago recognized this fact, and centered its attention on the wants and needs of the man in the bungalow.

The man in the bungalow and the man in the penthouse today have the same basic interests. What that revolutionary fact means to the whole economy: Both men have current earnings and probably savings in one form or another. Both are interested in seeing the dollar keep its purchasing power. To the extent that inflation develops, both men are robbed.

If you had $1,000 saved up in 1939, which you did not draw out to use until 1953, you really took a beating. Inflation had sneaked into your savings during those years and made off with $478. How? Because inflationary price rises during that time cut the purchasing value of the dollars you were saving, every minute of every day. When you drew out your $1,000 savings, inflation had stolen away with all but $522 of the purchasing power your dollars had when you put them aside in 1939.

This is a terrible thing to happen to a nation of people who are working and sweating and scrimping to put aside money for the education of their children, the purchase of a home, or to provide for their old age.

The man in the bungalow often tries, by purchasing insurance, to build up some security to leave to his wife and children in the event of his untimely death. It is a terrible thing to have the purchasing power of his insurance—the time that it will pay the rent and set the table for those that are left—cut nearly in half in just 15 years.

It is a heartless thing for a man and woman who put aside savings in a pension or retirement trust fund as they work during their lifetime to find on retirement that inflation has robbed them of nearly half of what they had invested to live on in their declining years.

We in the Eisenhower Administration have made halting inflation one of the principal goals of our Administration. In the last 20 months, the value of the dollar has changed only one-half of one cent. This means that we have kept inflation's hand out of your savings almost entirely. . . .

The man in the bungalow and the man in the penthouse have at least an equal interest in this fight. But, if there is any difference between them, it is the man in the bungalow who most needs protection. He can less afford to lose.

Now, it is the vast sum of the many smaller savings of the man in the bungalow on which our industrial and commercial system depends for its financing. The sum of all the little savings is funneled mainly into big investments by the savings banks, the building and loan associations, the insurance companies, investment trusts, pension funds, union and fraternal organizations, and others handling the savings of the man in the bungalow.

Business in this country is pouring nearly $27 billion of new investment into its plants and equipment this year. That tremendous amount must come from somebody's savings. Without it, the future's new jobs will never be born, nor will we get tomorrow's increase in productivity, as the result of new and better tools of production, bought by new investment.

Saving is important to the nation, and must be encouraged, because it strongly influences the security of the job you have, and your hopes for ever-better pay through continued increase in your productivity. Thus you can see how inflation can rob you not only of your personal savings but, in addition, steal away your pay increases and perhaps even your job.

We must have policies that put solid ground under our day-to-day evolution of continual betterment from the bottom up. Such policies must aim at everyone, spreading the riches throughout the land. There is only one way to have every one have more. The nation's treasures of goods and services must constantly increase by continually increasing individual productivity.

Our policies must result in giving the man in the bungalow ever more and more of the same things which the man in the penthouse also wants to have. And that can only be accomplished by an economy that constantly produces more of the comforts, conveniences and necessities of life. Such an economy will also be a beacon of progress in the whole free world, a sharp, attractive contrast to the smouldering darkness behind the Iron Curtain.

Our strong economy must—and can—carry the costs of fully adequate defense, and of indispensable public services, and at the same time continue its healthy growth. But it will only be able to do so if we balance the load correctly, so that it can be carried, and carried indefinitely, without a breakdown.

We are not the slave of any particular aspect of our flexible policies. We regard inflation as a public enemy of the worst type. But we have not hesitated, either, to ease or restrict the basis of credit when need was indicated. Under the new co-operation that exists in this Administration between the Treasury and the Federal Reserve, the full force of monetary policy has been made effective more promptly than ever before in the nation's history to better respond to natural demands.

We found, when we came to office, an overblown economy. It was harnessed with all sorts of artificial controls, dangerously dependent upon the uncertainties of defense spending, and inflationary pressures. It was borrowing from tomorrow's production and income at a prodigious rate, with unsound confiscatory taxation that still failed to provide for the profligate spending. This resulted in huge deficits that were passing the heavy burden of our excesses on for our children and grandchildren to bear. And sooner or later it was sure to result in complete downfall.

Correction of that situation has been well started. The whole economy, the livelihood of all the people, has been made more safe. This has been done by the timely use of monetary policy and credit in response to actual demand; by the return to the public of purchasing power through the biggest tax cut in the history of the nation, by cutting unjustified amounts from Government spending; and at the same time by timely encouragement to construction, home building, and needed improvements. . . .

In turning our faces resolutely from inflation and unrealistic spending, what have we turned toward? We have turned to you, to the 160 million people of America, with full confidence to a people that have demonstrated that you are industrious, saving, inventive, daring, progressive and self-reliant to an unprecedented degree. We believe in your capacity to go on providing yourselves with an ever better life, if we in government support your efforts where the general welfare calls for such support, and do not load you with unnecessary burdens, or take from you by excessive taxation the increase in your income that you might otherwise earn and save. . . . We will not be rising on the hot, uncertain air of inflation. We will be rising on the solid ground of these things:

Savings protected against shrinkage by a stable dollar;

Increased production and increased wages and earnings made possible by the investment of those savings in more, new and better tools of production;

Wide use, by Americans who are both workers and investors, of these tools of production for the creation of more jobs and new, better and cheaper goods, with ever-widening distribution among an ever-growing number of consumers as their earning power increases and the cost of the goods declines;

Use of the increased income from this increased production of the things you want—not to pay the bill for unneeded or unwise Government spending or as tribute to inflation.

We have turned our backs on artificial stimulants. We have turned our faces confidently to practical, natural methods for the creation of a better life for all of us.

Concerning the stock market

*Statement by Secretary Humphrey before the Senate
Banking and Currency Committee. Senator
J. William Fulbright, presiding.*

March 15, 1955

. . . I am not here today to say that the market is either too high or too low. I gave up years ago trying to figure out the stock market. But I am glad to consider with you the importance of a healthy stock market to a growing economy.

A healthy stock market is one of the evidences of a strong and growing nation. The 4.5 billion shares listed on the organized exchanges alone are impressive evidence of the effectiveness of markets throughout the country in meeting the needs of our dynamic economy. These 4.5 billion shares represent investment by millions of savers throughout the country. Many millions of them own stock directly. Many millions more have an interest in stock ownership through the pension plans where they work or through the financial institutions that handle their life insurance and other savings. Colleges, hospitals, religious and charitable institutions, scientific and other research centers, and many other endowed funds also rely heavily on stock ownership.

These billions of shares are truly shares in America. They represent the ownership of American business and property. They are the fountainhead of more and better jobs—the invested savings through which the inventive genius of America can find expression in the development of new products and methods.

Widespread ownership of American industry is to be encouraged. A dynamic economy is synonymous with increased emphasis on corporate financing through stock issuance rather than by going further and further into debt. And the success of new risk-taking enterprise is peculiarly dependent on equity financing. A healthy stock market is essential if the role of equity financing in corporate finance is to flourish.

Your committee's study presents an opportunity for increased public understanding of the market and its functions at a time when it is a matter of broad public interest. But I want to say just a word of caution with respect to that a little later. It is also an opportunity to define more clearly the Government's place in relation to the stock market's operations. The role of Government should be to do what it can to assist in making stock-market activity contribute to, rather than detract from, the soundness of our financial structure.

This takes two forms at present. Both are important.

The first involves the supervisory responsibilities of the Securities and Exchange Commission. These are designed, as we all know, to insure fair and honest markets in securities transactions on the organized exchanges, through adequate public information on proposed new security issues, adequate periodic company reports, and the regulation of trading on these exchanges.

The second involves Federal Reserve Board regulation of margin requirements, in order to help supply sufficient credit but not excessive credit in stock-market trading. . . .

Even more important to a healthy market, however, is governmental policy in assisting the achievement of a broad, sound financial base for economic development. Such a base must rest primarily on the continued stability of the dollar, with reasonably stable buying power. This means a budget that is under control and headed for balance. It means a public debt that is prudently managed. It means a tax system that is fair and equitable—one which minimizes tax barriers to the initiative of workers and investors alike. It means monetary and credit policies which will operate through the exercise of broad general powers rather than through a crushing maze of direct controls.

This is the way confidence in the future of America is built. Such confidence is the very lifeblood not only of a healthy stock market but of a vibrant, growing economy. Government action at best can only assist to influence the broad direction of healthy markets—whether they are for stocks, for bonds, or for commodities. The real success of these efforts must rest squarely upon the people of the United States—as investors, as managers of business enterprise, or as brokers or stock-exchange members. . . .

A healthy stock market can be visualized as one in which prices bear an appropriate relationship to earnings and to asset values, where stock yields have a reasonable spread in comparison to those of corporate bonds, where margin trading remains on a conservative basis, and where turnover is sufficient to maintain a broad, active market yet avoids excessive speculation.

The price rise that has taken place in the stock market during the last year and a half reflects many viewpoints of millions of people and conditions not only here at home but from abroad. It is in part the rebirth of confidence in the functioning of our free-enterprise system.

It is also perhaps reflecting a new phenomenon in our national life that is growing daily. The small savings of millions of Americans are being invested in securities in greater amounts than ever before. This wider investment is not just individual purchases in the market; it reflects the rapid growth of pension funds and other group investments. What it means is that millions of people working in industry today have $5 or $10 or some such amount deducted from each paycheck for their future retirement, and a good share of that goes into stocks and bonds. They often do not realize it, but these small savings multiply into hundreds of millions of dollars of security purchases, which is making millions of people investors in American industry who had never thought of doing it before. These purchases are largely for long-term investment and so tend to continually work to lessen the floating supply of the securities they buy.

We are watching attentively the conditions which the new higher level of the stock market is creating. Federal Reserve action in January in raising margin requirements was, we believe, a desirable thing. Buying on margin is not nearly as important as it used to be, but we want to be watchful to see that credit in the stock market—just like all other kinds of credit—does not exceed the reasonable demands. The Federal Reserve action simply served as a reminder that caution should be used in making commitments. The offering of the new Treasury 40-year bond in February may also have been helpful in offering an attractive alternative form of investment. . . .

Now I would like to add a short comment. There is just one word of caution that I want to leave with you. Confidence or lack of it has more to do with conduct of investors, businessmen, and the great mass of the people generally than any single thing. If there is confidence in the future, in the stability of the economy, and in the maintenance of jobs, the American people continue to buy the things they need and the things they want.

Most American families are in position today to buy more than the bare necessities of life. When they have confidence, they buy things they do not absolutely need, but they buy things that they want. If they lose confidence, they postpone or cancel those purchases. Businessmen either move forward with plant expansion, with the creation of new jobs, or they are cautious and restrained based on confidence. And investors are perhaps more sensitive than any in governing their conduct on the confidence that they have or that they lack.

Confidence is a subtle thing. It is built slowly and can be easily and quickly shaken. It manifests itself in many ways. A crowd leaving a theater at the close of a play will walk out in orderly fashion in short order, but if as the curtain goes down someone calls "Fire," terror can reign and great injury can result.

It has been said many times that this inquiry is a friendly study with the best intentions and only to obtain more knowledge. More knowledge never hurts any one. But as criticisms of the conduct of the affairs of the Government, as criticisms of conditions have been stated from day to day before this committee and in the public press, with discussion of restrictive action that Government agencies might or might not take or might or might not engage in, such criticisms can easily contribute to a questioning of confidence and uncertainty as to what the future may hold.

The feeling of confidence in the future has been strong and has moved up on a broad front for the past several months. Business activity has been expanding. And this month that we are in today may well be one of the highest months of activity we have ever had in our history. We are on sound economic grounds based on sound principles. There is no reason why we should not go forward unless confidence is injured or destroyed.

Cross-examination of Secretary Humphrey

THE CHAIRMAN. . . . . Is it fair to conclude that you believe these hearings have injured the confidence of the people in the economy of this country?

SEC. HUMPHREY. I do not know, Mr. Chairman, whether they have or not. I think that you are approaching a ground which is very difficult to express an opinion on. As I said, confidence grows very slowly. Confidence can be easily upset or destroyed. And I do not know how much speculation—public speculation on whether or not responsible Government agencies are doing their job or whether they should or should not move in or move out in matters that can affect credit and affect the confidence of people in purchasing or refraining from purchasing—can go on and not have some effect on public morale.

I refer particularly, to be very specific, to discussions as to whether or not the Federal Reserve Board should take further action or whether it should not. Now, the responsibility for that action is in the Federal Reserve Board. It is not in a committee of Congress. And to speculate as to whether they should or whether they should not may well raise some fears in some people's minds that they will or that they will not and may govern their conduct as to whether they will buy or whether they will not buy.

I think what conduct may be indulged in or withheld under such circumstances is very, very difficult to tell. . . . As I have said many times, more knowledge never hurt anyone. The line between knowledge and speculation as to what may happen that would hamper or aid in the future conduct is a very, very close line, and it is a very difficult thing to decide. I do not think that I would care to advise this committee on what its functions are and what it should do.

THE CHAIRMAN. I understood that last statement of yours to be advice to this committee. I was trying to elicit just what that advice is. There was a little uncertainty in my mind as to what you intended to convey to the committee by the last statement.

SEC. HUMPHREY. What I intended to convey is exactly what I said, Mr. Chairman. I intended to convey to you caution as to your conduct because of the effect it may have in one way or another, and I think that you should have that prominently in mind in determining what course you will follow. . . .

THE CHAIRMAN. One thing the committee is trying to do is to find out whether it is different or not. That is one of the objectives. You said in the beginning you did not think knowledge hurt anybody. I think you will agree that many of us on this committee are not experts in this field. We do not profess to be. But it is our duty I think to inform ourselves. It is very difficult for me to see what the answer to this criticism is. Should the committee simply ignore these matters and not hold hearings, or is it a criticism as to the manner in which the hearings are held?

SEC. HUMPHREY. No, I think, Mr. Chairman, as I say, I am not trying to be critical of the committee. What I am trying to do is give whatever facts I can in answer to your questions. I think that as relates to your statement about comparison of the conditions preceding 1929 and the conditions of today, those are matters of fact, and I think that it is not difficult to marshal the facts that obtained, the various factors that existed in the situation prior to 1929 and compare them with those that obtain today, and you will find a great difference. . . .

THE CHAIRMAN. Do you have any comment at all about the comparison between what happened or did not happen in 1928 and what this committee is seeking to do now?

SEC. HUMPHREY. I do not think the conditions obtaining in 1928 are conditions obtaining today at all. I think they are very different. . . . I think, Mr. Chairman, that insofar as the investigations of the committee go to the development of the facts, more knowledge of facts never hurt anyone. I think that to the extent that the inquiries of the committee speculate on the functions of governmental agencies and on future conduct and actions, things that may or may not be done to affect the economy, or criticisms of the base, perhaps you are laying the groundwork for conduct by people where you do not know how far it will go.

When you drop a stone in a quiet pool, those ripples go a long way. This stock market is a meeting place of ideas and all sorts of people, millions of people as I said, not only at home but from abroad, and those ideas develop over a very wide area. One of the reasons why you and I cannot guess what the stock market is going to do is because our knowledge of conditions which affect it is not broad enough to cover the whole field. We just do not know. We do not have an opportunity, any of us, to take into account all of the things and all of the ideas that may affect people in their conduct of purchasing and selling securities that may affect the confidence that they have in the future or the lack of it.

SENATOR HOMER E. CAPEHART (Indiana). Mr. Secretary, do you have any facts to prove that stock prices are too high? Are there any facts to prove that they are? Is it not the opposite—that all the facts prove they are not too high at the moment?

SEC. HUMPHREY. Oh, Mr. Capehart, I do not think that I want to attempt to guess whether the stock prices are too high or too low. I think that that is something that in my private life I learned long ago not to try to reach conclusions on. And I do not see why I should change in public now.

SENATOR CAPEHART. Do you know any facts or any statistics or proof that industry is not going to continue to be profitable in the United States? That it is not going to continue to even make bigger profits and go forward and grow and expand?

SEC. HUMPHREY. Well, again, I am not going to try to guess the future by looking into a crystal ball as to industry. I can give you some facts as to where we are right now. . . .

Steel production last week was at 93 per cent of capacity. That is a terrifically high rate. Tonnage produced was at the highest level since June of 1953.

Automobile production, cars and trucks, in the first two months of 1955 was at a record high for the period, 37 per cent above a year ago. New passenger-car sales reported to be as much as 40 per cent over a year ago. Dealers' stocks of new passenger cars at the end of February were about 13 per cent below where they were a year ago.

Construction expenditures in February were at a new record high annual rate of $40.7 billion. Construction contract awards in the first two months of 1955 were at a record high for the period, 30 per cent above a year ago.

Private housing starts in January were at a computed annual rate of over 1,400,000 units. The record calendar-year figure is 1,396,000. So the present computed rate appears to be higher than ever before.

Retail sales in the first two months of 1955 rose 7 per cent above a year earlier and are slightly above the previous record high for the period.

A new survey of consumer finances for 1955 indicates that consumers are more optimistic than a year ago and plan to buy homes, furniture, and appliances. Now, that last is extremely important with reference to what I said a minute ago. What the people of this country plan to do, whether they buy these things or whether they do not, depends, gentlemen, on confidence. It depends upon the confidence they have in the maintenance of their jobs, in the future of the economy, and the way things are going. They decide, 160 million Americans decide, either that they will go forward or that they will be cautious.

Unemployment in February was 300,000 below a year earlier, less unemployment than there was in February a year ago. Nonagricultural employment in February was about 500,000 above a year ago. Unemployment was lower; employment was higher. But total civilian employment was about 100,000 lower due to the decline in the agricultural employment. So that for the month of February we had 59,938,000 people employed as against 60 million and a few-odd in the previous year.

Personal income in January, amounting to an annual rate of $290,700 million, was only $700 million below the December 1954 record high and was about $6 billion above a year earlier.

Disposable personal income in the fourth quarter of 1954, the latest available, reached a record high, 2 per cent above a year earlier, the greatest disposable income we have ever had.

Average weekly earnings of factory workers in February rose to an all-time high, 5 per cent above a year ago.

Gross national product in the fourth quarter of 1954 rose $6.5 billion to an annual rate of $362 billion. A comparable increase is easily possible in the first quarter of 1955, which would raise it to close to the record peak by the time we get to the end of the first quarter. . . .

Now, where we go from here you can guess as well as I.

SENATOR CAPEHART. The average turnover or sale of stocks on the New York Exchange I think has been running about 3 million a day.

SEC. HUMPHREY. I think something like that.

SENATOR CAPEHART. Is that a large amount, a small amount, or a normal amount taking into consideration the fact that there are about four times as many shares listed today as there were in 1929?

SEC. HUMPHREY. Well, Senator, I am not an expert on the stock market. I really cannot tell you. I never in my life have paid much attention to the stock market. As to the stocks I have been interested in, I was interested as an investor, and I have never paid much attention to it. . . .

SENATOR HERBERT H. LEHMAN (New York). Mr. Secretary, you have referred to what you call group buying, and I will say that I have been talking about institutional buying. I think your term, group buying, is more descriptive than the term I have used, institutional buying, because it is all-inclusive.

That group buying has gone on, of course, at an increasing rate in the past years. The President of the stock exchange testified that today there were $66 billion of securities, listed securities, held by institutions, compared to $32 billion in 1949. He did point out that 80 per cent of this increase was accounted for by a rise in the market value, but, nonetheless, the fact remains that 28 per cent of all the securities listed on the exchanges are held by groups. . . .

You say these purchases continually work to lessen the floating supply of the securities they buy. If that is carried to a further limit, do you not think you destroy your free markets? Do you not create a situation where the floating supply is so small that it really does not reflect the actual value of the stock? ... If it is true that so large a proportion of the stock of these companies is now controlled by groups, is it not a relatively easy thing for these groups in time to get possession of a great many of the companies of this country, industrial companies, railroads, and commercial banks?

SEC. HUMPHREY. Well, now, as to your first question, Senator, of course the more stock of any company that is purchased and taken out of the market, the less supply there is to be available for future purchasers. But I think it is only within very narrow limits that that is effective—for two reasons.

In the first place, as you yourself have just pointed out, most of these group purchases are in a more limited number of the companies, and most of those companies are the companies with the largest amounts of shares outstanding. They are large companies with large amounts of stock outstanding. So that while it is possible as time goes on and over a long period of time that all of the stock of some particular company, United States Steel Corporation or General Motors might be owned by these groups of people with their pension funds or with insurance funds or something of that sort, it is a long ways away and I think quite improbable.

As to the operation of the law of supply and demand, it is simply this: The demand for the purchase of a security depends very largely upon its relative worth in the market. A large investor is more interested in the relative position of two stocks in the market than he is in the level of those two stocks with respect to the dollar.

There are two comparisons you have to make in thinking of the value of the stock. One is the value of the stock in comparison with the value of a dollar. ... The same thing is true if you buy or sell commodities.

The other consideration that an investor in securities has, has nothing to do or very little to do with the current relationship between the value of the stock and the value of the dollar. It has to do with the relative value of one stock as against the relative value of another stock. And in that case, if one stock gets higher relatively than another stock, then the tendency is for investors to sell that higher stock and purchase the lower stock, because one is overpriced at some point and the other is underpriced in the opinion of the investor.

So while you can follow this suggestion you have made through to a possible difficulty, I think in practice the field is so large and it involves so much money and so many people that I do not think you are going to run into a case except rarely where the value of the security is determined by a fictitious demand. And that is particularly true of the big companies.

In some smaller company with a limited amount of stock what you are really suggesting is: Can you get an old-fashioned corner in the stock? I think it is very difficult to get an old-fashioned corner in the stock, practically impossible in the big companies and very difficult in a small company.

SENATOR LEHMAN. I was wondering whether you do not think that the impact of this large group buying has had something to do or a considerable amount to do with the steady rise, and the very substantial rise in the security markets.

SEC. HUMPHREY. Well, I think that what this group buying is doing is supplying a steady demand for purchasing in a greater amount than we have ever had before. I think it is one of the greatest things that has ever happened to America. I think the fact that millions of Americans do not even know they are doing it is an unfortunate thing. If you told a lot of people, "I see that you bought five shares of steel common yesterday," he would be amazed. The fact is that what he did was to tell his employer to deduct so many dollars from his payroll over a period of time and that that amount which was deducted from his payroll went into a trustee's hands in a pension trust, and a pension trustee today bought so many shares of steel common of which his share was five shares. His money actually bought five shares of steel common today.

Now, the same thing is true with respect to buying insurance. You pay the premiums on an insurance policy, and that money, if you followed it around, you would find actually bought two shares of General Motors or something or other. . . . All that is a very healthy thing, I think, to have going on in America today.

SENATOR IRVING M. IVES (New York). Do you remember in 1928, quite a lot of talk began about the stock-market crash. Do you remember that?

SEC. HUMPHREY. I certainly do. I am an old man, Senator Ives, and I have been through a lot of these.

SENATOR IVES. Do you hear anything today about the stock market crash? Is there any talk about it at all?

SEC. HUMPHREY. I think aside from the comparison between 1929 and the present time as developed in the hearings of this committee, that is about the only conversation I have heard about it. . . . I think the indication is there is no impending crash. I do not know what you mean by a crash. Normal fluctuations of the market, or whether we are headed for another 1929? I think the only conversation I have heard is largely gossip; I do not think anybody believes we are headed for another 1929 today.

SENATOR IVES. You greatly favor having stock owned generally by the American people, and the broader that ownership, or the more holders there are of the stock, the better for all concerned. . . . Do you feel that these promotional activities on the part of the Stock Exchange are proper?

SEC. HUMPHREY. I think it is excellent, and just for this reason. In America today a man cannot earn a living with just his two hands. In America today a man can only earn a living when he has tools in his hands, and power in his hands, and you cannot get tools and power without investment. So that without investment a man just cannot have a job in America today. There has to be some investment back of him.

I want to be perfectly clear on this, because people say that means I cannot get a job. That is not true. Somebody has to have investments in transportation, and somebody has to have investments in all kinds of power developments, and somebody has to have investments in all sorts of tools, and somebody has to have investments in plants, and somebody has to have investments in factories, and somebody has to have investments in farm equipment. You have to have investments in highways and many things in order for a man to function.

A farmer today has to get his produce to market. It has to be marketed through storage. A newspaper reporter today who works with a pencil and a piece of paper—those are not the only tools he works with. Somebody has to own some forests, and somebody has to own some paper mills, and somebody has to own some newspaper establishments, and somebody has to have railroads to carry the stuff on. Somebody has to have delivery wagons and trucks. Somebody has to have the right methods, and the stores where papers can be sold, and so on.

So that everybody today, to earn a living, has to be backed up with an enormous amount of investment to permit him to do the things he is doing currently and sell his services and the goods he produces.

The wider that investment can be—the more that investment can be encouraged, the more we have available for tools with which people can work, and the more tools and power they have, the more they can get for their services; and the more they can produce as individuals, and the higher individual productivity goes, the higher goes our scale of living. That is what makes America. . . .

SENATOR IVES. You are the chief authority of the Government from the standpoint of taxation. I would like to ask you what you think—

SEC. HUMPHREY. The Ways & Means Committee are.

SENATOR IVES. We are leaving the Congress out of this. I would like to ask you the effect of the capital-gains tax on diminishing the floating supply of stock.

SEC. HUMPHREY. I think the capital-gains taxes undoubtedly have some restraining influence on the current sale of securities. I think, as I said a minute ago, the large investor or true investor is interested more in the relative merits of different securities than he is in the levels at which those securities are selling, because if he sells one he has to buy another, and he has to keep his funds invested.

If in the process of switching from one security to another he has to take a loss of part of his investment and pay it to the Government in taxes, then he has to be more sure that the security he is switching to is better than the one he has—more than he would be if he made an even trade. To that extent, it is a deterrent to the supply of stocks and to the ready sale of stocks.

I suppose the next question or the next thought is that if that is so why do you not recommend its repeal? I have not recommended its repeal. We have given a great deal of study to whether it should be scaled down, or whether it should be partially modified or repealed entirely. . . . I will say I think there is no question but that if the capital-gains tax were repealed today that the Treasury would probably get as much, and possibly more, money than it will with a half a tax than it would with the full tax we have today. I think that would continue for some little time, because I think the increase in volume would more than offset it for the reduction of some substantial amount in the rate.

The deterrent to repeal, and there are several of them, is this: That the great disparity between the tax on individual income and the tax on capital gains is a thing that is so wide and so great that it is influencing commercial transactions. Business people and individuals, and everybody in the country—you, me, and all the rest of us—determine or think very carefully and cautiously as to what we are going to do and how we are going to get it into a capital-gains field rather than into a current income field if it can be done. ... If you repeal the capital-gains tax you still further intensify that disparity and still further increase the incentive to manipulate yourself into a capital-gains operation.

I think that the complexities and difficulties, and the tremendous influence a tremendously high level of income-tax take has on business conduct is such—on the grade on which you have to operate—is such that I do not think it is a good thing for the country to increase that disparity. ...

SENATOR PAUL H. DOUGLAS (Illinois). Mr. Secretary, I would like to address a series of questions to you on the relationship of the tax changes in the 1954 act to the increase in stock-market prices. I would like to begin with the effect of the so-called accelerated depreciation provision in your tax bill of last year. ...

SEC. HUMPHREY. Well, Senator, in a word, what the changed depreciation provisions provide is that in the earlier years of the life of a depreciable item a greater amount of depreciation can be taken. Then it is graduated down to a lesser amount in the later years, rather than taking the—

SENATOR DOUGLAS. Starting out at double the straight-line rate. Is that right?

SEC. HUMPHREY. That is approximately right. It is the same total amount in the end, but it is more now and less later. ...

SENATOR DOUGLAS. Under the new declining balance method—and I omit the sum of the years method—the depreciation in the first year would be what?

SEC. HUMPHREY. I will have to check that.

SENATOR DOUGLAS. It would be $100,000, would it not? If the straight-line method were $50,000 and you have doubled the rate of depreciation in the initial year, then the deduction would be $100,000, would it not?

Sec. Humphrey. That is right, sir.

Senator Douglas. And the tax value of that depreciation charge would be $52,000. Am I correct?

Sec. Humphrey. That is right.

Senator Douglas. In other words, the company would save $26,000 in taxes in the first year by using this method.... In the second year, what would the depreciation allowance be? ... Are my figures correct? I have $46,800. According to my arithmetic the tax value of 52 per cent of that would be $46,800. Does that check with your figures?

Dan Smith (Deputy to the Secretary). It sounds substantially correct.

Senator Douglas. But, Mr. Secretary, if at that time the company buys another $1 million facility it will again save in taxes, will it not?

Sec. Humphrey. Each time you buy an item—

Senator Douglas. The savings in taxes will be greater than the amount of repayment with respect to the first facility. That is, you get your saving on your first facility and saving on the second before the first is really fully depreciated.

Sec. Humphrey. It would depend, of course, on when you bought it.

Senator Douglas. I understand. In fact, if the company continues to expand—and I presume that that is the purpose of this progression— its tax savings on new facilities will continue for some considerable time to stay ahead of the former tax savings it would have to give back as the facilities get older.

Sec. Humphrey. That could be.

Senator Douglas. In other words, what you are doing is eating into the future in the same way as was done under the Ruml plan and under section 462 of the 1954 Internal Revenue Code, about which there has been some discussion in recent days.... One eats into the future on the first new installation, and by the time the depreciation charges are less and the taxes would be more, then by developing other new facilities one is able to get a greater tax deduction.

Sec. Humphrey. Senator, do you not think that would be a good thing? ... Do you not think it is a good thing if I have had to buy one of those machines either to make a new job or a better job for a man to work at? ...

SENATOR DOUGLAS. I had not questioned its propriety. I have tried merely to understand its operation. Now, Mr. Secretary, these tax savings under accelerated depreciation in the early years of a new facility's life can be used to help pay for the equipment, or build up a fund with which to buy new equipment, can they not? ... These tax savings of 8 per cent of the cost of the facility would mean, if the company had to raise money from outside to finance the investment, it would have to raise 10 per cent less because of these tax provisions.

SEC. HUMPHREY. It would raise substantially less and have a much better chance to raise it.

SENATOR DOUGLAS. Therefore, is it not fair to assume, insofar as companies can take advantage of these accelerated depreciation provisions, that their dependence on the market for financing would be reduced?

SEC. HUMPHREY. I think to that extent, yes.

SENATOR DOUGLAS. So we might expect that companies will be offering fewer shares of new stocks than they would be if they did not have these tax savings? ... The effect of this accelerated depreciation seems to be that new issues of stock would fall off while demand increases and the price of shares goes up.

SEC. HUMPHREY. No. That is where you get into trouble. It is just the opposite. ... I think the stimulation of industry and stimulation of jobs—

SENATOR DOUGLAS. I do not see how you can avoid it. You have said "yes" to all of these previous questions. I do not see how you can balk at the final question; namely, that it makes possible greater internal financing without dependence on the stock market.

SEC. HUMPHREY. We will have more people working at better jobs and making more goods and collect more taxes.

SENATOR DOUGLAS. It increases the earnings of corporations at the same time it diminishes the amount of stock issues and increases the demand for stocks and diminishes the supply of stocks, and hence increases the price of stocks.

SEC. HUMPHREY. I am sorry. I just do not follow you and I do not think that is it. The trouble is, you have lost the logical sequence. ...

You leave out the fact that you have more people working at better jobs, and making more goods at better prices. . . .

THE CHAIRMAN. Has there been considerable fluctuation in the price of Government bonds since you have been Secretary?

SEC. HUMPHREY. Yes, there has.

THE CHAIRMAN. What caused that?

SEC. HUMPHREY. Different pressures and demands for money.

THE CHAIRMAN. Did some bonds go down as low as 90 cents on the dollar?

SEC. HUMPHREY. I believe so.

THE CHAIRMAN. Then they recovered?

SEC. HUMPHREY. Partially at least.

THE CHAIRMAN. Are any of them under par now?

SEC. HUMPHREY. I cannot tell you.

THE CHAIRMAN. You cannot tell me?

SEC. HUMPHREY. No.

THE CHAIRMAN. If you cannot, then I do not know who can.

SEC. HUMPHREY. I have not checked it.

THE CHAIRMAN. Do you think it would be improper to inquire about the effect of inflation upon the holders of Government bonds in a hearing like this?

SEC. HUMPHREY. What?

THE CHAIRMAN. Do you think it would be improper to inquire about the effect of inflation upon the holder of a Government bond in a hearing like this? Is that a subject that might affect the confidence of people in Government bonds?

SEC. HUMPHREY. I do not think so. . . . I think the effect of inflation is becoming pretty well known.

THE CHAIRMAN. If it was well known why do you think people buy bonds? . . .

SEC. HUMPHREY. I do not just quite get what it is you are seeking. I do not understand what it is you are driving at.

THE CHAIRMAN. Inflation destroys the purchasing power of money, does it not?

SEC. HUMPHREY. That is right.

THE CHAIRMAN. If you own a bond, it is to make up for the destruction of the purchasing power.

SEC. HUMPHREY. That is right.

THE CHAIRMAN. If a man bought a bond in 1939 or 1940, has he fared very well as the owner of a bond, contrasted to stocks, in the last 20 years?

SEC. HUMPHREY. No; I think not.

THE CHAIRMAN. I only use it as an illustration. It is difficult to talk about any of these things without raising this question of confidence. I do not know how one goes about trying to understand a simple thing like that without actually raising some question about it. I suppose you should not talk about it.

With respect to the stock market, I am unable to follow this argument that confidence is such a delicate thing that in one minute it can be destroyed....

SEC. HUMPHREY. I do not think that just conversation will do it, Senator. I think the thing that will affect confidences is fear of action at some time....

THE CHAIRMAN. We have certainly proposed no action here. We were inquiring about why action was taken. You in your own statement say that the increase in margin requirements was a desirable thing....

SEC. HUMPHREY. I thought so.

THE CHAIRMAN. Which, I assume, means there was too much credit in the market—speculative credit?

SEC. HUMPHREY. I thought it was beginning—I thought it was time to do that.

THE CHAIRMAN. Then to that extent it raises a red flag?

SEC. HUMPHREY. That is right.... I think an examination of facts is an entirely different thing. The examination of facts as I say—a study of what the facts are—is a perfectly proper method of procedure....

THE CHAIRMAN. The facts with regard to the existence of credit, for example? How much credit is in the market? Those are facts which were brought out, I think, in an accurate way. As far as I know there was no challenge to the facts that were brought out with regard to matters of that kind. One illustration, I think, of perhaps a justifiable inquiry, I think it was about two or three days after the matter was first mentioned in this committee, that the President himself requested the re-enactment of the renegotiation bill. I think maybe it was a coincidence, but it could have been a reminder.

SEC. HUMPHREY. No. That was just a pure happenso.

THE CHAIRMAN. A what?

SEC. HUMPHREY. A pure happenso that it happened to come at that time. That had nothing to do with this hearing.

THE CHAIRMAN. Why do you think it was not requested in the initial program of the President? Did he overlook it?

SEC. HUMPHREY. No. There was some discussion over in the Defense Department when they were examining contracts to see to what extent the matter could be covered by contracts. It was thought it possibly could be covered by contracts in the Defense Department and would not need to be a law. There was an examination made to see whether it could be effectively done, and it was decided that it could not be effectively worked that way. If it were, and the provisions were put in to be effective it would slow down activity.

That had absolutely nothing to do with this committee.

THE CHAIRMAN. I have just been handed a ticker tape which indicates that it seems this morning there was a big rally. Do you think we have caused that?

SEC. HUMPHREY. I would be very gratified if I caused it....

"Buy and build and improve"

*Speech by Secretary Humphrey to the annual
meeting of the American Petroleum Institute,
San Francisco.*

November 17, 1955

...We have turned our backs on artificial stimulants. We have turned our faces confidently to practical, natural methods for the creation of a better life for all of us—firm in the belief that continuation of the processes of the American evolution of self-betterment from the bottom up is second nature to our whole people.

The United States is now enjoying plenty—in peace. Americans are breaking all records in the number of people with jobs, the high wages they are receiving, and in the production of goods for people to enjoy. And they are enjoying this high prosperity while successfully resisting pressures toward inflation.

Whether this high prosperity will continue without getting into the excesses of inflation or deflation depends in very large part upon what 166 million Americans do. It depends upon you in this room this morning, and your associates in the economic life of America.

We hope for continued prosperity based, not on war scares or artificial government stimulants, but on steady spending by consumers, and investment by business. It has a broad and solid base. We have laid to rest the myth that a free enterprise system can thrive only in war. We have shown that free men in a free world can provide an abundance—can provide plenty in peace—far above the capacity of the government-run economies of the world.

The best that government can do to strengthen our economy is to provide a fertile field in which millions of Americans can work. The continued success of our economy depends, not upon government, but upon the efforts of all the people trying to do a little more for themselves and their loved ones. It is the sum total of all these individual efforts that makes our system superior to anything known in this world before. It is what makes America.

The continued prosperity of America is peculiarly a responsibility of a group such as the petroleum industry. For it is from such industries as yours that we constantly get the new products, and new uses for products which lead to the new jobs, higher income, and better living, which is the progress of America.

From the seemingly inexhaustible spring of American research flows a stream of new ideas and new products resulting in new opportunities and new wealth for everyone. Your industry is one which must continue to be a front-runner in nurturing progress from the spring of research.

If all Americans—workers, producers, businessmen, consumers, and investors—go ahead and buy and build and improve with confidence tempered with prudence, this nation will continue to be even more a nation of "haves" enjoying new peaks of prosperity in business, production, and wages, and constantly higher standards of living—for *all* the people.

✍ On this occasion the Secretary also repeated much of his New York "from the bottom up" speech; changing, however, his figure of speech from "the man in the bungalow and the man in the penthouse" to "the man in overalls and the man in the business suit."

"Our prosperity didn't just happen"

*Speech by Secretary Humphrey to the Centennial
Anniversary Dinner of the Mercantile Trust Company,
St. Louis.*

December 7, 1955

The future is promising—if we pull together. For three years, we have
been reshaping this Government's economic policies into the policies
required for a strong and forward-looking nation, its economy firmly
rooted and self-supporting; an economy that will pump a continuous
new flow of nourishment into the day-to-day American evolution of
self-betterment; an economy that will constantly generate new and
better-paying jobs for an ever-growing population.

At the same time our economy must provide an ever-higher standard
of living, plus the social services the people want and need, as well
as the men and the weapons we must have for our defense.

The peaceful evolution has resulted in a tremendous upheaval of this
nation's whole economy that has really created a different kind of a
nation, a unique nation of "haves" that needs an up-to-date way of
thinking about itself and up-to-date policies in keeping with its strength
and growth potential.

We have curbed inflation, avoided deflation and encouraged initiative and expansion which have developed into the greatest period of
prosperity that our fast-growing, now unhobbled economy has ever
known.

Barring unforeseen developments, we will have a balanced federal
budget in the present fiscal year. The anticipated deficit of the Government for fiscal 1956 was $1.7 billion at the time of the mid-year review
last July. If present estimates are realized, we will have a balanced
budget for this fiscal year ending June 30, 1956.

Our prosperity didn't just happen. It was brought about by the confidence of the American people in the Eisenhower Administration and
the favorable climate which has been created for 166 million free
Americans to exercise their own initiatives and endeavors to the full

limit of their abilities to improve and better the lives of their loved ones and themselves.

The Administration's program promised a new, a better day, not for any particular segment of the population but for all the people. We have seen that day dawn. It is just the beginning if we can continue to achieve national unity and improve the lot of the farmer, about the only large segment of our population still suffering from the overhanging effects of past unrealistic governmental programs.

We have the greatest productive machine the world has ever seen. It is expanding rapidly.... We have set new records in almost every way in which good times can be judged and measured. Employment last summer reached 65.5 million for the first time in history. Unemployment declined in October to 2.1 million. The dollar has been stable for three years; wage earners have been getting real wage increases instead of "the cost of living" wage increases of the previous several years....

If all Americans—workers, producers, businessmen, consumers, and investors—go ahead and work and buy and build and improve with confidence tempered with prudence, this nation will continue to be even more a nation of "haves" enjoying new peaks of prosperity in business, production, and wages and constantly higher standards of living—for all the people.

🖘 First cautious public commitment that the budget would be in balance the following July 1.

THE PRESIDENT

¶ President Eisenhower and his Secretary of the Treasury were particularly close because of the President's directness in depending on Secretary Humphrey for the immense financial task involved in an administration. In their first meeting they established an area of independence in which the Secretary would work, and during the Secretary's service no Presidential budget or economic report went forth without his guidance and impetus.

The inevitable fiscal considerations—the price or cost of any given policy—drew Secretary Humphrey almost automatically into every conference on statecraft, diplomacy, internal program, or emergency. The historian Merlo Pusey reports that the President, at the start, granted the one request as to their operations that the Secretary made. "When anyone talks to you about money," said Humphrey, "will you ask him if he has seen George? If he has not seen George, will you ask him to do so before any commitments are made?"

Thereby the President's administrative staff came to communicate and deal with the Secretary of the Treasury perhaps more than with any other department of the government, and he became advisor to the executive staff as well as to the President.

When in September, 1955, the President was unexpectedly stricken with a heart attack, there took place an immediate informal coalition of leadership initiated by Secretary of State Dulles, who had first news of the heart attack. It was composed of Secretary Dulles, Vice President Nixon, Attorney General Brownell, and Secretary Humphrey. They met in Secretary Humphrey's office to consider what necessities and possible emergencies confronted the Government. The first item in this section is the statement which they agreed Secretary Humphrey, for the Administration, should issue to the public, and for the first weeks of the President's convalescence at Denver the quadrumvirate conferred hourly and daily. It was an adequate team for the situation, and no national leadership was ever found lacking.

President Eisenhower spent three brief vacations at the Humphrey plantation at Thomasville, Ga., one shortly after leaving the hospital at Denver. (Even while in the Denver hospital bed, the President was considering ways and means of being able to shoot in the Thomasville thickets, and accomplished it by hunting wagon and the companionship of his physician.)

Secretary Humphrey's contributions to President Eisenhower's 1956 campaign for re-election were invariably reflections of his estimate of the President's personal achievements for peace and fiscal improvement. The Secretary's selection to give the opening speech in Madison Square Garden, New York, emphasized how close was his association with the President. A similar speech at St. Louis in which he questioned the genuineness of opposition to President Eisenhower is included.

"... But not of alarm"

Statement by Secretary Humphrey at the Treasury Department.

September 26, 1955

The whole world is concerned and distressed by the President's illness. But the best medical advice encourages us to hope it is temporary in character and that a complete recovery is probable. It is a cause of sadness, but not of alarm.

Our policies and programs are definite and firmly established. There is no reason to anticipate any change. We will carry on during his absence exactly as previously planned. There is no reason for others to do otherwise.

"A great tribute to the President"

Remarks by Secretary Humphrey at a press conference at Lowry Air Force Base, Denver.

October 15, 1955

JAMES C. HAGERTY (Press Secretary to the President). As you all know, the Secretary got to the hospital shortly after he arrived at Lowry. He talked to the doctors for a few minutes and then he was in with the President, I would say 15 or 20 minutes, and later talked with Mrs. Eisenhower. We have just left the hospital.

SEC. HUMPHREY. Well, the first thing I would like to tell you is that the President accepted Coleman Andrews' resignation. He regrets very much indeed that Coleman Andrews is leaving. I want to say that I regret it very much indeed, but Mr. Andrews has done a wonderful job for us. He took on the work to do a complete reorganization job, and he has done it with great distinction and effectiveness. He had other arrangements that he wanted to make that he had commitments on, and under the circumstances there was nothing we could do but very regretfully accept his resignation, to be effective the first of the month.

QUESTION. Could you discuss those commitments—those pressures—

SEC. HUMPHREY. I can't discuss them today. I think that they will be announced. I think that he will announce them as soon as this is announced. It's some arrangements that he had made, as I understand it, in Richmond. I frankly don't know exactly what they are.

QUESTION. Mr. Secretary, were you able to inform the President that we are going to have a balanced budget next year?

SEC. HUMPHREY. Well, I wonder if—I have here a memorandum that I thought maybe it would save time if I just pass this out and give it to you, and I will just read it through, and then I will get to your question, and answer that first.

"I had a good visit with the President and found him in fine spirits and keenly interested in affairs of the day."

I will just add to that by saying that I was just delighted at the way the President looked, and the very excellent spirits that he was in this morning. I—I—I can't tell you how pleased I was to see how very well he looked.

He is—this being out on the porch is—out under the sun—has given him some color and he just looks splendidly to me, and seemed in excellent spirits, and I just thoroughly enjoyed my visit with him.

"Just before the President became ill, I had planned to come to Denver to report to him on the annual meetings of the International Bank and the Monetary Fund in Istanbul, Turkey, from which I had just returned. I have now been able to make that report which was postponed on account of the President's illness.

"I told the President that we received reports of high prosperity from nearly all of the more than 50 free world nations represented at the Istanbul meetings. Representatives of some countries with whom we talked spoke of the reappearance of inflationary pressures in their countries. It is reassuring that the financial advisers of so many nations of the free world are aware of the dangers of possible excesses and pressures toward inflation which can accompany high prosperity. If these are not curbed, they can lay the foundations for reaction and the difficulties of a deflation that we would all deplore.

"Here in the United States, we are breaking all records in the number of people with jobs, the high wages they are receiving, and in the production of goods for people to enjoy. This prosperity is shared less in agriculture where the disposal of large surpluses has created situations we are earnestly seeking to improve. The great majority of Americans, however, are enjoying high prosperity while successfully resisting pressures toward inflation.

"The productive capacity of our country is so great that normal competitive conditions with our present high level of production should continue to keep prices relatively stable even with very high consumer demand.

"I assured the President that we in the Administration will continue to carry out his firmly established policies and programs. If all Americans—workers, producers, consumers, businessmen, and investors—go ahead with confidence tempered with prudence, there is every reason why this nation will continue to enjoy new peaks of prosperity in jobs, production, and wages, and increasingly higher standards of living for all the people as time goes on."

QUESTION. Mr. Secretary, was this statement written before you came out here?

SEC. HUMPHREY. It was, all but the first part which relates to my visit with the President. That I put in after I came here.

QUESTION. This last statement you have here, this assurance that with confidence we can continue to have prosperity, was that inspired in any way by the drop in stock prices in Wall Street?

SEC. HUMPHREY. Well, stock prices, as you know, for the last couple of weeks, have been moving sideways—back and forth—some days they are down and some days they are up.

There is nothing in the stock market at this time that occasions that. It is simply—this is my belief as to the situation at this time and conditions at this time.

QUESTION. Now, sir, were you concerned by the dip in the stock market or are you concerned about the loss—at least the paper loss, of many billions—

SEC. HUMPHREY. Oh, I think that the President's illness was a terrific shock to the world. You must remember that—I am sure that there is no man in the world—ever—ever—who has carried the hopes of as many millions of people on his shoulders as has the President of the United States. And when his illness was broadcast to the world, it was a great shock to the whole world.

I think personally that it was quite remarkable and a fine tribute to the good sense and the stability of the American people, after receiving such a shock, that the near panic was dissipated as rapidly as it was. I think that it is a great tribute to the President, to his associates and to the President himself as a great leader in having so established his programs and having them so well understood and having his associates so well trained that they could carry on in his absence with as little difficulty as there was—as there has been—over the past few weeks. It takes a great leader to do that, and I think it is a great tribute to the President that that occurred. And I think it is a great tribute to the President that the people of the country soon settled down to calmness rather than a panic under the shock, under the circumstances of such a shock.

QUESTION. Mr. Secretary, this is a complex question. You had a visit with the doctors today before you saw the President, is that correct, sir?

SEC. HUMPHREY. Just for a few minutes.

QUESTION. There are people in Ohio who say that last week or week before last that you said to them that the President's heart attack was so minor that if it happened to any one else it would not have occasioned much attention.

SEC. HUMPHREY. That is untrue. I never said it to anybody.

QUESTION. Mr. Secretary, there has been a sort of "Humphrey for President" boom in the country. I judge that from what we have been reading out here. In the event that President Eisenhower retired after this first term, would you be receptive to the Republican nomination?

SEC. HUMPHREY. I went into public life for just one purpose and that was to act as the Secretary of the Treasury. I am doing that to the best of my ability, and I have just one candidate for the President of the United States, and that man is now the President of the United States. He is the only candidate I have and the only candidate I have any interest in at any time.

QUESTION. Do you think he is going to run again—

QUESTION. Could we have—could you tell us what you were able to tell the President about the budget now?

SEC. HUMPHREY. Yes, I will be glad to. What I told the President about the budget was just what I said the night before last in Boston— I have said it a number of times: I am still very hopeful that we are going to balance the budget this year. And I mean 1956 budget, June 30th coming.

Now, that will be done, if it is done, it will be done by a combination of two circumstances. One will be somewhat higher revenues than we anticipated because of the continuation of good times that we are now enjoying, and the other will be because of the savings that have been made.

Every department in Washington—everybody in the Government is working honestly and religiously to try to reduce any unnecessary or wasteful or extravagant expenditure that they can find that will not either reduce our service to the people or our security.

Now, there has been a good deal of conversation about the situation between Mr. Wilson and myself, and I would just like to cover that at the same time I am doing this.

There is no controversy or problem between Mr. Wilson and myself at all. We had lunch together yesterday. There never has been any time when I wanted to or thought that there should be any change in the program of defense. That is a thing that is set—I do not set it— I don't have anything to do with it; and the program that is set for defense was never contemplated to be changed. And I never asked Mr. Wilson to do anything that would change that.

Mr. Wilson, on the other hand, has assured me and—and every one, in the letter that he wrote to Senator Johnson, and he has repeated it subsequently, that he is doing everything that he can do to try to eliminate unnecessary expenditures or unnecessary inventories, or any wasteful action that can be eliminated that will not change the program for defense and that will keep our effective defense at its peak levels.

Now, that's all I can ask. It's all I want. And I have known Mr. Wilson for a great many years—we have been associated for a long time, and I have a lot of confidence in him and his ability to get things done. And I hope that in his departments and in all the other departments—all put together—we will get enough savings so that, with the income that we have a chance to get, we will get a balanced budget.

QUESTION. Mr. Secretary, you spoke a moment ago about—

SEC. HUMPHREY. Excuse me just a second—I will be right there.

QUESTION. Did you discuss the prospects for a tax cut for next year with the President today?

SEC. HUMPHREY. No, I did not. We did not discuss it at all, but I will be very glad to tell you just how I feel about that. That will depend—and I have said this several times before—that will depend entirely upon how successful we are in the two fields that I have just mentioned, with respect to balancing the budget.

I am opposed to a tax cut until we can see where the money is coming from to pay it.

I am opposed to a tax cut that has to come out of borrowed money. I don't think that is a real tax cut.

On the other hand, I have said many times we don't have to actually have the money in the till before we agree to a tax cut because the tax cut comes along as the months go by. But I want to be able to see where the money is coming from so that it will be available as the time approaches when it will be returned to the people. Just as soon as we can see it, I am for the tax cuts. I believe we should have them, and I will be the first to advocate them, and I think they ought to be done as soon as we know how we are going to pay for them.

QUESTION. Mr. Secretary, you mentioned a moment ago that your candidate for the Presidency was the President himself.

SEC. HUMPHREY. President Eisenhower.

QUESTION. Two questions, sir. First, did you discuss that with him, and, second, do you believe he is going to run again?

SEC. HUMPHREY. We have never discussed it, either today or any other day. And I have no information nor knowledge more than you gentlemen or anybody else has, and I don't think anybody can tell until his recovery has much further progressed.

QUESTION. Mr. Secretary, do you have any idea what form your tax revisions might take?

SEC. HUMPHREY. No, and I have answered that before, and I have to say that exactly the same as I did before, which is this: That until we can get an idea, first, that we can give a tax cut, and second of how much money will be available for release to the people, that we can't decide how it shall fairly be distributed among the people. The amount involved makes quite a difference as to what you can do—what you can afford to do; until we can get some idea, I don't think there's any intelligent way to decide how it should be distributed to the people.

What we are trying to do—and taxes, gentlemen, are a very simple thing. When the Government decides how much money it is going to spend, then our job is to try to collect that amount of money in the fairest possible way—distributed among all the people, all classes of people, business and individuals, in the United States.

When we can reduce taxes, we have the same problem—how to fairly bring down the amount that is available and release it to the people that we would otherwise be collecting it from.

QUESTION. Mr. Secretary, you are saying, sir, that a balanced budget is not enough to justify the cut, that we have—beyond that we would have to have a surplus, or a surplus in sight, is that—

SEC. HUMPHREY. That is my opinion. We have to see where the money is coming from to pay it, and not pay it out of the deficit.

QUESTION. Mr. Secretary, do you—what is the present official estimated deficit—I mean the present estimated—

SEC. HUMPHREY. Now, before I answer that, let me just—I want you to be sure you understand this and on the other questions, boys—because I want everybody to understand it—I don't mean we have to have, if we are going to release any figure you want—two billion, or one, or three—whatever it may be—I don't mean we have to have that in the till before we will do it. I mean we have to see where it is coming from to be available at the time it will be released as we go along.

QUESTION. There is no question, though, that you want a balanced budget before—

SEC. HUMPHREY. Before a tax cut, that is correct.

QUESTION. Mr. Secretary, do you have a successor in mind for Mr. Andrews?

SEC. HUMPHREY. Not ready to announce, no.

QUESTION. What is the last figure on the budget deficit? I realize you hope to balance it, but what is the latest estimate?

SEC. HUMPHREY. A billion seven was the August figure, and there is no other figure at this time....

QUESTION. Mr. Secretary, even though you are not ready to announce it, did you discuss a possible successor for Mr. Andrews with the President?

SEC. HUMPHREY. No, I did not.

QUESTION. Mr. Secretary, aside from the international conference which you covered in this statement, can you tell us some of the things you did discuss with the President, sir?

SEC. HUMPHREY. Well, mostly we talked about general things, and

I was here as much for a visit with him as to discuss matters—to just bring him up to date on various things. I had no important or pressing problem that I came to get an answer on.

QUESTION. Did you talk to him about—

SEC. HUMPHREY. This was bringing him up to date and giving him information in a general way about what was going on.

QUESTION. Did you put any matter of a decision up to him?

SEC. HUMPHREY. Not me, no. There was nothing—I had nothing that required any decision of any kind.

QUESTION. Did you discuss the action of the—

SEC. HUMPHREY. Except if you want to call Andrews—but that wasn't really a matter for decision.

QUESTION. I was thinking about the budget.

SEC. HUMPHREY. No, there was no matter of decision. I hadn't any pending.

QUESTION. Mr. Secretary, you just informed him about Mr. Andrews?

SEC. HUMPHREY. That's right.

QUESTION. You did not discuss a successor?

SEC. HUMPHREY. No.

MR. HAGERTY. He physically signed the letter of acceptance to Mr. Andrews.

SEC. HUMPHREY. I changed that—I spoke of it simply because that was really a piece of definite business.

QUESTION. Did you discuss the action of the stock market over the past few weeks?

SEC. HUMPHREY. No. No.

QUESTION. Do you know whether the President is aware of the break in the stock market?

SEC. HUMPHREY. Well, I didn't mention it, so I don't know. I wouldn't know.

QUESTION. Did the President express any hopes of his own with respect to a balanced budget?

SEC. HUMPHREY. No. I think he—I know he has hopes of it, but he was—I honestly can't recall when I talked about it. He asked about how we are going, and I told him, and I can't recall whether he—I gathered he approved of it, I'll put it that way. I just really don't remember whether he said anything, whether he said "Good," or "I'm glad"— I just don't remember.

Mr. Hagerty. Refer them to all the statements he has made on that. . . .

Sec. Humphrey. I can assure you that he was not disappointed; at least, I couldn't detect it.

Question. Did you discuss the new budget?

Sec. Humphrey. No, no, the new budget is not ready for discussion.

Question. But you did discuss this year's?

Sec. Humphrey. This is the 1956 budget that I am talking about right now.

Question. Perhaps you meant, but I am not sure—you answered a question, and that was this: That in the event that President Eisenhower retires, would you be receptive to the Republican nomination?

Sec. Humphrey. I have just one candidate and I am going to stick with my candidate.

Question. Suppose the President personally asked you to be a candidate?

Sec. Humphrey. Well, now, boys, I think I have gone far enough on that.

Question. Mr. Secretary, there were reports that Andrews had planned to submit his resignation, I think two or three days after the President's heart attack. Do you know if he delayed it for three weeks because of the President's illness?

Sec. Humphrey. Well, this is not something that has come up out of a clear sky with Mr. Andrews at all. Mr. Andrews has been making plans and we have discussed it. I have known that Mr. Andrews had in contemplation the making of these other arrangements, and that this was a thing that was going to come up for some little time, and we have been making our plans accordingly.

Now, Mr. Andrews—as to just when it would be best to do it depended upon the developments in the service and a great many things. Mr. Andrews has been very considerate in his handling of the matter, as I think we have been with him.

Mr. Hagerty. Bob, that is spelled out in more details in Andrews' letter to the President and in the President's answer to Mr. Andrews and we are stenciling it now.

Question. Mr. Secretary, when you speak of hopeful, we are going to have a balanced budget this year, you are speaking of fiscal 1956—

Sec. Humphrey. Yes, sir, by June 30th coming.

Question. In other words, to wipe out that—

SEC. HUMPHREY. Billion seven.

QUESTION. Yes.

SEC. HUMPHREY. Yes, sir.

QUESTION. Mr. Secretary, if that came about, then, would you say that there was a pretty good chance that you could have a balanced budget for the future year, or a surplus?

SEC. HUMPHREY. Again, all I can say, boys, is the trend that would accomplish that is the trend toward a tax reduction. A further tax reduction. It's the doing of things that will accomplish that will lead the way toward a further tax reduction. Now, whether they will be sufficient or not, only time will tell.

QUESTION. Mr. Secretary, in your statement here, is this the first time you have commented on the Istanbul meeting?

SEC. HUMPHREY. Yes. You see, I was coming out to report to the President, and then it was all held up.

QUESTION. Mr. Secretary, there is some sentiment in this country for foregoing a tax reduction and really going to work on this great national debt. If we have a tax cut, I don't see how you are going to reduce the—

SEC. HUMPHREY. Well, now, I have explained my position on that several times, but just to make it perfectly clear, I will do it again so that you people will understand.

There is only one way that you can pay down on your debt and that is to collect more money from the people than the government is spending currently, so that you have some money left and that you use that money to pay down on the debt.

Now, I personally think—I am a great believer in paying your debts and in paying down on your debts, but I also think that you have to take into account a good many other conditions as to when and how you do it. And I personally think that our taxes are so high, and there is such a burden on our economic well-being, that we ought not to, at a time when our taxes are as high as they are now, have to pay down on our debt when our Nation's necessity for security—for military security—is as great as it is today.

There will come a time—I don't know when it will be—but there will come a time, as there has been in the past, when the expenses for security will not be as heavy as they are today, and when a substantial reduction in expenditures can be made. The time is going to come when there is going to be a much more solid peace in the world, a much better peaceful understanding in the world than there is today.

When the time comes that we are able to make very substantial reductions in our expenditures, then I am going to be in favor of paying down on our debt, as we more slowly reduce the taxes than we do our expenditures, and use the difference to pay on the debt.

QUESTION. Mr. Secretary, you say President Eisenhower is still your candidate. Do you think there is any prospect that the President will run again?

SEC. HUMPHREY. Well, I told you gentlemen I don't know any more about that than you do.

QUESTION. Mr. Secretary, to what do you attribute your optimism about the possibility of reducing expenses for military security in the future?

SEC. HUMPHREY. I think—and I think we all hope—and I think hope to the extent that we believe—and all past history indicates, that these periods of great tension in the world do lead—that you do get into periods of better understanding, and that you do not go ahead with these terrific expenditures that are burdening the whole world, as they are today. Every country in the world today has its economy seriously burdened with expenses for preparedness; and we are—and the whole world—devoting a very large share of everybody's earnings.

You boys don't realize it, but you get right down to brass tacks, every man in this room is devoting some number of hours every single day to make things for the defense of this country, or to having people for the defense of this country—we take the money away from you to provide it—you don't do it yourselves—but we take the money away from you in order to provide it—to build things that aren't doing you one bit of good so far as your scale of living is concerned—so far as the well-being of the American people is concerned.

Except for one thing: And that is to save them from attack by somebody else. Now, if we once get freed from the fear of attack from somebody else, then you fellows aren't going to have to give up as much money as we are now taking away from you to buy these things that are not doing us or you a bit of good except for that one thing. And that money can be used by you and by others to get more things for yourselves, the things you want, the things you need, and raise the scale of living of all of the people in this country and in the world.

QUESTION. This is a mechanical detail—when are you leaving?

SEC. HUMPHREY. I think tomorrow.

QUESTION. Mr. Secretary, getting back to that question of a tax cut following a balanced budget—the way you put it, as I understand it, is that there would be a trend in that direction?

SEC. HUMPHREY. That's right.

QUESTION. Could we put it that way, that, once the budget is balanced, the outlook for a tax reduction will be favorable or—

SEC. HUMPHREY. That's right. It will be much more favorable than it is now. If the trend has sufficient momentum, why, you are headed in the direction to accomplish it.

QUESTION. Can we stress your "hopeful" a little and say that you are hopeful for a balanced budget by the end of this fiscal year which would permit a tax cut?

SEC. HUMPHREY. Well, I don't know. I am hopeful for a balanced budget, and I—surely, you can say I hope for a tax cut. I believe our taxes ought to be cut just as soon as we can afford to cut them.

QUESTION. You hope for a balanced budget, which will permit a tax cut in the next fiscal year?

SEC. HUMPHREY. That's right, looking ahead—looking ahead.

QUESTION. Next calendar year?

SEC. HUMPHREY. Well, I don't know just when—depends on the progress—it depends entirely on the amount of progress.

QUESTION. During the year or afterwards?

SEC. HUMPHREY. That's right.

QUESTION. To sum it up, then, Mr. Secretary, you are hopeful for a balanced budget and a tax cut?

SEC. HUMPHREY. I am hopeful for a balanced budget June 30th. I am hopeful for a tax cut at some time. I—of course, I hope for it June 30th, but I am not hopeful to the extent that I want to say it is assured, or indicated we are going to have it, or anything of the kind.

QUESTION. You hope for a tax cut thereafter?

SEC. HUMPHREY. I am hoping for tax cuts—I think our taxes are too high and I hope we will be able to get them down.

MR. HAGERTY. On the mechanics—the Secretary is going to probably drop in to see the President tomorrow before he leaves here, but it will be just a purely social visit and not business, and he will leave sometime around noon. He also has an engagement this afternoon with Mrs. Doud and Mrs. Moore,—

SEC. HUMPHREY. Who are waiting out at the gate.

"Beautiful—and not a lame duck in the flight!"

Crockett in *The Washington Star*, 1956

MR. HAGERTY. . . . and he has to repeat these things for the cameras, so I wish you would—if you have any more questions—make them fast.

QUESTION. The question I had in mind was, sir, what could you tell us about the President's reaction to your report about the outlook for continued prosperity and budget balancing and the whole favorable picture?

SEC. HUMPHREY. The President seemed pleased and in good spirits and feeling very good about it when I was talking to him.

QUESTION. Thank you, sir.

SEC. HUMPHREY. Thank you, boys, very much.

◀ In this interview is the only intimation in the Humphrey Papers to considerable discussion over the country, following the President's heart attack and possibilities of immobilization, as to whether his Secretary of the Treasury might become a successor candidate for President. One partisan Republican weekly newspaper in Michigan at about this juncture published a banner-lined call to "draft" Secretary Humphrey for President. The Secretary paid no heed to any of it.

Early in 1956, before the President's availability for re-election was determined, the Gallup Poll counted the votes of 1,692 Republican county chairmen of the nation on a potential political successor. Secretary Humphrey received 70 votes.

"A wise, cool head . . . A firm hand"

◀ The largest audience ever to hear Secretary Humphrey gathered in Madison Square Garden, New York City, the night of January 21, 1956, at a "Citizens for Eisenhower" dinner, 13,000 strong. The Secretary was one of four speakers who celebrated President Eisenhower's recovery from the September heart attack and ability to go forward as chief executive. In recounting the glories of the first four years, Mr. Humphrey was assigned naturally to the boast of the first balance of the Budget.

Speech by Secretary Humphrey at Madison Square Garden, New York.

January 21, 1956

We are here tonight to salute the greatest American of our time—Dwight David Eisenhower. History may ultimately record him as the greatest man of many times, but it is clearly evident at the moment that he is beyond doubt the outstanding figure in the world today.

Never before in history have the hopes of so many millions of people throughout the world been centered on the shoulders of one man. Never before in history has a man stricken with illness had the fervent prayers for his recovery from so many millions of people all over the world.

One reason for this great attachment of so many millions to our

President is the fact that he has become a symbol for peace. A military man for most of his life, President Eisenhower has fought valiantly for peace and against war during the past three decades.

His military service in the Philippines and later in Africa and in Europe brought him into intimate contact with the people of many nations. His warm personality, remarkable good will, great wisdom, enormous patience, and devotion to duty have become well known to both the leaders and the ordinary citizens of many countries on a close personal basis.

In World War II he was the conquering hero who led the forces which repelled the armies of the dictators and eventually won peace and freedom for the overrun nations. He returned to Europe to head the drive for a NATO structure again to protect the free world from another threat to peace and freedom.

During the past three years as President of this great land, President Eisenhower has become increasingly in the eyes of the world the great hope for a just and lasting peace. He has become the embodiment of the fervent hopes of millions of the world's people for the eventual day of just peace among nations.

So I am humbly proud, and I know that you too are proud, to be among the vast numbers of American citizens who tonight are saluting President Eisenhower.

His character is reflected in the objectives he has held and worked for during his term of office, and the depth of his sincerity has imbued his associates with those same objectives and enthusiasm for their accomplishment. His objectives are few and simple. They can be characterized with but a single word—"progress"—steady, insistent, persistent progress in three fundamental directions:

Toward a just and lasting peace throughout the world.

Toward a widespread and continuing prosperity.

Toward greater freedom for the individual in his pursuit of happiness and protection from the ravages of adversity for all mankind.

His high ideals are firmly footed on the solid foundation of practicability. He is no idle dreamer. He wants and works for his dreams to come true. . . .

His accomplishments toward peace have recently been described at length in the State of the Union Message to the Congress. The problems are enormous. The broad highway to accomplishment is not clear and it is beset with frustrations and difficulties at every turn, but the bare fact remains that within a few months after he took office the shooting stopped in Korea and no American mothers have had to worry about their sons and daughters since then in a shooting war.

Crises continually beset us and will continue to do so, but we can all rest assured that we have a wise, cool head directing a firm hand on the tiller to steer our ship of state as carefully as it can be done between the rocks and shoals of war and aggression, but forward— always forward, pressing forward toward a just and lasting peace.

His accomplishments toward a widespread and continuing prosperity are here before our eyes to see on almost every hand. Only a part of our farm population is still suffering from the burdensome surpluses accumulated under past laws ill-devised to bring on anything but the very burdens which are now bearing so heavily on farm crops, production and prices in some fields. Practical, workable relief in that area is of first concern, and no problem is receiving greater attention. But it is the result of an accumulation of years of bad practice and cannot be soundly corrected all at once.

Everywhere else on almost every side we are having the greatest employment, the most jobs, the best pay, the lowest percentage of people unemployed, the highest earnings and the best times, by any measure, that this country has ever seen with new high records in almost every line.

It is no accident that this great economic achievement has come about under the leadership of President Eisenhower. We have achieved prosperity without the bloody cost of war, and without the false promise of inflation. The American people today enjoy not only a record economy but a sound one.

This achievement in economic integrity is no surprise to any one who knows the President. It reflects the integrity of the man. It is a subject, next to peace, that is closest to his heart, and closest *to your welfare.*

I am asked many times why we in the Eisenhower Administration have given such very great importance to balancing the budget and stopping inflation.

Balancing the budget in prosperous times is the prime requisite of financial integrity. We have made financial integrity and stability in the cost of living one of our foremost goals. We have not done this out of any academic concern. It isn't just a matter of accounting or book-keeping or business man's fetish.

Money has no value except as it affects people. We are so concerned about the value of the dollar because it is the people's money we are collecting, spending—and defending, and because stability in the cost of living so vitally affects each of us.

We are determined to avoid inflation, as well as to prevent deflation. Either can jeopardize the happiness, the hopes, and the well-being of all the 167 million people of this great nation.

Inflation can steal away your savings, your pension, and the value of your wages. Deflation can endanger millions of jobs.

The integrity—the staying power—of the value of the dollar is of primary importance to each and everyone of us no matter what our condition. Rich or poor—old or young—on a salary or a daily wage, or living on a pension or an insurance policy we are all concerned, not only as it affects our current cost of living but our very jobs are at stake.

A job is the most important thing in America. Whether you are working for yourself, in a profession or in a factory, in a mine, in transportation, in some form of service, or on a farm, it is all the same.

To have a job you must have tools, power and machines to work with; and some one must save and invest to supply them. We have a rapidly growing population and over a million new jobs must be created every year to supply our needs. That means new tools—new factories—new mines—new trucks and trains, and all kinds of things to work with.

That means more and more investment to buy them; and who will invest if the value of their money is uncertain? Who will buy the big bond issues? Who will make the mortgage loans? You all are involved. Not only is your job at stake but your home is also. Who will make the loans that permit you to buy your home or your car on time if the value of money is uncertain?

Moreover, millions of you are also investors. It is not the rich who supply the funds today. The great investors in this country are not only the millions of small individual investors but are the small savers who, through the insurance companies, the pension funds, the savings banks, union and fraternal funds, and the other ways of saving buy the stocks, bonds, and mortgages and make the other loans.

Sound money is the incentive that keeps men doing their best.

That spurs their imaginations to do research and make new inventions. That underlies our great industrial machine. That will modernize the old jobs and make the new jobs to make the new and better and cheaper things we all need to continually increase our scale of living. That will induce the savings and investment of savings of the millions of Americans who have confidence in our free system and the soundness of our finances.

These are the material reasons why a balanced budget, financial responsibility, and the soundness of the dollar are of fundamental importance to each and every one of us no matter who we are, nor where we are.

Bad money, like a bad apple, will rot the whole barrel. A government that adopts inflation as a policy to achieve its ends leads its people into a false land.

When you tinker with a value so basic as the value of money—when you induce inflation and make it a policy to give the people more and more income of less and less buying power—falseness in all other things must follow.

The government which adopts a policy of inflation must pre-empt to itself an ever growing web of other powers with which it can hide the falseness of its money and smother the complaints of the people as they see the buying power of their savings and life insurance being stolen away, as the prices of food, clothing and shelter rise faster than more false money can supply. False money leads to the slave state.

The buying power of the dollar dropped from 100 cents to only 52 cents in just fifteen years preceding the election of this Administration. But the long trend of inflation that had been eating away the value of your dollar has now been halted, and there has been no significant loss in the buying power of the dollar now for over three full years.

This means that when your incomes are increased—and they are now at record highs—you have a real raise, not merely a raise to match the higher cost of living that was for so long the order of the day. This has been a real "Eisenhower extra."

You all remember their slogans in the last campaign "You never had it so good" and "Don't let them take it away." You can ask them now "Who wants to go back?"

Now, how did this all happen? What were some of the specific moves by the Eisenhower Administration which contributed to this result?

Total Government spending was cut sharply. Spending now is $10 billion under three years ago, and $14 billion less than had been planned by the final budget of the previous Administration.

We at long last have balanced the budget, the surest index to thrifty management in a home, in a business, or in the Federal Government.

And we have made the largest dollar tax cut in the history of this country. This great tax reduction of almost $7.5 billion was a mighty assist in the transition from a war-time to a peace-time economy.

The Eisenhower Administration has also accomplished much toward greater freedom for the individual in his pursuit of happiness and from the ravages of adversity. Artificial controls, rationing, price fixing and all manner of directives and decisions from Washington were promptly removed in nearly everything but farm programs where rigid laws prevented.

Ten million additional people were included in social security benefits. The minimum wage was increased. Additional health research is assisting in the prevention and treatment of disease. Large scale integrated federal road and school building programs are proposed. The scale of living of 167 million Americans is higher than ever in our history. . . .

We can never take for granted the preservation of our free way of life. Only a people of high integrity can deserve freedom. No people, however great, can preserve integrity if it must transact its business, measure its worth, in a false, inflated currency. Prudence, thrift, honest work and honest government must all go hand in hand.

And make no mistake about it. It is no coincidence that, since the scourge of inflation was let loose on the modern world, slave states have multiplied.

In the slave state, men do things under the lash of the whip of "do it or else." They have been robbed of the honest values that spur men in the free world to work, to save, and to build a better life. We are determined here on preserving those values, so that in our country men will never lack the incentive to do the things in freedom that make for a fuller and better life—and do them far better than they can ever be done in any slave state.

These basic incentives to honesty, thrift, hard work, and production cannot fail to inspire—as they have inspired—thrifty, hard-working government. And they cannot fail to preserve among our people those qualities of prudence, thrift, industry, and spirit of self-betterment that have made them the greatest and best provided people on this earth.

In these times of deadly contest between our way of freedom and the reactionary ways of the communist slave state, it behooves us all to keep intact and vigorous all our qualities of greatness. Only if we do so can we remain a great beacon light of freedom and promise in the free world, an encouragement to all others to pursue our way of freedom, and avoid seduction into slavery.

The large measure of success in restoring freedom from war and financial integrity and progress in the pursuit of happiness for all the people are truly the proudest accomplishments of the great leader we salute tonight.

It reflects, as perhaps nothing else can, the basic honesty and high character of the President himself.

There is no more fitting time than this to pledge that we shall not falter in this great task, nor shall we ever be driven from it by men who would ignore tomorrow's doom for today's advantage.

The record and the critic

Speech by Secretary Humphrey to a Republican Dinner at the Chase Hotel, St. Louis.

October 22, 1956

. . . In accepting the Presidential nomination four years ago, Candidate Eisenhower said: "It is our aim to give our country a program of progressive policies drawn from our finest traditions; to unite us wherever we have been divided; to strengthen freedom wherever, among any group, it has weakened; to build a sure foundation for sound prosperity for all here at home and for a just and sure peace throughout the world."

After almost four years, a promise-and-performance box score on the three major areas into which President Eisenhower's pledges fell may be of interest.

First, he promised to wage peace after first establishing a mighty defense structure so that we could maneuver from a position of strength.

Second, he was determined to achieve solvency for this country through efficient fiscal and tax programs, economical administration, and a return to free enterprise and individual initiative.

Third, he pledged to promote the health and welfare of our people and a more abundant life for all.

The resolve to wage peace and win it was made in the shadow of a war in Korea, a war which those in control had been apparently powerless to end, yet unwilling to win.

Before his inauguration, President Eisenhower flew to Korea. Six months after President Eisenhower took office, the shooting was ended.

There still are many difficult problems for which solutions have not yet been found. But a system of treaties and mutual defense pacts has been created among our Allies, which has strengthened the position of the whole free world and lays a foundation for co-operative efforts to provide for an increasingly effective defense of the peace we are enjoying. . . .

Our defenses are at peak efficiency. Admiral Radford, Chairman of the Joint Chiefs of Staff, said recently: "I feel as of today that we are better prepared to meet an emergency than we ever have been during my forty years' service in the armed forces."

Yet President Eisenhower honored his promise to scrutinize the necessity for every expenditure and cut waste from each program. He has reduced planned spending without cutting into the "bone and muscle" of real and effective defense. Today, at less cost, we have an armed strength more efficient and better organized than ever before.

Our military might must be kept constantly in balance with what our economy can afford to maintain over an extended period of time. The foundation of our program is our unalterable belief that a sound economy is absolutely necessary to a strong defense over an extended period.

We have the world's key economy today. If it should crumble, our Allies would soon be in dire peril.

Our defenses, and our economy must both be kept at maximum development and in delicate balance, for the greatest bulwark of our security is the productive might of our magnificent economic machine.

The maintenance of this delicate balance is the most important task of any administration. This is so not only because our very lives are at stake, but because the continuation of good times and ever better living for all our people at home cannot be assured unless that balance is maintained. . . .

Now who is it who urges the American people to replace this foremost military leader in all this world? And who is the man who would replace him to guide us in making these most vital decisions?

Is it a man who has led the world's greatest armies to final victories?

Is it a man who has unified the policies of heads of state in a great crusade for human freedom?

Is it a man who has changed the entire direction of a nation away from a 20-year trend of centralization, inflation, and laxity in government?

Is it a man experienced in international affairs who has demonstrated superior ability to keep conflicting tensions from flaring into war?

It is not. . . .

Rather, it is a man whose reputation rests almost entirely upon words and phrases; one whose record is filled with things he says he *will* do, and almost entirely lacking in things he *has* done.

That President Eisenhower has fulfilled his promise to promote a more abundant life is apparent for every one to see. We have record high employment—more than 66 million people working at good jobs. We have record high wages. We have production of goods and services exceeding all previous records. . . .

The only group of our people who have not been sharing fully in this great prosperity is the farm group. They still feel the bad effects of past years of ill-advised legislation when farm laws were passed for politicians rather than farmers. But even the farm situation has already begun to improve.

Under President Eisenhower's health and welfare program, old-age and survivors' insurance has extended protection to over 10 million additional people.

A three-year program of federal aid to states for improved hospital service, greater facilities for the aged, chronically ill and disabled, and greater diagnostic and treatment facilities, and health research has been started.

Our problems today are—happily—the problems of great prosperity. They are nonetheless real and difficult and must be courageously faced.

We can't have high prosperity, abundant jobs at high pay, high confidence, high spending, and wide general expansion with cheap, unlimited money and a stable cost of living all at the same time.

We are prosperous, and that means we are working very close to the limits of our manpower and our materials. We are at peace, so there is no place for wartime controls or powers to ration work and materials. We are free and we want to stay free, so we do not want to dictate wages, prices or rents. We do not want to arbitrarily allocate materials and labor by Government order or decree.

But just because we are prosperous—in peace and in freedom—because the public in general has great confidence in the future, we all want to buy and expand.

We must keep the supply of money from growing beyond the supply of people and materials. That is the only way to avoid rapidly rising prices and inflation while maintaining prosperity with both peace and freedom.

We don't want to go the "easy" money road, the old familiar road to inflation. We don't want to go up only to come down. We want to let natural corrections and restraints operate freely.

This prosperity . . . didn't just happen. The President came to office near the peak of a "crash" preparedness program. Critics said that the transition from war to peace could not be achieved without an economic disaster. They filled the headlines and air waves at that time with gloomy forebodings and warnings of depression.

The President's program promised a new, a better day, not for any particular group in our population, but for all the people. We have seen that day dawn. It is just the beginning if we continue to carry forward his constructive policies. . . .

Interrupting "our close association"

Letter of resignation by Secretary Humphrey.

May 28, 1957

Dear Mr. President:

It is with sincere regret that I tender my resignation as Secretary of the Treasury, to be effective at the time which you determine will be best suited to the transfer of this office to my successor. I hope that this date may be no later than the close of the current Congressional session.

You know of the responsibilities which I left when I assumed this office. Because of the illness and recent retirement from business of one of my former partners, my resignation from your Cabinet is now an absolute necessity.

I want to express my deep appreciation for the warmth of the friendship which you and Mamie have given to Pam and to me and for the opportunity you have given us for the friendships we have made with the members of your official family, which we will cherish always.

I am most grateful for the privilege you have given me to assist you during these past four and a half years in developing financial plans and programs which you and I jointly have deemed to be in the best interests of our country.

I will be glad to assist with Congressional consideration of the various items of the budget, with particular reference to the defense and mutual assistance programs which so vitally affect the security of our country, and with such other matters now pending in which I can be helpful.

As you know, Randolph Burgess, who has served so effectively as Undersecretary, is planning to leave his present post to accept another Government appointment. At our request, he has also agreed to remain with the Treasury for the transition period.

The knowledge that you have asked Robert Anderson to succeed me allows me to leave with the assurance that the policies in which we believe will be continued. In our close association during the time of his previous service in your Administration, I learned of his great capacity at first hand and I know that it is his fixed determination to carry forward the plans and policies in our fiscal affairs which have

"And if you were
in my boots, George?"

Poinier in
The Detroit News, 1956

guided us continually during the time that I have been here with you.

It is hard to interrupt our close association, but you will know and will remember, I am sure, that I stand ready to help you and your Administration in the future in any way that I can.

With every good wish, I am

Yours very sincerely,
GEORGE M. HUMPHREY

The President's letter accepting Secretary Humphrey's resignation.

May 29, 1957

Dear George:

Although I have known for more than two years that your retirement from Government service could not be indefinitely postponed, the actual receipt of your letter of resignation fills me with profound

"It won't be the same without you, George!"

Haynie in
The Greensboro News,
1957

regret. Yet, because of your personal situation, which I fully under-stand, I, of course, accept your decision.

It would be idle to attempt expression of my feelings of gratitude for the extraordinary talents that more than four years ago you brought to the Treasury Department and for the loyal and tireless way in which you have, ever since, applied them to problems of the greatest import. It has been of real satisfaction to me that in working on these problems we have invariably found our conclusions and con-victions to be practically identical.

I thank you further for allowing me to designate the actual date of your separation from the federal service, with the commitment that such date will be no later than the close of the current Congressional session. There are a number of critical problems to be considered during this session, and, until the bulk of these have been satisfactorily solved, I deeply believe that your experience and the confidence that you enjoy everywhere in the Government, will be great assets in reach-ing the best answers. Consequently, the date you turn over your duties to your successor will, within the limits indicated, be dictated by circumstances.

I share your satisfaction that Robert Anderson has been able to accept my nomination as the individual to take over your duties in the Treasury Department. I am sending his name to the Senate today. I agree with you that he will continue to follow the general path that you have so clearly marked out. So long as you must leave the post, I can think of no other to whom I would rather entrust the responsibilities of that office.

Finally, I am grateful to you for your offer of future assistance to the Administration. From time to time I know we shall want to call upon you for advice and counsel, and have no doubt that such occasions will be of considerable frequency.

On the personal side, I cannot tell you what a sense of loss it is to Mamie and to me to know that you and Pam will shortly leave the intimate Cabinet family. But a friendship of the strength and depth of ours cannot suffer merely because of your departure from Washington.

With affectionate regard to you both,

As ever,

DWIGHT D. EISENHOWER

GENERAL AND

PERSONAL

Tribute by the home town

Remarks by Secretary Humphrey at a Civic Dinner in his honor at Saginaw, Michigan. Saginaw was the Secretary's boyhood home, and the whole city prepared this welcoming event for months. Secretary Humphrey was introduced by President Eisenhower over closed-circuit television from Washington.

November 10, 1953

Schoolmates, neighbors, and old friends and many newer friends:

I would like to laugh but I'm afraid I'm going to cry. If I do, don't pay any attention to it, just go right on. I think that really the events of today—seeing so many people I haven't seen for so long—having the pleasure of visiting with them—people who have come here since Pam and I left—there never has been and there never will be a day in our lives, for Pam and me, like this.

There's just one thing about it that makes it finer and that is that I've seen about 50 or maybe 100 people—it's been advertised as a homecoming for me—and I think there are about 50 or maybe 100 people who have had just as great a thrill as Pam and I have had because they've seen many of their old friends too.

I would like to stand here and reminisce about a lot of things that have gone on in the past. I'd just like to go over some things with pretty near everybody I see except for one thing—I might tell a lot of things they wouldn't want the rest of you to know.

I couldn't help but think as they put that picture of the bicycle horse on the screen of all the things that happen in this world in your lifetime. That horse I'll never forget as long as I live, I had a hard time riding it around, and Genesee Avenue was paved with cedar blocks, and the summer that I had that horse they tore up the cedar blocks and put in the asphalt pavement, and I rode it up and down that asphalt pavement. It was swell—it lasted a long time.

When Bud was a little boy, I tried to teach him how to play football, and I showed him how to hold the football and then would show him that this is the way Bottle Thompson used to do it and then kick it 75 yards. Then I would show him that this is the way Octie (now Dr. Albert C. Furstenberg, dean of the University of Michigan School of Medicine) used to play tackle and "Zip" Picard at quarter and Art Franke played end. I would tell him that that was the way they would run and everything and it made quite an impression until we came home for Christmas.

Some of my kind friends recalled the 1908 game when we were playing for the championship with Ann Arbor, and I was at the backfield for a few minutes. That was all I ever did get in. Some big guy by the name of Conklin was on the Ann Arbor team and he picked me up, ball and all, and started running for the goal.

And, of course, I went right out of the game.

Well, there is just one thing that has disturbed me a little bit tonight. I've always been told that one must beware of the power of a woman. I think if back in those days all of those fellows had thought that for a meeting they would catch you, Bottle, Art, and Octie here with me in the Arthur Hill High School, they would wonder what's going on. All I could ever remember about the Arthur Hill High School was 11 guys named Earl Wilson running around the end.

I can understand how as time goes on I'm getting used to seeing poor taxpayers getting it in the neck—that's common practice—with big beautiful buildings like this, but then I saw a great big case as I entered the building—all filled with cups and trophies. How in the world did Arthur Hill High School ever get all those? And also, when I entered, all I could think of was the wonderful little girls—all dressed up—that were guiding us along. I began to wonder if all the boys on the east side were over here now.

I thought that so long as Pam and I were working for all of you—now that you're our bosses—that perhaps it would be appropriate for me to make a little report to you as to what we're trying to do, and what we ran up against. I'm not going to bore you very long, but I thought that maybe you ought to have a little report, so I have written this down to read to you.

There are two great goals on which this Administration is determined. First, this nation must and will provide the military posture best designed to promote peace in the world. Second, this nation must and will maintain the sound economy and productive power which is the basis for that military strength and leadership for peace.

This Administration is soberly and sincerely committed to and working toward both these two goals. We no longer have the physical security of being protected by two broad oceans, and we must be guarded and protected against the forces which might bring about swift destruction. So, the goal of peace—real lasting peace—must always be continuously sought for the good of all. In the meantime and as a means to that end, we must be militarily strong, and at the same time maintain a healthy economy and a productive economy without which a strong defense is absolutely impossible. This must also command its full measure of consideration in all that we do.

Let us just look for a minute to the burden of inheritance in the physical and economic field with which we were left and with which we have to contend in attempting to keep ourselves militarily strong in our quest for peace. Our inheritance included huge public debts— $81 billion in COD orders—orders that were placed—one—two or three years ago that were to come this year, next year or the year after in the future and no money provided for payment. Extravagance in the Government, a staggering tax burden, rigidly controlled economy— this only eight months ago—controls on prices and wages. Orders from bureaus—directives and directions from Washington telling us—each one of us what to do from day to day. A war in stalemate—a war daily taking the lives of boys every day in Korea. These were just some of the burdens we fell heir to. We faced hard financial facts as indicated in President Eisenhower's State of the Union Address.

We found deficits and we have attempted to balance the budget. The first step toward balancing the budget was to get previously planned spending under control. A thorough review of civilian and military programs was immediately undertaken.

Through the help of the Appropriations Committee of Congress, this Administration was able to cut planned expenditures for the fiscal year of 1954 by more than $6 billion under the January estimate of the previous Administration. This has resulted in cutting a prospective deficit from more than $11 billion to less than $4 billion. This is an important turning point in Government finances because for the first time in recent years—estimates provide for less spending in the current year than before.

More than 70 per cent of our spending is for military defense or atomic programs. Under such circumstances the reason for not moving faster is that we are eager to make sure that savings are only made with extreme care—and to be protected during the great peril in which we live in this Atomic Age.

The second objective—meeting the cost of this defense. We wish to provide security tomorrow as well as today, thereafter until we find a way to lasting peace. We can and we must spend to protect ourselves. We also know, however, that real defense of America will not result simply from the spending of huge amounts of money. We know that any program for defense must be measured not by its cost but by its wisdom.

Now, the management of this huge debt. This Administration plans to do two things which will make this debt less inflationary.

At every appropriate time we will extend the maturity of debt by placing longer term issues. We must be careful not to dislocate the sense of economy. We cannot always move on both fronts at the same time. Our goal is clear, and we're looking toward it.

Every fractional new high in the Consumers Price Index of the cost of living receives interested public attention. From 1946 to 1952, this index increased from 80 to 114 or a total of 34 points in these six years. In marked contrast, during the past year it has increased only one point which is 1 per cent during the year. A temporary stability has been achieved on a high level of productivity.

This Administration is reducing taxes, because it has reduced expenses, and only because we have made this reduction can we end the excess profits tax on December 31, and make a 10 per cent reduction on individual income tax. No tax reduction whenever planned could be justified without these savings. Additional tax reduction is desired by all of the people and is essential to continued growth in this country—and so that this land may continue as a nation—a land of opportunity—with their youth interested and anxious to better themselves—for the young can't long endure as such under the stricter taxes.

Taxes can only be reduced as expenditures are reduced. This Administration believes that the average American can do more for himself if he is allowed to do so than the Government can do for him. They must be given the right to competitive enterprise and free initiative, courage to take a chance and the opportunity to better one's self. These have made America great.

The collective effort of 160 million Americans, each for himself, striving to improve his lot, advance his children and improve the position of each succeeding generation—that all taken together has been a power to create higher standards of living for all. Opportunity is the rightful heritage of our children. It must be protected, guarded and handed on. . . .

May Divine Providence ever guide us toward peace and give us the strength and wisdom and the courage to realistically face the facts as we see them and act vigorously with freedom toward them.

Thank you, friends, very much for the day.

I appreciate it more than I can say and so does Pam, don't you?

"I love any kind of a horse"

*Remarks by Secretary Humphrey to the annual
dinner of the Thoroughbred Racing Associations
of the United States at the Plaza Hotel, New York.*

December 3, 1953

Horse racing in the United States has grown tremendously in the past decade. This applies both to the trotters and the thoroughbreds. As a matter of fact, millions of Americans do not know the difference— horse racing is horse racing to them and that's all there is to it. There are, of course, many important and wide differences between the two, but we are concerned here tonight only with the racing of thoroughbreds.

The growth of thoroughbred racing, both as a sport and as a business during the past ten years, for which complete figures are available, can best be illustrated by the following comparisons for the years 1942 and 1952:

Year	Tracks	Starters	Racing Days	No. of Races	Purse Distribution	Attendance
1942	49	12,614	1,792	14,251	$16,548,492	10,611,759
1952	92	23,813	2,893	23,947	58,835,225	27,663,412

The figures for 1953, when finally compiled, will show even greater growth.

Thoroughbred racing is not only the world's oldest spectator sport that has continued to modern times, but it is today attended by more people than any other sport in this country, having surpassed all others in spectator attendance.

It had its beginnings in America in earliest colonial times. Its history in those days is fascinating. It flourished in the Carolinas, Virginia, and New York. It moved with the population into Tennessee and Kentucky and into New England. Importations of the best blooded stock were made at the earliest times for the improvement of the breed, and the leaders of the times, including General Washington himself, participated as both breeders and owners, as well as in the promotion of important matches and race meetings.

When Andrew Jackson was President, he kept some of his race horses in the White House stable. John Hervey, under the pen name of the great "Salvator," has written a most interesting history of both the horses and the famous people interested in them in colonial days.

Racing has had ups and downs during the years, but has continually gained in interest and participation, until today it is not only our leading spectator sport, but it is also an enormous business.

It represents today investments of something over $700 million. It employs some 65,000 persons with an estimated annual payroll of $235 million. Nearly 28 million people went to the races last year, and that figure will be increased when the statistics are available for this year. It is conducted in 24 states under regulatory laws, and paid to those states which sponsored it, something over $120 million in revenue in a single year.

This money paid to the several states has been used by them to build and operate schools, hospitals, and all sorts of improvements and benefits for old and young. It is an important item in their revenues. Indeed, so important that there is always the threat that efforts to increase it may seriously injure or even kill the goose that lays this enormous golden egg for them. Stakes and purses this year were estimated to total more than $59 million in the United States alone not including Canada, Mexico or Cuba, and the 19,000 horses that competed for that huge sum represent a capital investment of over $75 million.

There are more than 27,000 young horses, stallions, and brood mares on over 1,000 farms in this country valued at over $90 million for the stock alone, in addition to the value of the farms and all of the attendant items that are involved.

It is truly big sport, and it is truly big business. It has long been the sport of kings, and it still continues to be, in the sense that in this great free land of ours, every man is a king in his own right. To choose for himself how he will live, how he will worship and what he will do for his own pleasure and enjoyment. It is an old adage that "all men are equal in and under the turf," and racing is conducted in America on that basis with its wide appeal to the interests of all. It is enjoyed and participated in both by our leaders in industry and government, as well as by millions of other good honest Americans who find relaxation, health, and happiness in the sport.

The fact that it has grown to such proportions and is now so widely and favorably known is not just an accident. No small credit for its elevation in public esteem can be attributed to this fine organization that is our host tonight. The Jockey Club for years has led the way, but this young organization of Thoroughbred Racing Associations of the United States has done more than any other single influence to enforce high standards, and, in practical ways, with vigorous action, police and promote racing on the highest ethical plane. Its Thoroughbred Racing Protective Bureau, financed entirely by its member tracks, is second only to the FBI in public recognition for effective detection and correction of misconduct in its field. It has done a tremendous job in raising standards and eliminating many of the causes of criticism. No sport or no business in this country or elsewhere has done more for self-policing and practical enforcement of its highest standards.

It has been so effective and the results have been so obvious to the public, that it has had wide acclaim and is largely responsible for the increased public confidence in the ethical standards of the sport. It is, of course, a never-ending job which must be vigorously continued Its scope must be widened and it must continue to promptly detect and harshly crack down on every violation of its code.

In addition to all this, there has been a tremendous improvement in the comforts and conveniences for the race-going public. There are today, and, of course, always will be complaints about the inadequacy of facilities on some of the great gala days. That cannot be avoided. You never can build for the great day alone. But by and large, the increasing crowds are being better and better cared for, with more convenience, more comfort for enjoying the sport, than ever before.

Great as the strides have been thus far, with the development of this relatively young, but most effective organization, it cannot rest on its oars. It must progress, actively sponsored and continue to provide for the development and the improvement of this great business and sport.

I was particularly impressed reading an account the other evening of the remarks made by Alfred Vanderbilt a few weeks ago in Kentucky. He made several interesting suggestions that should be followed up. But the thing that impressed me most was the fact, which he pointed out, that no part of this great business can prosper alone. Each is dependent upon prosperity in the other branches. The breeding farms cannot grow and develop and import the best stock from abroad without good sales and high prices for yearlings. High prices for yearlings follow high purse and stake distribution. These in turn depend on good racing.

Good racing cannot be had without public support. And without good horses, clean and keen competition, the public will lose interest. From the foal at the farm until the last racing fan leaves the gate to go home, prosperity for one means prosperity for all. This great train of events carried on by so many people in so many places can only result from constant improvement being made all along the line.

The big stables and the big stakes and the occasional $700 horse that wins one-half million dollars get the screaming headlines, but the backbone of racing is supplied by those hundreds and hundreds of little owners and breeders who breed or buy and race a few horses each year, dreaming of the day when they may see the colt they bred covered with roses after he has won the Derby. They are not only the backbone of racing, they are almost its forgotten man. Their expenses have increased tremendously. If they are lucky enough to win a race, nearly everybody working at the track takes a cut before they get their share. It takes a pretty fair horse just to break even.

I suggest that more consideration for their problems might well be given by this Association and its affiliated organizations. Among their many problems, the taxation of their profits, if any, and losses is as important to them as it is to the bigger stables. It is hoped that the new tax bill to be considered by the Congress this coming spring, will more adequately clarify and simplify the tax procedures applicable to them.

There is one other aspect resulting from this tremendous increase in racing which I believe your fine organization may well begin to think about. The tremendous growth of racing itself is increasing the importance of this problem. What I have in mind is simply this. It's always possible to get too much of even a good thing. There is hardly a large population center in this country that has not, within an area of 50 miles, or so, one or more thoroughbred race tracks, with a trotting track or two in addition. The huge investment now required for the giving of all the comforts for the benefit of the public attending the races is so great that there is bound to be more and more pressure for the greater use of these facilities.

This means a great temptation to seek more and more days racing at each location. Continuous racing in any locality which draws upon a single area for its support with thoroughbreds running in the afternoon and trotters going at night can sow the seeds of growing trouble. Trouble in any one locality can rapidly spread to others. The way to stop it, is to never let it start.

Isn't it time, and might it not be well, for some committee of this great organization to study the facts, keep fully posted as to just what is going on in all of the various localities involved, and then consider such means as might be appropriate to give the public the sport they want, but not to surfeit them with it? Moderation may be difficult to fairly accomplish, but it alone will avoid the difficulties that may well follow excesses. The candy is always sweeter if there is just enough to go around, but not enough for indigestion.

I cannot tell you what a pleasure it has been for me to have this opportunity to be with you here tonight. I have owned, shown, hunted, bred and raced horses since early boyhood days, in one way or another. I like every branch of the sport and love any kind of a horse. For years and years, at times when problems have piled up so that I cannot go to sleep, I just start reading the last horse paper. Then all the problems disappear and I start thinking how to breed the mares the following spring, how the yearlings are doing, or when I will breed the horse that will win the triple crown. . . .

The first iron ore down the Seaway

Remarks by Secretary Humphrey on the arrival
of the first ship carrying ore from Labrador,
coming through the new St. Lawrence Seaway,
at East Ninth Street Municipal Pier, Cleveland.

September 4, 1954

This is a great day. . . . For all of us, this is a great thing. We have been waiting twelve years to see this, and here it is. . . .

This cargo of iron ore from northeastern Canada means a great deal to Cleveland and to the other communities on the Great Lakes. It is an important new source of an important raw material. It seems to me important, too, that it is coming from Canada to the United States; for in a world where jealousies and hatreds between other countries are so common, Canada and our country live as friends of one another along 3,000 miles of unprotected and unfortified border.

A great many persons will look at this iron ore and see only red dirt. But when I look at it I see great buildings which are constructed of the steel which comes out of this red iron ore—buildings like the Terminal Tower and the great Cleveland Stadium. I see all of the kinds of things we need and use which are made of steel, clear down to the needles and pins. Steel is a mighty important thing to our country and the whole world. We not only build and manufacture from it, we fought two World Wars with it, and those wars were won because of our superior production and quality and uses of steel. . . .

About a friend

Remarks by Secretary Humphrey to the annual
dinner of the Pennsylvania Society of New York
in presenting the Society's Gold Medal
to Richard K. Mellon of Pittsburgh. Waldorf-Astoria
Hotel, New York.

December 11, 1954

This is a most agreeable honor for me this evening. It is not often that the opportunity is presented to have the high privilege of honoring a distinguished citizen but also a life-long admired and devoted friend.

Richard K. Mellon is one of Pennsylvania's most outstanding citizens by ancestry and by right of his own many and varied accomplishments for the lasting benefit of his fellow man.

In work, in business and in sports for more than 30 years, we have been closely associated in a firm friendship that has brought enduring recollections of pleasure and happiness to us both.

So that now when it is my high privilege to be selected to present to him the highest award for distinguished citizenship from this great society of the people of his state, I do so not only with a great feeling of pride and honor in his accomplishments but with a real personal joy in participating in such a magnificent tribute to my good friend.

The Society's Gold Medal was founded on the tenth anniversary of the Society in 1908 as a means of recognizing "distinguished achievement." Over the years, each December the Society has gathered to honor an individual who has achieved eminence on the world scene.

The man to whom we pay tribute tonight has done outstanding service in furthering the free enterprise and initiative which have made this nation so great.

He is one of the nation's great leaders in banking and a wise counsellor in the affairs of many of our leading corporations. A native of Pittsburgh, he began his business career as a messenger in the Mellon National Bank in 1920. From assistant cashier in 1924 to a vice president in '28, he became president in '34 and chairman of the board of the Mellon National Bank & Trust Company in 1946. As you well know, he is now governor and president of T. Mellon and Sons, and a director of many leading corporations such as Aluminum Corporation of America, General Motors, the Koppers Company, Pittsburgh Plate Glass, Pennsylvania Railroad, and many more.

True to the traditions of great leaders who go into uniform in time of need, Dick Mellon became a student pilot in the Air Corps in 1918. He re-entered the service as a major in April of 1942 and came out as a colonel in 1945. He is now a major general in the Reserves.

But his greatest accomplishment and the one for which he will be long honored and remembered is his great work in leading civic development by the Pittsburgh Regional Planning Association and the Allegheny Conference on Community Development. In this he has helped to inspire and accomplish one of the greatest civic improvement programs that has ever been attempted. It has transformed the central business district and other congested areas of the city of Pittsburgh to the everlasting advantage of thousands of its citizens and has improved life in Pittsburgh for years to come.

He also has contributed much as a trustee of the American Museum of Natural History, Carnegie Institute, and countless other charitable enterprises for the great good of so many of his fellow men.

Fortunately for all, he is still a young man and, being a man of vision and energy, his accomplishments of the past are only evidence of his will and determination to improve the lot of others in continued progress for the future.

So it is that it is my privilege to ask my friend and your great fellow citizen to take his rightful place on the distinguished list of his predecessors as recipients of this Society's Gold Medal, which includes such illustrious names as Henry Ford, Marshal Foch, Herbert Hoover, Sr., General Marshall, Andrew Carnegie, Charles Dawes, President Eisenhower, the Senator here tonight—and his illustrious uncle, the great Secretary of the Treasury, Andrew W. Mellon. It is a great honor and a rare personal pleasure for me to ask Richard K. Mellon to join with these outstanding figures as a recipient of the Gold Medal of the Pennsylvania Society.

"Their entertaining works"

A preface by Secretary Humphrey to President Eisenhower's
Cartoon Book published in 1956 by Frederick Fell, Inc.,
for the National Cartoonists' Society in the interests of
the United States Savings Bonds program. Publication
was promoted by the Secretary. The cartoons were
unpublished original impressions of the President of 85
nationally known political cartoonists and authors of
comic strips.

The cartoons in this book were presented to President Eisenhower by the artists after he had been elected an honorary member of the National Cartoonists' Society in June, 1954. The President has consented to their publication as a permanent reminder of the great contribution of the members of the Society to the promotion of the United States Savings Bonds program.

Whoever and whatever encourages more Americans to buy and hold Savings Bonds helps bring peace, security, and continued prosperity. The cartoonists have salted their entertaining works with sound advice on savings for the multi-millions of their followers.

Partnership of philanthropy and government

Remarks by Secretary Humphrey at the dedication
of the Howard M. Hanna Pavilion of University
Hospitals, Cleveland.

April 14, 1956

Eleven years ago on the seventeenth day of last month the finest man I ever knew, Howard M. Hanna, died suddenly of a heart attack.

The shock to his family and large circle of friends was terrific. Our community, and in fact the whole country, had suddenly lost the great abilities, the wise counsel, and the devoted dedication to promotion of the general welfare of one of its finest citizens of all time.

University Hospitals and the Western Reserve School of Medicine had long been foremost in his thoughts and benefactions. For years he had spent long hours in collaborating and planning wisely for its future. Its pre-eminence was one of his most cherished objectives particularly in the development and expansion of research and the training of skilled men in all activities for the promotion of widespread, better health for our people.

On April 25, 1945, the Board of Trustees of University Hospitals adopted the following resolution:

"Howard Melville Hanna died while at the height of his service to the University Hospitals and to the closely affiliated Medical School of Western Reserve University. He had the keenest interest in the maintenance of standards and improvement of research and teaching in these institutions. Not merely a very generous giver, he was a wise and farsighted giver. Like his father in former years, he knew and analyzed the problems and the needs and gave freely to meet them. His financial support, however, was only a small part of what he did for the hospitals and the school. Even while spending his winters in the South, he continued to be in close touch and available for counsel and advice. He was extremely alive to the necessity of securing the right man for the right place and was always ready to help when opportunity arose to secure men of marked ability to serve on the staff. He preferred to take no conspicuous part in these matters, offering his suggestions from behind the scenes but no less effectively. He was a truly great, unostentatious, and farseeing friend of the institutions which we all so deeply prize. He cannot be replaced."

Howard M. Hanna had come by his devotion both to the promotion of better health and to these particular institutions naturally enough. His father before him had been equally devoted to both. In one of the most remarkable letters of advice ever written from a father to a son, his father had said in this letter written May 30, 1904, now over fifty years ago, and I quote:

"Be generous and liberal but with true generosity and liberality in helping the needy and worthy institutions rationally, intelligently, and thoughtfully. Thoughtless giving is more apt to be wicked and a curse than a benefit. I commend to you and Gertrude and Kate two institutions that I have considered worthy of support—the Lakeside Hospital and the Medical School of Western Reserve University. Poor and insufficient medical education is a crime. I have tried to help the Western Reserve Medical School to a position among the first."

The Hanna family in all its branches now for three generations have devoted themselves, their time, their thoughtful help and their gifts generously and liberally to the best interest, the growth, and the improvement of these institutions; and the opportunities for better health for our citizens to which both institutions and their staffs of loyal people have contributed so greatly over the years.

When the move from Lakeside was first made and the conception of the wonderful grouping of the present University Hospitals was first proposed, the Hanna family were participants. Hanna House, an important part of the original group, was the gift of Mrs. L. C. Hanna and Leonard in memory of his father, and he has been a stalwart supporter of the project right from the first, continuing to the present time, and participating substantially in the present building. This fine building which we are here to dedicate today is but another expression of this great interest in health and welfare in the long line of contributions which this family has made over the years. . . .

New preventive procedures, new scientific discoveries, and new and better approaches both to treatment and teaching always claimed his rapt attention. His objective always was to help provide the opportunity for imaginative investigation, then careful and painstaking analysis, and finally the creation of new and more effective ways of everyday application for the better education of people or for prevention or treatment of disease.

This building in his memory affords just such opportunities. It provides facilities for study and treatment in one of the newest fields of health treatment, where we hope great progress is in its infancy and where new facilities are most needed. It is a broad field in itself and may reach out into wide, new horizons for assistance and perhaps changes and improvement in treatment of some of the older methods.

Its possibilities would thrill him if he were here today.

He would be proud of the careful thought and painstaking care that have gone into its planning and construction over nearly ten years past. The work of the hospital staff, the officers and Trustees in perfecting the design, rearranging the layout time after time to provide the best possible advantages and in securing the governmental contributions took long and tedious hours of thought and days and months of study. Long trips were taken to study better methods wherever opportunity presented which all results in this fine building we will all see later today.

He would be most grateful for all that they have done and keenly interested and encouragingly impatient for proof of its useful future.

Above all he would be interested in the plans for teaching and the development of more highly skilled men. That was always his greatest interest; the making of better, more intelligent and skillful men. . . .

We know now from the medical profession that mental illness, like physical illness, can be treated and cured. The treatment of mental illness has become, in fact, a very important part of the work of the medical profession. The dedication of this Pavilion today underscores this growing awareness of how the use of surgery, radiology, drugs, and the other things we normally associate with physical illness can now be brought to bear upon the problems of the mentally ill and perhaps show new ways of treating physical ailments as well.

And so the donors of this fine memorial can feel a sense of satisfaction in having helped to provide an instrument for future betterment in health that will meet the requirements that he would demand.

The faculty of the medical school can accept the challenge that these facilities given in his memory present for them with full knowledge that only their most efficient and intelligent use would meet with his approval.

And the trustees of University Hospitals will, I am sure, administer this memorial with his high requirements always in mind for the promotion of greater service in the prevention and treatment of disease and the widespread benefits of better health. . . .

Now there is one other thought that dedication of this memorial brings to mind. It is largely the gift of the family and associates of Howard Hanna, but substantial contributions for construction and research were also made by Hill-Burton Act funds and the National Institutes of Health. This is the newer pattern that is growing in our civic life. Those of us who over the years have been interested in what then was of necessity private charity have watched this trend toward greater participation of public financing sometimes with a little concern as to just where it might lead. As for myself, I have less and less concern as time goes on. I believe that more and more people should and will be interested to assure the continuance of large private participation in charitable enterprises for the public good, and with the tax benefits that flow to the individual both on account of current income and in the distribution of estates both large and small there is added inducement to do so.

Only in this way can the advantages of private management be kept alive as a stimulant to better public management of our public institutions and public affairs. It is essential in our system which is based upon the dignity and free choice and initiative and drive of the free individual that this be done. Otherwise bureaucracy can take over with no competitive challenge to lethargy and all our vaunted individually dynamic system will lapse and die from lack of demonstration of its effective power.

We have gone some distance down this road but not so far as might be supposed. So long as a full and vitally active partnership is maintained with private participation and management I have no fears. . . .

But let all of us who are interested, and many, many more who should be, never forget that it is also our duty—not duty—our privilege, so long as our performance protects that privilege, to do our part in keeping up our end of this partnership affair. We can give our thought and our time and our ideas in helpful management but we can do so only if we also give our money to pay our partnership way. If once the money is all or even preponderantly public funds, the privilege of private management and its great benefits will be lost and bureaucracy will take over wholly.

So let us have this fine memorial, built with both public and private funds in ample proportion, stand not only as a worthy memorial to one of the finest citizens Cleveland ever had, but also as a constant reminder to those who follow him with his high principles and concrete, practical, never-failing financial support to keep the freedom of management of such partnership charity in private hands as an inspiration and competitive spur to better public management in all public institutions.

It will stand as an ever-present object lesson for following genera-tions to endure the sacrifices and assume the burdens necessary to carry on our great traditions of freedom for the individual in all his activities and in his precious heritage of freedom of choice. Free to worship; free to come and go; free to speak his mind; and free to exert his utmost endeavors, so long as he always respects the same rights for his neighbor, to advance himself and his loved ones to any position his industry and ability will permit him to attain.

Only in this way can we protect and pass on to future generations what our ancestors entrusted to us, a free America.

A kind word for two Democrats

Remarks by Secretary Humphrey before a Republican meeting at The Plains, Virginia.

October 14, 1956

. . . In keeping Government spending down to make it possible to balance the budget and reduce the debt, we have had the staunchest support from Virginia's outstanding two senators, Harry F. Byrd and A. Willis Robertson. We are everlastingly grateful to them for their unfailing support of our fiscal policies. They are great citizens of this state and of our country. . . .

Chronological List of Public Appearances and Statements

1953

January 19—Statement and testimony, Senate Finance Committee, on confirmation of his appointment.
January 24—Television panel interview, Meet the Press, Washington.
January 27—Message to Treasury employees.
February 8—Television panel interview, State of the Nation, Washington.
February 17—Remarks, luncheon of Cleveland Chamber of Commerce, Cleveland.
February 20—Announcement of Treasury staff organization.
April 1—Remarks, Advertising Council of America, Washington.
April 7—Testimony, Senate Appropriations Committee (executive).
April 13—Letter to House Government Appropriations Committee.
April 13—Letter to nine senators on new 3¼ per cent bonds.
April 13—Statement, Treasury Department, announcing thirty-year 3¼ per cent bond issue.
April 15—Testimony, Senate Foreign Relations Committee (executive).
April 16—Remarks, American Society of Newspaper Editors, Washington.
April 20—Speech, annual luncheon Associated Press, New York.
May 4—Statement to House Ways and Means Committee, Washington.
May 5—Statement to Senate Foreign Relations Committee.
May 5—Speech, White House Conference of Governors, Washington.
May 8—Testimony, Senate Foreign Relations Committee (executive).
May 21—News conference, Treasury.
May 24—Television panel interview, Meet the Press, Washington.
June 1–3—Statement and testimony, House Ways and Means Committee.
June 3—Remarks, television panel at White House with the President and three other cabinet members.
June 12—Article, U.S. News & World Report, "What Sound Money Will Mean."

June 21—Television panel interview, Man of the Week, Washington.
June 22—Radio panel interview, Reporters' Round-up, Washington.
June 24—Statement, Federal Reserve Board discount rate.
July 19—Statement, Treasury, analysis at end of fiscal year.
July 30—News conference, White House, debt limit.
August 4—Speech, National Conference of Governors, Seattle.
August 7—Interview, *U.S. News & World Report*, debt limit.
August 10—Interview, *Newsweek*, Washington.
August 10—Radio interview, Washington.
August 27—News conference, Treasury, budget.
September 9—Statement to International Monetary Fund and Bank
    for the U.S., Washington.
September 15—Statement, Capehart Government Study Commission,
    Washington.
September 16—Speech, National Press Club luncheon, Washington.
September 22—Speech, American Bankers Association, Washington.
September 30—Statement on Federal sales tax.
October 5—Speech, New York Clearing House Association, New York.
October 20—Speech, California Republican Finance Committee dinner,
    San Francisco.
October 23—Remarks [unpublished], Business Advisory Deparment of the
    Department of Commerce, Pebble Beach, California.
October 30—Speech, Union League Club, Philadelphia.
November 6—Speech, Georgia Republican State Finance Committee,
    Atlanta.
November 9—Speech, Economic Club, Detroit.
November 10—Remarks, civic dinner of Saginaw, Michigan; introduced on
    closed-circuit television by the President.
November 23—Speech, Republican finance dinner, Chicago.
December 1—Speech, Investment Bankers of America, Hollywood, Florida.
December 3—Remarks, dinner of Thoroughbred Racing Association,
    New York.
December 18–19—Statements [unpublished], Conference of Republican
    Legislative Leaders, White House.

1954

January 3—Article, *The Washington Post*, first year's progress.
January 4—Interview, *Newsweek*, Washington.
January 20—News conference, Treasury, analysis of 1954 budget.
February 2—Testimony, Joint Economic Committee.
February 7—Article, *Nation's Business*, Washington, fiscal progress.
February 9—Statement, Treasury, success of bond sales.
February 10—Statement, debt limit.
February 12—Testimony, Joint Economic Committee.

February 25—Statement, Treasury, tax exemption proposals.
February 28—Statement, Treasury, excise tax proposals.
March 1—Speech, League of Republican Women, Washington.
March 15—Article, *Life*, the tax revision bill.
March 17—Testimony, Senate Finance Committee (executive), excise taxes.
March 17—Letter to Speaker Joseph W. Martin, Jr., tax revision bill.
March 22—Testimony, Senate Appropriations Committee.
March 28—Television interview, Youth Wants to Know, Washington.
April 2—Article (with James C. Derieux), *Collier's*, Washington.
April 7—Testimony, Senate Finance Committee (executive).
April 7—Speech, Republican Women's Centennial Conference, Washington.
April 8—Letter to Senator Milliken, Chairman Senate Finance Committee.
April 15—Speech, American Society of Newspaper Editors, Washington.
April 27—Testimony, Senate Judiciary Committee; letter to Chairman William Langer opposing tax limitation.
April 30—Statement, Treasury, announcing new bond issues.
May 10—Letter to Secretary of State concerning Finland Exports.
May 11—Speech, Unemployment Conference of Congress of Industrial Organizations, Washington.
May 25—Speech, Farm-City Conference, New York.
June 1—Article, *U.S. Coast Guard Magazine*, "The Sound Dollar."
June 24—Remarks, breakfast National Cartoonists' Society, Washington.
June 27—Television panel interview, Meet the Press, Washington.
June 28—Speech, Republican finance dinner, Louisville, Kentucky.
July 6—Remarks, National Women's Planning Committee of Savings Bonds Division, Treasury.
July 14–15—Testimony, Senate Finance Committee (executive).
July 28—Article, *Pittsburgh Legal Journal*, Pittsburgh, "Our Savings Bonds."
August 4—Testimony, Senate Finance Committee (executive).
September 4—Remarks, welcome to first iron ore cargo through St. Lawrence Seaway, Cleveland.
September 14—News conference, Treasury, 1955 budget forecast.
September 15—Speech, Republican finance dinner, Minneapolis.
September 20—Statement, Treasury, deficit increase.
September 28—Panel discussion, meeting of International Monetary Fund and World Bank, Washington.
October 1—Speech, Tax Institute of University of Texas, Austin.
October 2—Article, *The Saturday Evening Post*, "What the New Tax Law Does for You."
October 2—Speech, Republican finance dinner, Tulsa.
October 7—Article, *The New York Herald-Tribune*, "Where Fiscal Government Stands."

October 19—Speech, American Bankers Association, Atlantic City.
October 20—Speech, Republican dinner, Newark.
October 21—Panel interview, *The New York Herald-Tribune* Forum, New York.
October 21—Speech, New York Investment Bankers Association, New York.
October 23—Speech, dinner Indiana Republican Editorial Association, Indianapolis.
November 1—Statement, Treasury, current economy.
November 18—Statement, Treasury, forecast of economic conference at Rio de Janeiro.
November 23—Speech, Inter-American Economic Conference, Rio de Janeiro.
December 6—News conference, Treasury, budget situation.
December 7—Statement, Joint Economic Committee.
December 11—Remarks, dinner Pennsylvania Society of New York, New York.
December 12—Presentation to President and Cabinet of mint medals.

1955

January 1—Article, *Nation's Business*, Washington.
January 2—Article, *The Washington Post and Times-Herald*, Washington.
January 6—Article, *The Philadelphia Inquirer*, Washington.
January 15—News conference, Treasury, budget, taxes.
January 18—Statement, House Ways and Means Committee.
January 30—Statement, Treasury, deference of corporation tax reduction.
February 16—Speech, dinner Greater Philadelphia Chamber of Commerce, Philadelphia.
February 19—Speech, National Canners' Association, Chicago.
February 21—Testimony, House Ways and Means Committee.
February 28—Testimony, Senate Finance Committee (executive).
March 2—Testimony, Senate Finance Committee (executive).
March 7—Letter to Chairman Jere Cooper of House Ways and Means Committee, tax reductions.
March 10—Testimony, House Ways and Means Committee, tax reductions.
March 15—Statement and testimony, Senate Banking Committee, Stock markets.
March 19—Statement, endorsing national reserve program.
March 22—Testimony, Senate Public Works Committee, gasoline taxes.
March 23—Testimony, Senate Appropriations Committee.
April 1—Article, *Fortune*, "The Future: Sound as a Dollar."
May 8—Remarks [unpublished], Business Advisory Committee of Department of Commerce, Hot Springs, Virginia.
May 11—Testimony, Senate Finance Committee (executive).

May 16—Testimony, House Public Works Committee, federal highway program.

June 6—Statement and testimony, Senate Banking Committee; international finance agency.

June 16—News conference, Treasury, Operation Alert.

June 24—Testimony, House Ways and Means Committee.

June 27—Testimony, House Ways and Means Committee.

July 12—Testimony, House Public Works Committee, highway program finance.

July 15—Testimony, House Appropriations Committee (executive).

July 18—Testimony, House Government Operations Committee, tax write-offs.

July 20—Statement, Treasury, analysis of 1956 budget deficit.

August 25—News conference, Treasury, budget prospect.

September 7—Statement, Treasury, dismissal of E. E. Hoppe.

September 12—Remarks, International Monetary Fund and World Bank meeting, Istanbul, Turkey.

September 26—Statement, Treasury, reassurance after the President's heart attack.

September 29—Statement, Treasury, prospect of budget balance.

September 29—Statement, on Senator Johnson—Secretary Wilson defense statements.

October 4—Speech, Republican finance dinner, Philadelphia.

October 12—Speech, Republican finanee dinner, Chicago.

October 13—Speech, Republican finance dinner, Boston.

October 15—Statement and news conference, Lowry Air Base, Denver, after visit with the President.

November 7—Speech, Cleveland Post, American Ordnance Association, Cleveland.

November 16—Speech, Republican finance dinner, Los Angeles.

November 17—Speech, American Petroleum Institute, San Francisco.

November 17—Speech, Republican finance dinner, Oakland.

November 19—Speech, National Grange, Cleveland.

December 7—Remarks, Mercantile Trust Company, centennial dinner, St. Louis.

December 30—Remarks, Rotary Club, Thomasville, Georgia.

1956

January 1—Article, *Tax Outlook*, New York, "What Makes America."

January 4—Article, *The Washington Post and Times Herald*, Washington.

January 14—News conference, Treasury, new budget.

January 21—Speech, Citizens' Salute to Eisenhower, Madison Square Garden, New York.

January 22—Television panel interview, Meet the Press, Washington.

February 3—Testimony, Joint Committee on Economic Report.

February 14—Statement and testimony, House Ways & Means
      Committee, highway financing.

February 22—Telecast speech to Institute of Mining and Metallurgical
      Engineers, New York, and American Good Government Society,
      Washington.

March 2—Testimony, House Ways & Means Committee, international
      trade.

March 9—Letter to Chairman J. Percy Priest of House Commerce
      Committee, tax exemptions.

March 21—Letter to Senate Finance Committee, tax exemptions.

March 25—Testimony, Senate Finance Committee (executive).

April 14—Speech, dedication of Hanna Pavilion of University Hospitals,
      Cleveland.

May 17—Testimony, Senate Finance Committee (executive).

May 21—Remarks [unpublished], Business Advisory Council of
      Department of Commerce, Hot Springs, Virginia.

May 24—Panel interview, National Press Club, Washington.

June 12—Testimony, Joint Economic Committee, current economy.

June 18—Speech, Republican finance dinner, Indianapolis.

June 19—Testimony, House Ways & Means Committee, debt limit.

June 26—Remarks (by telephone from Washington) to Chamber of
      Commerce of the Americas at Miami.

August 21—Remarks, Republican National Convention, San Francisco.

September 25—Speech, International Monetary Fund and World Bank
      Meeting, Washington.

October 8—Speech, Economic Club, Detroit.

October 14—Remarks, Republican meeting, The Plains, Virginia.

October 15—Television speech, inflation, debt, and taxes, Washington.

October 18—Speech, Republican meeting, Baltimore.

October 19—Speech, Republican meeting, Greenwich, Connecticut.

October 22—Speech, Republican finance dinner, St. Louis.

October 25—Speech, Associated Industries of Massachusetts, Boston.

November 2—Remarks, Associated Grocery Manufacturers Representatives,
      Cleveland.

December 8—Speech, Pennsylvania Society of New York, New York.

1957

January 12—Remarks, wreath laying at Alexander Hamilton Statue,
      Treasury.

January 15—Statement on budget and news conference, Treasury.

January 23—Testimony, House Appropriations Committee (executive).

January 27—Television panel interview, Meet the Press, Washington.

February 4—Testimony, Joint Economic Committee.

February 6—Statement, House Ways & Means Committee.

February 8—Interview, *U.S. News and World Observer*, taped.

March 3—Testimony, House Appropriations Committee, new budget.

March 6—Statement, Treasury, on signing amendment to Anglo-American Agreement of 1945.

March 6—Speech, Republican meeting, Masonic Auditorium, Detroit.

March 12—Testimony, Senate Finance Committee (executive).

March 15—Statement and testimony, Senate Banking Committee, Anglo-American loan terms.

March 18—Statement, House Foreign Affairs Committee, Anglo-American loan terms.

March 19—Statement, Senate Finance Committee, small business tax proposal.

March 22—Article, *U.S. News & World Report*, "Why the Budget is so Big."

April 18—Article, *Iron Age*, "Why We Must Limit Fast Write-offs."

April 18—Speech, National Industrial Conference Board, New York, the budget.

May 7—Testimony, Senate Finance Committee, tax write-offs.

May 7—Speech, Republican meeting, Des Moines.

May 27—Statement, House Judiciary Committee, vetoes by item.

May 28—Letter of resignation to President Eisenhower.

June 14—Testimony, Joint Economic Committee, taxation proposals.

June 18–July 10—Statement and testimony, Senate Finance Committee, financial condition of country.

June 24—Statement and testimony, House Post Office Committee.

Index

Advertising Council of America, 43, 46, 47
Agriculture, see Farm Problem
Aldrich, Winthrop W.: free trade, 423
Allen, Leo: mentioned, 36
Allen, Lois, 390–91
Allen, Thomas B.: quoted, 98
American Bankers Association, 118, 159
American Farm Bureau Federation, 388
American Federation of Labor, 185–86
American Institute of Mining and Metallurgical Engineers, 4
American Iron and Steel Institute, 4
American Petroleum Institute, 572
American Retail Federation, 388
Amortization, 244, 432, 434–42
    see also Depreciation; Tax write-offs
Anderson, Clinton P.
    mentioned, 348, 349
    Hells Canyon amortization, 439–42
Anderson, Robert: successor to Humphrey, 603, 606
Andrew, Marie, 392
Andrews, T. Coleman
    mentioned, 8, 359
    resignation, 580–81, 586, 587, 588
Appropriations
    defined, 81–82
    fixing, 28
    procedure in Congress, 108–10
Armco Steel Corporation, 19
Arthur, Chester A.: mentioned, 543
Assouan Dam, 485
Atomic energy: commercial possibilities, 271
Atomic Energy Commission, 442
Automobile production, 369, 561

Balanced budget, 15, 39, 51, 72, 77, 91, 93, 96–97, 111–12, 114, 138, 144, 182, 199, 362–63, 376, 384, 391, 540, 583–84
    achieved, 227–28, 303

Balanced budget—continued
    deficit, estimate of, 1955, 586
    Eisenhower Administration, goal of, 179
    excess profits tax extension, effect of, 59
    predicted by Humphrey, 62–63, 206–18, 574, 591
    prerequisites for, 218–19
    reasons not accomplished, 177, 401–2, 451–53
Banks, see Federal Reserve Banks
Bender, George H., 375
Bennett, Wallace F., 27, 30, 343–45, 347, 535
Benson, Ezra Taft, 524, 526
Bethlehem Steel Corporation, 19, 20
Black, Eugene R.
    mentioned, 457, 462
    quoted, 472
Boggs, Hale, 204, 205, 206
Bolling, Richard, 374, 375
Bonds, 62, 116–17
    interstate highway financing, 498–515
    long-term, 47–48, 86–88, 99, 107, 118, 123, 140, 166, 176, 184–85, 359–60, 364
    tax free, 339
    trust, 75–76
    see also Interest rates; United States Savings Bonds
Booth, Warren, 356
Bretton Woods Agreements Act, 480
Brookings Institution, 377
Brooks, Ned, 229, 254, 259, 260
Brownell, Herbert, 579
Brundage, Percival F., 242–43
Budget, 58–59, 82–83, 132
    fiscal year 1954, 63
    money, sound, basis of, 119–22
    policy, as prerequisite for sound money, 491
    procedure for establishing, 280
    receipts and expenditures, 1929–1958, 335

Budget—*continued*
  Truman Administration's, 39, 40, 80
  see also Balanced budget; Eisenhower
    Administration
Budget, Bureau of the, 283, 285
Burgess, Randolph, 8, 124, 205, 236, 304,
  355, 517, 539, 603
Bush, Prescott, 511–12
Business
  conditions improving, *1954*, 547
  record investment, 300
  tax relief proposed, 396
  see also Small Business Administration
Butler, R. A., 486
  mentioned, 457
  rules for British success in foreign in-
    vestment, 463
Byfield, Robert S., 418, 421
Byrd, Harry F., 8–10, 14, 513, 626
  mentioned, 12, 108, 154, 232, 434,
    526
  quoted, 311, 503–7
  chairman: Senate Finance Committee,
    298, 330–33, 350–51, 436–39, 442–
    43, 530–34, 536
  highway financing, 497, 499–500,
    503–9
  letter to, 333–35
Byrnes, John W., 73

Canada, 18–19, 454, 456, 459, 478, 618
Canada and Dominion Sugar Company, 4
Capehart, Homer E.
  mentioned, 131, 454, 455
  stock prices, 560–62
Capital-gains tax, 566–67
Carlson, Frank, 30
Carnegie, Andrew: mentioned, 620
Case, Francis, 509–10, 511
Chamber of Commerce of Cleveland, 37
Chamber of Commerce of Greater Phila-
  delphia, 173
Chamber of Commerce, International,
  U.S. Council, 4
Chamber of Commerce, United States:
  excess profits tax, 97
Childs, Marquis W., 94, 95–97, 254,
  255, 260, 261
Clayton Act, 314
Clearing House, New York, 128
Commerce, Bureau of Domestic, 511
Commerce, Department of, 4, 547
Commodity Credit Corporation, 120–21

Commonwealth Development Corpora-
  tion, 463
Conger Consolidated Gold Mines, 19
Congress of Industrial Organizations, Full
  Employment Conference, 398
Consumer Price Index, 337, 338, 612
Cooper, Jere, 71, 72, 73
  mentioned, 388
  chairman: House Ways & Means Com-
    mittee, 191, 201, 202
Corporate income tax, 211, 215, 257,
  375, 395
  extension, 95, 129, 387, 425
  Mills Plan, 113, 121, 197, 216
  reduction, 65, 66–67, 147
Cost of living, 128, 224, 300, 327, 521,
  541
Cotton, Felix, 210, 211, 217
Craig, May, 55, 56, 57, 62, 212
Credit, 308
  housing, 317–22
  stock market, 571
  United States reserve, 334
  see also Commodity Credit Corpora-
    tion; Federal Reserve Banks; Money
Credit policy: alternatives to, 313
Crowther, Rodney, 210
Currency, *see* Money
Curtis, Carl T., 73
Curtis, Thomas B., 197, 198, 199
Customs laws, 476–77
Customs Simplification Acts, 448, 469,
  476

Dale, Edwin, 254, 258, 259, 262, 263
Dawes, Charles: mentioned, 620
Debt, *see* National debt
Deductions, *see* Tax deductions
Defense, *see* National defense
Defense, Department of, 92, 122, 442,
  572
Defense industry: tax write-offs, 430–42
Defense Mobilization, Office of, 151,
  430, 433, 436, 437
Deficit
  annual, 37, 43, 50, 63, 64, 65, 72, 80–
    81, 82, 91, 101, 119, 139, 145, 153,
    156–57, 158, 177, 179, 184, 206,
    303, 363, 391
  financing, 46, 109, 116, 117, 119, 136,
    153, 266, 383, 401, 491, 531, 536–
    37
  highway program, 527
  Post Office, 249–50
  tax reduction, relation to, 248–49

Depreciation, 146–47, 567–69
  allowances, 358, 367, 373–74, 421, 431
  new provisions for, 408, 417
  see also Tax write-offs
Depression, 49, 98–99, 160, 258–59, 273–74, 357
  prediction, 252, 253
  prevention, 84
  see also Recession
Deshmukh, Chintaman
  mentioned, 457
  foreign investment in India, 463
Detroit Economic Club, 489
Dividends, *see* Taxation, double on dividends
Dodge, Joseph M.
  mentioned, 77, 102
  resignation, 390–91
Dollar, *see* Money
Doud, Mrs. John: mentioned, 591
Douglas, Paul H., 145, 167, 369–72, 377, 567–69
Douglas Report, *1950*, 164, 165
Dulles, John Foster
  mentioned, 449, 466, 474, 485, 579
  aid to Latin America, 464

Economic Cooperation Administration for Revision of Reparations and Dismantling of Plants in Germany, 4
Economic Development, Committee for, 4, 412
Economic Indicators, 340–341
Eden, Anthony, 485
Edson, Peter, 217
Egypt, 455, 484–85
Eisenhower Administration
  balancing budget, method, 598
  defense, attitude toward, 363
  farm problem, 524–26
  goals, 39, 42, 106–7, 137–38, 140–42, 153, 156, 174, 222, 238, 284–85, 303–7, 361–62, 379, 393, 448, 490, 493, 599–601, 611
  inflation, program to fight, 171–73, 316–17
  money policy, 111
  philosophy, 53
  problems faced by, 60, 101, 135–36, 302–3, 362, 375, 422–23, 451, 548–49, 553
  record in office, 138–42, 157–59, 161–62, 164, 168–71, 221, 225–27, 279,

Eisenhower Administration—*continued*
  289–90, 293–94, 298–329, 380, 574–75, 598, 600–2
  tax program, 129, 183, 355, 358–59
Eisenhower, Dwight David
  mentioned, 4, 46, 47, 54, 60, 63, 64, 68, 69, 102, 112, 148, 220, 224, 254, 262, 267, 270, 279, 284, 292, 330, 383, 387, 389, 451, 543, 609, 620, 621
  quoted, 44, 56, 65–67, 76–78, 162, 221, 238, 281, 310, 388, 464–65
  budget, 290
  candidate, 35, 585, 590
  debt, national, 358
  defense, 177, 181, 219
  farm problem, 524–25
  fiscal policy
    objectives, 362
    problems, 236–37
  heart attack, 219–20, 579, 580, 582
  Humphrey
    relations with, 579–606
    resignation of, 604–6
  International Finance Corporation, 477
  old age insurance tax, 200
  tax reform, 147, 406, 413
  tribute to, 593–95, 599
Eisenhower, Mrs. Dwight (Mamie):
  mentioned, 603, 606
Employment Act, 164
Employment and unemployment, 93, 148, 149, 151, 159–60, 186, 226, 299, 327–28, 374, 389–90, 521, 561–62, 575
  government spending, relation to, 402–3
  heavy industries, 223–24
  jobs, creation of, 399–400, 404
  money, relation to, 79
  transition from war to peace, 384
England, 449
  as investor, 463
  loan to, 252
  the pound
    convertibility of, 424–25
    maintenance of, 270, 272, 279
    Suez crisis, 486
  Suez crisis, 484–85
Erickson, O. W.: quoted, 98
Estate tax, 398
Europe
  economy, 270
  mutual security, 73

Excess profits tax, 15–16, 71–73, 92, 129, 215–16, 356, 394, 419, 431, 491, 493, 612
  expiration, 125, 136, 141
  extension, 35–36, 37, 59–60, 63–75, 78, 90, 94–95, 96, 97
Excise tax
  automobile, 512
  extension, 95, 129, 147, 265–66, 425
  gasoline, 512, 514
  highway program financing, 528–29, 537
  reduction, 57, 65, 67, 394, 419–20, 426
Exemptions, *see* Tax exemptions
Expenditures, *see* Government spending
Export-Import Bank, 272, 454–55, 471–72, 473, 474, 479

Fairless, Benjamin F., 260
Fairless Committee, 260
Farm problem
  interest rates, 325
  price supports, 151
  solution, 523–26
  surpluses, 369, 522–23
  taxation of cooperatives, 525
  tax revision for, 385, 396
Federal Highway Corporation, 515
Federal Housing Administration, 166, 167, 319, 320, 321
Federal National Mortgage Association, 285, 319
Federal Power Commission, 440
Federal Reserve Act, 342
Federal Reserve Banks, 128, 141, 306, 517–18
Federal Reserve Board, 87, 127, 131, 132, 149–50, 323, 337, 347, 556, 559
  accord of *1951*, 309
  bank credit policy, 318
  debt management, 304
  Eisenhower Administration supports, 317
  independence, 538–42
  inflation, 307–10
  interest rates, 57, 236, 538–42
  monetary policy, 233, 491–92
  reserve requirements, reduction of, 99–100
  Treasury, relation to, 30
  see also Monetary policy
Federal Reserve System, 111, 116, 118, 122–23, 164–65, 175

Federal spending, *see* Government spending
Felmly, Lloyd M., 356
Field, Marshall, Jr., 355
Financing, *see* Deficit; Highway financing
Flanders, Ralph E., 26, 27, 28, 264
  mentioned, 345
  chairman: Subcommittee on Economic Stabilization, 63, 167
Flemming, Arthur: quoted, 436
Foch, Marshal: mentioned, 620
Folsom, Marion B., 8, 355, 356, 358, 406, 413
Ford, Henry: mentioned, 620
Foreign aid, 83, 181–82, 476
  economic, 449
  Middle East, 251–52, 270–72
  objectives, 450
  repayable loans, 260
  see also Investment; Mutual Security Administration
France, 73, 449, 484–85
Franke, Art: mentioned, 610
Frear, J. Allen, Jr.
  mentioned, 22, 345
  quoted, 21
  rapid amortization, 439
Friendly, Alfred, 90, 92, 93
Fulbright, J. William, 369, 373, 374
  chairman: Senate Banking and Currency Committee, 555, 558–60, 570–72
Full Employment Act of *1946*, 404
Furstenberg, Dr. Albert C.: mentioned, 610

Gallup poll
  balanced budget and tax reduction, 93, 94
  excess profits tax, 96
  successor to Eisenhower, 593
Gasoline tax, federal, 512
Gemmill, Kenneth, 406, 413
George, Walter F., 392
Germany, 449
Gift tax, federal, 398
Glass, Carter, 538
Gold standard, 29, 356
Gore, Albert, 347, 348, 349, 496
  presiding: Subcommitte on Public Roads, 498–503
Gore Bill, 529–30
Government
  corporations, 509
  cost of, 229

Government debt, *see* National debt
Government spending, 52, 78, 112–13,
  124–25, 129, 182–83, 234, 291,
  294, 330–31
  allocation, 280–81
  compensatory, 248–49
  effect on money, 243
  Eisenhower Administration reduces,
    303, 365
  importance of controlling, 347–48
  inflation, 258, 263–64, 330
  reduction, 145–48, 149, 161, 179–80,
    183, 237–41, 254–65, 272, 275,
    277, 281–83, 311
  restraint of, 44–46
  security, 120
Grant, Ulysses S.: mentioned, 543
Gray, Mr., 437, 439, 440, 441
Gudin, Egenio
  mentioned, 457
  private investment abroad, 463

Hagerty, James C., 580, 587, 588, 591,
  592
Hanna Coal & Ore Corporation, 4, 31
Hanna, Howard M., *see* Hanna Pavilion
Hanna, Leonard C., 623
Hanna, Mrs. Leonard C., 623
Hanna, M. A., Company, 3, 4, 5, 17,
  18, 21
Hanna Pavilion, University Hospitals
  (Cleveland): dedicated, 621–26
Hauge, Gabriel: mentioned, 255
Hayden, Martin, 254, 255–56, 261, 263
Hayes, Rutherford B.: mentioned, 543
Heiskell, J. N., 356
Hells Canyon project, 439–41
Hensley, M. Stewart, 217, 218
Hervey, John: mentioned, 614
Highway financing, 496–515, 526–42
Hill-Burton Act, 624
Holmes, Hal, 202
Holmes, Jim, 389, 390
Holmes, Justice: quoted, 418
Hood, Clifford, 37
Hoover, Herbert, 154, 347, 620
Hoover, Herbert, Jr.: mentioned, 464
Hopkins, Mr.: mentioned, 271
Horse racing, *see* Thoroughbred racing
Housing
  credit, 319–22
  increase, 328
  mortgages, 151
  rising costs, effect of, 325–26

Hughes, Roland, 206, 207, 208, 210,
  213, 214, 216, 217
Hughes, Tom, 216
Humphrey, George M.
  America, views on
    charity, private and public, 624–25
    competition, importance of, 52–53,
      125–27
    confidence, importance of, 152,
      188–89, 557–58
    economic freedom, importance of,
      282–83, 286–92
    economy, 152, 360, 423, 494–95,
      572–73
    faith in people, 85, 230–31, 489
    free enterprise system, 130–32,
      467–68
    jobs, importance of, 152
    mass production, 144
    peace, 48–49, 137, 368
    threats to way of life, 50
  awards, 37, 152, 484
  biographical notes, 3–4
  businesses, 4
  Eisenhower, relations with, 579–606
  government
    compared to business, 267–68
    in economic affairs, 177–78, 468,
      490–93
    extravagance in, opposes, 135, 177
    goals of, 490
    power to tax, 331–32, 432
    responsibility of, 161
  philosophy of business, 61, 82, 89–90
  reminiscences, 609–10
  salary, 17, 26–27
  securities owned, 4–7
  Thomasville plantation, 486, 579
  Treasury post
    acceptance of, 13
    eligibility for, 14
    resignation from, 603–4
Humphrey, Mrs. George M. (Pamela
  Stark), 3, 13, 37, 38, 603, 606,
  609, 610, 613
Humphrey, Hubert H.: mentioned, 398

Idaho Power Company, 437
  see also Hells Canyon project
Income tax, *see* Individual income tax;
  Corporate income tax
India, 455, 463
Individual income tax, 92, 211, 257, 371,
  394, 491, 493, 612
  on earnings abroad, 359, 473, 474, 477

Individual income tax—*continued*
    rates, ceiling on proposed, 398
    reduction, 65, 67, 69, 83, 125,
        136, 141
Indo-China, 73
Industrial Rayon Corporation, 4
Industry
    agriculture, relation to, 524
    competition from Europe, 29
    double taxation, effect of, 366
    Internal Revenue Code of 1954,
        benefits from, 416–17
    plant investment, 373
    production decline, 340–41
    write-offs, effect of faster, 367
    see also Depreciation
Inflation, 39–40, 58, 116–17, 124, 140,
    158, 167, 185–86, 189, 249, 261, 263–
    65, 275, 296, 303, 307–8, 397, 421,
    467, 482, 483
    balanced with deflation, 334
    checked, 427
    effects of, 336–38, 551–52, 597, 598
    Eisenhower Administration fights,
        316–17, 552
    explanation of, 306–7
    government spending, 258
    importance of halting, 171–73, 176,
        235
    potential in highway program, 498
    way to check, 168–71, 238–40
    see also Money
Inland Waterways Corporation, 158
Insurance, *see* Old age insurance
Inter-American Economic and Social
    Council, 464
Interest rates, 79, 86–87, 88, 97–98,
    104, 106, 107, 115, 150, 235,
    305–6, 308–9, 360
    effects, 57–58, 323–26, 336, 492
    encourage savings, 274–75, 316
    manipulation of, 57
Internal Revenue, Bureau of, 359
Internal Revenue Code of 1954, 115,
    198, 216–17, 314, 387–89, 393–
    97, 405–18, 568
    benefits, 151–52, 223, 381
    importance, 382–83
    objectives, 146–47, 366
    revision of, 428–30
    see also Tax reduction
Internal Revenue, Commissioner of,
    7, 8, 9–10, 25
International Bank and Monetary Fund
    meeting of 1955, 581

International Bank for Reconstruction
    and Development, 447, 452, 454–55,
    457, 462, 472–74, 477, 479, 481–82
International Finance Corporation, 472–
    73, 474, 477, 478–79, 480, 481, 483
International Monetary Fund, 272, 447,
    452, 461, 481–82, 483, 486
International Trade, 423, 424
    extension, 448–49
    inter-American, 468–69
    see also Investment; Trade Agreements
        Program
Interstate Commerce Commission, 525
Interstate highway financing, *see* High-
    way financing
Investment
    foreign, 131, 452, 456, 457–62
    importance of, 116, 389, 396, 565–66
    see also Bonds
Investment Bankers Association of
    America, 138, 548
Investors League, 388
Iron Ore Company of Canada, 4, 18, 19
Israel, 484, 485
Ives, Irving M., 564, 565, 566

Jackson, Andrew: mentioned, 614
Jackson, Clarinda, 392
Jeffers, Mr.: mentioned, 509
Jenkins, Thomas A., 70
Jenner, William E., 349, 350
Jockey Club, The, 615
Johnson, Edwin C., 10, 11
Johnson, Lyndon B., 218, 219, 584
Jones, Day, Cockley, and Reavis, 7
Jones, Jesse: mentioned, 509

Karsten, Frank M., 192, 193, 194, 196,
    200, 201
Kean, Robert W., 196, 200
Keating, Kenneth B.: mentioned, 542
Kennedy, Robert, 356
Kerr, Robert S., 11–13, 15, 16, 23, 26,
    27, 335, 336, 338, 339, 531, 532,
    534–36, 539
Keyserling, Leon: quoted, 421
Kieft, van de, J.
    mentioned, 457
    quoted, 458–59
Korean War, 35, 49, 51, 72, 127, 142,
    148, 181, 193, 216, 221, 222, 380,
    413, 431, 495, 595

Labrador Mining & Exploration Com-
    pany, 19

Labrador ore, 18–20
Langer, William: mentioned, 398
Latin America, 454, 464–75, 478
Lawrence, David: mentioned, 254
Lawrence, William H., 90, 91, 93–94
Lehman, Herbert H., 562–63, 564
Lennartson, Nils A., 236
Lincoln, Abraham: quoted, 178
Lincoln, Murray D., 418, 419, 420, 421
Livingston, J. A.: quoted, 236
Long, Russell B., 15, 16, 17, 18, 19, 20, 21, 22, 23, 24, 536–41
Luce, Henry R., 418, 423

McCarthy, Eugene J., 202, 203, 204
McCarthy, Joseph: mentioned, 297
McCormick, Stephen: mentioned, 389
McDonald, David, 404
McGraw-Hill Publishing Company: survey of Department of Economics, 547
McKay, Douglas: mentioned, 442
McNamara, Patrick, 512
Malone, George W., 27, 28, 29, 30, 341–43
Mark, Ross F., 216
Marshall, George C.: mentioned, 620
Martin, Edward, 7, 22, 24, 25, 438, 531, 532
Martin, Joseph W.: letter to, 387–89
Martin, William M.: mentioned, 342, 539
Mason, Noah, 75, 196, 197
Maybank, Burnet R.: mentioned, 455
Mayo, Mr.: mentioned, 340
Mellon, Andrew W., 7, 74, 93, 620
Mellon, Richard K.: tribute to, 619–20
Mental illness, 624
Mercantile Trust Company, 574
Mexico, 455
Millikin, Eugene D.
  mentioned, 406, 413
  chairman: Senate Finance Committee, 3, 5–12, 14, 17, 21, 22, 26, 27, 31
  highways, 533
Mills Plan, 113, 121, 197, 216
Mills, Wilbur D., 74, 195, 196, 199, 201, 264
Monetary policy, 122–23, 149–50, 164–65, 232–36, 265, 268–69, 301, 307–10, 313, 323, 341–48
Money
  commodity, as a, 87

Money—*continued*
  convertibility, 424–25
  currency
    depreciation, 86–87, 153
    managed, 341, 342
    manipulation, 79, 80
    stabilization, 89
  dollar
    depreciation, 139, 249, 256, 308
    international trade, importance to, 475
    purchasing power, 343–44
    soundness, 189–90, 456
    value, 35, 39, 45, 49, 117, 158, 168, 171–72, 175, 357–58, 421–22, 541, 596, 597
  sound, 25, 29, 51, 53, 54, 69, 79–80, 97, 132, 140
    effects of, 89
    foundations of, 118–27
    importance of, 596–97
    savings, relation to, 104
    steps toward achieving, 116–18, 491–93
  see also Federal Reserve System; Gold standard; Inflation; Interest rates; Monetary policy; National debt
Monney, Richard E., 214, 215
Moore, Arthur L., 94, 95
Moore, Mrs.: mentioned, 591
Morris, John D., 94, 95, 96
Morse, Wayne: mentioned, 145
Mutual Security Administration, 73, 83
Mutual security program, 285
  expenditures (1955 & 1956), 182
  extension of recommended, 450–53
  Latin America, 466

Nasser, Gamal Abdel, 485
National American Legion, 389
National Association of Manufacturers, 97
National Association of Purchasing Agents, 547
National Canners Association, 178
National City Bank of Cleveland, 4, 416
National debt, 49, 106–8, 121–23, 140, 303, 327, 358, 540, 541
  interest rate, 242, 305
  limit, 333, 504–5
  management, 53, 88, 99, 117, 118, 123–24, 132, 141, 150, 163, 164–65, 304–5, 363–64, 492, 612
  payment of, 368–69, 589–90

National debt—*continued*
  raising limit, 102–3, 108–10, 113–14,
    134–35, 184, 191–206, 231–32,
    508–9
  reconstruction of, 162
  reduction of, 212, 229, 278
  steps to reduce danger of, 134
  structure of, 184–85
  see also Deficit; Government spending;
    Inflation
National defense, 61–62, 63, 64, 77,
  137, 140, 380
  dependence on world events, 494–95
  highways, importance of, 515
  industrial base of, 408–9, 417–18
  preparedness, 50, 273–74
  spending, 41, 51, 85, 180–81, 357,
    394, 612
  see also Mutual security program;
    National security
National Farm-City Conference, 152
National Grange, 521
National Housing Act, 319
National Industrial Conference Board,
  283
National Industrial Information Com-
  mittee, 4
National Institutes of Health, 624
National Municipal League, 543
National Press Club, 113
National security, 61–62, 121–22, 126,
  144, 179, 181, 199
  cost of, 139, 590
  expenditures, 120, 304
  importance of active economy, 600
  reason budget not balanced, 401–2
National Steel Corporation, 4, 19
NATO, *see* North Atlantic Treaty
  Organization
Newcomen Society of England, 4
New York Clearing House Association,
  127, 128, 131
New York Stock Exchange, 562
Nixon, Richard M., 579
Norman, John T., 216
North Atlantic Treaty Organization, 452
Nuttle, Ronald, 392

O'Brien, Frank, 55, 57, 58, 61, 62,
  208, 209, 214, 217
O'Brien, John, 90, 91
O'Connor, Happy, 391
O'Connor, P. J.: quoted, 98
Old age insurance, 62, 67, 200
  see also Social security

O'Leary, J. A., 215
Organization of the American States, 464
Overby, Andrew N.: mentioned, 8

Pan American Conference, Third, 465
Parsons, William W.: mentioned, 8
Patman Report of 1952, 164, 165
Patman, Wright, 166, 167, 263, 264,
  265, 368, 369, 373, 377
Pennsylvania Society of New York,
  484, 619
Pensions, 62, 395
  see also Old age insurance; Social
    security
Petty, Milburn, 214, 215
Phelps Dodge Corporation, 4
Picard, "Zip": mentioned, 610
Pittsburgh Consolidation Coal Company,
  3, 4
Political Science, Academy of, 4
Postal Pay Act, 295
Post Office, *see* United States Post Office
Public debt, *see* National debt
Pusey, Merlo, 579

Quebec-North Shore Exploration Company, 19

Radford, Arthur W.: quoted, 600
Rayburn, Sam, 283, 285, 392
Recession, 374–75, 384
  possibility of, 110
  steps to avert, 111
  see also Depression
Reciprocal trade, *see* Trade Agreements
  Act
Reconstruction Finance Corporation,
  158, 314, 509
Reed, Daniel A., 35, 36, 37, 90–93,
  406, 413
  mentioned, 60, 96, 383, 387
  quoted, 75
  chairman: House Ways & Means
    Committee, 63, 69, 70,
    74, 75
  excess profits tax, 94–95
Republic Steel Corporation, 19
Republican Women, League of, 519
Republican Women's Centennial
  Conference, 393
Reuther, Walter: mentioned, 398, 404
Riggs, Robert, 55, 56, 60
Rio Branco, Baron of: quoted, 466–67
Roberts, Roy A.: quoted, 54, 55